Integrating Artificial Intelligence in Cybersecurity and Forensic Practices

Marwan Omar
Illinois Institute of Technology, USA

Hewa Majeed Zangana
Duhok Polytechnic University, Iraq

Derek Mohammed
Saint Leo University, USA

IGI Global
Scientific Publishing
Publishing Tomorrow's Research Today

Vice President of Editorial — Melissa Wagner
Managing Editor of Acquisitions — Mikaela Felty
Managing Editor of Book Development — Jocelynn Hessler
Production Manager — Mike Brehm
Cover Design — Phillip Shickler

Published in the United States of America by
IGI Global Scientific Publishing
701 East Chocolate Avenue
Hershey, PA, 17033, USA
Tel: 717-533-8845
Fax: 717-533-8661
Website: https://www.igi-global.com E-mail: cust@igi-global.com

Library of Congress Cataloging-in-Publication Data

Names: Omar, Marwan, 1982- editor. | Zangana, Hewa Majeed, 1987- editor. | Mohammed, Derek, 1966- editor.
Title: Integrating artificial intelligence in cybersecurity and forensic practices / edited by Marwan Omar, Hewa Zangana, Derek Mohammed.
Description: Hershey, PA : IGI Global Scientific Publishing, 2025. | Includes bibliographical references and index. | Summary: "This book aims to bridge the gap between artificial intelligence (AI) innovations and their practical applications in cybersecurity and forensic practices, offering an interdisciplinary perspective that connects research with real-world implementation"-- Provided by publisher.
Identifiers: LCCN 2024054516 (print) | LCCN 2024054517 (ebook) | ISBN 9798337305882 (hardcover) | ISBN 9798337305899 (paperback) | ISBN 9798337305905 (ebook)
Subjects: LCSH: Computer security. | Digital forensic science. | Artificial intelligence.
Classification: LCC QA76.9.A25 I5526 2025 (print) | LCC QA76.9.A25 (ebook) | DDC 005.8--dc23/eng/20250124
LC record available at https://lccn.loc.gov/2024054516
LC ebook record available at https://lccn.loc.gov/2024054517

British Cataloguing in Publication Data
A Cataloguing in Publication record for this book is available from the British Library.

Table of Contents

Detailed Table of Contents

The integration of Artificial Intelligence (AI) in cybersecurity and forensic science represents a transformative shift in addressing today's complex digital security challenges. As cyber threats evolve in sophistication and frequency, AI-driven approaches provide a proactive and adaptive solution to enhance threat detection, prevention, and investigation capabilities. This chapter provides an overview of the role AI plays in advancing cybersecurity and forensic methodologies, with a focus on machine learning, deep learning, and natural language processing techniques. We examine the ways AI enhances traditional cybersecurity frameworks and forensic processes, such as anomaly detection, incident response, and digital evidence analysis. Additionally, we discuss the dual-use potential of AI, including both defensive and adversarial applications, as well as the ethical and privacy implications arising from its use in security-sensitive fields. By contextualizing the impact of AI in cybersecurity and forensic science,

In an increasingly digital world, the prevalence of cyber threats necessitates advanced solutions for effective threat detection and response. This chapter explores the critical role of machine learning (ML) and deep learning (DL) in enhancing cybersecurity practices. By leveraging algorithms that learn from data, these technologies enable the identification of anomalous patterns and behaviors that signify potential threats. The discussion encompasses various ML and DL techniques, their applications in threat detection, and the challenges faced in implementation. Furthermore, we analyze case studies demonstrating the efficacy of these technologies in real-world scenarios. Ultimately, this chapter underscores the significance of integrating ML and DL into cybersecurity frameworks to improve threat detection capabilities and foster a proactive security posture.

visuals are critical for identifying threats and verifying information. This chapter explores advanced AI-driven techniques for image denoising, emphasizing the role of deep learning, convolutional neural networks (CNNs), and generative models to enhance image clarity. By leveraging artificial intelligence, these methods adaptively reduce noise while preserving essential image features, improving both efficiency and reliability in digital forensic processes. Our examination includes a comparative analysis of traditional versus AI-based denoising approaches, assessing their applicability and effectiveness within cybersecurity and forensic environments. This chapter ultimately aims to provide a comprehensive overview of cutting-edge AI techniques that refine image quality, supporting better decision-making in complex, data-rich scenarios.

The integration of Artificial Intelligence (AI) in forensic investigations has transformed evidence collection and analysis, enabling quicker and more accurate assessments. This chapter examines the evolution and application of automated AI-driven tools in collecting, processing, and analyzing digital evidence. AI-based systems assist forensic experts by autonomously identifying, organizing, and categorizing massive datasets, thus accelerating traditional investigative workflows. Key AI methods discussed include machine learning algorithms for data classification, natural language processing for document analysis, and computer vision for image and video recognition. Additionally, we explore the implications of these technologies for the legal system, privacy concerns, and the accuracy and reliability of evidence derived through automation. This chapter also considers potential challenges, such as data integrity and bias, as well as future trends in AI applications within digital forensics.

In the increasingly complex cybersecurity landscape, human behavior plays a critical role in the efficacy of security measures within organizations. This author explores the integration of Human-Centered Cybersecurity (HCC), or usable security, practices, through the concepts of usability, education, and user engagement in security training programs to alleviate cybersecurity-induced friction. HCC emphasizes operational feasibility, advocating for training programs like Security Education, Training, and Awareness (SETA) that adapt to individual learning styles and roles, thereby fostering a culture of cybersecurity awareness. Some strategies to increase cybersecurity compliance include personalized training via hybrid interaction systems and gamification and a redefinition of employees' roles within an environment to shift to a security culture. This research calls for continuous evaluation and a multidimensional framework to incorporate human factors, aiming to strengthen Cybersecurity Culture (CSC) within organizations.

The operation of robust cybersecurity legislation plays a fundamental role in safeguarding data privacy in an increasingly unified digital terrain, providing a legal framework that sensitizes individuals on their rights and privileges as it relates to the protection of their data, regulates data handlers by stipulating applicable rules and regulations when handling the information of a data subject, and establishes enforceable measures when a breach occurs, thereby fostering a culture of trust and accountability in the digital landscape. Cybersecurity legislation covering data privacy requirements is critical in ensuring the safety and security of every individual's personal information.

Digital forensic data mining and pattern recognition are essential components in enhancing cybersecurity measures and forensic practices. This chapter explores the intersection of artificial intelligence and digital forensics, emphasizing the methodologies and technologies that enable the extraction of meaningful patterns from vast datasets. By leveraging advanced machine learning algorithms, investigators can identify anomalies, classify behaviors, and predict potential threats in real-time. The integration of AI enhances the efficiency and accuracy of forensic investigations, ultimately leading to improved decision-making and threat mitigation strategies. Case studies illustrate the practical applications of these techniques in various domains, underscoring the transformative potential of AI in digital forensics.

This chapter examines the evolution and integration of DevSecOps and Security Operations Centers (SOCs), emphasizing enhanced cybersecurity management

demonstrates that VulDetect achieves a vulnerability detection accuracy of up to 92.65%, surpassing SyseVR and VulDeBERT, two of the most advanced existing techniques for identifying software vulnerabilities.

Nation-sponsored cyberattacks pose a severe threat to national security, targeting critical infrastructure and disrupting essential services. Among the most impactful attacks on South Korea's banking sector and infrastructure was the DarkSeoul cyberattack, believed to have been conducted by North Korea state-sponsored hackers. Using spear phishing, DNS poisoning, and malware, this attack caused widespread disruption across critical systems. This paper presents an in-depth analysis of the DarkSeoul incident, detailing the techniques involved and offering insights and recommendations for the global cybersecurity community. The motivations and strategic objectives behind the attack are examined, as well as South Korea's response and the broader implications for cybersecurity policy. Our analysis highlights key vulnerabilities and underscores the urgency for enhanced defenses against state-sponsored cyber threats. This study emphasizes the necessity for robust national cybersecurity measures to counter such sophisticated attacks effectively.

Organizations continue to face a serious problem with insider threats, which frequently lead to data breaches, monetary losses, and harm to a brand's reputation. Because high-risk employee behaviors are complicated and usually subtle, traditional security measures often fail to uncover insider threats. By examining employee behavior patterns, this study explores the application of machine learning (ML) approaches to proactively identify possible insider threats. Our method simulates normal employee behavior and identifies deviations that point to unsafe behavior by combining supervised learning for classification with unsupervised learning for anomaly identification. Network activity logs, email content, access history, and system usage are among the data sources that are processed to produce a thorough picture of employee behavior.

Preface

The rapid evolution of technology has significantly transformed the landscape of cybersecurity and forensic science. As threats become increasingly sophisticated, the integration of Artificial Intelligence (AI) into these fields has emerged as a vital strategy for enhancing security measures and improving investigative processes. This book, **"Integrating Artificial Intelligence in Cybersecurity and Forensic Practices,"** compiles insights from leading experts in the field, exploring the myriad ways AI can be leveraged to address contemporary challenges.

In this volume, we delve into a variety of topics that illustrate the powerful intersection of AI with cybersecurity and forensic methodologies. By presenting both theoretical explorations and practical applications, we aim to equip readers with a comprehensive understanding of how AI can transform practices in these domains. Each chapter offers unique perspectives on the role of machine learning, natural language processing, and other AI technologies in enhancing threat detection, data analysis, and incident response.

Our objectives with this book are as follows:

- **Advance Knowledge in AI-Driven Cybersecurity:** We present innovative methodologies and case studies that expand the understanding of AI's application in threat detection and forensic analysis.
- **Encourage Interdisciplinary Collaboration:** This book unites experts from AI, cybersecurity, and forensic science, fostering collaborative research and holistic solutions to complex challenges.
- **Provide Practical Guidance:** Each chapter is designed to offer actionable insights, best practices, and tools for professionals looking to integrate AI into their security frameworks.
- **Identify Future Directions:** We highlight ongoing challenges and emerging opportunities in the integration of AI, inspiring future research and innovation.

This book is intended for a diverse audience, including cybersecurity professionals, forensic analysts, AI researchers, and students. Whether you are seeking to deepen your understanding of AI applications or looking for practical strategies to enhance your cybersecurity practices, this volume offers valuable insights.

ORGANIZATION OF THE BOOK

Chapter 1

Introduction to Artificial Intelligence in Cybersecurity and Forensic Science

This chapter introduces the foundational concepts of AI in the context of cybersecurity and forensic science, discussing its potential to transform traditional practices.

Chapter 2

The Role of Machine Learning and Deep Learning in Threat Detection

Explores how machine learning and deep learning techniques enhance the identification of cyber threats, focusing on their capabilities and applications.

Chapter 3

Using Natural Language Processing (NLP) for Phishing and Spam Detection

Covers the application of NLP techniques in detecting phishing attempts and spam, highlighting their effectiveness in safeguarding digital communications.

Chapter 4

Network Forensics and Traffic Analysis with Machine Learning

Discusses the integration of machine learning in network forensics, emphasizing its role in traffic analysis and anomaly detection.

Chapter 5

Image Denoising Techniques for Cybersecurity and Forensic Applications: AI-Driven Approaches

Examines AI-driven methods for image denoising, relevant in both cybersecurity and forensic contexts.

Chapter 6

Automated Evidence Collection and Analysis Using AI

Focuses on the automation of evidence collection processes through AI, enhancing the efficiency and accuracy of forensic investigations.

Chapter 7

How Human-Centered Cybersecurity (HCC) Training Fosters Organizational Cybersecurity Cultures (CSC)

Explores the importance of human-centered training approaches in cultivating a strong cybersecurity culture within organizations.

Chapter 8

The Role of Cybersecurity Legislation in Promoting Data Privacy

Analyzes how current legislation impacts data privacy and security, emphasizing the interplay between law and technology.

Chapter 9

Digital Forensic Data Mining and Pattern Recognition

Investigates the use of data mining and pattern recognition techniques in digital forensics, showcasing their effectiveness in uncovering insights.

Chapter 10

Improving AppSec Resiliency, Monitoring, Risk Assessment, and Compliance By Bridging DevSecOps with SOCs

Discusses strategies for enhancing application security resilience and compliance through the integration of DevSecOps practices.

Chapter 11

An In-Depth Investigation on Hardware Trojans Testing into Cyber Security Concerns Using Machine Learning Models

Examines the emerging threat of hardware trojans and the application of machine learning models in their detection and analysis.

Chapter 12

Source Code Analysis with Deep Neural Networks

Covers the utilization of deep neural networks in analyzing source code for vulnerabilities, highlighting advancements in this area.

Chapter 13

An In-depth Analysis of a Cyber Attack—Case Study and Security Insights

Presents a detailed case study of a significant cyber attack, providing insights into the security implications and lessons learned.

Chapter 14

Using Machine Learning to Identify High-Risk Employee Activity in Proactive Insider Threat Detection

Explores methods for leveraging machine learning to detect potential insider threats, focusing on risk assessment and mitigation strategies.

CONCLUSION

As we conclude "Integrating Artificial Intelligence in Cybersecurity and Forensic Practices," it is clear that AI is poised to play a transformative role in the future of these fields. Each chapter has underscored the potential of AI technologies to enhance security measures, streamline forensic investigations, and address the growing complexity of cyber threats.

The integration of AI not only offers advanced tools for threat detection and data analysis but also presents new challenges that must be navigated, including ethical considerations, model interpretability, and the need for robust security protocols. The discussions throughout this book highlight the importance of interdisciplinary collaboration in tackling these challenges, advocating for continuous innovation and responsible AI practices.

As we look forward, it is essential to remain committed to exploring the dynamic interplay between AI and cybersecurity. The insights and methodologies presented in this volume serve as a foundation for further research and application in real-world settings. By harnessing the power of AI, we can build more resilient, secure, and effective cybersecurity and forensic practices.

We hope this book inspires practitioners, researchers, and students alike to contribute to the ongoing evolution of these critical fields, ensuring that we are well-equipped to face the challenges of tomorrow.

Marwan Omar
Illinois Institute of Technology, USA

Hewa Majeed Zangana
Duhok Polytechnic University, Iraq

Derek Mohammed
Saint Leo University, USA

Chapter 1
Introduction to Artificial Intelligence in Cybersecurity and Forensic Science

Hewa Majeed Zangana
https://orcid.org/0000-0001-7909-254X
Duhok Polytechnic University, Iraq

Marwan Omar
Illinois Institute of Technology, USA

Derek Mohammed
Saint Leo University, USA

ABSTRACT

The integration of Artificial Intelligence (AI) in cybersecurity and forensic science represents a transformative shift in addressing today's complex digital security challenges. As cyber threats evolve in sophistication and frequency, AI-driven approaches provide a proactive and adaptive solution to enhance threat detection, prevention, and investigation capabilities. This chapter provides an overview of the role AI plays in advancing cybersecurity and forensic methodologies, with a focus on machine learning, deep learning, and natural language processing techniques. We examine the ways AI enhances traditional cybersecurity frameworks and forensic processes, such as anomaly detection, incident response, and digital evidence analysis. Additionally, we discuss the dual-use potential of AI, including both defensive and adversarial applications, as well as the ethical and privacy implications arising from its use in security-sensitive fields. By contextualizing the impact of AI

DOI: 10.4018/979-8-3373-0588-2.ch001

in cybersecurity and forensic science.

1. OVERVIEW OF ARTIFICIAL INTELLIGENCE IN CYBERSECURITY AND FORENSIC SCIENCE

Artificial Intelligence (AI) is transforming both cybersecurity and digital forensics by enhancing the ability to detect, prevent, and investigate cyber threats in increasingly complex and interconnected environments. As malicious actors adopt sophisticated attack strategies, traditional cybersecurity measures are often insufficient. In response, AI-powered tools provide dynamic, real-time threat analysis and response capabilities that go beyond static, rule-based systems, significantly strengthening cybersecurity postures (Tyagi et al., 2024; Dunsin et al., 2024).

In cybersecurity, AI aids in threat detection by leveraging machine learning algorithms to identify patterns and anomalies within large datasets, which are indicative of potential cyber attacks (Kaur, Gabrijelčič, & Klobučar, 2023; Zeadally et al., 2020). Machine learning (ML) techniques, such as neural networks and decision trees, are particularly adept at recognizing subtle, hard-to-detect signs of malicious activity, helping analysts uncover and mitigate threats more effectively than manual methods alone (Jarrett & Choo, 2021). Furthermore, AI models can learn from previous attacks to predict new ones, providing proactive rather than reactive defenses (Capuano et al., 2022; Rizvi et al., 2022).

AI also plays a crucial role in digital forensics, assisting in the analysis of digital evidence by automating processes that were previously time-intensive. By employing AI techniques, forensic analysts can process vast quantities of data rapidly, accurately pinpointing relevant evidence and potential threats (Moustafa, 2022; Faqir, 2023). For example, Natural Language Processing (NLP) can aid in analyzing textual data in investigations, while computer vision can assist in scrutinizing video or image-based evidence. Such applications enable investigators to handle complex digital cases with unprecedented efficiency (Du et al., 2020; Syed & ES, 2024).

AI-driven advancements are also evident in fields like incident response, where AI systems contribute by providing rapid, automated responses to cyber incidents, often faster than human analysts could achieve (Hassan & Ibrahim, 2023; Omar, 2022). In this context, AI is not merely a supplementary tool but a transformative force enabling more effective identification, containment, and mitigation of cyber threats, reinforcing organizational resilience against digital attacks (Bonfanti, 2022; Nair, Deshmukh, & Tyagi, 2024).

Despite these advantages, the integration of AI in cybersecurity and forensic science is not without challenges. Issues of explainability, bias, and data privacy raise ethical concerns, particularly when AI systems make critical security decisions (Sikos, 2021; Murphy, 2022). Additionally, there is a risk that attackers may exploit AI systems, necessitating ongoing efforts to secure AI algorithms and their underlying datasets (Ali, 2022; Omar & Zangana, 2024).

To better understand the role of AI in cybersecurity and forensic science, it is essential to visualize how AI techniques, such as machine learning and natural language processing, integrate within security frameworks. The diagram below outlines AI's contributions, highlighting its critical functions in real-time threat detection, anomaly detection, incident response, and evidence analysis.

Figure 1. AI integration in cybersecurity and forensic science

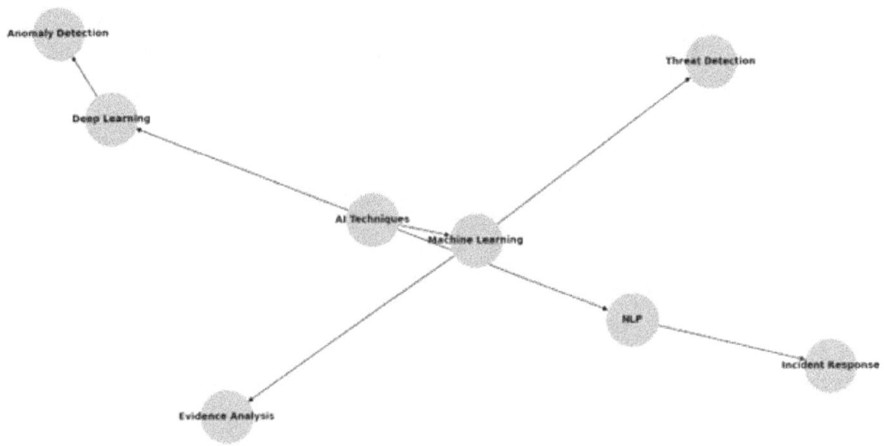

Overall, AI has become an indispensable component of modern cybersecurity and forensic science, pushing the boundaries of what is possible in detecting, responding to, and investigating cyber threats. As these fields continue to evolve, integrating advanced AI methodologies will be essential for maintaining effective defenses against emerging digital risks (Montasari, 2023; Mughal, 2019).

2. KEY CONCEPTS AND TECHNIQUES IN AI RELEVANT TO CYBERSECURITY AND FORENSICS

In the realm of cybersecurity and digital forensics, artificial intelligence (AI) is emerging as an essential toolkit, enabling faster response, enhanced detection accuracy, and more comprehensive data analysis.

Various AI techniques play distinct roles in cybersecurity and forensics. The chart below highlights popular techniques such as machine learning, deep learning, and natural language processing, with their specific applications. Understanding these distinctions helps in appreciating the nuanced contributions of AI to digital security.

Figure 2. Popular AI techniques in cybersecurity and their applications

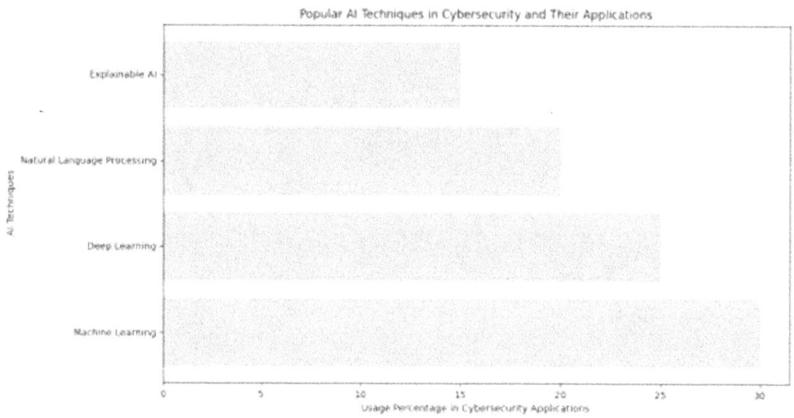

AI's rapid processing abilities and predictive models have significantly improved how security professionals detect and mitigate potential cyber threats, making it a cornerstone in the defense against increasingly sophisticated cyberattacks (Tyagi et al., 2024; Hassan & Ibrahim, 2023).

2.1 Machine Learning for Threat Detection and Analysis

Machine learning (ML) techniques, a subset of AI, are instrumental in identifying patterns and anomalies within large data sets, which is crucial for cybersecurity applications. Supervised and unsupervised ML algorithms aid in threat detection, differentiating between normal and suspicious activities by analyzing vast data streams in real time (Zeadally et al., 2020; Rizvi et al., 2022). These capabilities have revolutionized digital forensics by allowing forensic investigators to process enormous datasets more efficiently, flagging potential issues more accurately than traditional methods (Jarrett & Choo, 2021; Ghillani, 2022).

Deep learning, a more advanced ML technique, has shown particular promise in identifying and classifying malware. Deep neural networks (DNNs) can effectively differentiate between various types of malware by examining code patterns and behaviors, making them highly valuable in both cybersecurity and forensic analysis (Omar, 2022; Jones & Omar, 2024). Moreover, convolutional neural networks (CNNs) are being employed in tasks such as image and audio forensics, aiding in cases where evidence might be hidden in complex multimedia formats (Dunsin et al., 2024; Ali, 2022).

2.2 Natural Language Processing in Cybersecurity

Natural Language Processing (NLP), another key AI area, is transforming how security systems handle large volumes of textual data. Through NLP, AI systems can monitor communications on social media, emails, and forums to detect cyber threats, phishing schemes, and other forms of online fraud (Mughal, 2019; Samtani et al., 2020). This capability is crucial in digital forensics, where NLP assists in analyzing textual evidence, extracting relevant information from suspect conversations, and identifying language patterns indicative of criminal behavior (Sikos, 2021; Zangana & Omar, 2020).

2.3 Explainable AI and Forensic Accountability

Explainable AI (XAI) has emerged as a response to the opaque nature of many AI models, particularly in cybersecurity and forensics where transparency is critical. XAI allows forensic experts to better understand the AI's decision-making process, which is essential in courtroom scenarios where AI-driven evidence needs to be clear and interpretable (Capuano et al., 2022). XAI approaches enhance credibility and accountability, providing forensic experts and stakeholders with insights into the rationale behind AI's detection of anomalies or threats (Bonfanti, 2022; Kaur, Gabrijelčič, & Klobučar, 2023).

2.4 Incident Response and Automated Forensic Investigation

The AI-driven incident response process involves multiple stages that streamline threat detection and response, from identifying anomalies to resolving incidents. The flowchart below illustrates this workflow, demonstrating how AI enhances efficiency and accuracy throughout each step of incident response.

Figure 3. AI-driven incident response workflow

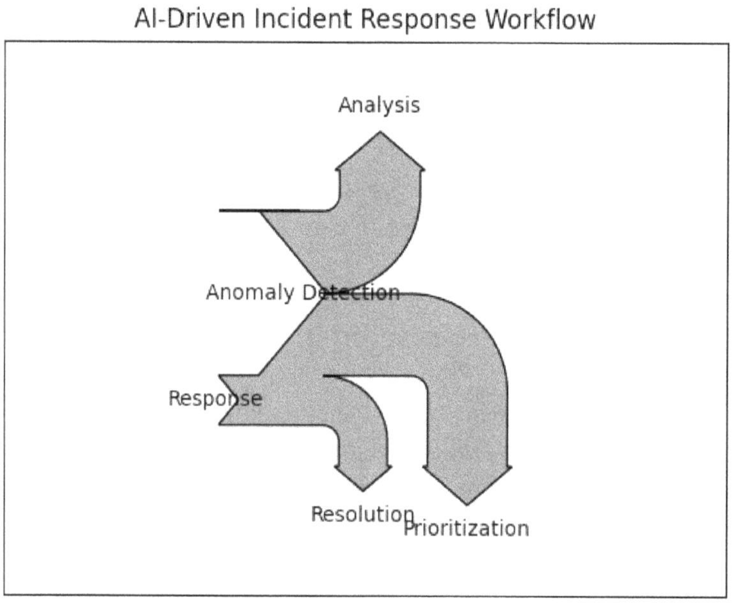

AI-driven automation has also been instrumental in enhancing incident response. Automated systems can initiate investigations immediately after detecting suspicious activity, allowing cybersecurity teams to respond faster and more effectively. This approach reduces the time it takes to identify, contain, and remediate threats, which is especially valuable in high-stakes environments like healthcare and finance (Montasari, 2023; Du et al., 2020). Automated forensic tools enable rapid evidence collection, reducing human error and enabling investigators to handle more complex cases (Hayes & Kyobe, 2020; Syed & ES, 2024).

2.5 AI in Digital Forensics: Future Potential and Challenges

As AI techniques continue to advance, their potential for digital forensics grows, albeit with significant challenges. AI's integration in digital forensics is still limited by issues of bias, data privacy, and the need for large datasets to train effective models (Tuli & Thaduri, 2023; Ukwen & Karabatak, 2021). Additionally, legal and ethical considerations arise, particularly regarding the reliability of AI-based evidence in courts, which calls for ongoing research into robust, fair, and explainable AI solutions for forensic applications (Murphy, 2022; Faqir, 2023).

The confluence of AI and cybersecurity presents new opportunities and demands for digital forensics, enabling proactive threat identification and more comprehensive investigative methods that keep pace with the evolving digital landscape. By leveraging these AI-driven techniques, cybersecurity and forensic experts can better defend against cyber threats and investigate digital crimes, providing a solid foundation for a more secure digital environment.

3. THE EVOLUTION OF AI APPLICATIONS IN CYBERSECURITY

Artificial intelligence (AI) has transformed the landscape of cybersecurity, offering new avenues for detecting, preventing, and responding to cyber threats. As the sophistication of cyber-attacks grows, AI's ability to process large datasets and identify patterns has proven invaluable. Early applications of AI in cybersecurity primarily focused on intrusion detection systems and antivirus software, which relied on machine learning to identify known threat signatures. However, as threat actors adapted and began using more complex, polymorphic malware, traditional approaches struggled to keep pace (Mughal, 2019; Ali, 2022).

In recent years, the integration of deep learning and neural networks into cybersecurity has enabled more advanced anomaly detection systems capable of identifying zero-day attacks and sophisticated threats in real time (Nair et al., 2024; Zeadally et al., 2020). For instance, convolutional neural networks (CNNs) and recurrent neural networks (RNNs) have been leveraged for detecting malicious network behavior by examining patterns and identifying anomalies that may indicate a breach (Capuano et al., 2022; Montasari, 2023).

AI's role has further expanded into domains like digital forensics and incident response, where it enhances the speed and accuracy of threat detection and helps forensic investigators analyze massive volumes of data efficiently (Tuli & Thaduri, 2023; Dunsin et al., 2024). The potential of AI in this field is especially evident in forensic accounting, where AI-driven tools are revolutionizing investigative practices by automating evidence collection and improving accuracy in identifying fraud (Syed & ES, 2024; Tuli & Thaduri, 2023). Moreover, digital forensics now incorporates AI to streamline data analysis processes in cybercrime investigations, enabling more thorough and timely responses (Moustafa, 2022; Murphy, 2022).

The application of AI in cybersecurity has also sparked advancements in specific areas such as network forensics, where techniques like network traffic analysis have evolved to detect complex threats and provide robust incident response solutions (Rizvi et al., 2022; Ghillani, 2022). Additionally, AI has facilitated the development of predictive analytics tools, enabling security professionals to foresee potential threats and strengthen their defenses proactively (Huff et al., 2023; Omar, 2024). This proactive stance is crucial in addressing threats like phishing and social engineering attacks, which have become increasingly sophisticated and difficult to counter using traditional measures (Zangana et al., 2024).

As AI technology continues to mature, its applications in cybersecurity are expected to become even more comprehensive, integrating with emerging technologies such as blockchain for secure timestamping in forensic investigations and large language models (LLMs) for real-time threat intelligence (Omar & Zangana, 2024; Wright et al., 2012). AI-driven advancements are also anticipated to address ethical and privacy concerns within cybersecurity, making systems not only more secure but also more transparent and accountable (Bonfanti, 2022; Samtani et al., 2020).

The ongoing evolution of AI applications in cybersecurity demonstrates its critical role in defending against today's cyber threats. AI's capabilities in big data analytics, threat prediction, and response automation are indispensable in creating a resilient cybersecurity infrastructure, paving the way for innovations that will continue to shape the field (Hayes & Kyobe, 2020; Jarrett & Choo, 2021; Hassan & Ibrahim, 2023).

4. COMMON AI TECHNIQUES IN CYBERSECURITY

Artificial intelligence (AI) has become pivotal in enhancing cybersecurity efforts, as its various techniques significantly improve threat detection, response, and forensics. Here, we explore some common AI methods widely applied in cybersecurity, including machine learning, deep learning, natural language processing (NLP), and explainable AI, each bringing unique capabilities and challenges to cybersecurity.

4.1. Machine Learning (ML)

Machine learning algorithms are highly effective in identifying patterns in vast datasets, making them suitable for intrusion detection and anomaly detection. By learning from historical data, ML models can differentiate between normal and suspicious activities, aiding in faster identification of potential threats (Jarrett & Choo, 2021; Moustafa, 2022). Supervised ML techniques, where algorithms learn from labeled data, are used extensively in malware detection and classification, while unsupervised techniques help identify unknown attacks by detecting outliers in network traffic (Hassan & Ibrahim, 2023; Zeadally et al., 2020). With advancements in ML, cybersecurity has seen more automated solutions that improve response times and accuracy (Jones et al., 2023; Omar, 2024).

4.2. Deep Learning (DL)

Deep learning, a subset of ML, uses multi-layered neural networks to process complex data structures, making it especially useful for image and text recognition tasks in cybersecurity, such as identifying phishing emails and malicious code (Bonfanti, 2022; Rizvi et al., 2022). DL models, such as convolutional neural networks (CNNs) and recurrent neural networks (RNNs), have been applied to analyze network behavior and detect anomalies indicative of cyber threats. However, deep learning models are typically resource-intensive, posing challenges in scalability and requiring advanced hardware setups (Capuano et al., 2022; Du et al., 2020).

4.3. Natural Language Processing (NLP)

NLP techniques are essential for processing and analyzing human language data, which is increasingly critical in cybersecurity for identifying social engineering attacks, parsing unstructured data, and scanning for malicious intent in text-based threats. For instance, NLP models can process emails, social media posts, and chat logs to detect phishing attempts and insider threats (Ali, 2022; Syed & ES, 2024). NLP is also central to analyzing large volumes of digital forensic data, enhancing the efficiency of investigations (Montasari, 2023; Gholami & Omar, 2023). Nonetheless, NLP-based models must handle the inherent ambiguity and diversity of human language, which can complicate threat detection efforts (Samtani et al., 2020).

4.4. Explainable AI (XAI)

Explainable AI focuses on making AI models' decision-making processes transparent, which is vital in cybersecurity where understanding why a model flagged an activity as suspicious is necessary for corrective actions (Kaur et al., 2023; Ghillani, 2022). XAI methods are particularly beneficial in regulated environments, like finance and healthcare, where cybersecurity decisions must be auditable. Techniques such as LIME (Local Interpretable Model-agnostic Explanations) and SHAP (SHapley Additive exPlanations) help elucidate model predictions, ensuring the AI's insights can be trusted and acted upon responsibly (Murphy, 2022; Dunsin et al., 2024).

4.5. Reinforcement Learning (RL)

Reinforcement learning enables cybersecurity systems to adapt dynamically by learning optimal actions through interaction with the environment. This approach is commonly applied in network security, where systems continuously learn and adjust strategies to mitigate attacks (Nair et al., 2024; Tyagi et al., 2024). RL-based agents can detect and respond to evolving threats, making them highly adaptable; however, they require extensive training and can be unpredictable without proper tuning (Tuli & Thaduri, 2023).

These AI techniques collectively represent the core of modern cybersecurity tools and strategies, each contributing specific strengths in data analysis, threat detection, and automated response. However, integrating these technologies effectively requires careful consideration of resource demands, ethical concerns, and potential regulatory compliance, as the nature of cyber threats continues to evolve (Zangana et al., 2024; Montasari, 2023).

5. AI IN DIGITAL FORENSICS

The integration of Artificial Intelligence (AI) in digital forensics has become a transformative force, enhancing the capacity to analyze, interpret, and manage vast amounts of digital evidence in real-time. The rapid progression in AI techniques, especially in machine learning and deep learning, enables more effective and accurate forensics processes by automating labor-intensive tasks, thereby accelerating incident response times and reducing human error (Tyagi et al., 2024; Jarrett & Choo, 2021). AI applications in digital forensics are especially useful in cybersecurity contexts, where detecting anomalies, tracing threat actors, and identifying malicious patterns is increasingly complex (Hassan & Ibrahim, 2023; Omar & Zangana, 2020).

In recent years, AI has enhanced network forensics, providing improved monitoring capabilities to detect intrusions and anomalies more precisely (Rizvi et al., 2022). These advancements allow forensic analysts to perform deep packet inspection and interpret logs with unprecedented accuracy, benefiting fields such as forensic accounting, healthcare, and digital policing (Tuli & Thaduri, 2023; Syed & ES, 2024). Moreover, AI's role in digital forensics extends to areas like natural language processing (NLP), used for analyzing unstructured data, emails, and social media content, which has been instrumental in investigating cyber-related crimes (Du et al., 2020; Hayes & Kyobe, 2020).

AI also contributes significantly to overcoming challenges associated with traditional forensics methods, particularly in handling encrypted data and processing massive datasets. Tools leveraging machine learning and deep learning enhance the accuracy of identifying relevant data points and linking evidence across multiple devices, leading to more effective outcomes (Moustafa, 2022; Dunsin et al., 2024). As a result, AI-driven forensics tools not only aid in timely response but also provide strategic insights that support predictive threat modeling (Gholami & Omar, 2023; Murphy, 2022).

Furthermore, AI's potential in digital forensics is also recognized for its role in legal and regulatory compliance. By establishing rigorous analysis protocols and standardized practices, AI facilitates adherence to legal frameworks, reducing the likelihood of evidence being deemed inadmissible in court due to procedural errors (Montasari, 2023). As the field progresses, the intersection of AI and digital forensics promises to create a robust, resilient framework that can address emerging cybersecurity challenges and improve investigative efficiency (Nair et al., 2024; Zeadally et al., 2020).

Looking ahead, as AI technologies such as explainable AI (XAI) are applied to digital forensics, they offer greater transparency, enabling forensics professionals and stakeholders to understand and trust AI-driven insights. This capability is particularly valuable for multidisciplinary investigations where the integration of diverse perspectives is crucial (Capuano et al., 2022; Ghillani, 2022). Consequently, the continued evolution of AI in digital forensics will shape future investigative methodologies, with broader implications for enhancing cybersecurity resilience across sectors (Ukwen & Karabatak, 2021; Alghamdi, 2021).

6. CHALLENGES AND LIMITATIONS OF AI IN CYBERSECURITY AND FORENSICS

Artificial Intelligence (AI) is transforming the landscape of cybersecurity and digital forensics, offering enhanced data analysis capabilities, anomaly detection, and automation in threat response. However, several challenges and limitations constrain its full potential within these fields.

1. Complexity and Accuracy of AI Models

Implementing sophisticated AI algorithms for cybersecurity requires handling large datasets and complex models. High-dimensional data processing in AI systems can lead to computational limitations and increase the likelihood of inaccuracies (Jarrett & Choo, 2021). Errors in these models could result in overlooked threats or false alarms, which may disrupt incident response and compromise cybersecurity effectiveness (Hassan & Ibrahim, 2023; Tyagi et al., 2024).

2. Ethical and Privacy Concerns

AI-powered tools in cybersecurity and forensics often analyze vast amounts of personal and organizational data, raising ethical and privacy concerns (Samtani et al., 2020; Faqir, 2023). This issue is especially pertinent in cases where data ownership and consent are ambiguous, leading to potential legal and regulatory challenges, especially with AI's predictive and behavioral analysis features (Zeadally et al., 2020).

3. **Adversarial Attacks on AI Systems**

AI models used in cybersecurity are vulnerable to adversarial attacks, where malicious actors can manipulate input data to deceive the model into misclassifying information (Rizvi et al., 2022). Techniques such as generating synthetic malicious data can bypass AI detection systems, highlighting the need for robust defensive mechanisms against adversarial threats (Capuano et al., 2022; Omar, 2024).

4. **Interpretability and Explainability Issues**

AI models, particularly deep learning networks, are often considered "black boxes" due to their complex internal processes. This lack of transparency limits forensic investigators' ability to understand and justify AI-driven decisions, which is crucial for both legal and investigatory processes (Du et al., 2020; Bonfanti, 2022). Developing explainable AI (XAI) solutions is essential to improve accountability in forensic investigations and foster trust among practitioners (Gholami & Omar, 2024).

5. **Resource-Intensive Requirements**

AI applications in cybersecurity and digital forensics can be resource-intensive, requiring significant computational power, storage, and maintenance. Such requirements often lead to increased costs, limiting AI adoption, particularly for smaller organizations (Kaur et al., 2023; Ali, 2022). Additionally, complex models require skilled personnel for management and continuous updates, presenting further challenges for scalability and adaptability (Murphy, 2022).

6. **Limitations in Real-Time Data Processing**

Cybersecurity environments demand real-time threat detection and response, which presents a significant challenge for AI algorithms. The latency in processing large-scale data and providing actionable insights can hinder incident response times, potentially leading to delayed threat mitigation (Moustafa, 2022). Ensuring that AI systems can operate effectively under time constraints is a critical area of ongoing research (Montasari, 2023).

7. **Dependence on High-Quality Data**

AI systems require vast amounts of high-quality, labeled data to perform accurately. However, gathering, curating, and managing this data in cybersecurity and forensics can be difficult due to the sensitive and heterogeneous nature of threat information (Tuli & Thaduri, 2023). Without high-quality data, AI models risk generating inaccurate or biased results, which can lead to inadequate threat assessments and compromised investigations (Hayes & Kyobe, 2020).

8. **Regulatory and Compliance Challenges**

AI implementation in cybersecurity is subject to various regulatory frameworks that govern data usage, privacy, and security standards. Compliance with these frameworks is complex, as the legal landscape surrounding AI in cybersecurity and forensics is evolving rapidly. This uncertainty can limit organizations' ability to deploy AI solutions effectively (Mughal, 2019; Syed & ES, 2024).

While AI offers transformative benefits in cybersecurity, it also comes with challenges that limit its full potential. This diagram illustrates some of the key challenges, including explainability, data privacy concerns, and resource requirements, providing a comprehensive view of areas where ongoing research is essential.

Figure 4. Challenges and limitations of AI in cybersecurity

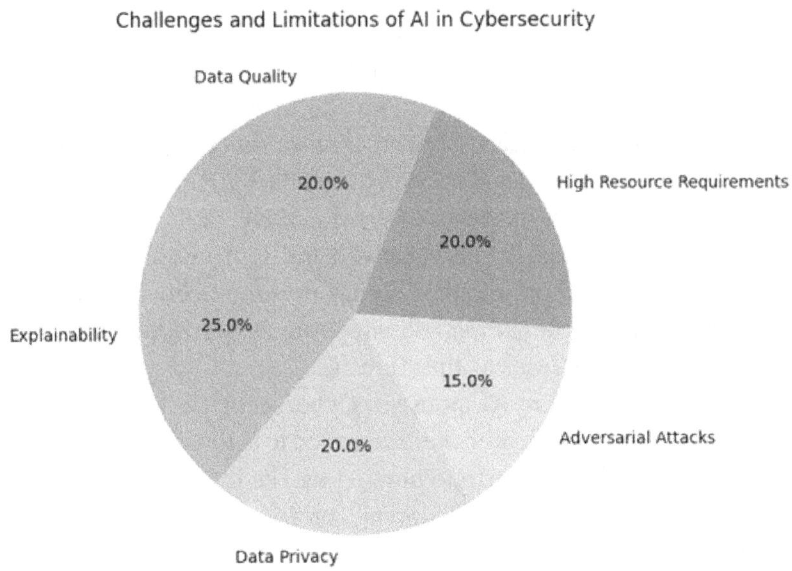

In summary, while AI offers transformative benefits for cybersecurity and digital forensics, its implementation is hindered by technical, ethical, and operational challenges. Addressing these limitations will require advancements in AI interpretability, resource optimization, and legal frameworks, ensuring that AI systems can operate securely and effectively within this critical domain.

7. CASE STUDIES ON AI APPLICATIONS IN CYBERSECURITY AND FORENSICS

The use of artificial intelligence (AI) in cybersecurity and digital forensics has rapidly expanded, offering novel solutions to address a range of modern threats. This section examines several case studies that demonstrate how AI is transforming both fields, highlighting the challenges, solutions, and opportunities that have emerged as AI tools become more deeply integrated into cybersecurity and forensic processes.

1. **Automating Forensic Investigations with AI**: The adoption of automation, driven by AI and machine learning, has allowed digital forensics to process large volumes of data more efficiently, thus speeding up investigations and increasing accuracy. Jarrett and Choo (2021) discuss how AI-based automation aids in digital forensics by minimizing human error and enabling real-time analysis, which is critical in handling large datasets in cyber investigations. Similarly, Du et al. (2020) explored AI's potential in forensic investigation, emphasizing advancements in automating repetitive tasks such as data parsing and malware detection.
2. **AI in Network Forensics**: Network forensics is crucial for monitoring and analyzing traffic to detect and prevent cyberattacks. Rizvi et al. (2022) underscore the application of AI in network forensics, particularly in identifying anomalous patterns and potential threats in network traffic. The integration of deep learning algorithms in network monitoring has proven effective in recognizing subtle patterns that traditional methods might miss, providing cybersecurity teams with proactive defenses against threats.
3. **AI-Powered Incident Response in Cybersecurity**: The role of AI in cybersecurity has extended beyond mere detection to active response strategies. Hassan and Ibrahim (2023) illustrate how AI assists in threat detection and incident response by processing vast amounts of data in real time, enabling faster and more accurate responses to cyber incidents. AI's capability to continuously learn and adapt makes it an invaluable tool for identifying emerging threats, as shown by Al-Hajri et al. (2023), who emphasized the critical role of AI-driven tools in digital forensics investigations to enhance accuracy and efficiency.

4. **AI-Enhanced Malware Detection and Analysis**: AI has become instrumental in combating advanced malware and zero-day attacks. For instance, Jones and Omar (2024) demonstrated the application of the GPT-2 Enhanced Attack Detection and Defense (GEADD) Method in detecting zero-day threats, showcasing AI's capability to analyze vast datasets, predict potential attacks, and reduce the likelihood of breaches. Additionally, Zangana and Omar (2020) highlighted the utility of AI in identifying and mitigating smartphone security threats, where AI-based algorithms can analyze behavioral patterns and detect unusual activity, making AI an essential tool in mobile forensics.
5. **AI's Role in Cyber Deception and Phishing Detection**: Cyber deception tactics, such as email phishing, remain prevalent threats. AI-based tools for phishing detection analyze email content, metadata, and sender patterns to identify phishing attempts effectively. Zangana et al. (2024) provided insights into how AI can detect deceptive tactics, especially in email phishing, by identifying behavioral patterns and linguistic cues often overlooked in manual reviews.
6. **Explainable AI in Forensic Analysis**: One significant challenge in applying AI in forensics is the need for explainable AI (XAI) to understand and justify the decisions made by AI systems. Capuano et al. (2022) emphasize the importance of XAI in cybersecurity, where interpretability is crucial for legal proceedings and audit trails. This is particularly relevant in digital forensics, where findings are often used as evidence in court, and the reasoning behind AI-driven conclusions must be clear and defensible.
7. **Machine Learning in Digital Forensics for Healthcare**: The healthcare sector faces unique challenges in cybersecurity, given the sensitivity of patient data. Syed and ES (2024) illustrate how AI-driven forensic tools can assist in investigating breaches in healthcare, identifying vulnerabilities, and mitigating data loss. The integration of machine learning in forensic analysis provides targeted insights that are essential for protecting sensitive medical information.
8. **AI for National Security and Cyberterrorism Countermeasures**: AI has also become a valuable tool for national security in countering cyberterrorism. Montasari (2023) discusses how AI enhances the capabilities of cybersecurity and digital forensics in countering cyberterrorism through proactive threat detection and response strategies. The use of AI-driven tools in cyber defense provides an additional layer of security by continuously scanning for suspicious activities and automating threat responses.
9. **AI in Financial and Accounting Forensics**: Beyond traditional cybersecurity, AI is increasingly used in forensic accounting to identify anomalies and fraud. Tuli and Thaduri (2023) discuss the application of AI in forensic accounting, where machine learning algorithms help detect fraudulent activities by analyzing transaction patterns, thus preventing financial cybercrimes.

These case studies collectively demonstrate the vast potential of AI in transforming cybersecurity and digital forensics. From enhancing incident response to advancing network and malware forensics, AI has proven invaluable in addressing today's cyber challenges. As AI technologies continue to evolve, so too will their applications in securing digital environments, safeguarding sensitive data, and ensuring resilience against an ever-growing landscape of cyber threats.

8. FUTURE PROSPECTS OF AI IN CYBERSECURITY AND FORENSICS

The potential of Artificial Intelligence (AI) to reshape cybersecurity and digital forensics continues to expand as both fields confront increasingly sophisticated cyber threats. As adversaries leverage AI to innovate their attack methods, defense mechanisms must similarly advance to maintain a robust cybersecurity posture. AI offers promising solutions in proactive threat detection, real-time response, and enhanced digital forensic capabilities, ultimately contributing to more resilient security infrastructures (Tyagi, Kumari, & Richa, 2024).

One of the most significant trends is the integration of AI with advanced data analytics to process and analyze large volumes of network data and digital artifacts quickly and efficiently. This capability is especially valuable in cybersecurity incident response and digital forensic investigations, where rapid, automated analysis is critical (Moustafa, 2022; Hassan & Ibrahim, 2023). AI-based tools are increasingly adept at detecting anomalies and identifying patterns indicative of malicious activity, which can facilitate the identification of advanced persistent threats (APTs) and zero-day vulnerabilities before they cause widespread harm (Jarrett & Choo, 2021).

Machine learning (ML) algorithms have demonstrated their utility in digital forensics by automating the identification of pertinent data within vast datasets, as seen in incident response cases involving complex malware. Techniques such as deep learning (DL) have shown particular promise, providing insights that guide investigators towards critical information faster than traditional methods (Dunsin et al., 2024; Kaur, Gabrijelčič, & Klobučar, 2023). Additionally, AI-enhanced digital forensics can support incident response by correlating disparate events across systems to establish a comprehensive understanding of an attack's scope and impact (Ali, 2022; Rizvi et al., 2022).

As digital forensics continues to evolve, explainable AI (XAI) is emerging as a key area of focus, addressing the need for transparency in AI-driven analyses. XAI can help forensic investigators understand and interpret AI's decisions, making it easier to justify conclusions in legal contexts. This trend aligns with growing regulatory expectations for accountability in forensic findings (Capuano et al., 2022).

Moreover, the development of hybrid AI models that combine rule-based reasoning with ML models offers enhanced detection capabilities, as these models can adapt to evolving cyber threats while preserving interpretable outcomes (Ghillani, 2022; Samtani, Kantarcioglu, & Chen, 2020).

Looking forward, the role of AI in cybersecurity and digital forensics is set to expand with the inclusion of advanced technologies like reinforcement learning and quantum computing. These technologies promise to provide substantial computational power and novel approaches to data analysis, potentially transforming areas like cryptography, threat prediction, and the analysis of encrypted data. Quantum computing, in particular, may revolutionize the ability to break complex encryption, thereby reshaping the landscape of digital forensic investigations and cybersecurity defenses (Nair, Deshmukh, & Tyagi, 2024; Murphy, 2022).

Incorporating AI into blockchain technologies for secure timestamping and data integrity verification is another promising direction. Blockchain can provide tamper-proof records of forensic data, offering an additional layer of reliability and security for forensic processes (Zangana, 2024; Bonfanti, 2022). With AI's expanding role, continued interdisciplinary research is essential to address new challenges, such as ethical considerations, bias in algorithms, and privacy concerns, which can complicate the implementation of AI-based tools in cybersecurity and forensics (Du et al., 2020; Ukwen & Karabatak, 2021).

In conclusion, as cybersecurity threats evolve, the integration of AI in both preventive and investigative capacities will likely continue to grow, enabling more resilient and adaptable security frameworks. The future of AI in cybersecurity and forensics is thus poised for substantial innovation, as researchers and practitioners work to refine and expand its applications to address emerging cyber challenges effectively (Hayes & Kyobe, 2020; Montasari, 2023).

9. CONCLUSION

The integration of artificial intelligence in cybersecurity and digital forensics is transformative, bringing unprecedented capabilities to address the complexities and challenges of modern cyber threats. As cyberattacks evolve, traditional defense mechanisms struggle to keep up with their scale and sophistication. AI-driven techniques, from machine learning to neural networks, provide a promising countermeasure, enabling faster detection, real-time response, and predictive analysis. However, the journey towards fully realizing AI's potential in these fields is fraught with challenges, including issues related to data privacy, interpretability, and the need for extensive, labeled data to train AI models effectively (Tyagi et al., 2024; Jarrett & Choo, 2021).

With its ability to uncover hidden patterns and perform sophisticated data analysis, AI enhances cyber forensics by supporting automated detection and helping to track down perpetrators more efficiently. This advancement reduces the manual burden on forensic investigators and boosts the accuracy of findings, thus fostering a safer digital environment. Nonetheless, as AI assumes a more critical role, the balance between automation and human oversight becomes essential to ensure reliability and accountability in forensic practices (Dunsin et al., 2024; Moustafa, 2022). The deployment of explainable AI is gaining traction, offering transparency in automated decision-making and building trust in AI-driven solutions across cybersecurity domains (Capuano et al., 2022; Sikos, 2021).

Furthermore, as we look toward the future, the convergence of AI with emerging technologies, such as blockchain and quantum computing, hints at new possibilities for building resilient cybersecurity infrastructures. These advancements could lead to robust security frameworks that leverage both predictive analytics and decentralized verification mechanisms, enhancing both preventive and reactive capabilities against cyber threats (Zangana & Omar, 2024; Bonfanti, 2022). Despite these prospects, the rapid deployment of AI in cybersecurity also calls for regulatory frameworks and ethical standards to mitigate risks associated with algorithmic biases and misuse of AI technologies in cyber warfare (Omar & Zangana, 2024; Montasari, 2023).

In summary, AI holds the key to a transformative era in cybersecurity and forensics, offering potent tools to address the rapidly evolving threat landscape. Yet, as these technologies advance, a balanced approach combining AI innovation with regulatory prudence and ethical considerations will be crucial. By fostering cross-disciplinary collaboration, investing in ethical AI research, and developing robust AI governance, stakeholders can ensure that AI-driven cybersecurity and forensic solutions remain both effective and trustworthy in safeguarding the digital ecosystem (Huff et al., 2023; Alghamdi, 2021).

REFERENCES

Ahmed Alaa El-Din, E. (2022). Artificial intelligence in forensic science: Invasion or revolution? *Egyptian Society of Clinical Toxicology Journal*, 10(2), 20–32. DOI: 10.21608/esctj.2022.158178.1012

Al-Hajri, S. M., Al-Thonayan, Z. J., Alqattan, M. M., Alalyani, N. A., Alali, N. D., & Alnaim, N. (2023). Maximizing the Potential of Artificial Intelligence in Digital Forensics Investigations.

Alghamdi, M. I. (2021). *Digital forensics in cyber security—recent trends, threats, and opportunities*. Cybersecurity Threats with New Perspectives. DOI: 10.5772/intechopen.94452

Ali, A. (2022). Cyber Crime Investigation and Forensics: Leveraging AI and Big Data for More Effective Solutions.

Bonfanti, M. E. (2022). *Artificial intelligence and the offence-defence balance in cyber security. Cyber Security: Socio-Technological Uncertainty and Political Fragmentation*. Routledge.

Capuano, N., Fenza, G., Loia, V., & Stanzione, C. (2022). Explainable artificial intelligence in cybersecurity: A survey. *IEEE Access : Practical Innovations, Open Solutions*, 10, 93575–93600. DOI: 10.1109/ACCESS.2022.3204171

CHILONGO, L., & KM, A. S. (2024). IMPACT OF ARTIFICIAL INTELLIGENCE ON CYBERSECURITY: A CASE OF INTERNET OF THINGS. *i-Manager's Journal on Digital Forensics & Cyber Security (JDF), 2*(1).

Du, X., Hargreaves, C., Sheppard, J., Anda, F., Sayakkara, A., Le-Khac, N. A., & Scanlon, M. (2020, August). SoK: Exploring the state of the art and the future potential of artificial intelligence in digital forensic investigation. In *Proceedings of the 15th international conference on availability, reliability and security* (pp. 1-10). DOI: 10.1145/3407023.3407068

Dunsin, D., Ghanem, M. C., Ouazzane, K., & Vassilev, V. (2024). A comprehensive analysis of the role of artificial intelligence and machine learning in modern digital forensics and incident response. *Forensic Science International Digital Investigation*, 48, 301675. DOI: 10.1016/j.fsidi.2023.301675

Faqir, R. S. (2023). Digital Criminal Investigations in the Era of Artificial Intelligence: A Comprehensive Overview. *International Journal of Cyber Criminology*, 17(2), 77–94.

Ghillani, D. (2022). Deep learning and artificial intelligence framework to improve the cyber security. *Authorea Preprints*. DOI: 10.22541/au.166379475.54266021/v1

Gholami, S., & Omar, M. (2023). Does Synthetic Data Make Large Language Models More Efficient? *arXiv preprint arXiv:2310.07830*.

Gholami, S., & Omar, M. (2024). Can a student large language model perform as well as its teacher? In *Innovations, Securities, and Case Studies Across Healthcare, Business, and Technology* (pp. 122-139). IGI Global. DOI: 10.4018/979-8-3693-1906-2.ch007

Hamza, Y. A., & Omar, M. D. (2013). Cloud computing security: Abuse and nefarious use of cloud computing. *International Journal of Computer Engineering Research*, 3(6), 22–27.

Hassan, S. K., & Ibrahim, A. (2023). The role of artificial intelligence in cyber security and incident response. *International Journal for Electronic Crime Investigation*, 7(2).

Hayes, D., & Kyobe, M. (2020, March). The adoption of automation in cyber forensics. In *2020 Conference on Information Communications Technology and Society (ICTAS)* (pp. 1-6). IEEE. DOI: 10.1109/ICTAS47918.2020.233977

Huff, A. J., Burrell, D. N., Nobles, C., Richardson, K., Wright, J. B., Burton, S. L., Jones, A. J., Springs, D., Omar, M., & Brown-Jackson, K. L. (2023). Management Practices for Mitigating Cybersecurity Threats to Biotechnology Companies, Laboratories, and Healthcare Research Organizations. In *Applied Research Approaches to Technology, Healthcare, and Business* (pp. 1-12). IGI Global.

Iqbal, S., & Alharbi, S. A. (2020). Advancing automation in digital forensic investigations using machine learning forensics. *Digital Forensic Science, 3*.

Jarrett, A., & Choo, K. K. R. (2021). The impact of automation and artificial intelligence on digital forensics. *WIREs Forensic Science*, 3(6), e1418. DOI: 10.1002/wfs2.1418

Jones, R., & Omar, M. (2024). Revolutionizing Cybersecurity: The GPT-2 Enhanced Attack Detection and Defense (GEADD) Method for Zero-Day Threats. *International Journal of Informatics* [INJIISCOM]. *Information System and Computer Engineering*, 5(2), 178–191.

Jones, R., Omar, M., Mohammed, D., Nobles, C., & Dawson, M. (2023). Harnessing the Speed and Accuracy of Machine Learning to Advance Cybersecurity. In *2023 Congress in Computer Science, Computer Engineering, & Applied Computing (CSCE)* (pp. 418-421). IEEE. DOI: 10.1109/CSCE60160.2023.00074

Kaur, R., Gabrijelčič, D., & Klobučar, T. (2023). Artificial intelligence for cybersecurity: Literature review and future research directions. *Information Fusion*, 97, 101804. DOI: 10.1016/j.inffus.2023.101804

Mohammed, D., Omar, M., & Nguyen, V. (2018). Wireless sensor network security: Approaches to detecting and avoiding wormhole attacks. *Journal of Research in Business. Economics and Management*, 10(2), 1860–1864.

Montasari, R. (2023). *Countering cyberterrorism: the confluence of artificial intelligence, cyber forensics and digital policing in US and UK national cybersecurity* (Vol. 101). Springer Nature. DOI: 10.1007/978-3-031-21920-7

Moustafa, N. (2022). *Digital Forensics in the Era of Artificial Intelligence*. CRC Press. DOI: 10.1201/9781003278962

Mughal, A. A. (2019). A comprehensive study of practical techniques and methodologies in incident-based approaches for cyber forensics. *Tensorgate Journal of Sustainable Technology and Infrastructure for Developing Countries*, 2(1), 1–18.

Murphy, J. P. (2022). *Digital Forensic Investigations and Automated and Artificial Intelligence Technologies* (Master's thesis, Utica University).

Nair, M. M., Deshmukh, A., & Tyagi, A. K. (2024). Artificial intelligence for cyber security: Current trends and future challenges. *Automated Secure Computing for Next-Generation Systems*, 83-114.

Nguyen, V., Mohammed, D., Omar, M., & Banisakher, M. (2018). The Effects of the FCC Net Neutrality Repeal on Security and Privacy. [IJHIoT]. *International Journal of Hyperconnectivity and the Internet of Things*, 2(2), 21–29. DOI: 10.4018/IJHIoT.2018070102

Omar, M. (2021). New insights into database security: An effective and integrated approach for applying access control mechanisms and cryptographic concepts in Microsoft Access environments.

Omar, M. (2022). *Machine Learning for Cybersecurity: Innovative Deep Learning Solutions*. Springer Brief. https://link.springer.com/book/978303115

Omar, M. (2024). From Attack to Defense: Strengthening DNN Text Classification Against Adversarial Examples. In *Innovations, Securities, and Case Studies Across Healthcare, Business, and Technology* (pp. 174-195). IGI Global.

Omar, M. (2024). Revolutionizing Malware Detection: A Paradigm Shift Through Optimized Convolutional Neural Networks. In *Innovations, Securities, and Case Studies Across Healthcare, Business, and Technology* (pp. 196-220). IGI Global. DOI: 10.4018/979-8-3693-1906-2.ch011

Omar, M., & Zangana, H. M. (Eds.). (2024). *Redefining Security With Cyber AI.* IGI Global., DOI: 10.4018/979-8-3693-6517-5

Piraianu, A. I., Fulga, A., Musat, C. L., Ciobotaru, O. R., Poalelungi, D. G., Stamate, E., Ciobotaru, O., & Fulga, I. (2023). Enhancing the evidence with algorithms: How artificial intelligence is transforming forensic medicine. *Diagnostics (Basel)*, 13(18), 2992. DOI: 10.3390/diagnostics13182992 PMID: 37761359

Tyagi, A. K., Kumari, S., & Richa. (2024). Artificial Intelligence-Based Cyber Security and Digital Forensics: A Review. *Artificial Intelligence-Enabled Digital Twin for Smart Manufacturing*, 391-419.

Rizvi, S., Scanlon, M., Mcgibney, J., & Sheppard, J. (2022). Application of artificial intelligence to network forensics: Survey, challenges and future directions. *IEEE Access : Practical Innovations, Open Solutions*, 10, 110362–110384. DOI: 10.1109/ACCESS.2022.3214506

Samtani, S., Kantarcioglu, M., & Chen, H. (2020). Trailblazing the artificial intelligence for cybersecurity discipline: A multi-disciplinary research roadmap. [TMIS]. *ACM Transactions on Management Information Systems*, 11(4), 1–19. DOI: 10.1145/3430360

Sikos, L. F. (2021). AI in digital forensics: Ontology engineering for cybercrime investigations. *WIREs Forensic Science*, 3(3), e1394. DOI: 10.1002/wfs2.1394

Stutz, D., de Assis, J. T., Laghari, A. A., Khan, A. A., Andreopoulos, N., Terziev, A., ... & Grata, E. G. (2024). Enhancing Security in Cloud Computing Using Artificial Intelligence (AI). *Applying Artificial Intelligence in Cybersecurity Analytics and Cyber Threat Detection*, 179-220.

Syed, F. M., & ES, F. K. (2024). AI-Driven Forensic Analysis for Cyber Incidents in Healthcare. *International Journal of Machine Learning Research in Cybersecurity and Artificial Intelligence*, 15(1), 473–499.

Tao, F., Akhtar, M. S., & Jiayuan, Z. (2021). The future of artificial intelligence in cybersecurity: A comprehensive survey. *EAI Endorsed Transactions on Creative Technologies*, 8(28), e3–e3. DOI: 10.4108/eai.7-7-2021.170285

Tuli, F. A., & Thaduri, U. R. (2023). The Integration of Artificial Intelligence in Forensic Accounting: A Game-Changer. *Asian Accounting and Auditing Advancement*, 14(1), 12–20.

Ukwen, D. O., & Karabatak, M. (2021, June). Review of NLP-based systems in digital forensics and cybersecurity. In *2021 9th International symposium on digital forensics and security (ISDFS)* (pp. 1-9). IEEE. DOI: 10.1109/ISDFS52919.2021.9486354

Wright, J., Dawson, M. E.Jr, & Omar, M. (2012). Cyber security and mobile threats: The need for antivirus applications for smartphones. *Journal of Information Systems Technology and Planning*, 5(14), 40–60.

Zangana, H. M. (2024). Exploring the Landscape of Website Vulnerability Scanners: A Comprehensive Review and Comparative Analysis. *Redefining Security With Cyber AI*, 111-129.

Zangana, H. M. (2024). Exploring Blockchain-Based Timestamping Tools: A Comprehensive Review. *Redefining Security With Cyber AI*, 92-110.

Zangana, H. M., Mohammed, A. K., Sallow, A. B., & Sallow, Z. B. (2024). Cybernetic Deception: Unraveling the Layers of Email Phishing Threats. [INJURATECH]. *International Journal of Research and Applied Technology*, 4(1), 35–47.

Zangana, H. M., & Omar, M. (2020). Threats, Attacks, and Mitigations of Smartphone Security. *Academic Journal of Nawroz University*, 9(4), 324–332. DOI: 10.25007/ajnu.v9n4a989

Zangana, H. M., Omar, M., Al-Karaki, J. N., & Mohammed, D. (2024). Comprehensive Review and Analysis of Network Firewall Rule Analyzers: Enhancing Security Posture and Efficiency. *Redefining Security With Cyber AI*, 15-36.

Zeadally, S., Adi, E., Baig, Z., & Khan, I. A. (2020). Harnessing artificial intelligence capabilities to improve cybersecurity. *IEEE Access : Practical Innovations, Open Solutions*, 8, 23817–23837. DOI: 10.1109/ACCESS.2020.2968045

Chapter 2
The Role of Machine Learning and Deep Learning in Threat Detection

Omar Ali
Embry-Riddle Aeronautical University, USA

ABSTRACT

In an increasingly digital world, the prevalence of cyber threats necessitates advanced solutions for effective threat detection and response. This chapter explores the critical role of machine learning (ML) and deep learning (DL) in enhancing cybersecurity practices. By leveraging algorithms that learn from data, these technologies enable the identification of anomalous patterns and behaviors that signify potential threats. The discussion encompasses various ML and DL techniques, their applications in threat detection, and the challenges faced in implementation. Furthermore, we analyze case studies demonstrating the efficacy of these technologies in real-world scenarios. Ultimately, this chapter underscores the significance of integrating ML and DL into cybersecurity frameworks to improve threat detection capabilities and foster a proactive security posture.

1. INTRODUCTION

The rapid evolution of technology has significantly transformed the landscape of cybersecurity, leading to an increase in the sophistication and frequency of cyber threats. Traditional methods of threat detection often fall short in combating these evolving threats, necessitating the integration of advanced techniques such as Ma-

DOI: 10.4018/979-8-3373-0588-2.ch002

chine Learning (ML) and Deep Learning (DL). These technologies leverage vast amounts of data to identify patterns, predict potential threats, and improve response times, thus enhancing overall security postures.

Machine Learning, a subset of artificial intelligence (AI), involves algorithms that learn from data and make predictions or decisions without explicit programming. By analyzing historical data, ML algorithms can uncover hidden patterns that might indicate a cyber threat. For instance, Tyagi, Kumari, and Richa (2024) emphasize the transformative potential of AI in cybersecurity, outlining its ability to process and analyze data at scales unachievable by human analysts. Similarly, Dunsin et al. (2024) provide a comprehensive analysis of how AI and ML are employed in modern digital forensics and incident response, highlighting their effectiveness in improving the accuracy and speed of threat detection.

Deep Learning, a more advanced branch of ML, utilizes neural networks with multiple layers to analyze complex data structures. This approach has proven particularly effective in areas such as image recognition and natural language processing, making it invaluable for cybersecurity applications. For instance, Ghillani (2022) discusses how deep learning frameworks enhance cybersecurity measures by improving the detection of malicious activities through advanced pattern recognition capabilities.

The increasing complexity of cyber threats, such as advanced persistent threats (APTs) and sophisticated malware, further underscores the necessity for automated threat detection systems. Kaur, Gabrijelčič, and Klobučar (2023) explore future research directions in AI for cybersecurity, emphasizing the need for developing systems capable of real-time analysis and adaptive learning to stay ahead of emerging threats.

Moreover, the integration of AI in digital forensics has led to a paradigm shift in how investigations are conducted. According to Jarrett and Choo (2021), automation and AI enhance digital forensic processes, enabling investigators to sift through vast datasets swiftly and efficiently. This capability not only expedites investigations but also increases the likelihood of identifying and mitigating threats before they escalate.

As organizations increasingly adopt cloud-based services and IoT devices, the attack surface expands, making traditional security measures inadequate. Zangana et al. (2024) discuss the implications of these technological advancements on cybersecurity, highlighting the need for innovative solutions that can adapt to the dynamic threat landscape. Additionally, Hassan and Ibrahim (2023) elaborate on the role of AI in incident response, asserting that ML and DL can streamline detection processes and improve response times to mitigate damage effectively.

To understand the context of cybersecurity, it's crucial to visualize the evolution of cyber threats over time. The following graph illustrates the increasing frequency and sophistication of cyber-attacks, highlighting the necessity for advanced detection techniques like Machine Learning (ML) and Deep Learning (DL).

Figure 1. Cyber threat evolution over time

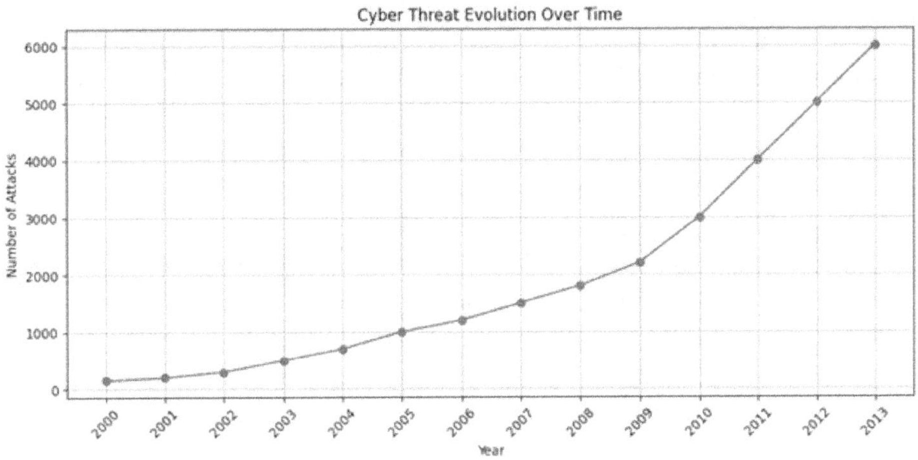

In summary, the convergence of machine learning and deep learning technologies plays a critical role in the future of threat detection and cybersecurity. By harnessing the power of AI, organizations can enhance their defense mechanisms, streamline forensic investigations, and respond to threats more effectively, ensuring a robust security framework in an increasingly complex digital environment.

2. FUNDAMENTAL CONCEPTS OF MACHINE LEARNING AND DEEP LEARNING IN CYBERSECURITY

In recent years, the integration of machine learning (ML) and deep learning (DL) into cybersecurity has revolutionized the way organizations approach threat detection, incident response, and digital forensics. These technologies leverage data-driven techniques to identify patterns and anomalies, providing proactive solutions to complex security challenges. This section outlines the fundamental concepts of ML and DL as they pertain to cybersecurity, exploring their roles, applications, and the emerging trends that shape this dynamic field.

2.1 Understanding Machine Learning in Cybersecurity

Machine learning is a subset of artificial intelligence that enables systems to learn from data and improve their performance over time without being explicitly programmed. In the context of cybersecurity, ML algorithms analyze vast amounts of data to detect suspicious activities, classify threats, and predict potential attacks. The primary types of ML used in cybersecurity include:

1. **Supervised Learning**: This involves training a model on labeled datasets, where the correct output is known. Supervised learning is commonly used for tasks such as spam detection and malware classification. For instance, Tyagi, Kumari, and Richa (2024) highlight how supervised learning models can effectively identify phishing attempts based on historical data.
2. **Unsupervised Learning**: Unlike supervised learning, unsupervised learning works with unlabeled data. It is often employed for anomaly detection, where the model identifies unusual patterns that deviate from the norm. For example, Kaur, Gabrijelčič, and Klobučar (2023) discuss the role of unsupervised learning in identifying zero-day vulnerabilities by analyzing traffic patterns.
3. **Reinforcement Learning**: This type of learning involves training algorithms to make decisions by rewarding desired outcomes. In cybersecurity, reinforcement learning can optimize defense mechanisms by learning from past incident responses (Dunsin et al., 2024).

The effectiveness of ML in cybersecurity lies in its ability to process large datasets rapidly and adapt to new threats. However, challenges such as data quality, feature selection, and the risk of adversarial attacks remain critical areas of focus (Hassan & Ibrahim, 2023).

2.2 The Role of Deep Learning in Cybersecurity

Deep learning, a more advanced subset of ML, utilizes neural networks with multiple layers to model complex patterns in data. This capability makes deep learning particularly effective in handling unstructured data, such as images and text, which are increasingly relevant in cybersecurity. Key applications of deep learning in cybersecurity include:

1. **Intrusion Detection Systems (IDS)**: Deep learning models can analyze network traffic to identify anomalies indicative of cyber intrusions. Moustafa (2022) emphasizes the advantages of deep learning in enhancing the accuracy and speed of IDS compared to traditional methods.
2. **Malware Analysis**: Deep learning algorithms can classify malware by learning from previous samples, effectively recognizing new strains even when they exhibit minor variations (Rizvi et al., 2022). This is crucial for developing robust anti-malware solutions that can keep pace with evolving threats.

3. **Digital Forensics**: As highlighted by Jarrett and Choo (2021), deep learning plays a significant role in digital forensics by automating the analysis of digital evidence, thereby streamlining investigations and improving the accuracy of findings. Tools powered by deep learning can sift through vast amounts of data, identifying relevant information more efficiently than human analysts.

2.3 Emerging Trends and Future Directions

The convergence of AI, ML, and DL in cybersecurity is driving significant innovations, but it also presents new challenges. For instance, the rise of AI-powered cyber threats necessitates the development of equally sophisticated defense mechanisms. As noted by Zangana and Omar (2020), organizations must stay ahead of adversaries by adopting proactive strategies that leverage AI for both offense and defense.

Moreover, the integration of AI into digital forensics is evolving rapidly, with researchers like Tuli and Thaduri (2023) advocating for a multidisciplinary approach that combines AI with traditional forensic methods. This integration not only enhances the capabilities of forensic investigators but also addresses the increasing complexity of cyber threats.

The need for explainable AI (XAI) in cybersecurity is another significant trend. As cybersecurity professionals seek to understand and trust the decisions made by AI systems, the development of interpretable models becomes essential (Capuano et al., 2022). The ability to explain the reasoning behind AI-driven decisions will foster greater acceptance and implementation of these technologies in critical security contexts.

The integration of various Machine Learning techniques is pivotal in enhancing threat detection capabilities. The chart below categorizes these techniques, illustrating their applications and effectiveness in identifying different types of cyber threats.

Figure 2. Machine learning techniques in cybersecurity

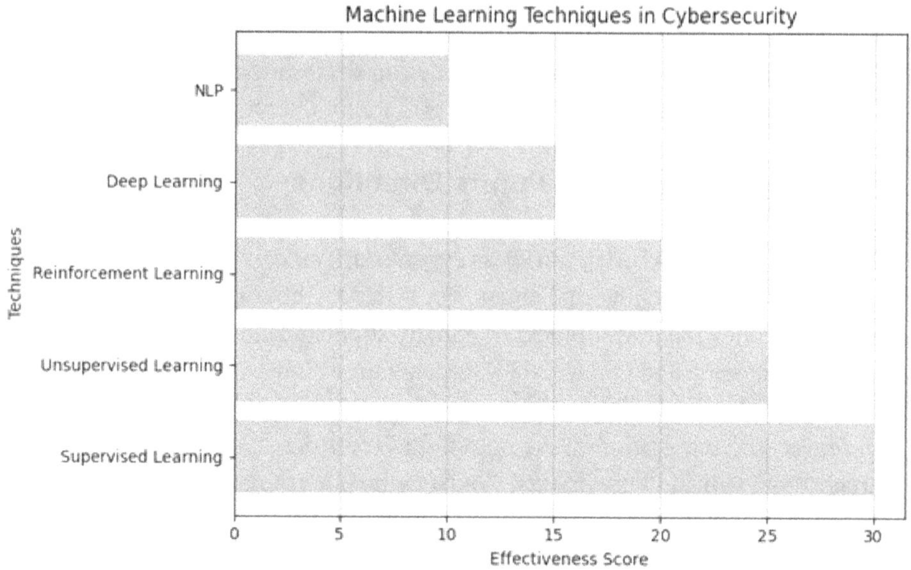

In conclusion, the integration of ML and DL into cybersecurity represents a paradigm shift in how organizations protect their assets and respond to threats. By harnessing the power of these technologies, cybersecurity professionals can enhance their threat detection capabilities, streamline forensic investigations, and ultimately create a more resilient security posture.

3. ML TECHNIQUES FOR THREAT DETECTION

Machine Learning (ML) has emerged as a transformative force in cybersecurity, particularly in threat detection. By analyzing vast amounts of data, ML algorithms can identify patterns and anomalies indicative of cyber threats. The integration of AI and ML techniques in cybersecurity has led to more robust and proactive defense mechanisms.

3.1 Supervised Learning Techniques

Supervised learning, a method where models are trained on labeled datasets, has shown great promise in threat detection. Common supervised learning algorithms used include decision trees, support vector machines (SVM), and neural networks. These algorithms can effectively classify data and predict potential threats based on historical patterns. For instance, Tyagi et al. (2024) discuss the application of supervised learning in identifying cyber threats, emphasizing its efficiency in managing extensive datasets.

3.2 Unsupervised Learning Techniques

Unsupervised learning techniques are equally important in detecting threats, particularly when labeled data is scarce. Algorithms such as clustering and anomaly detection are utilized to identify unusual patterns that may signify a security breach. Hassan and Ibrahim (2023) highlight the role of unsupervised learning in recognizing previously unknown threats, demonstrating how these techniques can uncover hidden anomalies in network traffic.

3.3 Deep Learning Approaches

Deep learning, a subset of ML, employs neural networks with multiple layers to analyze complex datasets. This approach has been particularly effective in threat detection due to its ability to process vast amounts of unstructured data. Moustafa (2022) notes that deep learning can enhance threat detection systems by enabling the identification of sophisticated attacks that traditional methods might overlook. For instance, convolutional neural networks (CNNs) have been applied to analyze network traffic and identify anomalies associated with cyber threats.

3.4 Natural Language Processing (NLP)

Natural Language Processing (NLP) techniques are becoming increasingly relevant in threat detection, especially in analyzing textual data from emails, social media, and other communication channels. NLP can help identify phishing attempts and other social engineering attacks by analyzing the language used in communications. Du et al. (2020) emphasize the potential of NLP in digital forensics, stating that it can significantly enhance the accuracy of threat detection systems by providing insights into the contextual nuances of communication.

3.5 Reinforcement Learning

Reinforcement learning (RL), where models learn through interactions with their environment, has also gained traction in cybersecurity. This technique allows systems to adapt and improve their threat detection capabilities over time based on feedback. The dynamic nature of cyber threats makes RL particularly valuable, as it can continuously refine its strategies to counter evolving tactics employed by cybercriminals. The integration of RL in threat detection is still in its early stages, but it holds promise for developing adaptive security measures (Samtani et al., 2020).

3.6 Ensemble Methods

Ensemble methods, which combine the predictions from multiple models to improve accuracy, are increasingly used in threat detection systems. These methods can enhance the robustness of detection systems by mitigating the limitations of individual algorithms. Dunsin et al. (2024) discuss how ensemble techniques can be leveraged to increase the reliability of threat detection, offering a comprehensive approach to cybersecurity.

3.7 Summary

The adoption of ML techniques in threat detection marks a significant advancement in the field of cybersecurity. By utilizing supervised and unsupervised learning, deep learning, NLP, reinforcement learning, and ensemble methods, organizations can enhance their defenses against a wide array of cyber threats. The continuous evolution of these technologies, as noted by Kaur et al. (2023), promises to strengthen cybersecurity measures and improve incident response capabilities in an increasingly digital world.

4. DEEP LEARNING TECHNIQUES IN ADVANCED THREAT DETECTION

Deep Learning models have revolutionized threat detection by providing sophisticated methods to analyze vast datasets. The following diagram summarizes the key types of deep learning architectures used in cybersecurity, depicting their unique applications in threat detection.

Figure 3. Deep learning models for threat detection

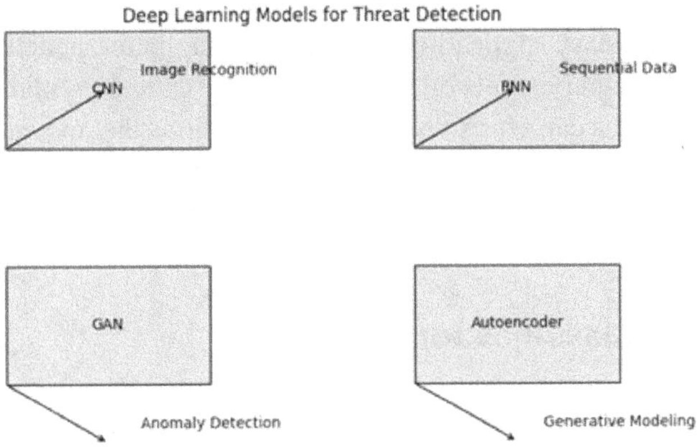

As cyber threats evolve in complexity and scale, traditional security measures often fall short. Deep learning (DL) techniques have emerged as a transformative force in the field of advanced threat detection, providing robust solutions capable of analyzing vast datasets, identifying patterns, and automating responses. This section delves into various deep learning approaches utilized in advanced threat detection, emphasizing their capabilities, challenges, and future prospects.

4.1 Overview of Deep Learning in Cybersecurity

Deep learning, a subset of machine learning, employs artificial neural networks to model and understand complex patterns in large datasets. In the context of cybersecurity, these techniques enable the automated detection of anomalies and potential threats in real-time. The adoption of deep learning algorithms, such as convolutional neural networks (CNNs), recurrent neural networks (RNNs), and generative adversarial networks (GANs), has significantly enhanced the capabilities of threat detection systems (Tyagi et al., 2024).

4.2 Anomaly Detection

One of the primary applications of deep learning in threat detection is anomaly detection. By training models on normal behavior patterns within a network, deep learning algorithms can effectively identify deviations that may indicate a security incident. For instance, Moustafa (2022) discusses the implementation of autoencoders for anomaly detection, which can reconstruct input data and flag discrepancies as potential threats.

4.3 Malware Classification

Deep learning has proven instrumental in the classification of malware. Traditional signature-based methods are increasingly ineffective against polymorphic and metamorphic malware. In contrast, deep learning techniques analyze the features of files and their behavior, enabling more accurate identification of malicious software (Zangana et al., 2024). CNNs are particularly effective in this domain, as they can extract hierarchical features from binary files, allowing for improved detection rates compared to conventional methods (Kaur et al., 2023).

4.4 Network Traffic Analysis

Deep learning algorithms are also applied in the analysis of network traffic to detect suspicious activity. By modeling network behavior using RNNs, cybersecurity systems can monitor real-time data streams and identify patterns indicative of attacks such as Distributed Denial of Service (DDoS) or man-in-the-middle attacks (Jarrett & Choo, 2021). These models can analyze temporal patterns and correlations in data, making them highly effective in identifying sophisticated threats that may evade traditional detection methods.

4.5 Phishing Detection

Phishing attacks remain one of the most prevalent threats in cybersecurity. Utilizing natural language processing (NLP) techniques combined with deep learning, systems can analyze emails and websites for signs of phishing attempts. For example, Ghillani (2022) highlights the effectiveness of deep learning models in analyzing textual content and metadata to classify communications as either legitimate or malicious.

4.6 Incident Response and Automation

The integration of deep learning into incident response systems allows for the automation of threat identification and remediation processes. Hassan and Ibrahim (2023) emphasize that AI-driven systems can analyze incident reports and logs to recommend actions or even execute responses autonomously, thus reducing the time taken to mitigate threats. This level of automation is crucial in environments where rapid response is necessary to prevent data breaches or other significant cyber incidents.

4.7 Challenges and Limitations

Despite the promising applications of deep learning in advanced threat detection, several challenges persist. The need for vast amounts of labeled data for training deep learning models can be a significant hurdle, especially in the context of cybersecurity, where obtaining labeled datasets may be difficult (Dunsin et al., 2024). Additionally, deep learning models can be susceptible to adversarial attacks, where malicious actors manipulate inputs to evade detection systems (Omar & Zangana, 2024).

7.8 Future Directions

Looking ahead, the continued evolution of deep learning in threat detection will likely focus on improving model explainability and robustness. As organizations seek to comply with regulatory standards, developing transparent models that can justify their decisions will be crucial (Capuano et al., 2022). Moreover, hybrid approaches that combine deep learning with traditional cybersecurity measures could enhance detection capabilities while mitigating the risks associated with solely relying on automated systems (Alghamdi, 2021).

In conclusion, deep learning techniques have revolutionized advanced threat detection, offering innovative solutions to combat the ever-evolving landscape of cyber threats. As the field matures, ongoing research and collaboration between cybersecurity professionals and data scientists will be essential in harnessing the full potential of deep learning technologies to safeguard digital assets.

5. FEATURE ENGINEERING AND DATA PREPROCESSING FOR EFFECTIVE DETECTION

In the field of cybersecurity and digital forensics, effective detection of threats and incidents heavily relies on well-structured feature engineering and meticulous data preprocessing. These steps are crucial in transforming raw data into a format that machine learning algorithms can process efficiently, thereby enhancing the accuracy of detection systems. This section outlines the significance of feature engineering and data preprocessing, the methodologies employed, and the impact of artificial intelligence (AI) in these processes.

5.1 Importance of Feature Engineering

Feature engineering is the process of selecting, modifying, or creating features from raw data to improve the performance of machine learning models. Effective feature engineering allows systems to better capture the underlying patterns and anomalies in the data that signify security threats. According to Tyagi, Kumari, and Richa (2024), feature engineering plays a pivotal role in optimizing AI models for cybersecurity applications by allowing for the extraction of relevant characteristics from large datasets.

Moreover, well-defined features can significantly reduce the dimensionality of the data, which not only enhances model performance but also decreases computational costs (Jarrett & Choo, 2021). For instance, transforming continuous data into categorical variables can make it easier for algorithms to interpret patterns associated with different types of attacks. Feature engineering methods often include:

1. **Normalization and Standardization**: Ensuring that features are on a comparable scale, which is essential for distance-based algorithms like k-nearest neighbors (KNN).
2. **Encoding Categorical Variables**: Utilizing techniques such as one-hot encoding or label encoding to convert categorical data into numerical format.
3. **Creating Interaction Features**: Combining existing features to capture relationships that may not be apparent in isolation.

5.2 Data Preprocessing Techniques

Data preprocessing is another critical step in preparing datasets for analysis. It involves cleaning the data and making it suitable for feature extraction. Key techniques in data preprocessing include:

- **Data Cleaning**: Identifying and rectifying errors or inconsistencies in the data, such as missing values, duplicate entries, and outliers. Moustafa (2022) emphasizes that a clean dataset is paramount for effective threat detection in digital forensics.
- **Data Transformation**: Applying mathematical transformations to data, such as logarithmic transformations or polynomial expansions, which can help reveal trends and patterns (Hassan & Ibrahim, 2023).
- **Data Reduction**: Techniques like Principal Component Analysis (PCA) and t-distributed Stochastic Neighbor Embedding (t-SNE) help reduce the volume of data while retaining its essential characteristics, making it easier to analyze (Ghillani, 2022).

5.3 Role of Artificial Intelligence in Feature Engineering and Data Preprocessing

The integration of AI into feature engineering and data preprocessing has revolutionized how cybersecurity professionals approach these tasks. Dunsin et al. (2024) highlight that AI techniques can automate the feature extraction process, reducing the manual effort and potential for human error. For instance, machine learning algorithms can automatically identify and prioritize relevant features from vast datasets, enabling quicker and more accurate detection of threats.

Additionally, AI can enhance the efficiency of data preprocessing. Algorithms trained on large datasets can learn to clean and transform data effectively, as seen in applications involving network forensics (Rizvi et al., 2022). Samtani, Kantarcioglu, and Chen (2020) suggest that employing AI in these preliminary steps can lead to the discovery of novel attack vectors and patterns that traditional methods might overlook.

5.4 Challenges in Feature Engineering and Data Preprocessing

Despite the advancements in feature engineering and data preprocessing, challenges remain. The dynamic nature of cyber threats necessitates continuous adaptation of feature sets and preprocessing methods. As highlighted by Kaur, Gabrijelčič, and Klobučar (2023), the rapid evolution of attack strategies means that features that were once effective may quickly become obsolete, necessitating ongoing research and development efforts.

Furthermore, the increasing complexity of data, particularly with the advent of Internet of Things (IoT) devices and cloud computing, adds layers of difficulty to these processes (Omar & Zangana, 2024). Addressing these challenges requires a collaborative approach, drawing insights from various disciplines to develop robust systems capable of evolving alongside emerging threats.

5.5 Summary

Effective feature engineering and data preprocessing are foundational components of successful threat detection systems in cybersecurity. The integration of AI technologies enhances these processes, allowing for automation and improved accuracy. As the landscape of cyber threats continues to evolve, ongoing research and innovation in these areas will be critical for developing resilient and effective detection mechanisms.

6. REAL-TIME THREAT DETECTION AND RESPONSE WITH ML AND DL

Understanding the workflow of real-time threat detection is essential for organizations to effectively respond to cyber threats. The flowchart below illustrates the key steps involved in the detection and response process, showcasing how ML and DL technologies integrate to enhance security measures.

Figure 4. Real-time threat detection workflow

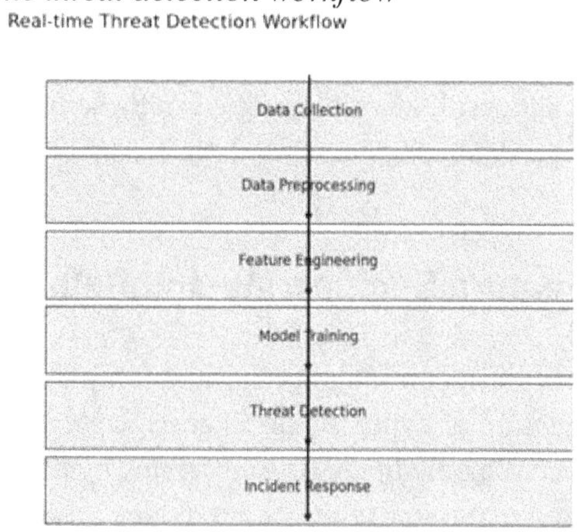

The increasing complexity of cyber threats necessitates advanced methods for threat detection and response. Machine Learning (ML) and Deep Learning (DL) have emerged as critical technologies in enhancing the capabilities of cybersecurity systems, particularly in real-time threat detection and response. By leveraging vast amounts of data, these technologies enable organizations to identify anomalies, predict potential attacks, and automate incident response, thereby improving overall security posture.

6.1. The Role of ML and DL in Threat Detection

Machine Learning algorithms excel in identifying patterns and anomalies within large datasets. Traditional rule-based systems often struggle to keep up with evolving threats. In contrast, ML models can learn from historical data, adapting to new patterns of behavior associated with cyber threats. For instance, Tyagi, Kumari, and Richa (2024) discuss the application of AI in cyber security, highlighting how these systems can continuously learn and improve their detection capabilities.

Deep Learning, a subset of ML, utilizes neural networks with multiple layers to analyze vast amounts of data. It has proven particularly effective in identifying complex patterns that may elude conventional algorithms. In the realm of cybersecurity, DL models can analyze network traffic, user behavior, and system logs to detect signs of potential breaches (Hassan & Ibrahim, 2023). For example, convolutional neural networks (CNNs) are often employed in analyzing network packets for malicious content, while recurrent neural networks (RNNs) can analyze time-series data to identify unusual user behavior.

6.2. Automated Incident Response

The automation of incident response is a significant advantage of integrating ML and DL into cybersecurity frameworks. Automated systems can respond to detected threats much faster than human analysts, minimizing damage and reducing response times. Dunsin et al. (2024) provide a comprehensive analysis of how AI can enhance incident response, emphasizing the importance of real-time data processing and decision-making.

Furthermore, by employing AI-driven solutions, organizations can not only detect and respond to threats but also predict them. Predictive analytics uses historical data to forecast potential future incidents, allowing for preemptive measures. For instance, Zangana and Omar (2020) discuss various smartphone security threats, emphasizing the importance of proactive measures in the evolving landscape of cyber threats.

6.3. Challenges and Future Directions

Despite the benefits, the integration of ML and DL in real-time threat detection and response faces challenges. One significant issue is the potential for false positives, where benign activities are misclassified as threats. This can lead to alarm fatigue among security teams and hinder their effectiveness (Kaur, Gabrijelčič, & Klobučar, 2023). Moreover, adversaries can exploit weaknesses in ML models, leading to adversarial attacks that manipulate model outputs (Jones & Omar, 2024).

To address these challenges, ongoing research is essential. Future directions should focus on developing more robust algorithms capable of handling diverse threat vectors and improving explainability to enhance user trust in automated systems (Capuano et al., 2022). The increasing reliance on AI in cybersecurity calls for a multidisciplinary approach, integrating insights from fields such as digital forensics and behavioral psychology (Samtani, Kantarcioglu, & Chen, 2020).

6.4. Case Studies and Practical Applications

Numerous case studies illustrate the effectiveness of ML and DL in real-time threat detection and response. For example, the application of AI in network forensics has been extensively documented by Rizvi et al. (2022), showcasing how automated systems can efficiently analyze network traffic and identify anomalies indicative of cyber threats. Furthermore, Moustafa (2022) discusses the implementation of AI-driven solutions in digital forensics, emphasizing the role of these technologies in enhancing investigative processes.

6.5. Summary

Real-time threat detection and response through ML and DL represents a transformative approach to cybersecurity. While challenges remain, ongoing advancements in these technologies promise to further enhance the efficacy of security measures. By continuously evolving and integrating these capabilities, organizations can better protect themselves against the ever-growing landscape of cyber threats.

7. CHALLENGES AND LIMITATIONS OF ML AND DL IN THREAT DETECTION

Machine learning (ML) and deep learning (DL) have revolutionized the landscape of cybersecurity by enhancing threat detection capabilities. However, these technologies are not without their challenges and limitations. Understanding these challenges is essential for developing robust cybersecurity solutions that leverage AI effectively.

While ML and DL technologies offer significant advancements in cybersecurity, they also face numerous challenges that can impact their effectiveness. The following chart highlights key challenges, categorizing them based on their influence on threat detection capabilities.

Figure 5. Challenges in ML and DL for cybersecurity

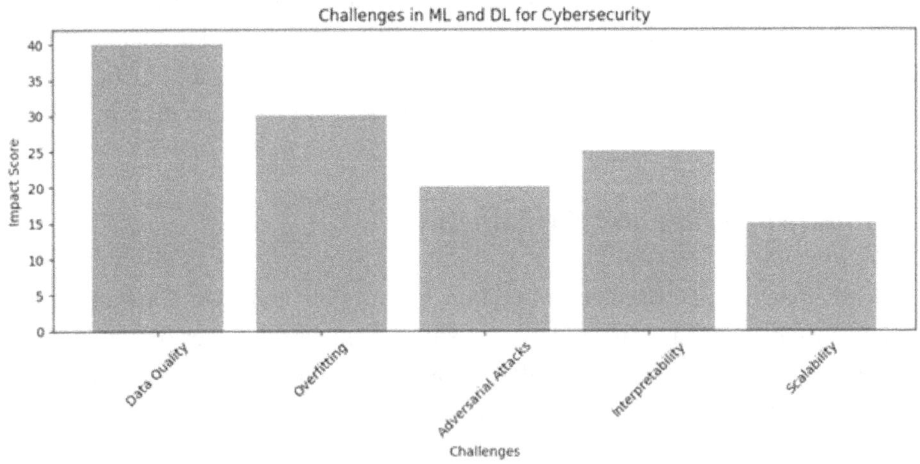

7.1. Data Quality and Availability

One of the primary challenges facing ML and DL in threat detection is the quality and availability of data. These algorithms rely heavily on large datasets for training, and the effectiveness of the models is contingent upon the quality of the input data. In many cases, the datasets may be incomplete, unbalanced, or contain noise, which can lead to inaccurate predictions (Jarrett & Choo, 2021; Tyagi, Kumari, & Richa, 2024). Additionally, in digital forensics, obtaining clean and representative datasets can be particularly difficult, given the sensitive nature of the information and privacy concerns (Hassan & Ibrahim, 2023; Dunsin et al., 2024).

7.2. Overfitting and Generalization Issues

Overfitting is another significant limitation of ML and DL models. These models can become too complex, capturing noise rather than the underlying patterns in the data. As a result, they may perform well on training datasets but poorly in real-world applications, where they encounter unseen data (Kaur, Gabrijelčič, & Klobučar, 2023; Moustafa, 2022). The ability to generalize across different environments and types of threats is crucial for effective threat detection, but overfitting undermines this ability.

7.3. Adversarial Attacks

The susceptibility of ML and DL models to adversarial attacks is a critical concern in cybersecurity. Attackers can manipulate the input data in subtle ways that lead to incorrect classifications, compromising the model's integrity (Omar, 2021; Gholami & Omar, 2023). For instance, slight alterations to a malicious file can evade detection, posing significant risks to security systems reliant on these technologies (Syed & ES, 2024).

7.4. Interpretability and Explainability

Another challenge is the black-box nature of many ML and DL algorithms, which complicates the understanding of how decisions are made. This lack of transparency can hinder trust among cybersecurity professionals and stakeholders (Capuano et al., 2022). In digital forensics, where understanding the rationale behind a decision is critical for legal and operational reasons, the inability to explain model outputs can be a significant limitation (Sikos, 2021; Ghillani, 2022).

7.5. Scalability and Computational Resource Requirements

As organizations scale their operations, the computational demands of ML and DL can become a bottleneck. These algorithms often require significant processing power and memory, making them challenging to deploy in resource-constrained environments (Zangana et al., 2024). The costs associated with acquiring the necessary hardware and software infrastructure can be prohibitive, particularly for smaller organizations (Al-Hajri et al., 2023; Rizvi et al., 2022).

7.6. Dynamic Nature of Cyber Threats

The ever-evolving landscape of cyber threats presents a formidable challenge for ML and DL solutions. Attackers continually adapt their techniques to bypass security measures, which can render previously trained models ineffective (Hassan & Ibrahim, 2023; Montasari, 2023). Regular updates and retraining of models are necessary to keep pace with new threats, which can be resource-intensive and time-consuming.

7.7. Regulatory and Compliance Issues

Finally, compliance with regulations regarding data privacy and security can complicate the implementation of ML and DL in threat detection. Organizations must navigate complex legal landscapes while ensuring their AI systems comply with applicable laws and regulations, which can limit data usage and sharing necessary for training effective models (Omar & Zangana, 2024). Failure to comply with these regulations can lead to severe penalties and damage to reputation.

7.8. Summary

While ML and DL offer significant advancements in threat detection, they also present several challenges that must be addressed. Data quality, overfitting, adversarial attacks, interpretability, scalability, the dynamic nature of threats, and regulatory compliance all pose obstacles that cybersecurity professionals must navigate to harness the full potential of these technologies. Future research and development must focus on mitigating these limitations to enhance the effectiveness of ML and DL in cybersecurity applications.

8. CASE STUDIES: SUCCESSFUL APPLICATIONS OF ML AND DL IN THREAT DETECTION

The rise of cyber threats necessitates innovative approaches to security, particularly through the application of Machine Learning (ML) and Deep Learning (DL) techniques. These technologies enhance threat detection capabilities by enabling real-time analysis and response to emerging security incidents. This section reviews several successful case studies that illustrate the effective integration of ML and DL in cybersecurity, particularly in threat detection, incident response, and digital forensics.

8.1. AI-Driven Cybersecurity Solutions

A. Automation in Digital Forensics

Jarrett and Choo (2021) discuss how automation and artificial intelligence (AI) revolutionize digital forensics. Their research highlights automated tools that use ML algorithms to process large volumes of data, identifying potential threats and anomalies efficiently. For instance, systems that automate the analysis of digital evidence can reduce the time required for investigations, allowing for quicker remediation of incidents.

B. Incident Response in Healthcare

Syed and ES (2024) present a case study on AI-driven forensic analysis in healthcare settings, demonstrating how ML algorithms can detect and respond to cyber incidents more effectively. The study reveals that AI tools significantly enhance the speed and accuracy of incident response by analyzing network traffic for unusual patterns indicative of breaches. This proactive approach mitigates risks associated with data theft and ensures compliance with healthcare regulations.

8.2. Enhanced Threat Detection Mechanisms

A. Network Forensics

Rizvi et al. (2022) conducted a comprehensive survey on the application of AI to network forensics, detailing the challenges and future directions of integrating ML models. Their findings indicate that ML techniques can identify intrusion attempts with high precision by learning from historical data. For example, anomaly detection systems utilizing neural networks have proven successful in flagging unusual patterns that signify potential attacks.

B. Phishing Detection

Zangana et al. (2024) explore the intricacies of cybernetic deception, particularly in email phishing. Their study shows how DL models trained on vast datasets of phishing emails can achieve high detection rates. These models analyze features such as sender reputation, email structure, and linguistic patterns to differentiate between legitimate communications and potential threats. The integration of these models into email systems has substantially reduced successful phishing attempts.

8.3. Digital Forensics Integration

A. AI in Digital Forensics

Moustafa (2022) discusses the role of AI in digital forensics, presenting various tools that leverage ML to enhance forensic investigations. For example, AI-enabled applications can automate the classification of digital evidence, allowing forensic experts to focus on analyzing critical data. This efficiency not only accelerates investigations but also increases the reliability of findings.

B. Cybercrime Investigations

Du et al. (2020) provide a thorough examination of the state of AI in digital forensic investigations. Their work highlights how AI techniques improve the accuracy of digital evidence analysis, particularly in complex cybercrime cases. By employing ML models that adapt to new threats, forensic investigators can uncover deeper insights from digital traces left by cybercriminals.

8.4. Comprehensive Security Strategies

A. Holistic Cybersecurity Framework

The integration of ML and DL into a comprehensive cybersecurity framework is critical for addressing evolving threats. Tyagi et al. (2024) emphasize the importance of adopting AI-based solutions for robust cybersecurity measures. Their study outlines a framework where AI tools are deployed for threat intelligence, allowing organizations to preemptively identify vulnerabilities and strengthen their defenses.

B. AI in Cybersecurity Research

Kaur et al. (2023) conducted a literature review on AI applications in cybersecurity, highlighting the diverse methods employed to enhance threat detection. Their findings suggest that collaborative approaches, where AI systems work alongside human analysts, yield the best results in identifying and mitigating threats. This hybrid model leverages the strengths of both AI and human intuition, fostering more resilient security postures.

8.5. Summary

The case studies outlined in this section illustrate the transformative impact of ML and DL on threat detection and cybersecurity as a whole. By automating processes, improving accuracy in forensic analysis, and providing proactive threat intelligence, these technologies are reshaping how organizations address cyber threats. Continued research and investment in AI-driven solutions will be crucial for staying ahead in the ever-evolving landscape of cybersecurity.

9. FUTURE DIRECTIONS FOR ML AND DL IN THREAT DETECTION

The integration of Machine Learning (ML) and Deep Learning (DL) in threat detection is a rapidly evolving field, with significant implications for cybersecurity and digital forensics. As cyber threats become increasingly sophisticated, leveraging AI technologies offers new strategies for enhancing threat detection capabilities. The future of this domain hinges on several key developments:

9.1. Enhanced Algorithmic Approaches

Future research should focus on developing advanced algorithms that improve the accuracy and efficiency of threat detection systems. Current ML and DL models can be further optimized by employing techniques such as transfer learning and ensemble methods, which can enhance model performance, particularly in low-data environments (Kaur, Gabrijelčič, & Klobučar, 2023). Moreover, integrating reinforcement learning into threat detection frameworks may allow systems to learn from past incidents and adapt dynamically to new threats (Zangana, H. M., 2024).

9.2. Explainable AI

As AI systems are increasingly adopted in critical security applications, the need for transparency and interpretability becomes paramount. Explainable AI (XAI) can facilitate understanding of model decision-making processes, enabling forensic analysts to validate results and trust automated systems (Capuano et al., 2022). Future research should prioritize the development of XAI frameworks within ML and DL models to foster greater accountability and user confidence in AI-driven threat detection systems (Dunsin et al., 2024).

9.3. Integration of Cybersecurity and Digital Forensics

The convergence of cybersecurity and digital forensics is vital for a comprehensive threat response. AI technologies can streamline forensic investigations by automating data analysis and identifying patterns indicative of malicious activity (Moustafa, 2022). Collaborating with forensic experts to refine ML algorithms can enhance the contextual understanding of cyber incidents, leading to more effective incident responses (Hassan & Ibrahim, 2023).

9.4. Adapting to Emerging Threat Landscapes

As cybercriminals evolve their tactics, it is crucial that ML and DL models are trained on diverse and up-to-date datasets reflective of current threat landscapes (Rizvi et al., 2022). Ongoing research should explore the implications of new attack vectors, such as those targeting IoT devices and critical infrastructure, ensuring that threat detection models remain relevant and robust against emerging risks (Ali, 2022). Continuous model retraining and adaptation to include the latest threat intelligence will be necessary to maintain the efficacy of these systems (Nair, Deshmukh, & Tyagi, 2024).

9.5. Ethical Considerations and Bias Mitigation

As AI systems are integrated into security frameworks, ethical considerations surrounding bias in ML algorithms must be addressed. There is a pressing need for research aimed at identifying and mitigating biases that could impact the fairness and effectiveness of threat detection systems (Omar, 2024). Establishing ethical guidelines for AI deployment in cybersecurity can help to ensure equitable treatment of all users and reduce potential discrimination (Bonfanti, 2022).

9.6. Collaboration Between Academia and Industry

Partnerships between academic researchers and industry practitioners are essential for advancing ML and DL applications in threat detection. Collaborative initiatives can foster innovation, drive practical applications, and facilitate knowledge transfer between theoretical advancements and real-world implementation (Samtani, Kantarcioglu, & Chen, 2020). Industry insights can guide research priorities, ensuring that academic contributions align with pressing cybersecurity challenges (Jarrett & Choo, 2021).

9.7. Focus on Resilience and Recovery

Future threat detection frameworks should also prioritize resilience and recovery. This involves not only detecting threats but also enabling rapid response and recovery from incidents (Tuli & Thaduri, 2023). Integrating predictive analytics and automated response mechanisms within ML and DL systems can enhance organizational resilience, allowing entities to recover swiftly from cyber incidents (Hayes & Kyobe, 2020).

9.8. Summary

The future of ML and DL in threat detection is promising, but it will require concerted efforts across multiple fronts. By focusing on enhanced algorithms, explainable AI, integration with digital forensics, adaptability to emerging threats, ethical considerations, industry collaboration, and resilience, stakeholders can leverage these technologies to create robust and effective cybersecurity frameworks. As research in this field continues to evolve, embracing these directions will be critical to advancing the capabilities of threat detection systems in the face of increasingly complex cyber threats.

10. CONCLUSION

The integration of machine learning (ML) and deep learning (DL) technologies into threat detection and digital forensics represents a pivotal shift in cybersecurity practices. As cyber threats continue to evolve in complexity and scale, traditional methods of detection and response are increasingly inadequate. The advanced capabilities of ML and DL enable organizations to not only improve the accuracy and speed of threat detection but also to automate and streamline the forensic analysis process. This evolution is crucial in addressing the rapidly changing landscape of cyber threats, where timely and precise incident response is essential.

The research has highlighted several promising directions for future developments in this field. For instance, the automation of digital forensic investigations, supported by AI algorithms, can significantly enhance the efficiency of data collection and analysis (Jarrett & Choo, 2021; Dunsin et al., 2024). Furthermore, the application of AI in analyzing vast amounts of data allows for more effective identification of anomalous behavior, leading to quicker and more effective responses to potential security incidents (Hassan & Ibrahim, 2023). This is particularly relevant in sectors like healthcare and financial services, where the repercussions of cyber incidents can be particularly severe.

Despite the potential benefits, challenges remain in the widespread adoption of these technologies. Issues related to data privacy, algorithmic bias, and the need for explainable AI solutions are pressing concerns that must be addressed to ensure the responsible deployment of AI in cybersecurity (Capuano et al., 2022; Kaur et al., 2023). Moreover, continuous advancements in the sophistication of cyber threats necessitate ongoing research and development to enhance the effectiveness of ML and DL models in threat detection (Nair et al., 2024; Tyagi et al., 2024).

In conclusion, the synergy between ML, DL, and digital forensics offers a promising avenue for bolstering cybersecurity measures. As organizations continue to embrace these technologies, collaborative efforts between academia, industry, and regulatory bodies will be essential to establish best practices, mitigate risks, and ultimately create a safer digital environment. The future of cybersecurity will undoubtedly be shaped by the innovative applications of AI, paving the way for more resilient and adaptive security frameworks.

REFERENCES

Ahmed Alaa El-Din, E. (2022). Artificial intelligence in forensic science: Invasion or revolution? *Egyptian Society of Clinical Toxicology Journal*, 10(2), 20–32. DOI: 10.21608/esctj.2022.158178.1012

Al-Hajri, S. M., Al-Thonayan, Z. J., Alqattan, M. M., Alalyani, N. A., Alali, N. D., & Alnaim, N. (2023). Maximizing the Potential of Artificial Intelligence in Digital Forensics Investigations.

Alghamdi, M. I. (2021). *Digital forensics in cyber security—recent trends, threats, and opportunities*. Cybersecurity Threats with New Perspectives. DOI: 10.5772/intechopen.94452

Ali, A. (2022). Cyber Crime Investigation and Forensics: Leveraging AI and Big Data for More Effective Solutions.

Bonfanti, M. E. (2022). *Artificial intelligence and the offence-defence balance in cyber security. Cyber Security: Socio-Technological Uncertainty and Political Fragmentation*. Routledge.

Capuano, N., Fenza, G., Loia, V., & Stanzione, C. (2022). Explainable artificial intelligence in cybersecurity: A survey. *IEEE Access : Practical Innovations, Open Solutions*, 10, 93575–93600. DOI: 10.1109/ACCESS.2022.3204171

CHILONGO, L., & KM, A. S. (2024). IMPACT OF ARTIFICIAL INTELLIGENCE ON CYBERSECURITY: A CASE OF INTERNET OF THINGS. *i-Manager's Journal on Digital Forensics & Cyber Security (JDF), 2*(1).

Du, X., Hargreaves, C., Sheppard, J., Anda, F., Sayakkara, A., Le-Khac, N. A., & Scanlon, M. (2020, August). SoK: Exploring the state of the art and the future potential of artificial intelligence in digital forensic investigation. In *Proceedings of the 15th international conference on availability, reliability and security* (pp. 1-10). DOI: 10.1145/3407023.3407068

Dunsin, D., Ghanem, M. C., Ouazzane, K., & Vassilev, V. (2024). A comprehensive analysis of the role of artificial intelligence and machine learning in modern digital forensics and incident response. *Forensic Science International Digital Investigation*, 48, 301675. DOI: 10.1016/j.fsidi.2023.301675

Faqir, R. S. (2023). Digital Criminal Investigations in the Era of Artificial Intelligence: A Comprehensive Overview. *International Journal of Cyber Criminology*, 17(2), 77–94.

Ghillani, D. (2022). Deep learning and artificial intelligence framework to improve the cyber security. *Authorea Preprints*. DOI: 10.22541/au.166379475.54266021/v1

Gholami, S., & Omar, M. (2023). Does Synthetic Data Make Large Language Models More Efficient? *arXiv preprint arXiv:2310.07830.*

Gholami, S., & Omar, M. (2024). Can a student large language model perform as well as its teacher? In *Innovations, Securities, and Case Studies Across Healthcare, Business, and Technology* (pp. 122-139). IGI Global. DOI: 10.4018/979-8-3693-1906-2.ch007

Hamza, Y. A., & Omar, M. D. (2013). Cloud computing security: Abuse and nefarious use of cloud computing. *International Journal of Computer Engineering Research*, 3(6), 22–27.

Hassan, S. K., & Ibrahim, A. (2023). The role of artificial intelligence in cyber security and incident response. *International Journal for Electronic Crime Investigation*, 7(2).

Hayes, D., & Kyobe, M. (2020, March). The adoption of automation in cyber forensics. In *2020 Conference on Information Communications Technology and Society (ICTAS)* (pp. 1-6). IEEE. DOI: 10.1109/ICTAS47918.2020.233977

Huff, A. J., Burrell, D. N., Nobles, C., Richardson, K., Wright, J. B., Burton, S. L., Jones, A. J., Springs, D., Omar, M., & Brown-Jackson, K. L. (2023). Management Practices for Mitigating Cybersecurity Threats to Biotechnology Companies, Laboratories, and Healthcare Research Organizations. In *Applied Research Approaches to Technology, Healthcare, and Business* (pp. 1-12). IGI Global.

Iqbal, S., & Alharbi, S. A. (2020). Advancing automation in digital forensic investigations using machine learning forensics. *Digital Forensic Science, 3.*

Jarrett, A., & Choo, K. K. R. (2021). The impact of automation and artificial intelligence on digital forensics. *WIREs Forensic Science*, 3(6), e1418. DOI: 10.1002/wfs2.1418

Jones, R., & Omar, M. (2024). Revolutionizing Cybersecurity: The GPT-2 Enhanced Attack Detection and Defense (GEADD) Method for Zero-Day Threats. *International Journal of Informatics* [INJIISCOM]. *Information System and Computer Engineering*, 5(2), 178–191.

Jones, R., Omar, M., Mohammed, D., Nobles, C., & Dawson, M. (2023). Harnessing the Speed and Accuracy of Machine Learning to Advance Cybersecurity. In *2023 Congress in Computer Science, Computer Engineering, & Applied Computing (CSCE)* (pp. 418-421). IEEE. DOI: 10.1109/CSCE60160.2023.00074

Kaur, R., Gabrijelčič, D., & Klobučar, T. (2023). Artificial intelligence for cybersecurity: Literature review and future research directions. *Information Fusion*, 97, 101804. DOI: 10.1016/j.inffus.2023.101804

Mohammed, D., Omar, M., & Nguyen, V. (2018). Wireless sensor network security: Approaches to detecting and avoiding wormhole attacks. *Journal of Research in Business. Economics and Management*, 10(2), 1860–1864.

Montasari, R. (2023). *Countering cyberterrorism: the confluence of artificial intelligence, cyber forensics and digital policing in US and UK national cybersecurity* (Vol. 101). Springer Nature. DOI: 10.1007/978-3-031-21920-7

Moustafa, N. (2022). *Digital Forensics in the Era of Artificial Intelligence*. CRC Press. DOI: 10.1201/9781003278962

Mughal, A. A. (2019). A comprehensive study of practical techniques and methodologies in incident-based approaches for cyber forensics. *Tensorgate Journal of Sustainable Technology and Infrastructure for Developing Countries*, 2(1), 1–18.

Murphy, J. P. (2022). *Digital Forensic Investigations and Automated and Artificial Intelligence Technologies* (Master's thesis, Utica University).

Nair, M. M., Deshmukh, A., & Tyagi, A. K. (2024). Artificial intelligence for cyber security: Current trends and future challenges. *Automated Secure Computing for Next-Generation Systems*, 83-114.

Nguyen, V., Mohammed, D., Omar, M., & Banisakher, M. (2018). The Effects of the FCC Net Neutrality Repeal on Security and Privacy. [IJHIoT]. *International Journal of Hyperconnectivity and the Internet of Things*, 2(2), 21–29. DOI: 10.4018/IJHIoT.2018070102

Omar, M. (2021). New insights into database security: An effective and integrated approach for applying access control mechanisms and cryptographic concepts in Microsoft Access environments.

Omar, M. (2022). *Machine Learning for Cybersecurity: Innovative Deep Learning Solutions*. Springer Brief. https://link.springer.com/book/978303115

Omar, M. (2024). From Attack to Defense: Strengthening DNN Text Classification Against Adversarial Examples. In *Innovations, Securities, and Case Studies Across Healthcare, Business, and Technology* (pp. 174-195). IGI Global.

Omar, M. (2024). Revolutionizing Malware Detection: A Paradigm Shift Through Optimized Convolutional Neural Networks. In *Innovations, Securities, and Case Studies Across Healthcare, Business, and Technology* (pp. 196-220). IGI Global. DOI: 10.4018/979-8-3693-1906-2.ch011

Omar, M., & Zangana, H. M. (Eds.). (2024). *Redefining Security With Cyber AI.* IGI Global., DOI: 10.4018/979-8-3693-6517-5

Piraianu, A. I., Fulga, A., Musat, C. L., Ciobotaru, O. R., Poalelungi, D. G., Stamate, E., Ciobotaru, O., & Fulga, I. (2023). Enhancing the evidence with algorithms: How artificial intelligence is transforming forensic medicine. *Diagnostics (Basel)*, 13(18), 2992. DOI: 10.3390/diagnostics13182992 PMID: 37761359

Tyagi, A. K., Kumari, S., & Richa. (2024). Artificial Intelligence-Based Cyber Security and Digital Forensics: A Review. *Artificial Intelligence-Enabled Digital Twin for Smart Manufacturing*, 391-419.

Rizvi, S., Scanlon, M., Mcgibney, J., & Sheppard, J. (2022). Application of artificial intelligence to network forensics: Survey, challenges and future directions. *IEEE Access : Practical Innovations, Open Solutions*, 10, 110362–110384. DOI: 10.1109/ACCESS.2022.3214506

Samtani, S., Kantarcioglu, M., & Chen, H. (2020). Trailblazing the artificial intelligence for cybersecurity discipline: A multi-disciplinary research roadmap. [TMIS]. *ACM Transactions on Management Information Systems*, 11(4), 1–19. DOI: 10.1145/3430360

Sikos, L. F. (2021). AI in digital forensics: Ontology engineering for cybercrime investigations. *WIREs Forensic Science*, 3(3), e1394. DOI: 10.1002/wfs2.1394

Stutz, D., de Assis, J. T., Laghari, A. A., Khan, A. A., Andreopoulos, N., Terziev, A., ... & Grata, E. G. (2024). Enhancing Security in Cloud Computing Using Artificial Intelligence (AI). *Applying Artificial Intelligence in Cybersecurity Analytics and Cyber Threat Detection*, 179-220.

Syed, F. M., & ES, F. K. (2024). AI-Driven Forensic Analysis for Cyber Incidents in Healthcare. *International Journal of Machine Learning Research in Cybersecurity and Artificial Intelligence*, 15(1), 473–499.

Tao, F., Akhtar, M. S., & Jiayuan, Z. (2021). The future of artificial intelligence in cybersecurity: A comprehensive survey. *EAI Endorsed Transactions on Creative Technologies*, 8(28), e3–e3. DOI: 10.4108/eai.7-7-2021.170285

Tuli, F. A., & Thaduri, U. R. (2023). The Integration of Artificial Intelligence in Forensic Accounting: A Game-Changer. *Asian Accounting and Auditing Advancement*, 14(1), 12–20.

Ukwen, D. O., & Karabatak, M. (2021, June). Review of NLP-based systems in digital forensics and cybersecurity. In *2021 9th International symposium on digital forensics and security (ISDFS)* (pp. 1-9). IEEE. DOI: 10.1109/ISDFS52919.2021.9486354

Wright, J., Dawson, M. E.Jr, & Omar, M. (2012). Cyber security and mobile threats: The need for antivirus applications for smartphones. *Journal of Information Systems Technology and Planning*, 5(14), 40–60.

Zangana, H. M. (2024). Exploring the Landscape of Website Vulnerability Scanners: A Comprehensive Review and Comparative Analysis. *Redefining Security With Cyber AI*, 111-129.

Zangana, H. M. (2024). Exploring Blockchain-Based Timestamping Tools: A Comprehensive Review. *Redefining Security With Cyber AI*, 92-110.

Zangana, H. M., Mohammed, A. K., Sallow, A. B., & Sallow, Z. B. (2024). Cybernetic Deception: Unraveling the Layers of Email Phishing Threats. [INJURATECH]. *International Journal of Research and Applied Technology*, 4(1), 35–47.

Zangana, H. M., & Omar, M. (2020). Threats, Attacks, and Mitigations of Smartphone Security. *Academic Journal of Nawroz University*, 9(4), 324–332. DOI: 10.25007/ajnu.v9n4a989

Zangana, H. M., Omar, M., Al-Karaki, J. N., & Mohammed, D. (2024). Comprehensive Review and Analysis of Network Firewall Rule Analyzers: Enhancing Security Posture and Efficiency. *Redefining Security With Cyber AI*, 15-36.

Zeadally, S., Adi, E., Baig, Z., & Khan, I. A. (2020). Harnessing artificial intelligence capabilities to improve cybersecurity. *IEEE Access : Practical Innovations, Open Solutions*, 8, 23817–23837. DOI: 10.1109/ACCESS.2020.2968045

Chapter 3
Using Natural Language Processing (NLP) for Phishing and Spam Detection

Yara Shamoo
https://orcid.org/0009-0004-2459-0807
Saint Leo University, USA

ABSTRACT

With the rapid advancement of digital communication, phishing and spam attacks have become pervasive cyber threats, targeting both individuals and organizations. This chapter explores the application of Natural Language Processing (NLP) in detecting and mitigating these malicious activities. By analyzing linguistic patterns and textual characteristics, NLP techniques can distinguish between legitimate and deceptive content, offering a robust, automated defense mechanism against a wide array of cyber threats. The chapter discusses various NLP-based methods, including text classification, feature extraction, sentiment analysis, and machine learning algorithms, that can effectively identify phishing and spam messages. Real-world case studies and practical implementations are also presented, providing insight into the operational efficacy of NLP in cybersecurity. The chapter concludes with future research directions, addressing the evolving tactics of cybercriminals and the potential of NLP to keep pace with emerging threats.

DOI: 10.4018/979-8-3373-0588-2.ch003

1. INTRODUCTION TO PHISHING AND SPAM DETECTION

Phishing and spam detection are critical components of modern cybersecurity practices, aiming to protect users and systems from malicious attacks disguised as legitimate communication. Phishing refers to deceptive attempts to obtain sensitive information, such as usernames, passwords, or financial details, by masquerading as a trustworthy entity, often through email, social media, or other digital platforms. In contrast, spam includes unsolicited, irrelevant messages typically sent in bulk to promote products or services, which can also contain malicious links or attachments that compromise user security. Both phishing and spam create vulnerabilities in digital ecosystems, exploiting human psychology and system weaknesses to infiltrate personal and corporate networks (Hassan & Ibrahim, 2023; Moustafa, 2022).

The volume of phishing and spam attacks has escalated significantly with the digital transformation, where increased online presence has provided new vectors for cybercriminals. Traditional methods for detecting these threats relied on manual inspection and rule-based systems, which are often inadequate in addressing the evolving sophistication of modern cyber threats (Samtani et al., 2020). As a result, artificial intelligence (AI), particularly natural language processing (NLP), has become instrumental in detecting phishing and spam more effectively. NLP techniques analyze the content and context of messages to distinguish between benign and malicious intent, making it a valuable tool for cybersecurity professionals (Dunsin et al., 2024; Tuli & Thaduri, 2023).

NLP algorithms, supported by machine learning (ML) models, enable automated identification and classification of phishing and spam. By analyzing patterns in text, metadata, and message behavior, NLP-based systems offer robust solutions that reduce human dependency and improve detection accuracy (Capuano et al., 2022; Jarrett & Choo, 2021). For example, supervised learning models trained on large datasets of spam and phishing emails can identify linguistic markers typical of these messages, allowing for faster response and containment of potential threats (Kaur et al., 2023). Moreover, NLP has advanced to recognize complex phishing tactics, such as spear-phishing and whaling, which target specific individuals or high-level executives by exploiting contextual relevance and personalized messages (Rizvi et al., 2022; Zangana et al., 2024).

Despite these advancements, phishing and spam detection through NLP face ongoing challenges, including adversarial attacks where cybercriminals craft messages to bypass detection filters (Bonfanti, 2022; Murphy, 2022). Moreover, the dynamic nature of language and the contextual subtleties in phishing content necessitate continuous training and refinement of NLP models (Omar, 2024). Ethical considerations, such as data privacy and the accuracy of predictive models, also play a crucial role in shaping the development and deployment of NLP-based detection tools (Sikos, 2021; Gholami & Omar, 2024).

The process of using Natural Language Processing (NLP) for phishing and spam detection involves several critical steps that allow systems to differentiate between benign and malicious messages. The following flowchart provides an overview of this NLP-based detection system, illustrating the sequence from data collection to classification. This framework helps visualize the automated workflow, from data preprocessing through advanced machine learning algorithms used to analyze text.

Figure 1. NLP-Based phishing detection system

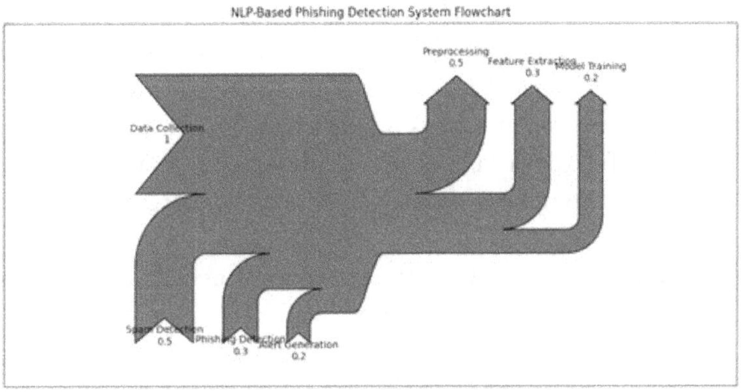

Through a discussion of the foundational principles, recent advancements, and challenges in phishing and spam detection using NLP, this chapter seeks to provide a comprehensive overview of this essential aspect of cybersecurity.

2. FUNDAMENTALS OF NLP IN CYBERSECURITY

Natural Language Processing (NLP) has emerged as a transformative technology in cybersecurity, aiding in the identification, analysis, and mitigation of various security threats. By leveraging the capabilities of NLP, cybersecurity professionals can enhance their ability to detect malicious activities, streamline digital forensic processes, and support incident response protocols. As cyber threats evolve, the application of NLP in areas like threat intelligence, malware analysis, and phishing detection has become vital, offering unique advantages in handling large-scale textual data and making sense of vast cyber environments (Omar, 2022).

NLP tools are particularly beneficial in processing unstructured data from various sources, such as threat intelligence reports, social media feeds, and log files, to identify patterns indicative of potential attacks. For instance, techniques such as sentiment analysis and text classification can aid in flagging malicious content and analyzing the language used by cybercriminals to craft phishing attacks. According to Kaur, Gabrijelčič, and Klobučar (2023), the role of NLP in extracting and analyzing key information from these text sources enhances the early detection of cyber threats, minimizing response time and improving overall resilience.

In digital forensics, NLP techniques are used to expedite the investigation process by enabling more efficient handling of textual evidence, including chat logs, emails, and other forms of communication. Moustafa (2022) emphasizes that AI-powered NLP tools facilitate automated analysis in forensic investigations, thereby reducing the workload on analysts and increasing the accuracy of findings. Similarly, tools that leverage NLP for keyword extraction, entity recognition, and topic modeling are essential for analyzing large datasets in a timely and organized manner (Jarrett & Choo, 2021).

The application of NLP extends to enhancing threat intelligence systems by enabling them to analyze the language used in malware, phishing emails, and social engineering tactics. This capability is crucial in dissecting how attackers manipulate language to deceive victims and bypass traditional security mechanisms (Samtani, Kantarcioglu, & Chen, 2020). Techniques such as semantic analysis and language modeling can reveal insights into attacker behavior, thereby enabling security teams to anticipate future threats and adapt their defenses accordingly (Zeadally et al., 2020).

The integration of NLP in cybersecurity also supports automated alert systems, enhancing incident response by prioritizing and categorizing alerts based on linguistic cues. These systems can parse through millions of data points to identify high-risk incidents, ensuring that security teams can focus on the most critical threats (Tyagi, Kumari, & Richa, 2024). NLP-driven solutions have the potential to revolutionize cybersecurity incident management by providing enhanced situational awareness, aiding in the real-time detection of cyber threats, and facilitating prompt mitigation (Dunsin et al., 2024).

Finally, in the context of emerging technologies, NLP is pivotal for analyzing the vast amounts of data generated by IoT devices, social media platforms, and other sources relevant to cybersecurity. With the rapid adoption of AI and NLP in cyber forensics, future research will likely focus on enhancing these systems to handle increasingly sophisticated threats and adapt to dynamic environments, paving the way for a more proactive approach to cybersecurity (Syed & ES, 2024; Ali, 2022).

3. TYPES OF PHISHING AND SPAM ATTACKS AND THEIR LINGUISTIC CHARACTERISTICS

Phishing and spam attacks are among the most prevalent forms of cyber threats, targeting individuals and organizations through deceptive communications aimed at obtaining sensitive information, disrupting operations, or spreading malware. These attacks are characterized by their ability to manipulate users linguistically, leveraging tactics rooted in psychology and language patterns to exploit trust and incite action. Various forms of phishing attacks include spear phishing, whaling, vishing, smishing, and social media phishing, each with distinct linguistic attributes tailored to their specific targets and intended outcomes.

1. **Spear Phishing**: Spear phishing targets specific individuals within an organization, often using personalized language to increase credibility. Attackers may reference the recipient's position or projects to create a sense of familiarity, making these messages more convincing (Zangana et al., 2024). Research shows that spear phishing often involves formal language and industry-specific jargon to make the email appear legitimate (Tyagi, Kumari, & Richa, 2024). Additionally, psychological cues, such as urgency and authority, are prominent in these messages to prompt a quick response from the target (Moustafa, 2022).
2. **Whaling**: Whaling is a type of spear phishing that targets high-profile individuals, such as executives. Given the high stakes involved, these messages are often meticulously crafted, using formal, authoritative language. Attackers may reference ongoing company operations or even impersonate other high-ranking officials (Du et al., 2020). The linguistic precision in whaling emails is intended to reduce suspicion and leverage the authority figures typically involved in decision-making roles (Hassan & Ibrahim, 2023).
3. **Vishing and Smishing**: Voice phishing (vishing) and SMS phishing (smishing) employ verbal and text communication channels, respectively. Vishing typically uses conversational language to create a sense of immediacy, whereas smishing employs short, directive language meant to evoke a quick response (Montasari, 2023). Both methods rely on emotional triggers, such as fear or urgency, and are increasingly using AI-driven text generation to mirror natural human speech patterns (Jarrett & Choo, 2021).
4. **Social Media Phishing**: With the rise of social media platforms, attackers have adapted their tactics to these environments, crafting messages that appear to come from trusted contacts or businesses. These messages often mimic informal social media language, making them blend seamlessly into the user's regular online interactions. They may include shortened URLs and direct language

to enhance credibility, thus reducing the likelihood of users questioning their authenticity (Samtani, Kantarcioglu, & Chen, 2020).

The linguistic characteristics of phishing attacks are evolving with advancements in AI and natural language processing (NLP). AI tools can analyze language patterns and adjust them to mirror genuine communication styles, making detection increasingly difficult (Ali, 2022). Linguistic analysis has shown that, while phishing messages may vary across attack types, they generally incorporate specific keywords, phrases, and tones designed to bypass users' skepticism and encourage action. These insights are crucial in developing AI-driven cybersecurity tools to counteract such threats effectively (Gholami & Omar, 2023; Rizvi et al., 2022).

Phishing attacks vary widely in their approach and target demographics. The following bar chart highlights several common types of phishing attacks, each with distinct linguistic characteristics that NLP algorithms can identify. These characteristics help NLP-based systems categorize the phishing type, thereby refining detection accuracy.

Figure 2. Different phishing types and their characteristics

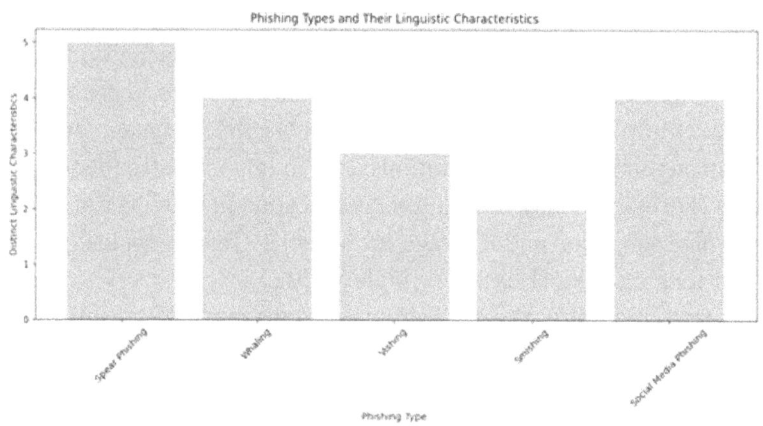

4. NLP TECHNIQUES FOR FEATURE EXTRACTION IN PHISHING AND SPAM DETECTION

Natural Language Processing (NLP) techniques have become pivotal in phishing and spam detection by automating the extraction of relevant linguistic and contextual features from email and web data. Advanced NLP models have streamlined the identification of deceptive language patterns, anomalous syntactic structures, and abnormal sentiment shifts indicative of phishing attempts. According to Tyagi, Kumari, and Richa (2024), NLP's integration with AI can enhance cybersecurity measures, especially for phishing and spam detection, by analyzing language patterns and sentiment shifts often associated with such threats.

One effective approach in NLP-based feature extraction is leveraging transformer models that can understand the syntactic and semantic intricacies of phishing emails (Jarrett & Choo, 2021). For example, transformers can capture unusual wording and grammatical inconsistencies that may be indicative of malicious intent, thus reducing the rate of false positives in spam detection systems. Hassan and Ibrahim (2023) emphasize the role of AI-driven NLP in enhancing the contextual understanding of content, which helps isolate phishing attempts by identifying inconsistencies in tone, grammar, and email structure.

Moreover, techniques such as tokenization and embedding play a crucial role in extracting linguistic features in phishing detection systems. Tokenization allows systems to break down text into manageable units, while embeddings, which convert words into numerical representations, help to capture relational context and word similarities, as suggested by Moustafa (2022). These techniques enable detection algorithms to identify phishing by focusing on subtle language cues and context-based anomalies.

Another relevant NLP application in feature extraction for phishing and spam detection is sentiment analysis, which identifies the emotional undertone of messages to detect potentially suspicious content. As Rizvi et al. (2022) highlight, sentiment analysis can effectively identify the manipulative tones often found in phishing emails, which typically aim to elicit urgency or fear. Techniques such as named entity recognition (NER) also assist in recognizing suspicious entities or names that often appear in phishing attempts (Samtani, Kantarcioglu, & Chen, 2020).

Deep learning models, particularly recurrent neural networks (RNNs) and their derivatives like Long Short-Term Memory (LSTM) networks, have shown effectiveness in detecting sequences or patterns in phishing emails over time (Du et al., 2020). These models are especially useful for tracking language use patterns across multiple messages, thereby identifying subtle variances in tone or content that might go unnoticed in individual messages.

Furthermore, Zangana and Omar (2020) discuss the importance of combining NLP techniques with domain-specific knowledge to enhance detection precision. In cases where phishing messages target specific organizations, NLP systems can be tuned to identify industry-specific terms or jargon that might be used to gain trust fraudulently.

NLP techniques use various feature extraction methods to analyze text for phishing detection. Each method provides unique insights that contribute to the overall classification of suspicious content. The pie chart below shows the most commonly used feature extraction techniques and their relative importance in phishing detection.

Figure 3. Feature extraction techniques in NLP for phishing detection

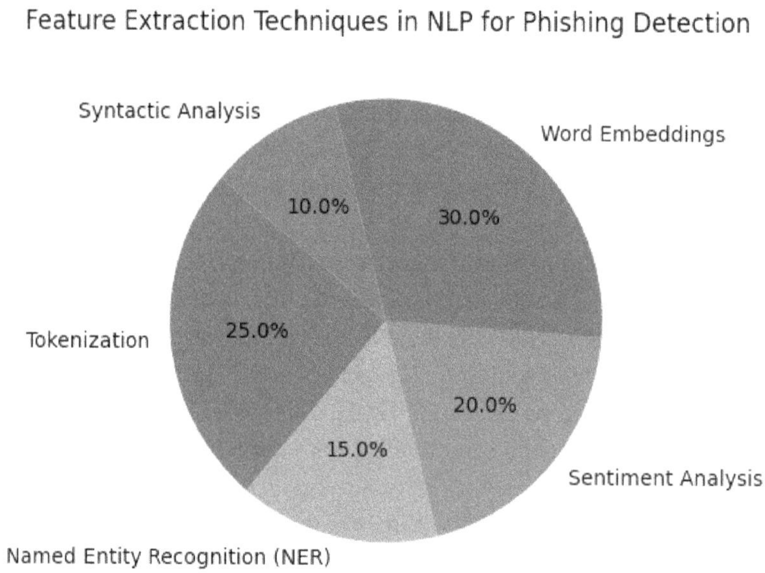

In conclusion, NLP techniques such as tokenization, sentiment analysis, NER, and deep learning-based sequence analysis are instrumental in phishing and spam detection. As automation and AI-driven systems continue to evolve, the role of NLP in extracting linguistic features becomes even more critical in building robust defenses against phishing and spam attacks. With the aid of these advanced NLP techniques, cybersecurity efforts can more effectively counter increasingly sophisticated phishing strategies, enhancing overall security resilience.

5. ML AND NLP APPROACHES FOR PHISHING AND SPAM DETECTION

Phishing and spam detection are crucial components of cybersecurity due to the persistent and evolving nature of social engineering attacks. Machine Learning (ML) and Natural Language Processing (NLP) have been instrumental in creating more resilient detection systems capable of adapting to new threats. By leveraging these advanced techniques, organizations can build systems that not only detect but also mitigate phishing and spam attempts with improved accuracy and speed.

ML models, particularly supervised learning algorithms, are extensively used to classify email content as legitimate or malicious. Techniques like Naive Bayes, Support Vector Machines (SVM), and deep learning methods, such as convolutional and recurrent neural networks, have shown significant success in this domain (Omar, 2024; Zangana et al., 2024). For instance, convolutional neural networks (CNNs) are particularly effective in identifying malicious patterns in images and text, making them suitable for phishing detection in multimedia-rich environments (Dunsin et al., 2024). Additionally, reinforcement learning approaches allow models to continuously improve by learning from real-time interactions, adapting to new phishing methods as they emerge (Moustafa, 2022).

In parallel, NLP techniques are employed to analyze the linguistic patterns in email content. NLP enables the detection of subtle anomalies in language that may indicate a phishing attempt. By using tokenization, sentiment analysis, and syntactic structure analysis, systems can detect the likelihood of malicious intent based on language irregularities (Hassan & Ibrahim, 2023). Text classification methods, powered by NLP, can also analyze the sender's intent, distinguishing phishing emails from legitimate communications through contextual understanding (Tyagi et al., 2024). Techniques such as term frequency-inverse document frequency (TF-IDF) and word embeddings help in understanding the semantic patterns within text data, making it easier to filter out phishing and spam messages effectively (Sikos, 2021).

The integration of ML and NLP in phishing and spam detection offers more robust, scalable solutions, especially when paired with real-time data processing capabilities in cloud environments. For instance, recent developments in federated learning allow organizations to collaborate on phishing detection models without sharing sensitive data, enhancing privacy while improving the model's effectiveness (Jarrett & Choo, 2021; Capuano et al., 2022). The application of adversarial machine learning in this context also helps improve resilience against adaptive attacks, which can attempt to fool detection models by subtly altering phishing content to evade detection (Du et al., 2020).

The effectiveness of machine learning (ML) models in phishing detection can improve over time as models are trained on larger datasets and updated to recognize newer phishing techniques. The following line chart illustrates the increase in accuracy of various ML models used for phishing detection as they undergo successive training cycles.

Figure 4. ML models' accuracy in phishing detection over time

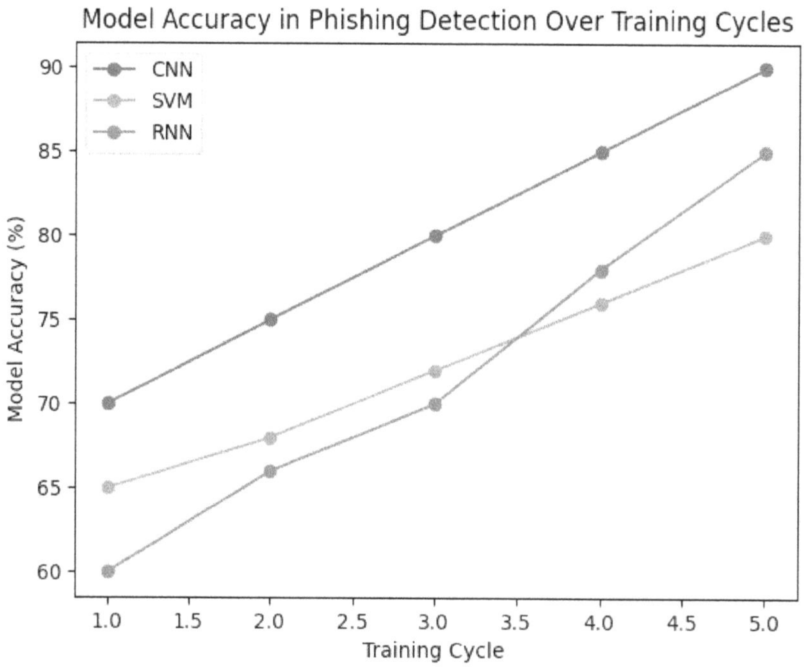

In summary, ML and NLP approaches provide significant advantages in combating phishing and spam. By utilizing these technologies, cybersecurity systems can achieve higher accuracy, adapt to new threats, and offer organizations more effective protection against the rising tide of phishing and spam attacks (Alghamdi, 2021; Bonfanti, 2022).

6. ADVANCED NLP MODELS FOR PHISHING AND SPAM DETECTION

The detection of phishing and spam messages has become increasingly critical as cyber threats evolve in sophistication, particularly in sectors reliant on digital communication. Advanced Natural Language Processing (NLP) models have been instrumental in detecting these threats by analyzing textual patterns, language usage, and behavioral indicators. Integrating NLP with cybersecurity helps to counter phishing attacks, which often exploit social engineering tactics to deceive users into revealing sensitive information.

One of the most promising applications of NLP in cybersecurity is leveraging large language models (LLMs) to analyze and detect subtle language features indicative of phishing or spam. For example, recent advancements in machine learning have facilitated automated methods for identifying phishing emails by recognizing suspicious patterns and anomalous language constructs (Zangana et al., 2024; Tyagi, Kumari, & Richa, 2024). Advanced NLP models can detect inconsistencies in syntax, structure, and tone, which are often hallmarks of fraudulent messages (Samtani, Kantarcioglu, & Chen, 2020; Kaur, Gabrijelčič, & Klobučar, 2023).

Furthermore, techniques such as deep learning and Transformer-based models, which are widely used in NLP, have shown significant potential in enhancing phishing detection systems. For instance, convolutional neural networks (CNNs) have been adapted to recognize patterns in email structures and sender metadata, helping to identify phishing attempts with greater accuracy (Omar, 2024; Bonfanti, 2022). Models that incorporate both linguistic and contextual analyses enable a more comprehensive approach to threat detection, where traditional rule-based methods might fall short (Du et al., 2020; Montasari, 2023).

Another advancement is the use of NLP to detect voice phishing (vishing) attempts by analyzing voice messages. This technology is particularly relevant in sectors like financial services, where attackers frequently use vishing to access customer data. These NLP-driven tools can assess tone, language, and pacing to detect signs of deception, which complements traditional security measures in identifying potential fraud (Murphy, 2022; Moustafa, 2022). Additionally, NLP models have been applied to improve user response by alerting them to phishing indicators, an approach that enhances situational awareness among users (Hassan & Ibrahim, 2023).

Incorporating NLP into a layered security framework aligns with modern cybersecurity strategies. By combining NLP-driven phishing detection with other artificial intelligence (AI)-based tools, organizations can reduce the incidence of successful phishing attacks and secure critical data (Jarrett & Choo, 2021; Zeadally et al., 2020). Enhanced NLP models not only bolster cybersecurity infrastructure but also improve incident response times, supporting a proactive rather than reactive approach to security (Tuli & Thaduri, 2023; Dunsin et al., 2024).

Given the potential of NLP in phishing detection, continued research is necessary to address evolving phishing techniques and ensure that AI-based solutions remain effective against sophisticated attacks (Faqir, 2023; Ali, 2022). The ongoing development of NLP techniques in this field promises further resilience in digital security efforts, making them essential tools in the fight against phishing and spam in cybersecurity.

7. CHALLENGES IN NLP FOR PHISHING AND SPAM DETECTION

Natural Language Processing (NLP) has emerged as a potent tool for identifying phishing and spam content. However, it faces several critical challenges in achieving accuracy and reliability, particularly due to the ever-evolving tactics used by attackers and the complexity of language nuances in malicious content. The primary challenges include the following:

1. **Evolving Language Patterns in Phishing Attacks**

Phishing and spam messages frequently change language patterns, making it difficult for static NLP-based models to keep up. Attackers exploit natural language variations, including grammar and spelling errors, context-specific jargon, and coded language to evade detection. Research by Zangana and Omar (2020) emphasizes that dynamic threats, such as smartphone security attacks, rely on varied linguistic patterns that traditional NLP tools may struggle to capture effectively.

2. **Data Imbalance and Labeling Complexity**

The imbalance in labeled datasets for phishing and non-phishing content poses a considerable challenge. While there is abundant data for benign content, phishing and spam data is often limited, resulting in models that are biased toward recognizing non-malicious content. Hassan and Ibrahim (2023) noted that this imbalance affects AI models' performance in cybersecurity tasks, such as phishing detection, where the scarcity of accurately labeled malicious samples impacts model generalization.

3. **Semantic Ambiguity and Contextual Understanding**

Accurate phishing and spam detection requires models to understand context, which is often challenging due to the ambiguity of language. For instance, seemingly benign phrases could hold malicious intent depending on the context. Tyagi, Kumari, and Richa (2024) discussed the importance of deep contextual comprehension in AI-based cyber forensics, a principle that also applies to NLP-driven phishing detection systems.

4. **Resistance to Adversarial Manipulations**

NLP models are vulnerable to adversarial attacks where slight alterations in text can deceive the model into classifying malicious content as benign. Jones and Omar (2024) highlighted the necessity of hardening AI-driven defenses against adversarial examples, an aspect equally critical in NLP for phishing, where attackers may use slight language modifications to bypass detection systems.

5. **High Computational Costs for Real-Time Detection**

Real-time spam and phishing detection require high computational resources, especially as NLP models become increasingly complex. Efficient resource management is crucial to maintain detection speed without sacrificing accuracy. Rizvi, Scanlon, McGibney, and Sheppard (2022) discussed the challenges of resource-intensive AI applications in digital forensics, which also resonate with real-time phishing detection efforts, where computational costs can hinder practical deployment.

6. **Privacy and Ethical Concerns in Data Collection**

Collecting and processing data for NLP models involves privacy concerns, especially when sensitive information is contained within messages. Privacy-preserving methods are essential but can limit the data available for effective model training. Kaur, Gabrijelčič, and Klobučar (2023) argue that balancing cybersecurity advancements with ethical data practices is a significant challenge, especially when handling user-generated content for phishing detection.

Addressing these challenges requires continuous adaptation of NLP models to account for the variability and evolution in phishing language. Combining NLP with advanced AI techniques, such as explainable AI (Capuano et al., 2022) and synthetic data generation (Gholami & Omar, 2023), may offer promising avenues for improving resilience and efficacy in phishing and spam detection systems.

8. CASE STUDIES: SUCCESSFUL NLP APPLICATIONS IN PHISHING AND SPAM DETECTION

Natural Language Processing (NLP) has proven to be a valuable tool in the field of cybersecurity, specifically in phishing and spam detection, where it can process and interpret vast amounts of textual data to identify malicious content effectively. This section explores real-world applications of NLP for phishing and spam detection, illustrating how these tools enhance security measures and streamline incident response processes.

NLP-based phishing detection systems primarily work by analyzing the language patterns within emails or messages, identifying typical phishing indicators like suspicious URLs, inappropriate requests for personal information, or irregular grammatical structures. As Tyagi, Kumari, and Richa (2024) discuss, these applications are essential for filtering out potential threats before they reach end users, safeguarding both personal and organizational data. This ability is especially relevant in modern cybersecurity frameworks, which rely heavily on automated systems to handle the sheer volume of digital communications (Jarrett & Choo, 2021).

In practical applications, artificial intelligence (AI)-driven NLP systems employ supervised and unsupervised machine learning methods to train on extensive datasets of phishing and spam messages. For example, research by Dunsin et al. (2024) highlights how AI models can learn the characteristics of phishing attempts and apply this knowledge to detect similar patterns in new messages. Additionally, Hassan and Ibrahim (2023) emphasize the importance of these systems in real-time response, enabling organizations to respond rapidly to potential threats.

Beyond detecting phishing content, these systems can also adapt to evolving threat patterns by employing techniques like reinforcement learning. Moustafa (2022) suggests that incorporating dynamic learning methods can significantly improve the accuracy and adaptability of phishing detection models, which is critical given that attackers constantly evolve their strategies to bypass conventional detection systems. Similarly, Zangana, Mohammed, Sallow, and Sallow (2024) point out the value of integrating AI into cybersecurity systems, enabling them to adaptively counter new phishing techniques as they emerge.

Advanced NLP systems also enhance spam detection by filtering out messages that contain unsolicited or malicious content, which otherwise could congest communication channels and expose users to various cyber threats. Samtani, Kantarcioglu, and Chen (2020) discuss how NLP-driven spam filters analyze contextual and semantic clues within emails to differentiate between legitimate and malicious messages effectively. This capability not only reduces the likelihood of successful phishing attempts but also improves the efficiency of communication systems by filtering out non-productive traffic.

The deployment of NLP techniques in phishing and spam detection represents a significant advancement in cybersecurity practices, allowing organizations to respond to threats in near real-time. By continually refining these systems based on incoming data, AI and NLP can help security teams maintain a high level of vigilance against sophisticated phishing attacks and spam campaigns (Du et al., 2020). Future research will likely focus on further integrating NLP with other AI-driven forensic tools, as illustrated by Rizvi et al. (2022), to create more comprehensive and adaptive cybersecurity systems.

In conclusion, NLP applications in phishing and spam detection have transformed how organizations protect their digital assets and users from malicious communications. These technologies continue to advance, offering promising avenues for future cybersecurity strategies as they become more embedded within AI-powered frameworks (Nair, Deshmukh, & Tyagi, 2024). By automating the detection of phishing and spam through NLP, organizations can maintain stronger defenses while streamlining their incident response workflows.

9. FUTURE DIRECTIONS AND EMERGING TRENDS IN NLP FOR THREAT DETECTION

As natural language processing (NLP) continues to evolve, its role in threat detection is increasingly vital. The convergence of NLP with advanced AI methodologies has opened new avenues for detecting cyber threats in real-time and with greater precision. Moving forward, several emerging trends and directions are anticipated to shape this field.

1. **Enhanced Contextual Understanding**

NLP models are advancing in their ability to understand context, allowing for more nuanced threat detection capabilities. Traditional methods relied on keyword-based recognition, which often missed context-sensitive cues in cyber threats. Newer models are leveraging deep contextual embeddings to distinguish between benign and malicious messages (Tyagi, Kumari, & Richa, 2024). These models utilize AI to assess language patterns and identify subtle markers of cyber threats across domains such as email phishing and social engineering attacks (Zangana et al., 2024).

2. **Explainable AI (XAI) in Threat Analysis**

As NLP models become more sophisticated, the need for transparency has led to a focus on explainable AI, particularly in cybersecurity contexts where accountability is essential. By integrating explainable models, cybersecurity professionals can better interpret NLP outputs, enhancing trust and reliability in threat detection (Capuano et al., 2022). This approach not only makes threat analysis more accessible but also aids in improving cybersecurity practices by identifying specific areas of vulnerability.

3. **Real-Time Incident Response and Forensic Analysis**

The integration of NLP in automated incident response is critical for real-time threat mitigation. NLP models are increasingly capable of parsing vast amounts of text from network logs, identifying suspicious activities, and suggesting mitigation steps instantaneously. For example, automated forensic analysis frameworks that utilize NLP for parsing logs and chat records have shown potential in speeding up cyber incident response (Moustafa, 2022; Ali, 2022). This allows organizations to detect and contain threats faster, thereby reducing potential damage (Syed & ES, 2024).

4. **NLP-Driven Behavioral Analytics**

Behavioral analytics using NLP involves assessing an individual's digital behavior patterns to detect anomalies that may indicate a cyber threat. This approach is particularly useful in identifying insider threats and social engineering attacks. By analyzing email content, social media interactions, and other communication forms, NLP-driven behavioral models can flag unusual language that diverges from a user's typical style, thus signaling potential threats (Huff et al., 2023; Du et al., 2020). Such analytics are increasingly critical in industries like finance and healthcare, where sensitive data requires robust protection.

5. **Multilingual Threat Detection**

Cyber threats are a global phenomenon, making multilingual NLP models essential. Future NLP systems will likely expand their multilingual capabilities to detect threats across languages and dialects, which is crucial in today's interconnected world (Kaur, Gabrijelčič, & Klobučar, 2023; Zeadally et al., 2020). This multilingual focus not only improves threat detection but also enhances collaboration in international cybersecurity efforts, especially as cross-border cyber threats increase in frequency and complexity.

6. **Integration with Digital Twins and Simulation Environments**

Digital twin technology, often used for predictive analysis, is beginning to merge with NLP and AI for cybersecurity applications. Digital twins that simulate real-world environments can use NLP models to predict cyber threats and their impacts, testing responses to simulated attacks before they occur in reality (Tuli & Thaduri, 2023; Gholami & Omar, 2024). This predictive capability provides a robust method for preparing against complex threats, particularly in critical infrastructure.

7. **AI-Augmented Digital Forensics**

Future NLP applications in cybersecurity are expected to play a more central role in digital forensics, where AI is already transforming how investigators analyze digital evidence. For instance, NLP can assist in understanding communications within criminal networks or identifying coordinated cyber-attacks, aiding forensic experts in uncovering hidden patterns within vast datasets (Jarrett & Choo, 2021; Alghamdi, 2021). AI-driven NLP also improves the efficiency of examining digital trails and strengthens the overall cybersecurity posture (Montasari, 2023).

In conclusion, the future of NLP in threat detection is characterized by increased contextual understanding, real-time response capabilities, and expanded multilingual support, among other advancements. As NLP models become more sophisticated, they offer promising tools for combating emerging cyber threats and bolstering digital forensics, thereby establishing a proactive approach to cybersecurity. The integration of NLP with AI and other technologies stands to significantly improve threat detection and response, paving the way for a safer digital future.

10. CONCLUSION

In summary, the integration of Natural Language Processing (NLP) within cybersecurity has emerged as a transformative force in enhancing threat detection and incident response. The proliferation of cyber threats necessitates innovative solutions that can analyze vast amounts of data in real time, making NLP an indispensable tool in this landscape. By leveraging techniques such as sentiment analysis, entity recognition, and text classification, organizations can proactively identify and mitigate threats, streamline investigations, and bolster overall security posture.

Moreover, the convergence of AI technologies with NLP paves the way for more robust and adaptive systems capable of evolving with emerging threats. As highlighted by Tyagi, Kumari, and Richa (2024), the synergy between artificial intelligence and digital forensics creates new avenues for addressing complex security challenges. The potential for NLP to enhance the accuracy and efficiency of threat detection mechanisms underscores its critical role in shaping the future of cybersecurity.

Additionally, the ongoing research into the ethical implications and limitations of NLP applications in cybersecurity must be prioritized. As noted by Jarrett and Choo (2021), the reliance on automated systems raises concerns about bias, transparency, and accountability. It is essential to develop frameworks that ensure the responsible use of NLP in cybersecurity, fostering trust and compliance within organizations.

Ultimately, the future of NLP in threat detection will be shaped by continuous advancements in technology and an emphasis on interdisciplinary collaboration. The insights provided by various studies, such as those from Kaur, Gabrijelčič, and Klobučar (2023) and Moustafa (2022), emphasize the need for ongoing exploration of innovative methodologies and techniques to stay ahead of cyber adversaries. By prioritizing research and development in this domain, organizations can not only enhance their cybersecurity measures but also contribute to a more secure digital ecosystem.

In conclusion, embracing the potential of NLP and AI in cybersecurity is crucial for navigating the complexities of modern threats. As we look to the future, it is imperative for stakeholders across industries to collaborate, share knowledge, and innovate in order to build resilient systems capable of addressing the evolving landscape of cyber threats effectively.

REFERENCES

Ahmed Alaa El-Din, E. (2022). Artificial intelligence in forensic science: Invasion or revolution? *Egyptian Society of Clinical Toxicology Journal*, 10(2), 20–32. DOI: 10.21608/esctj.2022.158178.1012

Al-Hajri, S. M., Al-Thonayan, Z. J., Alqattan, M. M., Alalyani, N. A., Alali, N. D., & Alnaim, N. (2023). Maximizing the Potential of Artificial Intelligence in Digital Forensics Investigations.

Alghamdi, M. I. (2021). *Digital forensics in cyber security—recent trends, threats, and opportunities*. Cybersecurity Threats with New Perspectives. DOI: 10.5772/intechopen.94452

Ali, A. (2022). Cyber Crime Investigation and Forensics: Leveraging AI and Big Data for More Effective Solutions.

Bonfanti, M. E. (2022). *Artificial intelligence and the offence-defence balance in cyber security. Cyber Security: Socio-Technological Uncertainty and Political Fragmentation*. Routledge.

Capuano, N., Fenza, G., Loia, V., & Stanzione, C. (2022). Explainable artificial intelligence in cybersecurity: A survey. *IEEE Access : Practical Innovations, Open Solutions*, 10, 93575–93600. DOI: 10.1109/ACCESS.2022.3204171

CHILONGO, L., & KM, A. S. (2024). IMPACT OF ARTIFICIAL INTELLIGENCE ON CYBERSECURITY: A CASE OF INTERNET OF THINGS. *i-Manager's Journal on Digital Forensics & Cyber Security (JDF), 2*(1).

Du, X., Hargreaves, C., Sheppard, J., Anda, F., Sayakkara, A., Le-Khac, N. A., & Scanlon, M. (2020, August). SoK: Exploring the state of the art and the future potential of artificial intelligence in digital forensic investigation. In *Proceedings of the 15th international conference on availability, reliability and security* (pp. 1-10). DOI: 10.1145/3407023.3407068

Dunsin, D., Ghanem, M. C., Ouazzane, K., & Vassilev, V. (2024). A comprehensive analysis of the role of artificial intelligence and machine learning in modern digital forensics and incident response. *Forensic Science International Digital Investigation*, 48, 301675. DOI: 10.1016/j.fsidi.2023.301675

Faqir, R. S. (2023). Digital Criminal Investigations in the Era of Artificial Intelligence: A Comprehensive Overview. *International Journal of Cyber Criminology*, 17(2), 77–94.

Ghillani, D. (2022). Deep learning and artificial intelligence framework to improve the cyber security. *Authorea Preprints*. DOI: 10.22541/au.166379475.54266021/v1

Gholami, S., & Omar, M. (2023). Does Synthetic Data Make Large Language Models More Efficient? *arXiv preprint arXiv:2310.07830.*

Gholami, S., & Omar, M. (2024). Can a student large language model perform as well as its teacher? In *Innovations, Securities, and Case Studies Across Healthcare, Business, and Technology* (pp. 122-139). IGI Global. DOI: 10.4018/979-8-3693-1906-2.ch007

Hamza, Y. A., & Omar, M. D. (2013). Cloud computing security: Abuse and nefarious use of cloud computing. *International Journal of Computer Engineering Research*, 3(6), 22–27.

Hassan, S. K., & Ibrahim, A. (2023). The role of artificial intelligence in cyber security and incident response. *International Journal for Electronic Crime Investigation*, 7(2).

Hayes, D., & Kyobe, M. (2020, March). The adoption of automation in cyber forensics. In *2020 Conference on Information Communications Technology and Society (ICTAS)* (pp. 1-6). IEEE. DOI: 10.1109/ICTAS47918.2020.233977

Huff, A. J., Burrell, D. N., Nobles, C., Richardson, K., Wright, J. B., Burton, S. L., Jones, A. J., Springs, D., Omar, M., & Brown-Jackson, K. L. (2023). Management Practices for Mitigating Cybersecurity Threats to Biotechnology Companies, Laboratories, and Healthcare Research Organizations. In *Applied Research Approaches to Technology, Healthcare, and Business* (pp. 1-12). IGI Global.

Iqbal, S., & Alharbi, S. A. (2020). Advancing automation in digital forensic investigations using machine learning forensics. *Digital Forensic Science, 3.*

Jarrett, A., & Choo, K. K. R. (2021). The impact of automation and artificial intelligence on digital forensics. *WIREs Forensic Science*, 3(6), e1418. DOI: 10.1002/wfs2.1418

Jones, R., & Omar, M. (2024). Revolutionizing Cybersecurity: The GPT-2 Enhanced Attack Detection and Defense (GEADD) Method for Zero-Day Threats. *International Journal of Informatics* [INJIISCOM]. *Information System and Computer Engineering*, 5(2), 178–191.

Jones, R., Omar, M., Mohammed, D., Nobles, C., & Dawson, M. (2023). Harnessing the Speed and Accuracy of Machine Learning to Advance Cybersecurity. In *2023 Congress in Computer Science, Computer Engineering, & Applied Computing (CSCE)* (pp. 418-421). IEEE. DOI: 10.1109/CSCE60160.2023.00074

Kaur, R., Gabrijelčič, D., & Klobučar, T. (2023). Artificial intelligence for cybersecurity: Literature review and future research directions. *Information Fusion*, 97, 101804. DOI: 10.1016/j.inffus.2023.101804

Mohammed, D., Omar, M., & Nguyen, V. (2018). Wireless sensor network security: Approaches to detecting and avoiding wormhole attacks. *Journal of Research in Business. Economics and Management*, 10(2), 1860–1864.

Montasari, R. (2023). *Countering cyberterrorism: the confluence of artificial intelligence, cyber forensics and digital policing in US and UK national cybersecurity* (Vol. 101). Springer Nature. DOI: 10.1007/978-3-031-21920-7

Moustafa, N. (2022). *Digital Forensics in the Era of Artificial Intelligence*. CRC Press. DOI: 10.1201/9781003278962

Mughal, A. A. (2019). A comprehensive study of practical techniques and methodologies in incident-based approaches for cyber forensics. *Tensorgate Journal of Sustainable Technology and Infrastructure for Developing Countries*, 2(1), 1–18.

Murphy, J. P. (2022). *Digital Forensic Investigations and Automated and Artificial Intelligence Technologies* (Master's thesis, Utica University).

Nair, M. M., Deshmukh, A., & Tyagi, A. K. (2024). Artificial intelligence for cyber security: Current trends and future challenges. *Automated Secure Computing for Next-Generation Systems*, 83-114.

Nguyen, V., Mohammed, D., Omar, M., & Banisakher, M. (2018). The Effects of the FCC Net Neutrality Repeal on Security and Privacy. [IJHIoT]. *International Journal of Hyperconnectivity and the Internet of Things*, 2(2), 21–29. DOI: 10.4018/IJHIoT.2018070102

Omar, M. (2021). New insights into database security: An effective and integrated approach for applying access control mechanisms and cryptographic concepts in Microsoft Access environments.

Omar, M. (2022). *Machine Learning for Cybersecurity: Innovative Deep Learning Solutions*. Springer Brief. https://link.springer.com/book/978303115

Omar, M. (2024). From Attack to Defense: Strengthening DNN Text Classification Against Adversarial Examples. In *Innovations, Securities, and Case Studies Across Healthcare, Business, and Technology* (pp. 174-195). IGI Global.

Omar, M. (2024). Revolutionizing Malware Detection: A Paradigm Shift Through Optimized Convolutional Neural Networks. In *Innovations, Securities, and Case Studies Across Healthcare, Business, and Technology* (pp. 196-220). IGI Global. DOI: 10.4018/979-8-3693-1906-2.ch011

Omar, M., & Zangana, H. M. (Eds.). (2024). *Redefining Security With Cyber AI.* IGI Global., DOI: 10.4018/979-8-3693-6517-5

Piraianu, A. I., Fulga, A., Musat, C. L., Ciobotaru, O. R., Poalelungi, D. G., Stamate, E., Ciobotaru, O., & Fulga, I. (2023). Enhancing the evidence with algorithms: How artificial intelligence is transforming forensic medicine. *Diagnostics (Basel)*, 13(18), 2992. DOI: 10.3390/diagnostics13182992 PMID: 37761359

Tyagi, A. K., Kumari, S., & Richa. (2024). Artificial Intelligence-Based Cyber Security and Digital Forensics: A Review. *Artificial Intelligence-Enabled Digital Twin for Smart Manufacturing*, 391-419.

Rizvi, S., Scanlon, M., Mcgibney, J., & Sheppard, J. (2022). Application of artificial intelligence to network forensics: Survey, challenges and future directions. *IEEE Access : Practical Innovations, Open Solutions*, 10, 110362–110384. DOI: 10.1109/ACCESS.2022.3214506

Samtani, S., Kantarcioglu, M., & Chen, H. (2020). Trailblazing the artificial intelligence for cybersecurity discipline: A multi-disciplinary research roadmap. [TMIS]. *ACM Transactions on Management Information Systems*, 11(4), 1–19. DOI: 10.1145/3430360

Sikos, L. F. (2021). AI in digital forensics: Ontology engineering for cybercrime investigations. *WIREs Forensic Science*, 3(3), e1394. DOI: 10.1002/wfs2.1394

Stutz, D., de Assis, J. T., Laghari, A. A., Khan, A. A., Andreopoulos, N., Terziev, A., ... & Grata, E. G. (2024). Enhancing Security in Cloud Computing Using Artificial Intelligence (AI). *Applying Artificial Intelligence in Cybersecurity Analytics and Cyber Threat Detection*, 179-220.

Syed, F. M., & ES, F. K. (2024). AI-Driven Forensic Analysis for Cyber Incidents in Healthcare. *International Journal of Machine Learning Research in Cybersecurity and Artificial Intelligence*, 15(1), 473–499.

Tao, F., Akhtar, M. S., & Jiayuan, Z. (2021). The future of artificial intelligence in cybersecurity: A comprehensive survey. *EAI Endorsed Transactions on Creative Technologies*, 8(28), e3–e3. DOI: 10.4108/eai.7-7-2021.170285

Tuli, F. A., & Thaduri, U. R. (2023). The Integration of Artificial Intelligence in Forensic Accounting: A Game-Changer. *Asian Accounting and Auditing Advancement*, 14(1), 12–20.

Ukwen, D. O., & Karabatak, M. (2021, June). Review of NLP-based systems in digital forensics and cybersecurity. In *2021 9th International symposium on digital forensics and security (ISDFS)* (pp. 1-9). IEEE. DOI: 10.1109/ISDFS52919.2021.9486354

Wright, J., Dawson, M. E.Jr, & Omar, M. (2012). Cyber security and mobile threats: The need for antivirus applications for smartphones. *Journal of Information Systems Technology and Planning*, 5(14), 40–60.

Zangana, H. M. (2024). Exploring the Landscape of Website Vulnerability Scanners: A Comprehensive Review and Comparative Analysis. *Redefining Security With Cyber AI*, 111-129.

Zangana, H. M. (2024). Exploring Blockchain-Based Timestamping Tools: A Comprehensive Review. *Redefining Security With Cyber AI*, 92-110.

Zangana, H. M., Mohammed, A. K., Sallow, A. B., & Sallow, Z. B. (2024). Cybernetic Deception: Unraveling the Layers of Email Phishing Threats. [INJURATECH]. *International Journal of Research and Applied Technology*, 4(1), 35–47.

Zangana, H. M., & Omar, M. (2020). Threats, Attacks, and Mitigations of Smartphone Security. *Academic Journal of Nawroz University*, 9(4), 324–332. DOI: 10.25007/ajnu.v9n4a989

Zangana, H. M., Omar, M., Al-Karaki, J. N., & Mohammed, D. (2024). Comprehensive Review and Analysis of Network Firewall Rule Analyzers: Enhancing Security Posture and Efficiency. *Redefining Security With Cyber AI*, 15-36.

Zeadally, S., Adi, E., Baig, Z., & Khan, I. A. (2020). Harnessing artificial intelligence capabilities to improve cybersecurity. *IEEE Access : Practical Innovations, Open Solutions*, 8, 23817–23837. DOI: 10.1109/ACCESS.2020.2968045

Chapter 4
Network Forensics and Traffic Analysis With Machine Learning

Yara Shamoo
https://orcid.org/0009-0004-2459-0807
Saint Leo University, USA

ABSTRACT

Network forensics plays a crucial role in identifying, monitoring, and analyzing network traffic to uncover malicious activities and provide evidence in cyber incidents. The integration of machine learning techniques into network forensics significantly enhances the ability to detect anomalies, identify patterns, and respond to threats in real-time. This chapter explores the application of machine learning algorithms in network traffic analysis, detailing various methodologies and their effectiveness in distinguishing between legitimate and malicious traffic. We examine case studies that demonstrate the advantages of these techniques over traditional methods, highlighting their potential for improving cybersecurity practices. Additionally, the challenges and future directions in the field of network forensics and traffic analysis using machine learning are discussed, emphasizing the need for continued innovation and adaptation to emerging threats.

1. INTRODUCTION TO NETWORK FORENSICS AND TRAFFIC ANALYSIS

In the rapidly evolving digital landscape, where cyber threats are becoming increasingly sophisticated, the fields of network forensics and traffic analysis have emerged as critical components in the cybersecurity domain. Network forensics

DOI: 10.4018/979-8-3373-0588-2.ch004

involves the capture, recording, and analysis of network packets to understand past events that occurred on a network, whereas traffic analysis focuses on the examination of the patterns and characteristics of data flowing through a network to identify anomalies and potential security incidents. This chapter delves into the integration of artificial intelligence (AI) and machine learning (ML) into network forensics and traffic analysis, showcasing their potential to enhance cybersecurity measures and forensic investigations.

1.1 Definition and Importance of Network Forensics

Network forensics is defined as the process of monitoring and analyzing computer network traffic for the purpose of information gathering, legal evidence collection, or intrusion detection (Dunsin et al., 2024). It plays a pivotal role in identifying security breaches, tracing the source of attacks, and collecting evidence necessary for legal proceedings. The significance of network forensics lies in its ability to provide organizations with insights into malicious activities, enabling timely responses to cyber threats.

The growing reliance on digital communication and the proliferation of internet-enabled devices have exacerbated security challenges. Cybercriminals employ a myriad of techniques, including malware, phishing, and denial-of-service attacks, which necessitate the adoption of robust network forensic techniques to mitigate risks (Hassan & Ibrahim, 2023). By leveraging AI and ML, network forensic investigations can be automated and enhanced, leading to faster and more accurate incident response.

1.2 Traffic Analysis: Techniques and Applications

Traffic analysis is a method used to observe and analyze data packets traversing a network to deduce patterns and behaviors. This process involves the collection of metadata, such as the size of packets, source and destination IP addresses, and transmission protocols. Traffic analysis can be broadly categorized into two types: passive analysis, where data is collected without altering the traffic flow, and active analysis, which may involve injecting data packets into the network (Tyagi, Kumari, & Richa, 2024).

The primary applications of traffic analysis include:

- **Anomaly Detection**: Identifying unusual patterns in network traffic that may indicate malicious activities.
- **Performance Monitoring**: Assessing the quality and speed of network services, allowing for proactive management of resources.

- **User Behavior Analysis**: Understanding user interactions and behavior patterns to detect insider threats or compromised accounts (Rizvi et al., 2022).

The integration of AI techniques into traffic analysis has shown promise in enhancing the efficiency and accuracy of these applications. For instance, machine learning algorithms can be trained to recognize normal traffic patterns, enabling the identification of anomalies in real-time (Jarrett & Choo, 2021).

To better understand the dynamics of network traffic, it is essential to visualize the flow of data packets within a network. The following graph illustrates typical traffic patterns, showcasing both legitimate and malicious activities. This visualization aids in recognizing anomalies and understanding the overall traffic behavior.

Figure 1. Network traffic flow analysis

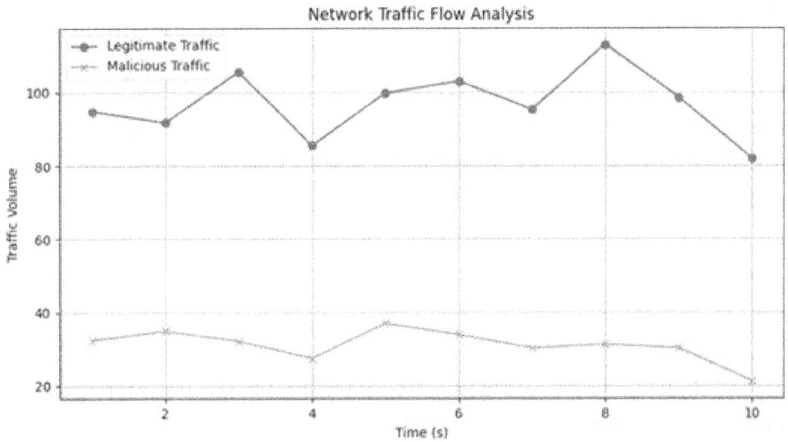

1.3 The Role of Artificial Intelligence in Enhancing Network Forensics and Traffic Analysis

Artificial intelligence has revolutionized various fields, including cybersecurity. In network forensics and traffic analysis, AI can automate complex analytical tasks, enabling security professionals to focus on strategic decision-making rather than routine data processing. AI-driven solutions can analyze vast amounts of network data at unprecedented speeds, leading to quicker identification of threats and more effective incident response (Moustafa, 2022).

The application of AI in network forensics can be seen in several areas:

- **Automated Packet Analysis**: AI systems can process and analyze large volumes of network packets, flagging suspicious activities for further investigation.
- **Predictive Analytics**: Machine learning models can predict potential future attacks based on historical data, allowing organizations to implement preventative measures (Nair, Deshmukh, & Tyagi, 2024).
- **Enhanced Reporting**: AI can generate comprehensive reports detailing network activities, facilitating better communication among stakeholders (Montasari, 2023).

As cyber threats become more sophisticated, the fusion of AI technologies with traditional network forensics and traffic analysis practices will be crucial in maintaining the integrity and security of digital systems.

1.4 Summary

In summary, network forensics and traffic analysis play a fundamental role in safeguarding digital environments against cyber threats. The integration of artificial intelligence and machine learning into these domains promises to enhance the effectiveness of investigations and improve the overall security posture of organizations. As we continue to explore the capabilities of AI in cybersecurity, it is vital to remain aware of the ethical considerations and potential limitations associated with these technologies (Omar & Zangana, 2024). The future of network forensics lies in the innovative convergence of AI techniques that enable proactive threat detection and efficient incident response, ensuring that organizations are well-equipped to confront the challenges of an increasingly digital world.

2. FUNDAMENTAL CONCEPTS OF NETWORK FORENSICS

Network forensics is a critical subfield of digital forensics, focusing on the monitoring, capturing, and analysis of network traffic to investigate security incidents and identify malicious activities. As cyber threats evolve and become more sophisticated, network forensics has gained prominence in both corporate and governmental cybersecurity frameworks. This section outlines fundamental concepts of network forensics, its processes, tools, and its intersection with emerging technologies such as artificial intelligence (AI).

2.1. Definition and Scope of Network Forensics

Network forensics refers to the process of capturing, recording, and analyzing network events in order to discover the source of security attacks and prepare evidence for legal proceedings. It involves the collection and analysis of data packets traveling over networks, enabling investigators to trace malicious activities and understand attack patterns. According to Tyagi, Kumari, and Richa (2024), network forensics plays a vital role in securing systems against unauthorized access and malicious threats by providing insights into the behavioral patterns of cybercriminals.

2.2. Key Processes in Network Forensics

The process of network forensics typically encompasses several stages:

- **Data Collection**: The initial phase involves gathering relevant network data. This can be achieved through various methods such as packet sniffing, flow analysis, and logging network activities (Moustafa, 2022).
- **Data Preservation**: Ensuring the integrity of collected data is crucial. This involves creating exact copies of the data while maintaining its original state to prevent tampering (Rizvi et al., 2022).
- **Data Analysis**: In this phase, forensic analysts utilize various tools and methodologies to examine the captured data for anomalies, unauthorized access, and attack signatures. The analysis may involve reconstructing sessions to understand the timeline of events leading to an incident (Hassan & Ibrahim, 2023).
- **Reporting and Presentation**: Finally, findings are compiled into comprehensive reports that outline the investigation process, analysis results, and recommendations. These reports are essential for legal proceedings and organizational improvements (Du et al., 2020).

2.3. Tools and Techniques

Several tools are employed in network forensics, ranging from open-source software to sophisticated commercial solutions. Some widely used tools include:

- **Wireshark**: A powerful network protocol analyzer that captures and displays packet data. It allows forensic analysts to filter and inspect packets in real-time (Jarrett & Choo, 2021).
- **NetFlow**: Utilized for collecting and analyzing network traffic flow data, enabling identification of patterns and anomalies (Zangana et al., 2024).

- **Snort**: An open-source intrusion detection system (IDS) that analyzes network traffic and generates alerts for suspicious activities (Syed & ES, 2024).

The integration of AI into these tools can significantly enhance their capabilities. As highlighted by Dunsin et al. (2024), AI can assist in identifying patterns and anomalies in vast amounts of data that would be challenging to detect manually.

2.4. Artificial Intelligence in Network Forensics

The convergence of AI and network forensics is transforming how investigations are conducted. AI-driven algorithms can automate the analysis of network traffic, improving detection rates of intrusions and reducing response times. For example, deep learning models can classify traffic patterns and identify potential threats by learning from historical data (Kaur, Gabrijelčič, & Klobučar, 2023).

As noted by Ghillani (2022), AI techniques such as machine learning and natural language processing are paving the way for more effective forensic analyses, enabling proactive measures against cyber threats. This includes not only real-time monitoring but also predictive analytics that forecast potential attack vectors based on emerging trends (Ali, 2022).

2.5. Challenges in Network Forensics

Despite the advancements in tools and methodologies, network forensics faces several challenges:

- **Data Volume**: The sheer amount of network data generated can overwhelm traditional forensic tools. This necessitates the development of more efficient processing and analysis techniques (Montasari, 2023).
- **Encryption**: The widespread use of encryption poses a significant barrier, as it complicates the analysis of network traffic. Investigators often struggle to decipher encrypted data during an investigation (Zangana & Omar, 2020).
- **Legal and Ethical Considerations**: Conducting network forensics raises privacy and legal concerns, particularly regarding data interception and surveillance. Establishing protocols that balance security needs with ethical considerations is vital (Bonfanti, 2022).

2.6. Future Directions

The field of network forensics is rapidly evolving, especially with the integration of AI and machine learning technologies. Future research directions should focus on developing advanced algorithms that can handle large datasets efficiently while maintaining ethical standards. As stated by Ukwen and Karabatak (2021), leveraging AI in digital forensics holds great promise for enhancing the effectiveness of investigations and reducing human error.

In summary, network forensics is an indispensable aspect of cybersecurity that enables organizations to investigate and respond to cyber incidents effectively. By harnessing the power of advanced technologies like AI, network forensics can continue to adapt and evolve, offering improved methods for protecting sensitive data and maintaining the integrity of information systems.

3. MACHINE LEARNING IN TRAFFIC ANALYSIS: AN OVERVIEW

Traffic analysis is an essential component of cybersecurity and digital forensics, as it involves monitoring and analyzing data packets traversing a network to detect malicious activities and anomalies. The integration of machine learning (ML) into traffic analysis enhances the effectiveness and efficiency of traditional methods by leveraging the power of data-driven approaches. This section explores the role of machine learning in traffic analysis, highlighting its applications, methodologies, challenges, and future directions.

3.1 The Role of Machine Learning in Traffic Analysis

Machine learning has emerged as a vital tool in traffic analysis due to its ability to process large volumes of data and identify patterns that may indicate security threats. Unlike conventional methods that rely on predefined rules, ML algorithms can learn from historical data, adapt to new threats, and improve their performance over time. This adaptability is particularly important in the ever-evolving landscape of cyber threats, where attackers continuously refine their techniques to evade detection.

1. **Applications of Machine Learning in Traffic Analysis**

Machine learning techniques are employed in various applications within traffic analysis, including intrusion detection systems (IDS), anomaly detection, and malware classification. For instance, researchers have demonstrated that supervised learning algorithms, such as support vector machines (SVM) and decision trees, can effectively classify network traffic as benign or malicious (Rizvi et al., 2022). Moreover, unsupervised learning techniques, such as clustering algorithms, are utilized for anomaly detection by identifying deviations from normal traffic patterns (Moustafa, 2022).

2. **Methodologies**

The methodologies for applying machine learning in traffic analysis typically involve data collection, preprocessing, feature extraction, model training, and evaluation. Initial steps include capturing traffic data from various sources, such as routers and switches, and preprocessing it to remove noise and irrelevant information. Feature extraction is crucial, as it transforms raw data into meaningful attributes that machine learning algorithms can analyze. Various techniques, including statistical analysis and dimensionality reduction, can be employed to enhance the performance of ML models (Tyagi et al., 2024).

Once the data is prepared, machine learning models can be trained using labeled datasets. Common algorithms used in traffic analysis include deep learning models, which excel in identifying complex patterns in large datasets, and ensemble methods that combine multiple models to improve accuracy (Hassan & Ibrahim, 2023). Evaluation metrics, such as precision, recall, and F1-score, are employed to assess the performance of the models and ensure their effectiveness in detecting malicious activities (Kaur et al., 2023).

3. **Challenges**

Despite the advantages of machine learning in traffic analysis, several challenges persist. One significant issue is the availability of high-quality labeled datasets, which are essential for training supervised models. Many organizations may lack the necessary resources to collect and annotate sufficient data (Dunsin et al., 2024). Additionally, the dynamic nature of network traffic means that models may become obsolete as new attack vectors emerge. Thus, continuous model retraining and updating are required to maintain efficacy (Alghamdi, 2021).

Another challenge is the interpretability of machine learning models. Many advanced algorithms, particularly deep learning models, operate as "black boxes," making it difficult for analysts to understand how decisions are made. This lack of transparency can hinder trust in automated systems, especially in critical areas such as cybersecurity (Capuano et al., 2022).

4. **Future Directions**

The future of machine learning in traffic analysis lies in enhancing its capabilities through advancements in technology and methodology. Integration of explainable AI (XAI) techniques can improve the interpretability of ML models, enabling security analysts to understand the rationale behind decisions made by algorithms (Ghillani, 2022). Additionally, leveraging transfer learning and federated learning can facilitate the sharing of knowledge between organizations while preserving data privacy and security (Nair et al., 2024).

Furthermore, combining machine learning with other technologies, such as blockchain for secure data sharing and edge computing for real-time analysis, presents significant opportunities for enhancing traffic analysis (Zangana et al., 2024). As cyber threats become more sophisticated, continuous research and collaboration among academia, industry, and government agencies will be crucial in developing innovative solutions that leverage machine learning for effective traffic analysis (Samtani et al., 2020).

The integration of machine learning into traffic analysis has proven to be a game changer in identifying anomalies. The following bar chart demonstrates the effectiveness of various machine learning algorithms in detecting anomalies within network traffic. This comparison underscores the importance of selecting appropriate techniques for optimal outcomes.

Figure 2. Machine learning application in anomaly detection

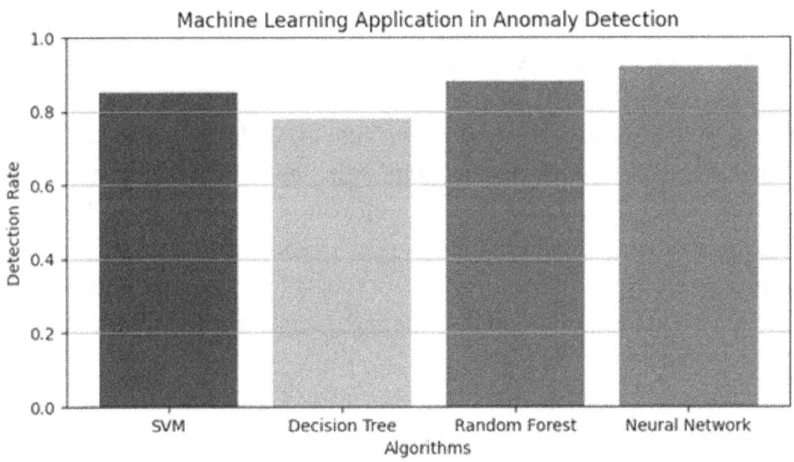

3.2 Summary

Machine learning plays a pivotal role in modern traffic analysis, offering innovative solutions to enhance cybersecurity and digital forensics. By automating the detection of malicious activities and adapting to evolving threats, machine learning significantly improves the effectiveness of traffic analysis. However, challenges such as data scarcity and model interpretability must be addressed to maximize the potential of ML in this domain. The future of traffic analysis will likely see further integration of machine learning with emerging technologies, fostering a more robust security posture against cyber threats.

4. FEATURE EXTRACTION AND DATA PREPROCESSING FOR NETWORK TRAFFIC ANALYSIS

In the context of network traffic analysis, feature extraction and data preprocessing play crucial roles in ensuring the accuracy and effectiveness of subsequent analysis and decision-making processes. These steps involve transforming raw network data into structured formats that can be effectively utilized by machine learning and artificial intelligence (AI) algorithms. This section delves into the methodologies and practices essential for effective feature extraction and data preprocessing in network traffic analysis, particularly within the realm of cybersecurity.

4.1 Importance of Feature Extraction

Feature extraction is the process of identifying and selecting relevant characteristics or features from raw data that can help in distinguishing between normal and malicious traffic. The choice of features significantly impacts the performance of machine learning models and their ability to detect anomalies or threats in network traffic. As highlighted by Rizvi et al. (2022), a robust feature extraction process can enhance the detection capabilities of AI systems by focusing on the most informative attributes of the data.

Common features extracted from network traffic include:

1. **Protocol Type**: Identifying whether the traffic is HTTP, TCP, UDP, etc., can help in understanding the nature of the communication.
2. **Packet Length**: Analyzing the size of packets can provide insights into potential data exfiltration or malicious activities.

3. **Source and Destination IP Addresses**: These features help in tracking communication patterns and identifying abnormal interactions between devices (Zangana et al., 2024).
4. **Traffic Volume**: Monitoring the amount of data being transmitted can reveal unusual spikes or drops that may indicate a security threat.

The extraction process often involves the use of automated tools and algorithms that can process vast amounts of data quickly and efficiently (Samtani, Kantarcioglu, & Chen, 2020). The increasing complexity of network environments necessitates advanced techniques to manage and analyze this data effectively.

Effective feature extraction is vital for successful network traffic analysis. The flowchart below illustrates the process of extracting relevant features from raw data, highlighting key steps such as data cleaning, normalization, and feature selection. This systematic approach ensures that only the most informative attributes are utilized in further analysis.

Figure 3. Feature extraction process

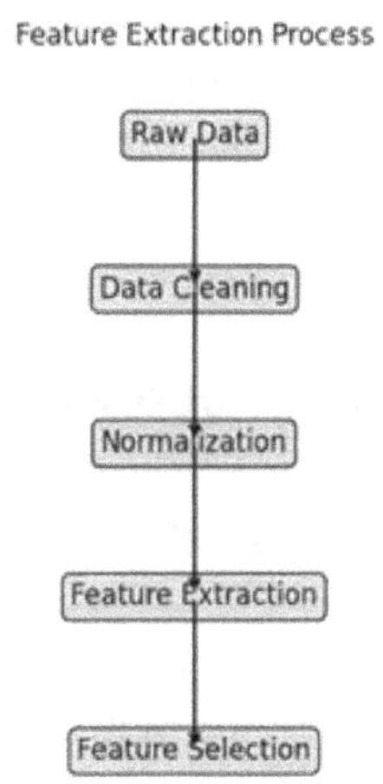

4.2 Data Preprocessing Techniques

Once features are extracted, the next critical step is data preprocessing, which prepares the data for analysis. This step typically includes several sub-processes:

1. **Data Cleaning**: This involves removing or correcting erroneous, incomplete, or irrelevant data. As noted by Dunsin et al. (2024), clean data is essential for ensuring the reliability of the analysis results.
2. **Normalization**: Normalizing features to a common scale helps in mitigating biases that may arise from varying scales across different features. For instance, numerical values can be scaled between 0 and 1, which can be particularly useful when different features have different units or ranges (Kaur, Gabrijelčič, & Klobučar, 2023).
3. **Encoding Categorical Variables**: Since many machine learning algorithms require numerical input, categorical variables (e.g., protocol types) need to be encoded. Techniques like one-hot encoding can be employed to convert these categories into a numerical format that maintains the categorical nature of the data (Ghillani, 2022).
4. **Feature Selection**: This process involves selecting the most relevant features from the extracted set to improve model performance. Techniques such as recursive feature elimination or feature importance scores from tree-based algorithms can be employed to identify key features that contribute significantly to the analysis (Tyagi, Kumari, & Richa, 2024).
5. **Handling Imbalanced Data**: In many cybersecurity applications, the dataset may be imbalanced, with significantly more instances of benign traffic compared to malicious traffic. Techniques such as oversampling the minority class or undersampling the majority class can be implemented to balance the dataset and enhance model performance (Hassan & Ibrahim, 2023).

4.3 Role of AI in Feature Extraction and Data Preprocessing

The integration of artificial intelligence in feature extraction and preprocessing processes has revolutionized network traffic analysis. AI algorithms can automate and optimize these tasks, allowing for the processing of large datasets in real time. For instance, advanced machine learning models can be trained to identify relevant features and preprocess data automatically, improving both efficiency and accuracy (Moustafa, 2022).

Moreover, as highlighted by Ali (2022), AI-driven approaches can continuously learn from incoming data, adapting their feature extraction and preprocessing techniques to evolving threats and patterns in network traffic. This adaptability is particularly crucial in the dynamic landscape of cybersecurity, where new attack vectors emerge frequently.

4.4 Summary

Feature extraction and data preprocessing are foundational components of network traffic analysis, significantly influencing the efficacy of threat detection and response mechanisms. Employing advanced techniques and AI-driven solutions can enhance the quality and relevance of data, leading to more effective cybersecurity measures. As the field continues to evolve, ongoing research and development in this area will be crucial for addressing emerging challenges in cybersecurity and digital forensics (Montasari, 2023).

5. SUPERVISED LEARNING TECHNIQUES FOR TRAFFIC CLASSIFICATION AND ANOMALY DETECTION

Supervised learning techniques have emerged as critical tools in traffic classification and anomaly detection within the realm of cybersecurity. These methods leverage labeled datasets to train models capable of identifying normal and anomalous traffic patterns in network environments. This section explores various supervised learning approaches, their applications, and their effectiveness in enhancing cybersecurity measures.

5.1 Overview of Supervised Learning

Supervised learning involves training algorithms on labeled data, where each input is associated with a known output. The algorithm learns to map inputs to outputs, enabling it to make predictions on unseen data. In traffic classification, these inputs can include packet data, flow records, and various network features, while outputs typically denote categories such as benign traffic or specific types of cyber threats.

5.2 Popular Supervised Learning Algorithms

1. **Support Vector Machines (SVM):** Support Vector Machines are effective for binary classification tasks, where they create hyperplanes to separate different classes in the feature space. In traffic classification, SVMs can differentiate between normal and malicious traffic based on predefined features, such as packet size, timing, and protocol types (Tyagi et al., 2024).
2. **Decision Trees:** Decision trees are intuitive models that recursively split the dataset based on feature values. They can be particularly useful in identifying complex patterns in traffic data. Decision trees can handle both numerical and

categorical data, making them versatile for various traffic classification tasks (Dunsin et al., 2024).

3. **Random Forests:** An extension of decision trees, random forests combine multiple decision trees to improve classification accuracy and robustness. This ensemble method reduces the risk of overfitting and is effective in handling large datasets typical in network traffic (Zangana et al., 2024).
4. **Neural Networks:** Neural networks, especially deep learning models, have gained popularity in recent years for their ability to learn hierarchical representations from data. Convolutional neural networks (CNNs) and recurrent neural networks (RNNs) can be particularly effective in capturing temporal and spatial patterns in traffic data, facilitating anomaly detection (Gholami & Omar, 2023; Omar, 2022).
5. **Gradient Boosting Machines (GBM):** GBMs build models incrementally by optimizing for errors made by previous models. This iterative approach enhances the performance of classifiers and is effective in dealing with imbalanced datasets often found in anomaly detection scenarios (Jarrett & Choo, 2021).

Supervised learning techniques are pivotal in classifying network traffic. The pie chart below illustrates the distribution of various algorithms used in traffic classification, providing insight into the most commonly employed methods. This visualization aids in understanding the landscape of machine learning applications in network forensics.

Figure 4. Supervised learning techniques for traffic classification

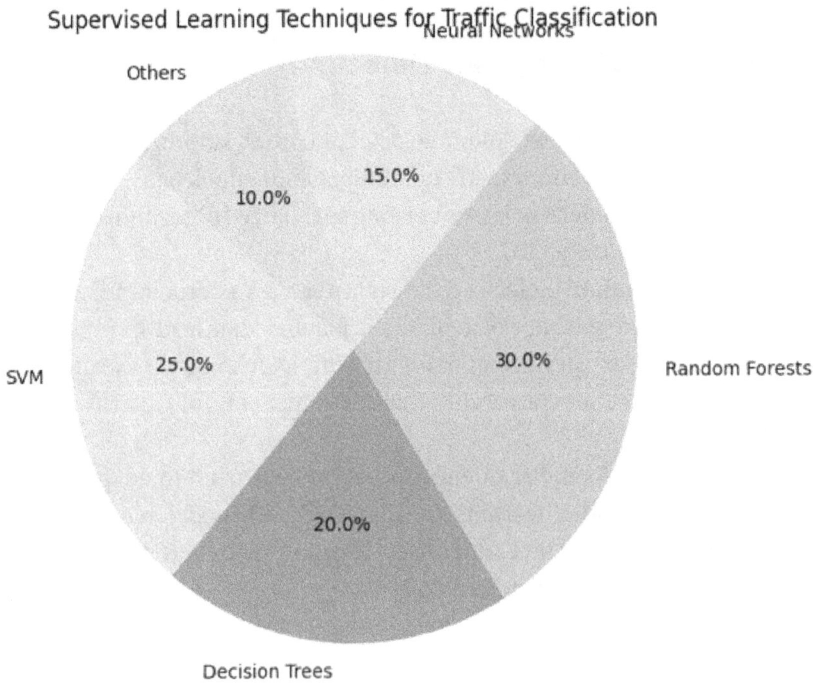

5.3 Application in Traffic Classification

Traffic classification involves categorizing network packets into various classes, such as benign, malicious, or suspicious. Supervised learning techniques play a vital role in this process. For instance, SVMs can be trained on historical traffic data to learn the characteristics of different types of traffic. Once trained, these models can quickly classify incoming packets, aiding in real-time threat detection (Rizvi et al., 2022).

5.4 Anomaly Detection

Anomaly detection focuses on identifying unusual patterns that deviate from established norms, often indicating potential security breaches. Supervised learning models can be trained using labeled datasets that include examples of both normal and anomalous traffic. Once a model is developed, it can flag traffic that significantly deviates from the learned patterns as suspicious, prompting further investigation (Hassan & Ibrahim, 2023; Samtani et al., 2020).

5.5 Challenges in Anomaly Detection

1. **Imbalanced Datasets:** Anomaly detection often suffers from class imbalance, where normal instances vastly outnumber anomalous ones. Techniques such as oversampling minority classes or using specialized algorithms can help mitigate this issue (Moustafa, 2022).
2. **Feature Selection:** Selecting the right features is crucial for effective model performance. Irrelevant or redundant features can lead to poor classification results. Employing dimensionality reduction techniques or feature engineering can enhance the model's ability to discern meaningful patterns (Al-Hajri et al., 2023).
3. **Adaptability:** As cyber threats evolve, models need to adapt to new types of attacks. Continuous learning mechanisms and model retraining on updated datasets can ensure that supervised learning models remain effective against emerging threats (Faqir, 2023).

5.6 Summary

Supervised learning techniques are integral to the fields of traffic classification and anomaly detection. By utilizing a variety of algorithms tailored to specific tasks, cybersecurity professionals can significantly enhance their capabilities in identifying and mitigating threats. As the landscape of cyber threats continues to evolve, ongoing research and development in supervised learning will be essential to maintaining robust security postures in network environments.

6. UNSUPERVISED AND SEMI-SUPERVISED LEARNING IN ANOMALY DETECTION

Anomaly detection plays a crucial role in various domains, including cybersecurity, healthcare, and finance, where the identification of rare events or patterns can prevent significant losses or damages. Traditional methods of anomaly detection rely heavily on labeled data, which can be scarce or expensive to obtain. Consequently, there has been a growing interest in leveraging unsupervised and semi-supervised learning approaches to enhance anomaly detection capabilities. These techniques enable the identification of unusual patterns without the need for extensive labeled datasets, making them particularly valuable in the context of digital forensics and cybersecurity.

6.1 Unsupervised Learning in Anomaly Detection

Unsupervised learning techniques analyze data without labeled outputs, making them suitable for scenarios where anomalies are rare and diverse. In this context, algorithms can learn from the intrinsic structure of the data to identify outliers. Common unsupervised methods include clustering techniques, principal component analysis (PCA), and autoencoders.

1. **Clustering Techniques**: Clustering algorithms like K-means, DBSCAN, and hierarchical clustering are used to group similar data points. Outliers can be identified as points that do not fit well into any cluster. For instance, Tyagi et al. (2024) highlight the effectiveness of clustering algorithms in cybersecurity applications, where unusual traffic patterns may indicate potential threats.
2. **Principal Component Analysis (PCA)**: PCA reduces the dimensionality of data while retaining variance, enabling the identification of anomalies that deviate from normal patterns in lower-dimensional space. PCA has been successfully applied in network intrusion detection, as discussed by Dunsin et al. (2024), emphasizing its role in identifying significant deviations from normal behavior.
3. **Autoencoders**: Autoencoders are neural network architectures that learn to reconstruct input data. During training, the model learns to minimize reconstruction error, allowing it to effectively highlight anomalies that exhibit a high reconstruction error. Moustafa (2022) notes the potential of autoencoders in digital forensics for identifying unusual patterns in large datasets.

6.2 Semi-Supervised Learning in Anomaly Detection

Semi-supervised learning approaches combine a small amount of labeled data with a larger pool of unlabeled data, leveraging both types of information to improve anomaly detection performance. This method is particularly advantageous when labeled data is scarce or expensive to acquire.

1. **Self-Training**: Self-training involves training a model on labeled data and then using it to label the most confident predictions on the unlabeled dataset. These newly labeled instances are subsequently added to the training set for further refinement. This approach is useful in cyber incident response, as noted by Hassan and Ibrahim (2023), where labeled examples of attacks can be complemented with vast amounts of unlabeled network traffic.

2. **Co-Training**: Co-training involves training two models on different feature sets. Each model labels instances for the other, leading to improved performance through the collaborative process. This method can be applied in digital forensics, allowing for better recognition of anomalous behaviors by leveraging various data sources (Ali, 2022).
3. **Generative Models**: Generative models, such as Generative Adversarial Networks (GANs), can also be employed in semi-supervised settings. These models learn the underlying distribution of the data, enabling them to generate synthetic examples that resemble normal instances. By augmenting the dataset with these synthetic examples, the detection of anomalies can be improved. Jarrett and Choo (2021) discuss the integration of such models in enhancing digital forensic investigations by simulating various attack scenarios.

6.3 Advantages of Unsupervised and Semi-Supervised Learning

The primary advantage of using unsupervised and semi-supervised learning techniques for anomaly detection lies in their ability to operate effectively with limited labeled data. This capability is particularly relevant in rapidly evolving fields like cybersecurity, where new threats continuously emerge. As noted by Kaur, Gabrijelčič, and Klobučar (2023), these methods provide flexibility and scalability, enabling organizations to adapt to the dynamic nature of cyber threats.

Additionally, these techniques often result in reduced computational costs associated with labeling data, making them attractive options for organizations facing resource constraints. The work of Zeadally et al. (2020) underscores the potential of AI in enhancing cybersecurity processes, emphasizing the need for methods that can efficiently detect anomalies without extensive human intervention.

6.4 Challenges and Future Directions

Despite their advantages, unsupervised and semi-supervised learning approaches face challenges, particularly in terms of model interpretability and the risk of false positives. Developing explainable models is crucial for gaining trust in automated anomaly detection systems, especially in sensitive domains like digital forensics (Capuano et al., 2022).

Future research should focus on enhancing the robustness of these methods, improving their ability to adapt to evolving threat landscapes, and integrating them with existing cybersecurity frameworks. As outlined by Montasari (2023), the confluence of AI and digital forensics presents significant opportunities for advancing anomaly detection techniques.

In conclusion, unsupervised and semi-supervised learning techniques offer valuable solutions for anomaly detection in various fields, particularly in cybersecurity and digital forensics. By leveraging these approaches, organizations can enhance their ability to identify and respond to unusual patterns and potential threats, ultimately improving their overall security posture.

7. DEEP LEARNING APPROACHES IN NETWORK FORENSICS

Network forensics, a crucial subfield of digital forensics, focuses on monitoring and analyzing computer network traffic to gather evidence and understand cyber incidents. With the increasing complexity of cyber threats, traditional methods often fall short in their capacity to efficiently analyze large volumes of data. Deep learning (DL) techniques, a subset of artificial intelligence (AI), have emerged as powerful tools in this domain, offering enhanced capabilities for data analysis, anomaly detection, and automated responses to cyber threats. This section explores the application of deep learning in network forensics, highlighting key methodologies, challenges, and future directions.

7.1. Understanding Deep Learning in Network Forensics

Deep learning refers to a class of machine learning algorithms based on artificial neural networks with multiple layers. These algorithms are particularly well-suited for identifying patterns and making predictions from vast amounts of unstructured data. In network forensics, deep learning can process and analyze network traffic data, identifying malicious activities with higher accuracy than traditional methods.

The primary DL techniques employed in network forensics include Convolutional Neural Networks (CNNs), Recurrent Neural Networks (RNNs), and Autoencoders. CNNs are effective for analyzing spatial data and are commonly used for intrusion detection. RNNs, particularly Long Short-Term Memory (LSTM) networks, excel at processing sequences of data, making them ideal for temporal analysis of network traffic. Autoencoders are valuable for anomaly detection, as they can learn the normal patterns of network traffic and identify deviations that may indicate malicious activities (Zangana et al., 2024).

7.2. Applications of Deep Learning in Network Forensics

7.2.1 Intrusion Detection Systems (IDS)

Deep learning has significantly improved the capabilities of IDS. Traditional IDS often rely on predefined rules, which can miss novel attack vectors. In contrast, DL-based IDS can learn from historical data, allowing them to adapt to new threats dynamically. For instance, Tyagi, Kumari, and Richa (2024) highlight that using deep learning algorithms enhances the accuracy and efficiency of intrusion detection, enabling quicker identification and mitigation of threats.

7.2.2 Malware Detection

Another critical application of deep learning in network forensics is malware detection. By analyzing traffic patterns and behavior, DL models can classify files and network packets as benign or malicious. Rizvi et al. (2022) conducted a survey on the application of AI in network forensics, indicating that deep learning techniques, particularly CNNs, are effective in detecting malware by recognizing patterns in network traffic that indicate compromise.

7.2.3 Anomaly Detection

Anomaly detection is a pivotal aspect of network forensics. Deep learning methods, such as Autoencoders, can learn the normal behavior of network traffic and identify deviations. This capability is crucial for identifying potential security breaches or data exfiltration attempts. Dunsin et al. (2024) emphasize that the integration of DL into anomaly detection systems leads to significant improvements in identifying sophisticated attacks that traditional methods may overlook.

7.3. Challenges in Implementing Deep Learning Approaches

Despite the advantages of deep learning in network forensics, several challenges persist:

7.3.1 Data Quality and Quantity

Deep learning models require large amounts of high-quality data for training. In the context of network forensics, obtaining labeled data can be challenging due to the dynamic nature of cyber threats. Additionally, noise and irrelevant data in network traffic can affect the model's performance (Kaur, Gabrijelčič, & Klobučar, 2023).

7.3.2 Interpretability

Deep learning models are often regarded as "black boxes," making it difficult to interpret their decision-making processes. This lack of transparency can hinder the acceptance of DL solutions in forensic investigations, where understanding the rationale behind decisions is crucial (Capuano et al., 2022).

3.3 Evasion Attacks

Cyber attackers continuously evolve their tactics to evade detection by DL-based systems. This arms race between attackers and defenders necessitates the continual refinement of DL models to maintain their efficacy against emerging threats (Zangana & Omar, 2020).

7.4. Future Directions

As the field of network forensics continues to evolve, several future directions for deep learning approaches can be identified:

7.4.1 Enhanced Model Interpretability

Research efforts are increasingly focused on improving the interpretability of deep learning models. Techniques such as Explainable AI (XAI) can help forensic investigators understand model predictions, leading to greater trust and usability in practical applications (Bonfanti, 2022).

7.4.2 Federated Learning

Federated learning is an emerging approach that allows models to be trained across multiple decentralized devices while keeping data localized. This method can enhance privacy and security in network forensics, as sensitive data does not need to be transmitted to a central server (Nair, Deshmukh, & Tyagi, 2024).

7.4.3 Integration with Traditional Methods

Combining deep learning with traditional forensic techniques can provide a more comprehensive approach to network security. By leveraging the strengths of both methodologies, practitioners can enhance detection capabilities and improve response times to incidents (Hassan & Ibrahim, 2023).

7.5. Summary

Deep learning has revolutionized network forensics, offering powerful tools for anomaly detection, malware classification, and intrusion detection. While challenges such as data quality and interpretability remain, ongoing research and advancements in AI technology promise to further enhance the effectiveness of deep learning in combating cyber threats. As organizations continue to embrace these technologies, the landscape of network forensics is set to transform, making it an essential area of study for cybersecurity professionals.

8. REAL-TIME NETWORK TRAFFIC ANALYSIS AND THREAT DETECTION

In today's increasingly digital landscape, the necessity for real-time network traffic analysis and threat detection has become paramount. Organizations are often vulnerable to various cyber threats that can compromise sensitive data, disrupt services, and lead to significant financial losses. Therefore, leveraging advanced technologies, particularly artificial intelligence (AI) and machine learning (ML), has become critical in identifying and mitigating these threats as they occur.

8.1 Understanding Network Traffic Analysis

Network traffic analysis involves the monitoring and inspection of data packets transmitted across networks to ensure their integrity, confidentiality, and availability. The analysis helps in identifying suspicious activities and potential security breaches. Traditional methods of network monitoring often struggle to keep pace with the volume and complexity of data, making them inadequate for timely threat detection. As a solution, AI and ML algorithms can enhance these processes by automating the analysis and enabling the rapid identification of anomalies within network traffic.

8.2 Role of AI in Threat Detection

Artificial intelligence plays a vital role in modern threat detection systems by improving the accuracy and efficiency of identifying potential threats. According to Hassan and Ibrahim (2023), AI facilitates real-time monitoring of network traffic, allowing for the swift identification of unusual patterns indicative of cyber threats. These AI-driven systems can learn from historical data, adapt to new threats, and reduce the number of false positives, thus ensuring a more reliable threat detection mechanism.

Furthermore, Moustafa (2022) emphasizes that AI enhances digital forensics capabilities, allowing for more thorough investigations into cyber incidents. This synergy between AI and digital forensics enables organizations to not only detect threats more efficiently but also to understand the nature of these threats, thereby improving their incident response strategies.

8.3 Advanced Detection Techniques

Recent studies highlight the integration of sophisticated detection techniques powered by AI, such as deep learning and anomaly detection algorithms. For instance, Rizvi et al. (2022) discuss the application of deep learning methods in network forensics, illustrating how these techniques can analyze vast amounts of data in real-time to identify previously unknown attack vectors. By employing such methodologies, organizations can enhance their cybersecurity posture and respond proactively to emerging threats.

Moreover, the work of Tyagi, Kumari, and Richa (2024) demonstrates that AI-based systems can significantly enhance digital forensics by automating data collection and analysis processes, thereby accelerating the investigative workflow and providing insights that would be challenging to uncover manually.

8.4 Challenges and Future Directions

While the adoption of AI in network traffic analysis offers substantial benefits, it is not without challenges. For example, the reliance on AI can introduce new vulnerabilities, including the potential for adversarial attacks that manipulate the algorithms themselves (Kaur, Gabrijelčič, & Klobučar, 2023). As the landscape of cyber threats evolves, it is crucial for organizations to continuously refine their AI systems and keep them updated to counteract these challenges.

As indicated by Dunsin et al. (2024), there is an ongoing need for interdisciplinary research that combines insights from cybersecurity, digital forensics, and AI. Such collaboration can pave the way for the development of more sophisticated systems that can adapt to the rapidly changing threat environment. This will not only improve real-time threat detection but also contribute to a holistic approach to cybersecurity that encompasses prevention, detection, and response.

8.5 Summary

In summary, real-time network traffic analysis and threat detection are vital components of a robust cybersecurity framework. The integration of AI technologies enhances the effectiveness and efficiency of these processes, enabling organizations to respond swiftly to cyber threats. However, as the field continues to evolve, ongoing research and adaptation are essential to address the inherent challenges and leverage the full potential of AI in cybersecurity and digital forensics.

9. CHALLENGES AND LIMITATIONS OF USING MACHINE LEARNING IN NETWORK FORENSICS

Machine Learning (ML) has transformed various domains, including cybersecurity and digital forensics. However, its integration into network forensics presents unique challenges and limitations. This section outlines these obstacles, emphasizing the need for a critical understanding of ML's role in this context.

9.1. Data Quality and Availability

One of the primary challenges in applying ML to network forensics is the quality and availability of data. For ML algorithms to function effectively, they require large, diverse, and high-quality datasets. However, obtaining such datasets in network forensics can be challenging due to privacy concerns, legal restrictions, and the proprietary nature of network traffic data (Dunsin et al., 2024). In many cases, forensic investigators rely on simulated datasets, which may not adequately reflect real-world scenarios, leading to models that perform poorly in practice (Rizvi et al., 2022).

9.2. Complexity of Network Traffic

Network traffic is inherently complex and can exhibit a wide variety of behaviors depending on numerous factors, including user activity, network configuration, and the presence of malicious actors (Moustafa, 2022). This complexity poses a significant challenge for ML models, which may struggle to generalize across different types of network environments or adapt to evolving threats. Furthermore, the dynamic nature of network traffic means that models trained on historical data may quickly become outdated, necessitating frequent retraining (Jarrett & Choo, 2021).

9.3. Interpretability and Explainability

Another critical limitation of ML in network forensics is the interpretability of the algorithms used. Many ML models, particularly deep learning techniques, function as "black boxes," making it difficult for forensic analysts to understand how decisions are made (Capuano et al., 2022). This lack of transparency can hinder the adoption of ML in legal contexts, where the ability to explain and justify findings is paramount (Sikos, 2021). Additionally, the need for interpretability becomes crucial in ensuring that forensic findings can be trusted and validated in court (Hayes & Kyobe, 2020).

9.4. High False Positive Rates

ML algorithms can often yield high false positive rates in network forensics, where benign activities may be mistakenly identified as malicious (Ghillani, 2022). This problem is exacerbated by the imbalance in training data, where normal behavior patterns may vastly outnumber malicious ones, leading to models that struggle to differentiate between the two accurately (Alghamdi, 2021). High false positive rates can result in unnecessary alerts, wasting valuable investigative resources and potentially causing alarm fatigue among cybersecurity personnel (Hassan & Ibrahim, 2023).

9.5. Evasion Tactics

Adversaries continuously evolve their tactics to evade detection by ML-based systems. Attackers can manipulate their behaviors to mimic legitimate users, rendering traditional anomaly detection techniques less effective (Zangana et al., 2024). As a result, forensic investigators may find it increasingly challenging to distinguish between legitimate and malicious activity in network traffic, undermining the effectiveness of ML-driven forensic tools (Al-Hajri et al., 2023).

9.6. Integration with Existing Systems

Integrating ML solutions into existing network forensic frameworks can be a complex and resource-intensive process. Organizations may face challenges related to compatibility with legacy systems, which can hinder the deployment of advanced ML models (Omar & Zangana, 2024). Additionally, the need for specialized skills to implement and maintain these systems can pose a barrier to widespread adoption, particularly in smaller organizations or those with limited resources (Mughal, 2019).

9.7. Ethical and Legal Concerns

The application of ML in network forensics raises ethical and legal questions, particularly regarding data privacy and surveillance. The use of personal data to train ML models may conflict with regulations such as the General Data Protection Regulation (GDPR), leading to potential legal repercussions for organizations (Nair et al., 2024). Moreover, the use of automated systems in sensitive investigations can lead to concerns about bias, accountability, and the potential for misuse of forensic findings (Zeadally et al., 2020).

9.8. Summary

While ML offers significant potential to enhance network forensics, it is essential to navigate its challenges and limitations carefully. Addressing issues related to data quality, interpretability, and integration with existing systems is crucial for the effective deployment of ML solutions in this field. Furthermore, ethical considerations must guide the development and application of ML technologies to ensure they serve the dual goals of enhancing security and upholding individual rights. As the landscape of cyber threats continues to evolve, ongoing research and innovation will be necessary to harness the full potential of ML in network forensics.

10. CASE STUDIES AND REAL-WORLD APPLICATIONS OF ML IN NETWORK FORENSICS

The integration of machine learning (ML) in network forensics has transformed the landscape of digital investigations. By automating the analysis of vast amounts of data and identifying patterns indicative of malicious activity, ML enhances the efficiency and accuracy of forensic investigations. This section discusses several case studies that highlight the practical applications of ML in network forensics, focusing on real-world incidents where these technologies have been pivotal.

10.1. Cybersecurity Incident Response in Healthcare

A notable case study is the implementation of AI-driven forensic analysis in healthcare cybersecurity incidents. Syed and ES (2024) explored how AI technologies can enhance forensic investigations following data breaches in healthcare settings. Their analysis indicated that ML algorithms effectively detected anomalies in network traffic that often go unnoticed by traditional methods. The integration of these tools allowed for faster incident response times, reducing the potential damage from cyberattacks. The findings underscore the necessity for healthcare organizations to adopt AI-enhanced methodologies to safeguard sensitive patient data.

10.2. Phishing Threat Detection

Zangana et al. (2024) conducted a study focusing on email phishing threats, utilizing ML to identify deceptive communications. By training algorithms on historical phishing data, the researchers were able to develop a model that significantly outperformed existing detection methods. Their work illustrated how machine learning could be applied to analyze email patterns and content, providing real-time alerts for potential phishing attempts. This case emphasizes the importance of using ML in network forensics to protect against social engineering attacks that target unsuspecting users.

10.3. Digital Forensics in Cybercrime Investigation

Moustafa (2022) provided insights into the role of ML in digital forensics, particularly in cybercrime investigations. The study reviewed various ML applications, such as anomaly detection and classification algorithms, which assist forensic analysts in identifying malicious activities. By leveraging ML, investigators could streamline the process of analyzing digital evidence, leading to quicker resolutions in cases involving data breaches and cyberattacks. This application of ML showcases its potential in transforming traditional forensic methodologies into more efficient systems.

10.4. The Role of AI in Network Traffic Analysis

Rizvi et al. (2022) explored the challenges and opportunities presented by AI in network forensics, focusing specifically on network traffic analysis. Their survey highlighted several case studies where ML algorithms successfully identified suspicious patterns within network traffic, thereby enabling forensic teams to detect potential intrusions before they escalated. The study emphasized that while traditional methods rely heavily on predefined signatures, ML approaches adaptively learn from evolving threats, making them more effective in real-time network monitoring.

10.5. Automation in Digital Forensic Investigations

Jarrett and Choo (2021) discussed the impact of automation and AI on digital forensics, particularly in streamlining investigation processes. Their findings indicated that incorporating AI-driven tools reduced the workload on forensic analysts, allowing them to focus on more complex investigative tasks. Case studies presented in their research illustrated how automated systems, combined with ML, enabled forensic teams to handle large volumes of data without compromising the quality of their analysis. This highlights the critical role of AI in enhancing operational efficiency within digital forensics.

10.6. AI in Cybersecurity: A Comprehensive Review

Tyagi, Kumari, and Richa (2024) conducted a comprehensive review of AI-based solutions in cybersecurity, emphasizing their applications in digital forensics. Their analysis included various case studies where AI tools played a vital role in incident detection and response. The review highlighted the growing reliance on ML to process and analyze digital evidence, underscoring the necessity for ongoing research and development in this field to enhance the capabilities of forensic investigations.

10.7. Advanced Cyber Forensic Techniques

Dunsin et al. (2024) provided a thorough examination of the advancements in AI and ML technologies applied to modern digital forensics. Their research included case studies that demonstrated the effectiveness of these technologies in real-world scenarios, such as identifying data exfiltration and detecting insider threats. The insights gained from these investigations illustrate the transformative potential of ML in developing more sophisticated forensic techniques that adapt to the evolving cyber threat landscape.

10.8. Summary

The case studies presented in this section highlight the significant impact of machine learning on network forensics, showcasing its ability to enhance detection capabilities, automate processes, and ultimately improve incident response times. As the cyber threat landscape continues to evolve, the integration of ML and AI technologies into forensic investigations will be crucial for staying ahead of emerging threats. Ongoing research and collaboration between academia and industry will further refine these technologies, ensuring they remain effective tools in the fight against cybercrime.

11. FUTURE DIRECTIONS FOR MACHINE LEARNING IN NETWORK FORENSICS AND TRAFFIC ANALYSIS

As the digital landscape evolves, the integration of machine learning (ML) in network forensics and traffic analysis is becoming increasingly vital. With the growing complexity and volume of cyber threats, leveraging AI and ML techniques offers promising avenues for enhancing the effectiveness and efficiency of forensic investigations. This section explores future directions for applying machine learning in network forensics and traffic analysis, focusing on advancements, challenges, and research opportunities.

11.1. Enhanced Predictive Analytics

One of the significant future directions for ML in network forensics is the development of advanced predictive analytics tools that can foresee potential security breaches and anomalies. By analyzing historical traffic patterns and utilizing deep learning algorithms, forensic analysts can build robust models to predict malicious activities before they occur. Research indicates that AI can significantly enhance predictive capabilities by utilizing vast datasets to identify emerging threat vectors (Jarrett & Choo, 2021; Hassan & Ibrahim, 2023). Tools that can process real-time data while adapting to evolving threats will be essential for proactive threat detection.

11.2. Integration of AI in Automated Response Systems

Automated incident response systems powered by AI will play a crucial role in network forensics. By integrating ML algorithms, these systems can autonomously analyze incidents, determine the best response strategies, and implement mitigation measures in real-time. This capability can significantly reduce response times and enhance the resilience of network systems against cyber-attacks. Future research should focus on developing intelligent agents capable of learning from past incidents and continuously improving their response strategies (Dunsin et al., 2024; Rizvi et al., 2022).

11.3. Multi-Modal Data Fusion

The future of network forensics will also involve the fusion of multiple data sources for comprehensive analysis. Combining data from various modalities, such as packet captures, logs, and user behavior analytics, can provide a more holistic view of network activities. Machine learning techniques can be employed to analyze and correlate these diverse data streams, thereby improving the accuracy of threat detection and response. This multi-modal approach has the potential to uncover sophisticated attack patterns that may not be apparent from isolated datasets (Kaur et al., 2023; Samtani et al., 2020).

11.4. Development of Explainable AI (XAI)

The growing reliance on AI in network forensics necessitates the development of explainable AI (XAI) methods that can provide insights into the decision-making processes of machine learning models. Ensuring transparency in AI systems is crucial for gaining trust among forensic analysts and legal entities. Future research should focus on creating XAI frameworks that elucidate how specific models arrive at their conclusions, thereby aiding in the legal admissibility of forensic evidence (Capuano et al., 2022; Moustafa, 2022).

11.5. Addressing Ethical and Privacy Concerns

As the integration of AI in network forensics expands, addressing ethical and privacy concerns will become paramount. Ensuring that ML algorithms respect user privacy while effectively analyzing network traffic is a critical challenge. Future directions should focus on developing privacy-preserving techniques that allow for effective forensic investigations without compromising individual rights (Zangana & Omar, 2020; Nair et al., 2024). This includes exploring federated learning approaches that enable model training on decentralized data without exposing sensitive information.

11.6. Cybersecurity Training and Skill Development

The rapid evolution of AI technologies necessitates ongoing training and skill development for forensic professionals. Future research should explore educational frameworks that incorporate AI and ML into forensic science curricula, ensuring that practitioners are equipped with the necessary skills to leverage these advanced tools effectively. Collaborative training programs that include practical exposure to AI-driven forensic tools can enhance the workforce's readiness to tackle emerging challenges in cybersecurity (Alghamdi, 2021; Ali, 2022).

11.7. Collaborative Research and Development

Finally, fostering collaboration between academia, industry, and law enforcement agencies will be essential for advancing the field of network forensics. Multi-disciplinary research initiatives can lead to innovative solutions that address real-world challenges in cybersecurity. By pooling resources and expertise, stakeholders can develop more robust ML models and forensic tools that are both effective and efficient (Montasari, 2023; Hayes & Kyobe, 2020).

11.8. Summary

The integration of machine learning in network forensics and traffic analysis represents a transformative opportunity to enhance cybersecurity measures. By focusing on predictive analytics, automated responses, data fusion, explainability, ethical considerations, skill development, and collaborative efforts, the future of this field holds great promise. Continued research and innovation will be crucial in harnessing the full potential of AI to combat the ever-evolving landscape of cyber threats.

12. CONCLUSION

The integration of machine learning (ML) into network forensics and traffic analysis represents a significant evolution in cybersecurity methodologies. As cyber threats become increasingly sophisticated, traditional techniques often fall short in addressing the complex dynamics of modern network environments. By leveraging ML algorithms, investigators can enhance their ability to detect anomalies, classify malicious activities, and respond to incidents with greater efficiency and accuracy. This chapter has explored various dimensions of this integration, highlighting the transformative potential of AI-driven approaches in digital forensics.

The future of machine learning in network forensics is not just about improving existing techniques; it is also about fostering innovation in the field. Emerging technologies, such as artificial intelligence (AI) and big data analytics, provide unprecedented opportunities to analyze vast amounts of traffic data in real-time. This capacity enables cybersecurity professionals to identify patterns and potential threats more swiftly, thereby significantly reducing response times and improving overall security posture. The continued exploration of these technologies will likely yield new insights and methodologies that can be adapted to various contexts, from enterprise networks to critical infrastructure.

However, the journey towards fully realizing the potential of ML in network forensics is not without challenges. Issues such as data privacy, algorithmic bias, and the interpretability of machine learning models require careful consideration. As highlighted by researchers like Jarrett and Choo (2021) and Dunsin et al. (2024), the implications of deploying automated and AI-driven forensic tools must be thoroughly examined to ensure ethical and effective use in cybersecurity practices.

Furthermore, as cyber threats evolve, so too must the tools and techniques employed to counter them. Continuous research and development will be essential to keep pace with these changes.

In conclusion, the intersection of machine learning and network forensics holds immense promise for enhancing the capabilities of cybersecurity professionals. As the field progresses, collaboration between researchers, practitioners, and policymakers will be crucial in shaping the future landscape of digital forensics. By embracing the advancements in AI and machine learning, we can pave the way for more resilient cybersecurity frameworks that not only respond to threats but also anticipate and mitigate them before they escalate. This proactive approach is vital in safeguarding our increasingly interconnected digital world.

REFERENCES

Ahmed Alaa El-Din, E. (2022). Artificial intelligence in forensic science: Invasion or revolution? *Egyptian Society of Clinical Toxicology Journal*, 10(2), 20–32. DOI: 10.21608/esctj.2022.158178.1012

Al-Hajri, S. M., Al-Thonayan, Z. J., Alqattan, M. M., Alalyani, N. A., Alali, N. D., & Alnaim, N. (2023). Maximizing the Potential of Artificial Intelligence in Digital Forensics Investigations.

Alghamdi, M. I. (2021). *Digital forensics in cyber security—recent trends, threats, and opportunities.* Cybersecurity Threats with New Perspectives. DOI: 10.5772/intechopen.94452

Ali, A. (2022). Cyber Crime Investigation and Forensics: Leveraging AI and Big Data for More Effective Solutions.

Bonfanti, M. E. (2022). *Artificial intelligence and the offence-defence balance in cyber security. Cyber Security: Socio-Technological Uncertainty and Political Fragmentation.* Routledge.

Capuano, N., Fenza, G., Loia, V., & Stanzione, C. (2022). Explainable artificial intelligence in cybersecurity: A survey. *IEEE Access : Practical Innovations, Open Solutions*, 10, 93575–93600. DOI: 10.1109/ACCESS.2022.3204171

CHILONGO, L., & KM, A. S. (2024). IMPACT OF ARTIFICIAL INTELLIGENCE ON CYBERSECURITY: A CASE OF INTERNET OF THINGS. *i-Manager's Journal on Digital Forensics & Cyber Security (JDF), 2*(1).

Du, X., Hargreaves, C., Sheppard, J., Anda, F., Sayakkara, A., Le-Khac, N. A., & Scanlon, M. (2020, August). SoK: Exploring the state of the art and the future potential of artificial intelligence in digital forensic investigation. In *Proceedings of the 15th international conference on availability, reliability and security* (pp. 1-10). DOI: 10.1145/3407023.3407068

Dunsin, D., Ghanem, M. C., Ouazzane, K., & Vassilev, V. (2024). A comprehensive analysis of the role of artificial intelligence and machine learning in modern digital forensics and incident response. *Forensic Science International Digital Investigation*, 48, 301675. DOI: 10.1016/j.fsidi.2023.301675

Faqir, R. S. (2023). Digital Criminal Investigations in the Era of Artificial Intelligence: A Comprehensive Overview. *International Journal of Cyber Criminology*, 17(2), 77–94.

Ghillani, D. (2022). Deep learning and artificial intelligence framework to improve the cyber security. *Authorea Preprints*. DOI: 10.22541/au.166379475.54266021/v1

Gholami, S., & Omar, M. (2023). Does Synthetic Data Make Large Language Models More Efficient? *arXiv preprint arXiv:2310.07830*.

Gholami, S., & Omar, M. (2024). Can a student large language model perform as well as its teacher? In *Innovations, Securities, and Case Studies Across Healthcare, Business, and Technology* (pp. 122-139). IGI Global. DOI: 10.4018/979-8-3693-1906-2.ch007

Hamza, Y. A., & Omar, M. D. (2013). Cloud computing security: Abuse and nefarious use of cloud computing. *International Journal of Computer Engineering Research*, 3(6), 22–27.

Hassan, S. K., & Ibrahim, A. (2023). The role of artificial intelligence in cyber security and incident response. *International Journal for Electronic Crime Investigation*, 7(2).

Hayes, D., & Kyobe, M. (2020, March). The adoption of automation in cyber forensics. In *2020 Conference on Information Communications Technology and Society (ICTAS)* (pp. 1-6). IEEE. DOI: 10.1109/ICTAS47918.2020.233977

Huff, A. J., Burrell, D. N., Nobles, C., Richardson, K., Wright, J. B., Burton, S. L., Jones, A. J., Springs, D., Omar, M., & Brown-Jackson, K. L. (2023). Management Practices for Mitigating Cybersecurity Threats to Biotechnology Companies, Laboratories, and Healthcare Research Organizations. In *Applied Research Approaches to Technology, Healthcare, and Business* (pp. 1-12). IGI Global.

Iqbal, S., & Alharbi, S. A. (2020). Advancing automation in digital forensic investigations using machine learning forensics. *Digital Forensic Science, 3.*

Jarrett, A., & Choo, K. K. R. (2021). The impact of automation and artificial intelligence on digital forensics. *WIREs Forensic Science*, 3(6), e1418. DOI: 10.1002/wfs2.1418

Jones, R., & Omar, M. (2024). Revolutionizing Cybersecurity: The GPT-2 Enhanced Attack Detection and Defense (GEADD) Method for Zero-Day Threats. *International Journal of Informatics* [INJIISCOM]. *Information System and Computer Engineering*, 5(2), 178–191.

Jones, R., Omar, M., Mohammed, D., Nobles, C., & Dawson, M. (2023). Harnessing the Speed and Accuracy of Machine Learning to Advance Cybersecurity. In *2023 Congress in Computer Science, Computer Engineering, & Applied Computing (CSCE)* (pp. 418-421). IEEE. DOI: 10.1109/CSCE60160.2023.00074

Kaur, R., Gabrijelčič, D., & Klobučar, T. (2023). Artificial intelligence for cybersecurity: Literature review and future research directions. *Information Fusion*, 97, 101804. DOI: 10.1016/j.inffus.2023.101804

Mohammed, D., Omar, M., & Nguyen, V. (2018). Wireless sensor network security: Approaches to detecting and avoiding wormhole attacks. *Journal of Research in Business. Economics and Management*, 10(2), 1860–1864.

Montasari, R. (2023). *Countering cyberterrorism: the confluence of artificial intelligence, cyber forensics and digital policing in US and UK national cybersecurity* (Vol. 101). Springer Nature. DOI: 10.1007/978-3-031-21920-7

Moustafa, N. (2022). *Digital Forensics in the Era of Artificial Intelligence*. CRC Press. DOI: 10.1201/9781003278962

Mughal, A. A. (2019). A comprehensive study of practical techniques and methodologies in incident-based approaches for cyber forensics. *Tensorgate Journal of Sustainable Technology and Infrastructure for Developing Countries*, 2(1), 1–18.

Murphy, J. P. (2022). *Digital Forensic Investigations and Automated and Artificial Intelligence Technologies* (Master's thesis, Utica University).

Nair, M. M., Deshmukh, A., & Tyagi, A. K. (2024). Artificial intelligence for cyber security: Current trends and future challenges. *Automated Secure Computing for Next-Generation Systems*, 83-114.

Nguyen, V., Mohammed, D., Omar, M., & Banisakher, M. (2018). The Effects of the FCC Net Neutrality Repeal on Security and Privacy. [IJHIoT]. *International Journal of Hyperconnectivity and the Internet of Things*, 2(2), 21–29. DOI: 10.4018/IJHIoT.2018070102

Omar, M. (2021). New insights into database security: An effective and integrated approach for applying access control mechanisms and cryptographic concepts in Microsoft Access environments.

Omar, M. (2022). *Machine Learning for Cybersecurity: Innovative Deep Learning Solutions*. Springer Brief. https://link.springer.com/book/978303115

Omar, M. (2024). From Attack to Defense: Strengthening DNN Text Classification Against Adversarial Examples. In *Innovations, Securities, and Case Studies Across Healthcare, Business, and Technology* (pp. 174-195). IGI Global.

Omar, M. (2024). Revolutionizing Malware Detection: A Paradigm Shift Through Optimized Convolutional Neural Networks. In *Innovations, Securities, and Case Studies Across Healthcare, Business, and Technology* (pp. 196-220). IGI Global. DOI: 10.4018/979-8-3693-1906-2.ch011

Omar, M., & Zangana, H. M. (Eds.). (2024). *Redefining Security With Cyber AI*. IGI Global., DOI: 10.4018/979-8-3693-6517-5

Piraianu, A. I., Fulga, A., Musat, C. L., Ciobotaru, O. R., Poalelungi, D. G., Stamate, E., Ciobotaru, O., & Fulga, I. (2023). Enhancing the evidence with algorithms: How artificial intelligence is transforming forensic medicine. *Diagnostics (Basel)*, 13(18), 2992. DOI: 10.3390/diagnostics13182992 PMID: 37761359

Tyagi, A. K., Kumari, S., & Richa. (2024). Artificial Intelligence-Based Cyber Security and Digital Forensics: A Review. *Artificial Intelligence-Enabled Digital Twin for Smart Manufacturing*, 391-419.

Rizvi, S., Scanlon, M., Mcgibney, J., & Sheppard, J. (2022). Application of artificial intelligence to network forensics: Survey, challenges and future directions. *IEEE Access : Practical Innovations, Open Solutions*, 10, 110362–110384. DOI: 10.1109/ACCESS.2022.3214506

Samtani, S., Kantarcioglu, M., & Chen, H. (2020). Trailblazing the artificial intelligence for cybersecurity discipline: A multi-disciplinary research roadmap. [TMIS]. *ACM Transactions on Management Information Systems*, 11(4), 1–19. DOI: 10.1145/3430360

Sikos, L. F. (2021). AI in digital forensics: Ontology engineering for cybercrime investigations. *WIREs Forensic Science*, 3(3), e1394. DOI: 10.1002/wfs2.1394

Stutz, D., de Assis, J. T., Laghari, A. A., Khan, A. A., Andreopoulos, N., Terziev, A., ... & Grata, E. G. (2024). Enhancing Security in Cloud Computing Using Artificial Intelligence (AI). *Applying Artificial Intelligence in Cybersecurity Analytics and Cyber Threat Detection*, 179-220.

Syed, F. M., & ES, F. K. (2024). AI-Driven Forensic Analysis for Cyber Incidents in Healthcare. *International Journal of Machine Learning Research in Cybersecurity and Artificial Intelligence*, 15(1), 473–499.

Tao, F., Akhtar, M. S., & Jiayuan, Z. (2021). The future of artificial intelligence in cybersecurity: A comprehensive survey. *EAI Endorsed Transactions on Creative Technologies*, 8(28), e3–e3. DOI: 10.4108/eai.7-7-2021.170285

Tuli, F. A., & Thaduri, U. R. (2023). The Integration of Artificial Intelligence in Forensic Accounting: A Game-Changer. *Asian Accounting and Auditing Advancement*, 14(1), 12–20.

Ukwen, D. O., & Karabatak, M. (2021, June). Review of NLP-based systems in digital forensics and cybersecurity. In *2021 9th International symposium on digital forensics and security (ISDFS)* (pp. 1-9). IEEE. DOI: 10.1109/ISDFS52919.2021.9486354

Wright, J., Dawson, M. E.Jr, & Omar, M. (2012). Cyber security and mobile threats: The need for antivirus applications for smartphones. *Journal of Information Systems Technology and Planning*, 5(14), 40–60.

Zangana, H. M. (2024). Exploring the Landscape of Website Vulnerability Scanners: A Comprehensive Review and Comparative Analysis. *Redefining Security With Cyber AI*, 111-129.

Zangana, H. M. (2024). Exploring Blockchain-Based Timestamping Tools: A Comprehensive Review. *Redefining Security With Cyber AI*, 92-110.

Zangana, H. M., Mohammed, A. K., Sallow, A. B., & Sallow, Z. B. (2024). Cybernetic Deception: Unraveling the Layers of Email Phishing Threats. [INJURATECH]. *International Journal of Research and Applied Technology*, 4(1), 35–47.

Zangana, H. M., & Omar, M. (2020). Threats, Attacks, and Mitigations of Smartphone Security. *Academic Journal of Nawroz University*, 9(4), 324–332. DOI: 10.25007/ajnu.v9n4a989

Zangana, H. M., Omar, M., Al-Karaki, J. N., & Mohammed, D. (2024). Comprehensive Review and Analysis of Network Firewall Rule Analyzers: Enhancing Security Posture and Efficiency. *Redefining Security With Cyber AI*, 15-36.

Zeadally, S., Adi, E., Baig, Z., & Khan, I. A. (2020). Harnessing artificial intelligence capabilities to improve cybersecurity. *IEEE Access : Practical Innovations, Open Solutions*, 8, 23817–23837. DOI: 10.1109/ACCESS.2020.2968045

Chapter 5

Image Denoising Techniques for Cybersecurity and Forensic Applications: AI-Driven Approaches

Hewa Majeed Zangana
https://orcid.org/0000-0001-7909-254X
Duhok Polytechnic University, Iraq

Firas Mahmood Mustafa
Duhok Polytechnic University, Iraq

ABSTRACT

With the proliferation of digital evidence in cybersecurity and forensic investigations, image denoising has become essential for accurate analysis, where high-quality visuals are critical for identifying threats and verifying information. This chapter explores advanced AI-driven techniques for image denoising, emphasizing the role of deep learning, convolutional neural networks (CNNs), and generative models to enhance image clarity. By leveraging artificial intelligence, these methods adaptively reduce noise while preserving essential image features, improving both efficiency and reliability in digital forensic processes. Our examination includes a comparative analysis of traditional versus AI-based denoising approaches, assessing their applicability and effectiveness within cybersecurity and forensic environments. This chapter ultimately aims to provide a comprehensive overview of cutting-edge AI techniques that refine image quality, supporting better decision-making in complex, data-rich scenarios.

DOI: 10.4018/979-8-3373-0588-2.ch005

1. INTRODUCTION TO IMAGE DENOISING IN CYBERSECURITY AND FORENSICS

In today's digital landscape, visual data plays a critical role in cybersecurity and forensic investigations. Image denoising, a process of removing noise from visual data, has emerged as a pivotal technique in enhancing the clarity of images, which is essential for accurate digital analysis and reliable decision-making. In cybersecurity, the importance of noise reduction extends beyond aesthetic improvement, serving as a foundational element in identifying, verifying, and documenting potential threats and evidence (Bharathiraja et al., 2023). For forensic applications, where visual clarity may determine the validity of digital evidence, efficient denoising is crucial for delivering unaltered, admissible imagery in investigative and legal contexts (Fayyaz et al., 2024).

Recent advancements in artificial intelligence (AI) have led to significant improvements in image denoising techniques, particularly through deep learning and generative models (Alotaibi, Williamson, & Khamis, 2023; Ali, Shah, & ElAffendi, 2024). Unlike traditional methods that rely on general smoothing techniques, AI-based denoising approaches employ algorithms that can adapt to the characteristics of specific types of noise. This adaptability enhances denoising efficiency by preserving essential image details, which is especially valuable in forensic contexts where image quality and detail integrity are paramount (Majeed & Hwang, 2023).

The growth of deep learning frameworks, such as convolutional neural networks (CNNs), has provided effective solutions for image restoration in complex cybersecurity environments (Gupta, Shreneter, & Sehgal, 2024; Khaleel et al., 2024). CNNs, generative adversarial networks (GANs), and other advanced AI models are able to differentiate between noise and relevant data, enabling more precise restoration of visual information. These technologies not only enhance forensic image processing but also contribute to emerging fields like IoT security and threat detection (Choi et al., 2020; Hewage et al., 2022).

Given the evolving nature of threats, there is an increasing demand for sophisticated denoising techniques that are both adaptable and robust across varied applications, from enhancing thermal imagery for secure access controls to ensuring the integrity of images in social media analyses (Almehdhar et al., 2024; Aslam, 2024). Through examining AI-driven denoising solutions, this chapter explores the role of image processing within cybersecurity and forensic domains, addressing the challenges and benefits of integrating advanced AI techniques for noise reduction and image clarity.

This introductory section sets the stage for a deeper examination of the methodologies and case studies that underscore the role of image denoising in modern cyber defense and forensic investigations. By bridging traditional approaches with

AI innovations, the following sections aim to highlight the transformative impact of AI on image denoising, underscoring its value for both practitioners and researchers in cybersecurity and digital forensics.

2. CHALLENGES IN IMAGE DENOISING FOR FORENSIC PURPOSES

Image denoising in forensic contexts poses unique challenges due to the necessity for high accuracy and image integrity preservation. Unlike general image enhancement, forensic denoising must ensure that no critical evidence is lost or distorted, making traditional noise reduction techniques, which often trade detail for clarity, unsuitable. AI-driven approaches, including deep learning and generative methods, offer powerful tools for forensic denoising, yet they also introduce several complex challenges.

2.1. Preservation of Image Integrity

In forensic applications, preserving the authenticity of the image is paramount, as any alteration may compromise its admissibility in court. Generative methods like GANs, while highly effective in reconstructing clean images, often introduce artifacts that may distort evidence (Das, 2024; Maheshwari & Paulchamy, 2024). This challenge is further amplified in cases involving synthetic or GAN-generated images, which may inadvertently alter original image features (Heidari et al., 2024). To address these issues, robust and explainable AI-based denoising frameworks are needed to ensure both noise reduction and the retention of crucial details (Majeed & Hwang, 2023).

2.2. Ethical and Privacy Concerns

Forensic image processing often involves sensitive and confidential data, where privacy concerns are heightened. AI-enhanced denoising can inadvertently expose private details or amplify irrelevant sections of an image, leading to ethical and legal implications (Golda et al., 2024). Privacy-preserving AI techniques are essential to maintain confidentiality in sensitive cases, and balancing these concerns with the need for accurate denoising remains a complex issue (Moustafa et al., 2023).

2.3. Handling Diverse Noise Types and Levels

Forensic images are often captured in challenging conditions, leading to various noise types, including Gaussian, salt-and-pepper, and motion blur. AI models trained on clean datasets may struggle to generalize across these noise variations (Bharathiraja et al., 2023). Moreover, forensic cases may involve images with compounded noise types, such as surveillance footage with low-light noise or blurred thermal images, demanding AI models that can handle diverse noise scenarios (Alotaibi et al., 2023; Almehdhar et al., 2024).

2.4. Training Data Limitations and Model Reliability

Deep learning models require large datasets for training, yet forensic images are often limited and difficult to obtain due to confidentiality. This scarcity of data affects the model's ability to generalize and may lead to biases in denoising results (Fu, Pasuksmit, & Tantithamthavorn, 2024). Synthetic data generation can alleviate this issue, but reliance on synthetic datasets introduces concerns about the realism and fidelity of denoising outcomes in actual forensic cases (Khaleel et al., 2024; Sindiramutty et al., 2025).

2.5. Adversarial Vulnerabilities and Model Robustness

AI-driven denoising models are susceptible to adversarial attacks, where small perturbations can significantly affect model output. In forensic applications, this vulnerability raises concerns about the reliability of AI-based denoising when used in adversarial environments (Khormali, 2022; Zhao et al., 2024). Model robustness remains a crucial focus, as adversarial attacks on forensic images can have severe repercussions, potentially obscuring evidence or misleading investigators (Ali, Shah, & ElAffendi, 2024; Dhayanidhi, 2022).

2.6. Detection and Handling of Deepfake Manipulations

As deepfake technologies evolve, forensic analysts face increasing challenges in distinguishing legitimate denoised images from manipulated content. AI-driven denoising techniques may sometimes struggle to detect deepfake alterations, making it imperative to integrate detection mechanisms that validate the integrity of denoised images (Lyu, 2024; Choi et al., 2020). This challenge underscores the need for a comprehensive approach that includes both denoising and deepfake detection capabilities within forensic workflows (Singla, 2024; Khimi et al., 2024).

2.7. Computational Resource Demands

Many advanced denoising models require significant computational resources, which may not be feasible in resource-constrained forensic settings (Tyagi & Addula, 2024). High-resolution forensic imagery often necessitates intensive processing, which can slow down investigations or limit the application of complex AI-based models (Rohatgi et al., 2023; Roshanaei, Khan, & Sylvester, 2024). Optimizing these models for efficiency without sacrificing quality remains a persistent challenge for researchers and forensic practitioners.

Image denoising in forensic applications poses multiple challenges, from maintaining image integrity to handling diverse noise types. Figure 1 visualizes these key challenges, highlighting areas such as model reliability and adversarial robustness, which require special attention in forensic contexts to preserve evidence accuracy and authenticity.

Figure 1. Challenges in forensic denoising

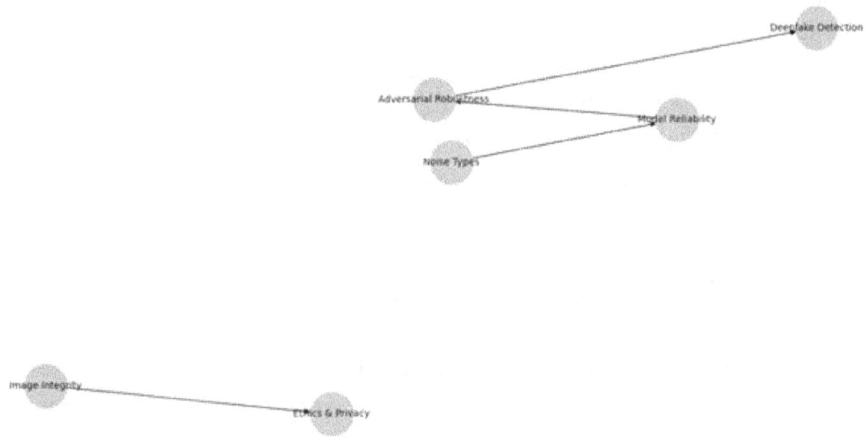

In conclusion, while AI-driven denoising techniques have introduced powerful capabilities to enhance forensic imaging, addressing these challenges is critical to advancing their reliability and effectiveness in legal and investigative contexts. Solutions that prioritize data integrity, ethical handling, and model robustness will be vital in ensuring that image denoising methods fulfill their potential in forensic applications.

3. TRADITIONAL VS. AI-BASED DENOISING TECHNIQUES

The evolution of image denoising methods has shifted from traditional statistical approaches to advanced artificial intelligence (AI)-based techniques. While both categories aim to reduce noise and improve image clarity, they differ significantly in approach, effectiveness, and adaptability to complex noise patterns.

3.1. Traditional Denoising Techniques

Traditional denoising methods, such as Gaussian smoothing, median filtering, and wavelet-based approaches, rely on predefined statistical models to eliminate noise. These techniques are effective for basic noise types, such as Gaussian and salt-and-pepper noise, and are often computationally inexpensive. However, they tend to blur fine image details, especially in high-noise scenarios, and may lack the adaptability needed for complex forensic applications (Fayyaz et al., 2024; Khaleel et al., 2024).

Wavelet-based denoising, for instance, has been widely used in forensic image processing due to its ability to separate noise from signal in different frequency bands. Yet, it often fails in cases of mixed or complex noise, where it can inadvertently remove relevant details along with the noise (Alotaibi et al., 2023). Traditional methods generally lack the flexibility to adapt to the wide array of noise types and levels found in diverse forensic contexts, where noise characteristics can vary greatly between cases (Bharathiraja et al., 2023).

3.2. AI-Based Denoising Techniques

AI-based denoising has introduced a paradigm shift, leveraging machine learning and deep learning models to achieve superior noise reduction while preserving fine image details. These methods, particularly convolutional neural networks (CNNs) and generative adversarial networks (GANs), can learn complex noise patterns and adapt to different noise types with minimal manual intervention (Gupta, Shreneter, & Sehgal, 2024; Dhayanidhi, 2022). Unlike traditional methods, AI-based approaches are capable of generalizing across different image types, including thermal and low-light images, commonly found in forensic contexts (Almehdhar et al., 2024).

Generative AI models, such as GANs, are especially powerful for denoising by generating high-quality, clean images that retain critical details. However, they also introduce ethical concerns, as the generative process can sometimes alter the image beyond mere noise reduction, potentially affecting its integrity as forensic evidence (Heidari et al., 2024; Majeed & Hwang, 2023). AI models can also be trained to handle adversarial attacks, offering additional robustness in cybersecurity and forensic applications (Ali, Shah, & ElAffendi, 2024).

3.3. Performance and Adaptability

AI-based techniques generally outperform traditional methods in denoising quality and adaptability, but they come with significant computational demands. Traditional methods are more accessible for real-time applications due to their low computational overhead, which remains an advantage in resource-limited forensic environments (Tyagi & Addula, 2024; Roshanaei, Khan, & Sylvester, 2024). However, AI-based models, once trained, can offer near-real-time processing capabilities, making them suitable for high-stakes forensic tasks (Choi et al., 2020; Sayyafzadeh, 2024).

Deep learning models are also notably better at handling mixed and complex noise patterns, as they are trained on diverse datasets that encompass a variety of noise types. The ability to customize AI models to specific noise types by training on specialized datasets offers an unparalleled level of flexibility that traditional methods lack (Maheshwari & Paulchamy, 2024; Aslam, 2024). Additionally, advancements in AI have led to explainable and transparent denoising models, addressing concerns about reliability and integrity in forensic applications (Moustafa et al., 2023).

3.4. Ethical and Security Implications

With the rise of generative AI in denoising, there are ethical concerns about the potential misuse of these technologies in creating forged or manipulated images, raising privacy and security issues (Golda et al., 2024; Takale, Mahalle, & Sule, 2024). While traditional methods are generally not prone to these issues, AI-based techniques necessitate strict oversight to ensure they are used responsibly, particularly in cybersecurity and forensic fields (Hewage et al., 2022; Rohatgi et al., 2023).

The comparison of traditional and AI-based denoising techniques provides insights into their strengths and limitations. While traditional methods, such as Gaussian smoothing, are computationally light, they often fall short in preserving details under high-noise conditions. In contrast, AI-driven methods like CNNs and GANs are more robust against complex noise but come with higher computational demands. Figure 2 illustrates the differences in efficiency, adaptability, and computational cost between these approaches.

Figure 2. Denoising techniques comparison

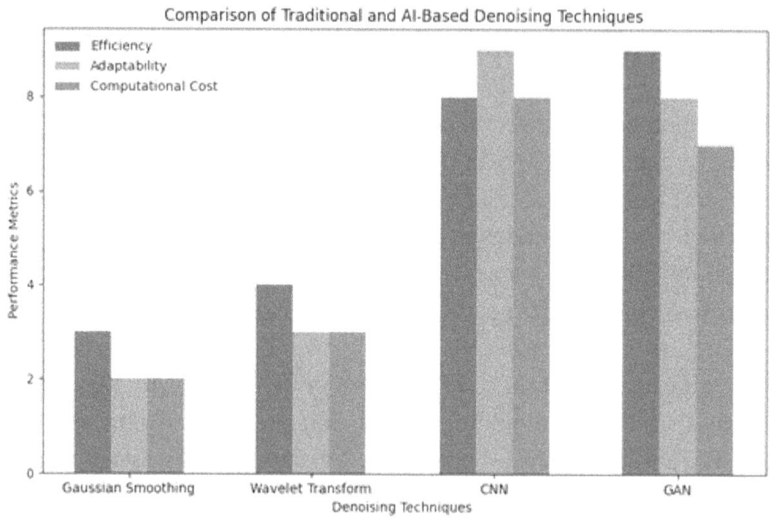

AI-based denoising processes typically follow a structured workflow involving data preprocessing, model training, and denoising application. Figure 3 illustrates a generalized workflow for AI-driven denoising techniques, from raw data input to model evaluation, highlighting steps crucial for maintaining image integrity in forensic applications.

Figure 3. AI denoising workflow

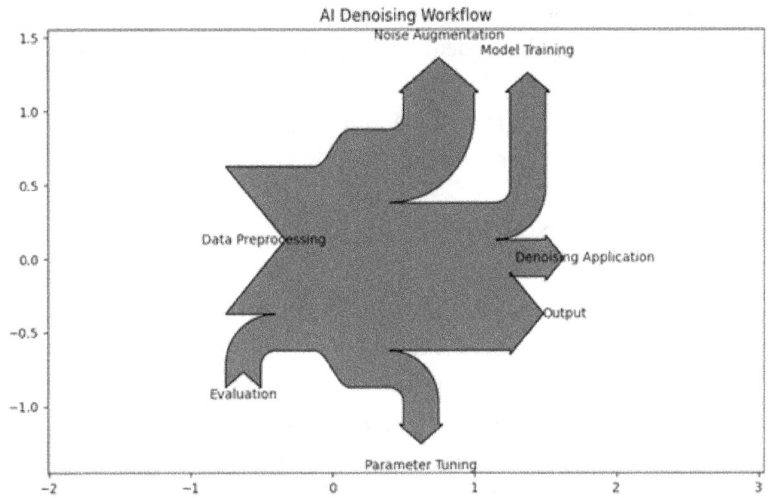

In conclusion, while traditional techniques still hold value for straightforward denoising tasks, AI-based methods are proving indispensable in advanced forensic applications due to their ability to handle complex noise and adapt to various scenarios. However, ethical and security considerations are essential to their application, especially as forensic and cybersecurity landscapes continue to evolve.

4. AI MODELS FOR IMAGE DENOISING

The integration of artificial intelligence in image denoising has led to significant advancements, especially in fields requiring high levels of accuracy, such as forensic analysis and cybersecurity. AI-driven denoising models excel by dynamically learning noise patterns, adapting to various image types, and retaining image details. This section explores the most prominent AI models used for image denoising and their application potential within cybersecurity and forensic domains.

4.1. Convolutional Neural Networks (CNNs)

CNNs are widely adopted in image denoising due to their capability to automatically learn and extract features at multiple layers. Through layered convolution and pooling operations, CNNs can effectively suppress noise while preserving essential image details. These models are particularly valuable for forensic applications, where image integrity and accuracy are crucial (Gupta, Shreneter, & Sehgal, 2024). By training CNNs on datasets that mimic various noise patterns, they can denoise images in real-time, making them ideal for high-speed environments, such as intrusion detection in intelligent vehicle networks (Almehdhar et al., 2024). CNN-based denoising has been instrumental in defending against adversarial noise attacks, enhancing resilience in cybersecurity contexts (Khaleel et al., 2024).

4.2. Denoising Autoencoders (DAEs)

Denoising autoencoders are another popular model, structured to learn robust representations of images by corrupting inputs with noise and then training the network to recover the original, noise-free image. DAEs use an encoder-decoder structure, where the encoder compresses the noisy input, and the decoder reconstructs the image. This structure has been highly effective in cybersecurity and forensic scenarios, as it can handle complex noise types and contribute to better anomaly detection (Fayyaz, Almehmadi, & El-Khatib, 2024). The adaptability of DAEs enables them to manage both simple and intricate noise patterns, proving valuable for forensic analysis of infotainment systems and other embedded systems prone to noise interference (Dhayanidhi, 2022; Aslam, 2024).

4.3. Generative Adversarial Networks (GANs)

GANs represent a transformative approach in denoising, involving two networks—a generator and a discriminator—that work in competition. The generator aims to create denoised images, while the discriminator evaluates them against real noise-free images, refining the denoising process iteratively. GANs have shown exceptional performance in restoring high-quality images from noisy data, making them suitable for sensitive forensic and cybersecurity applications (Lyu, 2024; Golda et al., 2024). While GANs provide unparalleled denoising quality, they also pose ethical and security challenges, as their generative capacity can lead to potential misuse, such as creating deepfake images for deception (Heidari et al., 2024; Khimi et al.).

The rise of GAN-based denoising in cybersecurity illustrates the dual role of generative models: enhancing data recovery and potentially being misused for image manipulation (Takale, Mahalle, & Sule, 2024). Thus, GANs require careful application, particularly in forensic fields, where authenticity is vital (Maheshwari & Paulchamy, 2024).

4.4. Recurrent Neural Networks (RNNs) and Long Short-Term Memory (LSTM) Networks

While RNNs and LSTM networks are more commonly associated with sequential data, they have recently been adapted for image denoising, especially in cases where images are part of video streams or multi-frame scenarios. RNNs and LSTMs can recognize temporal dependencies between frames, allowing for noise reduction in dynamic environments, such as live surveillance feeds, where consistency across frames is crucial (Alotaibi, Williamson, & Khamis, 2023). These models have the potential to strengthen incident response in cybersecurity by identifying and filtering noise from real-time images or video feeds (Ali, Shah, & ElAffendi, 2024; Moustafa et al., 2023).

4.5. Hybrid and Explainable AI Models

Hybrid models combining AI denoising techniques with traditional statistical methods are emerging as a powerful solution, integrating strengths from both approaches. For instance, explainable AI frameworks enhance transparency, helping analysts interpret model outputs and trust the denoising results in legal and forensic contexts (Roshanaei, Khan, & Sylvester, 2024; Choi et al., 2020). Such models also facilitate adaptive response mechanisms in systems like intrusion detection and data protection, providing higher accuracy without sacrificing interpretability (Rane, Choudhary, & Rane, 2024).

The integration of explainable AI in denoising not only enhances model reliability but also assists in mitigating risks associated with automated denoising systems, such as unintentional data alterations or over-denoising that could compromise critical details (Sayyafzadeh, 2024). This approach is especially beneficial in legal proceedings where digital evidence integrity is essential.

AI models utilized in denoising vary in complexity and application scope. This chart in Figure 4 summarizes popular models, such as Convolutional Neural Networks (CNNs), Denoising Autoencoders (DAEs), and Generative Adversarial Networks (GANs), emphasizing their specific attributes, applications, and effectiveness in forensic and cybersecurity settings.

Figure 4. AI models for denoising

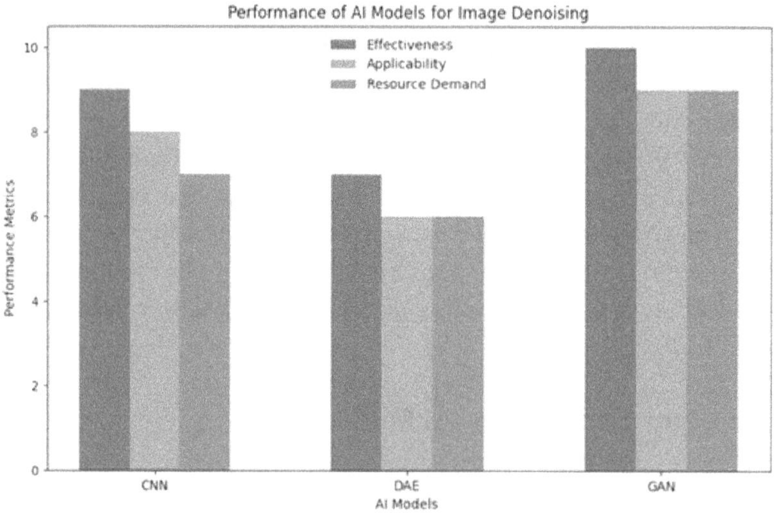

In summary, AI models like CNNs, DAEs, GANs, RNNs, and hybrid systems have set a new standard for image denoising. By leveraging these models, cybersecurity and forensic fields can benefit from enhanced accuracy, speed, and adaptability in noise removal, thereby strengthening data fidelity and forensic reliability. As these models advance, it is essential to balance their technical potential with ethical considerations, especially given the misuse risks in domains such as image forgery and misinformation (Sindiramutty et al., 2025; Das, 2024).

5. CASE STUDIES IN CYBERSECURITY AND FORENSIC IMAGE DENOISING

The application of AI-driven image denoising in cybersecurity and forensics is rapidly evolving, with case studies across various fields demonstrating its potential to enhance digital security, detect forgeries, and improve incident response accuracy. This section presents notable case studies that illustrate how AI-powered denoising technologies are being implemented to address specific cybersecurity and forensic challenges.

5.1. Enhancing Incident Response in Advanced Persistent Threats (APTs)

In cybersecurity, AI-driven denoising techniques have proven effective in enhancing Advanced Persistent Threat (APT) detection and incident response. For instance, the work by Ali, Shah, and ElAffendi (2024) demonstrates the potential of AI-optimized methods to process noisy image and signal data that APT detection systems generate. By applying image denoising, these systems reduce interference, allowing for faster and more accurate response times. This approach has been critical in filtering out irrelevant data within complex, multi-source threat environments, which often include corrupted or noisy digital evidence. The refined data supports timely decision-making, a significant advantage in high-stakes cyber incident management.

5.2. AI-Driven Denoising for Intelligent Vehicle Network Security

In the realm of intelligent vehicle networks, which require robust intrusion detection systems to protect against external attacks, AI models like convolutional neural networks (CNNs) and generative adversarial networks (GANs) have been applied to filter and analyze network traffic data (Almehdhar et al., 2024). These systems often encounter noise from numerous data sources, including GPS and in-vehicle communications, which can hinder the detection of malicious activities. Almehdhar et al. (2024) found that incorporating AI-based denoising enhances the system's capability to differentiate genuine security alerts from noise, thus optimizing real-time response mechanisms in these networks.

5.3. Forensic Analysis of Thermal Attacks and Data Privacy Risks

Thermal attacks on digital devices, such as keyboard interfaces, are a growing threat to privacy. The ThermoSecure study conducted by Alotaibi, Williamson, and Khamis (2023) highlights the application of AI-driven denoising in identifying and countering these attacks. In this context, image denoising helps to filter out thermal noise, making it easier to identify actual heat patterns left by keystrokes. This capability is essential for mitigating privacy breaches and unauthorized access, as well as for advancing forensic practices where heat signatures might be used to reconstruct input sequences without compromising personal data privacy (Majeed & Hwang, 2023).

5.4. Digital Forensics in Infotainment Systems

In forensic investigations, infotainment systems in vehicles present a unique challenge, as these systems generate a mixture of media content, often embedded with significant noise and interference. To address this, Fayyaz, Almehmadi, and El-Khatib (2024) developed a hybrid AI framework that integrates denoising algorithms for efficient processing of multimedia evidence within infotainment systems. By leveraging denoising capabilities, forensic analysts can extract and preserve critical information from audio and visual files, despite noise from internal or external sources, enhancing digital investigation accuracy in criminal or civil cases involving automotive evidence (Hewage et al., 2022).

5.5. Detecting and Preventing Deepfake Manipulations in Cybersecurity

The emergence of deepfake technologies poses substantial risks to digital content integrity, prompting the development of denoising techniques to detect and prevent misuse. Heidari et al. (2024) examine AI-based denoising as a critical element in deepfake detection, as it can differentiate authentic content from AI-generated forgeries. By filtering out noise in video and audio files, these techniques can reveal minute discrepancies that signify deepfake manipulation. Additionally, Maheshwari and Paulchamy (2024) highlight a hybrid approach combining denoising with explainable AI, which allows forensic investigators to understand the denoising process and validate the authenticity of digital media in legal contexts.

5.6. Addressing IoT and Edge Device Noise in Cybersecurity Defense

Internet of Things (IoT) devices and edge computing applications frequently encounter significant noise due to environmental factors and data transmission inconsistencies. Dhayanidhi (2022) discusses the application of AI models to denoise IoT data, facilitating clearer signal processing, which is crucial for detecting anomalies and unauthorized access attempts. In particular, Moustafa et al. (2023) demonstrate that denoising in IoT-based intrusion detection systems improves the quality of insights derived from low-quality sensor data, thereby enhancing overall network security. As IoT deployments continue to grow, implementing such denoising solutions will become increasingly relevant for safeguarding smart environments and reducing the risk of data breaches.

5.7. Digital Integrity and Forgery Detection in Cybersecurity

AI-driven denoising has also been applied to improve forgery detection in digital content, an area vulnerable to manipulation. Bharathiraja et al. (2023) outline how denoising techniques enhance the accuracy of image forgery detection, particularly in cases where noise can mask subtle manipulations. These approaches are particularly beneficial in verifying the authenticity of evidence for legal and forensic purposes. Furthermore, Gupta, Shreneter, and Sehgal (2024) demonstrated that denoising is essential for training CNN-based systems to recognize forged elements within images, thus supporting cyber defense efforts to mitigate risks associated with digital deception and misinformation.

5.8. Securing OSINT Data Through Denoising Techniques

Open Source Intelligence (OSINT) applications rely on large volumes of diverse and often noisy data, posing a challenge for extracting reliable intelligence. Oakley Browne, Abedin, and Chowdhury (2024) discuss AI-based denoising as a method to refine OSINT data, enabling more accurate analysis and reducing the likelihood of false positives. This approach is valuable for cybersecurity professionals who need to interpret and act upon OSINT data, which often contains noise from multiple, unstructured sources. Denoising ensures that only pertinent information is processed, enhancing the reliability of intelligence in cyber threat detection and situational awareness (Roshanaei, Khan, & Sylvester, 2024).

These case studies collectively underscore the versatility and effectiveness of AI-driven image denoising in enhancing digital security and forensic accuracy. As new threats emerge, continued advancements in denoising techniques will be instrumental in mitigating cyber risks and ensuring the integrity of digital content. These innovations not only bolster current cybersecurity practices but also establish a foundation for more resilient systems in future digital landscapes.

6. EVALUATION METRICS FOR DENOISING EFFECTIVENESS

Evaluating the effectiveness of image denoising techniques in cybersecurity and forensic applications requires specific metrics to measure how well noise reduction algorithms improve data quality without compromising essential information. Various metrics are applied across domains to quantify denoising performance, including signal fidelity, processing efficiency, and anomaly detection rates.

6.1. Peak Signal-to-Noise Ratio (PSNR)

Peak Signal-to-Noise Ratio (PSNR) is a widely used metric to assess image denoising quality. It calculates the ratio between the maximum possible pixel value of an image and the power of corrupting noise. High PSNR values indicate that the denoised image closely resembles the original, suggesting minimal information loss during noise reduction. PSNR is especially important in forensic applications where accuracy is critical, such as in digital image forgery detection (Bharathiraja et al., 2023). Higher PSNR values correlate with more reliable forensic analyses, as denoised images retain finer details that can be essential for distinguishing real from manipulated content (Heidari et al., 2024).

6.2. Structural Similarity Index Measure (SSIM)

Structural Similarity Index Measure (SSIM) is another crucial metric that evaluates the similarity between the original and denoised images based on luminance, contrast, and structure. SSIM scores range from -1 to 1, with higher values indicating greater similarity. In cybersecurity contexts, SSIM helps to verify that denoising processes preserve critical structural features necessary for accurate threat detection. For instance, in APT detection, Ali, Shah, and ElAffendi (2024) emphasize the importance of maintaining structural integrity during denoising, as distorted data structures could hinder threat response accuracy.

6.3. Mean Squared Error (MSE)

Mean Squared Error (MSE) quantifies the average squared difference between the original and denoised images, with lower MSE values indicating better denoising performance. MSE is commonly used in scenarios where preserving precise pixel values is crucial, such as detecting deepfakes. Maheshwari and Paulchamy (2024) emphasize MSE's relevance in AI-driven deepfake detection, where even small pixel inaccuracies could obscure subtle forgery indicators. MSE has also been applied in evaluating AI-enhanced digital forensics by Fayyaz, Almehmadi, and El-Khatib (2024) for analyzing infotainment system data, where precise recovery of noisy signals is essential for accurate investigation outcomes.

6.4. Information Entropy

Information entropy measures the complexity of information contained in an image, with higher values indicating greater detail and lower values suggesting simplification due to noise. Effective denoising should balance noise reduction with information retention, ensuring minimal loss in entropy. In scenarios like IoT-based intrusion detection, Dhayanidhi (2022) highlights the importance of preserving informational entropy to maintain accurate threat detection rates despite background noise. Moustafa et al. (2023) also discuss how information entropy aids in assessing denoising techniques in IoT and edge devices, where intricate patterns may signify potential cybersecurity threats.

6.5. Computational Efficiency and Processing Time

In addition to visual quality metrics, computational efficiency and processing time are crucial for real-time applications, especially in environments requiring rapid threat detection and response. Almehdhar et al. (2024) discuss the need for denoising algorithms that operate within limited processing windows in intelligent vehicle networks. Efficient denoising ensures that systems can maintain fast response rates, minimizing potential delays in detecting and addressing cybersecurity threats in high-speed, data-intensive environments.

6.6. Adversarial Robustness

With the rise of adversarial attacks, evaluating the robustness of denoising algorithms against these attacks has become critical. Robustness testing involves introducing adversarial noise or perturbations and assessing the denoising algorithm's ability to remove this noise without losing essential information. Alotaibi, Williamson, and Khamis (2023) highlight adversarial robustness in the context of thermal attack detection, where adversarial noise can obscure keystroke heat patterns. By maintaining robustness, denoising algorithms can prevent adversarial manipulations from compromising the accuracy of forensic and cybersecurity applications (Majeed & Hwang, 2023).

6.7. Precision and Recall in Anomaly Detection

Precision and recall are performance metrics for denoising algorithms integrated within anomaly detection systems. Precision measures the accuracy of detected anomalies, while recall assesses the system's ability to capture all true anomalies. These metrics are especially relevant in applications where noise removal must not interfere with anomaly detection, such as in OSINT and threat intelligence (Oakley Browne, Abedin, & Chowdhury, 2024). High precision and recall indicate that denoising processes effectively minimize false positives while identifying actual threats, an essential capability for reliable cybersecurity monitoring (Choi et al., 2020).

6.8. Human Visual Quality Assessment (HQA)

For applications involving human inspection, Human Visual Quality Assessment (HQA) is often used as a subjective metric, assessing the visual coherence of denoised images through human review. This metric is applied in fields like deepfake detection and image forgery analysis, where human judgment is essential in verifying the authenticity of denoised images (Gupta, Shreneter, & Sehgal, 2024). In cybersecurity applications, HQA helps validate whether denoising algorithms deliver visually accurate outputs, ensuring forensic reliability for legal investigations and content authenticity checks (Rane, Choudhary, & Rane, 2024).

Evaluating denoising performance is essential to ensure both noise reduction and detail preservation. Figure 5 provides an overview of common evaluation metrics, including PSNR, SSIM, and MSE, which are critical for assessing image quality and model performance, especially in forensic and security applications.

Figure 5. Evaluation metrics for denoising

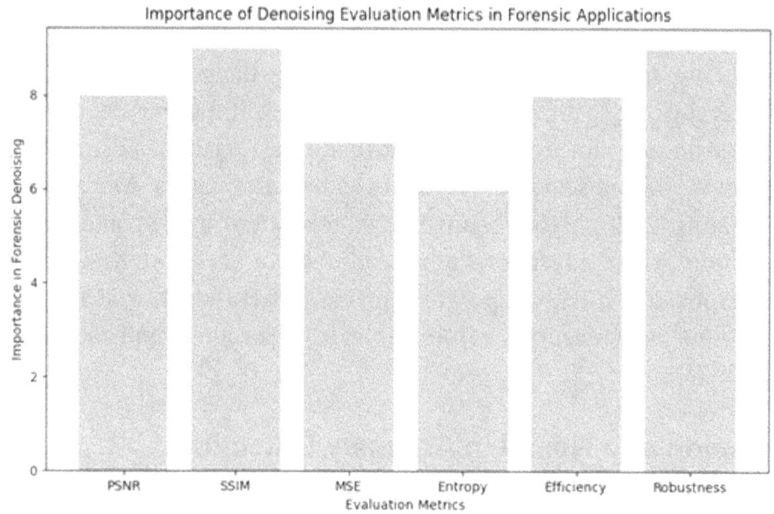

Each of these metrics offers unique insights into the effectiveness of denoising algorithms in cybersecurity and forensic contexts. By employing a combination of objective and subjective assessments, organizations can comprehensively evaluate how well these techniques balance noise reduction, fidelity, and computational efficiency—key factors in advancing secure and trustworthy digital environments.

7. FUTURE DIRECTIONS AND EMERGING TRENDS IN AI-BASED DENOISING

AI-based denoising techniques continue to advance, driven by the rising demand for effective noise reduction in complex cybersecurity and forensic applications. Emerging trends in this field aim to address challenges such as adversarial attacks, real-time processing, and ethical concerns, while promising innovations explore AI's potential to handle evolving threat landscapes and enhance system robustness. Below, key future directions and trends are outlined.

7.1. Adversarial Resilience in Denoising

Adversarial attacks remain a significant concern for AI-driven denoising applications, as malicious inputs can distort denoising processes, affecting image integrity and leading to potential misinterpretations. There is a growing emphasis on developing denoising algorithms that can withstand adversarial perturbations without compromising data quality (Khaleel et al., 2024). Techniques that integrate adversarial training and Explainable AI (XAI) frameworks, such as those proposed by Maheshwari and Paulchamy (2024), are anticipated to enhance resilience against adversarial distortions, particularly in areas like deepfake detection and anomaly identification.

7.2. Generative AI for Enhanced Noise Reduction

Generative AI models, including Variational Autoencoders (VAEs) and Generative Adversarial Networks (GANs), have shown promise in producing high-quality, denoised images by learning complex noise patterns. These models provide more accurate reconstructions, beneficial in scenarios requiring the restoration of visually and structurally accurate data (Singla, 2024). However, using generative AI for denoising also raises security and ethical concerns, especially regarding data privacy and the potential misuse of synthetic images in malicious applications (Golda et al., 2024).

7.3. Denoising in Edge Computing and IoT Environments

As IoT and edge computing continue to grow, there is an increasing need for denoising techniques that operate efficiently in resource-constrained environments. Almehdhar et al. (2024) highlight the critical role of denoising in enhancing the accuracy of intrusion detection within connected vehicle networks. Similarly, IoT-specific applications are focusing on lightweight AI models capable of performing real-time denoising at the edge, allowing for faster and more localized decision-making in threat detection (Dhayanidhi, 2022).

7.4. Explainability in AI-Based Denoising

The adoption of explainable AI (XAI) in denoising processes is essential for establishing trust, particularly in security-sensitive applications. XAI models can offer transparency in how denoising algorithms interpret and process data, which is crucial for applications in forensic analysis and regulatory compliance (Fayyaz, Almehmadi, & El-Khatib, 2024). By employing interpretable models, denoising techniques can ensure that stakeholders understand the noise removal process, thereby supporting reliable data analysis in legal contexts (Moustafa et al., 2023).

7.5. Real-Time Denoising for Incident Response

Real-time denoising capabilities are increasingly necessary for cybersecurity incident response and advanced threat detection (Ali, Shah, & ElAffendi, 2024). With advancements in deep learning, there is potential to create highly efficient denoising algorithms that can process large volumes of data instantaneously. Real-time denoising is particularly valuable for responding to Advanced Persistent Threats (APTs), as rapid data filtering can help detect suspicious activities faster and with higher accuracy (Aslam, 2024).

7.6. Cross-Disciplinary Applications of AI Denoising

Emerging applications of AI-driven denoising extend beyond traditional cybersecurity fields. For instance, thermal attack detection on keyboards, studied by Alotaibi, Williamson, and Khamis (2023), relies on precise image analysis for security in physical environments. Additionally, denoising techniques are now applied to secure image acquisition in OSINT, enhancing the fidelity of data gathered from public sources (Oakley Browne, Abedin, & Chowdhury, 2024). By adapting denoising methods to various fields, researchers can harness AI to secure an ever-expanding range of digital and physical data sources.

7.7. Ethical and Privacy Considerations in AI Denoising

The ethical and privacy implications of AI denoising have garnered increased attention, as denoised images and data carry sensitive information that could be exploited if mishandled (Majeed & Hwang, 2023). Future denoising techniques will likely incorporate privacy-preserving methodologies to ensure that data remains confidential and secure. Efforts are underway to address these concerns, with researchers like Roshanaei, Khan, and Sylvester (2024) advocating for ethical AI practices in cybersecurity that safeguard user privacy and mitigate risks associated with AI-based denoising.

7.8. Denoising for Deepfake and Image Forgery Detection

Denoising plays a crucial role in detecting deepfakes and image forgeries, where noise reduction can reveal subtle artifacts indicative of manipulation. Advanced denoising algorithms are being tailored to improve the detection of digitally manipulated content, as discussed by Gupta, Shreneter, and Sehgal (2024). Integrating denoising with deepfake detection models can enhance the robustness of forgery detection systems, further supported by explainable methodologies to maintain transparency (Khimi et al., 2024; Lyu, 2024).

7.9. AI Denoising and DevSecOps Integration

Integrating denoising within DevSecOps pipelines offers a proactive approach to threat prevention. Denoising algorithms can be employed to sanitize data inputs in real-time, ensuring that noise artifacts do not propagate through the development process (Fu, Pasuksmit, & Tantithamthavorn, 2024). As DevSecOps continues to evolve, AI-based denoising solutions can provide a first line of defense by filtering potentially harmful data at the source, which is particularly valuable for applications in secure software development and system maintenance.

As the field of AI-based denoising continues to evolve, several trends are emerging that are likely to shape future advancements. Figure 6 highlights key trends, including real-time processing, edge computing, adversarial resilience, and ethical considerations, underscoring their significance for both cybersecurity and forensic applications.

Figure 6. Future trends in AI-Based denoising

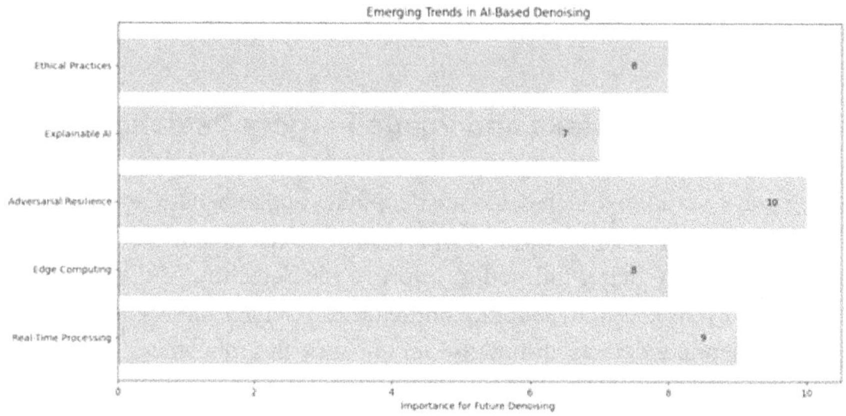

7.10. Summary

AI-based denoising techniques are rapidly evolving, with advancements spanning adversarial resilience, generative AI integration, and ethical practices. By focusing on real-time capabilities, explainability, and cross-disciplinary applications, researchers and practitioners are setting the stage for more sophisticated and robust denoising frameworks. As denoising methodologies advance, they will play an increasingly pivotal role in safeguarding digital assets, enhancing incident response, and promoting secure data management across cybersecurity and forensic domains.

8. CONCLUSION

The rapid advancements in AI-driven denoising techniques have opened up new avenues for enhanced cybersecurity and forensic practices. These sophisticated algorithms are no longer limited to traditional noise removal but are evolving into powerful tools capable of addressing a range of complex challenges, from adversarial resilience to real-time incident response. By combining deep learning, generative AI, and explainable models, modern denoising methods offer not only increased accuracy but also improved transparency, making them highly adaptable across various security and forensic applications.

AI-based denoising has also proven valuable in addressing specific challenges posed by emerging threats, such as deepfakes and image forgeries. The application of these techniques in detecting and analyzing digitally manipulated content underscores their importance in maintaining the integrity and reliability of digital evidence. Furthermore, the expansion of denoising into IoT and edge computing environments highlights its critical role in real-time security across a broad range of interconnected systems, where it can help identify and filter suspicious data closer to its source.

As the field continues to evolve, ethical considerations and privacy protection will play a more prominent role in shaping denoising technologies. With growing concerns over data misuse and privacy breaches, future advancements will likely incorporate safeguards to ensure the responsible use of denoising in sensitive applications. The integration of privacy-preserving techniques within denoising frameworks will help secure personal and proprietary data while still enabling robust analysis.

In summary, AI-based denoising has emerged as a vital component of modern cybersecurity and forensic workflows. By addressing a spectrum of challenges, from adversarial threats to ethical considerations, AI denoising solutions provide essential support in preserving data integrity and enabling secure digital environments. As the demand for more resilient and transparent cybersecurity tools grows, AI-driven denoising will continue to advance, offering valuable contributions to the protection and analysis of digital information.

REFERENCES

Ali, G., Shah, S., & ElAffendi, M. (2024). Enhancing Cybersecurity Incident Response: AI-Driven Optimization for Strengthened Advance Persistence Threat Detection.

Almehdhar, M., Albaseer, A., Khan, M. A., Abdallah, M., Menouar, H., Al-Kuwari, S., & Al-Fuqaha, A. (2024). Deep learning in the fast lane: A survey on advanced intrusion detection systems for intelligent vehicle networks. *IEEE Open Journal of Vehicular Technology*, 5, 869–906. DOI: 10.1109/OJVT.2024.3422253

Alotaibi, N., Williamson, J., & Khamis, M. (2023). ThermoSecure: Investigating the effectiveness of AI-driven thermal attacks on commonly used computer keyboards. *ACM Transactions on Privacy and Security*, 26(2), 1–24. DOI: 10.1145/3563693

Aslam, M. (2024). AI and cybersecurity: An ever-evolving landscape. *International Journal of Advanced Engineering Technologies and Innovations*, 1(1), 52–71.

Bharathiraja, S., Rajesh Kanna, B., Geetha, S., & Anusooya, G. (2023). Unmasking the digital deception-a comprehensive survey on image forgery and detection techniques. *The Australian Journal of Forensic Sciences*, •••, 1–49.

Choi, Y. H., Liu, P., Shang, Z., Wang, H., Wang, Z., Zhang, L., Zhou, J., & Zou, Q. (2020). Using deep learning to solve computer security challenges: A survey. *Cybersecurity*, 3(1), 1–32. DOI: 10.1186/s42400-020-00055-5

Das, R. (2024). *Generative AI: Phishing And Cybersecurity Metrics*. CRC Press. DOI: 10.1201/9781003503781

Dhayanidhi, G. (2022). Research on IoT threats & implementation of AI/ML to address emerging cybersecurity issues in IoT with cloud computing.

Fayyaz, Y., Almehmadi, A., & El-Khatib, K. (2024). A hybrid artificial intelligence framework for enhancing digital forensic investigations of infotainment systems. *Forensic Science International Digital Investigation*, 49, 301751. DOI: 10.1016/j.fsidi.2024.301751

Fu, M., Pasuksmit, J., & Tantithamthavorn, C. (2024). AI for DevSecOps: A Landscape and Future Opportunities. *arXiv preprint arXiv:2404.04839.*

Golda, A., Mekonen, K., Pandey, A., Singh, A., Hassija, V., Chamola, V., & Sikdar, B. (2024). Privacy and Security Concerns in Generative AI: A Comprehensive Survey. *IEEE Access : Practical Innovations, Open Solutions*, 12, 48126–48144. DOI: 10.1109/ACCESS.2024.3381611

Gupta, A. S., Shreneter, K. P., & Sehgal, S. (2024, March). Visual Veracity: Advancing AI-Generated Image Detection with Convolutional Neural Networks. In *2024 11th International Conference on Reliability, Infocom Technologies and Optimization (Trends and Future Directions)(ICRITO)* (pp. 1-6). IEEE.

Heidari, A., Jafari Navimipour, N., Dag, H., & Unal, M. (2024). Deepfake detection using deep learning methods: A systematic and comprehensive review. *Wiley Interdisciplinary Reviews. Data Mining and Knowledge Discovery*, 14(2), e1520. DOI: 10.1002/widm.1520

Hewage, C. T., Khattak, S. K., Ahmad, A., Mallikarachchi, T., Ukwandu, E., & Bentotahewa, V. (2022). Multimedia privacy and security landscape in the wake of ai/ml. *Social Media Analytics, Strategies and Governance*, 203-228.

Khaleel, Y. L., Habeeb, M. A., Albahri, A. S., Al-Quraishi, T., Albahri, O. S., & Alamoodi, A. H. (2024). Network and cybersecurity applications of defense in adversarial attacks: A state-of-the-art using machine learning and deep learning methods. *Journal of Intelligent Systems*, 33(1), 20240153. DOI: 10.1515/jisys-2024-0153

Khimi, W., Albarqi, K., Saif, K., & Elhag, S. A Systematic Review on Deep Fake Image Generation, Detection Techniques, Ethical Implications, and Overcoming Challenges.

Khormali, A. (2022). Advanced Deep Learning Methodologies for Deepfake Detection.

Lyu, S. (2024). *DeepFake the menace: mitigating the negative impacts of AI-generated content. Organizational Cybersecurity Journal: Practice*. Process and People.

Maheshwari, R. U., & Paulchamy, B. (2024). Securing online integrity: A hybrid approach to deepfake detection and removal using Explainable AI and Adversarial Robustness Training. *Automatika (Zagreb)*, 65(4), 1517–1532. DOI: 10.1080/00051144.2024.2400640

Majeed, A., & Hwang, S. O. (2023). When AI meets information privacy: The adversarial role of AI in data sharing scenario. *IEEE Access : Practical Innovations, Open Solutions*, 11, 76177–76195. DOI: 10.1109/ACCESS.2023.3297646

Moustafa, N., Koroniotis, N., Keshk, M., Zomaya, A. Y., & Tari, Z. (2023). Explainable intrusion detection for cyber defences in the internet of things: Opportunities and solutions. *IEEE Communications Surveys and Tutorials*, 25(3), 1775–1807. DOI: 10.1109/COMST.2023.3280465

Oakley Browne, T., Abedin, M., & Chowdhury, M. J. M. (2024). A systematic review on research utilising artificial intelligence for open source intelligence (OSINT) applications.

Rane, N., Choudhary, S., & Rane, J. (2024). Machine Learning and Deep Learning: a Comprehensive Review on Methods, Techniques, Applications, Challenges, and Future Directions. *Techniques, Applications, Challenges, and Future Directions (May 31, 2024).*

Rohatgi, S., Abinash, B., Joshi, S., Sushant, S., & Kumar, S. (2023). Introduction to Artificial Intelligence and Cybersecurity for Industry. In *Artificial Intelligence and Cyber Security in Industry 4.0* (pp. 1–22). Springer Nature Singapore. DOI: 10.1007/978-981-99-2115-7_1

Roshanaei, M., Khan, M. R., & Sylvester, N. N. (2024). Navigating AI Cybersecurity: Evolving Landscape and Challenges. *Journal of Intelligent Learning Systems and Applications*, 16(3), 155–174. DOI: 10.4236/jilsa.2024.163010

Sayyafzadeh, S. (2024). *Thumbnail Image Forensic Acquisition and Analysis in the Age of Artificial Intelligence* (Master's thesis, Florida Agricultural and Mechanical University).

Sindiramutty, S. R., Prabagaran, K. R. V., Akbar, R., Hussain, M., & Malik, N. A. (2025). Overview of Generative AI Techniques for Cybersecurity. *Reshaping CyberSecurity With Generative AI Techniques*, 1-52.

Singla, J. (2024). Safeguarding the Future: Advancements in Cybersecurity. *Utilizing Generative AI for Cyber Defense Strategies*, 421.

Takale, D. G., Mahalle, P. N., & Sule, B. (2024). Cyber Security Challenges in Generative AI Technology. *Journal of Network Security Computer Networks*, 10(1), 28–34.

Tyagi, A. K., & Addula, S. R. (2024). Artificial Intelligence for Malware Analysis: A Systematic Study. *Artificial Intelligence-Enabled Digital Twin for Smart Manufacturing*, 359-390.

Zhao, C., Du, H., Niyato, D., Kang, J., Xiong, Z., Kim, D. I., Shen, X., & Letaief, K. B. (2024). Generative AI for secure physical layer communications: A survey. *IEEE Transactions on Cognitive Communications and Networking*, 1. DOI: 10.1109/TCCN.2024.3438379

Chapter 6
Automated Evidence Collection and Analysis Using AI

Luay Albtosh
https://orcid.org/0009-0009-0338-9123
Capitol Technology University, USA & Houston Community College, USA

ABSTRACT

The integration of Artificial Intelligence (AI) in forensic investigations has transformed evidence collection and analysis, enabling quicker and more accurate assessments. This chapter examines the evolution and application of automated AI-driven tools in collecting, processing, and analyzing digital evidence. AI-based systems assist forensic experts by autonomously identifying, organizing, and categorizing massive datasets, thus accelerating traditional investigative workflows. Key AI methods discussed include machine learning algorithms for data classification, natural language processing for document analysis, and computer vision for image and video recognition. Additionally, we explore the implications of these technologies for the legal system, privacy concerns, and the accuracy and reliability of evidence derived through automation. This chapter also considers potential challenges, such as data integrity and bias, as well as future trends in AI applications within digital forensics.

1. INTRODUCTION TO AUTOMATED EVIDENCE COLLECTION AND ANALYSIS

Automated evidence collection and analysis using artificial intelligence (AI) represents a transformative development in cybersecurity and digital forensics. AI technologies facilitate a more efficient, accurate, and comprehensive approach

DOI: 10.4018/979-8-3373-0588-2.ch006

to handling digital evidence, overcoming limitations associated with traditional methods of forensic investigation. Manual forensic analysis, while thorough, is often labor-intensive and prone to delays, especially in environments dealing with high volumes of data and complex cybercrime patterns. As cyber threats evolve in sophistication and scale, integrating AI into digital forensic practices enables organizations to enhance their response to cyber incidents, reducing time to detection and response while ensuring thorough evidence processing (Tyagi, Kumari, & Richa, 2024; Hassan & Ibrahim, 2023).

The automation of forensic processes through AI has emerged as a priority in incident response and cybersecurity fields. Key benefits include rapid data parsing, real-time threat detection, and insights derived from advanced data analytics. AI's machine learning (ML) and deep learning (DL) models, when applied to digital forensics, are able to process large datasets, identify anomalies, and generate actionable intelligence much faster than human analysts alone. This capability not only accelerates investigation times but also reduces the risk of missing critical evidence, which can have severe implications for organizational security and legal proceedings (Jarrett & Choo, 2021; Samtani, Kantarcioglu, & Chen, 2020).

With the widespread integration of AI in forensic analysis, a multidisciplinary approach is often required to address the ethical, technical, and operational implications of these technologies. Issues such as data privacy, the interpretability of AI-driven conclusions, and the legal admissibility of evidence collected through AI-driven methods require careful consideration. As discussed by Moustafa (2022), the era of AI in digital forensics has introduced both opportunities and challenges, necessitating advancements in both the regulatory and technical aspects of evidence handling.

Furthermore, recent advancements emphasize the importance of automation in digital forensics, particularly in high-stakes domains such as healthcare, finance, and national security. Automation tools and platforms integrated with AI are now able to support forensic investigators in threat detection, anomaly analysis, and the categorization of complex data structures. Research by Dunsin et al. (2024) highlights the potential for AI-based solutions to revolutionize incident response processes by providing robust analytical capabilities, enhancing the identification of cyber threats, and supporting efficient data collection strategies.

The integration of AI into digital forensics has streamlined the process of evidence collection and analysis. The following flowchart illustrates the automated workflow, highlighting each stage from data acquisition to evidence classification and reporting.

Figure 1. AI-Driven forensic workflow

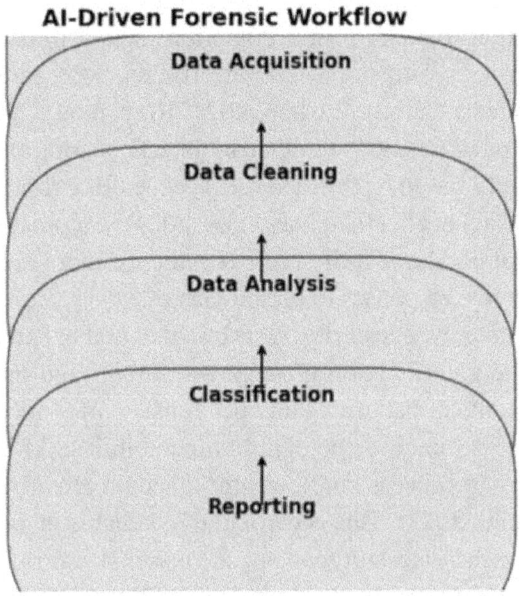

Overall, AI's role in automated evidence collection and analysis is a significant step forward in modern cybersecurity and forensic practices. The growing adoption of these tools indicates a shift toward more proactive and resilient approaches to cyber defense, empowering organizations to protect their assets and respond effectively to cyber incidents. This chapter delves into the technological, ethical, and practical aspects of AI-driven evidence collection, examining the implications for digital forensics and cybersecurity at large.

2. AI FUNDAMENTALS IN EVIDENCE COLLECTION AND ANALYSIS

The integration of artificial intelligence (AI) into evidence collection and analysis is rapidly transforming the digital forensics landscape, providing enhanced capabilities for processing and interpreting vast datasets associated with cyber incidents. Key areas where AI is having a significant impact include automation in digital forensics, improved detection and analysis of cybersecurity threats, and the application of machine learning for identifying and mitigating potential risks.

AI technologies are leveraged in digital forensics for a range of tasks, including anomaly detection, data pattern recognition, and automated incident response, providing forensic investigators with powerful tools to handle increasingly sophisticated cyber threats (Jarrett & Choo, 2021; Rizvi et al., 2022). Machine learning algorithms, for instance, can be trained to detect cyber intrusions and help analysts prioritize incidents based on threat severity, expediting response times and enhancing accuracy (Tyagi et al., 2024; Nair et al., 2024). Automated systems can analyze large amounts of data to identify critical evidence more rapidly, thereby enabling timely and effective responses to digital crimes.

In the domain of cybersecurity, AI is instrumental in handling various challenges, including the identification of unknown threats and the ability to adaptively learn from new attack patterns. Digital forensics often requires rapid analysis of complex datasets to uncover potential vulnerabilities; AI provides the analytical power necessary to process and interpret this data effectively (Kaur et al., 2023; Hassan & Ibrahim, 2023). This is particularly valuable in dynamic and high-stakes environments, such as law enforcement and national security, where timely insights can be pivotal (Moustafa, 2022; Montasari, 2023).

Additionally, deep learning and natural language processing (NLP) techniques are proving valuable for forensics, especially in cases involving unstructured data, such as emails and chat logs. These methods allow systems to interpret text, images, and video evidence, aiding in the classification of digital artifacts and linking disparate data points to provide a coherent narrative for investigators (Syed & ES, 2024; Du et al., 2020). Advanced applications of AI in digital forensics extend to blockchain-based timestamping and anomaly detection in encrypted data, ensuring data integrity and enhancing traceability within the digital evidence lifecycle (Zangana et al., 2024; Gholami & Omar, 2024).

Despite these advancements, AI in digital forensics also brings forward challenges. There is a need for explainability in AI algorithms to ensure that the decisions made by these systems are transparent and interpretable by human investigators (Capuano et al., 2022). Furthermore, continuous improvement and fine-tuning of AI models are essential to keep up with evolving cyber threats, as attackers adapt and find new ways to bypass security mechanisms (Samtani et al., 2020; Bonfanti, 2022).

As the field progresses, the role of AI in evidence collection and analysis is likely to expand, offering even more sophisticated tools for digital forensics professionals. This expansion promises not only to enhance the efficacy of investigations but also to redefine standards in cybersecurity and evidence handling across multiple sectors (Ali, 2022; Dunsin et al., 2024).

3. TYPES OF EVIDENCE SUITABLE FOR AUTOMATED COLLECTION

In digital forensics, the nature of evidence suitable for automated collection varies significantly, ranging from data logs and network traffic to application-specific metadata and user-generated files. Automated collection methods are especially useful in gathering time-sensitive data, such as log files, which capture timestamps, IP addresses, and user actions in real-time. For example, artificial intelligence (AI) techniques facilitate the rapid collection and analysis of these logs, identifying suspicious patterns or deviations in behavior that may indicate malicious activity (Tyagi, Kumari, & Richa, 2024; Rizvi et al., 2022).

Network traffic is another critical type of evidence, as it reveals patterns of data flow, potential intrusion points, and instances of unauthorized access. AI-driven tools, like machine learning algorithms, assist in collecting and examining large volumes of network traffic data, which would otherwise overwhelm human analysts (Rizvi et al., 2022; Kaur, Gabrijelčič, & Klobučar, 2023). These tools also help distinguish legitimate network behaviors from anomalies that suggest an intrusion, which is vital in incidents where attackers attempt to disguise their tracks (Syed & ES, 2024).

Metadata, such as email headers or document properties, also constitutes significant evidence in digital forensics. Automated systems can efficiently parse metadata from a variety of file types, allowing investigators to trace the origins of files, verify authorship, and establish timelines without needing manual examination. For example, in phishing investigations, metadata helps reveal the source and propagation of malicious emails, which is critical for reconstructing attack chains (Zangana et al., 2024).

User-generated files, including documents, images, and videos, provide additional context and may contain embedded or residual data that automated tools can extract and analyze. Advances in AI have enabled sophisticated content analysis on these files, allowing forensic tools to detect hidden information, such as steganography, or identify specific subjects within images through image recognition technologies (Bonfanti, 2022; Murphy, 2022).

AI techniques in digital forensics manage diverse evidence types, from network traffic to user files. The following bar chart depicts the common types of digital evidence processed through automated AI techniques, demonstrating its application across various data formats.

Figure 2. Evidence types processed by AI in digital forensics

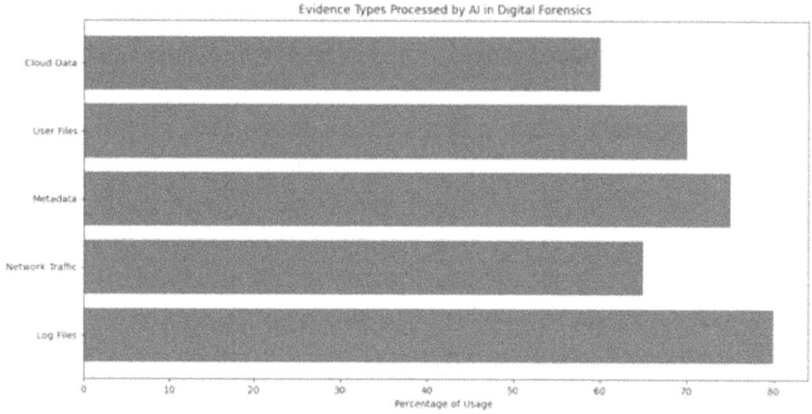

Finally, AI-driven automation has also been employed in the acquisition and examination of data from mobile devices, social media, and cloud-based environments. These areas are becoming increasingly relevant in modern digital forensics, given the rise in remote work and the prevalence of cloud storage solutions (Samtani, Kantarcioglu, & Chen, 2020; Mughal, 2019). Automated tools can navigate these complex digital environments, pulling data efficiently from diverse sources to provide investigators with a comprehensive view of the digital landscape surrounding a cyber incident (Alghamdi, 2021; Montasari, 2023).

4. AUTOMATED DATA ACQUISITION TECHNIQUES

Automated data acquisition is a fundamental component in modern digital forensics and cybersecurity, significantly enhancing efficiency, accuracy, and scope. As the volume of data generated across networks and devices continues to grow, automation helps mitigate the challenges associated with manual data collection. Recent advances in artificial intelligence (AI) and machine learning (ML) have further propelled the capabilities of automated tools, which can now sift through vast amounts of data, pinpoint critical information, and expedite the decision-making process (Jarrett & Choo, 2021; Tyagi et al., 2024).

Automated data acquisition often leverages AI to handle unstructured data, such as logs, network traffic, and multimedia files, enabling real-time processing and analysis. This advancement is crucial in cyber forensics, where investigators require both speed and accuracy to detect and respond to potential threats effectively (Hassan

& Ibrahim, 2023). For example, tools using AI algorithms are capable of identifying suspicious patterns in data, such as abnormal login attempts or data transfer activities, which may indicate cyber attacks or data breaches (Dunsin et al., 2024).

Additionally, in cybersecurity incident response, AI-driven automation assists in the systematic collection of forensic evidence, which is vital for tracking threat actors and preserving data integrity (Montasari, 2023; Moustafa, 2022). AI's role extends beyond mere acquisition; it also assists in the intelligent filtering of data to prioritize critical information, reducing noise and allowing analysts to focus on high-priority alerts. Such approaches are increasingly vital, especially with the integration of IoT devices and cloud services, which contribute to a complex and dispersed data environment (Alghamdi, 2021; Zangana et al., 2024).

AI's application in automation also strengthens digital forensics by improving accuracy in identifying and acquiring relevant data, thus mitigating human errors. This ensures that data handling during investigations remains reliable and unbiased, which is essential in scenarios requiring stringent compliance with legal standards (Rizvi et al., 2022; Tuli & Thaduri, 2023). Furthermore, automated data acquisition tools provide cybersecurity professionals with rapid insights by utilizing machine learning techniques to classify data in real time, aligning with the goal of preemptive threat mitigation in cybersecurity frameworks (Kaur et al., 2023; Omar & Zangana, 2024).

In sum, automated data acquisition techniques, powered by AI, represent a transformative shift in digital forensics and cybersecurity. By enabling precise, fast, and scalable data handling, these techniques not only streamline investigations but also offer a robust defense against increasingly sophisticated cyber threats (Faqir, 2023; Murphy, 2022).

5. AI IN EVIDENCE PRESERVATION AND INTEGRITY VERIFICATION

The use of artificial intelligence (AI) in evidence preservation and integrity verification is reshaping the field of digital forensics. AI methods bring new capabilities for securing the integrity of digital evidence from the point of acquisition to final analysis. This section discusses how AI tools and algorithms contribute to preserving digital evidence and verifying its integrity, particularly in the dynamic and challenging landscape of cyber forensics.

5.1 Ensuring Evidence Integrity with AI Tools

Maintaining the integrity of evidence throughout the forensic process is paramount for reliable results and admissibility in legal contexts. AI techniques like machine learning and neural networks are increasingly applied to detect any tampering with digital artifacts, such as metadata changes or content manipulation (Rizvi et al., 2022; Dunsin et al., 2024). These approaches analyze vast datasets and identify anomalies that may indicate an alteration, helping forensic analysts flag suspicious data promptly (Jarrett & Choo, 2021). Moreover, blockchain technology, integrated with AI for timestamping and verification, offers additional security against unauthorized alterations of data (Zangana, 2024; Al-Hajri et al., 2023).

5.2 AI-Enhanced Evidence Preservation

The preservation of evidence involves ensuring that the digital evidence collected is stored and managed without compromise. AI-enhanced forensic methods, such as AI-driven automated acquisition systems, optimize the handling of large volumes of data, which is critical in cloud and IoT environments. These systems leverage machine learning algorithms to assess data relevance, reducing the potential for data loss or accidental modification during acquisition (Tyagi et al., 2024; Hassan & Ibrahim, 2023). Additionally, AI enables automated tracking and logging, supporting a comprehensive chain of custody for every data interaction, thereby strengthening the traceability of evidence handling (Moustafa, 2022; Capuano et al., 2022).

5.3 Application of AI for Real-Time Verification

AI is also proving valuable in real-time integrity verification, where digital evidence is authenticated and validated as it is gathered. This is particularly useful in fast-paced environments where data volatility requires immediate validation to prevent data corruption. For example, explainable AI (XAI) models allow forensic experts to understand and justify how evidence integrity is assessed, promoting transparency in forensic processes (Kaur et al., 2023; Capuano et al., 2022). As cyber threats grow more sophisticated, integrating XAI tools aids in justifying forensic decisions and fortifying the trustworthiness of digital evidence handling.

5.4 Overcoming Challenges in Evidence Verification

AI-driven evidence verification comes with challenges, such as balancing accuracy with explainability and ensuring compliance with legal standards. Despite these challenges, AI continues to streamline forensic processes, making digital forensics more resilient against manipulative threats like deepfakes and altered metadata (Samtani et al., 2020; Bonfanti, 2022). Research also indicates that the hybrid use of AI with traditional cryptographic methods improves evidence integrity checks, thereby addressing potential vulnerabilities in automated systems (Omar & Zangana, 2024; Murphy, 2022).

AI has transformed evidence preservation and integrity verification in digital forensics, offering enhanced accuracy, efficiency, and reliability. By combining machine learning, blockchain, and explainable models, AI continues to fortify the integrity of digital evidence, thus contributing to more robust and defensible forensic outcomes.

6. DATA PROCESSING AND PREPROCESSING FOR EVIDENCE ANALYSIS

Data processing and preprocessing are essential steps in evidence analysis, particularly when dealing with vast amounts of digital information. Digital forensic investigations rely on these processes to extract, clean, and format data for efficient analysis and accurate interpretation. As the volume and complexity of data continue to grow, particularly in cybersecurity contexts, automation and artificial intelligence (AI) play increasingly significant roles in refining these stages, enabling more thorough insights and efficient workflows (Tyagi, Kumari, & Richa, 2024).

Data preprocessing is vital in digital forensics to ensure accurate and reliable evidence analysis. The following flowchart outlines the main stages, including data collection, filtering, cleaning, transformation, and validation.

Figure 3. Data preprocessing stages

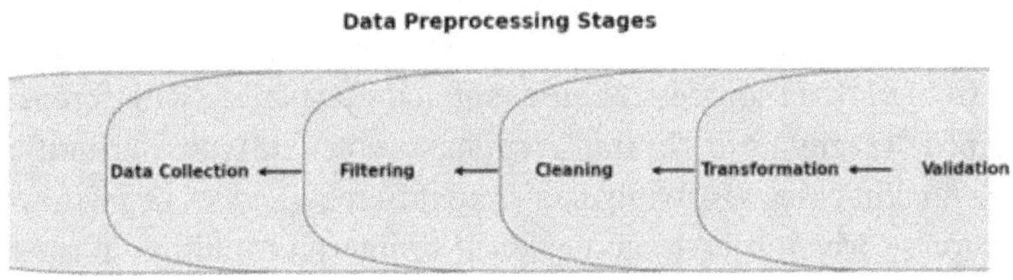

6.1 Data Collection and Filtering

Data collection in digital forensics involves gathering digital artifacts from various sources, such as devices, networks, and storage systems. The collected data often contains a mix of structured and unstructured information, which can include log files, emails, images, and application data. Effective filtering is crucial to ensure the data remains relevant to the investigation. AI-driven solutions are advantageous here, as they allow forensic investigators to automate the identification and extraction of pertinent data, reducing manual effort and time (Hassan & Ibrahim, 2023; Moustafa, 2022). For instance, automated tools can prioritize data from known threat signatures or filter data based on predefined investigation parameters, enabling a more focused and efficient analysis (Jarrett & Choo, 2021).

6.2 Data Cleaning and Noise Reduction

Once collected, the data often contains noise—irrelevant or redundant information that may obscure critical evidence. Data cleaning techniques, supported by machine learning and AI, are deployed to remove such noise and enhance data quality. Noise reduction is particularly critical in the cybersecurity domain, where false positives can mislead investigators. Techniques such as clustering and anomaly detection can help in isolating relevant data while reducing the amount of redundant information (Dunsin et al., 2024). Additionally, advanced methods like deep learning models enable effective pattern recognition within large datasets, making it possible to highlight anomalies that could indicate security breaches or unauthorized access (Zangana & Omar, 2020; Du et al., 2020).

6.3 Data Standardization and Transformation

Standardizing data formats is another fundamental step in preprocessing, ensuring that data from various sources is consistent and compatible with forensic analysis tools. AI models facilitate this by transforming diverse data types into unified formats, a task essential in cases involving data from different devices or platforms. Digital forensics tools, driven by AI, are designed to interpret multiple formats, making it easier to process and compare data effectively. Tools such as AI-driven parsers can automatically convert data, for example, from proprietary logs to standardized formats (Zeadally et al., 2020; Mughal, 2019). This standardization aids in cross-referencing evidence and improves interoperability between forensic systems (Kaur, Gabrijelčič, & Klobučar, 2023).

6.4 Data Validation and Integrity Verification

To ensure the validity and reliability of the evidence, data integrity verification is critical. Methods such as hashing and blockchain-based timestamping are utilized to validate the data's authenticity and protect it from tampering throughout the forensic process. Recent developments in AI and blockchain integration offer robust solutions for data integrity verification, providing immutable records that maintain the evidential quality of digital artifacts (Zangana, 2024; Omar & Zangana, 2024). Additionally, deep learning techniques are used to detect any tampering or unauthorized modifications to the data, thereby ensuring that the forensic evidence remains intact (Ali, 2022; Tuli & Thaduri, 2023).

6.5 Preprocessing Challenges and Future Directions

The adoption of AI-driven preprocessing techniques has improved the efficiency of digital forensic investigations, but challenges remain. For instance, managing the diversity of data sources and formats requires continuous advancements in AI tools to ensure adaptability and accuracy. Moreover, the implementation of explainable AI (XAI) is needed to enhance transparency in preprocessing steps, allowing investigators to understand and trust the decisions made by AI systems (Capuano et al., 2022; Syed & ES, 2024). Future advancements are likely to focus on integrating more sophisticated AI algorithms that not only automate preprocessing but also adapt dynamically to new data patterns and forensic needs (Rizvi et al., 2022; Montasari, 2023).

In summary, effective data processing and preprocessing are foundational to reliable evidence analysis in digital forensics. AI and machine learning technologies enable significant efficiencies in collecting, filtering, cleaning, and validating data, allowing forensic investigators to focus on more complex interpretative tasks and ensuring that the evidence remains both relevant and credible for legal proceedings.

7. USING MACHINE LEARNING FOR EVIDENCE ANALYSIS AND CLASSIFICATION

Machine learning (ML) has become instrumental in digital forensics, offering innovative methods for efficiently analyzing and classifying evidence. Its application has revolutionized traditional digital forensic processes by automating labor-intensive tasks and improving the accuracy of threat detection, data recovery, and evidence classification. This section explores key machine learning models and methods used in evidence analysis, drawing on advancements and current implementations within digital forensic science.

Machine learning in digital forensics supports real-time evidence analysis, a critical factor given the increasing complexity and volume of data in cyber investigations. Tyagi, Kumari, and Richa (2024) highlight that ML-driven digital forensic tools can process massive datasets to identify patterns and correlations that would otherwise go unnoticed, thus expediting incident response. Similarly, automation, as explored by Jarrett and Choo (2021), has greatly improved the scalability of forensic investigations by enabling continuous, automated threat assessment and facilitating faster evidence classification.

A range of ML algorithms, including supervised, unsupervised, and deep learning techniques, are applied to enhance digital forensics, from identifying anomalies in data (Hassan & Ibrahim, 2023) to classifying types of cyberattacks based on historical data. For instance, the integration of deep learning models in digital forensics, as suggested by Moustafa (2022), helps detect complex attack patterns and classify evidence with a higher accuracy rate, especially in sophisticated cybercrime investigations.

Furthermore, neural networks and convolutional neural networks (CNNs) have demonstrated significant efficacy in classifying large datasets, particularly for image recognition and natural language processing in digital forensics (Dunsin et al., 2024). These algorithms help digital investigators sift through vast data sets to detect traces of cyber incidents, thus enhancing the precision and reliability of digital evidence.

Another prominent application is AI's role in filtering and categorizing evidence, as noted by Kaur, Gabrijelčič, and Klobučar (2023), which allows investigators to prioritize critical data points efficiently. This automation is not only time-saving but also enhances the consistency of forensic analysis, reducing potential biases in manual evidence review. The ability to predict and classify based on historical cases is also facilitated by AI, as discussed by Rizvi et al. (2022), enabling more proactive forensic methodologies.

Additionally, the deployment of AI in digital forensics aids in addressing the dynamic nature of cyber threats, including new methods of cyber deception like email phishing and other advanced persistent threats, as explored by Zangana, Mohammed, Sallow, & Sallow (2024). Machine learning techniques are also instrumental in identifying previously unknown attack vectors through predictive analysis, which is vital in rapidly evolving cyber environments (Du et al., 2020).

The potential for machine learning to advance digital forensic methodologies continues to expand, underscored by the importance of AI in evidence extraction, data preservation, and real-time analytics (Zeadally et al., 2020). As digital forensics grows more complex, these machine learning advancements promise to streamline and enhance the accuracy of investigative processes, as well as offer a more agile response to emerging cyber threats.

By utilizing ML for evidence analysis and classification, digital forensic science can achieve unprecedented levels of efficiency and effectiveness, transforming the landscape of modern cybersecurity and digital investigations. This chapter continues with a deeper analysis of ML applications in digital forensics, expanding on specific case studies, technical implementations, and future directions in ML for evidence classification.

8. NATURAL LANGUAGE PROCESSING (NLP) FOR TEXT-BASED EVIDENCE ANALYSIS

The application of Natural Language Processing (NLP) in digital forensics has transformed the way investigators analyze and interpret vast amounts of text-based evidence. NLP techniques enable automated parsing, understanding, and contextualization of unstructured data, making it a crucial tool for modern forensics (Kaur, Gabrijelčič, & Klobučar, 2023). By leveraging advanced NLP algorithms, digital forensic investigators can detect patterns and correlations across datasets, aiding in uncovering hidden connections that would be difficult to recognize manually (Tyagi, Kumari, & Richa, 2024).

One of the significant benefits of NLP in forensic analysis is its capability to handle large volumes of data from diverse sources, such as emails, social media posts, and other textual communications. This capability is essential for cyber investigations, where evidence is often hidden within textual data, requiring robust language models for context-based analysis (Samtani, Kantarcioglu, & Chen, 2020). The use of NLP for automated text classification, sentiment analysis, and entity recognition has been further augmented by advancements in AI and machine learning, which improve the precision of identifying relevant content within large datasets (Rizvi et al., 2022).

NLP also plays a critical role in countering cyber threats by assisting in the rapid identification of malicious language or intent in communications. For example, NLP models can be designed to recognize threatening keywords or identify trends in language that may indicate an imminent security threat (Montasari, 2023). Furthermore, in cases involving cybercrime, NLP can aid in detecting anomalies or inconsistent behavior within digital communications, offering insights into potential insider threats or compromised accounts (Faqir, 2023).

Moreover, NLP facilitates automated reporting, an essential feature for forensic analysis as it enables investigators to generate comprehensive reports based on textual evidence efficiently (Zaedally et al., 2020). Automated summarization techniques allow for quick extraction of key points from extensive texts, streamlining the review process and ensuring that investigators focus on the most pertinent information (Capuano et al., 2022). Advanced NLP techniques, particularly those that incorporate explainable AI, also enable investigators to trace how conclusions are derived, enhancing transparency and reliability in digital forensic reporting (Gholami & Omar, 2024).

In summary, NLP serves as a foundational technology in modern forensic investigations, equipping analysts with the tools needed to swiftly interpret text-based evidence and support broader cybersecurity measures. As AI and NLP continue to evolve, their integration in digital forensics will become increasingly refined, providing more precise and actionable insights to combat cybercrime (Omar & Zangana, 2024).

9. COMPUTER VISION FOR IMAGE AND VIDEO EVIDENCE ANALYSIS

The rise of computer vision in digital forensics has transformed how evidence is analyzed, particularly in processing image and video data. As artificial intelligence (AI) capabilities have matured, computer vision techniques can now handle massive volumes of multimedia content efficiently and accurately, making it crucial in investigating digital evidence from diverse sources. These techniques support the extraction of valuable insights from unstructured visual data, enhancing forensic capabilities and facilitating more effective incident response (Jarrett & Choo, 2021; Hassan & Ibrahim, 2023).

One major advantage of computer vision in forensic analysis lies in its ability to automate image and video processing. Automation reduces the time spent on manual inspection and minimizes human error, crucial for high-stakes investigations (Hayes & Kyobe, 2020; Tyagi et al., 2024). Advanced AI models, especially convolutional neural networks (CNNs) and deep learning frameworks, have proven effective in tasks such as facial recognition, object detection, and scene reconstruction (Moustafa, 2022; Dunsin et al., 2024). For instance, deep learning methods can automatically tag objects and events in videos, significantly aiding investigators in identifying relevant evidence quickly (Capuano et al., 2022).

Computer vision also offers substantial advancements in authenticity verification. Techniques such as AI-driven image forensics assess the originality and integrity of multimedia files by detecting alterations, a process integral to ensuring evidence credibility (Ali, 2022; Syed & ES, 2024). As image tampering methods become increasingly sophisticated, the reliance on computer vision has grown to ensure the reliability of digital evidence (Bonfanti, 2022; Montasari, 2023). These advancements underscore the importance of robust AI frameworks in safeguarding evidence integrity.

Moreover, computer vision techniques can enhance incident response by providing automated surveillance and anomaly detection, enabling faster identification of suspicious activities and aiding law enforcement and cybersecurity teams in real-time monitoring (Samtani et al., 2020; Zangana et al., 2024). By integrating with existing AI-driven security frameworks, these techniques provide a more comprehensive approach to digital forensics (Rizvi et al., 2022; Ukwen & Karabatak, 2021).

In summary, the role of computer vision in analyzing image and video evidence has become indispensable in modern digital forensics. The integration of AI-based solutions, including deep learning and automated analysis, offers powerful tools for quickly and accurately extracting critical information, verifying evidence authenticity, and enabling proactive monitoring. These advancements set the foundation for a more efficient, reliable, and scalable approach to handling digital evidence in cybersecurity investigations (Ghillani, 2022; Faqir, 2023).

10. AUTOMATED REPORT GENERATION AND DOCUMENTATION OF EVIDENCE

In the evolving landscape of digital forensics, the integration of automation and artificial intelligence (AI) has revolutionized how evidence is collected, analyzed, and documented. Automated report generation systems leverage AI to streamline the documentation process, significantly enhancing efficiency and accuracy. This transformation is pivotal as traditional manual reporting can be time-consuming and prone to human error, which can compromise the integrity of forensic investigations (Jarrett & Choo, 2021).

Automated report generation involves the systematic compilation of data collected from various sources during an investigation. By employing natural language processing (NLP) and machine learning techniques, these systems can automatically produce comprehensive reports that encapsulate all relevant findings in a structured format. This not only accelerates the reporting process but also ensures that all critical information is consistently included, thereby reducing the likelihood of oversight (Tyagi, Kumari, & Richa, 2024).

The role of AI in digital forensics extends beyond mere report generation. It encompasses the ability to analyze large volumes of data quickly, identify patterns, and even predict potential future incidents based on historical data (Dunsin et al., 2024; Moustafa, 2022). These capabilities are essential in incidents where time is of the essence, such as in cases of ongoing cyberattacks, where immediate responses are necessary to mitigate damage (Hassan & Ibrahim, 2023).

Documentation of evidence is another critical area where AI technologies have made significant strides. Automated systems ensure that evidence is not only collected but also cataloged and preserved in a manner that maintains its integrity. These systems can automatically tag evidence with timestamps, origin details, and handling records, creating a robust chain of custody that is vital in legal contexts (Zangana & Omar, 2020). Furthermore, the automation of documentation reduces the workload on forensic analysts, allowing them to focus on more complex analytical tasks (Ali, 2022).

Additionally, the incorporation of AI tools in digital forensics aids in enhancing the reliability of evidence. For instance, AI can assist in validating the authenticity of digital evidence, which is paramount in legal proceedings. Techniques such as blockchain-based timestamping are increasingly being explored to provide immutable records of evidence handling (Zangana, 2024). This innovation ensures that any evidence presented in court is verifiable and has not been tampered with, thus bolstering its admissibility (Al-Hajri et al., 2023).

Moreover, automated systems can facilitate collaboration among forensic teams by providing a centralized platform for evidence sharing and report generation. This collaborative environment ensures that all stakeholders have access to the same information, which is crucial for coordinated responses in complex investigations (Nair, Deshmukh, & Tyagi, 2024).

In conclusion, the advent of automated report generation and documentation of evidence through AI is reshaping the field of digital forensics. By enhancing efficiency, accuracy, and reliability, these technologies not only improve the investigative process but also ensure that digital evidence can withstand the scrutiny of legal examinations. As the field continues to advance, ongoing research and development will be essential to fully harness the potential of AI in digital forensics, ultimately leading to more effective incident response and enhanced cybersecurity measures (Samtani, Kantarcioglu, & Chen, 2020; Gholami & Omar, 2023).

11. CHALLENGES AND LIMITATIONS IN AUTOMATED EVIDENCE COLLECTION AND ANALYSIS

The integration of artificial intelligence (AI) in digital forensics has introduced significant advancements in evidence collection and analysis, enhancing efficiency and accuracy. However, several challenges and limitations accompany this technological evolution.

11.1. Data Quality and Integrity

One of the primary challenges in automated evidence collection is ensuring data quality and integrity. AI algorithms rely heavily on the data fed into them, and poor-quality data can lead to inaccurate conclusions. Issues such as incomplete data, data corruption, or data that lacks context can compromise the reliability of forensic analyses (Moustafa, 2022; Tyagi, Kumari, & Richa, 2024). In some cases, automated systems may misinterpret or overlook critical details, especially if the data is unstructured or lacks proper tagging (Hassan & Ibrahim, 2023).

11.2. Complexity of Cyber Attacks

Cybercriminals continuously evolve their tactics to exploit vulnerabilities in digital systems, making it difficult for automated systems to keep pace. The complexity of modern cyber threats requires advanced analytical capabilities, often beyond the scope of current AI technologies. As Hassan and Ibrahim (2023) note, the ability of AI to accurately predict or respond to new attack vectors remains limited, necessitating ongoing human intervention for effective incident response.

11.3. Legal and Ethical Considerations

The legal landscape surrounding digital forensics is constantly changing, raising ethical concerns about the use of AI in evidence collection and analysis. Issues such as privacy rights, data protection laws, and the admissibility of AI-generated evidence in court pose significant challenges (Zangana & Omar, 2020; Rizvi et al., 2022). The ambiguity in regulations can hinder the deployment of automated systems, as organizations fear legal repercussions from potential misuses of AI technologies (Montasari, 2023).

11.4. Dependence on Technical Expertise

While automation aims to simplify forensic processes, it also creates a dependency on technical expertise for the setup, operation, and maintenance of AI systems. The skills gap in cybersecurity and digital forensics is a critical limitation, as professionals may lack the necessary training to effectively use automated tools (Dunsin et al., 2024; Kaur, Gabrijelčič, & Klobučar, 2023). As a result, organizations may struggle to fully leverage the capabilities of AI in their forensic investigations.

11.5. Bias in AI Algorithms

AI systems can perpetuate existing biases present in training data, leading to skewed results in forensic investigations. Bias can arise from various sources, including historical data that reflects systemic prejudices or from human error during data labeling (Samtani, Kantarcioglu, & Chen, 2020). Such biases can compromise the fairness and objectivity of investigations, potentially resulting in wrongful accusations or overlooked evidence (Du et al., 2020).

11.6. Resource Constraints

The implementation of AI technologies often requires substantial financial and computational resources, which can be a significant barrier for many organizations, particularly smaller ones (Hayes & Kyobe, 2020; Ali, 2022). Without adequate investment in infrastructure and tools, organizations may find it challenging to effectively adopt automated forensic solutions.

11.7. Summary

While the potential of AI to transform digital forensics is immense, addressing these challenges is essential to ensure effective and reliable evidence collection and analysis. Continuous advancements in AI must be complemented by robust legal frameworks, ethical guidelines, and training programs to fully realize the benefits of automation in digital forensics (Gholami & Omar, 2023; Omar & Zangana, 2024). As the field progresses, collaborative efforts between technologists, legal experts, and practitioners will be crucial to overcoming these limitations and maximizing the impact of AI in digital investigations.

12. CASE STUDIES: APPLICATIONS OF AI IN EVIDENCE COLLECTION AND ANALYSIS

The application of Artificial Intelligence (AI) in evidence collection and analysis has transformed digital forensics, enhancing the efficiency, accuracy, and scope of investigations. Various studies highlight how AI technologies contribute to different aspects of forensic investigations, including cybersecurity incidents, digital crime analysis, and incident response.

12.1 Automated Evidence Collection

Automated evidence collection systems utilize AI to efficiently gather and categorize digital evidence from various sources. For example, Tyagi et al. (2024) emphasize that AI-driven tools can autonomously sift through large volumes of data to identify relevant information, significantly reducing the time required for forensic analysis. This automation not only expedites investigations but also minimizes human error, leading to more reliable outcomes.

In the realm of cybersecurity, the role of AI in incident response is critical. Hassan and Ibrahim (2023) discuss how AI algorithms can predict potential security breaches and respond in real time. These AI systems analyze network traffic and user behavior to detect anomalies, allowing for immediate intervention. By integrating AI with traditional digital forensics, organizations can create a more robust security posture, effectively preventing data breaches before they escalate.

12.2 Enhanced Analysis Techniques

AI algorithms, particularly machine learning models, enhance the analysis of collected evidence by identifying patterns that may not be immediately apparent to human analysts. Dunsin et al. (2024) explore the use of machine learning in analyzing digital evidence, noting that these technologies can process and categorize data at unprecedented speeds. This capability is crucial in cases involving complex data sets, such as those encountered in cybercrime investigations.

Furthermore, Moustafa (2022) highlights how deep learning techniques can improve image and video analysis in digital forensics. For instance, AI systems can automatically recognize and extract critical elements from video footage, aiding investigators in establishing timelines and identifying suspects. This application is particularly useful in cases involving online harassment or cyberstalking, where visual evidence plays a pivotal role.

12.3 Cybersecurity Applications

AI's integration into cybersecurity has led to significant advancements in threat detection and response. Rizvi et al. (2022) provide a comprehensive survey on the application of AI in network forensics, discussing how machine learning models can be trained to identify malicious patterns in network traffic. This capability allows cybersecurity teams to respond to threats more swiftly and effectively, thereby minimizing potential damage.

Moreover, studies by Zangana et al. (2024) illustrate the importance of AI in understanding and countering phishing attacks, a common cybersecurity threat. By employing natural language processing (NLP) techniques, AI systems can analyze emails for characteristics typical of phishing attempts, thereby aiding in the timely detection of such threats.

12.4 AI in Forensic Accounting

The integration of AI in forensic accounting represents a transformative approach to detecting financial crimes. Tuli and Thaduri (2023) assert that AI tools can analyze financial transactions and detect anomalies that suggest fraudulent activities. This capability is particularly beneficial for organizations looking to enhance their internal auditing processes. By automating the analysis of financial data, AI reduces the potential for oversight, thus improving the chances of identifying fraudulent activities early.

12.5 Future Directions

As AI continues to evolve, its applications in digital forensics and cybersecurity will expand further. Ali (2022) argues that leveraging AI and big data in forensic investigations will lead to more effective solutions, enabling analysts to uncover hidden patterns and correlations within vast datasets. This potential for enhanced insights paves the way for future research aimed at optimizing AI technologies for even greater efficacy in forensic contexts.

In conclusion, the application of AI in evidence collection and analysis is revolutionizing the field of digital forensics. From automating evidence collection to enhancing analysis techniques, AI technologies significantly improve the efficiency and effectiveness of forensic investigations. Continued advancements in AI will likely yield even more sophisticated tools and methodologies, making digital forensics more robust and responsive to the challenges posed by evolving cyber threats.

13. FUTURE DIRECTIONS IN AI-POWERED EVIDENCE COLLECTION AND ANALYSIS

The integration of artificial intelligence (AI) into evidence collection and analysis marks a transformative shift in digital forensics and cybersecurity. As cyber threats evolve in complexity, leveraging AI to enhance investigative processes and incident response capabilities is becoming increasingly vital. This section discusses potential future directions for AI in this domain, highlighting emerging trends, opportunities for innovation, and the critical challenges that lie ahead.

AI applications in digital forensics are expanding, with significant advances in automation, analysis, and predictive capabilities. The pie chart below highlights the primary focus areas for AI integration, showcasing its growing role in each forensic function.

Figure 4. AI applications in forensics

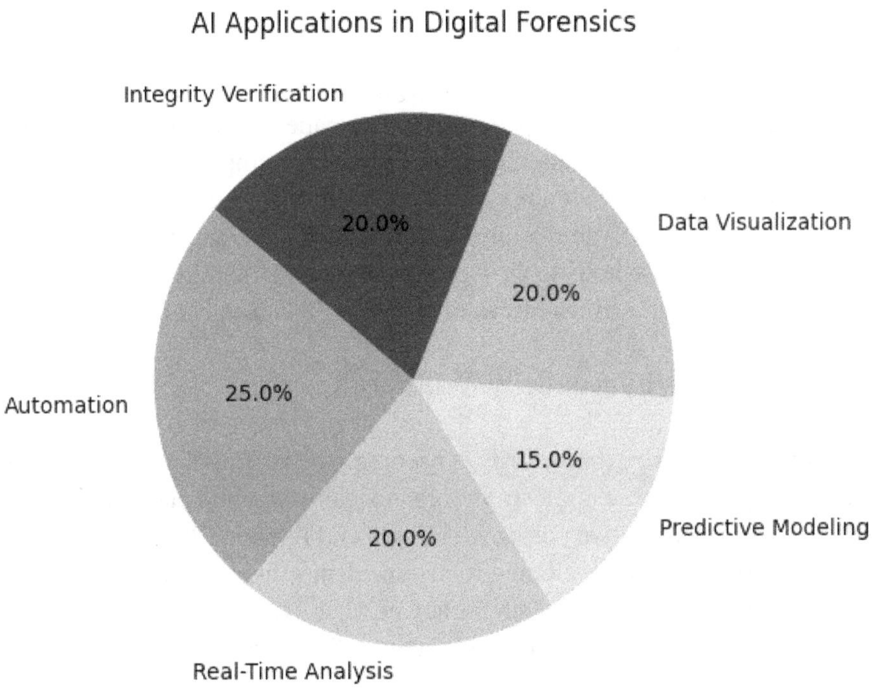

13.1 Enhanced Automation in Digital Forensics

Automation is set to play a crucial role in digital forensics, improving the speed and efficiency of evidence collection and analysis. Recent studies suggest that automated systems, powered by AI, can significantly reduce the time required to process digital evidence. For instance, Jarrett and Choo (2021) argue that automation can streamline workflows in digital forensics, enabling investigators to focus on more complex analytical tasks rather than routine data collection. The adoption of automated digital forensic tools will likely accelerate as new AI methodologies are developed, allowing for real-time data processing and analysis (Hayes & Kyobe, 2020).

13.2 Intelligent Data Analysis

The future of evidence analysis will be driven by AI algorithms that enhance the capabilities of traditional forensic methodologies. AI-powered systems can analyze large volumes of data, identifying patterns and anomalies that human analysts might overlook. For instance, Moustafa (2022) emphasizes the importance of employing machine learning techniques to improve data classification and anomaly detection in forensic investigations. Additionally, AI can facilitate the integration of disparate data sources, providing a holistic view of incidents and aiding in the identification of connections between various pieces of evidence (Zangana et al., 2024).

13.3 Proactive Cybersecurity Measures

AI's role in proactive cybersecurity is becoming more pronounced. By utilizing predictive analytics and machine learning, organizations can anticipate potential cyber threats and initiate preventive measures. Hassan and Ibrahim (2023) highlight that AI can be instrumental in developing robust incident response strategies, enabling organizations to mitigate threats before they escalate. This proactive approach not only enhances security but also minimizes the need for reactive forensic investigations, ultimately leading to a more resilient cybersecurity posture.

13.4 Challenges in AI Implementation

Despite the promising benefits of AI in digital forensics, several challenges must be addressed to ensure effective implementation. One significant concern is the ethical implications of using AI for evidence analysis. The potential for bias in AI algorithms can lead to wrongful conclusions or misinterpretation of evidence (Kaur, Gabrijelčič, & Klobučar, 2023). Additionally, as AI systems become more complex, the transparency and explainability of their decision-making processes become critical (Capuano et al., 2022). Future research must focus on developing frameworks that ensure the ethical use of AI in forensic investigations while maintaining accountability and transparency (Zangana, 2024).

13.5 Integration of Advanced Technologies

The convergence of AI with other advanced technologies, such as blockchain and the Internet of Things (IoT), offers new avenues for enhancing digital forensics. For example, Zangana and Omar (2020) explore how blockchain technology can improve the integrity and traceability of digital evidence, thereby bolstering the reliability of forensic investigations. Moreover, the integration of AI with IoT devices can facilitate real-time data collection and analysis, significantly enhancing the responsiveness of forensic systems (Syed & ES, 2024).

13.6 Research and Development Focus

As the landscape of digital forensics continues to evolve, future research should prioritize the development of AI tools tailored to specific forensic challenges. Dunsin et al. (2024) suggest a comprehensive analysis of the intersection of AI, machine learning, and digital forensics to identify key areas for innovation. This includes the exploration of deep learning techniques to enhance image and video analysis capabilities in forensic investigations (Ghillani, 2022). Additionally, there is a growing need for interdisciplinary collaboration to advance AI methodologies that are applicable across various forensic domains (Samtani, Kantarcioglu, & Chen, 2020).

13.7 Summary

The future of AI-powered evidence collection and analysis holds significant promise for enhancing the capabilities of digital forensics and cybersecurity. By embracing automation, intelligent data analysis, and proactive measures, organizations can improve their investigative processes and incident response strategies. However, addressing the ethical implications and ensuring the integration of advanced technologies will be essential for maximizing the benefits of AI in this critical field. Continued research and development will play a pivotal role in shaping the future of AI in digital forensics, paving the way for innovative solutions to emerging challenges in cybersecurity.

14. CONCLUSION

The integration of artificial intelligence (AI) into digital forensics and cybersecurity represents a transformative shift in how professionals approach evidence collection, analysis, and incident response. As cyber threats become increasingly sophisticated, the traditional methods of forensic investigation are often insufficient. AI technologies, including machine learning and deep learning, have shown remarkable promise in enhancing the speed, accuracy, and efficiency of digital forensic processes. By automating repetitive tasks and providing advanced analytical capabilities, AI empowers forensic investigators to focus on more complex aspects of their work, ultimately leading to faster and more effective resolutions of cyber incidents.

Furthermore, the role of AI extends beyond mere automation; it introduces new paradigms for evidence interpretation and decision-making. AI algorithms can process vast amounts of data, identify patterns, and generate actionable insights that would be challenging for human analysts to discern. This capability not only improves the chances of successful investigations but also fosters a more proactive stance against emerging cyber threats. Organizations that adopt AI-driven tools are better equipped to anticipate vulnerabilities, streamline their incident response strategies, and enhance overall cybersecurity resilience.

Despite the numerous advantages, the integration of AI into digital forensics also presents significant challenges, including ethical considerations, data privacy issues, and the potential for algorithmic bias. As AI technologies evolve, it is crucial for professionals in the field to remain vigilant about these concerns and to develop frameworks that ensure responsible use. Collaboration between technologists, legal experts, and policymakers will be essential in establishing guidelines that balance innovation with ethical standards.

In conclusion, the future of digital forensics and cybersecurity is intricately linked to the advancement of AI technologies. By harnessing the power of AI, the field can move toward more effective and efficient investigative processes, ultimately enhancing security measures across various sectors. Continued research and development in this domain will not only advance the capabilities of forensic analysis but also contribute to a safer digital environment for all users. The journey ahead will require a collective effort to address challenges, embrace opportunities, and adapt to the rapidly evolving landscape of technology and cyber threats.

REFERENCES

Abbasi, R., Bashir, A. K., Mateen, A., Amin, F., Ge, Y., & Omar, M. “Efficient Security and Privacy of Lossless Secure Communication for Sensor-based Urban Cities,” *IEEE Sensors Journal*, vol. 2023.

Ahmed, H., Rasheed, H., Bashir, A. K., & Omar, M. (2023). Rasheed, A. K. Bashir, and M. Omar, “Millimeter-wave Channel Modeling in a VANETs Using Coding Techniques,”. *PeerJ. Computer Science*, 9, e1374. DOI: 10.7717/peerj-cs.1374 PMID: 37346660

Ahmed, N., Mohammadani, K., Bashir, A. K., Omar, M., Jones, A., & Hassan, F. “Secure and Reliable Routing in the Internet of Vehicles Network: AODV-RL with BHA Attack Defense,” *CMES-Computer Modeling in Engineering & Sciences*, vol. 139, no. 1, 2024.

Ahmed Alaa El-Din, E. (2022). Artificial intelligence in forensic science: Invasion or revolution? *Egyptian Society of Clinical Toxicology Journal*, 10(2), 20–32. DOI: 10.21608/esctj.2022.158178.1012

Al-Hajri, S. M., Al-Thonayan, Z. J., Alqattan, M. M., Alalyani, N. A., Alali, N. D., & Alnaim, N. (2023). Maximizing the Potential of Artificial Intelligence in Digital Forensics Investigations.

Al Harthi, S., Al Balushi, M. Y., Al Badi, A. H., Al Karaki, J., & Omar, M. *“Metaverse Adoption in UAE Higher Education: A Hybrid SEM-ANN Approach,” in 98 Mohammad Daradkeh, Boshra Aldhanhani, Amjad Gawanmeh, Shadi Atalla and Sami Miniaoui. Applied Research Approaches to Technology, Healthcare, and Business*. IGI Global.

Al-Karaki, J. N., Omar, M., Gawanmeh, A., & Jones, A. “Advancing CyberSecurity Education and Training: Practical Case Study of Running Capture the Flag (CTF) on the Metaverse vs. Physical Settings,” in *2023 International Conference on Intelligent Metaverse Technologies & Applications (iMETA)*, pp. 1-7, IEEE, 2023. DOI: 10.1109/iMETA59369.2023.10294722

Al Kinoon, M., Omar, M., Mohaisen, M., & Mohaisen, D. “Security Breaches in the Healthcare Domain: A Spatiotemporal Analysis,” in *Computational Data and Social Networks: 10th International Conference, CSoNet 2021, Virtual Event, November 15-17, 2021, Proceedings*, Springer International Publishing, pp. 171-183, 2021. DOI: 10.1007/978-3-030-91434-9_16

Al-Sanjary, O. I., Ahmed, A. A., Jaharadak, A. A. B., Ali, M. A., & Zangana, H. M. "Detection Clone an Object Movement Using an Optical Flow Approach," in *2018 IEEE Symposium on Computer Applications & Industrial Electronics (ISCAIE)*, pp. 388-394, 2018. DOI: 10.1109/ISCAIE.2018.8405504

O. I. Al-Sanjary, A. A. Ahmed, H. M. Zangana, M. Ali, S. Aldulaimi, and M. Alkawaz, "An Investigation of the Characteristics and Performance of Hybrid Routing Protocol in (MANET)," *International Journal of Engineering & Technology*, vol. 7, no. 4.22, pp. 49-54, 2018.

Alghamdi, M. I. (2021). *Digital forensics in cyber security—recent trends, threats, and opportunities*. Cybersecurity Threats with New Perspectives. DOI: 10.5772/intechopen.94452

Ali, A. (2022). Cyber Crime Investigation and Forensics: Leveraging AI and Big Data for More Effective Solutions.

Alturki, N., Altamimi, A., Umer, M., Saidani, O., Alshardan, A., Alsubai, S., Omar, M., & Ashraf, I. "Improving Prediction of Chronic Kidney Disease Using KNN Imputed SMOTE Features and TrioNet Model," *CMES-Computer Modeling in Engineering & Sciences*, vol. 139, no. 3, 2024. DOI: 10.32604/cmes.2023.045868

Arulappan, G. (2023). Raja, A. K. Bashir, A. Mahanti, and M. Omar, "ZTMP: Zero Touch Management Provisioning Algorithm for the On-boarding of Cloud-native Virtual Network Functions,". *Mobile Networks and Applications*, •••, 1–13.

Ayub, M., Li, X., Mahmood, K., Shamshad, S., Saleem, M. A., & Omar, M. (2023). Secure Consumer-centric Demand Response Management in Resilient Smart Grid as Industry 5.0 Application with Blockchain-based Authentication. *IEEE Transactions on Consumer Electronics*.

M. Banisakher, D. Mohammed, and M. Omar, "A Cloud-Based Computing Architecture Model of Post-Disaster Management System," *International Journal of Simulation--Systems, Science & Technology*, vol. 19, no. 5, 2018.

Banisakher, M., Omar, M., & Clare, W. (2019). Critical Infrastructure—Perspectives on the Role of Government in Cybersecurity. *Journal of Computer Sciences and Applications*, 7(1), 37–42. DOI: 10.12691/jcsa-7-1-6

Banisakher, M., Omar, M., Hong, S., & Adams, J. (2020). A Human-centric Approach to Data Fusion in Post-Disaster Management. *Jurnal of Business Management and Science*, 8(1), 12–20.

Basharat, M., & Omar, M. "Adapting to Change: Assessing the Longevity and Resilience of Adversarially Trained NLP Models in Dynamic Spam Detection Environments," in *Innovations, Securities, and Case Studies Across Healthcare, Business, and Technology*, pp. 157-173, IGI Global, 2024. DOI: 10.4018/979-8-3693-1906-2.ch009

Basharat, M., & Omar, M. (2024). Harnessing GPT-2 for Feature Extraction in Malware Detection: A Novel Approach to Cybersecurity. *Land Forces Academy Review*, 29(1), 74–84. DOI: 10.2478/raft-2024-0008

M. Basharat and M. Omar, "SecuGuard: Leveraging Pattern-exploiting Training in Language Models for Advanced Software Vulnerability Detection," *International Journal of Mathematics and Computer in Engineering*, 2024.

Bonfanti, M. E. (2022). *Artificial intelligence and the offence-defence balance in cyber security. Cyber Security: Socio-Technological Uncertainty and Political Fragmentation*. Routledge.

Burrell, D. N., Nobles, C., Cusak, A., Omar, M., & Gillesania, L. (2022). Cybercrime and the Nature of Insider Threat Complexities in Healthcare and Biotechnology Engineering Organizations. *Journal of Crime and Criminal Behavior*, 2(2), 131–144. DOI: 10.47509/JCCB.2022.v02i02.04

Burrell, D. N., Nobles, C., Richardson, K., Wright, J. B., Jones, A. J., Springs, D., & Brown-Jackson, K. (2023). Allison Huff. In *Applied Research Approaches to Technology, Healthcare, and Business*. IGI Global. DOI: 10.4018/979-8-3693-1630-6

Capuano, N., Fenza, G., Loia, V., & Stanzione, C. (2022). Explainable artificial intelligence in cybersecurity: A survey. *IEEE Access : Practical Innovations, Open Solutions*, 10, 93575–93600. DOI: 10.1109/ACCESS.2022.3204171

CHILONGO, L., & KM, A. S. (2024). IMPACT OF ARTIFICIAL INTELLIGENCE ON CYBERSECURITY: A CASE OF INTERNET OF THINGS. *i-Manager's Journal on Digital Forensics & Cyber Security (JDF), 2*(1).

Davis, L., Dawson, M., & Omar, M. (2016). Systems Engineering Concepts with Aid of Virtual Worlds and Open Source Software: Using Technology to Develop Learning Objects and Simulation Environments. In *Handbook of Research on 3-D Virtual Environments and Hypermedia for Ubiquitous Learning* (pp. 483–509). IGI Global. DOI: 10.4018/978-1-5225-0125-1.ch020

Dawson, M. (2015). A Brief Review of New Threats and Countermeasures in Digital Crime and Cyber Terrorism. In *New Threats and Countermeasures in Digital Crime and Cyber Terrorism* (pp. 1–7). IGI Global. DOI: 10.4018/978-1-4666-8345-7.ch001

Dawson, M., Al Saeed, I., Wright, J., & Omar, M. "Technology enhanced learning with open source software for scientists and engineers," in *INTED2013 Proceedings*, IATED, 2013, pp. 5583–5589.

Dawson, M., Davis, L., & Omar, M. (2019). Developing learning objects for engineering and science fields: Using technology to test system usability and interface design. *Int. J. Smart Technol. Learn.*, 1(2), 140–161. DOI: 10.1504/IJSMARTTL.2019.097951

Dawson, M., Eltayeb, M., & Omar, M. (2016). *Security solutions for hyperconnectivity and the Internet of things*. IGI Global.

Dawson, M., Omar, M., & Abramson, J. (2015). Understanding the methods behind cyber terrorism. In *Encyclopedia of Information Science and Technology* (3rd ed., pp. 1539–1549). IGI Global.

Dawson, M., Omar, M., Abramson, J., & Bessette, D. (2014). *Information security in diverse computing environments*. Academic Press.

Dawson, M., Omar, M., Abramson, J., & Bessette, D. (2014). The future of national and international security on the internet. In *Information security in diverse computing environments* (pp. 149–178). IGI Global. DOI: 10.4018/978-1-4666-6158-5.ch009

Dawson, M., Omar, M., Abramson, J., Leonard, B., & Bessette, D. (2017). Battlefield cyberspace: Exploitation of hyperconnectivity and Internet of Things. In *Developing Next-Generation Countermeasures for Homeland Security Threat Prevention* (pp. 204–235). IGI Global. DOI: 10.4018/978-1-5225-0703-1.ch010

Dawson, M., Wright, J., & Omar, M. (2015). Mobile devices: The case for cyber security hardened systems. In *New Threats and Countermeasures in Digital Crime and Cyber Terrorism* (pp. 8–29). IGI Global. DOI: 10.4018/978-1-4666-8345-7.ch002

Dayoub and M. Omar. (2024). Advancing IoT security posture K-Means clustering for malware detection. In *Innovations, Securities, and Case Studies Across Healthcare, Business, and Technology* (pp. 221–239). IGI Global.

Dong, H., Wu, J., Bashir, A. K., Pan, Q., Omar, M., & Al-Dulaimi, A. "Privacy-preserving EEG signal analysis with electrode attention for depression diagnosis: Joint FHE and CNN approach," in *GLOBECOM 2023-2023 IEEE Global Communications Conference*, IEEE, 2023, pp. 4265–4270. DOI: 10.1109/GLOBECOM54140.2023.10436783

Du, X., Hargreaves, C., Sheppard, J., Anda, F., Sayakkara, A., Le-Khac, N. A., & Scanlon, M. (2020, August). SoK: Exploring the state of the art and the future potential of artificial intelligence in digital forensic investigation. In *Proceedings of the 15th international conference on availability, reliability and security* (pp. 1-10). DOI: 10.1145/3407023.3407068

Dunsin, D., Ghanem, M. C., Ouazzane, K., & Vassilev, V. (2024). A comprehensive analysis of the role of artificial intelligence and machine learning in modern digital forensics and incident response. *Forensic Science International Digital Investigation*, 48, 301675. DOI: 10.1016/j.fsidi.2023.301675

Faqir, R. S. (2023). Digital Criminal Investigations in the Era of Artificial Intelligence: A Comprehensive Overview. *International Journal of Cyber Criminology*, 17(2), 77–94.

Fawzi, D., & Omar, M. (n.d.). *New insights to database security: An effective and integrated approach to applying access control mechanisms and cryptographic concepts in Microsoft access environments*. Academic Press.

Ghillani, D. (2022). Deep learning and artificial intelligence framework to improve the cyber security. *Authorea Preprints*. DOI: 10.22541/au.166379475.54266021/v1

Gholami, S. (2024). Can pruning make large language models more efficient? In *Redefining Security With Cyber AI* (pp. 1–14). IGI Global. DOI: 10.4018/979-8-3693-6517-5.ch001

Gholami, S. (2024). Do generative large language models need billions of parameters? In *Redefining Security With Cyber AI* (pp. 37–55). IGI Global. DOI: 10.4018/979-8-3693-6517-5.ch003

Gholami, S., & Omar, M. (2023). Does Synthetic Data Make Large Language Models More Efficient? *arXiv preprint arXiv:2310.07830.*

Gholami, S., & Omar, M. "Does synthetic data make large language models more efficient?" *arXiv preprint arXiv:2310.07830*, 2023.

Gholami, S., & Omar, M. (2024). Can a student large language model perform as well as its teacher? In *Innovations, Securities, and Case Studies Across Healthcare, Business, and Technology* (pp. 122-139). IGI Global. DOI: 10.4018/979-8-3693-1906-2.ch007

Gholami, S., & Omar, M. (2024). Can a student large language model perform as well as its teacher? In *Innovations, Securities, and Case Studies Across Healthcare, Business, and Technology* (pp. 122–139). IGI Global. DOI: 10.4018/979-8-3693-1906-2.ch007

Hamza, Y. A., & Omar, M. D. (2013). Cloud computing security: Abuse and nefarious use of cloud computing. *International Journal of Computer Engineering Research*, 3(6), 22–27.

Hamza, Y. A., & Omar, M. D. (2013). Cloud computing security: Abuse and nefarious use of cloud computing. *International Journal of Computer Engineering Research*, 3(6), 22–27.

Hassan, S. K., & Ibrahim, A. (2023). The role of artificial intelligence in cyber security and incident response. *International Journal for Electronic Crime Investigation*, 7(2).

Hayes, D., & Kyobe, M. (2020, March). The adoption of automation in cyber forensics. In *2020 Conference on Information Communications Technology and Society (ICTAS)* (pp. 1-6). IEEE. DOI: 10.1109/ICTAS47918.2020.233977

Huff, A. J., Burrell, D. N., Nobles, C., Richardson, K., Wright, J. B., Burton, S. L., Jones, A. J., Springs, D., Omar, M., & Brown-Jackson, K. L. (2023). Management Practices for Mitigating Cybersecurity Threats to Biotechnology Companies, Laboratories, and Healthcare Research Organizations. In *Applied Research Approaches to Technology, Healthcare, and Business* (pp. 1-12). IGI Global.

Huff, J., Burrell, D. N., Nobles, C., Richardson, K., Wright, J. B., Burton, S. L., Jones, A. J., Springs, D., Omar, M., & Brown-Jackson, K. L. (2023). Management practices for mitigating cybersecurity threats to biotechnology companies, laboratories, and healthcare research organizations. In *Applied Research Approaches to Technology, Healthcare, and Business* (pp. 1–12). IGI Global. DOI: 10.4018/979-8-3693-1630-6.ch001

Iqbal, S., & Alharbi, S. A. (2020). Advancing automation in digital forensic investigations using machine learning forensics. *Digital Forensic Science, 3*.

Jabbari, H. Khan, S. Duraibi, I. Budhiraja, S. Gupta, and M. Omar, "Energy maximization for wireless powered communication enabled IoT devices with NOMA underlaying solar powered UAV using federated reinforcement learning for 6G networks," *IEEE Trans. Consum. Electron.*, 2024.

Jarrett, A., & Choo, K. K. R. (2021). The impact of automation and artificial intelligence on digital forensics. *WIREs Forensic Science*, 3(6), e1418. DOI: 10.1002/wfs2.1418

Jones, A., & Omar, M.Jones and M. Omar. (2024). Codesentry: Revolutionizing real-time software vulnerability detection with optimized GPT framework. *Land Forces Acad. Rev.*, 29(1), 98–107. DOI: 10.2478/raft-2024-0010

Jones, M., & Omar, M. (2023). *"Detection of Twitter spam with language models: A case study on how to use BERT to protect children from spam on Twitter," in 2023 Congress in Computer Science, Computer Engineering, & Applied Computing (CSCE)*. IEEE.

Jones, M., & Omar, M. (2023). *"Measuring the impact of global health emergencies on self-disclosure using language models," in 2023 Congress in Computer Science, Computer Engineering, & Applied Computing (CSCE)*. IEEE.

Jones, M., & Omar, M. (2023). *"Studying the effects of social media content on kids' safety and well-being," in 2023 Congress in Computer Science, Computer Engineering, & Applied Computing (CSCE)*. IEEE.

Jones, R., & Omar, M. "Detecting IoT Malware with Knowledge Distillation Technique," in *2023 Congress in Computer Science, Computer Engineering, & Applied Computing (CSCE)*, pp. 131-135, IEEE, 2023. DOI: 10.1109/CSCE60160.2023.00026

Jones, R., & Omar, M. (2024). Revolutionizing Cybersecurity: The GPT-2 Enhanced Attack Detection and Defense (GEADD) Method for Zero-Day Threats. *International Journal of Informatics* [INJIISCOM]. *Information System and Computer Engineering*, 5(2), 178–191.

Jones, R., & Omar, M. (2024). Codeguard: Utilizing Advanced Pattern Recognition in Language Models for Software Vulnerability Analysis. *Land Forces Academy Review*, 29(1), 108–118. DOI: 10.2478/raft-2024-0011

Jones, R., & Omar, M. (2024). Revolutionizing Cybersecurity: The GPT-2 Enhanced Attack Detection and Defense (GEADD) Method for Zero-Day Threats [INJIISCOM]. *International Journal of Informatics, Information System and Computer Engineering*, 5(2), 178–191. DOI: 10.34010/injiiscom.v5i2.12741

Jones, R., Omar, M., & Mohammed, D. "Harnessing the Power of the GPT Model to Generate Adversarial Examples," in *2023 Congress in Computer Science, Computer Engineering, & Applied Computing (CSCE)*, pp. 1699-1702, IEEE, 2023. DOI: 10.1109/CSCE60160.2023.00279

Jones, R., Omar, M., Mohammed, D., & Nobles, C. "IoT Malware Detection with GPT Models," in *2023 Congress in Computer Science, Computer Engineering, & Applied Computing (CSCE)*, pp. 1749-1752, IEEE, 2023. DOI: 10.1109/CSCE60160.2023.00288

Jones, R., Omar, M., Mohammed, D., Nobles, C., & Dawson, M. (2023). Harnessing the Speed and Accuracy of Machine Learning to Advance Cybersecurity. In *2023 Congress in Computer Science, Computer Engineering, & Applied Computing (CSCE)* (pp. 418-421). IEEE. DOI: 10.1109/CSCE60160.2023.00074

Jones, R., Omar, M., Mohammed, D., Nobles, C., & Dawson, M. "Harnessing the Speed and Accuracy of Machine Learning to Advance Cybersecurity," in *2023 Congress in Computer Science, Computer Engineering, & Applied Computing (CSCE)*, pp. 418-421, IEEE, 2023. DOI: 10.1109/CSCE60160.2023.00074

Jones and M. Omar. (2023). *"Harnessing the efficiency of reformers to detect software vulnerabilities," in 2023 Congress in Computer Science, Computer Engineering, & Applied Computing (CSCE)*. IEEE.

Jones and M. Omar. (2023). *"Optimized decision trees to detect IoT malware," in 2023 Congress in Computer Science, Computer Engineering, & Applied Computing (CSCE)*. IEEE.

Jun, W., Iqbal, M. S., Abbasi, R., Omar, M., & Huiqin, C. "Web-Semantic-Driven Machine Learning and Blockchain for Transformative Change in the Future of Physical Education," *International Journal on Semantic Web and Information Systems (IJSWIS)*, vol. 20, no. 1, pp. 1-16, IGI Global, 2024. DOI: 10.4018/IJSWIS.337961

Kaur, R., Gabrijelčič, D., & Klobučar, T. (2023). Artificial intelligence for cybersecurity: Literature review and future research directions. *Information Fusion*, 97, 101804. DOI: 10.1016/j.inffus.2023.101804

Khan, S. A., Alkawaz, M. H., & Zangana, H. M. "The use and abuse of social media for spreading fake news," in *2019 IEEE International Conference on Automatic Control and Intelligent Systems (I2CACIS)*, pp. 145-148, IEEE, 2019. DOI: 10.1109/I2CACIS.2019.8825029

V. A. Kumar, S. Surapaneni, D. Pavitra, R. Venkatesan, M. Omar, and A. K. Bashir, "An Internet of Medical Things-Based Mental Disorder Prediction System Using EEG Sensor and Big Data Mining," *Journal of Circuits, Systems and Computers*, vol. 2450197, World Scientific Publishing Company, 2024.

Majeed, H. (2020). Watermarking Image Depending on Mojette Transform for Hiding Information. *International Journal on Computer Science and Engineering*, 8, 8–12.

Mohammed, D., Omar, M., & Nguyen, V. (2018). Wireless sensor network security: Approaches to detecting and avoiding wormhole attacks. *Journal of Research in Business. Economics and Management*, 10(2), 1860–1864.

Mohammed, M. O., & Nguyen, V. (2017). Enhancing Cyber Security for Financial Industry through Compliance and Regulatory Standards. In *Security Solutions for Hyperconnectivity and the Internet of Things* (pp. 113–129). IGI Global. DOI: 10.4018/978-1-5225-0741-3.ch005

Mohammed, M. O., & Nguyen, V. (2018). Wireless Sensor Network Security: Approaches to Detecting and Avoiding Wormhole Attacks. *Journal of Research in Business, Economics and Management*, 10(2), 1860–1864.

Mohammed and M. Omar. "Decision Trees Unleashed: Simplifying IoT Malware Detection With Advanced AI Techniques," in *Innovations, Securities, and Case Studies Across Healthcare, Business, and Technology*, pp. 240-258, IGI Global, 2024.

Montasari, R. (2023). *Countering cyberterrorism: the confluence of artificial intelligence, cyber forensics and digital policing in US and UK national cybersecurity* (Vol. 101). Springer Nature. DOI: 10.1007/978-3-031-21920-7

Moustafa, N. (2022). *Digital Forensics in the Era of Artificial Intelligence*. CRC Press. DOI: 10.1201/9781003278962

Mughal, A. A. (2019). A comprehensive study of practical techniques and methodologies in incident-based approaches for cyber forensics. *Tensorgate Journal of Sustainable Technology and Infrastructure for Developing Countries*, 2(1), 1–18.

Murphy, J. P. (2022). *Digital Forensic Investigations and Automated and Artificial Intelligence Technologies* (Master's thesis, Utica University).

Nair, M. M., Deshmukh, A., & Tyagi, A. K. (2024). Artificial intelligence for cyber security: Current trends and future challenges. *Automated Secure Computing for Next-Generation Systems*, 83-114.

Nguyen, V., Mohammed, D., Omar, M., & Banisakher, M. (2018). The Effects of the FCC Net Neutrality Repeal on Security and Privacy. [IJHIoT]. *International Journal of Hyperconnectivity and the Internet of Things*, 2(2), 21–29. DOI: 10.4018/IJHIoT.2018070102

V. Nguyen, D. Mohammed, M. Omar, and M. Banisakher, "The Effects of the FCC Net Neutrality Repeal on Security and Privacy," *International Journal of Hyperconnectivity and the Internet of Things (IJHIoT)*, vol. 2, no. 2, pp. 21-29, IGI Global, 2018.

V. Nguyen, M. Omar, and D. Mohammed, "A Security Framework for Enhancing User Experience," *International Journal of Hyperconnectivity and the Internet of Things (IJHIoT)*, vol. 1, no. 1, pp. 19-28, IGI Global, 2017.

Nguyen, V., Omar, M., Mohammed, D., & Dean, P. "Net Neutrality Around the Globe: A Survey," in *2020 3rd International Conference on Information and Computer Technologies (ICICT)*, pp. 480-488, IEEE, 2020. DOI: 10.1109/ICICT50521.2020.00083

Omar, M. *Smartphone Security: Defending Android-based Smartphone Against Emerging Malware Attacks* (Doctoral dissertation, Colorado Technical University), 2012.

Omar, M. "Insider Threats: Detecting and Controlling Malicious Insiders," in *New Threats and Countermeasures in Digital Crime and Cyber Terrorism*, pp. 162-172, IGI Global, 2015. DOI: 10.4018/978-1-4666-8345-7.ch009

Omar, M. "Cloud Computing Security: Abuse and Nefarious Use of Cloud Computing," in *Handbook of Research on Security Considerations in Cloud Computing*, pp. 30-38, IGI Global, 2015. DOI: 10.4018/978-1-4666-8387-7.ch002

Omar, M. (2019). A World of Cyber Attacks. *Survey (London, England).*

Omar, M. (2021). New insights into database security: An effective and integrated approach for applying access control mechanisms and cryptographic concepts in Microsoft Access environments.

M. Omar, "New Insights into Database Security: An Effective and Integrated Approach for Applying Access Control Mechanisms and Cryptographic Concepts in Microsoft Access Environments," 2021.

Omar, M. (2022). *Machine Learning for Cybersecurity: Innovative Deep Learning Solutions*. Springer Brief. https://link.springer.com/book/978303115

Omar, M. "Application of Machine Learning (ML) to Address Cybersecurity Threats," in *Machine Learning for Cybersecurity: Innovative Deep Learning Solutions*, pp. 1-11, Springer International Publishing Cham, 2022. DOI: 10.1007/978-3-031-15893-3_1

Omar, M. *Machine Learning for Cybersecurity: Innovative Deep Learning Solutions*, Springer Brief, 2022. https://link.springer.com/book/978303115

Omar, M. "Malware Anomaly Detection Using Local Outlier Factor Technique," in *Machine Learning for Cybersecurity: Innovative Deep Learning Solutions*, pp. 37-48, Springer International Publishing Cham, 2022. DOI: 10.1007/978-3-031-15893-3_3

Omar, M. "VulDefend: A Novel Technique Based on Pattern-Exploiting Training for Detecting Software Vulnerabilities Using Language Models," in *2023 IEEE Jordan International Joint Conference on Electrical Engineering and Information Technology (JEEIT)*, pp. 287-293, IEEE, 2023. DOI: 10.1109/JEEIT58638.2023.10185860

Omar, M. (2024). From Attack to Defense: Strengthening DNN Text Classification Against Adversarial Examples. In *Innovations, Securities, and Case Studies Across Healthcare, Business, and Technology* (pp. 174-195). IGI Global.

Omar, M. (2024). Revolutionizing Malware Detection: A Paradigm Shift Through Optimized Convolutional Neural Networks. In *Innovations, Securities, and Case Studies Across Healthcare, Business, and Technology* (pp. 196-220). IGI Global. DOI: 10.4018/979-8-3693-1906-2.ch011

Omar, M. "From Attack to Defense: Strengthening DNN Text Classification Against Adversarial Examples," in *Innovations, Securities, and Case Studies Across Healthcare, Business, and Technology*, pp. 174-195, IGI Global, 2024. DOI: 10.4018/979-8-3693-1906-2.ch010

Omar, M. "Revolutionizing Malware Detection: A Paradigm Shift Through Optimized Convolutional Neural Networks," in *Innovations, Securities, and Case Studies Across Healthcare, Business, and Technology*, pp. 196-220, IGI Global, 2024. DOI: 10.4018/979-8-3693-1906-2.ch011

Omar, M. *Defending Cyber Systems through Reverse Engineering of Criminal Malware*, Springer Brief, [n.d.][n.d.].https://link.springer.com/book/9783031116278

M. Omar, *Latina Davis Morgan State University 1700 E Cold Spring Ln. Baltimore, MD 21251, USA E-mail: latinaedavis@ hotmail.com*, [n.d.][n.d.].

M. Omar, *Machine Learning for Cybersecurity*, [n.d.][n.d.].

Omar, M.. (2024). Committee Members. *Journal of Physics: Conference Series*, 2711, 011001.

M. Omar and D. Burrell, "From Text to Threats: A Language Model Approach to Software Vulnerability Detection," *International Journal of Mathematics and Computer in Engineering*, 2023.

Omar, M., & Burrell, D. N. "Organizational Dynamics and Bias in Artificial Intelligence (AI) Recruitment Algorithms," in *Evolution of Cross-Sector Cyber Intelligent Markets*, pp. 269-290, IGI Global, 2024.

Omar, M., Choi, S., Nyang, D., & Mohaisen, D. "Quantifying the Performance of Adversarial Training on Language Models with Distribution Shifts," in *Proceedings of the 1st Workshop on Cybersecurity and Social Sciences*, pp. 3-9, 2022. DOI: 10.1145/3494108.3522764

Omar, M., Choi, S., Nyang, D., & Mohaisen, D. (2022). Robust Natural Language Processing: Recent Advances, Challenges, and Future Directions. *IEEE Access : Practical Innovations, Open Solutions*, 10, 86038–86056. DOI: 10.1109/ACCESS.2022.3197769

Omar, M., & Dawson, M. "Research in Progress-Defending Android Smartphones from Malware Attacks," in *2013 Third International Conference on Advanced Computing and Communication Technologies (ACCT)*, pp. 288-292, IEEE, 2013. DOI: 10.1109/ACCT.2013.69

Omar, M., Gouveia, L. B., Al-Karaki, J., & Mohammed, D. "Reverse-Engineering Malware," in *Cybersecurity Capabilities in Developing Nations and Its Impact on Global Security*, pp. 194-217, IGI Global, 2022. DOI: 10.4018/978-1-7998-8693-8.ch010

Omar, M., Jones, R., Burrell, D. N., Dawson, M., Nobles, C., & Mohammed, D. "Harnessing the Power and Simplicity of Decision Trees to Detect IoT Malware," in *Transformational Interventions for Business, Technology, and Healthcare*, pp. 215-229, IGI, 2023. DOI: 10.4018/979-8-3693-1634-4.ch013

Omar, M., & Mohaisen, D. "Making Adversarially-Trained Language Models Forget with Model Retraining: A Case Study on Hate Speech Detection," in *Companion Proceedings of the Web Conference 2022*, pp. 887-893, 2022. DOI: 10.1145/3487553.3524667

Omar, M., Mohammed, D., & Nguyen, V. (2017). Defending Against Malicious Insiders: A Conceptual Framework for Predicting, Detecting, and Deterring Malicious Insiders. *International Journal of Business Process Integration and Management*, 8(2), 114–119. DOI: 10.1504/IJBPIM.2017.083794

Omar, M., Mohammed, D., Nguyen, V., Dawson, M., & Banisakher, M. "Android Application Security," in *Research Anthology on Securing Mobile Technologies and Applications*, pp. 610-625, IGI Global, 2021. DOI: 10.4018/978-1-7998-8545-0.ch034

Omar, M., & Shiaeles, S. "VulDetect: A Novel Technique for Detecting Software Vulnerabilities Using Language Models," in *2023 IEEE International Conference on Cyber Security and Resilience (CSR)*, IEEE. https://ieeexplore.ieee.org/document/10224924

Omar, M., & Sukthankar, G. "Text-Defend: Detecting Adversarial Examples Using Local Outlier Factor," in *2023 IEEE 17th International Conference on Semantic Computing (ICSC)*, pp. 118-122, IEEE, 2023. DOI: 10.1109/ICSC56153.2023.00026

Omar, M., & Zangana, H. M. (Eds.). (2024). *Redefining Security With Cyber AI.* IGI Global., DOI: 10.4018/979-8-3693-6517-5

Omar, M., & Zangana, H. M. (2024). *Redefining Security With Cyber AI.* IGI Global., DOI: 10.4018/979-8-3693-6517-5

Pauu, K. T., Pan, Q., Wu, J., Bashir, A. K., & Omar, M. "IRS-Aided Federated Learning with Dynamic Differential Privacy for UAVs in Emergency Response," *IEEE Internet of Things Magazine*, vol. 7, no. 4, pp. 108-115, IEEE, 2024. DOI: 10.1109/IOTM.001.2400021

Peng, Y.. (2024). *"An Intelligent Resource Allocation Strategy with Slicing and Auction for Private Edge Cloud Systems," Future Generation Computer Systems* (Vol. 160). North-Holland.

Piraianu, A. I., Fulga, A., Musat, C. L., Ciobotaru, O. R., Poalelungi, D. G., Stamate, E., Ciobotaru, O., & Fulga, I. (2023). Enhancing the evidence with algorithms: How artificial intelligence is transforming forensic medicine. *Diagnostics (Basel)*, 13(18), 2992. DOI: 10.3390/diagnostics13182992 PMID: 37761359

Rajesh, R.. (2024). Threat Detection and Mitigation for Tactile Internet Driven Consumer IoT-Healthcare System. *IEEE Transactions on Consumer Electronics.*

Tyagi, A. K., Kumari, S., & Richa. (2024). Artificial Intelligence-Based Cyber Security and Digital Forensics: A Review. *Artificial Intelligence-Enabled Digital Twin for Smart Manufacturing*, 391-419.

Rizvi, S., Scanlon, M., Mcgibney, J., & Sheppard, J. (2022). Application of artificial intelligence to network forensics: Survey, challenges and future directions. *IEEE Access : Practical Innovations, Open Solutions*, 10, 110362–110384. DOI: 10.1109/ACCESS.2022.3214506

Saleem, M. A.. (2023). Provably Secure Conditional-Privacy Access Control Protocol for Intelligent Customers-Centric Communication in VANET. *IEEE Transactions on Consumer Electronics.*

Samtani, S., Kantarcioglu, M., & Chen, H. (2020). Trailblazing the artificial intelligence for cybersecurity discipline: A multi-disciplinary research roadmap. [TMIS]. *ACM Transactions on Management Information Systems*, 11(4), 1–19. DOI: 10.1145/3430360

Sikos, L. F. (2021). AI in digital forensics: Ontology engineering for cybercrime investigations. *WIREs Forensic Science*, 3(3), e1394. DOI: 10.1002/wfs2.1394

Stutz, D., de Assis, J. T., Laghari, A. A., Khan, A. A., Andreopoulos, N., Terziev, A., ... & Grata, E. G. (2024). Enhancing Security in Cloud Computing Using Artificial Intelligence (AI). *Applying Artificial Intelligence in Cybersecurity Analytics and Cyber Threat Detection*, 179-220.

Sun, Y., Xu, T., Bashir, A. K., Liu, J., & Omar, M. "BcIIS: Blockchain-Based Intelligent Identification Scheme of Massive IoT Devices," in *GLOBECOM 2023-2023 IEEE Global Communications Conference*, pp. 1277-1282, IEEE, 2023. DOI: 10.1109/GLOBECOM54140.2023.10437203

Syed, F. M., & ES, F. K. (2024). AI-Driven Forensic Analysis for Cyber Incidents in Healthcare. *International Journal of Machine Learning Research in Cybersecurity and Artificial Intelligence*, 15(1), 473–499.

Tao, F., Akhtar, M. S., & Jiayuan, Z. (2021). The future of artificial intelligence in cybersecurity: A comprehensive survey. *EAI Endorsed Transactions on Creative Technologies*, 8(28), e3–e3. DOI: 10.4108/eai.7-7-2021.170285

Tao, Y., Wu, J., Pan, Q., Bashir, A. K., & Omar, M. (2024). O-RAN-Based Digital Twin Function Virtualization for Sustainable IoV Service Response: An Asynchronous Hierarchical Reinforcement Learning Approach. *IEEE Transactions on Green Communications and Networking*, 8(3), 1049–1060. DOI: 10.1109/TGCN.2024.3435796

Tiwari, N., Ghadi, Y., & Omar, M. "Analysis of Ultrasound Images in Kidney Failure Diagnosis Using Deep Learning," in *Transformational Interventions for Business, Technology, and Healthcare*, pp. 45-74, IGI Global, 2023. DOI: 10.4018/979-8-3693-1634-4.ch004

Tiwari, N., Omar, M., & Ghadi, Y. "Brain Tumor Classification From Magnetic Resonance Imaging Using Deep Learning and Novel Data Augmentation," in *Transformational Interventions for Business, Technology, and Healthcare*, pp. 392-413, IGI Global, 2023. DOI: 10.4018/979-8-3693-1634-4.ch023

Tuli, F. A., & Thaduri, U. R. (2023). The Integration of Artificial Intelligence in Forensic Accounting: A Game-Changer. *Asian Accounting and Auditing Advancement*, 14(1), 12–20.

Ukwen, D. O., & Karabatak, M. (2021, June). Review of NLP-based systems in digital forensics and cybersecurity. In *2021 9th International symposium on digital forensics and security (ISDFS)* (pp. 1-9). IEEE. DOI: 10.1109/ISDFS52919.2021.9486354

Umer, M., Aljrees, T., Karamti, H., Ishaq, A., Alsubai, S., Omar, M., Bashir, A. K., & Ashraf, I. (2023). Heart Failure Patients Monitoring Using IoT-Based Remote Monitoring System. *Scientific Reports*, 13(1), 19213. DOI: 10.1038/s41598-023-46322-6 PMID: 37932424

Vitianingsih, V., Firmansyah, D., Maukar, A. L., Kacung, S., & Zangana, H. M. (2024, August). Recommendation System for Determining the Best Banner Supplier Using Profile Matching and TOPSIS Methods. *Intensif Jurnal Ilmiah Penelitian Teknologi Dan Penerapan Sistem Informasi*, 8(2), 246–262. DOI: 10.29407/intensif.v8i2.21635

Wright, J., Dawson, M. E.Jr, & Omar, M. (2012). Cyber security and mobile threats: The need for antivirus applications for smartphones. *Journal of Information Systems Technology and Planning*, 5(14), 40–60.

Wright, J., Dawson, M. E.Jr, & Omar, M. (2012). Cyber Security and Mobile Threats: The Need for Antivirus Applications for Smartphones. *Journal of Information Systems Technology and Planning*, 5(14), 40–60.

Xu, X., Wu, J., Bashir, A. K., & Omar, M. (2024). Machine Learning and Zero Knowledge Empowered Trustworthy Bitcoin Mixing for Next-G Consumer Electronics Payment. *IEEE Transactions on Consumer Electronics*, 70(1), 2210–2223. DOI: 10.1109/TCE.2024.3361690

H. M. Zangana, "A New Skin Color Based Face Detection Algorithm by Combining Three Color Model Algorithms," *IOSR Journal of Computer Engineering*, vol. 17, pp. 06-125, 2015.

H. M. Zangana, "A new algorithm for shape detection," *IOSR Journal of Computer Engineering (IOSR-JCE)*, vol. 19, no. 3, pp. 71-76, 2017.

H. M. Zangana, "Library Data Quality Maturity (IIUM as a Case Study)," *IOSR-JCE*, vol. 29, Mar. 2017.

Zangana, H. M. (2017). Watermarking System Using LSB. *IOSR Journal of Computer Engineering*, 19(3), 75–79. DOI: 10.9790/0661-1903027579

Zangana, H. M. (2018). Design an information management system for a pharmacy. *International Journal of Advanced Research in Computer and Communication Engineering*, 7(10), 52–55. DOI: 10.17148/IJARCCE.2018.71012

Zangana, H. M. "Developing Data Warehouse for Student Information System (IIUM as a Case Study)," *International Organization of Scientific Research*, vol. 20, no. 1, pp. 09-14, 2018.

H. M. Zangana, "Implementing a System for Recognizing Optical Characters," 2018.

H. M. Zangana, "Issues of Data Management in the Library: A Case Study," 2019.

H. M. Zangana, "ITD Data Quality Maturity (A Case Study)," *International Journal Of Engineering And Computer Science*, vol. 8, no. 10, 2019.

Zangana, H. M. (2020). Mobile Device Integration in IIUM Service. *International Journal (Toronto, Ont.)*, 8(5).

Zangana, H. M. (2021). The Global Financial Crisis from an Islamic Point Of View. *Qubahan Academic Journal*, 1(2), 55–59. DOI: 10.48161/qaj.v1n2a39

Zangana, H. M. (2022). Creating a Community-Based Disaster Management System. *Academic Journal of Nawroz University*, 11(4), 234–244. DOI: 10.25007/ajnu.v11n4a1485

Zangana, H. M. (2022). Implementing New Interactive Video Learning System for IIUM. *Academic Journal of Nawroz University*, 11(2), 23–29. DOI: 10.25007/ajnu.v11n2a1281

H. M. Zangana, "Improving The Web Services for Remittance Company: Express Remit as a Case Study," *Academic Journal of Nawroz University (AJNU)*, vol. 11, no. 3, 2022.

Zangana, H. M. (2024). Exploring the Landscape of Website Vulnerability Scanners: A Comprehensive Review and Comparative Analysis. *Redefining Security With Cyber AI*, 111-129.

Zangana, H. M. (2024). Exploring Blockchain-Based Timestamping Tools: A Comprehensive Review. *Redefining Security With Cyber AI*, 92-110.

Zangana, H. M. (2024). *Exploring Blockchain-Based Timestamping Tools: A Comprehensive Review*. Redefining Security With Cyber AI. DOI: 10.4018/979-8-3693-6517-5.ch006

Zangana, H. M. (2024). *Exploring the Landscape of Website Vulnerability Scanners: A Comprehensive Review and Comparative Analysis*. Redefining Security With Cyber AI. DOI: 10.4018/979-8-3693-6517-5.ch007

H. M. Zangana, "CHALLENGES AND ISSUES of MANET," 2024.

Zangana, H. M., & Abdulazeez, A. M. (2023). Developed Clustering Algorithms for Engineering Applications: A Review [INJIISCOM]. *International Journal of Informatics, Information System and Computer Engineering*, 4(2), 147–169. DOI: 10.34010/injiiscom.v4i2.11636

Zangana, H. M., & Al-Shaikhli, I. F. (2013). A new algorithm for human face detection using skin color tone. *IOSR Journal of Computer Engineering*, 11(6), 31–38. DOI: 10.9790/0661-1163138

Zangana, H. M., Al-Shaikhli, I. F., & Graha, Y. I. (2013). The Ethical Dilemma of Software Piracy: An Inquiry from an Islamic Perspective. *Creative Communication and Innovative Technology Journal*, 7(1), 59–76. DOI: 10.33050/ccit.v7i1.171

Zangana, H. M., Bazeed, S. M. S., Ali, N. Y., & Abdullah, D. T. (2024). Navigating Project Change: A Comprehensive Review of Change Management Strategies and Practices. *Indonesian Journal of Education and Social Sciences*, 3(2), 166–179. DOI: 10.56916/ijess.v3i2.735

Zangana, H. M., Graha, Y. I., & Al-Shaikhli, I. F. (2024). Blogging: A New Platform For Spreading Rumors! *Creative Communication and Innovative Technology Journal*, 9(1), 71–76.

Zangana, H. M., Khalid Mohammed, A., & Zeebaree, S. R. (2024). Systematic Review of Decentralized and Collaborative Computing Models in Cloud Architectures for Distributed Edge Computing. *Sistemasi: Jurnal Sistem Informasi*, 13(4), 1501–1509. DOI: 10.32520/stmsi.v13i4.4169

Zangana, H. M., Mohammed, A. K., & Mustafa, F. M. (2024). Advancements and Applications of Convolutional Neural Networks in Image Analysis: A Comprehensive Review. *Jurnal Ilmiah Computer Science*, 3(1), 16–29.

Zangana, H. M., Mohammed, A. K., & Mustafa, F. M. (2024). Advancements in Edge Detection Techniques for Image Enhancement: A Comprehensive Review [IJAIR]. *International Journal of Artificial Intelligence & Robotics*, 6(1), 29–39. DOI: 10.25139/ijair.v6i1.8217

Zangana, H. M., Mohammed, A. K., Sallow, A. B., & Sallow, Z. B. (2024). Cybernetic Deception: Unraveling the Layers of Email Phishing Threats. [INJURATECH]. *International Journal of Research and Applied Technology*, 4(1), 35–47.

Zangana, H. M., Mohammed, A. K., Sallow, A. B., & Sallow, Z. B. (2024). Cybernetic Deception: Unraveling the Layers of Email Phishing Threats [INJURATECH]. *International Journal of Research and Applied Technology*, 4(1), 35–47.

Zangana, H. M., Mohammed, A. K., Sallow, Z. B., & Mustafa, F. M. (2024). Exploring Image Representation and Color Spaces in Computer Vision: A Comprehensive Review. *The Indonesian Journal of Computer Science*, 13(3). Advance online publication. DOI: 10.33022/ijcs.v13i3.3998

Zangana, H. M., & Mustafa, F. M. (2024). From Classical to Deep Learning: A Systematic Review of Image Denoising Techniques. *Jurnal Ilmiah Computer Science*, 3(1), 50–65.

Zangana, H. M., & Mustafa, F. M. (2024). Review of Hybrid Denoising Approaches in Face Recognition: Bridging Wavelet Transform and Deep Learning. *The Indonesian Journal of Computer Science*, 13(4). Advance online publication. DOI: 10.33022/ijcs.v13i4.4209

Zangana, H. M., & Mustafa, F. M. (2024). Surveying the Landscape: A Comprehensive Review of Object Detection Algorithms and Advancements. *Jurnal Ilmiah Computer Science*, 3(1), 1–15.

Zangana, H. M., & Omar, M. (2020). Threats, Attacks, and Mitigations of Smartphone Security. *Academic Journal of Nawroz University*, 9(4), 324–332. DOI: 10.25007/ajnu.v9n4a989

Zangana, H. M., & Omar, M. (2020). Threats, Attacks, and Mitigations of Smartphone Security. *Academic Journal of Nawroz University*, 9(4), 324–332. DOI: 10.25007/ajnu.v9n4a989

Zangana, H. M., Omar, M., Al-Karaki, J. N., & Mohammed, D. (2024). Comprehensive Review and Analysis of Network Firewall Rule Analyzers: Enhancing Security Posture and Efficiency. *Redefining Security With Cyber AI*, 15-36.

Zangana, H. M., Omar, M., Al-Karaki, J. N., & Mohammed, D. (2024). *Comprehensive Review and Analysis of Network Firewall Rule Analyzers: Enhancing Security Posture and Efficiency*. Redefining Security With Cyber AI. DOI: 10.4018/979-8-3693-6517-5.ch002

Zangana, H. M., Omar, M., & Ali, N. Y. (2024). Harnessing Artificial Intelligence in Modern Marketing: Strategies, Benefits, and Challenges [BAMJ]. *Business, Accounting and Management Journal*, 02(02), 70–82.

Zangana, H. M., Sallow, Z. B., Alkawaz, M. H., & Omar, M. "Unveiling the Collective Wisdom: A Review of Swarm Intelligence in Problem Solving and Optimization," *Inform: Jurnal Ilmiah Bidang Teknologi Informasi dan Komunikasi*, vol. 9, no. 2, pp. 101-110, 2024.

Zangana, H. M., & Zeebaree, S. R. (2024). Distributed Systems for Artificial Intelligence in Cloud Computing: A Review of AI-Powered Applications and Services [INJIISCOM]. *International Journal of Informatics, Information System and Computer Engineering*, 5(1), 11–30. DOI: 10.34010/injiiscom.v5i1.11883

Zeadally, S., Adi, E., Baig, Z., & Khan, I. A. (2020). Harnessing artificial intelligence capabilities to improve cybersecurity. *IEEE Access : Practical Innovations, Open Solutions*, 8, 23817–23837. DOI: 10.1109/ACCESS.2020.2968045

Zhang, H., Wu, J., Pan, Q., Bashir, A. K., & Omar, M. (2024). Toward Byzantine-Robust Distributed Learning for Sentiment Classification on Social Media Platform. *IEEE Transactions on Computational Social Systems*, 1–11. DOI: 10.1109/TCSS.2024.3361465

Zhou, S., Ali, A., Al-Fuqaha, A., Omar, M., & Feng, L. (2024). Robust Risk-Sensitive Task Offloading for Edge-Enabled Industrial Internet of Things. *IEEE Transactions on Consumer Electronics*, 70(1), 1403–1413. DOI: 10.1109/TCE.2023.3323146

Chapter 7
How Human-Centered Cybersecurity (HCC) Training Fosters Organizational Cybersecurity Cultures (CSC)

Zealous Irwin Godwin
Illinois Institute of Technology, USA

ABSTRACT

In the increasingly complex cybersecurity landscape, human behavior plays a critical role in the efficacy of security measures within organizations. This author explores the integration of Human-Centered Cybersecurity (HCC), or usable security, practices, through the concepts of usability, education, and user engagement in security training programs to alleviate cybersecurity-induced friction. HCC emphasizes operational feasibility, advocating for training programs like Security Education, Training, and Awareness (SETA) that adapt to individual learning styles and roles, thereby fostering a culture of cybersecurity awareness. Some strategies to increase cybersecurity compliance include personalized training via hybrid interaction systems and gamification and a redefinition of employees' roles within an environment to shift to a security culture. This research calls for continuous evaluation and a multidimensional framework to incorporate human factors, aiming to strengthen Cybersecurity Culture (CSC) within organizations.

DOI: 10.4018/979-8-3373-0588-2.ch007

HOW HUMAN-CENTERED CYBERSECURITY (HCC) TRAINING FOSTERS ORGANIZATIONAL CYBERSECURITY CULTURES (CSC)

Since the early 1900s, the study of humans within the workplace has been a topic of many psychologists. This is called Industrial Organizational Psychology (I/O psychology). A large part of this subsection of psychology has focused on leadership, training, stress, performance, recruitment, and teams. Recently, the topic of culture has come to light within the workplace and this section of psychology. Culture is the "system in which individuals share meanings and common ways of viewing events and objects" (Conte & Landy, 2019). When culture moves into the workplace and the members of an organization, it is seen as organizational culture. Organizational culture is important for many reasons; these can include increased satisfaction, commitment, and engagement as well as cohesive values and behaviors. The main factors in fostering an organizational culture are structure, leadership, vision, mission, environment, and communication (Chalmers, 2023).

Within an organizational culture, there are also sub-cultures. One of these sub-cultures is the organizational cybersecurity culture (CSC). CSC is the combined attitudes, norms, assumptions, and values within an organization regarding cyber-security and further how that affects people's behavior toward security (inclusive of information security and security culture). When building a CSC, several key components need to be considered. These include mindset, leadership, training and awareness, performance management, and technical and policy reinforcement (NICE, 2018). Additionally, with the quickly changing and ever-adapting threat landscape, this concept is more important than ever.

These cultures may be a second thought for many organizations, but they are incredibly important to maintain a robust cybersecurity system and framework. Along with other cultures, the CSC influences the effectiveness and the deployment of resources that support the organization's policy (Choudhry et al., 2007). Without the change in mindset to support the protective efforts, behaviors towards new systems will lack luster and be less supportive of the goal objective. According to Herath & Rao (2009), the positive attitude towards security policy has a significant effect on response efficacy and will significantly decrease the chance that a cyber-attack is successful (Willie, 2023). When put into practice, Liberty Mutual, through continuous learning and a strengthened belief and values system, created a culture of organizational citizenship behaviors (OCB) where any perceived attacks are reported or responded to accordingly with utmost accuracy (Huang & Pearlson, 2019).

An organizational culture, either cybersecurity-based or not, tends to increase the number of OCBs. OCBs are actions that individuals take, outside of their defined job tasks, through their discretion. They are generally categorized into seven types. These include "helping behaviors, sportsmanship, organizational loyalty, organizational compliance, individual initiative, civic virtue, and self-development" (Pickford, 2024). Increasing organizational citizenship behavior regarding security (OCB-S) decreases non-malicious counterproductive computer security behaviors (CCSB) (computer use that goes against the organization's values) as civic virtue and helping increases, increases participation through the social exchange in clearly defined roles, and increases organizational safety as a sense of belonging increases (Ifenedo, 2015) (Turel 2017).

Many factors go into building and maintaining an organizational CSC. These can include leadership techniques, policies, procedures, a new change, general beliefs towards cybersecurity, and training. Additionally, with cybersecurity being such a new department, risk, and worry, many organizations have fallen behind with cybersecurity techniques, training, and knowledge from within. Then, even if these companies introduce new policies and procedures to the people within the organization, it may not be enough to prevent risk to the organization. Since human factors are the weakest link in most cybersecurity scenarios, organizations need to target this link to reduce the largest section of risk the organization has. It seems having these training and information sessions may not be enough protection since in 2023, 74% of data breaches involve human factors, like social engineering, mistakes, and purposeful mistreatment of the system (2023 Data breach investigations report, 2023). This has made the focus within cybersecurity education shift to human-centered cybersecurity (HCC) training.

HCC connects employees or people with their technology to lessen the number of human errors. The training approaches human behaviors and limitations concerning technology while designing the program to educate employees. The HCC technique places humans at the center of the cybersecurity posture of an organization's strategy. Various organizations have different approaches to tackling the human issue within cybersecurity training. In the past, many cybersecurity efforts have focused on an approach that addresses humans as the problem, not the solution. Similarly, these trainings were widely off-the-shelf general training that did not target individuals or their roles and responsibilities within and outside of an organization. Currently, some of the most successful ways to tackle cybersecurity through the human-centered lens include individualized training, defined roles, and a mindset change. Therefore to foster, maintain, and improve an organizational culture that supports the growing need for a robust cybersecurity framework, organizations need to use human-centered security training through individualized training, a shift in mindset toward humans within cybersecurity, and clearly defined roles and responsibilities in security.

HUMAN-CENTERED CYBERSECURITY (HCC) TRAINING

To explore the practice of human behavior, understanding, and beliefs on cybersecurity, multiple disciplines, including Information Technology, Cybersecurity, Human-Computer Interaction (HCI), and Business, investigate HCC. This can also be called "usable security" (Haney et al., 2024). The biggest goal of HCC-designed security programs is to reduce cybersecurity-induced friction and increase usability components (Howley, 2023). This friction is the frustration and lack of understanding towards security measures that may protect the organization but cause perceived difficulty within the system that can lead to general non-compliance. The concept of cybersecurity-induced friction also fits into operational feasibility. The friction of cybersecurity activities will be lessened if the extent of acceptance of a solution within an organizational culture is feasible (Witman, 2018). Effectiveness, whether a task can be completed, efficiency, how much time and resources a task takes to be completed, and satisfaction, the combination of a physical and mental response to a system or service, are the core usability components that can influence a user's view of a system (Haney, 2023). By decreasing these factors, the sense of community and acceptance of new change within an organization increases.

One of the many current training programs is Security Education, Training, and Awareness (SETA) which supports an organization's effort to tackle human factors in cybersecurity. This program starts by identifying security shortfalls, educating individuals through a multifaceted approach with various delivery methods, evaluating effectiveness, and then repeats. An example of a current market program is KnowBe4. The current market leader in cybersecurity training is KnowBe4 security awareness training (SAT) (Witts, 2024). It offers free and paid digital training with lectures, presentations, quizzes, and more with insight and effectiveness tracking. KnowBe4, like many other out-of-the-box training programs, can be effective for some individuals, but for others, it may not be as effective. Because of the lack of customizability, the training may not be relevant for all students taking the course. To make the SETA training more effective the training should be individualized, have a shift in mindset, clearly defined roles, and promote continuous learning environments.

Individualized Training

These SAT and SETA programs have many forms of use for organizations and individuals. Firstly, they can be digital or paper-based. Although paper-based training is less common with the emergence of the internet and the surge of work from home from the COVID-19 pandemic, some companies will still decide to use it. Secondly, there is in-person, online synchronous, and online asynchronous training. The difference between the asynchronous and synchronous versions of online training is whether an individual can complete it at their leisure or at a designated time. The training can be divided by department, skill level, and functional background, and further by department, job function, or main tasks (Witman, 2018). Lastly, there are generalized out-of-the-box training that an organization buys and distributes to the organization and custom training that is made specifically for the organization's dynamic.

Within all of the different mix-and-match options, there is a decision that can be made to make the training more effective. That is making the training individualized or using Personalized Learning Theory (PLT). Targeting what an employee needs to know and its specific audience makes training the most effective (Nieles et al., 2017). For example, a general user may just need to know how to lock their computers or change their passwords, but a technical user may need to know the standard for protecting files or data in a system.

Since individualization of learning needs to occur to make the program the most effective, ways to cater to that need should be decided upon. One form of individualization is a hybrid interaction system (HIS). This is a decision within training modules where the human and the digital systems work in tandem and become the center of attention during training (Terloth et al., 2020). Both the human and computer in these systems are active actors, instead of static learning devices and learners. HIS focuses on interaction. One of the main points of HIS cybersecurity training is the gamification of what needs to be learned. Gamification is the process of combining game mechanics into an interactive learning environment. This usually involves short and frequent cybersecurity games with a reward system like passing a level, getting in-game rewards, etc. Gamification of a cybersecurity learning module can improve knowledge retention by 40% (Vijga, 2023). This format also offers other learning benefits. These include immediate feedback, collaboration and teamwork, familiarization with the organization's security systems, and scalable progression. All of these factors make learning more individualized since the employees can return to old levels, move on when they feel ready, and feel more motivated to change or do something new.

Another way to achieve individualization is by adjusting the training to a person's learning style. Using mixed media, for example, a lecture and a simulation or lab environment together, is more effective than using a singular form of teaching. In an expository study on cybersecurity training, Workman (2021) found that classroom or lab teaching ($\mu = 233.19$, $\sigma = 0.34$) would be improved with cybersecurity simulations ($\mu = 301.11$, $\sigma = 0.26$, $F = 7.88$, $p < 0.00$, $\eta 2 = 0.29$) and would be improved with both simulations and live activity together ($\mu = 233.19$, $\sigma = 0.34$, $F = 11.29$, $p < 0.00$, $\eta 2 = 0.31$).

Table 1. Pretest means and Pearson correlations and posttest means, f-scores, f-scores and eta squared for hypothesis

Pretest Means and Pearson Correlations Among Groups Prior to Training							
Group	**Study Condition**	**μ**	**σ**	**1**	**2**	**3**	**4**
1	Classroom/Labs	114.17	1.11	--			
2	Simulations	109.83	1.26	-.64**	--		
3	Live Activity	116.19	1.57	.68**	.62**	--	
4	Simulations + Activity	112.32	1.34	-.60**	.69**	-.63**	--
Posttest Means, F-Scores, F-scores and Eta Squared for Hypothesis							
Hypothesis	Study Condition	μ	σ	F	η2		
	Classroom/Labs	233.19	0.34	--	--		
H1	Simulations	301.11	0.26	7.88***	0.29		
H2	Live Activity	256.19	0.84	1.88	0.14		
H3	Simulations + Activity	388.88	0.4	11.29***	0.31		

N=209. *p<.05, **p<.01, ***p<.001

Note. This table is adapted from Workman (2021). It shows the Pre and Post-test data from the experiment involving mixed media for teaching cybersecurity.

Where μ is the posttest mean, σ statistical significance through standard deviation, F is the proportion of variance, η2 ratio of variance in an outcome variable controlled by predictors, and the p-value is the probability of the null hypothesis being true given the data that was obtained. The test that was completed was a pretest and post-test on analytical and procedural skills. Out of the two improvements, the classroom, live activity, and simulation combination improved the pretest scores the most with the 209-person test. Workman's tests for the activities were completed with what were current educational programs.

Individualization of training can be completed in many ways. One of the most effective forms of individualized training is having a mixed media approach to learning, whether that be through the gamification of knowledge and tasks or simulations, labs, and lectures. Having multiple approaches to learning will increase the likelihood that the individual taking the course will retain the information from their preferred mode of learning. Having this individualized approach can make the employee feel seen and appreciated within the organization and therefore increase motivation. Lastly, not only does individualized training increase effectiveness and knowledge retention, but it can also change their attitude toward cybersecurity. All of these effects can improve and make the CSC more robust.

Clearly Defined Roles and Responsibilities in Security

All jobs have roles and responsibilities, as well as tasks that the employee is trained on, told to do, and completed. These are necessary for finding new recruits as well as instructing what current employees should complete with accuracy. Without these clearly defined roles, or having role ambiguity, effectiveness and efficiency for said employee are decreased. Having clearly defined roles in the workplace, or role clarity, causes employees who have it to be "53% more efficient and 27% more effective… than employees who have role ambiguity" (Pijnacker, 2019). Similarly, work performance improves by 25% with defined roles and responsibilities (Pijnacker, 2019). This is because the worker would feel autonomous and not need to stop working to ask questions or clarify responsibilities.

This phenomenon does not only occur for managing individuals at an organization. This also applies to new roles and responsibilities for every employee to tackle within the realm of cybersecurity. Clearly defined responsibilities are necessary for ensuring the wanted cybersecurity best practices that occur on an individual basis to support the needs and ideology of the organization. These roles are defined job tasks that are needed for the employee to perform their job correctly. When these roles are defined in the operation of cybersecurity and the requirements of training and support are met, users will "effectively and economically integrate… into the cybersecurity system" (Boyce et al., 2011). When the cybersecurity roles are built into the job, employees will not see them as a secondary task to complete, it will be a task that needs to be completed, alone. This is especially important in a time-sensitive scenario. When completing a time valuable task, humans tend to focus on their perceived most important task of the immediate goal (West, 2008). If instead, security is now moved to the forefront and made a part of the task at hand as a necessity to complete, it will no longer interrupt that task.

Viewing security as an important job task and not a secondary action to be taken will improve the CSC as a whole. Since culture is defined on three cognitive levels: artifacts and behaviors, exposed values, and basic underlying assumptions, the task shift would affect values and assumptions (Millerd, 2019). The actual task would not change, but the norms, what is acceptable to do or say, related to the task change to become the focus of attention. With security being the unspoken norm, the culture improves. Secondly, the assumptions, and underlying beliefs brought from values, also change (Conte & Landy., 2019). Once the tasks become second nature to the individual, their assumptions change. Therefore, once security, the priority task, becomes normal for the individual to complete, it will further improve the CSC.

Shift in Mindset Toward Humans Within Cybersecurity

Since the start of the internet, hackers have been attempting to exploit web systems. Since the start of the Russia-Ukraine conflict in 2022, 97% of companies have reported an increase in cyber attacks (Sobers, 2024). Additionally, there was a 68% increase in data breaches from 1,108 in 2020 to 1,862 in 2021 (Fowler, 2022). During any intelligent hacking endeavors, the "weakest link" of a system is targeted and exploited. The "weakest link" is the least protected or most insecure element within an information system. The amount of security the link has is the same amount of security the entire system has because of the effort to exploit the easiest targets. The subsequent question then becomes what is the "weakest link" and how should their security be improved (Pan et al., 2015).

In general, most organizations and stakeholders in cybersecurity consider humans to be the issue in many of these scenarios, for good reason. In 2023, 74% of data breaches involved a human element (Sobers, 2024). Many of the current solutions for human behaviors act as containers for them and automatically treat all users of a system as threat actors. Many of the solutions to the human issue in cybersecurity include creating more resistance to tasks that employees need to perform. Additionally, it can reduce an employee to a cog in the machine of security as a rule follower with only punishment reinforcement for bad behaviors (Zimmermann & Renaud, 2019). Punishment reinforcement is when someone or an employee does something wrong, they are punished per policy or contingencies placed on the employee.

Having too much security resistance, causes people to develop insecure actions to make their job easier. This can be seen when people write passwords on sticky notes to remember them if the password is too complex or changes too often. Similarly, even with resistance, companies still fall victim to cybersecurity attacks. In a survey of over 3,600 security and IT professionals, 59% of organizations had over 30 security tools in place and only 5% had less than 10 security tools, yet 51% reported a significant data breach and 61% paid a ransomware attack (Cyber Resilient Organization Study 2021, 2021). Punishment reinforcement can cause many negative side effects. It can cause the punished negative emotions toward the company or punisher which can lead to counterproductive work behaviors, the opposite of OCBs. It is also difficult to scale the severity of the punishment and repeatable punishments may not be as effective because of the inconsistency with repetition (Gordan, 2014).

Renaud & Zimmermann (2019) suggest that an alternative to the "human-as-problem" approach is switching to a "human-as-solution" mindset. The current system of human treatment within cybersecurity focuses on preventing errors, rigorous policy and training, containing employees, and a root cause analysis of who during a cyber incident. Further, it needs to change to focus on learning, expertise, communication, cooperation, successes, and having ongoing reviews and cyber incident reviews on why something occurred. This theoretical approach to cybersecurity relies on the fact that the problem is not just the technology, it is the socio-technical relationship between the users and the system. There is not one single failing component because of this. This theory focuses on the technical expertise of different cybersecurity threats. For example, for the threat of phishing, Renaud and Zimmerman (2019) recommend instead of focusing on the negative consequences of a successful phishing, to focus on successfully identifying anomalies in the emails and turn reporting them to the organization.

Achieving the change in training will shift employees' assumptions and values in the CSC. They will see themselves as a part of the solution, someone who can protect others. Further, employees would be more likely to see themselves as part of the vulnerable that are affected by a cybersecurity attack, see cybersecurity threats as having actual risk, and have self-efficacy, the belief the employee, themself, can handle risk, regarding security (Sulaiman et al., 2022). As per the Protection Motivation Theory (PMT), the idea that people are motivated to protect themselves based on the perceived threat and perceived coping mechanism, employees are more likely to complete cybersecurity-related tasks because of the change in mindset (Shillair R., 2020). This is because the employees will want to protect themselves in the face of a perceived danger or threat against them. Instead of ostracizing humans for being the biggest threat, include them in the organization and give them many ways to solve a problem, whether that be through communication, basic security solutions, or making someone with more expertise know about the threat. Inclusion will increase the likelihood that a culture can be fostered by employees as well as increase the chance that the employees will want to protect themselves and the organization. Therefore, the individual will have the motivation and the facilities to be a part of a culture and uphold the CSC.

ANALYSIS

Although the identification of a shift in mindset is important, it needs to be supported by a framework, training, and continuous efforts. These three sections of HCC training and practices cannot work alone. Each section has one side of human-centered training. Humans are ever-changing and adapting to new work environments, this means that the training that is given must fit this form of growth. It is known that not every form of learning fits every individual learner perfectly.

This means that multiple efforts and learning adjustments need to occur to produce the best outcome possible.

Not only do multiple efforts need to be made, but the efforts need to be continuously supported. As stated previously, a CSC is a socio-technical relationship and environment, in turn, a multidimensional continuous framework should be put in place to match the environment that is being fostered (Malatji et al., 2019). The guide needs to be continuously reassessed to best fit the needs of the company while it is being utilized. Through this socio-technical network, frequent rapid prototyping needs to occur to reassess the needs of the organization. Through a combination of the ADDIE model and rapid prototyping, this can be done. The ADDIE model, or the Analyze, Design, Develop, Implement, and Evaluate model, involves those five steps to be used one step at a time and continuously during an institutional course. These steps can take a long time to fully complete to move on to the next step. Therefore, it should be combined with rapid prototyping efforts. This means that throughout each step there is constant evaluation and feedback with the prototyping of the design process. This change to the ADDIE model gives the framework a chance to respond to the ever-changing cybersecurity landscape and the current threats an organization faces. With constant feedback, the lessons learned by the users of the framework will feel more relevant to the organization. This gives the users a reason to learn and use the methods and techniques taught. Having a reason increases the likelihood of the employee using the technique and thereby strengthening the CSC.

Even though there would be a framework put into place, the organization should treat it as a framework, not a set of instructions to follow. This is because the CSC needs to be cultivated and fostered, not "rigidly designed" (Bada et al., 2021). The concept of HCC should be used as a guide to push training and awareness to be more useful to a wider range of skilled employees. Multiple frameworks have been developed and suggested for use, but very few of them have been tested outside of a theoretical academic approach. Chowdhury, Gkioulos, and Katsikas (2022) suggested a framework with HCC in mind. It combines the various HCC training techniques with continuous monitoring, accessibility to all users, and feedback loops.

Figure 1. Conceptual cybersecurity framework from Chowdhury, Gkioulos, and Katsikas (2022)

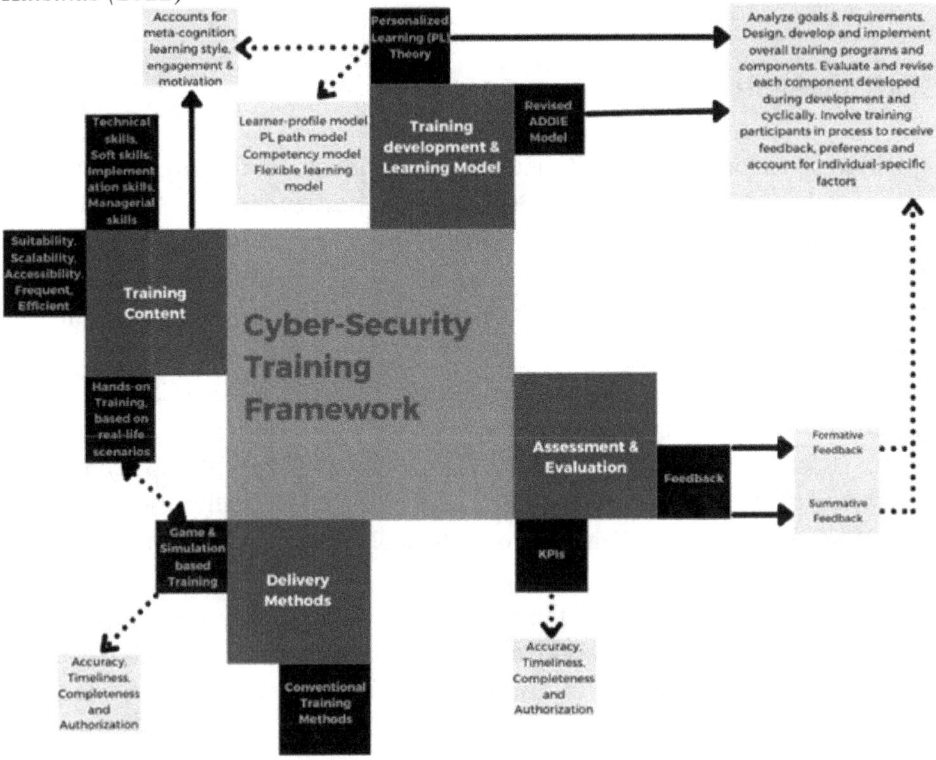

Note. The Delphi model is a theoretical framework that combines a revised ADDIE model, with its design phases, and motivation theory with technical skill, soft skill, and real-life techniques training. Lastly, it involves regular evaluation of its success through actual use of the techniques learned and feedback from the users (Chowdhury N. et al., 2022).

This framework guides hands-on timely training through a continuous feedback and improvement model that focuses on human factors and motivations within the workplace. The theoretical approach to training and awareness has been proven, in each separate part, to work, but not together as a whole. Still, capturing complex human feelings, actions, and mindsets within a framework of an ever-changing system, needs a continuously improving and prototyping framework, like the Delphi model suggested.

Further, HCC, although a new concept within the span of training and I/O psychology, has already proven to be increasingly effective for users. Some of the conclusions already made include Robinson's (2022) finding that HCC training decreases cognitive overload and increases the awareness of behavioral analysis techniques, Callari et. al. (2021) finding having the individualized multidisciplinary approach and making cybersecurity all person responsibilities creates a culture with less friction for security measures, and Cunningham et al. (2022) finding that human factor engineering is essential in the future of cybersecurity training and culture.

CONCLUSION

Different factors within HCC including individualized training, a shift to a human-as-the-solution mindset, continuous monitoring, and having clearly defined roles and responsibilities all increase the quality of cybersecurity training and culture separately. From the preliminary research, surveys, and findings from a collection of research papers for each factor affecting cybersecurity, it can be preliminarily concluded that HCC does positively affect CSC.

To clearly state that human-centered training, in its entirety, affects CSC positively, all factors within HCC need to be tested together. This research should, first, test pairs of HCC factors and then further into larger groups. This will help to conclude how each of the factors relate to and affect each other. Additionally, research within cybersecurity and Industrial Organizational Psychology needs to be conducted within both fields. This is because the training for cybersecurity affects all businesses and organizations within the current threat landscape that businesses face. Therefore, both industry professionals in workplace culture and dynamics as well as the effectiveness of cybersecurity need to research the effectiveness of training. This will give multiple perspectives into cybersecurity and separate training, which may be able to improve other necessary training that users need to take, outside the realm of cybersecurity as well.

Initiating a new form of cybersecurity mindset is difficult, but it begins with research. The development of a framework model for cybersecurity and all types of people within an organization takes time, funding, and more research to develop it. After its development, it needs to go through rigorous testing with human actors of many different technical skill levels and managerial roles. As said previously, further research will be needed to test the sanctity of HCC as it relates to the CSC.

REFERENCES

Addams, A., & Sasse, M. A. (1999). Users Are Not The Enemy. []. essay, CACM.]. *Communications of the ACM*, 42(12), 41–46.

Aksoy, C. (2024). Building a cyber security culture for resilient organizations against Cyber Attacks. *İşletme Ekonomi ve Yönetim Araştırmaları Dergisi, 7*(1), 96–110. DOI: 10.33416/baybem.1374001

Alyami, A., Sammon, D., Neville, K., & Mahony, C. (2023). Critical success factors for Security Education, training and awareness (SETA) programme effectiveness: An empirical comparison of practitioner perspectives. *Information and Computer Security*, 32(1), 53–73. DOI: 10.1108/ICS-08-2022-0133

Ani, U. D., He, H., & Tiwari, A. (2019). Human factor security: Evaluating the cybersecurity capacity of the Industrial Workforce. *Journal of Systems and Information Technology*, 21(1), 2–35. DOI: 10.1108/JSIT-02-2018-0028

Boyce, M. W., Duma, K. M., Hettinger, L. J., Malone, T. B., Wilson, D. P., & Lockett-Reynolds, J. (2011). Human performance in cybersecurity: A research agenda. *Proceedings of the Human Factors and Ergonomics Society Annual Meeting*, 55(1), 1115–1119. DOI: 10.1177/1071181311551233

Chalmers, R. (2023, May 22). *Organizational culture*. StatPearls [Internet]. https://www.ncbi.nlm.nih.gov/books/NBK560543/

Charness, N., & Boot, W. R. (2016). Technology, gaming, and Social Networking. *Handbook of the Psychology of Aging, Eighth ed.*, 389–407. DOI: 10.1016/B978-0-12-411469-2.00020-0

Choudhry, R. M., Fang, D., & Mohamed, S. (2007). The nature of safety culture: A survey of the state-of-the-art. *Safety Science*, 45(10), 993–1012. DOI: 10.1016/j.ssci.2006.09.003

Chowdhury, N., Katsikas, S., & Gkioulos, V. (2022). Modeling effective cybersecurity training frameworks: A delphi method-based study. *Computers & Security*, 113, 102551. Advance online publication. DOI: 10.1016/j.cose.2021.102551

Conte, J., & Landy, F. (2019). *Work in the 21st Century: An Introduction to Industrial and Organizational Psychology* (6th ed.). Wiley.

Cyber Resilient Organization Study 2021. IBM. (2021). https://www.ibm.com/resources/guides/cyber-resilient-organization-study/

2023. *Data breach investigations report.* Verizon Business. (2023). https://www.verizon.com/business/resources/reports/dbir/

Fowler, B. (2022, January 24). *Data breaches break record in 2021.* CNET. https://www.cnet.com/news/privacy/record-number-of-data-breaches-reported-in-2021-new-report-says/

Gordan, M. (2014). A Review of B. F. Skinner's 'Reinforcement Theory of Motivation'. *International Journal of Research in Education Methodology*, 5(3), 680–688. DOI: 10.24297/ijrem.v5i3.3892

Haney, J. (2023), Users Are Not Stupid: Six Cyber Security Pitfalls Overturned, Cyber Security: A Peer-Reviewed Journal, [online], https://tsapps.nist.gov/publication/get_pdf.cfm?pub_id=935795

Haney, J., Cunningham, C., & Furman, S. M. (2024). Towards Integrating Human-Centered Cybersecurity Research Into Practice: A Practitioner Survey. *Symposium on Usable Security and Privacy (USEC) 2024*, 1–16. https://doi.org/DOI: 10.14722/usec.2024.23xxx

He, W., & Zhang, Z. (2019). Enterprise cybersecurity training and awareness programs: Recommendations for Success. *Journal of Organizational Computing and Electronic Commerce*, 29(4), 249–257. DOI: 10.1080/10919392.2019.1611528

Herath, T., & Rao, H. R. (2009). Protection motivation and deterrence: A framework for security policy compliance in organisations. *European Journal of Information Systems*, 18(2), 106–125. DOI: 10.1057/ejis.2009.6

Howley, C. (2023, April 12). *Gartner identifies the top cybersecurity trends for 2023.* Gartner. https://www.gartner.com/en/newsroom/press-releases/04-12-2023-gartner-identifies-the-top-cybersecurity-trends-for-2023

Huang, K., & Pearlson, K. (2019). For what technology can't fix: Building a model of organizational cybersecurity culture. *Proceedings of the Annual Hawaii International Conference on System Sciences*, 6398–6407. DOI: 10.24251/HICSS.2019.769

Ifinedo, P. (2015). Effects of Organizational Citizenship Behavior and Social Cognitive Factors on Employees' Non-Malicious Counterproductive Computer Security Behaviors: An Empirical Analysis. *CONF-IRM 2015 PROCEEDINGS,* 1–13. https://aisel.aisnet.org/confirm2015/36/

Malatji, M., Von Solms, S., & Marnewick, A. (2019). Socio-Technical Systems Cybersecurity Framework. *Information and Computer Security*, 27(2), 233–272. DOI: 10.1108/ICS-03-2018-0031

Marikyan, D., & Papagiannidis, S. (2023). Technology Acceptance Model: A review. In Papagiannidis, S. (Ed.), *TheoryHub Book.*, Available at https://open.ncl.ac.uk /

McNeese, M., Cooke, N. J., D'Amico, A., Endsley, M. R., Gonzalez, C., Roth, E., & Salas, E. (2012). Perspectives on the role of cognition in Cyber Security. *Proceedings of the Human Factors and Ergonomics Society Annual Meeting*, 56(1), 268–271. DOI: 10.1177/1071181312561063

Millerd, P. (2022, June 7). *Edgar Schein - organizational culture: Artifacts, values & assumptions*. Boundless by Paul Millerd. https://think-boundless.com/edgar-scheins-anxiety-assumptions-powerful-ideas-on-culture/

National Institute for Cybersecurity Education Working Group (NICE). (2018). Cybersecurity is everyone's job. National Institute of Standards and Technology. Retrieved from https://www.nist.gov/system/files/documents/2018/10/15/cybersecurity_is_everyones_job_v1.0.pdf

Nieles, M., Dempsey, K., & Pillitteri, V. Y. (2017). An introduction to information security. *NIST SP 800-12 Rev. 1*. DOI: 10.6028/NIST.SP.800-12r1

Nobles, C., Robinson, N., Cunningham, M., & Cunningham, M. (2022). Straight from the Human Factors Professionals' mouth: The need to teach human factors in cybersecurity. *Proceedings of the 23rd Annual Conference on Information Technology Education*, 157–158. DOI: 10.1145/3537674.3555782

Pan, C., Zhong, W., & Mei, S. (2015). Finding the weakest link in the interdependent security chain using the analytic hierarchy process. *Journal of Advances in Computer Networks*, 3(4), 320–325. DOI: 10.18178/JACN.2015.3.4.190

Patrascu, P. (2019). Promoting cybersecurity culture through education. *eLearning and Software for Education, Vol. II*. DOI: 10.12753/2066-026X-19-108

Pavlou, C. (2023, October 26). *The psychology of gamification: Motivating employees during Cybersecurity training*. eLearning Industry. https://elearningindustry.com/the-psychology-of-gamification-motivating-employees-during-cybersecurity-training

Pelgrin, W. (2014). A Model For Positive Change: Influencing Positive Change in Cyber Security Strategy, Human Factor, and Leadership. *Best Practices in Computer Network Defense: Incident Detection and Response*, 107–137. DOI: 10.3233/978-1-61499-372-8-107

Pickford, H. (2024, March 12). *Organizational citizenship behaviours: Definitions and dimensions*. Economics of Mutuality Alliance. https://eom.org/literature-reviews/organizational-citizenship-behaviours/

Pijnacker, L. (2023, September 19). *HR analytics: Role clarity impacts performance.* Effectory. https://www.effectory.com/knowledge/hr-analytics-role-clarity-impacts-performance/

Pollini, A., Callari, T. C., Tedeschi, A., Ruscio, D., Save, L., Chiarugi, F., & Guerri, D. (2021). Leveraging human factors in cybersecurity: An integrated methodological approach. *Cognition Technology and Work*, 24(2), 371–390. DOI: 10.1007/s10111-021-00683-y PMID: 34149309

Prümmer, J., van Steen, T., & van den Berg, B. (2024). A systematic review of current cybersecurity training methods. *Computers & Security*, 136, 103585. Advance online publication. DOI: 10.1016/j.cose.2023.103585

Reegard, K., Blackett, C., & Katta, V. (2019). Proceedings of the 29th European Safety and Reliability Conference (ESREL). *Proceedings of the 29th European Safety and Reliability Conference*, 4036–4043. DOI: 10.3850/978-981-11-2724-3_0761-cd

Robinson, N. (2023). Human Factors Security Engineering: The future of cybersecurity teams. *EDPACS*, 67(5), 1–17. DOI: 10.1080/07366981.2023.2211429

Ron, F., & Porod, C. (2021). Motivating employees and organizations to adopt a cybersecurity-focused culture. *Journal of Organizational Psychology*, 21(1), 114–131. DOI: 10.33423/jop.v21i1.4030

Sadiq Nasir, S. N., & Nasir, S. (2023). Exploring the effectiveness of cybersecurity training programs: Factors, best practices, and future directions. *Advances in Multidisciplinary and Scientific Research Journal Publication*, 2(1), 151–160. DOI: 10.22624/AIMS/CSEAN-SMART2023P18

Shillair, R. (2020a). Protection motivation theory. *The International Encyclopedia of Media Psychology*, 1–3. DOI: 10.1002/9781119011071.iemp0188

Shillair, R. (2020b). Protection motivation theory. *The International Encyclopedia of Media Psychology*, 1–3. DOI: 10.1002/9781119011071.iemp0188

Sobers, R. (2024, January 4). *161 cybersecurity statistics and trends [updated 2023].* Varonis. https://www.varonis.com/blog/cybersecurity-statistics

Sulaiman, N. S., Fauzi, M. A., Hussain, S., & Wider, W. (2022). Cybersecurity behavior among government employees: The role of protection motivation theory and responsibility in mitigating cyberattacks. *Information (Basel)*, 13(9), 413. DOI: 10.3390/info13090413

Terfloth, L., Budde, L., & Schulte, C. (2020). Combining ideas and artifacts: An interaction-focused view on computing education using a cybersecurity example. *Koli Calling '20:Proceedings of the 20th Koli Calling International Conference on Computing Education Research*. DOI: 10.1145/3428029.3428052

Turel, O., Xu, Z., & Guo, K. (2017). Organizational Citizenship Behavior Regarding Security: Leadership Approach Perspective. *Journal of Computer Information Systems*, 60(1), 61–75. DOI: 10.1080/08874417.2017.1400928

Uchendu, B., Nurse, J. R. C., Bada, M., & Furnell, S. (2021). Developing a cyber security culture: Current practices and future needs. *Computers & Security*, 109, 102387. Advance online publication. DOI: 10.1016/j.cose.2021.102387

Vijga, L. (2024, February 12). *Cybersecurity gamification: Winning the cyberwar through play*. BYVI. https://byvi.co/2023/10/01/cybersecurity-gamification/

West, R. (2008). The Psychology of Security. In *Communications of the ACM* (Vol. Vol. 51, Ser. No. 4, pp. 34–41). essay, Association of Computing Machinery. DOI: 10.1145/1330311.1330320

Whitman, M. (2018). *Management of Information Security* (6th ed.)., https://bookshelf .vitalsource.com/books/9781337671545

Willie, M. M. (2023). The role of Organizational Culture in cybersecurity: Building a security-first culture. *Journal of Research* [JoRIT]. *Innovation and Technologies*, 2(16), 179–198. DOI: 10.57017/jorit.v2.2(4).05

Witts, J. (2024, March 21). *The top 10 security awareness training platforms*. Expert Insights. https://expertinsights.com/insights/the-top-security-awareness-training -platforms-for-businesses/

Workman, M. (2021). An exploratory study of mode efficacy in cybersecurity training. *Journal of Cybersecurity Education, Research and Practice, Volume*, 2021(1), 1–12. https://digitalcommons.kennesaw.edu/jcerp/vol2021/iss1/2/. DOI: 10.62915/2472-2707.1075

Zimmermann, V., & Renaud, K. (2019). Moving from a 'human-as-problem" to a 'human-as-solution" cybersecurity mindset. *International Journal of Human-Computer Studies*, 131, 169–187. DOI: 10.1016/j.ijhcs.2019.05.005

Chapter 8
The Role of Cybersecurity Legislation in Promoting Data Privacy

Ngozi Tracy Aleke
https://orcid.org/0009-0005-2328-5680
Illinois Institute of Technology, USA

ABSTRACT

The operation of robust cybersecurity legislation plays a fundamental role in safeguarding data privacy in an increasingly unified digital terrain, providing a legal framework that sensitizes individuals on their rights and privileges as it relates to the protection of their data, regulates data handlers by stipulating applicable rules and regulations when handling the information of a data subject, and establishes enforceable measures when a breach occurs, thereby fostering a culture of trust and accountability in the digital landscape. Cybersecurity legislation covering data privacy requirements is critical in ensuring the safety and security of every individual's personal information.

INTRODUCTION

Background and Context of Cybersecurity Legislation

The importance of the security of personal data and information is constantly being emphasized. Within a few decades of its discovery, information technology has become an essential part of the lives of most Americans and other global citizens. Unusually, this will call for the proliferation of government policies affecting information technologies in multiple agencies under multiple authorities, often with

DOI: 10.4018/979-8-3373-0588-2.ch008

little or no organization (Grant, 2010). In the United States, the nudge to create policies affecting cybersecurity originally emanated from the White House through the White House Cyberspace Policy Review, which recognized that the priority in pursuing cybersecurity is to establish a one-point leadership system within the federal government. To achieve this goal, the White House sought support from Congress.

With matters relating to the emergence of the internet and its rapid growth, increasing dependence on information technology by the government, both the public and private institutions, the very right ingrained in the Bill of Rights – The right to be let alone. High-profile cyber incidents experienced by companies such as the 2017 Equifax data breach and the 2014 Sony picture hacks have also shared a significant need for the states to be involved in cyber security protections through legislation. Cybersecurity ordinarily is the governance, development, management, and use of information security, information technology security, operating technology security, techniques and tools of achieving regulatory compliance, defending and securing assets from and compromising the assets of adversaries to keep our data safe (Brustolin, 2019).

Purpose and Significance of the Study

In this new digital era, our daily lives are increasingly and continuously interwoven with technology. Information gathered through these technologies is constantly being stored and processed by various entities. Data including personal information, online activities, shopping preferences and style, and our financial transactions are some of the information affected by these activities. For some people this information, though personal may not mean much, for others, it means a lot, and compromise may become deadly. The purpose and significance of this study is to shed more light on the impact of legislation in the protection of personal data and how this has made an average user of technology protected from fear of breach or compromise of their data when having a good faith transaction on the internet.

Emergence of Digital Technology

Humans have always at one time, or the other, tried to create equipment and technologies to attempt to make life better. The first of these tools were created during the Stone Age. These tools were the earliest technological development by humans. From stones, work tools such as axes, hammers, arrowheads, knives, and even the ignition of fire through the use of stones were invented. Human societies have transitioned through phases to get to where it is today, that is the "Digital Age". From the Paleolithic period, through the digital age, one thing that has been common to all men is the desire to create tools that make life better and chores easier.

This quest for comfort and convenience has given room to the emergence of various technologies around the world, from automobiles to industrial technologies and most recent information technologies. Technological help makes the world fairer, just, and peaceful. Bringing this to the workplace, technology makes producing work decent and stress-free. The advancement of digital technology has reached around 50% of the developing world's population in barely two decades, making digital technology the topmost advanced innovation in the world's history (UN, 2020).

Proliferation of Mainframe Computers and Early Network Systems

We cannot talk about the evolution of information technology without referring to Mainframe Computers. These machines were first developed in 1944 (Prasad, 1989) and have undergone various alterations and advancements both in their functionality and design. Before going further, it is trite to first understand what mainframe computers are. The IBM Dictionary of Computing defines a mainframe as a large computer, one to which other computers can be connected so that they can share facilities the mainframe provides (McDaniel, 1994). The first generation of digital computers was first developed in 1944 by IBM in collaboration with Harvard University. It was an electromechanical machine, and it was known as the Automatic Sequence Controlled Calculator. Additions were performed in one-third of a second while multiplication was done within six seconds (McDaniel, 1994). Over the next few years, smaller but faster and more versatile machines were created. The most popular at that time was the IBM 701. These innovative changes to the mainframe have continued through the years and for over 50 years, the mainframe computers have served as the backbone of large-scale computing. It has adapted and adopted new technological requirements. The mainframe is used in today's world in ways that were unfathomable when it was first created.

While the first mainframe computer was created in the 1940s, the internet did not start until the 1960s. Though the mainframe made work easier and faster, information could not easily be shared among people not currently in the same physical location. Postal mail and physical presence were the only available options. The computers on the other hand were large and heavy and could not be easily moved around. This inability to share information was what necessitated the creation of the internet, as government researchers wanted ways to share information without having to go through the hustle of long waits or lost or diverted mail. Additionally, states and international relationships and conflicts played a big role in the creation of the Internet. For example, the launch of the Sputnik satellite by the then USSR spurred the U.S. Department of Defense to consider ways of continued dissemination of information even after a nuclear attack.

Figure 1. History of cybersecurity

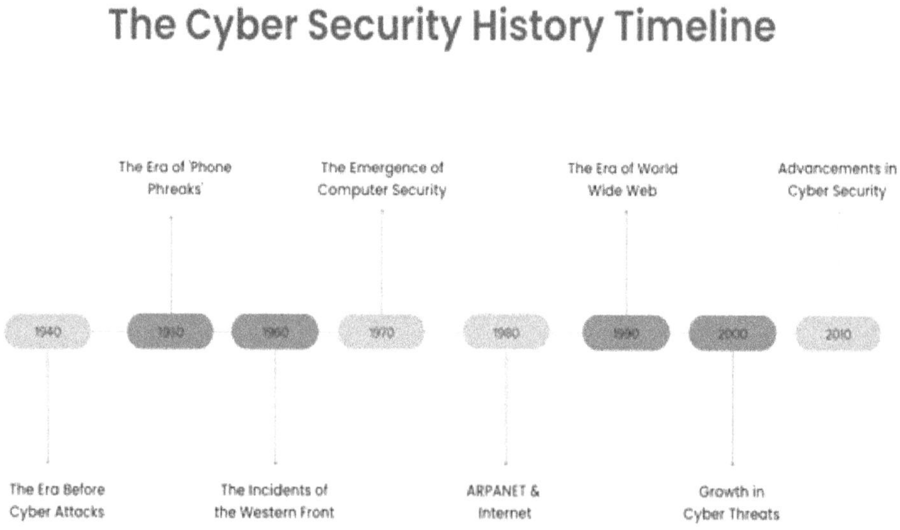

Source: https://www.theknowledgeacademy.com/blog/history-of-cyber-security/

The development of the Advanced Research Project Agency Network (ARPANET), the network that ultimately evolved into what is now known as the internet was formed based on this curiosity (University System of Georgia, 2023). Even though the ARPANET was created for information sharing, access was limited to certain academics and research organizations that had contracts with the Department of Defense. On January 1, 1983, a new communication protocol called Transfer Control Protocol/Internetwork protocol (TCP/IP) was established. TCP/IP allowed for different kinds of computers on different networks to communicate with each other.

Figure 2. Importance of data privacy in the digital age

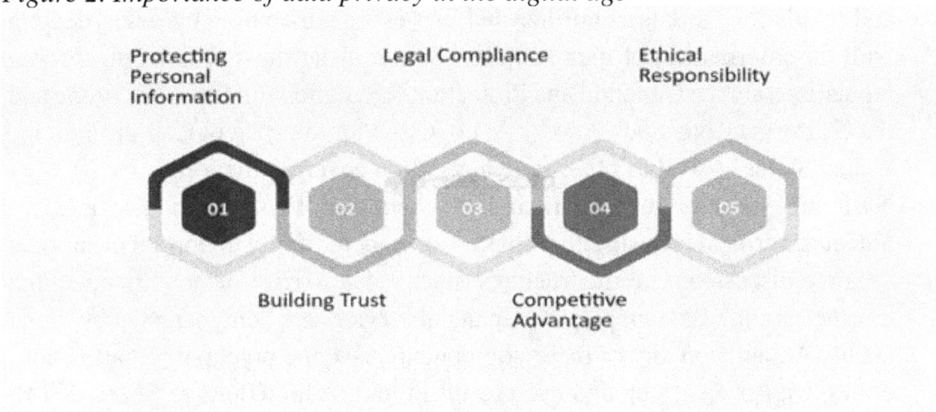

The Future of Data Protection in the Digital Age - EIDV and GDPR: Ensuring Data Protection in the Digital Age

Before going further, we must first understand what is meant by "Privacy". Warren & Brandeis (1890) defined privacy as the right to be left alone. Consequently, Privacy according to the International Association of Privacy Professionals (2020) is defined as the desire of people to freely choose the circumstances and the degree to which their attitude and behavior would be exposed to the public. The principle of privacy is used to protect an individual's dignity, independence, and integrity. The major aim of data privacy is to ensure that individuals always have the authority to determine what happens to their data. How it is collected, processed, and shared, is a principle that also extends to not just "the person" but anything they own including their personal, financial, educational, health information and otherwise. Data privacy is of great importance for many reasons, a few are listed below.

a). **Preservation of Individual Autonomy:** Privacy gives an individual an autonomous authority to determine what happens to their personal information. It affords an individual the ability to exercise a sense of control over their digital identities and personal lives.

b). **Ethical Considerations and HumanDignity:** Respecting the privacy of an individual is an ethical requirement. Every person is entitled to the right to their private life and human dignity and organizations must ensure that right is always upheld by ensuring data protection, transparency, and due and informed consent is sought and always gotten in their data handling practices.

c). **Legal Compliance and Accountability:** Though the digital age and cyberspace are still relatively young, precedents on data breaches have shown how enormous and radical a breach can be. For this reason, many jurisdictions around the world have invested a lot into data protection by enacting data privacy laws and regulations a data controller and processor must abide by when dealing with the information of data subjects. Some of the most prominent of these regulations are the General Data Protection Regulation (GDPR) for Europe and the California Consumer Privacy Act (CCPA) for the state of California in the United States as well as other state legislation covering the feed.

d). **National Security and Critical Infrastructure Protection:** The need to Safeguard critical infrastructures has become increasingly important in national security discussions. Infrastructures such as electricity, telecommunication, transportation, water supply, and financial services are being targeted by threat actors. Assaults on any of these components have the potential to harm economies, trigger disasters, and even result in loss of life (Betts & Sezer, 2014). Given the reliance by contemporary societies, these infrastructures have become susceptible to threats from organized crime and acts of terrorism. Thus, ensuring their security is paramount for both national security interests and the safety of the public. The Department of Homeland Security through the Department of Cybersecurity and Infrastructure Security Agency (CISA) is responsible for protecting the United States from any attack on Critical Infrastructure protected data. Some of the ways they do this are by protecting the government's computer network, strengthening the security of critical infrastructure, and studying the latest technology for risks (www.dhs.gov). In March 2022, Congress approved the Cyber Incident Reporting for Critical Infrastructure Act of 2022 (CIRCIA) which mandates entities within the critical infrastructure sector to report "significant cyber incidents" and any ransom payments made by organizations to CISA. The act also provided those specific areas, such as which entities are covered by the provisions of the law, and what types of incidents necessitate reporting, would be clarified through rulemaking (McNicholas & Angle, 2022). Additionally, the federal government has released sector-specific guidelines for operators of critical infrastructure. Sectors including nuclear, chemical, electrical, government contracting, and transportation have comprehensive statutory and regulatory obligations that each operator must abide by.

e). **Global Business Operations and Cross-Border Data Flows:** According to Marwala (2023), Data is the lifeblood of modern business. Data transcends the engagements of two entities, neither is data just a consequence of a transaction. Data should be seen as an asset, a substance of innovation, and a vital element of the global economy that must be protected. The flow of data influences anything it comes across; it flows beyond borders and fuels anything it comes across from personalized customer experiences to artificial intelligence and predictive analytics. Cross-border data flow refers to the sharing of information across international borders. This may either be through multinational corporations sharing employee data between offices in different countries, a cloud computing company storing information for organizations in different countries, or simply a user in one country viewing a video in another. These data flow streams are enormous, and they help build efficiency in business, innovation, and scalability. With these flows, one can boast of a variety of content technology and services for consumers. However, with these flows comes a great deal of challenges for the government. Threats to national security, infrastructures, privacy, and economic interest are only but a few that a government could face.

Understanding the Concept of Cybersecurity Legislation

There are quite a few cybersecurity legislations and regulations that have been put in place to curb cybersecurity issues at the federal level of government. This law protects and provides the requirements for the security of the information system of the United States Government in conjunction with the sharing of information between governments, and private sectors versus the government. The major objectives of these laws are to prevent cybercrimes and at the same time protect sensitive government and corporate information. Some examples of recent Federal Cybersecurity Legislation include the Federal Information Security Modernization Act (FISMA), the Cybersecurity Information Sharing Act (CISA), and the Computer Fraud and Abuse Act (CFAA), The Federal Trade Commission (“FTC”), The Health Insurance Portability and Accountability Act (“HIPAA”) he Gramm-Leach-Bliley Act (“GLBA”).

At the State level, most states in the United States have one form of cyber security legislation or another. The most prominent of these legislations is New York's SHIELD Act, which requires that a data controller or processor puts in place reasonable security for personal information while also specifying measures that may be put in place. The California Consumer Privacy Act (“CCPA”) (expanded by the California Consumer Privacy Rights Act beginning in 2023) provides for a data breach right action for residents of California with statutory specific amounts if the data subject whose personal information has been breached can prove that the impacted business failed to implement reasonable security measures to protect their personal information. Other states such as Colorado, Connecticut, Virginia, and Utah have Data protection laws that also require appropriate or reasonable security procedures to be put in place by a business that in one way or another deals with individuals' data.

WHAT IS CYBERSECURITY LEGISLATION?

Definition and Scope

Cybersecurity legislation is a body of laws, rules, policies, guidelines, and principles put in place for the administration and governance of the activities carried out within cyberspace. These laws cover various aspects of cybersecurity from computer systems protections – both hardware and software, to network securities, to data protection from theft, damage, or unauthorized access to general online behavior. The presence of Cyber legislation in this new technological dispensation cannot be jettisoned. Despite the various shortcomings of these legislations, its presence has made carrying out activities in cyberspace more secure and less cumbersome. Cybersecurity legislation regulates a wide range of cyber activities including data privacy and protection, online behavior, network and information security practices, and legal frameworks for addressing cybercrimes such as incident reporting and response, intellectual property protections, e-commerce and consumer protection, national security, and cybersecurity strategies, regulation of critical infrastructure, as well as educational and sensitization initiative. Overall, cyber legislation plays a critical role in establishing legal frameworks that govern and protect activities in the digital space. Its scope is broad and multifaceted, reflecting the complex and evolving nature of cyber threats in today's interconnected world. These measures help to reduce and manage cyber risks, protect individuals and organizations from cyber threats and attacks, and maintain the integrity and security of digital systems and information.

HISTORICAL EVOLUTION OF CYBERSECURITY LEGISLATION

a) Pre-Internet Era

Decades after the creation of the first computer, there was no need for cyber legislation as carrying out cyberattacks was quite tricky. Most individuals did not have access to electronic machines due to the huge size of these machines, and access was limited to a very small number of people. Meanwhile, only a handful of people knew how to work on these machines, so threats were non-existent (Chadd, 2020). However, cybersecurity as a separate field of study began in 1972 through a research initiative on ARPANET, a precursor to today's internet. It all started when a researcher Bob Thomas developed a program named Creeper that could traverse ARPANET, leaving a trace of its movements with the message "I'm the creeper, catch me if you can." This program which in today's world would have been known as a virus. Even though the extent of the damage caused by Creeper is unspecified, most people claim that this program was a source of annoyance to them as it will replicate itself in the system to the extent of clogging out other programs in an affected system. To this end, Ray Tomlinson, the email inventor, created Reaper, which pursued and eradicated Creeper. Reaper not only marked the inception of antivirus software but also stood as the initial self-replicating program, constituting the earliest computer worm. Protecting these promising technologies' vulnerabilities became crucial as organizations increasingly utilized telecommunication for remote networks. Every connected piece of hardware introduced a potential 'entry point' that required safeguarding.

During the early 1970s, the increasing reliance on computers and expanding networks led governments to recognize the critical need for security measures. The potential consequences of unauthorized access to data and systems were deemed potentially catastrophic. This period witnessed a significant surge in discussions on computer security, primarily within academic circles and published papers from 1972 to 1974. Initiatives in computer security were jointly undertaken by ESD, ARPA, the U.S. Air Force, and other organizations. They collaborated on designing a security kernel for the Honeywell Multics (HIS level 68) computer system. Concurrently, similar projects were pursued at UCLA and the Stanford Research Institute. ARPA's Protection Analysis project focused on the security of operating systems, aiming to identify automated methods for detecting vulnerabilities in software.

b) 1980s – 1990s: Pioneering Legislation

In the 1980s, there was a surge in notable cyberattacks, including incidents at National CSS, AT&T, and Los Alamos National Laboratory. It was also the year when terms like Trojan Horse and Computer Virus were first coined. During the Cold War era, the risk of cyber espionage became more pronounced. In 1985, the US Department of Defense issued the Trusted Computer System Evaluation Criteria, also known as The Orange Book. This document offered guidance on Evaluating the level of trust that can be attributed to software handling classified or sensitive data and specifying the security features that manufacturers should incorporate into their commercial products. It was at this time that the US government enacted the first known cybersecurity law, the Computer Fraud and Abuse Act (CFAA), enacted in 1986. The CFAA was designed to address computer-related crimes and unauthorized access to computer systems. It criminalized various activities, including unauthorized access to protected computers, exceeding authorization, obtaining information without authorization, and causing damage to computer systems.

c) Lates 1990s – Early 2000s: Globalization of the Internet and the Emergence of New Threats- Key Contributing Legislations

In this era are the executive orders signed by President Bill Clinton and George W. Bush. On February 11, 1997, President Clinton signed Executive Order 13035, marking the first significant step in addressing cybersecurity concerns. This order established the Advisory Committee on High-Performance Computing and Communications, Information Technology, and the Next Generation Internet. Comprising non-federal members, this committee aimed to guide advanced computing, communications, and the development of the Next Generation Internet. Its role included evaluating the progress of initiatives in these areas. The Department of Defense was tasked with providing financial and administrative support for the committee's operations. President Clinton further expanded the framework by signing Executive Order 13133 on August 5, 1999. This order established the Working Group on Unlawful Conduct on the Internet, which was tasked with evaluating the sufficiency of existing federal laws in dealing with unlawful activities on the Internet. The order also sought input on new technological resources that might be required for effective investigation and prosecution of internet-related unlawful behavior, as well as available tools for public education and prevention of such conduct. Despite these initiatives, there was notable resistance in the initial efforts to coordinate federal efforts in this domain.

President George W. Bush took a significant step by enacting Executive Order 13231 on October 16, 2001. Titled "Critical Infrastructure Protection in the Information Age," its objective was to promote ongoing efforts in securing information systems critical for infrastructure, including emergency communication preparedness and the physical assets supporting these systems. The order established the "President's Critical Infrastructure Protection Board," tasked with recommending policies and programs to ensure the security and continuity of national security information systems. To achieve this, the Board would collaborate closely with the private sector, State, and local governments to establish and sustain systems capable of sharing threat warnings, conducting analyses, and facilitating recovery efforts. There was also resistance both from within and outside the administration against this executive order.

d) Early 2000s: Focus on Critical Infrastructure Protection

In the early 2000s, the need for cybersecurity legislation became extremely pressing even though there was the CFAA and various executive orders, there was still an urgent need for new legislation. President Obama acknowledged the urgency of improving cybersecurity and issued Executive Order 13691, titled "Promoting Private Sector Cybersecurity Information Sharing," on February 13, 2015. This directive aimed to enhance information sharing, urging collaboration between private sector companies and the federal government to identify cyber threats. It encouraged the voluntary establishment of organizations focused on sharing cyber-security information, to continuously improve their capabilities and functions and foster partnerships with the Federal Government voluntarily. The Department of Homeland Security (DHS) was entrusted with creating a non-profit organization to establish voluntary standards for these information-sharing groups (ISAOs) and create information-sharing agreements with them. Additionally, the order addressed privacy concerns, instructing private sector ISAOs to abide by voluntary privacy protection standards when sharing information.

Nevertheless, to augment presidential capabilities, President Obama signed Executive Order 13694, "Blocking the Property of Certain Persons Engaging in Significant Malicious Cyber-Enabled Activities," on April 1, 2015. This order responded to recent cyber threats as a national security crisis and authorized the imposition of sanctions on individuals involved in cyber activities likely to pose a significant threat to national security, foreign policy, or economic stability. These activities included causing substantial disruptions to computer systems or networks, or misappropriating funds, trade secrets, or financial information for economic or competitive advantage. The order also allowed sanctions on those knowingly using or receiving stolen trade secrets through cyber activities for financial gain, when the theft jeopardizes national security, foreign policy, or financial stability. (Russo & Rishikof, 2016)

The Mid-2000s – Present: Comprehensive Cybersecurity Legislation

The Cybersecurity Act of 2015 is a compilation of 3 different Legislations. The Act included an iteration of the Cybersecurity Information Sharing Act ("CISA") and components of both the Protecting Cyber Networks Act ("PCNA") and the National Cybersecurity Protection Advancement Act ("NCPAA"). This act and various other state, publications, and self-regulatory guidelines act as a guild in today's cyberspace.

ETHICAL HACKING AND VULNERABILITY DISCLOSURE

The internet's rapid expansion has brought numerous benefits like e-commerce, vast educational resources, collaborative tools, email, and enhanced information sharing. Given that a significant portion of work now occurs online, safeguarding data on the internet is paramount. However, alongside technological progress, hacking has emerged as a concerning issue. Hacking involves exploiting system vulnerabilities for personal gain. As online activities such as shopping, banking, and sharing sensitive information have become commonplace, protecting against hacking has become crucial. Ethical hacking, on the other hand, serves as a defense mechanism against illegal cyberattacks. It involves identifying system weaknesses to enhance security and prevent data breaches. Accordingly, Maurushat (2019) defined Ethical hacking as the non-violent use of technology in pursuit of a cause, political or otherwise, which is often legally and morally ambiguous. Studying ethical hacking aims to assess the security of target systems. (Sinha & Arora, 2020).

Vulnerability disclosure is the act of notifying the creators of computer software or hardware about any security weaknesses found. This can be done by security experts, internal development teams, third-party developers, and others who interact with the affected systems. It is imperative to allow software or hardware providers to rectify these vulnerabilities before they can be discovered and exploited by malicious individuals. Recognizing these weaknesses is of such significance that organizations often implement bug bounties or vulnerability rewards programs, which compensate researchers for discovering these flaws. These programs are typically conducted in conjunction with internal code examinations and penetration tests as part of an organization's strategy for managing vulnerabilities. The best practice guidelines for a vulnerability disclosure process are mostly based on international standards ISO/IEC 29147:2018, Information technology – Security techniques -- Vulnerability disclosure and ISO/IEC 30111:2019 Information technology — Security techniques — Vulnerability handling processes.

Public-Private Partnership in Cybersecurity

In an era defined by digital interconnectivity, safeguarding our virtual landscapes has become a paramount concern. As cyber threats continue to evolve in sophistication and scale, the imperative for collaborative efforts between the public and private sectors has never been more critical. This dynamic synergy, often referred to as a Public-Private Partnership (PPP) in Cybersecurity, represents a strategic alliance between government agencies, industry leaders, and stakeholders. Together, they unite their resources, expertise, and intelligence to fortify our digital infrastructure, preemptively identify and mitigate threats, and collectively respond to emerging cyber challenges. Moore (2019) opined that cybersecurity areas where PPP could be applied ought to be divided into four main areas: areas relating to online identity theft, botnets, protection of critical infrastructure, and industrial cyber espionage.

Considering the impact on international experiences, PPP mechanisms give hope for the success and growth of public and private sector cooperation strategies in cybersecurity (Kruhlov et al., 2021). According to Linder (2000), The PPP outcome is seen as a combined result of sharing inventive resource utilization and applying managerial expertise in a way that optimally enables the attainment of objectives for all involved parties, particularly when these objectives cannot be met without engaging these participants. On the other hand, the need for a commercial approach to PPP cooperation in cybersecurity is a way of ensuring national security (Carr, 2016). Furthermore, to ensure transactions that align with the provisions of the law, during PPP processes, security responsibilities are delegated to private organizations per market principles (Bures, 2017).

DEFINING DATA PRIVACY

Data privacy is the right for one's data or personal information to be left alone. It is the right of a data subject to freely choose the circumstance and degree to which their data could be exposed to another.

Personal and Non-Personal and Sensitive Data

The term personal information is often used to describe information covered by privacy law. They are usually information that could be used to identify a data subject. Examples include Social Security number, name, passport number, email address, street address, telephone number, etc. Non-personal information is not generally covered by privacy laws as the element of making a data subject identifiable is not present. However, sensitive data is usually considered as a subset of personal information. In the United States, the definition of sensitive data varies from within jurisdictions. Nevertheless, this information requires additional privacy and security to collect.

Figure 3. Sensitive and non-sensitive data

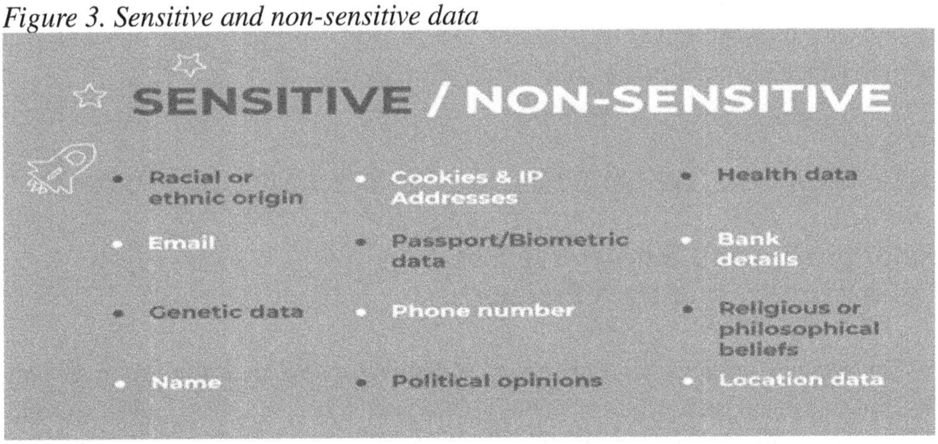

GDPR is underway: Are you collecting your data securely? https://www.netmatters.co.uk/gdpr-is-underway-are-you-collecting-your-data-securely retrieved October 28, 2024

Examples are SSN, driver's license, health information, and financial information. (Swire & Kennedy-Mayo, 2020). Personal Information can be sourced from public records, which includes information collected and maintained by a government entity, publicly available information, for instance, information that is generally available to the public, and nonpublic records which is information that is not generally available to the public due to custom.

Fair Information Practices

The definition of Fair Information Practices (FIP) or Fair Information Privacy Practices (FIPP) varies across jurisdictions; however, it is generally the principles and guidelines designed to ensure that personal information is handled in a fair, transparent, and responsible manner. These practices are meant to protect individuals' privacy and provide them with control over their data (Swire & Kennedy-Mayo, 2020). FIP generally includes two fields of principle.

- The rights of an individual include the right to notice, choice, and consent, and the right to have access to data.
- Control on the information – organizations should focus control on the security of the information, data integrity and purpose limitation, and accountability and oversight.

These guidelines serve as the foundation for privacy legislation in numerous nations globally. They offer a structure for organizations to manage personal data in a responsible and morally sound manner. Following Fair Information Practices fosters trust between individuals and entities, a vital aspect in an age where there is a growing accumulation and utilization of personal data.

INTERPLAY BETWEEN CYBERSECURITY AND DATA PRIVACY

Relationship and Similarities Between Cybersecurity and Data Privacy

Privacy and security differ primarily in that privacy pertains to the control and utilization of your data, whereas security safeguards this data. It's possible to have security without privacy, but the opposite is not true. Both computer security and privacy are equally vital for handling personal and sensitive information. Generally, privacy relates to personal information and how an individual chooses to disclose it, whereas security shields one from potential risks. Consequently, cybersecurity focuses on protecting data from unauthorized access or usage.

Concerning data, privacy directly addresses how companies collect, manage, store, and govern the utilization of the data provided by an individual. While personal privacy has historically been seen as a privilege not accessible to all, security has always been regarded as indispensable. Although public security has often been prioritized over privacy, a deficiency in personal privacy can evolve into a public security concern. Despite their distinctions, both security and privacy necessitate vigilant upkeep (Okta, 2023).

Figure 4. Privacy and cybersecurity: related and distinct fields

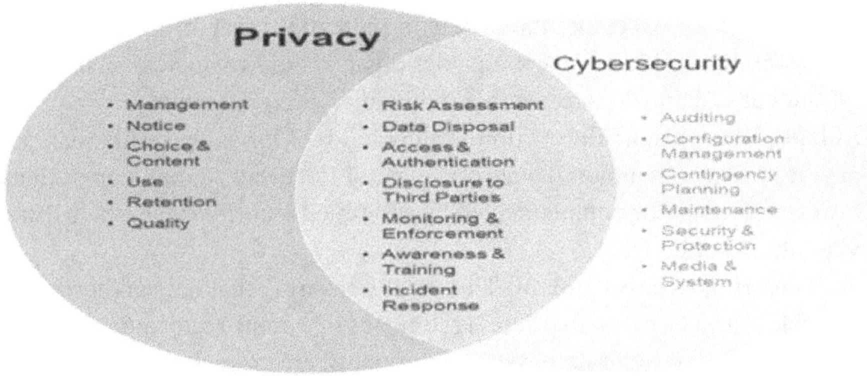

North Carolina Office of Privacy & Data Protection https://it.nc.gov/programs/privacy-data-protection/about-office-privacy-data-protection

The relationship between cybersecurity and data protection cannot be overemphasized. They are two sides of the same coin (Wiewiórowski, 2023). For any organization to excel in its data protection drive, it must integrate the principles of data protection into its cybersecurity strategies through collaborations between the data protection officers and the IT security department. This collaboration will give room to the protection of the organization's assets, its people, and the people whose data they process. Integrating data protection and cybersecurity is crucial because, in the pursuit of safeguarding communications and data, there is often a necessity to handle personal data. Therefore, data protection and cybersecurity should serve as complementary benchmarks, each enhancing their respective standards. An organization responsible for safeguarding individuals' privacy and personal data should not only ensure the implementation of measures to prevent cyberattacks and mitigate associated risks but also guarantee compliance with both state and federal data protection laws, including the ePrivacy directive governing privacy and electronic communications. In practice, this entails an ongoing evaluation of cybersecurity measures to ascertain the necessity of processing personal data for their implementation and whether the same goal can be achieved through less intrusive means.

Another illustration of the reciprocal reinforcement between cybersecurity and data protection lies in the crucial role played by cryptography and encryption. These elements are essential for preserving the confidentiality and integrity of personal data, forming the fundamental components of advanced techniques that enhance privacy.

i. **Achieving Balance:** Achieving a balance between cybersecurity and privacy necessitates a comprehensive approach, encompassing the implementation of suitable security measures while upholding individual privacy rights. Here are some methods to strike this balance.
ii. **Conducting Risk Assessments:** Evaluating potential threats to data security and privacy through risk assessments enables organizations to implement measures that safeguard data while respecting individuals' privacy rights.
iii. **Utilizing Encryption:** Encryption is a crucial tool for safeguarding data privacy. It prevents unauthorized access, even in the event of data compromise. However, it should be complemented by additional security measures to thwart cyber-attacks effectively.
iv. **Implementing Access Control:** This entails ensuring that only authorized individuals can access sensitive data. Techniques like multi-factor authentication, password policies, and role-based access control are crucial.
v. **Adopting Privacy by Design:** This concept emphasizes integrating privacy considerations into the entire design and development process of a system or application. By doing so, organizations embed data protection and privacy right from the system's inception.
vi. **Establishing Data Retention Policies:** These policies delineate how long data will be retained and when it will be deleted. Setting appropriate data retention policies minimizes the risk of data breaches and ensures personal information isn't retained longer than necessary.
vii. **Embracing Transparent Data Practices:** This involves informing individuals about how their data will be utilized and affording them control over its collection, use, and sharing.
viii. **Providing Options:** Providing options for individuals to opt out of data sharing or limiting the extent of data collected is part of this approach.

CHALLENGES IN BALANCING SECURITY AND PRIVACY

Striking a balance between security and user experience presents a major dilemma for organizations. While robust security measures safeguard data, they can also create inconvenience for users. Hence, organizations must aim for an equilibrium between security and ease of use to ensure users remain engaged with their services or systems.

a) **Adhering to regulatory requirements is crucial.** Organizations must navigate a complex landscape of data privacy and security regulations that vary by country and region. The dynamic nature of regulations further compounds the challenge, making it demanding for organizations to stay compliant.
b) **The escalating intricacy of systems and networks adds complexity to the task.** Implementing effective security measures while upholding privacy becomes a formidable task as systems grow more interconnected. This elevated interconnectivity heightens the risk of data breaches and cybersecurity threats, posing a challenge to the efficient management of data privacy and security.
c) **Insider threats pose a substantial risk.** Employees or contractors with access to sensitive data can, intentionally or unintentionally, compromise data security and privacy. This underscores the importance for organizations to enforce stringent access control and monitoring policies.
d) **The advent of emerging technologies like artificial intelligence and the Internet of Things (IoT) introduces fresh hurdles to data privacy and security.** These technologies amass extensive volumes of data, prompting concerns about how this data is used and safeguarded.
e) **Although finding the right balance between cybersecurity and privacy is a demanding task, it is imperative for robust data protection.** By conducting thorough risk assessments, implementing appropriate access controls, and integrating privacy considerations into the design process, organizations can navigate this challenge effectively and safeguard data proficiently.

IMPACT ASSESSMENT OF CYBERSECURITY LEGISLATION ON DATA PRIVACY

Fundamentals of Incident Management for Data Breaches

Every organization should put in place procedures for managing data breaches. This procedure is not a method of detecting or preventing data breaches, but how the organization reacts after a data breach has occurred. The aim of every organization at the point of breach should be tailored towards containment and stoppage of the breach. Most states in the United States have also created breach notification laws that companies must adhere to. Below are the steps to take when faced with a data breach to manage the incident.

Figure 5. Data breach incident response: 5-step methodology

Dilmegani & Palazoğlu (2024), Data Breach Incident Response: 5-Step Methodology, AI Multiple Research retrieved October 28, 2024

a) Preparation
b) Determine or identification of the breach
c) Containment and analysis of the incidence
d) Notification of the affected parties and other regulatory bodies as required by the law
e) Implementation and review of interventions

When it comes to managing an incident, organizations may engage in different approaches, however, the fundamentals are usually the same. For example, the notification laws depending on each state may either give a stipulated date upon which an organization must notify parties and stakeholders of the breach or must do so without “undue delay”. Not adhering to these laws would lead to non-compliance, which is usually not the goal of any responsible organization.

Analyzing Legislation's Role in Mitigating Risk

Legislation, as a foundation of cybersecurity and data protection, provides the necessary legal infrastructure needed to establish and enforce standards. It provides protections for individuals' privacy and holds organizations accountable for securing sensitive information without consent. In an era defined by digital interconnectivity, the role of legislation in mitigating cyber risks cannot be overstated. It stands as a critical component in the comprehensive strategy to protect our digital landscapes. The Legislation sets standards and frameworks with sanctions when a breach occurs for data protection and handling. Organizations have no choice but to abide by the rules stated in this legislation. For example, the GDPR rule of handling data belonging to European citizens applies to both organizations operating in Europe, or operating outside of Europe. The Sanction for breach includes a 20 million euro fine or 4% of the year's profit, whichever is greater (GDPR, 2018).

Other ways legislations mitigate risk is by mandating breach notification laws. Even though there is no Federal law regulating breach notification, all 50 states with California being the first, and the District of Columbia, Puerto Rico, and the US Virgin Islands as of 2018 all have in place breach notification laws that create a guideline on who to notify, how notification should be made, when and what the notification should include. Also, with the help of legislation, specific industries can be regulated. For example, the Health Insurance Portability and Accountability Act (HIPAA) in the U.S., addresses unique risks and requirements for specific sectors handling sensitive information, and FERPA. Protects the educational record of any person in a public or private elementary school, secondary or post-secondary school, it also applies to any state or local education agency that receives funds under an applicable US program. These regulations ensure tailored protection measures for distinct industries.

COMPLIANCE AND ENFORCEMENT MECHANISM

Studies have shown that it is not enough to enact a law, compliance with a law can only be assured if there are sanctions and punishment for violation. Enforcement can sometimes be tedious if the right mechanisms are not put in place. Some mechanisms include the creation of regulatory authorities that would act as specialized agencies or bodies responsible for overseeing and enforcing compliance with cybersecurity and data protection laws. These authorities have the power to investigate violations, impose fines, and take legal action against non-compliant organizations. Another means of ensuring compliance is through audits and assessments, regular audits, and assessments of organizations' cybersecurity and data protection practices to verify compliance with legal requirements. This sometimes involves interviews, site inspections, and reviews of documentation for compliance.

Figure 6. Why comply with data privacy regulations?

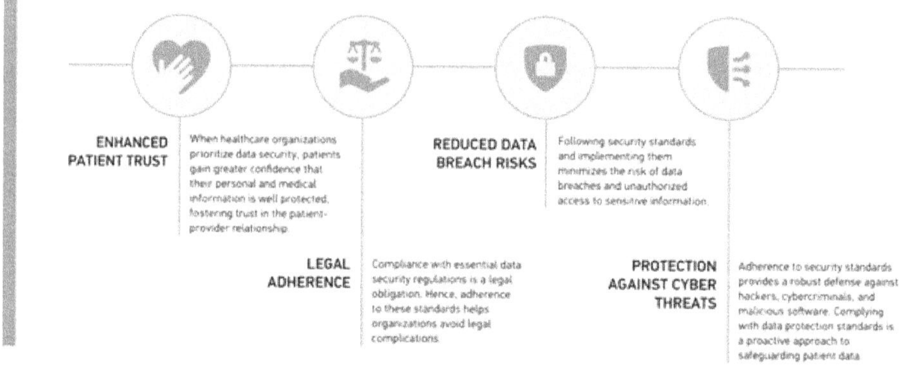

Source: https://kodjin.com/blog/the-value-of-data-privacy-in-healthcare/

Financial penalties could be imposed on organizations found in violation of cybersecurity and data protection laws. The severity of these penalties varies based on the extent and nature of the violation. Other compliance and enforcement mechanisms include Injunctions and cease-and-desist Orders, data breach notification and reporting requirements that require affected companies to report a breach promptly, protection for employees who want to act as whistle-blowers when there is a potential violation, and continuous education and guidance. To help organizations understand and implement compliance requirements effectively.

PENALTIES AND SANCTIONS FOR NON-COMPLIANCE

The following are some of the penalties an organization could face for non-compliance.

a) Public Disclosure of Violations
b) Suspension or revocation of licenses or certifications
c) Civil litigation
d) Criminal prosecution
e) Financial penalty

CHALLENGES AND LIMITATIONS CYBERSECURITY LEGISLATION

Cybersecurity legislation and data privacy laws play a crucial role in safeguarding digital landscapes and protecting sensitive information. However, these legislations are usually faced with several challenges and limitations. Below is a table that describes the likely challenges faced by cybersecurity legislation.

Table 1. Challenges and limitations cybersecurity legislation

Item	Challenges	Limitation
Rapidly Evolving Threat Landscape	Cyber threats are constantly evolving, with attackers finding new techniques and vulnerabilities. Legislation sometimes struggles to keep up with emerging threats.	Laws might become outdated quickly, potentially leaving gaps in protection against novel cyber threats.
Global Nature of Cyber Attacks	Cyber-attacks often originate from and target multiple jurisdictions. Coordinated international efforts are necessary to combat cybercrime effectively.	lack of coordinated legislation across borders.
Compliance and Enforcement	Ensuring compliance with cybersecurity and data privacy laws across a diverse range of organizations, from small businesses to large multinational corporations, can be challenging.	Limited resources and enforcement capabilities may hinder monitoring and enforcing compliance effectively.
Resource Constraints	Small and medium-sized enterprises (SMEs) may lack the resources and expertise to implement robust cybersecurity measures, despite legal requirements.	Compliance costs can be burdensome for smaller organizations, potentially leading to a gap in cybersecurity practices.
Technological Advancements	Rapid technological advancements, such as AI, IoT, and blockchain, present new challenges for legislation. Adapting laws to address these emerging technologies is complex.	Legislation may struggle to keep up with the pace of technological innovation, potentially leaving regulatory gaps.
Balancing Security and Privacy	Striking the right balance between security measures and individual privacy rights is a delicate task. Overemphasis on security may infringe on privacy, and vice versa.	Achieving a harmonious equilibrium between security and privacy can be challenging, and legislative efforts may face criticism from various stakeholders.
Global Data Flows	Data flows across international borders are common in today's digital economy. Legislation must address how data is handled and protected in cross-border transactions.	Resolving conflicts between different jurisdictions' data protection laws and ensuring the free flow of information can be complex
Education and Awareness:	Ensuring that individuals and organizations are aware of their responsibilities and rights under cybersecurity and data privacy laws is crucial.	Limited public awareness and understanding of these laws can hinder their effectiveness.

continued on following page

Table 1. Continued

Item	Challenges	Limitation
Adaptability of Legislation	Legislation must be adaptable to changing circumstances and technologies. Rigidity in legal frameworks may hinder their effectiveness.	Revising and updating laws can be a lengthy and complex process, potentially delaying responses to emerging threats.
Emerging Threats like Deepfakes and AI-driven Attacks:	New threats like deep fakes and AI-driven attacks present unique challenges that may not be adequately addressed by current legislation.	Adapting laws to effectively combat these emerging threats requires a deep understanding of the technology and its implications.

While cybersecurity legislation and data privacy laws are crucial in protecting digital assets, they face ongoing challenges in adapting to a dynamic and complex cybersecurity landscape. Balancing security with privacy, ensuring global cooperation, and staying abreast of technological advancements are key areas that legislators must navigate.

CONCLUSION

Technology Solutions and Best Practices

Technology Solutions and Best Practices encompass a range of strategies and tools designed to enhance cybersecurity and data privacy. These include Firewalls and Intrusion Detection Systems (IDS), encryption of data, use of access control and least privilege, regular and continuous software patches and updates, the use of multi-factor authentication (MFA), incident response and disaster recovery plans, integrating privacy by design and default, security awareness training, security auditing, and logging, the use of artificial intelligence, etc.

By adopting a combination of these technology solutions and best practices, organizations can significantly enhance their cybersecurity posture and protect sensitive data from evolving cyber threats.

IMPLICATIONS FOR THE FUTURE OF CYBERSECURITY AND DATA PRIVACY

The implications for the future of cybersecurity and data privacy are profound. As technology continues to advance, so do the complexities and sophistication of cyber threats. This demands a proactive and adaptive approach to legislation and regulations. Striking the right balance between security measures and individual privacy rights will be paramount. Additionally, global cooperation and harmonization of laws will be essential to combat cybercrime effectively. The emergence of new technologies like artificial intelligence and IoT will necessitate continuous updates to legal frameworks. Ultimately, the future of cybersecurity and data privacy hinges on agile, informed, and collaborative legislative efforts to safeguard digital landscapes and protect sensitive information.

REFERENCES

Abbasi, R., Bashir, A. K., Mateen, A., Amin, F., Ge, Y., & Omar, M. "Efficient Security and Privacy of Lossless Secure Communication for Sensor-based Urban Cities," *IEEE Sensors Journal*, vol. 2023.

Ahmed, H., Rasheed, H., Bashir, A. K., & Omar, M. (2023). Rasheed, A. K. Bashir, and M. Omar, "Millimeter-wave Channel Modeling in a VANETs Using Coding Techniques,". *PeerJ. Computer Science*, 9, e1374. DOI: 10.7717/peerj-cs.1374 PMID: 37346660

Ahmed, N., Mohammadani, K., Bashir, A. K., Omar, M., Jones, A., & Hassan, F. "Secure and Reliable Routing in the Internet of Vehicles Network: AODV-RL with BHA Attack Defense," *CMES-Computer Modeling in Engineering & Sciences*, vol. 139, no. 1, 2024.

Al Harthi, S., Al Balushi, M. Y., Al Badi, A. H., Al Karaki, J., & Omar, M. *"Metaverse Adoption in UAE Higher Education: A Hybrid SEM-ANN Approach," in 98 Mohammad Daradkeh, Boshra Aldhanhani, Amjad Gawanmeh, Shadi Atalla and Sami Miniaoui. Applied Research Approaches to Technology, Healthcare, and Business*. IGI Global.

Al-Karaki, J. N., Omar, M., Gawanmeh, A., & Jones, A. "Advancing CyberSecurity Education and Training: Practical Case Study of Running Capture the Flag (CTF) on the Metaverse vs. Physical Settings," in *2023 International Conference on Intelligent Metaverse Technologies & Applications (iMETA)*, pp. 1-7, IEEE, 2023. DOI: 10.1109/iMETA59369.2023.10294722

Al Kinoon, M., Omar, M., Mohaisen, M., & Mohaisen, D. "Security Breaches in the Healthcare Domain: A Spatiotemporal Analysis," in *Computational Data and Social Networks: 10th International Conference, CSoNet 2021, Virtual Event, November 15-17, 2021, Proceedings*, Springer International Publishing, pp. 171-183, 2021. DOI: 10.1007/978-3-030-91434-9_16

Al-Sanjary, O. I., Ahmed, A. A., Jaharadak, A. A. B., Ali, M. A., & Zangana, H. M. "Detection Clone an Object Movement Using an Optical Flow Approach," in *2018 IEEE Symposium on Computer Applications & Industrial Electronics (ISCAIE)*, pp. 388-394, 2018. DOI: 10.1109/ISCAIE.2018.8405504

O. I. Al-Sanjary, A. A. Ahmed, H. M. Zangana, M. Ali, S. Aldulaimi, and M. Alkawaz, "An Investigation of the Characteristics and Performance of Hybrid Routing Protocol in (MANET)," *International Journal of Engineering & Technology*, vol. 7, no. 4.22, pp. 49-54, 2018.

Alturki, N., Altamimi, A., Umer, M., Saidani, O., Alshardan, A., Alsubai, S., Omar, M., & Ashraf, I. "Improving Prediction of Chronic Kidney Disease Using KNN Imputed SMOTE Features and TrioNet Model," *CMES-Computer Modeling in Engineering & Sciences*, vol. 139, no. 3, 2024. DOI: 10.32604/cmes.2023.045868

Arulappan, G. (2023). Raja, A. K. Bashir, A. Mahanti, and M. Omar, "ZTMP: Zero Touch Management Provisioning Algorithm for the On-boarding of Cloud-native Virtual Network Functions,". *Mobile Networks and Applications*, •••, 1–13.

Ayub, M., Li, X., Mahmood, K., Shamshad, S., Saleem, M. A., & Omar, M. (2023). Secure Consumer-centric Demand Response Management in Resilient Smart Grid as Industry 5.0 Application with Blockchain-based Authentication. *IEEE Transactions on Consumer Electronics*.

M. Banisakher, D. Mohammed, and M. Omar, "A Cloud-Based Computing Architecture Model of Post-Disaster Management System," *International Journal of Simulation--Systems, Science & Technology*, vol. 19, no. 5, 2018.

Banisakher, M., Omar, M., & Clare, W. (2019). Critical Infrastructure—Perspectives on the Role of Government in Cybersecurity. *Journal of Computer Sciences and Applications*, 7(1), 37–42. DOI: 10.12691/jcsa-7-1-6

Banisakher, M., Omar, M., Hong, S., & Adams, J. (2020). A Human-centric Approach to Data Fusion in Post-Disaster Management. *Journal of Business Management and Science*, 8(1), 12–20.

Basharat, M., & Omar, M. "Adapting to Change: Assessing the Longevity and Resilience of Adversarially Trained NLP Models in Dynamic Spam Detection Environments," in *Innovations, Securities, and Case Studies Across Healthcare, Business, and Technology*, pp. 157-173, IGI Global, 2024. DOI: 10.4018/979-8-3693-1906-2.ch009

Basharat, M., & Omar, M. (2024). Harnessing GPT-2 for Feature Extraction in Malware Detection: A Novel Approach to Cybersecurity. *Land Forces Academy Review*, 29(1), 74–84. DOI: 10.2478/raft-2024-0008

M. Basharat and M. Omar, "SecuGuard: Leveraging Pattern-exploiting Training in Language Models for Advanced Software Vulnerability Detection," *International Journal of Mathematics and Computer in Engineering*, 2024.

Betts, J., & Sezer, S. (2014, May). Ethics and privacy in national security and critical infrastructure protection. In *2014 IEEE International Symposium on Ethics in Science, Technology, and Engineering* (pp. 1-7). IEEE. DOI: 10.1109/ETHICS.2014.6893417

Brustolin, V. (2019). Comparative analysis of regulations for cybersecurity and cyber defense in the United States and Brazil. *Revista Brasileira de Estudos de Defesa, 6*(2).

Bures, O. (2017). Contributions of private business to the provision of security in the EU: Beyond public-private partnerships. *Crime, Law, and Social Change*, 67(3), 289–312. DOI: 10.1007/s10611-016-9650-6

Burrell, D. N., Nobles, C., Cusak, A., Omar, M., & Gillesania, L. (2022). Cybercrime and the Nature of Insider Threat Complexities in Healthcare and Biotechnology Engineering Organizations. *Journal of Crime and Criminal Behavior*, 2(2), 131–144. DOI: 10.47509/JCCB.2022.v02i02.04

Burrell, D. N., Nobles, C., Richardson, K., Wright, J. B., Jones, A. J., Springs, D., & Brown-Jackson, K. (2023). Allison Huff. In *Applied Research Approaches to Technology, Healthcare, and Business*. IGI Global. DOI: 10.4018/979-8-3693-1630-6

Carr, M. (2016). Public-private partnerships in national cyber-security strategies. *International Affairs*, 92(1), 43–62. DOI: 10.1111/1468-2346.12504

Chadd, K. (2020) The History of Cybercrime and Cybersecurity, 1940-2020, Cybercrime Magazine https://cybersecurityventures.com/the-history-of-cybercrime-and-cybersecurity-1940-2020/ retrieved November 2, 2023

Davis, L., Dawson, M., & Omar, M. (2016). Systems Engineering Concepts with Aid of Virtual Worlds and Open Source Software: Using Technology to Develop Learning Objects and Simulation Environments. In *Handbook of Research on 3-D Virtual Environments and Hypermedia for Ubiquitous Learning* (pp. 483–509). IGI Global. DOI: 10.4018/978-1-5225-0125-1.ch020

Dawson, M. (2015). A Brief Review of New Threats and Countermeasures in Digital Crime and Cyber Terrorism. In *New Threats and Countermeasures in Digital Crime and Cyber Terrorism* (pp. 1–7). IGI Global. DOI: 10.4018/978-1-4666-8345-7.ch001

Dawson, M., Al Saeed, I., Wright, J., & Omar, M. "Technology enhanced learning with open source software for scientists and engineers," in *INTED2013 Proceedings*, IATED, 2013, pp. 5583–5589.

Dawson, M., Davis, L., & Omar, M. (2019). Developing learning objects for engineering and science fields: Using technology to test system usability and interface design. *Int. J. Smart Technol. Learn.*, 1(2), 140–161. DOI: 10.1504/IJSMART-TL.2019.097951

Dawson, M., Eltayeb, M., & Omar, M. (2016). *Security solutions for hyperconnectivity and the Internet of things*. IGI Global.

Dawson, M., Omar, M., & Abramson, J. (2015). Understanding the methods behind cyber terrorism. In *Encyclopedia of Information Science and Technology* (3rd ed., pp. 1539–1549). IGI Global.

Dawson, M., Omar, M., Abramson, J., & Bessette, D. (2014). *Information security in diverse computing environments*. Academic Press.

Dawson, M., Omar, M., Abramson, J., & Bessette, D. (2014). The future of national and international security on the internet. In *Information security in diverse computing environments* (pp. 149–178). IGI Global. DOI: 10.4018/978-1-4666-6158-5.ch009

Dawson, M., Omar, M., Abramson, J., Leonard, B., & Bessette, D. (2017). Battlefield cyberspace: Exploitation of hyperconnectivity and Internet of Things. In *Developing Next-Generation Countermeasures for Homeland Security Threat Prevention* (pp. 204–235). IGI Global. DOI: 10.4018/978-1-5225-0703-1.ch010

Dawson, M., Wright, J., & Omar, M. (2015). Mobile devices: The case for cyber security hardened systems. In *New Threats and Countermeasures in Digital Crime and Cyber Terrorism* (pp. 8–29). IGI Global. DOI: 10.4018/978-1-4666-8345-7.ch002

Day, J., Kearney, P., Moor, J., Marshall, R., Bott, A., & Poyner, I. (2021). Vulnerability Disclosure: Best Practice Guidelines. IoT Security Foundation website.

Dayoub and M. Omar. (2024). Advancing IoT security posture K-Means clustering for malware detection. In *Innovations, Securities, and Case Studies Across Healthcare, Business, and Technology* (pp. 221–239). IGI Global.

Dong, H., Wu, J., Bashir, A. K., Pan, Q., Omar, M., & Al-Dulaimi, A. "Privacy-preserving EEG signal analysis with electrode attention for depression diagnosis: Joint FHE and CNN approach," in *GLOBECOM 2023-2023 IEEE Global Communications Conference*, IEEE, 2023, pp. 4265–4270. DOI: 10.1109/GLOBECOM54140.2023.10436783

Exec. Order No. 13035, 62 Fed. Reg. 7131 (Feb. 14, 1997), http://www.gpo.gov/fdsys/pkg/FR-1997-02-14/pdf/97-3992.pdf [https://perma.cc/D5WB-R4GJ].

Exec. Order No. 13133, 64 Fed. Reg. 43895 (Aug. 5, 1999), http://www.gpo.gov/fdsys/pkg/FR-1999-08-11/pdf/99-20924.pdf [https://perma.cc/W458-2QGZ]. 20 Id. 21 Exec. Order No. 13231, 3 C.F.R. § 13231 (2002), https://fas.org/irp/offdocs/eo/eo13231.htm [https://perma.cc/QAA4-ZF6T].

Fawzi, D., & Omar, M. (n.d.). *New insights to database security: An effective and integrated approach to applying access control mechanisms and cryptographic concepts in Microsoft access environments*. Academic Press.

Gholami, S. (2024). Can pruning make large language models more efficient? In *Redefining Security With Cyber AI* (pp. 1–14). IGI Global. DOI: 10.4018/979-8-3693-6517-5.ch001

Gholami, S. (2024). Do generative large language models need billions of parameters? In *Redefining Security With Cyber AI* (pp. 37–55). IGI Global. DOI: 10.4018/979-8-3693-6517-5.ch003

Gholami, S., & Omar, M. "Does synthetic data make large language models more efficient?" *arXiv preprint arXiv:2310.07830*, 2023.

Gholami, S., & Omar, M. (2024). Can a student large language model perform as well as its teacher? In *Innovations, Securities, and Case Studies Across Healthcare, Business, and Technology* (pp. 122–139). IGI Global. DOI: 10.4018/979-8-3693-1906-2.ch007

Grant, J. (2010). Will there be cybersecurity legislation? *J. Nat'l Sec. L. & Pol'y*, 4, 103. https://www.dhs.gov/employee-resources/securing-cyberspace-and-critical-infrastructure and https://www.okta.com/identity-101/privacy-vs-security/

Hamza, Y. A., & Omar, M. D. (2013). Cloud computing security: Abuse and nefarious use of cloud computing. *International Journal of Computer Engineering Research*, 3(6), 22–27.

Huff, J., Burrell, D. N., Nobles, C., Richardson, K., Wright, J. B., Burton, S. L., Jones, A. J., Springs, D., Omar, M., & Brown-Jackson, K. L. (2023). Management practices for mitigating cybersecurity threats to biotechnology companies, laboratories, and healthcare research organizations. In *Applied Research Approaches to Technology, Healthcare, and Business* (pp. 1–12). IGI Global. DOI: 10.4018/979-8-3693-1630-6.ch001

ISO/IEC 29147:2018, Information technology -- Security techniques -- Vulnerability disclosure

Jabbari, H. Khan, S. Duraibi, I. Budhiraja, S. Gupta, and M. Omar, "Energy maximization for wireless powered communication enabled IoT devices with NOMA underlaying solar powered UAV using federated reinforcement learning for 6G networks," *IEEE Trans. Consum. Electron.*, 2024.

Jones, A., & Omar, M.Jones and M. Omar. (2024). Codesentry: Revolutionizing real-time software vulnerability detection with optimized GPT framework. *Land Forces Acad. Rev.*, 29(1), 98–107. DOI: 10.2478/raft-2024-0010

Jones, M., & Omar, M. (2023). *"Detection of Twitter spam with language models: A case study on how to use BERT to protect children from spam on Twitter," in 2023 Congress in Computer Science, Computer Engineering, & Applied Computing (CSCE)*. IEEE.

Jones, M., & Omar, M. (2023). *"Measuring the impact of global health emergencies on self-disclosure using language models," in 2023 Congress in Computer Science, Computer Engineering, & Applied Computing (CSCE)*. IEEE.

Jones, M., & Omar, M. (2023). *"Studying the effects of social media content on kids' safety and well-being," in 2023 Congress in Computer Science, Computer Engineering, & Applied Computing (CSCE)*. IEEE.

Jones, R., & Omar, M. "Detecting IoT Malware with Knowledge Distillation Technique," in *2023 Congress in Computer Science, Computer Engineering, & Applied Computing (CSCE)*, pp. 131-135, IEEE, 2023. DOI: 10.1109/CSCE60160.2023.00026

Jones, R., & Omar, M. (2024). Codeguard: Utilizing Advanced Pattern Recognition in Language Models for Software Vulnerability Analysis. *Land Forces Academy Review*, 29(1), 108–118. DOI: 10.2478/raft-2024-0011

Jones, R., & Omar, M. (2024). Revolutionizing Cybersecurity: The GPT-2 Enhanced Attack Detection and Defense (GEADD) Method for Zero-Day Threats [INJIIS-COM]. *International Journal of Informatics, Information System and Computer Engineering*, 5(2), 178–191. DOI: 10.34010/injiiscom.v5i2.12741

Jones, R., Omar, M., & Mohammed, D. "Harnessing the Power of the GPT Model to Generate Adversarial Examples," in *2023 Congress in Computer Science, Computer Engineering, & Applied Computing (CSCE)*, pp. 1699-1702, IEEE, 2023. DOI: 10.1109/CSCE60160.2023.00279

Jones, R., Omar, M., Mohammed, D., & Nobles, C. "IoT Malware Detection with GPT Models," in *2023 Congress in Computer Science, Computer Engineering, & Applied Computing (CSCE)*, pp. 1749-1752, IEEE, 2023. DOI: 10.1109/CSCE60160.2023.00288

Jones, R., Omar, M., Mohammed, D., Nobles, C., & Dawson, M. "Harnessing the Speed and Accuracy of Machine Learning to Advance Cybersecurity," in *2023 Congress in Computer Science, Computer Engineering, & Applied Computing (CSCE)*, pp. 418-421, IEEE, 2023. DOI: 10.1109/CSCE60160.2023.00074

Jones and M. Omar. (2023). *"Harnessing the efficiency of reformers to detect software vulnerabilities," in 2023 Congress in Computer Science, Computer Engineering, & Applied Computing (CSCE)*. IEEE.

Jones and M. Omar. (2023). *"Optimized decision trees to detect IoT malware," in 2023 Congress in Computer Science, Computer Engineering, & Applied Computing (CSCE).* IEEE.

Jun, W., Iqbal, M. S., Abbasi, R., Omar, M., & Huiqin, C. "Web-Semantic-Driven Machine Learning and Blockchain for Transformative Change in the Future of Physical Education," *International Journal on Semantic Web and Information Systems (IJSWIS)*, vol. 20, no. 1, pp. 1-16, IGI Global, 2024. DOI: 10.4018/IJSWIS.337961

Khan, S. A., Alkawaz, M. H., & Zangana, H. M. "The use and abuse of social media for spreading fake news," in *2019 IEEE International Conference on Automatic Control and Intelligent Systems (I2CACIS)*, pp. 145-148, IEEE, 2019. DOI: 10.1109/I2CACIS.2019.8825029

Kruhlov, V., Latynin, M., Horban, A., & Petrov, A. (2019). Public-Private Partnership in Cybersecurity. In *CybHyg* (pp. 619-628).

V. A. Kumar, S. Surapaneni, D. Pavitra, R. Venkatesan, M. Omar, and A. K. Bashir, "An Internet of Medical Things-Based Mental Disorder Prediction System Using EEG Sensor and Big Data Mining," *Journal of Circuits, Systems and Computers*, vol. 2450197, World Scientific Publishing Company, 2024.

Majeed, H. (2020). Watermarking Image Depending on Mojette Transform for Hiding Information. *International Journal on Computer Science and Engineering*, 8, 8–12.

Maurushat, A. (2019). *Ethical hacking*. University of Ottawa Press.

McDaniel, G. (Ed.). (1994). *IBM Dictionary of computing*.

McNicholas, E., & Angle, K. (2022) Cybersecurity Laws and Regulations USA 2023, ICLG 2022-11-14 https://iclg.com/practice-areas/cybersecurity-laws-and-regulations/usa

Mohammed, M. O., & Nguyen, V. (2017). Enhancing Cyber Security for Financial Industry through Compliance and Regulatory Standards. In *Security Solutions for Hyperconnectivity and the Internet of Things* (pp. 113–129). IGI Global. DOI: 10.4018/978-1-5225-0741-3.ch005

Mohammed, M. O., & Nguyen, V. (2018). Wireless Sensor Network Security: Approaches to Detecting and Avoiding Wormhole Attacks. *Journal of Research in Business, Economics and Management*, 10(2), 1860–1864.

Mohammed and M. Omar. "Decision Trees Unleashed: Simplifying IoT Malware Detection With Advanced AI Techniques," in *Innovations, Securities, and Case Studies Across Healthcare, Business, and Technology*, pp. 240-258, IGI Global, 2024.

Moore, T. Introducing the Economics of Cybersecurity: Principles and Policy Options. Deterring Cyberattacks: Informing Strategies and Developing Options for U. S. Policy, https://www.nap.edu/read/12997/chapter/3, last accessed 2019/10/23.

V. Nguyen, D. Mohammed, M. Omar, and M. Banisakher, "The Effects of the FCC Net Neutrality Repeal on Security and Privacy," *International Journal of Hyperconnectivity and the Internet of Things (IJHIoT)*, vol. 2, no. 2, pp. 21-29, IGI Global, 2018.

V. Nguyen, M. Omar, and D. Mohammed, "A Security Framework for Enhancing User Experience," *International Journal of Hyperconnectivity and the Internet of Things (IJHIoT)*, vol. 1, no. 1, pp. 19-28, IGI Global, 2017.

Nguyen, V., Omar, M., Mohammed, D., & Dean, P. "Net Neutrality Around the Globe: A Survey," in *2020 3rd International Conference on Information and Computer Technologies (ICICT)*, pp. 480-488, IEEE, 2020. DOI: 10.1109/ICICT50521.2020.00083

Omar, M. *Smartphone Security: Defending Android-based Smartphone Against Emerging Malware Attacks* (Doctoral dissertation, Colorado Technical University), 2012.

Omar, M. "Insider Threats: Detecting and Controlling Malicious Insiders," in *New Threats and Countermeasures in Digital Crime and Cyber Terrorism*, pp. 162-172, IGI Global, 2015. DOI: 10.4018/978-1-4666-8345-7.ch009

Omar, M. "Cloud Computing Security: Abuse and Nefarious Use of Cloud Computing," in *Handbook of Research on Security Considerations in Cloud Computing*, pp. 30-38, IGI Global, 2015. DOI: 10.4018/978-1-4666-8387-7.ch002

Omar, M. (2019). A World of Cyber Attacks. *Survey (London, England).*

M. Omar, "New Insights into Database Security: An Effective and Integrated Approach for Applying Access Control Mechanisms and Cryptographic Concepts in Microsoft Access Environments," 2021.

Omar, M. "Application of Machine Learning (ML) to Address Cybersecurity Threats," in *Machine Learning for Cybersecurity: Innovative Deep Learning Solutions*, pp. 1-11, Springer International Publishing Cham, 2022. DOI: 10.1007/978-3-031-15893-3_1

Omar, M. *Machine Learning for Cybersecurity: Innovative Deep Learning Solutions*, Springer Brief, 2022. https://link.springer.com/book/978303115

Omar, M. "Malware Anomaly Detection Using Local Outlier Factor Technique," in *Machine Learning for Cybersecurity: Innovative Deep Learning Solutions*, pp. 37-48, Springer International Publishing Cham, 2022. DOI: 10.1007/978-3-031-15893-3_3

Omar, M. "VulDefend: A Novel Technique Based on Pattern-Exploiting Training for Detecting Software Vulnerabilities Using Language Models," in *2023 IEEE Jordan International Joint Conference on Electrical Engineering and Information Technology (JEEIT)*, pp. 287-293, IEEE, 2023. DOI: 10.1109/JEEIT58638.2023.10185860

Omar, M. "From Attack to Defense: Strengthening DNN Text Classification Against Adversarial Examples," in *Innovations, Securities, and Case Studies Across Healthcare, Business, and Technology*, pp. 174-195, IGI Global, 2024. DOI: 10.4018/979-8-3693-1906-2.ch010

Omar, M. "Revolutionizing Malware Detection: A Paradigm Shift Through Optimized Convolutional Neural Networks," in *Innovations, Securities, and Case Studies Across Healthcare, Business, and Technology*, pp. 196-220, IGI Global, 2024. DOI: 10.4018/979-8-3693-1906-2.ch011

Omar, M. *Defending Cyber Systems through Reverse Engineering of Criminal Malware*, Springer Brief, [n.d.][n.d.].https://link.springer.com/book/9783031116278

M. Omar, *Latina Davis Morgan State University 1700 E Cold Spring Ln. Baltimore, MD 21251, USA E-mail: latinaedavis@ hotmail.com*, [n.d.][n.d.].

M. Omar, *Machine Learning for Cybersecurity*, [n.d.][n.d.].

Omar, M.. (2024). Committee Members. *Journal of Physics: Conference Series*, 2711, 011001.

M. Omar and D. Burrell, "From Text to Threats: A Language Model Approach to Software Vulnerability Detection," *International Journal of Mathematics and Computer in Engineering*, 2023.

Omar, M., & Burrell, D. N. "Organizational Dynamics and Bias in Artificial Intelligence (AI) Recruitment Algorithms," in *Evolution of Cross-Sector Cyber Intelligent Markets*, pp. 269-290, IGI Global, 2024.

Omar, M., Choi, S., Nyang, D., & Mohaisen, D. "Quantifying the Performance of Adversarial Training on Language Models with Distribution Shifts," in *Proceedings of the 1st Workshop on Cybersecurity and Social Sciences*, pp. 3-9, 2022. DOI: 10.1145/3494108.3522764

Omar, M., Choi, S., Nyang, D., & Mohaisen, D. (2022). Robust Natural Language Processing: Recent Advances, Challenges, and Future Directions. *IEEE Access : Practical Innovations, Open Solutions*, 10, 86038–86056. DOI: 10.1109/ACCESS.2022.3197769

Omar, M., & Dawson, M. "Research in Progress-Defending Android Smartphones from Malware Attacks," in *2013 Third International Conference on Advanced Computing and Communication Technologies (ACCT)*, pp. 288-292, IEEE, 2013. DOI: 10.1109/ACCT.2013.69

Omar, M., Gouveia, L. B., Al-Karaki, J., & Mohammed, D. "Reverse-Engineering Malware," in *Cybersecurity Capabilities in Developing Nations and Its Impact on Global Security*, pp. 194-217, IGI Global, 2022. DOI: 10.4018/978-1-7998-8693-8.ch010

Omar, M., Jones, R., Burrell, D. N., Dawson, M., Nobles, C., & Mohammed, D. "Harnessing the Power and Simplicity of Decision Trees to Detect IoT Malware," in *Transformational Interventions for Business, Technology, and Healthcare*, pp. 215-229, IGI Global, 2023. DOI: 10.4018/979-8-3693-1634-4.ch013

Omar, M., & Mohaisen, D. "Making Adversarially-Trained Language Models Forget with Model Retraining: A Case Study on Hate Speech Detection," in *Companion Proceedings of the Web Conference 2022*, pp. 887-893, 2022. DOI: 10.1145/3487553.3524667

Omar, M., Mohammed, D., & Nguyen, V. (2017). Defending Against Malicious Insiders: A Conceptual Framework for Predicting, Detecting, and Deterring Malicious Insiders. *International Journal of Business Process Integration and Management*, 8(2), 114–119. DOI: 10.1504/IJBPIM.2017.083794

Omar, M., Mohammed, D., Nguyen, V., Dawson, M., & Banisakher, M. "Android Application Security," in *Research Anthology on Securing Mobile Technologies and Applications*, pp. 610-625, IGI Global, 2021. DOI: 10.4018/978-1-7998-8545-0.ch034

Omar, M., & Shiaeles, S. "VulDetect: A Novel Technique for Detecting Software Vulnerabilities Using Language Models," in *2023IEEE International Conference on Cyber Security and Resilience (CSR)*, IEEE. https://ieeexplore.ieee.org/document/10224924

Omar, M., & Sukthankar, G. "Text-Defend: Detecting Adversarial Examples Using Local Outlier Factor," in *2023 IEEE 17th International Conference on Semantic Computing (ICSC)*, pp. 118-122, IEEE, 2023. DOI: 10.1109/ICSC56153.2023.00026

Omar, M., & Zangana, H. M. (2024). *Redefining Security With Cyber AI*. IGI Global., DOI: 10.4018/979-8-3693-6517-5

Pauu, K. T., Pan, Q., Wu, J., Bashir, A. K., & Omar, M. "IRS-Aided Federated Learning with Dynamic Differential Privacy for UAVs in Emergency Response," *IEEE Internet of Things Magazine*, vol. 7, no. 4, pp. 108-115, IEEE, 2024. DOI: 10.1109/IOTM.001.2400021

Peng, Y.. (2024). *"An Intelligent Resource Allocation Strategy with Slicing and Auction for Private Edge Cloud Systems," Future Generation Computer Systems* (Vol. 160). North-Holland.

Prasad, N. S. (1989). *IBM mainframes: architecture and design*. McGraw-Hill, Inc.

Rajesh, R.. (2024). Threat Detection and Mitigation for Tactile Internet Driven Consumer IoT-Healthcare System. *IEEE Transactions on Consumer Electronics*.

Regulation, G. D. P. (2018). General Data Protection Regulation (GDPR). *Intersoft Consulting, Accessed in October, 24*(1).

Russo, K., & Rishikof, H. Cybersecurity: Executive Orders, Legislation, Cyberattacks, and Hot Topics, 19 Chap. L. Rev. 421 (2016). Available at: https://digitalcommons.chapman.edu/chapman-law-review/vol19/iss2/4

Saleem, M. A.. (2023). Provably Secure Conditional-Privacy Access Control Protocol for Intelligent Customers-Centric Communication in VANET. *IEEE Transactions on Consumer Electronics*.

Sinha, S., & Arora, D. Y. (2020). Ethical hacking: the story of a white hat hacker. *International Journal of Innovative Research in Computer Science & Technology (IJIRCST), ISSN*, 2347-5552.

Sun, Y., Xu, T., Bashir, A. K., Liu, J., & Omar, M. "BcIIS: Blockchain-Based Intelligent Identification Scheme of Massive IoT Devices," in *GLOBECOM 2023-2023 IEEE Global Communications Conference*, pp. 1277-1282, IEEE, 2023. DOI: 10.1109/GLOBECOM54140.2023.10437203

Tao, Y., Wu, J., Pan, Q., Bashir, A. K., & Omar, M. (2024). O-RAN-Based Digital Twin Function Virtualization for Sustainable IoV Service Response: An Asynchronous Hierarchical Reinforcement Learning Approach. *IEEE Transactions on Green Communications and Networking*, 8(3), 1049–1060. DOI: 10.1109/TGCN.2024.3435796

Tiwari, N., Ghadi, Y., & Omar, M. "Analysis of Ultrasound Images in Kidney Failure Diagnosis Using Deep Learning," in *Transformational Interventions for Business, Technology, and Healthcare*, pp. 45-74, IGI Global, 2023. DOI: 10.4018/979-8-3693-1634-4.ch004

Tiwari, N., Omar, M., & Ghadi, Y. “Brain Tumor Classification From Magnetic Resonance Imaging Using Deep Learning and Novel Data Augmentation,” in *Transformational Interventions for Business, Technology, and Healthcare*, pp. 392-413, IGI Global, 2023. DOI: 10.4018/979-8-3693-1634-4.ch023

Tshilidzi, M. “Data Is the Lifeblood of the Global Economy, but Restrictions on Cross-border Data Flows Are a Reality,” United Nations University, UNU Centre, 2023-08-17, https://unu.edu/article/data-lifeblood-global-economy-restrictions-cross-border-data-flows-are-reality

Umer, M., Aljrees, T., Karamti, H., Ishaq, A., Alsubai, S., Omar, M., Bashir, A. K., & Ashraf, I. (2023). Heart Failure Patients Monitoring Using IoT-Based Remote Monitoring System. *Scientific Reports*, 13(1), 19213. DOI: 10.1038/s41598-023-46322-6 PMID: 37932424

United States Department of Justice https://www.justice.gov/jm/jm-9-48000-computer-fraud#:~:text=The%20Department's%20goals%20for%20CFAA%20enforcement%20are%20to%20promote%20privacy,stored%20in%20their%20information%20systems

Vitianingsih, V., Firmansyah, D., Maukar, A. L., Kacung, S., & Zangana, H. M. (2024, August). Recommendation System for Determining the Best Banner Supplier Using Profile Matching and TOPSIS Methods. *Intensif Jurnal Ilmiah Penelitian Teknologi Dan Penerapan Sistem Informasi*, 8(2), 246–262. DOI: 10.29407/intensif.v8i2.21635

Warren, S., & Brandeis, L. D. (1890, December 15). The right to privacy. *Harvard Law Review*, 4(5), 193. https://groups.csail.mit.edu/mac/class/6.805/articles/privacy/privacy_brand_warr2.html. DOI: 10.2307/1321160

Wiewiorowski, W. (2023) Cybersecurity and Data Protection: a necessary and powerful duo. European Data Protection Supervisorhttps://edps.europa.eu/press-publications/press-news/blog/cybersecurity-and-data-protection-necessary-and-powerful-duo_en

Wright, J., Dawson, M. E.Jr, & Omar, M. (2012). Cyber Security and Mobile Threats: The Need for Antivirus Applications for Smartphones. *Journal of Information Systems Technology and Planning*, 5(14), 40–60.

Xu, X., Wu, J., Bashir, A. K., & Omar, M. (2024). Machine Learning and Zero Knowledge Empowered Trustworthy Bitcoin Mixing for Next-G Consumer Electronics Payment. *IEEE Transactions on Consumer Electronics*, 70(1), 2210–2223. DOI: 10.1109/TCE.2024.3361690

H. M. Zangana, “A New Skin Color Based Face Detection Algorithm by Combining Three Color Model Algorithms,” *IOSR Journal of Computer Engineering*, vol. 17, pp. 06-125, 2015.

H. M. Zangana, “A new algorithm for shape detection,” *IOSR Journal of Computer Engineering (IOSR-JCE)*, vol. 19, no. 3, pp. 71-76, 2017.

H. M. Zangana, “Library Data Quality Maturity (IIUM as a Case Study),” *IOSR-JCE*, vol. 29, Mar. 2017.

Zangana, H. M. (2017). Watermarking System Using LSB. *IOSR Journal of Computer Engineering*, 19(3), 75–79. DOI: 10.9790/0661-1903027579

Zangana, H. M. (2018). Design an information management system for a pharmacy. *International Journal of Advanced Research in Computer and Communication Engineering*, 7(10), 52–55. DOI: 10.17148/IJARCCE.2018.71012

Zangana, H. M. “Developing Data Warehouse for Student Information System (IIUM as a Case Study),” *International Organization of Scientific Research*, vol. 20, no. 1, pp. 09-14, 2018.

H. M. Zangana, “Implementing a System for Recognizing Optical Characters,” 2018.

H. M. Zangana, “Issues of Data Management in the Library: A Case Study,” 2019.

H. M. Zangana, “ITD Data Quality Maturity (A Case Study),” *International Journal Of Engineering And Computer Science*, vol. 8, no. 10, 2019.

Zangana, H. M. (2020). Mobile Device Integration in IIUM Service. *International Journal (Toronto, Ont.)*, 8(5).

Zangana, H. M. (2021). The Global Financial Crisis from an Islamic Point Of View. *Qubahan Academic Journal*, 1(2), 55–59. DOI: 10.48161/qaj.v1n2a39

Zangana, H. M. (2022). Creating a Community-Based Disaster Management System. *Academic Journal of Nawroz University*, 11(4), 234–244. DOI: 10.25007/ajnu.v11n4a1485

Zangana, H. M. (2022). Implementing New Interactive Video Learning System for IIUM. *Academic Journal of Nawroz University*, 11(2), 23–29. DOI: 10.25007/ajnu.v11n2a1281

H. M. Zangana, “Improving The Web Services for Remittance Company: Express Remit as a Case Study,” *Academic Journal of Nawroz University (AJNU)*, vol. 11, no. 3, 2022.

Zangana, H. M. (2024). *Exploring Blockchain-Based Timestamping Tools: A Comprehensive Review*. Redefining Security With Cyber AI. DOI: 10.4018/979-8-3693-6517-5.ch006

Zangana, H. M. (2024). *Exploring the Landscape of Website Vulnerability Scanners: A Comprehensive Review and Comparative Analysis*. Redefining Security With Cyber AI. DOI: 10.4018/979-8-3693-6517-5.ch007

H. M. Zangana, "CHALLENGES AND ISSUES of MANET," 2024.

Zangana, H. M., & Abdulazeez, A. M. (2023). Developed Clustering Algorithms for Engineering Applications: A Review [INJIISCOM]. *International Journal of Informatics, Information System and Computer Engineering*, 4(2), 147–169. DOI: 10.34010/injiiscom.v4i2.11636

Zangana, H. M., & Al-Shaikhli, I. F. (2013). A new algorithm for human face detection using skin color tone. *IOSR Journal of Computer Engineering*, 11(6), 31–38. DOI: 10.9790/0661-1163138

Zangana, H. M., Al-Shaikhli, I. F., & Graha, Y. I. (2013). The Ethical Dilemma of Software Piracy: An Inquiry from an Islamic Perspective. *Creative Communication and Innovative Technology Journal*, 7(1), 59–76. DOI: 10.33050/ccit.v7i1.171

Zangana, H. M., Bazeed, S. M. S., Ali, N. Y., & Abdullah, D. T. (2024). Navigating Project Change: A Comprehensive Review of Change Management Strategies and Practices. *Indonesian Journal of Education and Social Sciences*, 3(2), 166–179. DOI: 10.56916/ijess.v3i2.735

Zangana, H. M., Graha, Y. I., & Al-Shaikhli, I. F. (2024). Blogging: A New Platform For Spreading Rumors! *Creative Communication and Innovative Technology Journal*, 9(1), 71–76.

Zangana, H. M., Khalid Mohammed, A., & Zeebaree, S. R. (2024). Systematic Review of Decentralized and Collaborative Computing Models in Cloud Architectures for Distributed Edge Computing. *Sistemasi: Jurnal Sistem Informasi*, 13(4), 1501–1509. DOI: 10.32520/stmsi.v13i4.4169

Zangana, H. M., Mohammed, A. K., & Mustafa, F. M. (2024). Advancements and Applications of Convolutional Neural Networks in Image Analysis: A Comprehensive Review. *Jurnal Ilmiah Computer Science*, 3(1), 16–29.

Zangana, H. M., Mohammed, A. K., & Mustafa, F. M. (2024). Advancements in Edge Detection Techniques for Image Enhancement: A Comprehensive Review [IJAIR]. *International Journal of Artificial Intelligence & Robotics*, 6(1), 29–39. DOI: 10.25139/ijair.v6i1.8217

Zangana, H. M., Mohammed, A. K., Sallow, A. B., & Sallow, Z. B. (2024). Cybernetic Deception: Unraveling the Layers of Email Phishing Threats [INJURATECH]. *International Journal of Research and Applied Technology*, 4(1), 35–47.

Zangana, H. M., Mohammed, A. K., Sallow, Z. B., & Mustafa, F. M. (2024). Exploring Image Representation and Color Spaces in Computer Vision: A Comprehensive Review. *The Indonesian Journal of Computer Science*, 13(3). Advance online publication. DOI: 10.33022/ijcs.v13i3.3998

Zangana, H. M., & Mustafa, F. M. (2024). From Classical to Deep Learning: A Systematic Review of Image Denoising Techniques. *Jurnal Ilmiah Computer Science*, 3(1), 50–65.

Zangana, H. M., & Mustafa, F. M. (2024). Review of Hybrid Denoising Approaches in Face Recognition: Bridging Wavelet Transform and Deep Learning. *The Indonesian Journal of Computer Science*, 13(4). Advance online publication. DOI: 10.33022/ijcs.v13i4.4209

Zangana, H. M., & Mustafa, F. M. (2024). Surveying the Landscape: A Comprehensive Review of Object Detection Algorithms and Advancements. *Jurnal Ilmiah Computer Science*, 3(1), 1–15.

Zangana, H. M., & Omar, M. (2020). Threats, Attacks, and Mitigations of Smartphone Security. *Academic Journal of Nawroz University*, 9(4), 324–332. DOI: 10.25007/ajnu.v9n4a989

Zangana, H. M., Omar, M., Al-Karaki, J. N., & Mohammed, D. (2024). *Comprehensive Review and Analysis of Network Firewall Rule Analyzers: Enhancing Security Posture and Efficiency*. Redefining Security With Cyber AI. DOI: 10.4018/979-8-3693-6517-5.ch002

Zangana, H. M., Omar, M., & Ali, N. Y. (2024). Harnessing Artificial Intelligence in Modern Marketing: Strategies, Benefits, and Challenges [BAMJ]. *Business, Accounting and Management Journal*, 02(02), 70–82.

Zangana, H. M., Sallow, Z. B., Alkawaz, M. H., & Omar, M. "Unveiling the Collective Wisdom: A Review of Swarm Intelligence in Problem Solving and Optimization," *Inform: Jurnal Ilmiah Bidang Teknologi Informasi dan Komunikasi*, vol. 9, no. 2, pp. 101-110, 2024.

Zangana, H. M., & Zeebaree, S. R. (2024). Distributed Systems for Artificial Intelligence in Cloud Computing: A Review of AI-Powered Applications and Services [INJIISCOM]. *International Journal of Informatics, Information System and Computer Engineering*, 5(1), 11–30. DOI: 10.34010/injiiscom.v5i1.11883

Zhang, H., Wu, J., Pan, Q., Bashir, A. K., & Omar, M. (2024). Toward Byzantine-Robust Distributed Learning for Sentiment Classification on Social Media Platform. *IEEE Transactions on Computational Social Systems*, 1–11. DOI: 10.1109/TCSS.2024.3361465

Zhang, H., Wu, J., Pan, Q., Bashir, A. K., & Omar, M. (2024). Toward Byzantine-Robust Distributed Learning for Sentiment Classification on Social Media Platform. *IEEE Transactions on Computational Social Systems*, 1–11. DOI: 10.1109/TCSS.2024.3361465

Zhou, S., Ali, A., Al-Fuqaha, A., Omar, M., & Feng, L. (2024). Robust Risk-Sensitive Task Offloading for Edge-Enabled Industrial Internet of Things. *IEEE Transactions on Consumer Electronics*, 70(1), 1403–1413. DOI: 10.1109/TCE.2023.3323146

Zhou, S., Ali, A., Al-Fuqaha, A., Omar, M., & Feng, L. (2024). Robust Risk-Sensitive Task Offloading for Edge-Enabled Industrial Internet of Things. *IEEE Transactions on Consumer Electronics*, 70(1), 1403–1413. DOI: 10.1109/TCE.2023.3323146

Chapter 9
Digital Forensic Data Mining and Pattern Recognition

Luay Albtosh
https://orcid.org/0009-0009-0338-9123
Capitol Technology University, USA & Houston Community College, USA

ABSTRACT

Digital forensic data mining and pattern recognition are essential components in enhancing cybersecurity measures and forensic practices. This chapter explores the intersection of artificial intelligence and digital forensics, emphasizing the methodologies and technologies that enable the extraction of meaningful patterns from vast datasets. By leveraging advanced machine learning algorithms, investigators can identify anomalies, classify behaviors, and predict potential threats in real-time. The integration of AI enhances the efficiency and accuracy of forensic investigations, ultimately leading to improved decision-making and threat mitigation strategies. Case studies illustrate the practical applications of these techniques in various domains, underscoring the transformative potential of AI in digital forensics.

1. INTRODUCTION TO DATA MINING AND PATTERN RECOGNITION IN DIGITAL FORENSICS

The rise of digital technologies has significantly transformed the landscape of forensic investigations, presenting both challenges and opportunities. As cybercriminal activities become increasingly sophisticated, the need for effective methods to analyze and interpret digital evidence has grown. Data mining and pattern recognition have

DOI: 10.4018/979-8-3373-0588-2.ch009

emerged as critical techniques in this context, enabling forensic analysts to extract valuable insights from vast amounts of data generated in digital environments.

1.1 Data Mining in Digital Forensics

Data mining refers to the process of discovering patterns and extracting meaningful information from large datasets. In digital forensics, this involves analyzing data from various sources, such as computers, mobile devices, and networks, to uncover hidden information that may be crucial for investigations. The integration of artificial intelligence (AI) has further enhanced data mining capabilities, allowing for automated analysis and the identification of anomalies that human analysts might overlook.

Machine learning algorithms, a subset of AI, play a pivotal role in this process. By employing techniques such as supervised learning, unsupervised learning, and reinforcement learning, forensic investigators can classify data, detect unusual behaviors, and predict potential security breaches (Dunsin et al., 2024). For instance, as Tyagi, Kumari, and Richa (2024) note, AI-based systems can learn from historical data to improve their predictive accuracy, thus streamlining the forensic investigation process.

1.2 Pattern Recognition in Digital Forensics

Pattern recognition involves identifying regularities and trends in data, which is particularly useful in forensic contexts where establishing connections between different pieces of evidence is crucial. This technique can aid in recognizing digital signatures, user behaviors, and even potential links between various cybercrime incidents. By leveraging pattern recognition algorithms, forensic experts can sift through complex data sets to pinpoint relevant information, significantly reducing the time and effort required for investigations.

The effectiveness of pattern recognition in digital forensics has been underscored by studies indicating its ability to enhance investigative outcomes. For example, Jarrett and Choo (2021) highlight the impact of automation and AI on digital forensic methodologies, emphasizing the potential for AI-driven pattern recognition to improve the accuracy of investigations. Furthermore, as Moustafa (2022) elaborates, the fusion of AI with traditional forensic techniques facilitates a more comprehensive analysis, enabling investigators to connect the dots across various data sources effectively.

1.3 Challenges and Considerations

Despite the promise of data mining and pattern recognition, several challenges persist in their application within digital forensics. The sheer volume of data generated in today's digital landscape can overwhelm traditional forensic tools and methodologies. Moreover, ensuring the integrity and authenticity of digital evidence remains a critical concern, as any manipulation of data can compromise the validity of forensic findings (Zangana & Omar, 2020).

Furthermore, ethical considerations related to privacy and data protection must be addressed. The use of AI and data mining techniques raises questions about the extent to which individuals' data can be analyzed without infringing on their rights. As Hassan and Ibrahim (2023) discuss, balancing the need for effective forensic investigations with the protection of civil liberties is paramount in maintaining public trust.

1.4 Summary

The integration of data mining and pattern recognition into digital forensics represents a significant advancement in the field, driven by the capabilities of artificial intelligence. While these techniques offer promising tools for enhancing investigative efficiency and accuracy, it is essential to navigate the associated challenges and ethical considerations carefully. By fostering a deeper understanding of these methodologies and their implications, the forensic community can better leverage AI to address the evolving threats posed by cybercrime.

In conclusion, as we move further into an era where digital evidence plays an increasingly vital role in investigations, embracing innovative approaches such as data mining and pattern recognition will be essential for maintaining effective and efficient forensic practices (Ghillani, 2022; Rizvi et al., 2022; Ukwen & Karabatak, 2021).

2. FUNDAMENTALS OF DIGITAL FORENSIC DATA MINING

Digital forensic data mining is an emerging field that integrates digital forensics with advanced data analysis techniques to extract meaningful information from vast amounts of digital data. This approach plays a crucial role in cybercrime investigations, incident response, and evidence collection. The core components of digital forensic data mining encompass data acquisition, data processing, analysis, and reporting, each of which relies on specific methodologies and technologies, particularly in the context of artificial intelligence (AI) and machine learning (ML).

To provide a clear understanding of the digital forensic data mining process, the following flowchart illustrates the core stages, from data acquisition to reporting. Each step outlines the necessary procedures and technologies, highlighting the integration of AI to enhance the efficiency of these processes.

Figure 1. Digital forensic data mining process

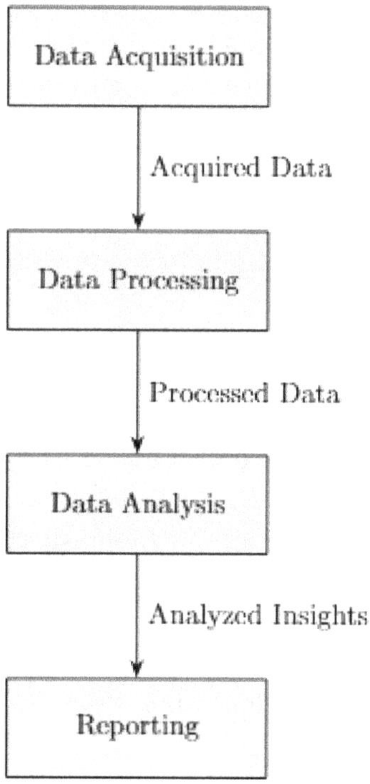

2.1. Data Acquisition

The first step in digital forensic data mining involves the acquisition of data from various digital sources. This includes hard drives, mobile devices, cloud storage, and network logs. Proper acquisition techniques ensure that data integrity is maintained, allowing for reliable analysis later. Automated tools can streamline the data acquisition process, reducing the time needed to gather evidence (Murphy, 2022). The integration of AI in this phase helps identify relevant data faster and more efficiently, enhancing the overall effectiveness of forensic investigations (Hassan & Ibrahim, 2023).

2.2. Data Processing

Once data is acquired, it must be processed to prepare it for analysis. This involves data cleaning, normalization, and transformation. During this phase, irrelevant or redundant information is removed, and the remaining data is organized into a structured format that facilitates analysis. Advanced algorithms, including those based on AI and ML, can significantly improve data processing by automating the identification of patterns and anomalies within the data (Tyagi et al., 2024; Dunsin et al., 2024).

2.3. Data Analysis

Data analysis in digital forensics focuses on uncovering patterns and insights that can aid in investigations. Traditional analysis methods often involve manual review, which can be time-consuming and prone to human error. However, the adoption of AI technologies can enhance the analytical capabilities of forensic investigators by enabling automated anomaly detection, predictive analytics, and clustering of data points (Dunsin et al., 2024; Kaur, Gabrijelčič, & Klobučar, 2023). AI-driven analytics can identify suspicious behaviors or trends that may indicate malicious activities, thereby expediting the investigative process (Jarrett & Choo, 2021).

2.4. Reporting

The final step in digital forensic data mining involves reporting the findings in a clear and comprehensive manner. Reports must be understandable to both technical and non-technical stakeholders and should adhere to legal and regulatory standards. AI tools can assist in generating reports by automating the documentation process, ensuring that all relevant details are captured accurately (Iqbal & Alharbi, 2020). Furthermore, visualizations produced through AI can help communicate complex data insights effectively (Hassan & Ibrahim, 2023).

2.5. Challenges and Future Directions

Despite its advantages, digital forensic data mining faces several challenges, including data privacy concerns, the rapid evolution of technology, and the increasing sophistication of cyber threats (Moustafa, 2022). As cybercriminals become more adept at concealing their activities, the need for advanced analytical tools and techniques grows. Future research should focus on enhancing the integration of AI in digital forensics to improve the accuracy and speed of investigations while addressing ethical considerations and compliance issues (Tuli & Thaduri, 2023; Zangana et al., 2024).

2.6. Summary

Digital forensic data mining is a vital component of modern cyber investigations, leveraging AI and machine learning to streamline processes from data acquisition to reporting. As this field continues to evolve, ongoing research and development will be essential to overcoming current challenges and enhancing the capabilities of digital forensic practitioners.

3. DATA COLLECTION AND PREPROCESSING FOR FORENSIC MINING

In the realm of digital forensics, effective data collection and preprocessing are crucial for the integrity and accuracy of forensic analysis. This section outlines the methodologies and best practices for gathering and preparing data in forensic mining, emphasizing the integration of artificial intelligence (AI) technologies to enhance the process.

Digital forensic investigations rely on diverse data sources to extract relevant evidence. The following pie chart visualizes the proportion of data typically acquired from various sources, such as hard drives, mobile devices, network logs, and cloud storage, in digital forensic processes.

Figure 2. Forensic data sources

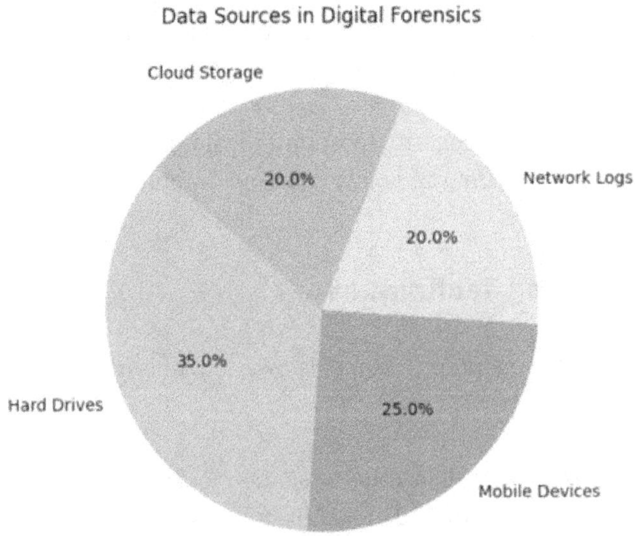

3.1. Data Collection Methods

Data collection in digital forensics can be categorized into several methods, each suited to specific environments and types of data. The primary methods include:

- **Live Data Collection**: This involves acquiring data from active systems, such as volatile memory and running processes. Techniques such as RAM imaging are used to capture live data before it is lost. As noted by Jarrett and Choo (2021), live data collection is essential in cases of active cyber incidents, where immediate action is required.
- **Static Data Collection**: This method is employed when dealing with devices that can be powered down without loss of critical data. Techniques include disk imaging and file system extraction. According to Moustafa (2022), static data provides a stable snapshot of a system, allowing for thorough analysis post-incident.
- **Network Traffic Capture**: Capturing data packets flowing through a network is vital for analyzing potential breaches or unauthorized activities. Tools like

Wireshark are commonly used in this context. Rizvi et al. (2022) emphasize the importance of network forensics in tracing attack vectors and understanding the methodologies employed by cybercriminals.

- **Cloud Data Collection**: With the rise of cloud computing, forensic investigations often require data from cloud storage solutions. This presents unique challenges due to the distributed nature of cloud services. Zangana et al. (2024) highlight the necessity for robust legal frameworks to govern data collection from cloud environments, ensuring compliance with data protection laws.

3.2. Preprocessing Techniques

Once data is collected, preprocessing is essential to prepare it for analysis. This involves several key steps:

- **Data Cleaning**: Raw data often contains noise and irrelevant information that can obscure important details. Techniques such as filtering and deduplication are employed to ensure that only relevant data is analyzed. Moustafa (2022) notes that effective data cleaning is critical to minimizing false positives during forensic analysis.
- **Data Transformation**: This step involves converting data into a suitable format for analysis. For instance, converting logs into a structured format like JSON or CSV facilitates easier querying and manipulation. The integration of AI can automate this transformation process, enhancing efficiency (Dunsin et al., 2024).
- **Feature Extraction**: Extracting relevant features from data is crucial for machine learning applications in digital forensics. This can include identifying specific keywords in documents or extracting metadata from files. Kaur, Gabrijelčič, and Klobučar (2023) emphasize the importance of feature extraction in improving the accuracy of AI models in forensic investigations.
- **Data Normalization**: Normalizing data ensures consistency across datasets, which is vital for comparative analysis. This involves standardizing formats and scales, making it easier to draw meaningful conclusions from diverse data sources.
- **Data Anonymization**: Protecting sensitive information during the analysis process is paramount. Techniques such as data masking or pseudonymization help maintain privacy while allowing investigators to work with the data (Hassan & Ibrahim, 2023).

3.3. AI Integration in Data Collection and Preprocessing

The incorporation of AI technologies into the data collection and preprocessing phases significantly enhances the capabilities of digital forensic investigations. AI algorithms can automate the identification of anomalies in large datasets, streamline the data cleaning process, and improve the accuracy of feature extraction. For example, machine learning models can be trained to recognize patterns indicative of cyber threats, as outlined by Samtani, Kantarcioglu, and Chen (2020).

Moreover, AI can assist in real-time data collection, enabling investigators to respond more swiftly to incidents. Tyagi, Kumari, and Richa (2024) discuss how AI-driven tools can adaptively collect and analyze data as incidents unfold, providing timely insights that are crucial for incident response.

3.4. Summary

Data collection and preprocessing are foundational steps in forensic mining that significantly impact the overall effectiveness of digital forensic investigations. By leveraging AI technologies, practitioners can enhance their methodologies, ensuring that the data analyzed is both relevant and accurately represents the events being investigated. As the field continues to evolve, the integration of these advanced technologies will play a vital role in shaping the future of digital forensics.

4. MACHINE LEARNING AND PATTERN RECOGNITION ALGORITHMS IN DIGITAL FORENSICS

In the rapidly evolving landscape of digital forensics, machine learning (ML) and pattern recognition algorithms play a crucial role in automating and enhancing investigative processes. As cyber threats become more sophisticated, the application of these technologies allows forensic analysts to analyze vast amounts of data efficiently, identify patterns indicative of criminal behavior, and streamline the collection and examination of digital evidence.

4.1 The Role of Machine Learning in Digital Forensics

Machine learning encompasses a variety of techniques that enable systems to learn from data and make predictions or decisions without explicit programming. In digital forensics, ML is utilized for various applications, including malware detection, network traffic analysis, and data recovery from corrupted devices. For instance, Tyagi et al. (2024) emphasize the integration of AI in digital forensics, highlighting its potential to improve the accuracy and speed of investigations. By leveraging algorithms capable of recognizing patterns in historical data, forensic experts can identify anomalies that may signify cyber crimes.

4.2 Pattern Recognition Algorithms

Pattern recognition is a key component of machine learning that focuses on classifying input data into categories based on its characteristics. In the context of digital forensics, these algorithms can analyze file signatures, user behaviors, and system logs to detect fraudulent activities or breaches. Dunsin et al. (2024) discuss how modern ML techniques, such as supervised and unsupervised learning, can be effectively employed to enhance forensic investigations. For example, supervised learning algorithms can be trained on labeled datasets of malicious and benign behaviors, allowing them to classify new data accurately.

4.3 Automation and Efficiency

The adoption of automation in digital forensics through AI and machine learning technologies significantly enhances investigative efficiency. Jarrett and Choo (2021) describe the impact of automation on digital forensic processes, noting that ML can automate repetitive tasks, such as data sorting and analysis, which traditionally required substantial manual effort. This not only accelerates the investigation process but also reduces the likelihood of human error. Additionally, with the capability of real-time analysis, forensic teams can respond promptly to emerging threats, thereby improving incident response times (Hassan & Ibrahim, 2023).

4.4 Challenges and Considerations

Despite the promising benefits, the integration of machine learning in digital forensics is not without challenges. Issues related to the interpretability of ML models, the potential for biased data, and the need for robust training datasets must be addressed to ensure reliable outcomes. For instance, Moustafa (2022) emphasizes the importance of developing transparent algorithms that can be easily understood and validated by forensic professionals. Moreover, the risk of adversarial attacks on ML systems necessitates ongoing research and development to safeguard against manipulation (Zangana et al., 2024).

4.5 Future Directions

Looking ahead, the future of machine learning and pattern recognition in digital forensics appears promising. Researchers are exploring innovative methodologies to enhance the robustness and adaptability of ML algorithms in various forensic contexts. As highlighted by Kaur et al. (2023), future research should focus on the intersection of AI and forensic science, paving the way for new applications and frameworks that can effectively address evolving cyber threats. Furthermore, continuous collaboration between academia and industry will be essential to develop practical solutions that can be deployed in real-world forensic investigations.

4.6 Summary

In conclusion, machine learning and pattern recognition algorithms are transforming digital forensics by providing advanced tools and methodologies that enhance investigative capabilities. As the field continues to evolve, the successful integration of these technologies will depend on addressing existing challenges and fostering innovation through interdisciplinary collaboration. By leveraging AI-driven techniques, forensic experts can improve their ability to detect, analyze, and respond to cyber threats in a timely and efficient manner.

5. ANOMALY DETECTION TECHNIQUES IN FORENSIC DATA MINING

Anomaly detection is a crucial component of forensic data mining, particularly in the context of cybersecurity, where identifying unusual patterns can be indicative of malicious activities. These techniques leverage statistical and machine learning methods to sift through vast amounts of data, pinpointing deviations from expected behavior. As the digital landscape evolves, so do the tools and methodologies used in anomaly detection, making it imperative for cybersecurity professionals to stay updated on the latest advancements.

The bar chart below categorizes the primary anomaly detection techniques used in digital forensics, including statistical, machine learning, deep learning, and hybrid approaches. Each technique's unique attributes contribute to forensic investigations by detecting patterns that may indicate cybercriminal activity.

Figure 3. Types of anomaly detection techniques

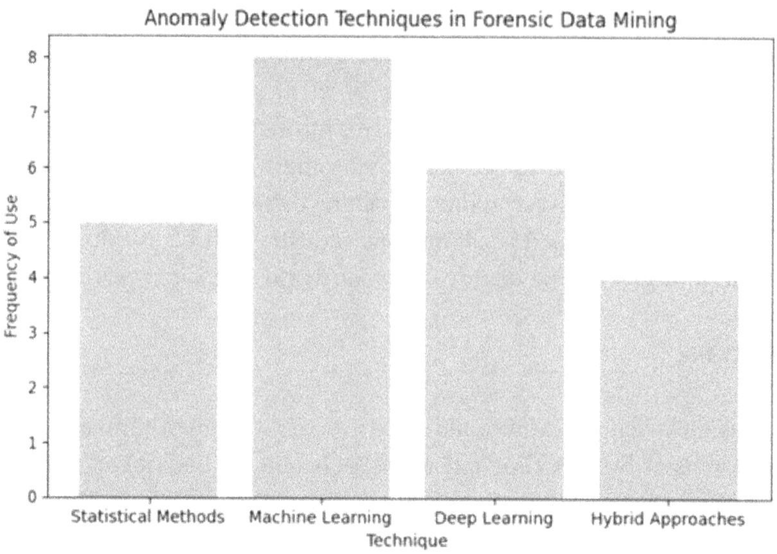

Anomaly detection plays a critical role in identifying unusual activities within digital forensic data. The heatmap below displays the intensity of detected anomalies across different types of forensic data sources, including network logs, application logs, user activity, and file integrity.

Figure 4. Anomaly detection in digital forensics

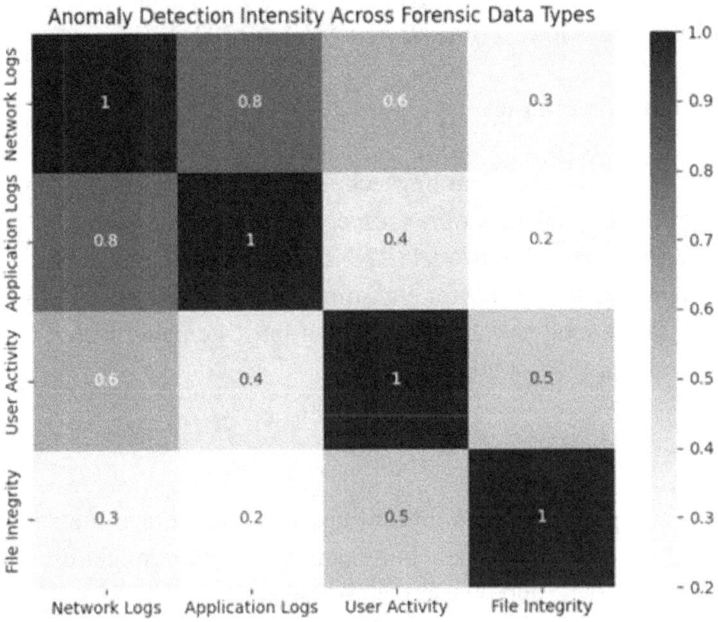

5.1 Types of Anomaly Detection Techniques

1. **Statistical Methods**

Statistical anomaly detection techniques utilize models based on historical data to establish a baseline of normal behavior. Any significant deviation from this baseline is flagged as an anomaly. Common approaches include Z-score analysis, where data points are transformed into standard deviations from the mean, and control charts, which monitor data over time to detect shifts. These methods are foundational in forensic analysis as they provide a straightforward way to assess data integrity (Zangana & Omar, 2020).

2. **Machine Learning Approaches**

Machine learning algorithms have gained prominence in anomaly detection due to their ability to adapt and learn from new data. Supervised learning techniques, such as decision trees and support vector machines, require labeled datasets to train models on what constitutes normal versus anomalous behavior. In contrast, unsupervised learning methods, including clustering algorithms like k-means and density-based spatial clustering (DBSCAN), do not require labeled data and can identify novel anomalies in real time (Jarrett & Choo, 2021).

3. **Deep Learning Techniques**

With the rise of big data, deep learning techniques have emerged as powerful tools for anomaly detection. Neural networks, especially convolutional neural networks (CNNs) and recurrent neural networks (RNNs), can model complex relationships within data, making them effective for high-dimensional data types like images and sequential logs. These models excel in detecting intricate patterns that traditional methods may overlook (Moustafa, 2022).

4. **Hybrid Approaches**

Combining multiple techniques, hybrid approaches leverage the strengths of different anomaly detection methods. For example, a system might use statistical methods for initial filtering and then apply machine learning algorithms for deeper analysis. This layered strategy enhances detection accuracy and reduces false positives, crucial in forensic investigations (Dunsin et al., 2024).

5.2 Applications in Cybersecurity

Anomaly detection plays a pivotal role in various cybersecurity domains. In network forensics, these techniques are used to identify unusual traffic patterns that may indicate data breaches or unauthorized access (Rizvi et al., 2022). In digital forensics, they assist investigators in uncovering hidden anomalies in file systems or databases that may suggest tampering or illicit activities (Hassan & Ibrahim, 2023).

5.3 Challenges and Future Directions

Despite their effectiveness, anomaly detection techniques face challenges, such as high false positive rates and the need for extensive labeled datasets for supervised learning. As cyber threats evolve, so too must the methods used to detect them. Future research is increasingly focused on enhancing the robustness of these techniques through the integration of artificial intelligence (AI) and machine learning (Tyagi et al., 2024). Continuous advancements in AI will likely provide more sophisticated models capable of adapting to new types of anomalies, thereby improving the efficacy of forensic investigations (Alghamdi, 2021).

5.4 Summary

Anomaly detection techniques are essential for modern forensic data mining, providing the tools needed to identify and respond to cyber threats effectively. As the landscape of digital forensics continues to change, the development of innovative methods that harness the power of AI and machine learning will be crucial in ensuring robust cybersecurity measures are in place (Kaur et al., 2023; Samtani et al., 2020). The ongoing evolution of these technologies signifies a proactive approach to securing digital environments against increasingly sophisticated cyber threats.

6. ASSOCIATION RULE MINING FOR UNCOVERING RELATIONSHIPS IN EVIDENCE

Association rule mining (ARM) is a fundamental technique used in data mining to uncover interesting relationships and patterns within large datasets. Originally popularized through applications in market basket analysis, where it helps identify products frequently purchased together, ARM has found significant relevance in various fields, including digital forensics and cybersecurity. The method enables investigators to analyze complex data, such as logs, transaction records, or network activity, to identify associations that can suggest potential criminal activities or security breaches.

6.1 Mechanism of Association Rule Mining

ARM operates on two primary components: **support** and **confidence**. Support measures the frequency of an itemset appearing in the dataset, while confidence indicates the likelihood of the occurrence of an associated itemset given the presence of another. For example, if a dataset contains records of cyber incidents, an ARM algorithm could identify that if a particular malware is present, there is a high probability that a specific vulnerability is also exploited.

The general formulation of an association rule is expressed as A⇒BA \Rightarrow BA⇒B, where AAA represents the antecedent and BBB the consequent. The effectiveness of ARM in practical scenarios hinges on various algorithms, with the Apriori and FP-Growth algorithms being among the most widely used. These algorithms systematically explore item sets to derive rules that satisfy predefined thresholds for support and confidence.

6.2 Application in Digital Forensics

In the realm of digital forensics, ARM can be utilized to analyze forensic data from compromised systems, log files, or communication channels. For instance, investigators can apply ARM to network traffic logs to uncover relationships between different types of network anomalies and corresponding indicators of compromise (IoCs). By establishing patterns, forensic analysts can generate hypotheses regarding the methods employed by attackers and the nature of the compromises.

Research indicates that the integration of artificial intelligence (AI) with ARM enhances its capabilities in digital forensics. Tyagi, Kumari, and Richa (2024) highlight the advantages of AI-driven methods in identifying complex patterns in cybersecurity and digital forensics. The combination of AI with ARM techniques enables automated detection of relationships that may not be evident through manual analysis, significantly improving the efficiency of investigations (Jarrett & Choo, 2021).

6.3 Identifying Cyber Threats

ARM can also be instrumental in identifying emerging cyber threats. By mining historical data of cyber incidents, forensic investigators can uncover frequent co-occurrences of attack vectors, tools, and exploited vulnerabilities. Dunsin et al. (2024) discuss how these associations can inform security practitioners about potential risks and guide proactive measures in incident response.

Moreover, the ability of ARM to manage vast datasets allows for the analysis of patterns across different environments, such as healthcare systems or financial networks, which are often targeted by cybercriminals. For instance, the work of Syed and ES (2024) emphasizes the importance of AI-driven forensic analysis in healthcare, where ARM can help uncover relationships between malware incidents and data breaches, enhancing the overall security posture.

6.4 Challenges and Future Directions

Despite its promise, the application of ARM in digital forensics faces challenges, including the complexity of data, evolving attack strategies, and the need for real-time processing capabilities. Moustafa (2022) notes that the integration of AI with ARM presents a pathway to overcome these obstacles by enabling dynamic learning and adaptation to new threats.

Future research directions should focus on enhancing the scalability of ARM algorithms to handle increasing volumes of data in digital forensics. Additionally, exploring hybrid models that combine ARM with other machine learning techniques may lead to more robust detection capabilities and improved incident response times (Kaur, Gabrijelčič, & Klobučar, 2023).

6.5 Summary

Association rule mining serves as a powerful tool in uncovering relationships in forensic evidence, providing insights that can significantly aid investigations. The synergy between ARM and artificial intelligence is set to revolutionize the field of digital forensics, enabling more efficient and effective identification of cyber threats. By continuing to explore this integration, researchers and practitioners can enhance their approaches to cybersecurity and incident response, ultimately leading to a more secure digital landscape.

7. TEMPORAL PATTERN ANALYSIS IN DIGITAL FORENSICS

Temporal pattern analysis plays a crucial role in digital forensics, as it enables investigators to understand the sequence and timing of events related to cyber incidents. This approach focuses on analyzing time-related data to establish a timeline, identify patterns, and uncover connections between different pieces of evidence. With the advent of artificial intelligence (AI) and machine learning, temporal pattern analysis has become more sophisticated, allowing forensic experts to extract insights that were previously difficult to obtain.

7.1 The Importance of Temporal Analysis

In digital forensics, understanding the timing of events can be pivotal in reconstructing a narrative surrounding a cyber incident. Temporal analysis assists in answering key questions: When did a breach occur? What actions were taken immediately before or after a significant event? Establishing timelines can provide critical context, helping to determine motives, methods, and even potential perpetrators. Tyagi, Kumari, and Richa (2024) emphasize that AI-based tools can automate the analysis of large datasets, making it easier to visualize and interpret temporal patterns.

7.2 Techniques for Temporal Pattern Analysis

Several techniques can be employed in temporal pattern analysis, including:

1. **Event Log Analysis**: Automated tools can analyze system and application logs to identify sequences of events leading up to an incident. Jarrett and Choo (2021) highlight the role of automation in enhancing the efficiency of log analysis, allowing forensic experts to quickly pinpoint anomalies.
2. **Time Series Analysis**: This method involves analyzing data points collected over time to identify trends or cyclic patterns. Dunsin et al. (2024) discuss how machine learning algorithms can be applied to time series data to detect deviations that may indicate malicious activity.
3. **Temporal Data Mining**: This involves discovering patterns from temporal data by applying various algorithms. Moustafa (2022) notes that temporal data mining can help uncover relationships between different events, which is critical in understanding the context of a cybercrime.
4. **Graph-Based Analysis**: Temporal data can be represented as graphs, where nodes represent events and edges represent the relationships between them. Kaur, Gabrijelčič, and Klobučar (2023) suggest that graph-based methods enable investigators to visualize complex temporal relationships, making it easier to identify critical events.

7.3 Challenges in Temporal Pattern Analysis

Despite its advantages, temporal pattern analysis faces several challenges:

- **Data Volume**: The sheer volume of data generated in digital environments can overwhelm traditional analysis methods. As noted by Rizvi et al. (2022), AI technologies can alleviate this issue by automating data processing and highlighting significant temporal patterns.
- **Data Integrity**: Ensuring the integrity of temporal data is vital, as any alterations can skew the analysis. Zangana and Omar (2020) emphasize the importance of maintaining unaltered timestamps and using verified sources to ensure accurate conclusions.
- **Dynamic Environments**: Cyber environments are continually changing, making it difficult to maintain up-to-date temporal models. Ali (2022) suggests that adaptive algorithms can help address this challenge by continuously learning from new data.

7.4 Applications in Incident Response

Temporal pattern analysis is not limited to forensic investigations; it also plays a vital role in incident response. By understanding the timeline of an incident, organizations can improve their response strategies and enhance overall security posture. For example, Al-Hajri et al. (2023) advocate for integrating temporal analysis into incident response protocols, allowing teams to act swiftly based on evidence-driven insights.

7.5 Future Directions

The integration of AI and machine learning into temporal pattern analysis in digital forensics presents exciting possibilities. Emerging technologies can facilitate more efficient and accurate analyses, enabling forensic experts to derive insights from complex datasets. As suggested by Montasari (2023), a multidisciplinary approach that combines AI, cybersecurity, and forensic science will be essential for advancing this field.

In conclusion, temporal pattern analysis is a vital component of digital forensics, providing essential insights into cyber incidents. As AI technologies continue to evolve, their integration into temporal analysis will undoubtedly enhance the capabilities of forensic investigations, ultimately leading to more effective responses to cyber threats.

8. TEXT MINING FOR FORENSIC INVESTIGATION

Text mining plays a pivotal role in forensic investigations, particularly in the realm of cybercrime. This process involves extracting valuable information from vast amounts of unstructured text data, such as emails, chat logs, and social media posts. As cybercriminals increasingly utilize digital platforms for illicit activities, the ability to efficiently analyze and interpret this information is crucial for investigators.

8.1 The Role of Text Mining in Cyber Forensics

Text mining techniques help forensic analysts uncover patterns, identify relationships, and extract relevant data that can aid in the investigation of cybercrimes. By leveraging natural language processing (NLP) and machine learning algorithms, investigators can automate the analysis of large datasets, significantly reducing the time required to identify pertinent evidence. For example, sentiment analysis can be employed to gauge the emotional tone of communications, which may indicate intent or state of mind during criminal activities (Iqbal & Alharbi, 2020).

In the context of cybersecurity, text mining is particularly beneficial in detecting phishing attempts, fraud schemes, and social engineering tactics. By analyzing textual features, such as language style and structure, forensic tools can flag suspicious communications that may indicate a cyber threat (Zangana et al., 2024).

Moreover, the integration of AI-driven text mining systems enhances the accuracy and efficiency of investigations, enabling analysts to focus on more complex tasks that require human judgment (Hassan & Ibrahim, 2023).

8.2 Challenges and Solutions in Text Mining for Forensics

Despite its advantages, text mining in forensic investigations presents several challenges. One major issue is the variability of language, including slang, jargon, and different linguistic styles that can obscure meaning. Moreover, the sheer volume of data generated in digital environments poses a significant hurdle for analysts. To address these challenges, advanced machine learning algorithms, particularly those utilizing deep learning techniques, can be deployed to improve the robustness of text mining applications (Moustafa, 2022; Dunsin et al., 2024).

Another challenge is ensuring the integrity and authenticity of the mined data. Forensic investigations require strict adherence to protocols to maintain the chain of custody. Solutions such as blockchain technology can provide a secure and tamper-proof method for logging the analysis process and the data used, ensuring that the findings can withstand scrutiny in a court of law (Zangana, 2024).

8.3 Future Directions in Text Mining for Digital Forensics

The future of text mining in forensic investigations is poised for significant advancements, particularly with the integration of AI and machine learning. As noted by Tyagi et al. (2024), the evolution of artificial intelligence is expected to drive more sophisticated text mining tools that can learn from previous investigations and adapt to emerging threats. These tools will not only improve detection capabilities but also enable predictive analytics, helping investigators anticipate potential cyber threats before they occur.

Furthermore, the application of explainable AI in text mining can enhance transparency in forensic processes, allowing investigators to understand how algorithms reach conclusions. This is crucial for maintaining trust in automated systems and ensuring that findings can be effectively communicated in legal contexts (Capuano et al., 2022).

8.4 Summary

In summary, text mining represents a powerful tool in the arsenal of digital forensic investigators. By effectively harnessing the capabilities of AI and machine learning, forensic professionals can significantly enhance their investigative processes, addressing the challenges posed by the ever-increasing volume and complexity of data in cyber environments. As technologies continue to evolve, the integration of text mining into forensic methodologies will be essential for staying ahead of cyber threats and ensuring justice in the digital age.

9. VISUALIZATION TECHNIQUES FOR FORENSIC PATTERN RECOGNITION

In the realm of digital forensics, effective visualization techniques are paramount for understanding complex data patterns and enhancing the overall investigative process. As the volume of digital evidence grows, traditional analytical methods often fall short in efficiently conveying critical insights. Therefore, leveraging advanced visualization techniques is essential for forensic analysts to interpret data effectively, identify anomalies, and derive actionable intelligence.

To illustrate relationships within forensic data, the following node-link diagram demonstrates how visual analytics can reveal connections between digital evidence. This is particularly useful in complex cases where identifying links between entities such as IP addresses or file origins is crucial.

Figure 5. Network visualization of data relationships using node-link diagram

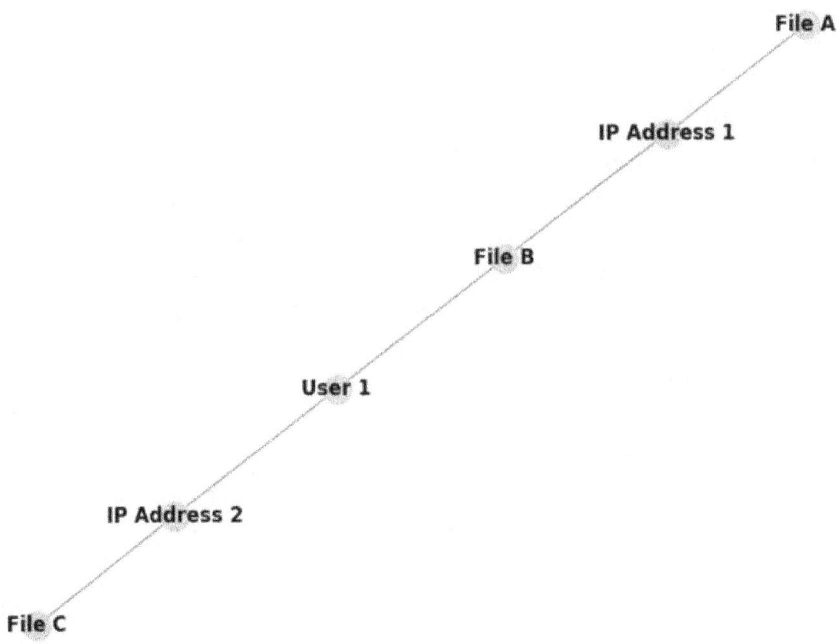

9.1. Importance of Visualization in Digital Forensics

Visualization plays a crucial role in digital forensics, allowing practitioners to transform raw data into understandable graphical representations. These techniques help forensic investigators discern patterns and relationships that may not be immediately apparent from numerical data alone. By utilizing visual analytics, forensic analysts can:

- Identify trends and anomalies within datasets.
- Communicate findings more effectively to stakeholders.
- Enhance decision-making processes during investigations.

As Tyagi et al. (2024) emphasize, the integration of artificial intelligence in visualization techniques provides a significant advantage in digital forensics, enabling more sophisticated analyses of complex data.

9.2. Types of Visualization Techniques

Various visualization techniques can be applied in digital forensic investigations, including:

- **Graphs and Charts**: Simple yet effective, graphs and charts provide a clear overview of data distributions and relationships. These visual tools are particularly useful for summarizing large datasets, as highlighted by Dunsin et al. (2024).
- **Heat Maps**: Heat maps visually represent data density and variations across different dimensions, aiding in the identification of hotspots or areas of interest within datasets. This technique is valuable in network forensics, where analyzing traffic patterns is crucial (Rizvi et al., 2022).
- **Node-Link Diagrams**: These diagrams illustrate relationships between entities, making them ideal for visualizing social networks, communication patterns, and potential connections in cybercrime investigations (Hassan & Ibrahim, 2023).
- **Time-Series Analysis**: By visualizing data over time, analysts can detect patterns, trends, and anomalies. This technique is particularly beneficial in incident response scenarios, where understanding the timeline of events is critical (Kaur et al., 2023).

9.3. Integrating AI into Visualization Techniques

The integration of artificial intelligence into visualization techniques has revolutionized digital forensics. AI algorithms can enhance the visualization process by automatically detecting patterns, categorizing data, and providing predictive insights. For instance, machine learning models can identify suspicious behaviors within datasets, as discussed by Samtani et al. (2020), enabling faster and more accurate forensic analyses.

Moreover, explainable AI frameworks can assist investigators in understanding the rationale behind AI-generated insights, fostering trust and transparency in the decision-making process (Capuano et al., 2022). This aspect is particularly vital in legal contexts, where the admissibility of evidence may hinge on its interpretability.

9.4. Challenges in Visualization

Despite the advantages of visualization techniques, several challenges persist. One significant hurdle is the complexity of the data itself, which can lead to information overload if not managed appropriately. Effective visualization requires a balance between detail and clarity, ensuring that critical information is not obscured (Iqbal & Alharbi, 2020).

Additionally, as Moustafa (2022) notes, the rapid evolution of cyber threats necessitates that visualization tools remain adaptive and responsive to new data types and formats. Continuous development and innovation in visualization methodologies are essential to keep pace with the dynamic landscape of digital forensics.

9.5. Future Directions

Looking ahead, the future of visualization in digital forensics will likely be shaped by advancements in AI and machine learning. As technologies evolve, the development of more intuitive and user-friendly visualization tools will enhance analysts' capabilities to interpret data effectively (Zangana et al., 2024). Furthermore, the exploration of interactive visualization platforms that allow users to manipulate data and explore different scenarios will facilitate deeper insights and understanding.

In conclusion, effective visualization techniques are vital for enhancing forensic pattern recognition in digital forensics. The integration of artificial intelligence and machine learning is transforming the field, providing powerful tools to detect patterns and anomalies within vast datasets. As the landscape of cyber threats continues to evolve, the continuous refinement of these techniques will be essential for maintaining robust investigative capabilities.

10. REAL-TIME DATA MINING AND PATTERN RECOGNITION IN DIGITAL FORENSICS

Digital forensics is increasingly relying on real-time data mining and pattern recognition technologies, significantly enhancing the capability to analyze large volumes of data swiftly and accurately. This integration of artificial intelligence (AI) and machine learning (ML) into digital forensic processes not only expedites investigations but also improves the accuracy of identifying patterns and anomalies that could indicate cybercriminal activities.

10.1 Importance of Real-Time Data Processing

The necessity for real-time data processing in digital forensics stems from the growing complexity and volume of data generated in the digital landscape. Investigators often confront massive datasets that require efficient handling to uncover relevant evidence. AI technologies, particularly data mining techniques, facilitate this process by enabling the extraction of useful information from unstructured data sources, such as emails, social media interactions, and file systems (Jarrett & Choo, 2021).

Real-time data mining allows forensic analysts to identify patterns and correlations within the data as they occur, rather than relying solely on post-event analysis. This immediacy can be crucial in preventing further criminal activity or mitigating damage during ongoing attacks. As Tyagi et al. (2024) highlight, AI-enabled tools can significantly enhance the speed and effectiveness of forensic investigations by automatically flagging suspicious behaviors in real time.

10.2 Pattern Recognition Techniques

Pattern recognition is a critical aspect of digital forensics, involving the identification of significant data patterns that may indicate malicious activities. Techniques such as supervised learning, unsupervised learning, and neural networks are increasingly employed to develop models that can recognize complex patterns in data. These methods can classify data as benign or malicious, predict potential security breaches, and provide insights into the behavior of cybercriminals (Dunsin et al., 2024).

For instance, machine learning algorithms can analyze historical data to learn the characteristics of normal user behavior. When deviations from this behavior occur, the system can alert investigators to potential security incidents (Hassan & Ibrahim, 2023). This proactive approach not only aids in immediate response efforts but also contributes to building a more robust security framework through continuous learning and adaptation (Kaur, Gabrijelčič, & Klobučar, 2023).

10.3 AI's Role in Cybersecurity and Digital Forensics

The integration of AI into digital forensics is revolutionizing traditional approaches. AI systems can process vast amounts of data from multiple sources, uncovering hidden connections and extracting insights that may not be immediately apparent to human analysts (Moustafa, 2022). These capabilities are vital in scenarios where time is of the essence, such as during active cyber incidents where immediate action is required to mitigate threats (Rizvi et al., 2022).

Furthermore, as noted by Ghillani (2022), AI enhances the effectiveness of forensic investigations by reducing human error and bias. AI-driven analysis allows for a more objective evaluation of evidence, ensuring that critical information is not overlooked. This capability is particularly important in cases involving complex digital crimes, where the sheer volume of data can be overwhelming (Omar & Zangana, 2024).

10.4 Challenges and Future Directions

While the potential of AI in digital forensics is substantial, challenges remain. The ever-evolving nature of cyber threats requires continuous updates to AI models and algorithms to maintain effectiveness (Montasari, 2023). Additionally, ethical considerations regarding privacy and data protection must be carefully navigated, as the use of AI in investigations could potentially infringe on individual rights if not managed properly (Faqir, 2023).

Future research must focus on enhancing the interpretability of AI systems in digital forensics. As AI continues to evolve, the need for transparent and explainable algorithms becomes crucial, especially in legal contexts where forensic evidence may be scrutinized (Capuano et al., 2022). Advancements in explainable AI could bridge the gap between complex algorithmic decisions and human understanding, fostering trust in AI-enhanced forensic processes (Stutz et al., 2024).

In conclusion, real-time data mining and pattern recognition are transforming the landscape of digital forensics, providing investigators with powerful tools to combat cybercrime effectively. As AI technology continues to develop, its role in digital forensics will likely expand, offering new methodologies and approaches to enhance security and protect against future threats. Embracing these advancements while addressing the accompanying challenges will be essential for the future of digital forensic investigations (Zangana et al., 2024; Ali, 2022).

11. CASE STUDIES AND APPLICATIONS OF DATA MINING IN DIGITAL FORENSICS

Data mining has emerged as a critical component in digital forensics, allowing investigators to extract valuable information from vast amounts of data. This section explores various case studies and applications where data mining techniques have significantly enhanced digital forensic investigations.

11.1. Introduction to Data Mining in Digital Forensics

Data mining involves the analysis of large datasets to discover patterns and extract useful information. In digital forensics, these techniques help in identifying, preserving, and analyzing digital evidence. The integration of artificial intelligence (AI) and machine learning (ML) in data mining has further revolutionized this field, enabling more efficient and effective investigations (Hassan & Ibrahim, 2023).

11.2. Case Study: Cybersecurity Incident Response

One notable case involved a significant cybersecurity breach where data mining techniques were employed to analyze network logs. By applying clustering algorithms, investigators identified patterns of unauthorized access that were previously unnoticed. This analysis not only facilitated the immediate incident response but also informed future security measures (Dunsin et al., 2024). Such applications highlight the importance of automation and AI in enhancing digital forensic processes (Jarrett & Choo, 2021).

11.3. Application: Email Phishing Threats

Email phishing remains a prevalent threat, and data mining techniques have been effectively used to combat this issue. A comprehensive analysis of phishing emails revealed specific linguistic patterns and metadata characteristics common among phishing attempts. By utilizing these patterns, machine learning models were trained to classify and filter potential phishing emails in real-time (Zangana et al., 2024). This proactive approach has significantly reduced the success rate of phishing attacks.

11.4. Case Study: Digital Forensic Investigation in Healthcare

In the healthcare sector, a case study demonstrated the application of AI-driven forensic analysis to detect anomalies in electronic health records (EHR). Data mining algorithms were employed to analyze access patterns and user behaviors, leading to the identification of potential breaches and unauthorized access to sensitive patient information. This integration of AI not only streamlined the investigation process but also enhanced compliance with healthcare regulations (Syed & ES, 2024).

11.5. Application: Network Forensics

Network forensics has benefited immensely from data mining techniques. For example, researchers have applied anomaly detection algorithms to analyze traffic data and identify potential intrusions. By correlating various data points, such as IP addresses, timestamps, and packet sizes, forensic analysts were able to pinpoint malicious activities, thereby improving response times and mitigation strategies (Rizvi et al., 2022).

11.6. Case Study: Automated Digital Forensics

Automation has become a cornerstone of modern digital forensics. In a recent study, the implementation of AI-based automation tools in digital investigations significantly reduced the time required for data analysis. These tools utilized data mining techniques to sift through terabytes of data, automatically categorizing evidence and prioritizing it for further investigation (Moustafa, 2022). Such advancements underscore the importance of leveraging AI to enhance efficiency in forensic investigations.

11.7. Future Directions

The future of data mining in digital forensics looks promising, particularly with the continued evolution of AI technologies. Ongoing research aims to explore new methodologies that integrate data mining with emerging technologies such as blockchain and IoT devices. These innovations hold the potential to further enhance the accuracy and reliability of forensic investigations (Kaur et al., 2023; Nair et al., 2024).

11.8. Summary

The integration of data mining techniques in digital forensics has proven invaluable across various sectors, from cybersecurity to healthcare. As technology continues to advance, the applications of data mining in digital forensics are expected to expand, offering new solutions to combat cyber threats and streamline investigative processes. Future research should focus on refining these techniques and exploring their applicability in increasingly complex digital environments.

12. CHALLENGES AND LIMITATIONS IN FORENSIC DATA MINING AND PATTERN RECOGNITION

Forensic data mining and pattern recognition have become integral components in the field of digital forensics, particularly with the increasing sophistication of cybercrime. However, despite significant advancements, there are several challenges and limitations that hinder the effectiveness of these technologies.

12.1. Data Quality and Integrity

One of the primary challenges in forensic data mining is ensuring data quality and integrity. In many instances, data may be incomplete, corrupted, or unstructured, which complicates the extraction of relevant patterns. Tyagi, Kumari, and Richa (2024) emphasize that the reliability of insights drawn from data mining processes hinges on the quality of the input data. Poor data quality can lead to misleading conclusions, which is particularly detrimental in forensic investigations.

12.2. Evolving Cyber Threat Landscape

The rapid evolution of cyber threats poses a significant challenge for forensic data mining. Cybercriminals continuously adapt their tactics, techniques, and procedures (TTPs), making it difficult for forensic systems to keep pace. Dunsin et al. (2024) highlight that as attackers leverage artificial intelligence (AI) to execute sophisticated cyberattacks, the effectiveness of traditional pattern recognition techniques diminishes. This necessitates ongoing updates and improvements in forensic methodologies to detect and respond to new types of threats.

12.3. Complexity of Algorithms

The complexity of algorithms used in forensic data mining can also be a barrier. While advanced algorithms can process vast amounts of data and identify intricate patterns, they often require significant computational resources and expertise to implement. As Jarrett and Choo (2021) note, the lack of understanding and accessibility to these sophisticated algorithms can limit their application in practical forensic settings. This complexity may also hinder timely responses in critical investigations.

12.4. Ethical and Privacy Concerns

The use of AI and data mining in forensic investigations raises ethical and privacy concerns. The potential for misuse of personal data during investigations can lead to violations of privacy rights. As discussed by Kaur, Gabrijelčič, and Klobučar (2023), there is an ongoing debate regarding the balance between effective forensic analysis and the protection of individual privacy. This tension can complicate the implementation of data mining techniques in real-world scenarios.

12.5. Integration with Existing Systems

Integrating forensic data mining tools with existing systems poses another challenge. Many organizations may have legacy systems that are not compatible with modern forensic technologies. This can create gaps in data collection and analysis, ultimately hampering the effectiveness of forensic investigations (Moustafa, 2022). Seamless integration is essential for ensuring that forensic capabilities are fully utilized across various platforms.

12.6. Interpretability of Results

Another critical limitation is the interpretability of results generated by AI-driven forensic data mining tools. Many AI models, particularly deep learning approaches, function as "black boxes," providing little insight into how decisions are made. This lack of transparency can be problematic in forensic contexts where the ability to explain findings is crucial (Sikos, 2021). The challenge lies in developing models that not only perform well but also offer interpretable outputs that can be communicated effectively to stakeholders.

12.7. Resource Constraints

Resource constraints, including funding, manpower, and technical expertise, can significantly impact the implementation of forensic data mining and pattern recognition systems. Many organizations may struggle to allocate sufficient resources for the continuous training and development required to keep pace with advancements in technology (Al-Hajri et al., 2023). As a result, the potential of these technologies may remain underutilized.

12.8. Legal and Regulatory Issues

Legal and regulatory frameworks surrounding digital forensics are often not well-defined, which can create uncertainties in the application of data mining techniques. Issues related to the admissibility of evidence gathered through AI-driven methods can complicate investigations and prosecutions (Zangana et al., 2024). The lack of clear guidelines can deter organizations from fully embracing advanced forensic techniques.

12.9. Summary

In conclusion, while forensic data mining and pattern recognition offer substantial potential for enhancing digital forensics, several challenges and limitations must be addressed. Improving data quality, adapting to evolving threats, simplifying algorithms, ensuring ethical practices, facilitating integration, enhancing interpretability, overcoming resource constraints, and clarifying legal frameworks are essential steps toward maximizing the effectiveness of these technologies. As the field continues to evolve, a collaborative approach involving researchers, practitioners, and policymakers will be crucial in overcoming these obstacles.

13. FUTURE DIRECTIONS IN FORENSIC DATA MINING AND PATTERN RECOGNITION

The integration of artificial intelligence (AI) in forensic data mining and pattern recognition presents an ultimate opportunity to revolutionize digital investigations. As cyber threats evolve, traditional forensic methodologies must adapt to harness AI's capabilities, enhancing efficiency and accuracy in data analysis. For instance, automated systems can process vast amounts of data in real-time, facilitating quicker responses to incidents (Jarrett & Choo, 2021; Dunsin et al., 2024).

Future research should focus on developing explainable AI models that can provide insights into decision-making processes, thereby improving trust in automated forensic tools (Capuano et al., 2022). Enhanced machine learning algorithms are essential for identifying complex patterns in data that may indicate malicious activities (Moustafa, 2022). The role of AI in cybersecurity extends to predictive analytics, where anticipating potential breaches can significantly mitigate risks (Hassan & Ibrahim, 2023).

Moreover, multidisciplinary approaches combining AI, digital forensics, and incident response will yield robust frameworks capable of addressing emerging cyber threats (Samtani et al., 2020; Tuli & Thaduri, 2023). Collaboration among academia, industry, and law enforcement is crucial for developing comprehensive training datasets that reflect current cyber landscapes (Nair et al., 2024).

As the field progresses, ethical considerations surrounding AI deployment in forensics will become paramount. Research should address the implications of biased algorithms and the need for regulatory standards to guide AI applications in forensic contexts (Gholami & Omar, 2023; Alghamdi, 2021). The exploration of AI-driven solutions in various domains, such as healthcare cybersecurity, further exemplifies the transformative potential of these technologies (Syed & ES, 2024).

In summary, the future of forensic data mining and pattern recognition lies in embracing AI to enhance investigative capabilities while navigating ethical complexities and fostering interdisciplinary collaboration. As articulated by Tyagi et al. (2024), the synergy of AI and digital forensics can unlock new avenues for tackling cybercrime effectively and efficiently.

14. CONCLUSION

The integration of artificial intelligence into forensic data mining and pattern recognition signifies a transformative shift in how digital investigations are conducted. As cyber threats continue to evolve in complexity and scale, traditional forensic methods are often insufficient to keep pace. AI technologies offer advanced analytical capabilities that can process vast amounts of data quickly and accurately, enabling investigators to identify patterns and anomalies that may indicate criminal activity.

Moreover, the application of AI in digital forensics fosters enhanced predictive analytics, allowing organizations to anticipate potential breaches before they occur. This proactive approach is crucial in an era where timely responses to incidents can significantly mitigate damage and enhance overall cybersecurity posture. The development of explainable AI models will also play a vital role in building trust among users, ensuring that automated systems can be understood and scrutinized.

As we look to the future, it is essential to address the ethical implications associated with AI in forensics. Issues such as algorithmic bias and data privacy must be carefully considered to ensure that these technologies are used responsibly. Interdisciplinary collaboration among academia, industry, and law enforcement will be crucial in developing robust frameworks and standards for AI applications in digital forensics.

In conclusion, the synergy between artificial intelligence and forensic data mining presents a promising frontier for enhancing the effectiveness and efficiency of digital investigations. By embracing these advancements, we can better equip ourselves to combat cybercrime and safeguard the integrity of digital environments. The journey ahead will require a balance between innovation and ethical considerations, ensuring that the tools we develop serve the greater good in an increasingly digital world.

REFERENCES

Abbasi, R., Bashir, A. K., Mateen, A., Amin, F., Ge, Y., & Omar, M. "Efficient Security and Privacy of Lossless Secure Communication for Sensor-based Urban Cities," *IEEE Sensors Journal*, vol. 2023.

Ahmed, H., Rasheed, H., Bashir, A. K., & Omar, M. (2023). Rasheed, A. K. Bashir, and M. Omar, "Millimeter-wave Channel Modeling in a VANETs Using Coding Techniques,". *PeerJ. Computer Science*, 9, e1374. DOI: 10.7717/peerj-cs.1374 PMID: 37346660

Ahmed, N., Mohammadani, K., Bashir, A. K., Omar, M., Jones, A., & Hassan, F. "Secure and Reliable Routing in the Internet of Vehicles Network: AODV-RL with BHA Attack Defense," *CMES-Computer Modeling in Engineering & Sciences*, vol. 139, no. 1, 2024.

Ahmed Alaa El-Din, E. (2022). Artificial intelligence in forensic science: Invasion or revolution? *Egyptian Society of Clinical Toxicology Journal*, 10(2), 20–32. DOI: 10.21608/esctj.2022.158178.1012

Al-Hajri, S. M., Al-Thonayan, Z. J., Alqattan, M. M., Alalyani, N. A., Alali, N. D., & Alnaim, N. (2023). Maximizing the Potential of Artificial Intelligence in Digital Forensics Investigations.

Al Harthi, S., Al Balushi, M. Y., Al Badi, A. H., Al Karaki, J., & Omar, M. *"Metaverse Adoption in UAE Higher Education: A Hybrid SEM-ANN Approach," in 98 Mohammad Daradkeh, Boshra Aldhanhani, Amjad Gawanmeh, Shadi Atalla and Sami Miniaoui. Applied Research Approaches to Technology, Healthcare, and Business*. IGI Global.

Al-Karaki, J. N., Omar, M., Gawanmeh, A., & Jones, A. "Advancing CyberSecurity Education and Training: Practical Case Study of Running Capture the Flag (CTF) on the Metaverse vs. Physical Settings," in *2023 International Conference on Intelligent Metaverse Technologies & Applications (iMETA)*, pp. 1-7, IEEE, 2023. DOI: 10.1109/iMETA59369.2023.10294722

Al Kinoon, M., Omar, M., Mohaisen, M., & Mohaisen, D. "Security Breaches in the Healthcare Domain: A Spatiotemporal Analysis," in *Computational Data and Social Networks: 10th International Conference, CSoNet 2021, Virtual Event, November 15-17, 2021, Proceedings*, Springer International Publishing, pp. 171-183, 2021. DOI: 10.1007/978-3-030-91434-9_16

Al-Sanjary, O. I., Ahmed, A. A., Jaharadak, A. A. B., Ali, M. A., & Zangana, H. M. “Detection Clone an Object Movement Using an Optical Flow Approach,” in *2018 IEEE Symposium on Computer Applications & Industrial Electronics (ISCAIE)*, pp. 388-394, 2018. DOI: 10.1109/ISCAIE.2018.8405504

O. I. Al-Sanjary, A. A. Ahmed, H. M. Zangana, M. Ali, S. Aldulaimi, and M. Alkawaz, “An Investigation of the Characteristics and Performance of Hybrid Routing Protocol in (MANET),” *International Journal of Engineering & Technology*, vol. 7, no. 4.22, pp. 49-54, 2018.

Alghamdi, M. I. (2021). *Digital forensics in cyber security—recent trends, threats, and opportunities*. Cybersecurity Threats with New Perspectives. DOI: 10.5772/intechopen.94452

Ali, A. (2022). Cyber Crime Investigation and Forensics: Leveraging AI and Big Data for More Effective Solutions.

Alturki, N., Altamimi, A., Umer, M., Saidani, O., Alshardan, A., Alsubai, S., Omar, M., & Ashraf, I. “Improving Prediction of Chronic Kidney Disease Using KNN Imputed SMOTE Features and TrioNet Model,” *CMES-Computer Modeling in Engineering & Sciences*, vol. 139, no. 3, 2024. DOI: 10.32604/cmes.2023.045868

Arulappan, G. (2023). Raja, A. K. Bashir, A. Mahanti, and M. Omar, “ZTMP: Zero Touch Management Provisioning Algorithm for the On-boarding of Cloud-native Virtual Network Functions,”. *Mobile Networks and Applications*, •••, 1–13.

Ayub, M., Li, X., Mahmood, K., Shamshad, S., Saleem, M. A., & Omar, M. (2023). Secure Consumer-centric Demand Response Management in Resilient Smart Grid as Industry 5.0 Application with Blockchain-based Authentication. *IEEE Transactions on Consumer Electronics*.

M. Banisakher, D. Mohammed, and M. Omar, “A Cloud-Based Computing Architecture Model of Post-Disaster Management System,” *International Journal of Simulation--Systems, Science & Technology*, vol. 19, no. 5, 2018.

Banisakher, M., Omar, M., & Clare, W. (2019). Critical Infrastructure—Perspectives on the Role of Government in Cybersecurity. *Journal of Computer Sciences and Applications*, 7(1), 37–42. DOI: 10.12691/jcsa-7-1-6

Banisakher, M., Omar, M., Hong, S., & Adams, J. (2020). A Human-centric Approach to Data Fusion in Post-Disaster Management. *Jurnal of Business Management and Science*, 8(1), 12–20.

Basharat, M., & Omar, M. "Adapting to Change: Assessing the Longevity and Resilience of Adversarially Trained NLP Models in Dynamic Spam Detection Environments," in *Innovations, Securities, and Case Studies Across Healthcare, Business, and Technology*, pp. 157-173, IGI Global, 2024. DOI: 10.4018/979-8-3693-1906-2.ch009

Basharat, M., & Omar, M. (2024). Harnessing GPT-2 for Feature Extraction in Malware Detection: A Novel Approach to Cybersecurity. *Land Forces Academy Review*, 29(1), 74–84. DOI: 10.2478/raft-2024-0008

M. Basharat and M. Omar, "SecuGuard: Leveraging Pattern-exploiting Training in Language Models for Advanced Software Vulnerability Detection," *International Journal of Mathematics and Computer in Engineering*, 2024.

Bonfanti, M. E. (2022). *Artificial intelligence and the offence-defence balance in cyber security. Cyber Security: Socio-Technological Uncertainty and Political Fragmentation*. Routledge.

Burrell, D. N., Nobles, C., Cusak, A., Omar, M., & Gillesania, L. (2022). Cybercrime and the Nature of Insider Threat Complexities in Healthcare and Biotechnology Engineering Organizations. *Journal of Crime and Criminal Behavior*, 2(2), 131–144. DOI: 10.47509/JCCB.2022.v02i02.04

Burrell, D. N., Nobles, C., Richardson, K., Wright, J. B., Jones, A. J., Springs, D., & Brown-Jackson, K. (2023). Allison Huff. In *Applied Research Approaches to Technology, Healthcare, and Business*. IGI Global. DOI: 10.4018/979-8-3693-1630-6

Capuano, N., Fenza, G., Loia, V., & Stanzione, C. (2022). Explainable artificial intelligence in cybersecurity: A survey. *IEEE Access : Practical Innovations, Open Solutions*, 10, 93575–93600. DOI: 10.1109/ACCESS.2022.3204171

CHILONGO, L., & KM, A. S. (2024). IMPACT OF ARTIFICIAL INTELLIGENCE ON CYBERSECURITY: A CASE OF INTERNET OF THINGS. *i-Manager's Journal on Digital Forensics & Cyber Security (JDF), 2*(1).

Davis, L., Dawson, M., & Omar, M. (2016). Systems Engineering Concepts with Aid of Virtual Worlds and Open Source Software: Using Technology to Develop Learning Objects and Simulation Environments. In *Handbook of Research on 3-D Virtual Environments and Hypermedia for Ubiquitous Learning* (pp. 483–509). IGI Global. DOI: 10.4018/978-1-5225-0125-1.ch020

Dawson, M. (2015). A Brief Review of New Threats and Countermeasures in Digital Crime and Cyber Terrorism. In *New Threats and Countermeasures in Digital Crime and Cyber Terrorism* (pp. 1–7). IGI Global. DOI: 10.4018/978-1-4666-8345-7.ch001

Dawson, M., Al Saeed, I., Wright, J., & Omar, M. "Technology enhanced learning with open source software for scientists and engineers," in *INTED2013 Proceedings*, IATED, 2013, pp. 5583–5589.

Dawson, M., Davis, L., & Omar, M. (2019). Developing learning objects for engineering and science fields: Using technology to test system usability and interface design. *Int. J. Smart Technol. Learn.*, 1(2), 140–161. DOI: 10.1504/IJSMART-TL.2019.097951

Dawson, M., Eltayeb, M., & Omar, M. (2016). *Security solutions for hyperconnectivity and the Internet of things*. IGI Global.

Dawson, M., Omar, M., & Abramson, J. (2015). Understanding the methods behind cyber terrorism. In *Encyclopedia of Information Science and Technology* (3rd ed., pp. 1539–1549). IGI Global.

Dawson, M., Omar, M., Abramson, J., & Bessette, D. (2014). *Information security in diverse computing environments*. Academic Press.

Dawson, M., Omar, M., Abramson, J., & Bessette, D. (2014). The future of national and international security on the internet. In *Information security in diverse computing environments* (pp. 149–178). IGI Global. DOI: 10.4018/978-1-4666-6158-5.ch009

Dawson, M., Omar, M., Abramson, J., Leonard, B., & Bessette, D. (2017). Battlefield cyberspace: Exploitation of hyperconnectivity and Internet of Things. In *Developing Next-Generation Countermeasures for Homeland Security Threat Prevention* (pp. 204–235). IGI Global. DOI: 10.4018/978-1-5225-0703-1.ch010

Dawson, M., Wright, J., & Omar, M. (2015). Mobile devices: The case for cyber security hardened systems. In *New Threats and Countermeasures in Digital Crime and Cyber Terrorism* (pp. 8–29). IGI Global. DOI: 10.4018/978-1-4666-8345-7.ch002

Dayoub and M. Omar. (2024). Advancing IoT security posture K-Means clustering for malware detection. In *Innovations, Securities, and Case Studies Across Healthcare, Business, and Technology* (pp. 221–239). IGI Global.

Dong, H., Wu, J., Bashir, A. K., Pan, Q., Omar, M., & Al-Dulaimi, A. "Privacy-preserving EEG signal analysis with electrode attention for depression diagnosis: Joint FHE and CNN approach," in *GLOBECOM 2023-2023 IEEE Global Communications Conference*, IEEE, 2023, pp. 4265–4270. DOI: 10.1109/GLOBECOM54140.2023.10436783

Du, X., Hargreaves, C., Sheppard, J., Anda, F., Sayakkara, A., Le-Khac, N. A., & Scanlon, M. (2020, August). SoK: Exploring the state of the art and the future potential of artificial intelligence in digital forensic investigation. In *Proceedings of the 15th international conference on availability, reliability and security* (pp. 1-10). DOI: 10.1145/3407023.3407068

Dunsin, D., Ghanem, M. C., Ouazzane, K., & Vassilev, V. (2024). A comprehensive analysis of the role of artificial intelligence and machine learning in modern digital forensics and incident response. *Forensic Science International Digital Investigation*, 48, 301675. DOI: 10.1016/j.fsidi.2023.301675

Faqir, R. S. (2023). Digital Criminal Investigations in the Era of Artificial Intelligence: A Comprehensive Overview. *International Journal of Cyber Criminology*, 17(2), 77–94.

Fawzi, D., & Omar, M. (n.d.). *New insights to database security: An effective and integrated approach to applying access control mechanisms and cryptographic concepts in Microsoft access environments*. Academic Press.

Ghillani, D. (2022). Deep learning and artificial intelligence framework to improve the cyber security. *Authorea Preprints*. DOI: 10.22541/au.166379475.54266021/v1

Gholami, S. (2024). Can pruning make large language models more efficient? In *Redefining Security With Cyber AI* (pp. 1–14). IGI Global. DOI: 10.4018/979-8-3693-6517-5.ch001

Gholami, S. (2024). Do generative large language models need billions of parameters? In *Redefining Security With Cyber AI* (pp. 37–55). IGI Global. DOI: 10.4018/979-8-3693-6517-5.ch003

Gholami, S., & Omar, M. (2023). Does Synthetic Data Make Large Language Models More Efficient? *arXiv preprint arXiv:2310.07830.*

Gholami, S., & Omar, M. "Does synthetic data make large language models more efficient?" *arXiv preprint arXiv:2310.07830*, 2023.

Gholami, S., & Omar, M. (2024). Can a student large language model perform as well as its teacher? In *Innovations, Securities, and Case Studies Across Healthcare, Business, and Technology* (pp. 122-139). IGI Global. DOI: 10.4018/979-8-3693-1906-2.ch007

Gholami, S., & Omar, M. (2024). Can a student large language model perform as well as its teacher? In *Innovations, Securities, and Case Studies Across Healthcare, Business, and Technology* (pp. 122–139). IGI Global. DOI: 10.4018/979-8-3693-1906-2.ch007

Hamza, Y. A., & Omar, M. D. (2013). Cloud computing security: Abuse and nefarious use of cloud computing. *International Journal of Computer Engineering Research*, 3(6), 22–27.

Hassan, S. K., & Ibrahim, A. (2023). The role of artificial intelligence in cyber security and incident response. *International Journal for Electronic Crime Investigation*, 7(2).

Hayes, D., & Kyobe, M. (2020, March). The adoption of automation in cyber forensics. In *2020 Conference on Information Communications Technology and Society (ICTAS)* (pp. 1-6). IEEE. DOI: 10.1109/ICTAS47918.2020.233977

Huff, J., Burrell, D. N., Nobles, C., Richardson, K., Wright, J. B., Burton, S. L., Jones, A. J., Springs, D., Omar, M., & Brown-Jackson, K. L. (2023). Management practices for mitigating cybersecurity threats to biotechnology companies, laboratories, and healthcare research organizations. In *Applied Research Approaches to Technology, Healthcare, and Business* (pp. 1–12). IGI Global. DOI: 10.4018/979-8-3693-1630-6.ch001

Iqbal, S., & Alharbi, S. A. (2020). Advancing automation in digital forensic investigations using machine learning forensics. *Digital Forensic Science, 3.*

Jabbari, H. Khan, S. Duraibi, I. Budhiraja, S. Gupta, and M. Omar, "Energy maximization for wireless powered communication enabled IoT devices with NOMA underlaying solar powered UAV using federated reinforcement learning for 6G networks," *IEEE Trans. Consum. Electron.*, 2024.

Jarrett, A., & Choo, K. K. R. (2021). The impact of automation and artificial intelligence on digital forensics. *WIREs Forensic Science*, 3(6), e1418. DOI: 10.1002/wfs2.1418

Jones, A., & Omar, M.Jones and M. Omar. (2024). Codesentry: Revolutionizing real-time software vulnerability detection with optimized GPT framework. *Land Forces Acad. Rev.*, 29(1), 98–107. DOI: 10.2478/raft-2024-0010

Jones, M., & Omar, M. (2023). *"Detection of Twitter spam with language models: A case study on how to use BERT to protect children from spam on Twitter," in 2023 Congress in Computer Science, Computer Engineering, & Applied Computing (CSCE).* IEEE.

Jones, M., & Omar, M. (2023). *"Measuring the impact of global health emergencies on self-disclosure using language models," in 2023 Congress in Computer Science, Computer Engineering, & Applied Computing (CSCE).* IEEE.

Jones, M., & Omar, M. (2023). *"Studying the effects of social media content on kids' safety and well-being," in 2023 Congress in Computer Science, Computer Engineering, & Applied Computing (CSCE).* IEEE.

Jones, R., & Omar, M. "Detecting IoT Malware with Knowledge Distillation Technique," in *2023 Congress in Computer Science, Computer Engineering, & Applied Computing (CSCE)*, pp. 131-135, IEEE, 2023. DOI: 10.1109/CSCE60160.2023.00026

Jones, R., & Omar, M. (2024). Revolutionizing Cybersecurity: The GPT-2 Enhanced Attack Detection and Defense (GEADD) Method for Zero-Day Threats. *International Journal of Informatics* [INJIISCOM]. *Information System and Computer Engineering*, 5(2), 178–191.

Jones, R., & Omar, M. (2024). Codeguard: Utilizing Advanced Pattern Recognition in Language Models for Software Vulnerability Analysis. *Land Forces Academy Review*, 29(1), 108–118. DOI: 10.2478/raft-2024-0011

Jones, R., & Omar, M. (2024). Revolutionizing Cybersecurity: The GPT-2 Enhanced Attack Detection and Defense (GEADD) Method for Zero-Day Threats [INJIISCOM]. *International Journal of Informatics, Information System and Computer Engineering*, 5(2), 178–191. DOI: 10.34010/injiiscom.v5i2.12741

Jones, R., Omar, M., & Mohammed, D. "Harnessing the Power of the GPT Model to Generate Adversarial Examples," in *2023 Congress in Computer Science, Computer Engineering, & Applied Computing (CSCE)*, pp. 1699-1702, IEEE, 2023. DOI: 10.1109/CSCE60160.2023.00279

Jones, R., Omar, M., Mohammed, D., & Nobles, C. "IoT Malware Detection with GPT Models," in *2023 Congress in Computer Science, Computer Engineering, & Applied Computing (CSCE)*, pp. 1749-1752, IEEE, 2023. DOI: 10.1109/CSCE60160.2023.00288

Jones, R., Omar, M., Mohammed, D., Nobles, C., & Dawson, M. (2023). Harnessing the Speed and Accuracy of Machine Learning to Advance Cybersecurity. In *2023 Congress in Computer Science, Computer Engineering, & Applied Computing (CSCE)* (pp. 418-421). IEEE. DOI: 10.1109/CSCE60160.2023.00074

Jones and M. Omar. (2023). *"Harnessing the efficiency of reformers to detect software vulnerabilities," in 2023 Congress in Computer Science, Computer Engineering, & Applied Computing (CSCE).* IEEE.

Jones and M. Omar. (2023). *"Optimized decision trees to detect IoT malware," in 2023 Congress in Computer Science, Computer Engineering, & Applied Computing (CSCE).* IEEE.

Jun, W., Iqbal, M. S., Abbasi, R., Omar, M., & Huiqin, C. "Web-Semantic-Driven Machine Learning and Blockchain for Transformative Change in the Future of Physical Education," *International Journal on Semantic Web and Information Systems (IJSWIS)*, vol. 20, no. 1, pp. 1-16, IGI Global, 2024. DOI: 10.4018/IJSWIS.337961

Kaur, R., Gabrijelčič, D., & Klobučar, T. (2023). Artificial intelligence for cybersecurity: Literature review and future research directions. *Information Fusion*, 97, 101804. DOI: 10.1016/j.inffus.2023.101804

Khan, S. A., Alkawaz, M. H., & Zangana, H. M. "The use and abuse of social media for spreading fake news," in *2019 IEEE International Conference on Automatic Control and Intelligent Systems (I2CACIS)*, pp. 145-148, IEEE, 2019. DOI: 10.1109/I2CACIS.2019.8825029

V. A. Kumar, S. Surapaneni, D. Pavitra, R. Venkatesan, M. Omar, and A. K. Bashir, "An Internet of Medical Things-Based Mental Disorder Prediction System Using EEG Sensor and Big Data Mining," *Journal of Circuits, Systems and Computers*, vol. 2450197, World Scientific Publishing Company, 2024.

Majeed, H. (2020). Watermarking Image Depending on Mojette Transform for Hiding Information. *International Journal on Computer Science and Engineering*, 8, 8–12.

Mohammed, D., Omar, M., & Nguyen, V. (2018). Wireless sensor network security: Approaches to detecting and avoiding wormhole attacks. *Journal of Research in Business. Economics and Management*, 10(2), 1860–1864.

Mohammed, M. O., & Nguyen, V. (2017). Enhancing Cyber Security for Financial Industry through Compliance and Regulatory Standards. In *Security Solutions for Hyperconnectivity and the Internet of Things* (pp. 113–129). IGI Global. DOI: 10.4018/978-1-5225-0741-3.ch005

Mohammed, M. O., & Nguyen, V. (2018). Wireless Sensor Network Security: Approaches to Detecting and Avoiding Wormhole Attacks. *Journal of Research in Business, Economics and Management*, 10(2), 1860–1864.

Mohammed and M. Omar. "Decision Trees Unleashed: Simplifying IoT Malware Detection With Advanced AI Techniques," in *Innovations, Securities, and Case Studies Across Healthcare, Business, and Technology*, pp. 240-258, IGI Global, 2024.

Montasari, R. (2023). *Countering cyberterrorism: the confluence of artificial intelligence, cyber forensics and digital policing in US and UK national cybersecurity* (Vol. 101). Springer Nature. DOI: 10.1007/978-3-031-21920-7

Moustafa, N. (2022). *Digital Forensics in the Era of Artificial Intelligence*. CRC Press. DOI: 10.1201/9781003278962

Mughal, A. A. (2019). A comprehensive study of practical techniques and methodologies in incident-based approaches for cyber forensics. *Tensorgate Journal of Sustainable Technology and Infrastructure for Developing Countries*, 2(1), 1–18.

Murphy, J. P. (2022). *Digital Forensic Investigations and Automated and Artificial Intelligence Technologies* (Master's thesis, Utica University).

Nair, M. M., Deshmukh, A., & Tyagi, A. K. (2024). Artificial intelligence for cyber security: Current trends and future challenges. *Automated Secure Computing for Next-Generation Systems*, 83-114.

Nguyen, V., Mohammed, D., Omar, M., & Banisakher, M. (2018). The Effects of the FCC Net Neutrality Repeal on Security and Privacy. [IJHIoT]. *International Journal of Hyperconnectivity and the Internet of Things*, 2(2), 21–29. DOI: 10.4018/IJHIoT.2018070102

V. Nguyen, M. Omar, and D. Mohammed, "A Security Framework for Enhancing User Experience," *International Journal of Hyperconnectivity and the Internet of Things (IJHIoT)*, vol. 1, no. 1, pp. 19-28, IGI Global, 2017.

Nguyen, V., Omar, M., Mohammed, D., & Dean, P. "Net Neutrality Around the Globe: A Survey," in *2020 3rd International Conference on Information and Computer Technologies (ICICT)*, pp. 480-488, IEEE, 2020. DOI: 10.1109/ICICT50521.2020.00083

Omar, M. *Smartphone Security: Defending Android-based Smartphone Against Emerging Malware Attacks* (Doctoral dissertation, Colorado Technical University), 2012.

Omar, M. "Insider Threats: Detecting and Controlling Malicious Insiders," in *New Threats and Countermeasures in Digital Crime and Cyber Terrorism*, pp. 162-172, IGI Global, 2015. DOI: 10.4018/978-1-4666-8345-7.ch009

Omar, M. "Cloud Computing Security: Abuse and Nefarious Use of Cloud Computing," in *Handbook of Research on Security Considerations in Cloud Computing*, pp. 30-38, IGI Global, 2015. DOI: 10.4018/978-1-4666-8387-7.ch002

Omar, M. (2019). A World of Cyber Attacks. *Survey (London, England).*

M. Omar, "New Insights into Database Security: An Effective and Integrated Approach for Applying Access Control Mechanisms and Cryptographic Concepts in Microsoft Access Environments," 2021.

Omar, M. (2022). *Machine Learning for Cybersecurity: Innovative Deep Learning Solutions*. Springer Brief. https://link.springer.com/book/978303115

Omar, M. "Application of Machine Learning (ML) to Address Cybersecurity Threats," in *Machine Learning for Cybersecurity: Innovative Deep Learning Solutions*, pp. 1-11, Springer International Publishing Cham, 2022. DOI: 10.1007/978-3-031-15893-3_1

Omar, M. *Machine Learning for Cybersecurity: Innovative Deep Learning Solutions*, Springer Brief, 2022. https://link.springer.com/book/978303115

Omar, M. "Malware Anomaly Detection Using Local Outlier Factor Technique," in *Machine Learning for Cybersecurity: Innovative Deep Learning Solutions*, pp. 37-48, Springer International Publishing Cham, 2022. DOI: 10.1007/978-3-031-15893-3_3

Omar, M. "VulDefend: A Novel Technique Based on Pattern-Exploiting Training for Detecting Software Vulnerabilities Using Language Models," in *2023 IEEE Jordan International Joint Conference on Electrical Engineering and Information Technology (JEEIT)*, pp. 287-293, IEEE, 2023. DOI: 10.1109/JEEIT58638.2023.10185860

Omar, M. (2024). From Attack to Defense: Strengthening DNN Text Classification Against Adversarial Examples. In *Innovations, Securities, and Case Studies Across Healthcare, Business, and Technology* (pp. 174-195). IGI Global.

Omar, M. (2024). Revolutionizing Malware Detection: A Paradigm Shift Through Optimized Convolutional Neural Networks. In *Innovations, Securities, and Case Studies Across Healthcare, Business, and Technology* (pp. 196-220). IGI Global. DOI: 10.4018/979-8-3693-1906-2.ch011

Omar, M. "From Attack to Defense: Strengthening DNN Text Classification Against Adversarial Examples," in *Innovations, Securities, and Case Studies Across Healthcare, Business, and Technology*, pp. 174-195, IGI Global, 2024. DOI: 10.4018/979-8-3693-1906-2.ch010

Omar, M. "Revolutionizing Malware Detection: A Paradigm Shift Through Optimized Convolutional Neural Networks," in *Innovations, Securities, and Case Studies Across Healthcare, Business, and Technology*, pp. 196-220, IGI Global, 2024. DOI: 10.4018/979-8-3693-1906-2.ch011

Omar, M. *Defending Cyber Systems through Reverse Engineering of Criminal Malware*, Springer Brief, [n.d.][n.d.].https://link.springer.com/book/9783031116278

M. Omar, *Latina Davis Morgan State University 1700 E Cold Spring Ln. Baltimore, MD 21251, USA E-mail: latinaedavis@ hotmail.com*, [n.d.][n.d.].

M. Omar, *Machine Learning for Cybersecurity*, [n.d.][n.d.].

Omar, M.. (2024). Committee Members. *Journal of Physics: Conference Series*, 2711, 011001.

M. Omar and D. Burrell, "From Text to Threats: A Language Model Approach to Software Vulnerability Detection," *International Journal of Mathematics and Computer in Engineering*, 2023.

Omar, M., & Burrell, D. N. "Organizational Dynamics and Bias in Artificial Intelligence (AI) Recruitment Algorithms," in *Evolution of Cross-Sector Cyber Intelligent Markets*, pp. 269-290, IGI Global, 2024.

Omar, M., Choi, S., Nyang, D., & Mohaisen, D. "Quantifying the Performance of Adversarial Training on Language Models with Distribution Shifts," in *Proceedings of the 1st Workshop on Cybersecurity and Social Sciences*, pp. 3-9, 2022. DOI: 10.1145/3494108.3522764

Omar, M., Choi, S., Nyang, D., & Mohaisen, D. (2022). Robust Natural Language Processing: Recent Advances, Challenges, and Future Directions. *IEEE Access : Practical Innovations, Open Solutions*, 10, 86038–86056. DOI: 10.1109/ACCESS.2022.3197769

Omar, M., & Dawson, M. "Research in Progress-Defending Android Smartphones from Malware Attacks," in *2013 Third International Conference on Advanced Computing and Communication Technologies (ACCT)*, pp. 288-292, IEEE, 2013. DOI: 10.1109/ACCT.2013.69

Omar, M., Gouveia, L. B., Al-Karaki, J., & Mohammed, D. "Reverse-Engineering Malware," in *Cybersecurity Capabilities in Developing Nations and Its Impact on Global Security*, pp. 194-217, IGI Global, 2022. DOI: 10.4018/978-1-7998-8693-8.ch010

Omar, M., Jones, R., Burrell, D. N., Dawson, M., Nobles, C., & Mohammed, D. "Harnessing the Power and Simplicity of Decision Trees to Detect IoT Malware," in *Transformational Interventions for Business, Technology, and Healthcare*, pp. 215-229, IGI, 2023. DOI: 10.4018/979-8-3693-1634-4.ch013

Omar, M., & Mohaisen, D. "Making Adversarially-Trained Language Models Forget with Model Retraining: A Case Study on Hate Speech Detection," in *Companion Proceedings of the Web Conference 2022*, pp. 887-893, 2022. DOI: 10.1145/3487553.3524667

Omar, M., Mohammed, D., & Nguyen, V. (2017). Defending Against Malicious Insiders: A Conceptual Framework for Predicting, Detecting, and Deterring Malicious Insiders. *International Journal of Business Process Integration and Management*, 8(2), 114–119. DOI: 10.1504/IJBPIM.2017.083794

Omar, M., Mohammed, D., Nguyen, V., Dawson, M., & Banisakher, M. "Android Application Security," in *Research Anthology on Securing Mobile Technologies and Applications*, pp. 610-625, IGI Global, 2021. DOI: 10.4018/978-1-7998-8545-0.ch034

Omar, M., & Shiaeles, S. "VulDetect: A Novel Technique for Detecting Software Vulnerabilities Using Language Models," in *2023 IEEE International Conference on Cyber Security and Resilience (CSR)*, IEEE. https://ieeexplore.ieee.org/document/10224924

Omar, M., & Sukthankar, G. "Text-Defend: Detecting Adversarial Examples Using Local Outlier Factor," in *2023 IEEE 17th International Conference on Semantic Computing (ICSC)*, pp. 118-122, IEEE, 2023. DOI: 10.1109/ICSC56153.2023.00026

Omar, M., & Zangana, H. M. (Eds.). (2024). *Redefining Security With Cyber AI*. IGI Global., DOI: 10.4018/979-8-3693-6517-5

Omar, M., & Zangana, H. M. (2024). *Redefining Security With Cyber AI*. IGI Global., DOI: 10.4018/979-8-3693-6517-5

Pauu, K. T., Pan, Q., Wu, J., Bashir, A. K., & Omar, M. "IRS-Aided Federated Learning with Dynamic Differential Privacy for UAVs in Emergency Response," *IEEE Internet of Things Magazine*, vol. 7, no. 4, pp. 108-115, IEEE, 2024. DOI: 10.1109/IOTM.001.2400021

Peng, Y.. (2024). *"An Intelligent Resource Allocation Strategy with Slicing and Auction for Private Edge Cloud Systems," Future Generation Computer Systems* (Vol. 160). North-Holland.

Piraianu, A. I., Fulga, A., Musat, C. L., Ciobotaru, O. R., Poalelungi, D. G., Stamate, E., Ciobotaru, O., & Fulga, I. (2023). Enhancing the evidence with algorithms: How artificial intelligence is transforming forensic medicine. *Diagnostics (Basel)*, 13(18), 2992. DOI: 10.3390/diagnostics13182992 PMID: 37761359

Rajesh, R.. (2024). Threat Detection and Mitigation for Tactile Internet Driven Consumer IoT-Healthcare System. *IEEE Transactions on Consumer Electronics*.

Tyagi, A. K., Kumari, S., & Richa. (2024). Artificial Intelligence-Based Cyber Security and Digital Forensics: A Review. *Artificial Intelligence-Enabled Digital Twin for Smart Manufacturing*, 391-419.

Rizvi, S., Scanlon, M., Mcgibney, J., & Sheppard, J. (2022). Application of artificial intelligence to network forensics: Survey, challenges and future directions. *IEEE Access : Practical Innovations, Open Solutions*, 10, 110362–110384. DOI: 10.1109/ACCESS.2022.3214506

Saleem, M. A.. (2023). Provably Secure Conditional-Privacy Access Control Protocol for Intelligent Customers-Centric Communication in VANET. *IEEE Transactions on Consumer Electronics*.

Samtani, S., Kantarcioglu, M., & Chen, H. (2020). Trailblazing the artificial intelligence for cybersecurity discipline: A multi-disciplinary research roadmap. [TMIS]. *ACM Transactions on Management Information Systems*, 11(4), 1–19. DOI: 10.1145/3430360

Sikos, L. F. (2021). AI in digital forensics: Ontology engineering for cybercrime investigations. *WIREs Forensic Science*, 3(3), e1394. DOI: 10.1002/wfs2.1394

Stutz, D., de Assis, J. T., Laghari, A. A., Khan, A. A., Andreopoulos, N., Terziev, A., ... & Grata, E. G. (2024). Enhancing Security in Cloud Computing Using Artificial Intelligence (AI). *Applying Artificial Intelligence in Cybersecurity Analytics and Cyber Threat Detection*, 179-220.

Sun, Y., Xu, T., Bashir, A. K., Liu, J., & Omar, M. "BcIIS: Blockchain-Based Intelligent Identification Scheme of Massive IoT Devices," in *GLOBECOM 2023-2023 IEEE Global Communications Conference*, pp. 1277-1282, IEEE, 2023. DOI: 10.1109/GLOBECOM54140.2023.10437203

Syed, F. M., & ES, F. K. (2024). AI-Driven Forensic Analysis for Cyber Incidents in Healthcare. *International Journal of Machine Learning Research in Cybersecurity and Artificial Intelligence*, 15(1), 473–499.

Tao, F., Akhtar, M. S., & Jiayuan, Z. (2021). The future of artificial intelligence in cybersecurity: A comprehensive survey. *EAI Endorsed Transactions on Creative Technologies*, 8(28), e3–e3. DOI: 10.4108/eai.7-7-2021.170285

Tao, Y., Wu, J., Pan, Q., Bashir, A. K., & Omar, M. (2024). O-RAN-Based Digital Twin Function Virtualization for Sustainable IoV Service Response: An Asynchronous Hierarchical Reinforcement Learning Approach. *IEEE Transactions on Green Communications and Networking*, 8(3), 1049–1060. DOI: 10.1109/TGCN.2024.3435796

Tiwari, N., Ghadi, Y., & Omar, M. "Analysis of Ultrasound Images in Kidney Failure Diagnosis Using Deep Learning," in *Transformational Interventions for Business, Technology, and Healthcare*, pp. 45-74, IGI Global, 2023. DOI: 10.4018/979-8-3693-1634-4.ch004

Tiwari, N., Omar, M., & Ghadi, Y. "Brain Tumor Classification From Magnetic Resonance Imaging Using Deep Learning and Novel Data Augmentation," in *Transformational Interventions for Business, Technology, and Healthcare*, pp. 392-413, IGI Global, 2023. DOI: 10.4018/979-8-3693-1634-4.ch023

Tuli, F. A., & Thaduri, U. R. (2023). The Integration of Artificial Intelligence in Forensic Accounting: A Game-Changer. *Asian Accounting and Auditing Advancement*, 14(1), 12–20.

Ukwen, D. O., & Karabatak, M. (2021, June). Review of NLP-based systems in digital forensics and cybersecurity. In *2021 9th International symposium on digital forensics and security (ISDFS)* (pp. 1-9). IEEE. DOI: 10.1109/ISDFS52919.2021.9486354

Umer, M., Aljrees, T., Karamti, H., Ishaq, A., Alsubai, S., Omar, M., Bashir, A. K., & Ashraf, I. (2023). Heart Failure Patients Monitoring Using IoT-Based Remote Monitoring System. *Scientific Reports*, 13(1), 19213. DOI: 10.1038/s41598-023-46322-6 PMID: 37932424

Vitianingsih, V., Firmansyah, D., Maukar, A. L., Kacung, S., & Zangana, H. M. (2024, August). Recommendation System for Determining the Best Banner Supplier Using Profile Matching and TOPSIS Methods. *Intensif Jurnal Ilmiah Penelitian Teknologi Dan Penerapan Sistem Informasi*, 8(2), 246–262. DOI: 10.29407/intensif.v8i2.21635

Wright, J., Dawson, M. E.Jr, & Omar, M. (2012). Cyber Security and Mobile Threats: The Need for Antivirus Applications for Smartphones. *Journal of Information Systems Technology and Planning*, 5(14), 40–60.

Xu, X., Wu, J., Bashir, A. K., & Omar, M. (2024). Machine Learning and Zero Knowledge Empowered Trustworthy Bitcoin Mixing for Next-G Consumer Electronics Payment. *IEEE Transactions on Consumer Electronics*, 70(1), 2210–2223. DOI: 10.1109/TCE.2024.3361690

H. M. Zangana, "A New Skin Color Based Face Detection Algorithm by Combining Three Color Model Algorithms," *IOSR Journal of Computer Engineering*, vol. 17, pp. 06-125, 2015.

H. M. Zangana, "A new algorithm for shape detection," *IOSR Journal of Computer Engineering (IOSR-JCE)*, vol. 19, no. 3, pp. 71-76, 2017.

H. M. Zangana, "Library Data Quality Maturity (IIUM as a Case Study)," *IOSR-JCE*, vol. 29, Mar. 2017.

Zangana, H. M. (2017). Watermarking System Using LSB. *IOSR Journal of Computer Engineering*, 19(3), 75–79. DOI: 10.9790/0661-1903027579

Zangana, H. M. (2018). Design an information management system for a pharmacy. *International Journal of Advanced Research in Computer and Communication Engineering*, 7(10), 52–55. DOI: 10.17148/IJARCCE.2018.71012

Zangana, H. M. "Developing Data Warehouse for Student Information System (IIUM as a Case Study)," *International Organization of Scientific Research*, vol. 20, no. 1, pp. 09-14, 2018.

H. M. Zangana, "Implementing a System for Recognizing Optical Characters," 2018.

H. M. Zangana, "Issues of Data Management in the Library: A Case Study," 2019.

H. M. Zangana, "ITD Data Quality Maturity (A Case Study)," *International Journal Of Engineering And Computer Science*, vol. 8, no. 10, 2019.

Zangana, H. M. (2020). Mobile Device Integration in IIUM Service. *International Journal (Toronto, Ont.)*, 8(5).

Zangana, H. M. (2021). The Global Financial Crisis from an Islamic Point Of View. *Qubahan Academic Journal*, 1(2), 55–59. DOI: 10.48161/qaj.v1n2a39

Zangana, H. M. (2022). Creating a Community-Based Disaster Management System. *Academic Journal of Nawroz University*, 11(4), 234–244. DOI: 10.25007/ajnu.v11n4a1485

Zangana, H. M. (2022). Implementing New Interactive Video Learning System for IIUM. *Academic Journal of Nawroz University*, 11(2), 23–29. DOI: 10.25007/ajnu.v11n2a1281

H. M. Zangana, "Improving The Web Services for Remittance Company: Express Remit as a Case Study," *Academic Journal of Nawroz University (AJNU)*, vol. 11, no. 3, 2022.

Zangana, H. M. (2024). Exploring the Landscape of Website Vulnerability Scanners: A Comprehensive Review and Comparative Analysis. *Redefining Security With Cyber AI*, 111-129.

Zangana, H. M. (2024). Exploring Blockchain-Based Timestamping Tools: A Comprehensive Review. *Redefining Security With Cyber AI*, 92-110.

Zangana, H. M. (2024). *Exploring Blockchain-Based Timestamping Tools: A Comprehensive Review*. Redefining Security With Cyber AI. DOI: 10.4018/979-8-3693-6517-5.ch006

Zangana, H. M. (2024). *Exploring the Landscape of Website Vulnerability Scanners: A Comprehensive Review and Comparative Analysis*. Redefining Security With Cyber AI. DOI: 10.4018/979-8-3693-6517-5.ch007

H. M. Zangana, "CHALLENGES AND ISSUES of MANET," 2024.

Zangana, H. M., & Abdulazeez, A. M. (2023). Developed Clustering Algorithms for Engineering Applications: A Review [INJIISCOM]. *International Journal of Informatics, Information System and Computer Engineering*, 4(2), 147–169. DOI: 10.34010/injiiscom.v4i2.11636

Zangana, H. M., & Al-Shaikhli, I. F. (2013). A new algorithm for human face detection using skin color tone. *IOSR Journal of Computer Engineering*, 11(6), 31–38. DOI: 10.9790/0661-1163138

Zangana, H. M., Al-Shaikhli, I. F., & Graha, Y. I. (2013). The Ethical Dilemma of Software Piracy: An Inquiry from an Islamic Perspective. *Creative Communication and Innovative Technology Journal*, 7(1), 59–76. DOI: 10.33050/ccit.v7i1.171

Zangana, H. M., Bazeed, S. M. S., Ali, N. Y., & Abdullah, D. T. (2024). Navigating Project Change: A Comprehensive Review of Change Management Strategies and Practices. *Indonesian Journal of Education and Social Sciences*, 3(2), 166–179. DOI: 10.56916/ijess.v3i2.735

Zangana, H. M., Graha, Y. I., & Al-Shaikhli, I. F. (2024). Blogging: A New Platform For Spreading Rumors! *Creative Communication and Innovative Technology Journal*, 9(1), 71–76.

Zangana, H. M., Khalid Mohammed, A., & Zeebaree, S. R. (2024). Systematic Review of Decentralized and Collaborative Computing Models in Cloud Architectures for Distributed Edge Computing. *Sistemasi: Jurnal Sistem Informasi*, 13(4), 1501–1509. DOI: 10.32520/stmsi.v13i4.4169

Zangana, H. M., Mohammed, A. K., & Mustafa, F. M. (2024). Advancements and Applications of Convolutional Neural Networks in Image Analysis: A Comprehensive Review. *Jurnal Ilmiah Computer Science*, 3(1), 16–29.

Zangana, H. M., Mohammed, A. K., & Mustafa, F. M. (2024). Advancements in Edge Detection Techniques for Image Enhancement: A Comprehensive Review [IJAIR]. *International Journal of Artificial Intelligence & Robotics*, 6(1), 29–39. DOI: 10.25139/ijair.v6i1.8217

Zangana, H. M., Mohammed, A. K., Sallow, A. B., & Sallow, Z. B. (2024). Cybernetic Deception: Unraveling the Layers of Email Phishing Threats. [INJURATECH]. *International Journal of Research and Applied Technology*, 4(1), 35–47.

Zangana, H. M., Mohammed, A. K., Sallow, A. B., & Sallow, Z. B. (2024). Cybernetic Deception: Unraveling the Layers of Email Phishing Threats [INJURATECH]. *International Journal of Research and Applied Technology*, 4(1), 35–47.

Zangana, H. M., Mohammed, A. K., Sallow, Z. B., & Mustafa, F. M. (2024). Exploring Image Representation and Color Spaces in Computer Vision: A Comprehensive Review. *The Indonesian Journal of Computer Science*, 13(3). Advance online publication. DOI: 10.33022/ijcs.v13i3.3998

Zangana, H. M., & Mustafa, F. M. (2024). From Classical to Deep Learning: A Systematic Review of Image Denoising Techniques. *Jurnal Ilmiah Computer Science*, 3(1), 50–65.

Zangana, H. M., & Mustafa, F. M. (2024). Review of Hybrid Denoising Approaches in Face Recognition: Bridging Wavelet Transform and Deep Learning. *The Indonesian Journal of Computer Science*, 13(4). Advance online publication. DOI: 10.33022/ijcs.v13i4.4209

Zangana, H. M., & Mustafa, F. M. (2024). Surveying the Landscape: A Comprehensive Review of Object Detection Algorithms and Advancements. *Jurnal Ilmiah Computer Science*, 3(1), 1–15.

Zangana, H. M., & Omar, M. (2020). Threats, Attacks, and Mitigations of Smartphone Security. *Academic Journal of Nawroz University*, 9(4), 324–332. DOI: 10.25007/ajnu.v9n4a989

Zangana, H. M., & Omar, M. (2020). Threats, Attacks, and Mitigations of Smartphone Security. *Academic Journal of Nawroz University*, 9(4), 324–332. DOI: 10.25007/ajnu.v9n4a989

Zangana, H. M., Omar, M., Al-Karaki, J. N., & Mohammed, D. (2024). Comprehensive Review and Analysis of Network Firewall Rule Analyzers: Enhancing Security Posture and Efficiency. *Redefining Security With Cyber AI*, 15-36.

Zangana, H. M., Omar, M., Al-Karaki, J. N., & Mohammed, D. (2024). *Comprehensive Review and Analysis of Network Firewall Rule Analyzers: Enhancing Security Posture and Efficiency*. Redefining Security With Cyber AI. DOI: 10.4018/979-8-3693-6517-5.ch002

Zangana, H. M., Omar, M., & Ali, N. Y. (2024). Harnessing Artificial Intelligence in Modern Marketing: Strategies, Benefits, and Challenges [BAMJ]. *Business, Accounting and Management Journal*, 02(02), 70–82.

Zangana, H. M., Sallow, Z. B., Alkawaz, M. H., & Omar, M. "Unveiling the Collective Wisdom: A Review of Swarm Intelligence in Problem Solving and Optimization," *Inform: Jurnal Ilmiah Bidang Teknologi Informasi dan Komunikasi*, vol. 9, no. 2, pp. 101-110, 2024.

Zangana, H. M., & Zeebaree, S. R. (2024). Distributed Systems for Artificial Intelligence in Cloud Computing: A Review of AI-Powered Applications and Services [INJIISCOM]. *International Journal of Informatics, Information System and Computer Engineering*, 5(1), 11–30. DOI: 10.34010/injiiscom.v5i1.11883

Zeadally, S., Adi, E., Baig, Z., & Khan, I. A. (2020). Harnessing artificial intelligence capabilities to improve cybersecurity. *IEEE Access : Practical Innovations, Open Solutions*, 8, 23817–23837. DOI: 10.1109/ACCESS.2020.2968045

Zhang, H., Wu, J., Pan, Q., Bashir, A. K., & Omar, M. (2024). Toward Byzantine-Robust Distributed Learning for Sentiment Classification on Social Media Platform. *IEEE Transactions on Computational Social Systems*, 1–11. DOI: 10.1109/TCSS.2024.3361465

Zhang, H., Wu, J., Pan, Q., Bashir, A. K., & Omar, M. (2024). Toward Byzantine-Robust Distributed Learning for Sentiment Classification on Social Media Platform. *IEEE Transactions on Computational Social Systems*, 1–11. DOI: 10.1109/TCSS.2024.3361465

Zhou, S., Ali, A., Al-Fuqaha, A., Omar, M., & Feng, L. (2024). Robust Risk-Sensitive Task Offloading for Edge-Enabled Industrial Internet of Things. *IEEE Transactions on Consumer Electronics*, 70(1), 1403–1413. DOI: 10.1109/TCE.2023.3323146

Chapter 10
Improving AppSec Resiliency, Monitoring, Risk Assessment, and Compliance by Bridging DevSecOps With SOCs

Angel Justo Jones
https://orcid.org/0009-0007-9740-6611
University of Virginia, USA

ABSTRACT

This chapter examines the evolution and integration of DevSecOps and Security Operations Centers (SOCs), emphasizing enhanced cybersecurity management through collaborative models. This study explores the theoretical underpinnings of DevSecOps using the Development and Cybersecurity Adoption Model (DCAM) and the Information Systems Development Acceptance Model (ISDAM), derived from the Theory of Planned Behavior (TPB). It investigates how these models facilitate the adoption of DevSecOps in SOCs, aiming to reduce vulnerabilities and enhance operational efficiency. The quantitative analysis focuses on identifying barriers to DevSecOps implementation and evaluating the effectiveness of bridging DevSecOps with SOCs in organizational settings. Results suggest that integrated approaches can significantly mitigate cybersecurity risks and foster a resilient digital infrastructure. This chapter contributes to academic and practical knowledge of cybersecurity by highlighting the benefits of merging development, operations, and security practices within organizational cybersecurity strategies.

DOI: 10.4018/979-8-3373-0588-2.ch010

INTRODUCTION

In 2004, Google's company leadership made an extraordinary decision. Instead of assigning network management responsibility to an information technology (IT) team, which constituted the standard best practice of the day, Google delegated this critical task to their development team (Mao et al., 2020; Maroukian & Gulliver, 2020; Rajapakse et al., 2021). The development team, a group of site reliability engineers (SREs), automated all repetitive infrastructure tasks that were error-prone and provided little value to the company's future (Rafi et al., 2020; Rowse & Cohen, 2021; Trihinas et al., 2018). The SREs termed those tasks "toil" and started a movement that would not have a name for another six years: DevOps, which combines development and operations teams into one cohesive unit. According to Marini-Wear (2019), DevOps is a process that enables continuous software enhancements via fast deployment cycles and facilitates intense automation and collaborative team interactions. In contrast, DevSecOps, the topic of the current study, not only integrates development and operations groups but also includes security personnel so that the DevOps process includes cybersecurity practices (Computer Security Division, 2020). DevSecOps serves as an updated process that automatically generates cybersecurity and compliance artifacts throughout the DevOps process (Computer Security Division, 2020).

DevSecOps is a philosophy emphasizing the need to incorporate cybersecurity principles into DevOps (Mao et al., 2020). DevSecOps is merely an expansion of the process-driven DevOps to include measures related to cybersecurity (Mao et al., 2020; Maroukian & Gulliver, 2020; Rajapakse et al., 2021). DevSecOps aims to provide safe and secure applications and infrastructure, making the application or infrastructure ready for users' demands and less vulnerable to outside attacks (Maroukian & Gulliver, 2020). As such, the primary objective of DevSecOps is to safeguard application development by integrating cybersecurity and operations group members into the DevOps team, allowing for collaboration with the development team from the start and throughout the project lifecycle (Mao et al., 2020). This notion leads to the DevSecOps methodology, which, according to Mao et al. (2020), focuses on bonding the usually siloed functions of cybersecurity, operations, and development into a cooperative, shared responsibility setting.

DevSecOps adoption provides various benefits to cybersecurity, operations, and development teams. According to Mao et al. (2020), the effective adoption of DevSecOps culture provides a competitive advantage over an institution's competitors by facilitating rapidly innovative business products faster and more securely than traditional software development approaches. With DevSecOps, software development teams will likely identify and avoid vulnerabilities instead of encountering potential data losses uncovered only after application deployment (Myrbakken & Colomo-

Palacios, 2017). DevSecOps implementation is automatic, shifting cybersecurity from earlier developments as a requirement in the application development, thereby addressing the vulnerabilities within the application for cyberattacks (Myrbakken & Colomo-Palacios, 2017). In DevSecOps, the configuration of safety consoles creates time for cybersecurity personnel to manage other concerns, which increases their overall speed and agility. DevSecOps does not require cybersecurity professionals when implementing automation, leaving these personnel to address other problems in an interdisciplinary environment (Rajapakse et al., 2021).

DevSecOps contributes to corporate value and benefits via resources and money saved related to the value stream, reduced vulnerabilities, threats, enhanced operations, increased quality, and described rework through automated testing and delivery of products on time or early (Zaydi & Nassereddine, 2020). These benefits indicate that DevSecOps is a significant component that organizations can implement, particularly in the cybersecurity division. Importantly, models exist for shifting from traditional software development to a DevSecOps culture. Early results show that DevSecOps, when appropriately implemented, further improves communication and teamwork among members from different divisions (Rajapakse et al., 2021). Rajapakse et al. (2021) indicated another critical benefit of DevSecOps adoption is adaptability in handling abrupt improvements during a project life cycle. DevSecOps is only half of the overall picture. While these studies show the promise of DevSecOps, more research is required to understand the nuances of how DevSecOps interacts with SOCs, the next layer of security operations. Before integrating DevSecOps it is crucial to evaluate the organization's current cybersecurity posture, data preparedness, and technical capabilities. This requires a thorough assessment of existing cybersecurity tools, the volume and quality of available data, and the skillset within the cybersecurity team (Jones & Jones, 2024).

Historically, traditional software development approaches create software in separate departments, comprising development and operations functions. The developer's role is to code and test software, while the operations department is responsible for deploying the software (Rajapakse et al., 2021). Like other operations departments within an organization, SOCs experience challenges monitoring infrastructure due to shifting operations from traditional software engineering approaches to DevSecOps (Mao et al., 2020; Maroukian & Gulliver, 2020; Rajapakse et al., 2021). A SOC is a centralized function within a business that integrates individuals, technology, and procedures to continuously monitor and enhance an organization's cybersecurity posture while averting, detecting, evaluating, and reacting to cybersecurity threats (Pandey, 2019). In a traditional DevSecOps setup, a SOC takes telemetry data from DevSecOps environments to monitor vulnerabilities and malicious activity. In this way, the SOC can respond to threats targeted toward the DevSecOps environment and prevent or minimize the risk of a security breach (Mao et al., 2020; Maroukian

& Gulliver, 2020). Due to the significant roles of SOCs, cybersecurity experts are the primary staff in SOCs, as they monitor and assess information that flows within and across a corporate infrastructure (Fearer, 2020). Factors influencing the collaboration between software developers and SOCs in a DevSecOps setting were examined.

The present exploratory quantitative study investigated the barriers to implementation and the significance of bridging monitoring DevSecOps environments within SOCs. This research effort, founded on the collaboration between development and operations, also known as DevOps, further expands the DCAM. DCAM, developed by Masombuka and Mnkandla (2018), aims to identify factors impacting the adoption of DevSecOps and how DevOps collaboration attributes influence developers' and operators' acceptance of DevOps, highlighting the possibility that the DevOps environment hinders DevSecOps. The information systems development acceptance model (ISDAM) is the foundation of DCAM. ISDAM derives from the theory of planned behavior (TPB) and provides DCAM with three components, which include: (a) perceived behavioral control, (b) subjective norm, and (c) attitude. Developed by Icek Ajzen, TPB predicts that behaviors determine behavioral intentions, influenced primarily by an individual's attitude toward a behavior, the subjective norms encasing the execution of the behavior, and the individual's perception of their control over the behavior (Ajzen, 1991). TPB denotes a psychological concept linking behavior to beliefs. This study was built upon DCAM by expanding TPB to determine factors affecting the adoption and collaboration of DevSecOps at SOCs.

Gaps In Literature

The current study adds to the existing body of knowledge concerning the issues of technology acceptance by organizations. It is important to note that there are limited research addressing the integration of DevSecOps with SOCs to enhance cybersecurity. Existing studies only highlight the roles of SOCs and DevSecOps, in silos, without exploring the complexities in their implementation when applied in an integrated environment. No researcher has examined this integration of DevSecOps and SOCs through the lens of DCAM. John Willis, one of the authors of "The DevOps Handbook," remarked in an interview in March 2021 that individuals taking part in the DevOps movement felt they made a tremendous achievement but seemed oblivious to concerns regarding security issues. The present study identified a gap in the literature regarding the problems of technology acceptance by organizations on integrating DevSecOps with SOCs through the DCAM as the conceptual framework.

PROBLEM STATEMENT

A significant problem highlighted in scholarly literature is the challenges an organization experiences in transitioning from traditional software engineering approaches to DevSecOps adoption (Duque Anton et al., 2020; Sánchez-Gordón & Colomo-Palacios, 2020; Tomas et al., 2019). Limited research addresses the integration of DevSecOps into SOCs thus, researchers have called for further research on the barriers to adopting DevSecOps in security operations (Mao et al., 2020; Maroukian & Gulliver, 2020; Rajapaksea et al., 2021).

Introducing DevSecOps methodology to organizations is complicated and typically features errors during implementation, primarily addressing cybersecurity concerns in distinct phases without considering their interdependence (Duque Anton et al., 2020). Traditionally, software security and software engineering differ, making the integration of DevSecOps in cybersecurity operations a challenge (Tomas et al., 2019). The development and operations teams lack the knowledge and training to effectively utilize automated cybersecurity tools, making the implementation process even more challenging (Tomas et al., 2019). The cybersecurity aspects of DevSecOps and SOCs are different, meaning that the various organizational units and the organizations themselves will often find the deployment process challenging (Sánchez-Gordón & Colomo-Palacios, 2020). Finally, Marini-Wear (2019) stated that although DevOps are rapidly deployed in organizations, security operation teams are not involved in this adoption. Since DevSecOps is an extension of DevOps, the same issues apply to the collaboration and adoption of DevSecOps (Mao et al., 2020). Trepidation in the adoption of DevSecOps, in turn, impacts the collaboration between DevSecOps and SOCs. While the job of a SOC is to take telemetry data from DevSecOps environments to monitor vulnerabilities and malicious activity, this does not generally occur or practice, as many SOCs often miss telemetry data from DevSecOps. Consequently, potentially introducing vulnerabilities whereby advisories can exploit undetected, further highlighting the need to understand the status of coordination between DevSecOps and SOCs.

PURPOSE OF THE STUDY

The purpose of this exploratory qualitative study is to examine the DevSecOps collaboration culture and the significance of bridging DevSecOps with SOCs in organizations that have already adopted the DevSecOps methodology. This study will build upon DCAM by expanding TPB. DCAM suggests that managers or colleagues can influence the software developers' intentions to adopt new processes (Masombuka & Mnkandla, 2018). Additionally, this study will identify organizational cultural impacts between DevSecOps and SOCs and if these beliefs and behaviors affect collaboration and acceptability.

SIGNIFICANCE OF THE STUDY

The study contributes to the existing knowledge and highlight barriers in implementing application cybersecurity controls and methodology, thereby highlighting the importance of bridging DevSecOps and SOCs. The researcher attempted to address the gaps in the literature regarding the integration of SOCs with DevSecOps. Organizational managers and cybersecurity personnel may utilize the findings from this study to devise approaches for adopting DevSecOps monitoring in SOCs. Corporate leaders and cybersecurity personnel will attain the benefits linked to the implementation of DevSecOps, such as increased awareness of development personnel of operational cybersecurity vulnerabilities, increased accountability for deployments, and increased responsibility for quality assurance (Rowse & Cohen, 2021).

The study findings may enable organizations' leaders and cybersecurity professionals to mitigate the barriers encountered in the adoption of monitoring DevSecOps in SOCs. Overcoming such obstacles becomes possible only by addressing insufficient research on integrating DevSecOps with SOCs to enhance cybersecurity. Other similar gaps in the literature include a lack of DevSecOps knowledge among cybersecurity teams, inadequate tools, and a conceptual gap between software development and cybersecurity operation teams (Valani, 2018). Using the findings of this study, organizations' managers may devise new and preferable approaches for DevSecOps adoption and collaboration with SOCs. DevSecOps engineers may identify obstacles hindering SOCs from adopting DevSecOps and formulate potential solutions from this study's findings. Cybersecurity and DevSecOps engineers can establish a coherent framework to support an influential collaborative culture in a DevSecOps setting.

SOC personnel are the key beneficiaries of this study as they glean insights on improving aspects of Masombuka and Mnkandla's (2018) DCAM model that illuminates positive attributes for the SOCs personnel to acquire. Collectively, these attributes can improve the significant function of SOCs, including overseeing the well-being of a company's workforce, locations, brand, reputation, and assets. OC, RE, TR, OU, and internal behavioral control are essential in creating teamwork and collaboration while enhancing job satisfaction and productivity (Masombuka & Mnkandla, 2018). SNs are similarly significant attributes since most individuals require norms to direct and guide their conduct, create a sense of understanding of one another's actions, and give order and predictability to social associations

(Masombuka & Mnkandla, 2018). The attribute of roles and RR implies that the entire team should be rewarded for their efforts and take accountability for any failures that may occur.

THEORIES THAT GUIDE THE STUDY

The theoretical framework chosen to underpin the study was the TPB. The TPB was the basis for the DCAM instrument utilized in the study, making this theory a logical choice for analysis of the study's results. The TPB intends to explain all the behaviors over which individuals have the ability to exercise self-control (Ajzen, 1991). The primary construct of the theory is behavioral intent, which Ajzen posited to be influenced by an individual's attitude regarding whether a particular behavior will produce the desired and expected outcome (Ajzen, 1991). TPB also accounts for an individual's subjective evaluation of the risks and benefits associated with a particular behavior and outcome (Ajzen, 1991, 2012). The TPB states that an individual's behavior depends on intention, motivation, ability, or behavioral control (Ajzen, 2020). Significantly, TPB distinguishes between different types of beliefs, including behavioral, normative, and control, which leads to the six constructs of the theory that together account for an individual's actual control over behavior. Figure 1 shows these six constructs and the relationships between them.

Figure 1. Graphical representation of the theory of planned behavior

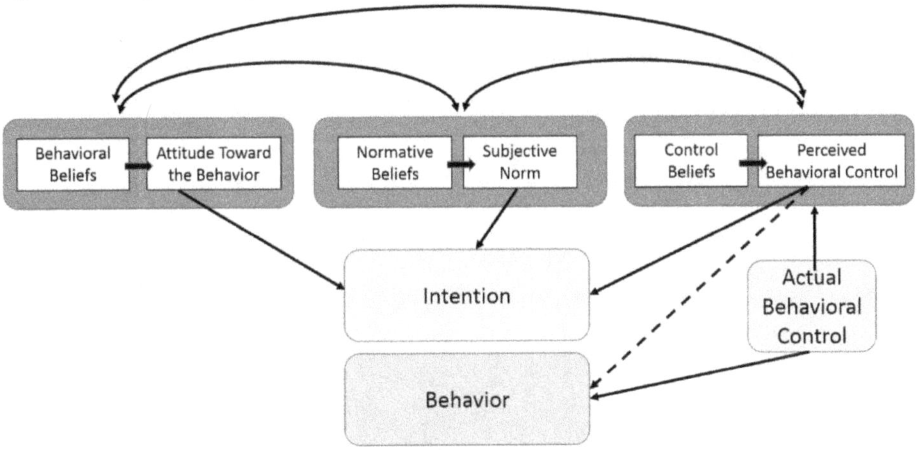

Note. This figure was taken from LaMorte (2019).

Each of the individual constructs of the TPB are described in detail later in Chapter One in the theoretical framework section of the literature review.

Significantly, the TPB has been utilized extensively in analyzing cybersecurity threats and responses. For example, researchers used the TPB to explain that over 85% of cybersecurity issues were due to human-derived security weaknesses (Nobles, 2018). Given that humans are perhaps the weakest link in cybersecurity, researchers utilize the TPB to design interventions that address cybersecurity risks (Briggs et al., 2017), as well as predict behaviors of individuals and groups in the context of cybersecurity (Alanazi et al., 2022; Maalem Lahcen et al., 2020; Redmiles et al., 2015). As such, there is a plethora of precedence in the utilization of TPB in the analysis of cybersecurity-related decision-making. The researcher employed TPB in the current study.

Conceptual Model

The researcher based the conceptual framework on Masombuka and Mnkandla's (2018) DCAM. DCAM aims to determine the factors that significantly influence the adoption of DevSecOps in security operations (Masombuka & Mnkandla, 2018). The aim of employing the DCAM model as the conceptual framework highlights the individual factors affecting the acceptability of DevSecOps in several security operation centers. As described earlier in the chapter and each sub-research question, this framework comprises eight variables to operationalize the adoption of DevSecOps (Masombuka & Mnkandla, 2018). The researcher explored the eight factors operationalized within the DCAM model. Figure 2 depicts the operationalization of the DCAM as the conceptual framework for this study.

Figure 2. The DCAM conceptual framework

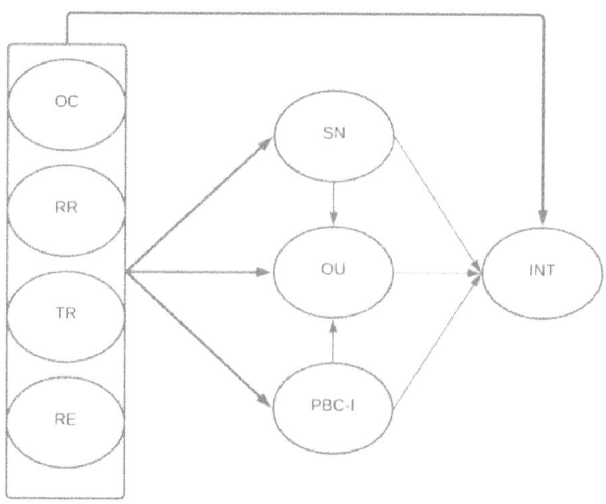

This exploratory quantitative study builds upon DCAM by expanding the TPB to determine the factors affecting the acceptance of DevSecOps at SOCs. Perceived behavioral control, subjective norm, and attitude provide the theory with some essential components (Hardgrave & Johnson, 2003). DCAM intends to utilize a new information systems development (ISD) process with three critical components defined earlier in the chapter. Hossain et al. (2020) described OU as the usefulness of the ISD approach, as perceived by the developer. SN indicates developers' intentions to accept a system, either indirectly via OU or directly due to the influence of managers and colleagues. Lastly, PBC-I describes an individual impediment to conducting a particular behavior.

DCAM is a suitable conceptual framework for the current study due to the software development contexts, and, as a result, DCAM encompasses the organizational culture. The present research fosters the integration of DevSecOps with SOCs to enhance cybersecurity DCAM suggests that the software developers' intentions to adopt ISD can influence their managers or colleagues (Masombuka & Mnkandla, 2018). Organizational culture impacts these beliefs and behaviors.

The commonly adopted technology acceptance model (TAM; McCord, 2007) application is unsuitable for this study. TAM is related to the current research in that it highlights the challenges faced while attempting to enhance cybersecurity protocols by integrating DevSecOps with the technology-use approaches of SOCs. Hardgrave and Johnson (2003) indicated that TAM, TAM2, TPB, and goal-setting frameworks do not explain accepting ISD procedures and complicated technological products or processes. ISDAM is an improved model to explain the acceptance of complex IS development methodologies. ISDAM replaces TAM, TAM2, TPB, and goal-setting frameworks as the conventional models, making technological acceptance and corporate integration by DevSecOps and SOC personnel more efficient. Unlike other technology acceptance models, developers' environments were the intended environment for ISDAM. The suggested framework, DCAM, adapts Masombuka and Mnkandla's (2018) study. It is an extension of ISDAM, where DevOps culture is a factor in determining practitioners' intentions - both software developers and software operators - to accept a new IS. DCAM suggests that the software developers' intentions to adopt IS influence the decisions of managers and the acceptance by colleagues (Masombuka & Mnkandla, 2018).

Rajapakse et al. (2021) posited that companies consider it significant to bridge DevOps with the security operation centers, but various challenges hinder this bridging process. This study bridges this gap by revealing feasible solutions by determining the challenges hindering the implementation of DevSecOps in SOCs. The research expanded DCAM and TPB to help determine the factors affecting the acceptability of DevSecOps at the security operation centers. The researcher describes these factors as the barriers and significance of bridging DevSecOps with SOCs

THEORETICAL FRAMEWORK

The TPB was chosen as the theoretical framework for the study. The TPB began as the theory of reasoned action (TRA) developed by Ajzen and Fishbein (1975). This predecessor to the TPB focused on the observation of two variables. First, attitudes are defined as positive or negative feelings when considered in the context of achieving an objective. Second, subjective norms represent the individual's perception of the ability to achieve those goals (Ajzen & Fishbein, 1975). The TRA suggests an individual's intention to perform determines the individual's behavior; this intention is, in turn, a function of the person's attitude toward the behavior and subjective norms (Ajzen & Fishbein, 1975). Ajzen and Fishbein (1975) highlighted multiple boundary conditions that affect the magnitude of the relationship between intention and behavior, one of which is the degree to which carrying out the purpose is under the deliberate control of the individual. According to Ajzen and Fishbein (1975), variables external to the TRA model are assumed to influence the intentions of an individual, but only to the extent that these external factors affect either attitudes or subjective norms and, therefore, voluntary control.

The TPB (Ajzen, 1985) extends the notion of voluntary control specified by the TRA by including beliefs regarding an individual's possession of the requisite knowledge and resources required to perform a specific behavior. In particular, the more resources, opportunities, and understanding an individual believes they possess, the greater they should have perceived behavioral control over a behavior. As such, the TPB intends to explain all behaviors over which individuals can exert self-control. Six constructs collectively representing an individual's actual control over behavior comprise the TPB (see Figure 1). Each of these six constructs will be discussed.

The six constructs of the TPB are: (a) attitudes, (b) behavioral intention, (c) subjective norms, (d) normative beliefs, (e) perceived power, and (f) perceived behavioral control. The construct of attitudes does not differ significantly from its original conceptualization in the TRA (Ajzen, 1985; Ajzen & Fishbein, 1975). The attitudes construct refers to the degree an individual perceives the behavior under examination positively or negatively. This construct includes an analysis of the potential outcomes that result from performing a behavior (Ajzen, 1985; Ajzen & Fishbein, 1975). Behavioral intention refers to the motivational factors influencing an individual to perform a specific behavior at a given time and place. As discussed earlier, this construct was not present in the original TRA model. Generally, the stronger the intention to perform a behavior, the more likely the individual will perform the behavior (Ajzen, 1985).

Subjective norms, present in both TRA and TPB, refer to the belief about whether most people approve or disapprove of the behavior. Subjective norms relate to an individual's beliefs about whether peers and other individuals of influence believe the individual should engage in the behavior (Ajzen, 1985; Ajzen & Fishbein, 1975). The fourth construct, SNs, refers to the codes of conduct that society or groups of people consider within a larger cultural context. The normative, or standard, behaviors dictated by society are called SNs (Ajzen, 1985). The fifth construct, perceived power, refers to the perceived presence of external factors that can facilitate or impede a behavior's performance. Perceived power contributes to an individual's perceived behavioral control. Lastly, and perhaps most important, perceived behavioral control is an individual's perception of the ease of performing a particular behavior. Perceived behavioral control varies across situations and actions, which results in an individual having varying perceptions of behavioral control depending on the situation (Ajzen, 1985). In the present study, these constructs were analyzed within the context of cybersecurity with the behavior under examination communication between DevSecOps and SOCs to seamlessly integrate development, security, and operations into a cohesive organization.

Application of TPB to Cybersecurity

A rich diversity of studies has utilized the TPB to analyze different aspects and issues of cybersecurity. Of particular importance to the current research, researchers applied information security management to the TPB (Kim et al., 2014), an explicit goal of DevSecOps and SOC environments. In a study by Alanazi et al. (2022), the authors examined the cyber security behaviors of individuals aged 18–30 under the lens of the TPB to identify measures and factors that can help reduce cyber threats. The study's results demonstrated that specific constructs of the TPB, namely attitude, subjective norm, and perceived behavioral control, influence the participants' intentions to practice cybersecurity behaviors (Alanazi et al., 2022). In another study, van Steen and Deeleman (2021) attempted to create a cybersecurity training module as a game to understand cybersecurity's behavioral aspect. The authors then tested the game's effectiveness experimentally against one that did not contain cybersecurity information; the TPB constructs served as the experiment's measures. Notably, the results showed that the cybersecurity game resulted in higher self-reported scores on attitudes, perceived behavioral control, intentions, and overall behavior compared to non-cybersecurity games (van Steen & Deeleman, 2021). Of particular importance to the current study, previous information security management studies applied the TPB (Kim et al., 2014), which the researcher similarly did in the examination of integrating DevSecOps and SOC environments.

CONCEPTUAL FRAMEWORK

The conceptual foundation of the present study centers on defining development and operations, also known as DevOps, and sought further to expand the DCAM. DCAM, developed by Masombuka and Mnkandla (2018), aims to identify factors impacting the adoption of DevSecOps and how DevOps collaboration attributes influence developers' and operators' acceptance of DevOps. The ISDAM framework is the foundation and predecessor of DCAM. ISDAM derives from the TPB and provides DCAM with an additional three components, which include: (a) perceived behavioral control, (b) subjective norm, and (c) attitude. As described above, the TPB predicts an individual's attitude toward a behavior, the subjective norms encasing the execution of the behavior, and the individual's perception of their control over the behavior determine an individual's behavioral intentions (Ajzen, 1991). TPB denotes a psychological concept linking behavior to beliefs. Generally, TPB holds that the three core aspects – perceived behavioral control, subjective norms, and attitude – function to change an individual's behavioral intentions (Alam & Sayuti, 2011). In the present study, the researcher built upon DCAM by expanding it to include TPB to determine factors affecting the adoption and collaboration of DevSecOps at SOCs. The researcher built upon DCAM by expanding TPB to determine factors affecting the adoption and union of DevSecOps at SOCs regarding cybersecurity.

Researchers have utilized the DCAM framework in IS and other fields related to DevSecOps. For instance, Hossain et al. (2020) attempted to build upon DCAM by expanding TPB to determine the acceptance of IS by software developers. Hossain et al. (2020) formulated the ISDAM framework based on the TPB. Initial findings obtained by Hossain et al. (2020) indicated that perceived behavioral control, subjective norm, and attitude provide the theory with essential components relevant to software developers. Hossain et al. (2020) discovered that the usefulness of the ISDAM framework in ISD, as predicated by developer perceptions, was that colleagues extensively influenced the intentions of their co-workers about their acceptance of new IS approaches.

The ability of the framework components to address the challenges experienced in transitioning from traditional software engineering approaches to DevSecOps adoption is the justification for the selected conceptual and theoretical frameworks (see Duque Anton et al., 2020) by exploring the barriers associated with bridging monitoring DevSecOps environments within SOCs. The DCAM model constitutes components serving as variables in the present study, including OC, RE, SN, roles, and RR, TR, OU, and PBC-I. Notably, these are all positive attributes for the SOCs' personnel to acquire and can collectively help improve the significant function of SOCs, which is overseeing the wellbeing of a company's workforces, locations, brand, reputation, and assets (Masombuka & Mnkandla, 2018). Additionally, the DCAM framework justifies its use in the current study due to its applicability in software development contexts. Notably, DCAM suggests that the software developers' intentions to adopt ISD can influence their managers or colleagues (Masombuka & Mnkandla, 2018).

ASSUMPTIONS, LIMITATIONS, and DELIMITATIONS

The conceptual foundation of the present study centers on defining development and operations, also known as DevOps, and sought further to expand the DCAM. DCAM, developed by Masombuka and Mnkandla (2018), aims to identify factors impacting the adoption of DevSecOps and how DevOps collaboration attributes influence

The Nature of SOC Operations

As defined by Lin et al. (2018), a SOC is a command center that monitors the IS that an enterprise uses for its IT infrastructure, which may include the business's websites, databases, servers, applications, networks, desktops, data centers, and a variety of endpoints. From a similar point of view, Feng et al. (2017) stated that a SOC cybersecurity group performs various functions. Some of these functions include: (a) monitoring each element of the infrastructure, (b) assessing the current health of these infrastructure elements by identifying potential and existing threats, (c) responding to threats, and (d) setting up information security measures and protocols designed to prevent future threats. SOCs perform many of the responsibilities of on-site security operations teams. According to Bartnes et al. (2016), such functionalities constitute monitoring, detecting, investigating, and responding to threats. More importantly, an SOC is responsible for safeguarding the organization's digital assets, such as employees' data, intellectual property, brand-related assets, and business systems.

On the other hand, it is critical to note that SOC operations are more efficient when executed in team contexts. Blum (2020) stated that while implementing the organization's security protocols and threat response fabric, a SOC could facilitate collaboration between different departments and individuals to ensure a unified approach to monitoring, assessing, and defending against cyber threats. Typically, a SOC's design uses a centralized hub-and-spoke setup, with the SOC being the hub and other divisions and departments being the spokes that form essential interactions with the centralized SOC (Akbar et al., 2022). Expounding on this point of view, Bartnes et al. (2016) recorded that SOC operations often involve a security information and event management (SIEM) system, which collects and correlates data that stream from security feeds. Depending on the needs of an organization's network, such activities involve several different tools. Some tools may include risk and compliance systems, governance protocols, vulnerability assessment, endpoint detection and remediation, threat-intelligence platforms, and behavior analytics of individual users and business entities (Shutock & Dietrich, 2022). These combined perspectives necessitate the acquisition of further insight into SOCs operations and standardized functions.

Standard SOC Functions and Operations: Taking Stock of Available Resources, Resource Protection, and Use Allocation

In general, the SOC manages two resource categories. One encompasses the devices, applications, and processes the SOC must protect, whereas the other involves the tools the SOC uses to safeguard these assets (Jbair, 2019). The asset landscape denotes that the SOC can protect many essential resources, depending on the organization's IT needs. Guillén et al. (2019) indicated that such assets include every component that comprises the network, constituting a variety of mobile and desktop endpoints. Adding value to this statement, Lubis et al. (2020) noted that the landscape assets may also involve cloud resources that either serve the organization's customers or support internal operations and applications. In some situations, the SOC devises protections for Internet-of-things (IoT) devices, including everything from kitchen microwaves to warehouse scanners.

SOCs manage not only the devices, applications, and processes of an organization but also the tools required to safeguard the organization's assets. It is important to note that the key to protecting the network is adequate visibility, without which there may be potentially dangerous blind spots that attackers can utilize successfully in cyberattacks. As such, one of the SOC's primary objectives is to gain complete visibility of all endpoints, software, and servers, which includes in-house components and anything that connects to the organization's network (Jbair, 2019). Henneberg (2019) noted that, at times, this means accounting for the endpoints that clients and partners may use to interface with the network for meetings or professional collaboration. To adequately protect this vast array of systems and devices, SOCs must have a broad and deep understanding of the tools at their disposal. Additionally, a SOC needs intricate knowledge regarding the workflows within the organization, including how individual departments and teams work and how they address threats on a day-to-day basis (Shutock & Dietrich, 2022).

Preparation and Preventative Maintenance

It is virtually impossible to prevent all cyber-related problems despite adequate training and preparations for any IT or cybersecurity team, as cybersecurity threats continuously inundate an organization's systems in one way or another and from various angles (Orazi et al., 2020). Feng et al. (2017) indicated that a SOC, when adequately prepared, can effectively and efficiently mitigate many of the efforts of attackers, often vanquishing these threats completely. Such a point of view brings to light the need for utilizing combined preparation and preventative maintenance approaches. As indicated by Nabil et al. (2017), the first step to preparedness is for the SOC to keep abreast of the security innovations at their disposal, which is crucial because remediating the latest threats requires the latest threat detection and response technologies. With IoT device usage increasing, the protection landscape is ever expanding, underscoring the need for continuous threat detection and response training.

A thorough understanding of how each IoT device category works and its vulnerabilities requires that modern-day organizations delineate one of their primary objectives to safeguard their customer's privacy and security (Lubis et al., 2020). According to Han et al. (2019), preparation involves taking stock of the tools available and the threats that could arise and then devising a roadmap that details how to meet each challenge. Settanni et al. (2017) cautioned that this plan should be thorough yet flexible, mainly because new threats constantly arise, forcing a need to incorporate disaster recovery measures into the roadmap. In confirming this statement's validity, Grünewald (2022) noted that if an attacker successfully infiltrates the system, these measures can make the difference between hours and days of downtime. Consequently, the disaster recovery roadmap must also account for the disasters that impact an organization's IT infrastructure in unpredictable, asymmetrical ways.

According to Kumar and Goyal (2020), the SOC perspective on preventative maintenance focuses on ensuring that attacks fail, or, at the very least, SOCs attempt to limit the damage cyber-attacks inflict, making necessary changes to preventive maintenance a regularity and a necessity. Preventative maintenance is not about preventing attacks because cybersecurity personnel understand that attacks will continue. Developers and security personnel must constantly update organizational security systems so that organizations can keep up with ever evolving cyberattack methodologies. As indicated by Shutock and Dietrich (2022), coevolving with cyber criminals involve ensuring that network firewall policies are constantly up to date, identifying vulnerabilities, and patching them. Shutock and Dietrich (2022) also emphasized a need to choose which sites an organization deems vital to whitelist and blacklist, followed by regular critical evaluation of the places in both categories.

Kumar and Goyal (2020) noted that preventative maintenance also involves ensuring the applications that interact with organizational networks are secure. Congruent with this view, Amaro et al. (2022) said that applications have become an increasingly popular attack surface, implying that by securing the application or its environment, organizations can limit the effectiveness of the attacks. In summary, while SOCs have many functions, some of the most critical functions require constant evolution with the continuous adaptation of cyber criminals. These vital functions require creativity, a quality primed for teamwork.

Continuous Proactive Monitoring Through SOC Evolution

Constant monitoring is key to maximizing the visibility of cyberattacks. According to Donaldson et al. (2015), for organizations to ensure that their monitoring system is effective, the SOC team must be capable of implementing tools that scan their networks, looking for anything that appears suspicious. Such suspicious activity includes obvious threats and abnormal activity that may or may not pose a danger (Guillén et al., 2019). In contrast, some activities will be easily identifiable as malicious because the data fits a pre-identified threat profile. Other activities may be suspicious but ultimately not overtly dangerous. For example, an application system log-on that occurs outside business hours would be considered suspicious but not necessarily dangerous. Proactively handling even mildly suspicious threats is paramount and may involve sandboxing the data or enacting security protocols to protect exposed devices.

Developers invented several new tools to address this possibility. For instance, tools like a SIEM or endpoint detection and response (EDR) system can be the centerpieces of the SOC team's approach (Ask et al., 2021). According to Ask et al. (2021), advanced SIEM and EDR systems incorporate artificial intelligence to help learn the behavior of both users and the endpoints, which implies that if something seems out of the ordinary, preventative steps can contain or eliminate the danger. This notion explains why Donaldson et al. (2015) noted that within the monitoring process, systems should exist that automatically and immediately alert the SOC team of emerging threats not yet identified or encountered by the system, as it is common to get hundreds or thousands of alerts every day.

Alert Ranking, Management, and Threat Response

Security personnel must vet system-generated alerts to prevent wasting the IT team's time or unnecessarily disrupting the workflow of employees or management. As indicated by Kumar and Goyal (2019), the SOC team is responsible for examining each alert and filtering the false positives that could unnecessarily consume time and resources. These findings indicate that if a security team identifies an actual threat, the SOC team must first determine the aggressiveness of the danger while determining the type of threat and ascertaining which areas of the network the threat is targeting. Filtering false positives and creating a rank order list of the aggressiveness of threats allows the SOC to handle each potential threat efficiently and effectively in terms of urgency (Shukla et al., 2022).

On the other hand, addressing an emerging threat is one of the pivotal activities of a SOC. According to Antonucci et al. (2020), when a threat manifests, the SOC responds to it. It takes appropriate action to protect the network and its users, which may often involve shutting down endpoints completely or disconnecting them from the network. In some cases, a SOC must further isolate an endpoint to ensure the threat does not spread to other network branches and endpoints. Herardian (2019) stated that the SOC's threat response could also involve identifying and terminating affected processes. Affirming this point of view, Antonucci et al. (2020) noted that with some threats, malicious software might use legitimate software to execute attacks on other connected devices; as such, termination of the affected process can protect an array of other endpoints on the network. In different situations, files may need to be deleted from specific network components to protect other users (Guillén et al., 2019). As the SOC responds to the threat, it should focus on providing a comprehensive solution while minimizing user activity disruption, ensuring continuity, and ensuring the organization's safety.

Log Management, Recovery, and Remediation

A log provides a baseline snapshot of the system in a healthy state (Bartnes et al., 2016). Although automatically generated, logs are an essential but often overlooked tool, as they contain a plethora, perhaps an overload, of helpful information about the system, including possible infiltrations. The SOC team must carefully collect, maintain, and review logged activity. According to Han et al. (2019), comparing two logs side by side, a threat may readily reveal itself, mainly if the second log differs from the baseline snapshot. Lubis et al. (2020) noted that the logs help remediate a security incident. Primary to remediation is engaging in a forensic examination of log data, which often reveals essential information about the nature of a threat and its targets (Bartnes et al., 2016).

Notably, different endpoints, firewalls, and operating systems connected to the network create several logs simultaneously, allowing for further comparison of logs to examine the impact of a security incident. Since every device on a network produces its log, it is essential to devise a system for evaluating logs in a timely, efficient manner. Thus, a SOC may use a SIEM tool for the aggregation and correlation of the data, which streamlines the log analysis process (Settanni et al., 2017). Once an organization's network and functions return to baseline following an incident, the SOC is responsible for returning the organization's operations to full functionality. According to Peterson et al. (2018), this may involve recovering lost data or examining potentially compromised data. During this procedure, each endpoint potentially within the attack vector requires careful examination to ensure the endpoint's safety because numerous network areas are interconnected. As indicated by Lubis et al. (2020), in the case of a ransomware attack, the SOC may have to identify system backups made before the attack, which can then be crucial to restoring the devices that needed to be erased, effectively restoring the device and the network to their states before the incident.

Application DCAM: Importance of OC, RE, and SNs on DevSecOps Engineers' and SOCs Personnel

The preceding literature review section included a discussion of the responsibilities and functions of SOCs and personnel. This information is critical for understanding how SOC and DevSecOps teams can collaborate and cooperate to enhance an organization's development, security, and operations. In the following sections of the literature review, the researcher discusses studies that have analyzed different aspects of the DCAM model. It is important to note that the studies presented in the literature review only examined certain parts of the DCAM model for DevSecOps, SOCs, or both and did not explicitly analyze all facets of the model. As such, this highlights an essential contribution of the present study because the researcher examined and will discuss all seven aspects of the DCAM model (see Figure 2) in the research findings. In the section that follows, literature that focuses on three DCAM items including: (a) OC, (b) RE, and (c) SNs, which were analyzed for cooperation between DevSecOps and SOCs.

Kumar and Goyal (2020) undertook a study in which they explored modeling continuous security utilizing a conceptual model for automated DevSecOps using open-source software over cloud (ADOC). The investigation stemmed from the literature-based realization that the combination of agile software development methodology and DevOps is critical in helping businesses achieve agility and velocity in delivering time-to-market applications and services through the aid of SOCs and DevSecOps engineers. OC, RE, and appropriate SNs are essential among DevSecOps engineers and SOCs personnel to foster agility in service delivery and efficient monitoring. Using the TPB framework, the researchers hypothesized that the absence of appropriate SNs, especially concerning OC, impeded the quest for agility, velocity, user data security, and privacy assurance (Kumar & Goyal, 2020).

Notably, the latter often receive a lower prioritization, as SOC personnel perceive privacy assurance as a time-consuming activity requiring specialized people, processes, and technology. According to Kumar and Goyal (2020), problems surrounding OC and RE were vital to address to help integrate security in DevOps processes, given that security for DevOps transformed into DevSecOps, with practical considerations for specific business contexts. Kumar and Goyal (2020) utilized these findings to propose a conceptual security model, ADOC, to facilitate improved OC and RE-driven norms, helping adopt DevSecOps for the business processes capitalizing on operational support systems (OSS) over the cloud. Findings from Kumar and Goyal (2020) indicated that OC, RE, and appropriate SNs were essential for the integration development, security, and operation activities by automating security controls using OSS over the cloud.

These findings are consistent with the results obtained by Díaz et al. (2019) after engaging in a study investigating the necessity of OC and RE for other employee inputs in matters related to self-service cybersecurity monitoring as an enabler for DevSecOps. Diaz et al. (2019) based the study on the discovery that current IoT systems are highly distributed systems that integrate cloud, edge, and fog computing approaches depending on where security personnel allocate intelligence and processing capabilities. According to Díaz et al. (2019), this distribution and heterogeneity make development and deployment pipelines complex and fragmented, with multiple delivery endpoints above hardware. Thus, Diaz et al. (2019) suggested that the absence of OC, RE, and appropriate SNs prevents rapid development and makes the operation and monitoring of production systems a difficult and tedious task, including cybersecurity event monitoring.

Findings obtained by Díaz et al. (2019) indicated that OC and SNs were crucial to facilitate fast and continuous feedback from operations to development by providing a flexible monitoring infrastructure so that teams can configure their monitoring and alerting services. Diaz et al. (2019) concluded that communication improvements were essential to foster augmented self-service monitoring and warning systems. Communication, in turn, allows for the breaking of silos between the development, operations, and security teams by opening access to critical security metrics, enabling a collaborative culture that fosters continuous improvement.

The DCAM components of OC, SNs, and RE are essential in facilitating improvements in privacy and data security. Grünewald (2022) engaged in a study investigating cloud native privacy engineering through a department known as DevPrivOps, a combination of development, privacy, and operations teams. The literature-based realization drove the study that cloud-native IS engineering enables scalable, resilient software architectures that power major online offerings built following agile development practices. From this perspective, Grünewald focused on the necessity of OC, RE, and appropriate SNs to ensure that cybersecurity personnel can meet the growing demand for privacy-friendly services, as articulated by societal norms and legislative policies. Grünewald identified conceptual dimensions of cloud-native privacy engineering relying on OC and SNs to bring together cloud-computing fundamentals and privacy regulation. Grünewald further proposed an integrative approach to address and overcome the shortcomings of existing privacy-enhancing technologies in practice by evaluating existing system designs. The study's findings indicate that augmentations in OC among cybersecurity personnel and adhering to appropriate SNs and RE open critical advances to the state-of-the-art privacy-by-design, which, by default, utilizes the latest emerging technologies.

The DCAM elements of OC, SNs, and RE are fundamental in helping cybersecurity personnel achieve higher dimensions in terms of security solutions, security operations, and security compliance considering modern-day challenges through adopting emerging measures. Kumar and Goyal (2019) investigated data security and privacy assurance in the cloud utilizing a three-dimensional perspective. The researchers indicated that since cloud-based data security and privacy is witnessing exponential growth, the forecast for further growth suggests a positive tendency in the attitude and mood of the typical business user for adopting cloud services (Kumar & Goyal, 2019). Kumar and Goyal (2019) further hypothesized that enhanced communication, RE, and adherence to SNs were necessary among cybersecurity personnel to meet the challenges associated with the evolution of cybersecurity, especially changes that are related to confidence in cybersecurity and privacy solutions for the cloud computing environment. Kumar and Goyal (2020) utilized a literature review approach to present a three-dimensional conceptual model describing the relationships between factors contributing to this increasing confidence in the cloud. Findings obtained by Kumar and Goyal indicated that OC, RE, and adherence to SNs are essential to modern-day cybersecurity personnel. These DCAM constructs allow SOCs to meet the growing demands associated with security solutions, security operations, and security compliance, all of which are elements of security assurance.

Shukla et al. (2022) corroborated these findings after investigating enterprise security with a particular focus on modern challenges and emerging measures. According to Shukla et al., the increasing dependence on technology brought about security and privacy concerns requiring cybersecurity personnel to develop standards to combat cyber threats and vulnerabilities by eliminating TR issues for businesses and enterprises. Shukla et al. attempted to explain the phenomenon by first describing the importance of augmented OC among cybersecurity personnel within the changing cyber ecosystem, due in large to the ramifications of extreme digitalization, as evidenced by the latest trends in cyber-attacks. The researchers discovered that improved OC was the key to helping cybersecurity personnel overcome modern-day security and privacy threats and foster their ability to address the cyber threats' consequences (Shukla et al., 2022). Shukla et al. concluded that in the presence of appropriate SNs and RE for emerging threats, OC improvements are critical to ensuring that enterprise security is more proactive, cognitive, automated, connected, invisible, and risk aware.

OC and appropriate SNs are also fundamental for resiliency and career development among DevSecOps engineers and SOC personnel. Onwubiko (2020) focused on the recovery aspects of cyber resilience, stating that the technological advances and emerging cyber security tactics, techniques, and procedures advanced the landscape for malicious purposes, as evidenced by the heightened number of cyber incidents and data breaches. With the realization that cyber incidents are likely unavoidable, Onwubiko (2020) hypothesized that improvements in cyber resilience through enhanced communication are cornerstones of any comprehensive and reliable cybersecurity strategy. Onwubiko sought to develop and present a comprehensive cyber recovery operational framework based on OC among cybersecurity personnel and RE for SNs. Onwubiko found that when embodied into frameworks, OC and RE for SNs made cybersecurity frameworks robust and helpful in developing resilience among cybersecurity personnel.

These findings are consistent with the results of Antonucci et al. (2020) after they investigated career development frameworks among cybersecurity personnel to develop a cybersecurity workforce through research-based career development frameworks. Antonucci et al. (2020) hypothesized that OC was necessary for cultivating resilience and promoting effective and sustainable career development frameworks that would improve resiliency among cybersecurity workers. The framework proposed by Antonucci et al. utilized the OC and RE for SNs aspect of the DCAM model to highlight and describe the current and prospects of the critical work required of cybersecurity workings in business and technical areas of manufacturing. The authors profiled the roles of these DCAM components concerning cybersecurity personnel proficiencies, particularly those in the manufacturing enterprise. Findings from the study indicated that OC and RE for SNs could augment resiliency among cybersecurity personnel when incorporated into frameworks for career development in cybersecurity. These findings, taken together, indicate that some aspects of DCAM, namely OC and RE for SNs, may serve as essential components of cybersecurity frameworks. This study aims to understand how other aspects of the DCAM, IS-DAM, and TPB models impact the collaboration between DevSecOps and SOCs, making these studies particularly relevant for the topic at hand.

Team functionalities and the ability to deal with cyber threat situations among DevSecOps engineers and SOCs personnel can improve by focusing on OC and fostering personnel RE for SNs. Brown et al. (2016) explored incidence response teams in IT operations centers with a particular focus on the tailor-made teams in operation centers model of team functionality. The researchers studied the nature of incident response teams in seven operations centers of varying sizes and types, including service providers, a SOC, a Data Center, and two military training operations centers (Brown et al., 2016). Utilizing a qualitative methodology, Brown et al. (2016) deployed questionnaires requiring 129 participants to respond concerning the context of incident response work, the modeling of incident response work, components needed to improve incident response work, and implications for tool developers. Brown et al. (2016) also conducted 38 interviews and facilitated 11 meetings with executives of these operations centers. Findings from the study indicated that the respondents were concerned about the absence of focus on communication training in their improvement programs. Brown et al. (2016) found that the respondents were optimistic that the inclusion of training on RE for SNs could improve their effectiveness in executing incident response work.

These findings are further consistent with the results of Ask et al. (2021), who investigated human-human communication in cyber threat situations. Notably, the researchers focused on the communication component concerning the decision-making processes required of cyber security personnel when faced with cyber security threats (Ask et al., 2021). According to Ask et al. (2021), such situations require human communication entailing technical complexity, time pressure, interdisciplinary factors, and, often, an insufficient information basis. This finding implies that OC in cyber threat situations can be challenging and has various implications for decision-making. Ask et al. reviewed human-to-human communication in cyber threat situations, intending to understand how communication in cybersecurity settings illuminates potential areas to develop common standards for information exchange in collaborative environments and to provide guidance for future research efforts. Ask et al. (2021) found that OC was critical in improving collaboration between cyber defense exercise organizers and cognitive scientists.

In summary, the findings indicate that OC, RE, and SNs, which are tenets of the DCAM conceptual framework, improve instances in which multiple teams collaborate to prevent cyberattacks and intervene when cyberattacks occur. These fundamental tenets are critical for all aspects of cybersecurity and numerous types of cybersecurity teams, including DevSecOps and SOCs. The researcher examined these tenets in detail in Chapter 3. In the next section of the literature review, the researcher discusses studies that examined the bridging of DevSecOps with SOCs, focusing on the functional improvements derived from the merging of the two sects of security personnel.

Significance of Bridging DevSecOps with SOCs: Improving Resiliency, Monitoring, Risk Assessment, and Compliance

Bridging DevSecOps with SOCs can help improve cloud security by developing new problem views and effective and timely cybersecurity solutions. Herardian (2019) investigated the soft belly of cybersecurity. Herardian was concerned with establishing the need for collaboration between DevSecOps and SOCs personnel to identify and deal with issues associated with weak links in cybersecurity. Herardian (2019) ultimately noted that cybersecurity regulatory compliance and cloud operations are interdependent. The researcher proposed that this interdependence was critical in improving cloud security (Herardian, 2019). Taking advantage of emerging technologies and regulatory trends could bridge the gap between the two groups of personnel. Findings from the study indicated that the inability to meet the growing cloud security concerns is extensively associated with the lack of bridging and collaboration among DevSecOps and SOCs personnel, leading to the persistent weak links in cloud security.

These findings are consistent with the results of Shutock and Dietrich (2022), who investigated the functionalities of SOCs, aiming to find a holistic viewpoint regarding existing issues and potential solutions. According to Shutock and Dietrich (2022), since the first implementation of SOCs, the operational gap between SOC and DevSecOps personnel has limited the efforts of both groups to combat cyber threats. Shutock and Dietrich (2022) hypothesized that SOCs struggle with changes and upgrades to their foundational elements of people, processes, and technology in pursuit of evolvability, despite having evolved to become as effective and efficient at dealing with the currently existing cybersecurity threats. In part, SOCs continue to struggle because researchers have not provided details on how companies can bridge the gap between SOC and DevSecOps personnel. Findings from the study indicate that bridging the operational gap between SOC and DevSecOps personnel can facilitate the current and future challenges of SOCs and their ability to combat future problems by developing sustainable and workable solutions (Shutock & Dietrich, 2022).

Evidence of the significance of bridging SOC and DevSecOps exists because establishing a workable bridge can improve resiliency and monitoring strategies, which are critical for building effective operation centers. Onwubiko and Ouazzane (2022) explored the challenges of building an effective cybersecurity operations center (CSOC). The researchers indicated the increasing dependency of modern society on IT systems and infrastructures for essential services such as internet banking, vehicular network, and health-IT, coupled with the growing number of cyber incidents and security vulnerabilities, have made CSOC undoubtedly vital. SOCs are responsible for continuously and proactively monitoring business services, IT systems, and infrastructures to identify vulnerabilities, detect cyber-attacks, security breaches, and policy violations, and respond to cyber incidents swiftly (Onwubiko & Ouazzane, 2022). SOCs must collaborate with DevSecOps personnel to ensure that security events and alerts are triaged and analyzed while coordinating and managing cyber incidents to resolution. Findings obtained from the study indicated that the absence of operational bridges between SOC and DevSecOps has contributed to heightened factors contributing to cybersecurity inefficiencies.

These findings are consistent with the results obtained by Jbair (2019), who explored security monitoring strategies associated with operational technology (OT) infrastructures. As indicated by Jbair (2019), cybersecurity threats are an ever-increasing risk to industrial control systems, implying that by considering the impact of cyberattacks as part of improvements in OT, infrastructure resiliency serves the goal of minimizing production downtime. The researcher hypothesized that organizations could reduce downtime by considering flexible and innovative security monitoring strategies, incorporating a SOC, and bridging the gap between SOC and DevSecOps operations. The findings obtained from the study were diverse. Jbair (2019) found that bridging the operational gap improved monitoring mechanisms, leading to OT infrastructure benefits. Such benefits include enhancing incident response management, threat, and vulnerability management, asset inventory and management, network flow monitoring, security logs monitoring, and correlation, as well as the core function of defense against cyberattacks. Jbair found that bridging the operational gap could prove vital in helping deploy resiliency-based best practices for security monitoring and protection used by different industry sectors. Jbair found the bridge between the operations of SOCs and DevSecOps could benefit the OT security community by providing general guidance, future vision, and required information to build a functional security strategy for critical national infrastructure by considering the security life cycle starting from monitoring, through detection, to response and reporting.

The bridge between SOC and DevSecOps operations is suitable for augmenting software development and improving the capabilities and practices of cybersecurity personnel. Akbar et al. (2022) studied how organizations can enhance their successes with DevSecOps software development. The researchers hypothesized that DevOps is limited in automating the continuous delivery of new software to reduce the development life cycle and produce quality software due partly to a lack of collaboration with SOC personnel (Akbar et al., 2022). Findings obtained from the study indicated that bridging the operational gap between the two cybersecurity personnel groups could augment automation in software development by bringing on board bi-faceted concepts that integrate security methods into a DevOps process.

These findings are consistent with other results, such as those obtained by Amaro et al. (2022). This research group performed a multivocal literature review to investigate capabilities and practices in DevOps. The study's impetus was the literature-based realization that a problem existed in bridging the gap between SOC and DevSecOps personnel, which led to issues incorporating the elements of culture, process, measurements, and techniques in business cybersecurity software. Findings obtained from the study indicated that merging the proficiencies of SOC and DevSecOps personnel could help augment software development by reinforcing team collaboration and communication. Amaro et al. (2022) aimed to acquire community consensus on the relationship between capabilities and practices about the proficiencies of the two personnel factions to enhance cybersecurity software development for businesses.

Bridging the operational gap between SOC and DevSecOps personnel can also prove helpful in augmenting root-cause analysis, which leads to cyber security refinement and improvement. Peterson et al. (2018) sought to address threats and risks associated with cybersecurity. The researchers focused on the necessity of answering questions that are critical in the aftermath of cybersecurity incidents (Peterson et al., 2018). Peterson et al. (2018) further hypothesized that a workable merger between the proficiencies of SOC and DevSecOps personnel could help utilize log data to determine how threats penetrated organizational security systems. Peterson et al. (2018) conducted extensive fieldwork for 2.5 years in Norwegian electric power companies to identify challenges for improving information security incident-management practices relying on semi-structured interviews, document analysis, a survey, and participant observations. The researchers ultimately found that bridging the activities of the two cyber security personnel groups was critical in utilizing log data to determine how the threat penetrated the system and where it entered, and from where it came (Peterson et al., 2018). Peterson et al. (2018) concluded that bridging the gap between SOC and DevSecOps personnel will prevent similar threats from penetrating systems.

To further argue that SOC and DevSecOps personnel should pursue collaboration, Bartnes et al. (2016) investigated cybersecurity issues by assessing the role of cooperation among cyber security personnel in addressing the pertinent risks and threats. Bartnes et al. (2016) hypothesized that merging the proficiencies of SOC and DevSecOps personnel was the key to incorporating sustainable and workable data security into organizational strategic plans to address the constantly changing threat landscape. Bartnes et al. (2016) also noted that without collaboration between the two cyber security personnel departments, cybersecurity refinements and improvements would continue to lack the ability to meet the security challenges posed by the current and dynamic cyberspace environment. Findings from the study indicated that the bridge between SOC and DevSecOps personnel is critical to help organizations overcome the dynamic problems presented by the capability of cybercriminals to refine and update their operations. Bartnes et al. (2016) found that bridging the gap between SOC and DevSecOps personnel is expedient in allowing modern-day organizations to continually improve their security measures and technology to remain abreast and ahead of the latest tools used by hackers and other bad actors.

Bridging the operational gap between SOC and DevSecOps personnel has been associated with improving compliance management. Rajapakse et al. (2022) explored the challenges and solutions when adopting DevSecOps by focusing on establishing collaboration between SOC and DevSecOps personnel and the need to improve compliance. According to Rajapakse et al. (2022), although DevOps has become one of the fastest-growing software development paradigms, this trend also comes with challenges, namely ensuring secure software delivery while maintaining the compliance of DevOps and collaboration with SOC personnel. Rajapakse et al. noted that compliance requirements come in two forms. In one form, external governmental agencies dictate best practices for an organization. Compliance with governmental regulations is standard in various industries, particularly in the medical, financial, legal, and law enforcement arenas. Using a systematic review approach, Rajapakse et al. accounted for the possible influences of bridging SOC and DevSecOps personnel operations on compliance matters. Findings obtained from the study indicated that bridging the operational gap between the two groups of cyber security personnel can heighten regulation compliance and help mitigate emerging cyber security challenges.

Other researchers corroborated these findings. Mao et al. (2020) explored DevSecOps collaboration with SOC personnel with an emphasis on adherence to compliance. According to the researchers, emerging from the agile culture, DevOps particularly emphasizes development and deployment speed to achieve rapid value delivery (Mao et al., 2020). This celerity brings some security risks to the software development process due to issues related to compliance and collaboration among cybersecurity personnel. Using the Google search engine to collect articles on DevSecOps and SOC personnel, the researchers conducted a grey literature review (Mao et al., 2020). Findings obtained from the study indicated that, despite the existence of three significant software security risks in DevOps, the establishment of a DevOps pipeline provides opportunities for software security activities but poses critical compliance issues due to the lack of collaboration between SOC and DevSecOps personnel operations (Mao et al., 2020). Mao et al. (2020) concluded that although DevSecOps is getting increasing attention in various industries, it is still in its infancy and needs promoting by augmenting collaboration between the two cybersecurity personnel factions to foster compliance.

Several other studies have further corroborated these findings. According to Carturan and Goya (2019) and Mohan and Othmane (2016), some regulations commonly affect the compliance considerations of organizations, including the General Data Protection Regulation, the Health Insurance Portability and Accountability Act, and the Payment Card Industry Data Security Standard. Bobbert and Chtepen (2021) noted that heightening compliance with these regulations protects both the system from dangers and the organization from potentially expensive litigation by bridging the operations gap between SOC and DevSecOps personnel. Mohan and Othmane (2016) stated that an effective SOC and DevSecOps collaboration could enhance compliance by taking control of these measures and ensuring agreement with legislative standards. Carturan and Goya (2019) further affirmed the validity of these statements noting that jointly tasking SOC and DevSecOps teams with taking existing measures and implementing them according to organizational policy achieved the objectives. If an organization's compliance framework is incomplete, then the collaboration helps determine the organization's best practices and, through adherence to compliance regulations, turns these best practices into a replicable and actionable protocol (Anjaria & Kulkarni, 2021).

Leadership in Cybersecurity

Leadership in cybersecurity is essential for ensuring the safety and security of an organization's digital assets. To effectively manage and mitigate cyber threats, leaders in this profession must possess a combination of technical expertise and strong communication skills (Yusif & Hafeez-Baig, 2021). Several leadership styles, including transformational, transactional, and adaptive, can be effective in cybersecurity. For example, transformational leaders motivate and inspire their followers to reach their maximum potential, whereas transactional leaders focus on accomplishing specific objectives through rewards and punishments (Bass & Riggio, 2006). On the other hand, adaptive leaders can swiftly adapt to changing conditions and navigate complex, uncertain environments effectively (DeRue, 2011). Each leadership style can be effective in cybersecurity, depending on an organization's unique requirements and challenges.

Transformational Leadership

Transformational leadership is an influential style of leadership that inspires and motivates individuals to realize their maximum potential. Bass and Riggio (2006) explained that transformational leaders have a clear vision for the future and convey it effectively to their adherents, igniting a sense of shared purpose and direction. Their passion, enthusiasm, and ability to create a positive and motivating work environment inspire others (Siangchokyoo et al., 2020). Transformational leaders also demonstrate genuine concern for the needs and growth of their adherents, nurturing personal development and empowerment (Bass & Riggio, 2006; Philip, 2021). Additionally, transformational leaders can transform individuals and organizations through visionary thinking, inspirational motivation, and individualized consideration, propelling exceptional performance and accomplishing extraordinary results (Siangchokyoo et al., 2020).

Transformational leaders can motivate and inspire cybersecurity professionals to excel in their positions, foster innovation, and drive continuous improvement (Siangchokyoo et al., 2020). For example, transformational leaders foster a shared sense of purpose and commitment to protecting vital data and systems by articulating a clear vision of a secure digital landscape (Bass & Riggio, 2006; Klimoski & Murray, 2016). In a cybersecurity setting, transformational leaders can encourage their teams to think creatively, adapt to new challenges, and remain current with the most recent cybersecurity practices and technologies (Hasib, 2022; Klimoski & Murray, 2016). Philip (2021) explained that transformational leaders impart a profound sense of responsibility and commitment to safeguarding sensitive data (Hasib, 2022) and ensuring the resilience of organizational infrastructure through their inspirational motivation.

For an organization to become more resilient, top management must recognize that cyber-attacks will likely intensify in the coming years. As a result, cyber security must be situated within the context of strategic cyber security management (Trim & Lee, 2022). In a study examining sociocultural intelligence and artificial intelligence and its relationship to organizational cyber security provisions, Trim and Lee (2022) described that it was evident that organizational learning, transformational leadership, organizational restructuring, crisis management, and corporate intelligence emerged as the most critical management considerations for top management to take into account, as they collectively provided insights into how threat intelligence was viewed and managed. Furthermore, by nurturing a supportive and collaborative workplace, these leaders establish a culture of trust in which individuals feel valued and empowered to contribute their best to the cybersecurity mission (Bass & Riggio, 2006; Philip, 2021; Siangchokyoo et al., 2020). Transformative influence not only strengthens the cybersecurity posture of organizations, but also cultivates a competent and passionate workforce able to address emergent threats proactively.

Transactional Leadership

Transactional leadership is a style of leadership that emphasizes maintaining stability and attaining predetermined objectives through a system of rewards and punishments (Sarros & Santora, 2001). Transactional leaders establish clear expectations and provide detailed instructions to their followers, delineating the tasks, deadlines, and repercussions for noncompliance (Khan, 2017). Khan (2017) explained that transactional leaders emphasize the significance of meeting objectives, adhering to established procedures, and observing organizational structures. Additionally, transactional leaders closely monitor performance, provide feedback, and administer rewards or punishments based on results (Sarros & Santora, 2001). While this leadership style can effectively maintain order and ensure task completion, Yusif and Hafeez-Baig (2021) argued that it frequently lacks the transformative and inspirational elements required to drive innovation and adaptability in dynamic fields like cybersecurity.

To maintain security protocols and mitigate risks, transactional leadership in cybersecurity involves establishing explicit expectations and protocols and instituting rewards and consequences. Transactional leaders in cybersecurity concentrate on ensuring compliance with established security policies and procedures, emphasizing the significance of adhering to established protocols and guidelines to safeguard sensitive data and systems (Almeida et al., 2022). In addition, transactional leaders closely monitor performance and provide feedback to ensure that duties and responsibilities related to cybersecurity are carried out effectively and efficiently (Klimoski & Murray, 2016; Sarros & Santora, 2001). Transactional leadership can help maintain discipline and order within cybersecurity teams and ensure the observance of established security measures. However, Almeida et al. (2022) posited that addressing the rapidly evolving nature of cyber threats may need to be improved, necessitating proactive and innovative strategies to remain clear of malicious actors.

Adaptive Leadership

Adaptive leadership is a leadership style that emphasizes the capacity to navigate and flourish in complex and swiftly changing environments (DeRue, 2011). It requires adaptability, resilience, and responsiveness to obstacles and opportunities. Adaptive leaders encourage innovation, foster collaboration, and delegate problem-solving and decision-making authority to individuals and teams (Ali et al., 2020; Heifetz et al., 2009). According to Ali et al. (2020), adaptive leaders place a premium on learning and development and are willing to adapt their strategies and methods as necessary. Furthermore, Ali et al., (2020) argued that adaptive leadership is crucial in today's dynamic world, where organizations and individuals must adapt and evolve to remain relevant and succeed in a constantly shifting environment.

In cybersecurity, adaptive leadership is indispensable for effectively addressing the ever-changing threat and vulnerability landscape (Burrell et al., 2021). In addition, adaptive leadership recognizes the need for continuous learning and to keep abreast of recent industry trends, technologies, and best practices (Ali et al., 2020; DeRue,

2011). Burrell et al. (2021) explained that by cultivating a culture of adaptability, adaptive leaders encourage their teams to remain nimble, to think critically, and to come up with inventive solutions to combat cyber threats.

Adaptive leadership in cybersecurity involves cross-functional collaboration and communication (Ali et al., 2020; Heifetz et al., 2009). Cybersecurity issues frequently necessitate the input and expertise of multiple departments within an organization (Hasib, 2022). Therefore, adaptive leaders must facilitate the effective exchange of information between teams, dismantling silos and fostering collaboration (Ali et al., 2020). Burrell et al. (2021) explained that successful adaptive leaders recognize that cybersecurity is not exclusively the responsibility of the IT department but rather necessitates participation from all employees. Finally, successful adaptive leadership requires facilitation of collective problem-solving and improve the organization's overall security posture by fostering a collaborative environment (Ali et al., 2020; Heifetz et al., 2009).

REFERENCES

Ajzen, I. (1985). From intentions to actions: A theory of planned behavior. In Kuhland, J., & Beckman, J. (Eds.), *Action control: From cognition to behavior* (pp. 11–39). Springer. DOI: 10.1007/978-3-642-69746-3_2

Ajzen, I. (1991). The theory of planned behavior. *Organizational Behavior and Human Decision Processes*, 50(2), 179–211. DOI: 10.1016/0749-5978(91)90020-T

Ajzen, I. (2020). The theory of planned behavior: Frequently asked questions. *Human Behavior and Emerging Technologies*, 2(4), 314–324. https://publons.com/publon/10.1002/hbe2.195. DOI: 10.1002/hbe2.195

Ajzen, I., & Fishbein, M. (1975). A Bayesian analysis of attribution processes. *Psychological Bulletin*, 82(2), 261–277. Advance online publication. DOI: 10.1037/h0076477

Akbar, M. A., Smolander, K., Mahmood, S., & Alsanad, A. (2022). Toward successful DevSecOps in software development organizations: A decision-making framework. *Information and Software Technology*, 147, 106894. Advance online publication. DOI: 10.1016/j.infsof.2022.106894

Alam, S. S., & Sayuti, N. M. (2011). Applying the theory of planned behavior (TPB) in halal food purchasing. *International Journal of Commerce and Management*, 21(1), 8–20. DOI: 10.1108/10569211111111676

Alanazi, M., Freeman, M., & Tootell, H. (2022). Exploring the factors that influence the cybersecurity behaviors of young adults. *Computers in Human Behavior*, 136, 107376. Advance online publication. DOI: 10.1016/j.chb.2022.107376

Almeida, M. C., Yoshikuni, A. C., Dwivedi, R., & Larieira, C. L. C. (2022). Do leadership styles influence employee information systems security intention? A study of the banking industry. Global Journal of Flexible Systems Management, 1–16. https://doi.org/DOI: 10.1007/s40171-022-00320-1

Amaro, R. M. D., Pereira, R., & da Silva, M. M. (2022). Capabilities and practices in DevOps: A multivocal literature review. *IEEE Transactions on Software Engineering*. Advance online publication. DOI: 10.1109/TSE.2022.3166626

Anjaria, D., & Kulkarni, M. **(2021).** Effective DevSecOps implementation: A systematic literature review. Revista Geintec-Gestao Inovacao E Tecnologias, 11(4), 4931–4945. http://revistageintec.net/wp-content/uploads/2022/03/2514.pdf

Antonucci, L., Kowalski, R., & Garamoni, M. (2020). *Manufacturing cyber security workforce and career development framework*. ManpowerGroup Milwaukee United States.

Ask, T. F., Lugo, R. G., Knox, B. J., & Sütterlin, S. (2021, July). Human-human communication in cyber threat situations: A systematic review. In *International Conference on Human-Computer Interaction* (pp. 21–43). Springer, Cham. https://doi.org/DOI: 10.1007/978-3-030-90328-2_2

Bartnes, M., Moe, N. B., & Heegaard, P. E. (2016). The future of information security incident management training: A case study of electrical power companies. *Computers & Security*, 61, 32–45. DOI: 10.1016/j.cose.2016.05.004

Bass, B. M., & Riggio, R. E. (2006). *Transformational leadership*. Lawrence Erlbaum Associates. DOI: 10.4324/9781410617095

Blum, D. (2020). Institute resilience through detection, response, and recovery. In *Rational cybersecurity for business* (pp. 259–295). Apress., DOI: 10.1007/978-1-4842-5952-8_9

Bobbert, Y., & Chtepen, M. (2021). Research findings in the domain of CI/CD and DevOps on security compliance. In *Strategic approaches to digital platform security assurance* (pp. 286–307). IGI Global., DOI: 10.4018/978-1-7998-7367-9.ch008

Briggs, P., Jeske, D., & Coventry, L. (2017). Behavior change interventions for cybersecurity. In *Behavior change research and theory* (pp. 115–136). Academic Press., DOI: 10.1016/B978-0-12-802690-8.00004-9

Brown, J. M., Greenspan, S., & Biddle, R. (2016). Incident response teams in IT operations centers: The T-TOCs model of team functionality. *Cognition Technology and Work*, 18(4), 695–716. DOI: 10.1007/s10111-016-0374-2

Burrell, D. N., Aridi, A. S., McLester, Q., Shufutinsky, A., Nobles, C., Dawson, M., & Muller, S. R. (2021). Exploring system thinking leadership approaches to the healthcare cybersecurity environment. [IJEACH]. *International Journal of Extreme Automation and Connectivity in Healthcare*, 3(2), 20–32. DOI: 10.4018/IJEACH.2021070103

Carturan, S. B. G., & Goya, D. H. (2019, September). A systems-of-systems security framework for requirements definition in cloud environment. In *Proceedings of the 13th European Conference on Software Architecture-Volume 2* (pp. 235–240). https://doi.org/DOI: 10.1145/3344948.3344977

Computer Security Division. I. T. L. (2020, October 21). DevSecOps | CSRC. *CSRC | NIST*. https://csrc.nist.gov/projects/devsecops

Díaz, J., Pérez, J. E., Lopez-Peña, M. A., Mena, G. A., & Yagüe, A. (2019). Self-service cybersecurity monitoring as enabler for devsecops. *IEEE Access : Practical Innovations, Open Solutions*, 7, 100283–100295. DOI: 10.1109/ACCESS.2019.2930000

Donaldson, S. E., Siegel, S. G., Williams, C. K., & Aslam, A. (2015). Enterprise cybersecurity and the cloud. In *Enterprise cybersecurity* (pp. 105–117). Apress., DOI: 10.1007/978-1-4302-6083-7_6

Duque Anton, S. D., Fraunholz, D., Krohmer, D., Reti, D., Schotten, H. D., Selgert, F., Marosvölgyi, M., Larsen, M., Sudhakar, K., Koch, T., Witt, T., & Bassem, C. (2020, September 8). Creating it from SCRATCh: A practical approach for enhancing the security of IoT-systems in a DevOps-enabled software development environment. In *International Conference on Computer Safety, Reliability, and Security* (pp. 266–281). Springer, Cham. https://doi.org/DOI: 10.1007/978-3-030-55583-2_20

Fearer, M. D. (2020). How to communicate to the C-level suite the need for security operations centers in fortune 1000 environments (Publication No. 28152440) [Doctoral dissertation, Capital Technology University]. ProQuest Dissertations and Theses Global.

Feng, C., Wu, S., & Liu, N. (2017, July). A user-centric machine learning framework for cyber security operations center. In *2017 IEEE International Conference on Intelligence and Security Informatics (ISI)* (pp. 173–175). IEEE. https://doi.org/DOI: 10.1109/ISI.2017.8004902

Guillén, J. H., Del Rey, A. M., & Casado-Vara, R. (2019). Security countermeasures of a SCIRAS model for advanced malware propagation. *IEEE Access : Practical Innovations, Open Solutions*, 7, 135472–135478. DOI: 10.1109/ACCESS.2019.2942809

Han, C. H., Park, S. T., & Lee, S. J. (2019). The enhanced security control model for critical infrastructures with the blocking prioritization process to cyber threats in power system. *International Journal of Critical Infrastructure Protection*, 26, 100312. Advance online publication. DOI: 10.1016/j.ijcip.2019.100312

Hardgrave, B. C., & Johnson, R. A. (2003). Toward an information systems development acceptance model: The case of object-oriented systems development. *IEEE Transactions on Engineering Management*, 50(3), 322–336. DOI: 10.1109/TEM.2003.817293

Hasib, M. (2022). *Cybersecurity leadership: Powering the modern organization* (Vol. 1). Tomorrow's Strategy Today.

Hays, D. G., & McKibben, W. B. (2021). Promoting rigorous research: Generalizability and qualitative research. *Journal of Counseling and Development*, 99(2), 178–188. DOI: 10.1002/jcad.12365

Heifetz, R. A., Heifetz, R., Grashow, A., & Linsky, M. (2009). *The practice of adaptive leadership: Tools and tactics for changing your organization and the world.* Harvard Business Press.

Henneberg, A. (2019). ADDRR: A counter kill chain cyber security model. Cyber Security: A Peer-Reviewed Journal, 3(3), 233–255. https://www.ingentaconnect.com/content/hsp/jcs/2019/00000003/00000003/art00005

Hossain, S. A., Bao, Y., Hasan, N., & Islam, M. F. (2020). Perception and prediction of intention to use online banking systems: An empirical study using extended TAM. International Journal of Research in Business and Social Science (2147-4478), 9(1), 112–116. https://doi.org/DOI: 10.20525/ijrbs.v9i1.591

Jbair, M. (2019). Security monitoring strategies for your OT infrastructure. Cyber Security: A Peer-Reviewed Journal, 3(3), 265–274. https://www.ingentaconnect.com/content/hsp/jcs/2019/00000003/00000003/art00007

Jones, R. K., & Jones, A. J. (2024). Integration of LLMs With Traditional Security Tools. In *Application of Large Language Models (LLMs) for Software Vulnerability Detection* (pp. 295–334). IGI Global., DOI: 10.4018/979-8-3693-9311-6.ch008

Khan, N. (2017). Adaptive or transactional leadership in current higher education: A brief comparison. International Review of Research in Open and Distributed Learning, 18(3), 178¬–¬183. https://doi.org/DOI: 10.19173/irrodl.v18i3.3294

Kim, S. H., Yang, K. H., & Park, S. (2014). An integrative behavioral model of information security policy compliance. *TheScientificWorldJournal*, 2014, 1–12. Advance online publication. DOI: 10.1155/2014/463870 PMID: 24971373

Klimoski, R., & Murray, J. (2016). Cyber security executive leadership. In *Psychosocial dynamics of cyber security* (pp. 165–196). Routledge.

Kumar, R., & Goyal, R. (2020). Modeling continuous security: A conceptual model for automated DevSecOps using open-source software over cloud (ADOC). *Computers & Security*, 97, 101967. Advance online publication. DOI: 10.1016/j.cose.2020.101967

LaMorte, W. W. (2019). Behavioral change models: The theory of planned behavior. https://sphweb.bumc.bu.edu/otlt/mphmodules/sb/behavioralchangetheories/BehavioralChangeTheories3.html

Lubis, M., Wardana, C., & Widjajarto, A. (2020, December). The development of information system security operation centre (SOC): Case study of auto repair company. In 2020 6th International Conference on Interactive Digital Media (ICIDM) (pp. 1–8). IEEE. https://doi.org/DOI: 10.1109/ICIDM51048.2020.9339678

Maalem Lahcen, R. A., Caulkins, B., Mohapatra, R., & Kumar, M. (2020). Review and insight on the behavioral aspects of cybersecurity. *Cybersecurity*, 3(1), 1–18. DOI: 10.1186/s42400-020-00050-w

Mao, R., Zhang, H., Dai, Q., Huang, H., Rong, G., Shen, H., Chen, L., & Lu, K. (2020, December). Preliminary findings of DevSecOps from grey literature. In *2020 IEEE 20th International Conference on Software Quality, Reliability and Security (QRS)* (pp. 450-457). IEEE. https://doi.org/DOI: 10.1109/QRS51102.2020.00064

Maroukian, K., & Gulliver, S. (2020). Exploring the link between leadership and DevOps practice and principle adoption. *Advanced Computing: An International Journal*, 11(4), 1–18. DOI: 10.5121/acij.2020.11401

Masombuka, T., & Mnkandla, E. (2018, September). A DevOps collaboration culture acceptance model. In *Proceedings of the Annual Conference of the South African Institute of Computer Scientists and Information Technologists* (pp. 279-285). DOI: 10.1145/3278681.3278714

McCord, M. (2007). Technology acceptance model. In *Handbook of research on electronic surveys and measurements* (pp. 306–308). IGI Global. DOI: 10.4018/978-1-59140-792-8.ch038

Mehta, P. D., & Neale, M. C. (2005). People are variables too: Multilevel structural equation modeling. *Psychological Methods*, 10(3), 259–284. DOI: 10.1037/1082-989X.10.3.259 PMID: 16221028

Myrbakken, H., & Colomo-Palacios, R. (2017, October). DevSecOps: A multivocal literature review. In *International conference on software process improvement and capability determination* (pp. 17-29). Springer, Cham._DOI: 10.1007/978-3-319-67383-7_2

Nabil, M., Soukainat, S., Lakbabi, A., & Ghizlane, O. (2017, May). SIEM selection criteria for an efficient contextual security. In 2017 international symposium on networks, computers and communications (ISNCC) (pp. 1–6). IEEE. DOI: 10.1109/ISNCC.2017.8072035

Nobles, C. (2018). Botching human factors in cybersecurity in business organizations. *HOLISTICA–Journal of Business and Public Administration*, 9(3), 71–88. DOI: 10.2478/hjbpa-2018-0024

Onwubiko, C. (2020, June). Focusing on the recovery aspects of cyber resilience. In *2020 International Conference on Cyber Situational Awareness, Data Analytics and Assessment (CyberSA)* (pp. 1–13). IEEE. https://doi.org/DOI: 10.1109/CyberSA49311.2020.9139685

Orazi, G., Vallittu, K., Sainio, P., & Virtanen, S. (2020). Enhancing and integration of security testing in the development of a microservices environment. https://www.utupub.fi/bitstream/handle/10024/150701/orazi_master_thesis.pdf?sequence=1

Pandey, A. (2019, June 14). Why do enterprises need Security operations center? https://www.proquest.com/magazines/why-do-enterprises-need-security-operations/docview/2239621832/se-2

Peterson, D. C., Adams, A., Sanders, S., & Sanford, B. (2018). Assessing and addressing threats and risks to cybersecurity. *Frontiers of Health Services Management*, 35(1), 23–29. DOI: 10.1097/HAP.0000000000000040 PMID: 30124511

Philip, J. (2021). Viewing digital transformation through the lens of transformational leadership. *Journal of Organizational Computing and Electronic Commerce*, 31(2), 114–129. DOI: 10.1080/10919392.2021.1911573

Rafi, S., Yu, W., & Akbar, M. A. (2020). Towards a hypothetical framework to secure DevOps adoption: Grounded theory approach. In *Proceedings of the evaluation and assessment in software engineering* (pp. 457-462). https://doi.org/DOI: 10.1145/3383219.3383285

Rajapakse, R. N., Zahedi, M., Babar, M. A., & Shen, H. (2021). Challenges and solutions when adopting DevSecOps: A systematic review. *Information and Software Technology*, 141, 106700. Advance online publication. DOI: 10.1016/j.infsof.2021.106700

Redmiles, E., Malone, A., & Mazurek, M. L. (2015). How I learned to be secure: Advice sources and personality factors in cybersecurity. In *Proceedings of the 2016 ACM SIGSAC conference on computer and communications security* (pp. 666–677). https://doi.org/DOI: 10.1108/K-05-2018-0226

Rowse, M., & Cohen, J. (2021, January). A Survey of DevOps in the South African software context. In Proceedings of the 54th Hawaii international conference on system sciences (p. 6785). http://hdl.handle.net/10125/71435

Sánchez-Gordón, M., & Colomo-Palacios, R. (2020, June). Security as culture: A systematic literature review of DevSecOps. In *Proceedings of the IEEE/ACM 42nd international conference on software engineering workshops* (pp. 266–269). https://doi.org/DOI: 10.1145/3387940.3392233

Sarros, J. C., & Santora, J. C. (2001). The transformational-transactional leadership model in practice. *Leadership and Organization Development Journal*, 22(8), 383–394. DOI: 10.1108/01437730110410107

Settanni, G., Shovgenya, Y., Skopik, F., Graf, R., Wurzenberger, M., & Fiedler, R. (2017, June). Acquiring cyber threat intelligence through security information correlation. In 2017 3rd IEEE international conference on cybernetics (CYBCONF) (pp. 1–7). IEEE. https://doi.org/DOI: 10.1109/CYBConf.2017.7985754

Shukla, M., Tupsamudre, H., & Lodha, S. (2022). Enterprise security: Modern challenges and emerging measures. In *Research anthology on business aspects of cybersecurity* (pp. 441–470). IGI Global., DOI: 10.4018/978-1-6684-3698-1.ch021

Shutock, M., & Dietrich, G. (2022, January). Security operations centers: A holistic view on problems and solutions. In Proceedings of the 55th Hawaii international conference on system sciences. http://hdl.handle.net/10125/80249

Siangchokyoo, N., Klinger, R. L., & Campion, E. D. (2020). Follower transformation as the linchpin of transformational leadership theory: A systematic review and future research agenda. *The Leadership Quarterly*, 31(1), 101341. Advance online publication. DOI: 10.1016/j.leaqua.2019.101341

Tomas, N., Li, J., & Huang, H. (2019, June). An empirical study on culture, automation, measurement, and sharing of DevSecOps. In 2019 International conference on cyber security and protection of digital services (cyber security) (pp. 1–8). IEEE. https://doi.org/DOI: 10.1109/CyberSecPODS.2019.8884935

Trihinas, D., Tryfonos, A., Dikaiakos, M. D., & Pallis, G. (2018). DevOps as a service: Pushing the boundaries of microservice adoption. *IEEE Internet Computing*, 22(3), 65–71. DOI: 10.1109/MIC.2018.032501519

Trim, P. R., & Lee, Y. (2022). Combining sociocultural intelligence with artificial intelligence to increase organizational cyber security provision through enhanced resilience. *Big Data and Cognitive Computing*, 6(4), 110. Advance online publication. DOI: 10.3390/bdcc6040110

Valani, A. (2018, September). Rethinking secure DevOps threat modeling: The need for a dual velocity approach. In 2018 IEEE cybersecurity development (SecDev) (pp. 136). IEEE. DOI: 10.1109/SecDev.2018.00032

van Steen, T., & Deeleman, J. R. (2021). Successful gamification of cybersecurity training. *Cyberpsychology, Behavior, and Social Networking*, 24(9), 593–598. DOI: 10.1089/cyber.2020.0526 PMID: 34491845

Yusif, S., & Hafeez-Baig, A. (2021). A conceptual model for cybersecurity governance. *Journal of Applied Security Research*, 16(4), 490–513. DOI: 10.1080/19361610.2021.1918995

Zaydi, M., & Nassereddine, B. (2020). DevSecOps practices for an agile and secure IT service management. Journal of Management Information and Decision Sciences, 23(2), 1–16. https://www.proquest.com/openview/8fdf6472c3a73b00fed8ec83a3e97b76/1?pq-origsite=gscholar&cbl=38743\ 74.

Chapter 11
An In-Depth Investigation on Hardware Trojans Testing Into Cyber Security Concerns Using Machine Learning Models

S. Hariharasitaraman
VIT Bhopal University, India

Ajinkya Bhanpurkar
VIT Bhopal University, India

Madhu Singh
https://orcid.org/0009-0000-0289-9169
VIT Bhopal University, India

Nilamadhab Mishra
https://orcid.org/0000-0002-1330-4869
VIT Bhopal University, India

ABSTRACT

The current study comprehensively investigates hardware Trojan testing using traditional and machine learning models. It highlights the challenge posed by the uniqueness of each Hardware Trojan and emphasizes the need for reliable solutions. The study recommends using machine learning models with feature extraction to

DOI: 10.4018/979-8-3373-0588-2.ch011

detect patterns in different Hardware Trojans. However, the study also identifies limitations in the existing models, including reliance on the XGBoost algorithm. The study suggests exploring hybrid mechanisms and newer languages, such as LightBGM, for model development as potential areas for further research. The study also underscores the significance of addressing security concerns in IoT technology.

1. INTRODUCTION

In recent times, the rapid integration and proliferation of electronic systems across critical sectors have raised substantial concerns about the vulnerability of hardware to malicious attacks. Among these threats, Hardware Trojans have emerged as particularly stealthy and insidious, capable of compromising the integrity and functionality of integrated circuits. Their potential insertion during the fabrication process or at any stage of the supply chain poses significant risks to the reliability and security of electronic devices, making them a crucial issue for end users, manufacturers, and designers alike (Blum, A. et al., 2020; DiMaggio, A. R., 2021).

This paper aims to thoroughly analyze diverse security technologies employed as defense mechanisms against Hardware Trojans. It delves into the intricate nature of these Trojans, their potential impacts on systems, and the current landscape of security solutions. By examining a spectrum of methodologies, including cryptographic techniques, hardware-based solutions, and verification strategies, this study aims to give a complete knowledge of several techniques' strengths, limits, and efficacy for minimizing Hardware Trojan risks. Furthermore, the paper intends to assess these security measures' adaptability to various design scenarios, cost implications, performance overhead, and practicality in real-world applications. A thorough analysis aims to provide valuable insights into the changing strategies necessary to strengthen hardware systems against the ongoing and developing threat posed by Hardware Trojans. Ultimately, this research endeavor seeks to contribute to the ongoing discourse on Hardware Trojans and their countermeasures by consolidating a perspective on the efficacy of various security technologies. It seeks to provide a complete overview of their possible consequences for assuring the integrity and trustworthiness of modern electronic systems.

2. LITERATURE REVIEW

Chen Dong et al. (Dong et al., 2019) introduced RG-Secure, a multi-layer system that protects the Internet of Things perception layer from hardware Trojans. The primary goal is to merge trustworthy design methodologies from third-party intellectual property with scan-chain netlist feature analysis software. This model was based on Hardware Trojan structural features and could detect both register transfer-level and gate-level Hardware Trojans. The approach provides quick processing of high-dimensional circuit feature data, significantly improving the efficiency and efficacy of hardware Trojan identification.

Tao Han et al. (Han et al., 2019) May suggested a machine learning-based detection approach for RTLs in integrated circuits that detects the presence of any HT. The machine learning model was trained using a training database and a gradient boost approach. A server-client approach was utilized to keep the detection system up to date on new threat classifications. The authors employed 21 circuits from Trust-Hub benchmark tests to determine the efficiency of their proposed architecture.

Hasegawa, K. et al. (Hasegawa, K., Shi, Y., & Togawa, N., 2018) provided Trojan characteristics, which were then examined using the Minimum Redundancy Maximum Relevance (mRMR) feature selection approach, yielding recommended feature combinations. The most effective method for categorizing Trojan and normal branches was then determined by testing the feature combinations using various machine-learning approaches. The method relied solely on direct static data extraction to affirm the presence of Trojans without necessitating additional logic simulation or model testing for confirmation.

Joseph Clements et al. (Clements, J., & Lao, Y., 2018) introduced a new HT attack and its defense mechanism in the scope of neural networks. The proposed attack specifically targeted the hardware circuitry of the neural network without altering any weights. Unlike many common Trojans, the HT was inserted in the supply chain, where it is done in the application phase.

Rozhin Yasaei et al. (Yasaei, R., Chen, L., Yu, S. Y., & Al Faruque, M. A., 2022) proposed a cutting-edge pre-silicon HT detection approach that uses powerful machine learning algorithms to understand circuit functioning without a golden reference. This method successfully identified potentially suspicious or malicious Trojans within the design. Furthermore, the study produced Directed Acyclic Graphs (DFG) for both Register-Transfer Level (RTL) codes and gate-level netlists, using a graph data format to represent the hardware architecture.

Tatsuki Kurihara et al. (Kurihara, T., Hasegawa, K., & Togawa, N., 2020) presented a machine learning-based HT detection method that used neural networks and random forests to 24 gate-level netlists. They evaluated the efficacy of gate-level IP cores with thousands of nets in learning 11 attributes for each net in a specific netlist. They used the newly learned classifiers to separate the nets into normal and Trojan nets and benchmarked them.

Hawzhin Mohammed et al. (Mohammed, H., Hasan, S. R., & Awwad, F. (2020); Mohammed, H., Howell, J., Hasan, S. R., Guo, N., Khalid, F., & Elkeelany, O., 2018) provide a method for dealing with IoT-ED embedded HTs, which might pose major privacy, security, and availability issues for IoT-based HANs. The researchers investigated five types of HT-based assaults against HANs. Power profiling and network traffic data were collected from various sources and processed to build a machine-learning model to detect Trojans based on known patterns. A modular test bed design encompassing multiple conceivable hardware-specific HAN assaults was utilized to implement three types of attacks, and the findings are reported in the study. The authors created a test bed with an interface designed to manage and simulate various necessary network behaviors as needed.

Xingyu Meng et al. (Meng, X., Hassan, R., Dinakrrao, S. M. P., & Basu, K., 2021) developed an overclocking-driven method for producing various bit-flip patterns on both unmodified and Trojan-inserted Integrated Circuits (ICs). They also developed a machine learning system capable of analyzing a dataset of bit flips to determine the existence of any Hardware Trojans within the targeted IC. The proposed approach was especially effective at detecting the presence of Hardware Trojans that were placed off of a critical path.

Ayush Jain et al. (Jain, A., Zhou, Z., & Guin, U., 2021) compared combinational, sequential, and analog Trojans and related defense mechanisms to provide valuable insights. The authors compared logic and optical-based Trojan detection techniques and found that optical-based techniques are better at detecting the presence of Trojan on given pieces of hardware. The researchers also proposed a practical approach for detecting the presence of Trojans on a piece of hardware using the categorization of EOFM images of an IoT chip.

Vivek Venugopalan et al. (Venugopalan, V., & Patterson, C. D., 2018) discovered that academic, business, defense authorities, and governmental institutions paid close attention to the continued research on IoT-based CPS security. Most of the research focuses on the system as a whole rather than hardware like sensors or processors, which are exposed and easily subject to an attack.

Shamik Kundu et al. (Kundu, S., Meng, X., & Basu, K., 2021) studied the cutting-edge machine learning-based defense techniques used for HT detection. The researchers aimed to investigate the prowess of the latest Trojan detection mechanisms in bolstering the security of a system for which the researchers analyzed the efficiency of each algorithm and underlined a few key problems with these existing Trojan detection approaches.

Kento Hasegawa et al. (Hasegawa, K., Shi, Y., & Togawa, N., 2018) discussed the latest machine-learning techniques for HT detection. The research also analyses various machine learning-based methods for finding HT. Specific netlist nets were separated into two groups to correctly and successfully detect HT: regular nets and Trojan nets, followed by feature extraction.

Yipei Yang et al. (Yang, Y., Ye, J., Cao, Y., Zhang, J., Li, X., Li, H., & Hu, Y., 2020) concentrated on techniques for detecting HTs at the gate level. They divided HT detection strategies into three categories based on the criteria below: search-based, threshold-based, and machine learning-based. Each technique was then thoroughly tested against the others regarding detection range, classification criteria, and feature selection. The researchers concluded that most of the latest detection approaches were based on HTs' low trigger probability aspect.

Liakos et al. (Liakos, K. G., Georgakilas, G. K., Moustakidis, S., Karlsson, P., & Plessas, F. C., 2019) conducted a detailed analysis and literature research on machine learning-based methods for detecting HTs in integrated circuits. The researchers reviewed twenty articles under five categories. The categories were: Golden Model-Free Approaches, Real-Time Detection, Gate-Level Netlists, Reverse Engineering Improvement and Classification approaches and pointed out the shortcomings in each.

Chen Dong et al. (Dong, C., He, G., Liu, X., Yang, Y., & Guo, W., 2019) used the XGBoost algorithm to test and score the 51 pre-existing features of Trojan circuits and list 49 effective ones. Thus providing increased effectiveness in the training of HT classifiers. The researchers also introduced five new features. They emphasized the detection of a Trojan net' in the process of detecting a whole HT to maximize the Recall.

Shichao Yu et al. (Yu, S., Gu, C., Liu, W., & O'Neill, M., 2020) suggested a novel method for collecting HT characteristics from gate-level circuit netlists to solve the challenges experienced by machine learning-based HT detection models. Instead of using statistical analysis as was done in earlier research efforts, the HT traits were retrieved from the circuit topology. A support vector machine (SVM)--based Hardware Trojan detection model was trained and tested using characteristics collected from Hardware Trojan benchmarks from open-source libraries and HT-generating platforms.

Taifeng Hu et al. (Hu, T., Wu, L., Zhang, X., Yin, Y., & Yang, Y., 2019) proposed using machine learning principles to identify HTs in Integrated Circuits, including SCA and SVM. Reverse Engineering and Logic Testing pathways were plagued with inefficiencies and sometimes complete disruption of the Integrated Circuit, on the other hand, SCA along with the SVM classifier provided promising results with both Trojan detection rate and decent classification accuracy.

Chen Dong et al. (Dong, C., Liu, Y., Chen, J., Liu, X., Guo, W., & Chen, Y., 2020) visualized the distributional characteristics of regular nets versus Trojan nets, highlighting disparities to condense the feature set dimensions. The team then presented an unsupervised hardware Trojan detection approach called PL-HTD, which combines Principal Component Analysis (PCA) and Local Outlier Factor (LOF) methods. This approach aimed to identify Hardware Trojans by leveraging these combined techniques. The aberrant nets were picked and then evaluated by specialists to see if they were true Trojans compared to the host circuit, allowing for identification based on each net's outliers. The testing results show that the proposed technique can efficiently detect hardware Trojans while lowering the cost of human secondary detection.

Chee Hoo Kok et al. (Kok, C. H., Ooi, C. Y., Inoue, M., Moghbel, M., Dass, S. B., Choo, H. S., ... & Hussin, F. A., 2019) proposed an HT detection strategy at the gate level netlist that evaluates each net and builds supervised classifiers utilizing testability metrics and net structural aspects as features. The researchers found that the inclusion of Trojan nets in Register Transfer Level (RTL) or gate-level designs, independent of the manner of insertion (e.g., scripting, synthesis via EDA tools, or integrating external IP cores with Hardware Trojans), was expected to be identifiable. This assertion stemmed from their approach's capability to identify anomalous or suspicious nets, thus hinting at the potential discovery of such modifications.

Table 1(a). Review summary of the existing works

Author, Year	Key Contribution	Gate-Level Netlists	Register Transfer	True Positive Rate (80 percent)	True Negative Rate (80 percent)
Chen Dong et al., (2019)	Proposed multi-layer HT protection architecture aimed primarily at IoT chips.	Yes	Yes	Yes	No
Kindt, J. (2024)	The suggested approach can identify five distinct forms of HT-based assaults that go unnoticed during IC design and testing of IoT devices.	No	No	No	No
Ayush Jain et al., (2021)	Proposed an EOFM technique to secure devices against HT attacks.	No	No	No	No
Vivek Venu-Gopalan et al., (2018)	Proposes that security primitives and countermeasures applicable to a CPS are not always appropriate for IoT systems.	No	No	No	No
Joseph Clements et al., (2018)	Introduces a new HT attack that specifically targets the hardware circuitry of the neural network without altering any weights.	No	No	No	No
Shamik Kundu et al., (2021)	They proposed that future research should increase the performance of these machine learning algorithms and safeguard them from specific attacks.	No	No	No	No

continued on following page

Table 1(a). Continued

Author, Year	Key Contribution	Gate-Level Netlists	Register Transfer	True Positive Rate (80 percent)	True Negative Rate (80 percent)
Chen Dong et al., (2019)	We proposed a machine learning-based approach for detecting HT in gate-level netlists, as well as five novel Trojan network characteristics.	Yes	No	Yes	Yes
Choo, H. S., et al., (2020)	Proposed a testbed implementation to simulate HT and investigate its impact on HAN security.	No	No	No	No
Kundu, S. et al., (2021)	The suggested method is particularly successful in detecting the presence of HT that are positioned outside of a critical route.	No	No	No	No
K. Hasegawa et al., (2018)	Elucidates the traits of HTs and displays the taxonomy of methods for detecting them during the design phase.	No	No	Yes	Yes
Y. Yang et al., (2020)	The previous research on feature selection methods, data balancing strategies, and classification criteria was summarized, with a focus on HT detection for gate-level netlists.	Yes	No	No	No
Rozhin Yasaei et al., (2022)	They created two models that infer the existence of HT from the produced graphs in RTL and gate-level netlist codes, as well as DFGs for both.	Yes	Yes	No	No
Liakos, K. G. et al., (2019)	Points out that there has been a lot of variability in the different types of benchmark tests used by researchers.	Yes	No	No	No
Tao Han et al., (2019)	We proposed a machine learning-based approach for detecting RTLs in integrated circuits (ICs).	No	Yes	Yes	Yes
Sankaran, S. et al., (2021)	A machine learning-based HT detection method was proposed, which use neural networks and random forests to analyze 24 gate-level netlists.	Yes	No	Yes	Yes
Yu, S et al., (2020)	Proposed an SVM-based novel feature extraction technique based on circuit topology.	Yes	No	No	No

continued on following page

Table 1(a). Continued

Author, Year	**Key Contribution**	**Gate-Level Netlists**	**Register Transfer**	**True Positive Rate (80 percent)**	**True Negative Rate (80 percent)**
Hu, T. et al., (2019)	Proposed a methodology to use machine learning concepts in the detection of HTs within ICs using SCA and SVM classifiers.	No	No	Yes	Yes
Naveenkumar, R., & Sivamangai, N. M. (2024).	Demonstrated four branching statement-related features and an approach for detecting RTL Trojans using mRMR.	No	Yes	Yes	Yes
Chen Dong et al., (2020)	An extracted useful set of 16 Trojan-net features Using the XGBoost algorithm's scoring system, we conducted a thorough comparison.	Yes	No	No	No
Chen, M. et al., (2024)	We detected gate-level netlists, using SCOAP values in conjunction with netlist structural features as HT features.	Yes	Yes	Yess	Yes

Table 1(b). Review summary of the existing works

Neural Networks	**Home- Area Networks**	**Machine Learning**	**Electro-Optical Frequency Mapping**	**Feature Extraction**
No	No	No	No	No
No	Yes	Yes	No	No
No	No	No	Yes*	No
No	No	Yes*	No	No
Yes	No	No	No	No
No	No	Yes*	No	No
No	No	Yes	No	Yes
No	Yes	No	No	No
No	No	Yes	No	No
No	No	Yes*	No	No
No	No	Yes*	No	Yes
Yes	No	Yes	No	No
No	No	Yes*	No	No

continued on following page

Table 1(b). Continued

Neural Networks	Home- Area Networks	Machine Learning	Electro-Optical Frequency Mapping	Feature Extraction
No	No	Yes	No	No
Yes	No	Yes	No	Yes
No	No	Yes	No	Yes
No	No	Yes	No	No
No	No	Yes	No	Yes
No	No	Yes	No	Yes
No	No	Yes	No	Yes

3. METHODOLOGY

3.1 Background

3.1.1 History

The word "Trojan" or "Trojan Horse" originates from an event that occurred in ancient Greek mythology. The Greek army built a wooden horse-like structure to infiltrate the city of Troy (Blum, A., Hopcroft, J., & Kannan, R., 2020). Epeius, a brilliant craftsman and warrior, created the horse. As the Greeks feigned to abandon the fight and sail to the nearby island of Tenedos, Sinon (a Greek soldier) duped the officials of Troy by informing them that the horse was a sacrifice to Athena (the goddess of war), which would render Troy impenetrable. The horse was permitted to enter Troy's city gates. Later that night, Greek troops emerged from the horse and opened the gates, allowing the reconstituted Greek army to enter, thereby winning the battle of Troy (DiMaggio, A. R., 2021). When discussing computer Trojan Horses, a few aspects of the narrative support the name:

The Trojan horse serves as a countermeasure to the target's defenses. In the original story, the city of Troy had been under siege for ten years, but the attackers could not destroy it. They were ultimately able to get access owing to the Trojan horse. A Trojan Horse can bypass powerful defenses by masquerading as beneficial software.

The Trojan Horse has the appearance of being a real gift. A computer Trojan is similar in appearance to legal software. The Trojan Horse's soldiers were in command of the city's defenses. When a Trojan virus infects a computer, it takes control, possibly exposing the system to other "invaders". A Trojan horse is any software that deceives people about its purpose in computers. The word is taken from the Ancient Greek myth of the deceitful Trojan Horse, which contributed to the destruction of Troy (Mondal, A., Karmakar, S., Mahalat, M. H., Roy, S., Sen, B., & Chattopadhyay, A., 2022). Trojans may usually be divided into two categories: Software Trojans are harmful pieces of code that can take control of a system. It is used to steal from or otherwise harm the victim's computer. It tricks the user into loading and running itself on the device. Once it runs, this gives adversary access to the user's computer and gives him/her the ability to do things like delete and edit data from files.

Hardware Trojans: Hardware Trojan is used to modify an IC chip's circuitry with malicious intent. The chips or the circuitry are modified without the knowledge of the personnel it was designed. This usually happens at the fabrication stage of chips used in various hardware components. The Hardware Trojan awakens at random intervals and engages in malicious or destructive behavior that is also unpredictable from the user's perspective.

Figure 1. Working of hardware trojan

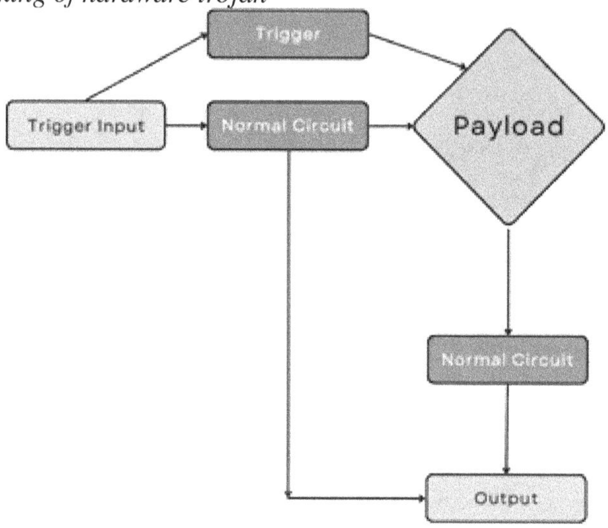

3.2 Hardware Trojan Security Detection

Popular security measures against Hardware Trojans that are primarily focused on detecting the presence of HTs in an IC chip can be classified as follows: Destructive: The efficiency of these techniques is jeopardized by the nature of destructive Hardware Trojan detection methods, which damage the studied Integrated Circuit (IC). Non-destructive: Non-destructive hardware Trojan detection techniques can be classified as intrusive or non-invasive since they do not cause damage to the integrated circuit under investigation. While intrusive approaches modify the design to include aspects that aid in Trojan detection, non-invasive solutions leave the system unaltered.

Figure 2. Types of hardware trojan detection techniques

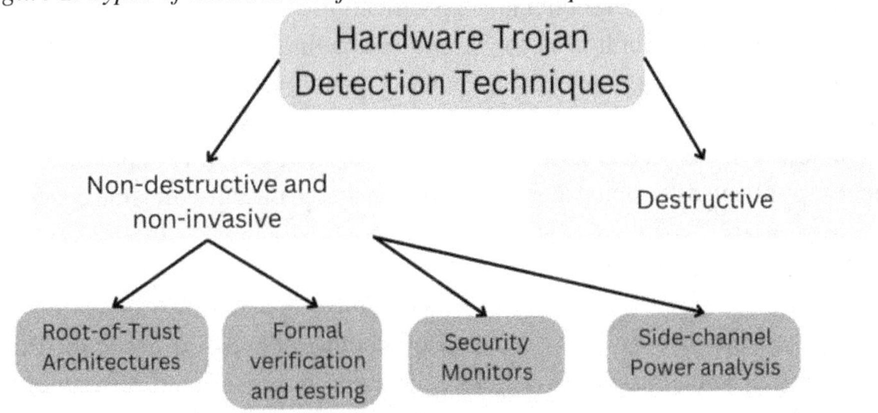

3.3 Countermeasures

Popular countermeasures against Hardware Trojans can be classified as follows:

Data Cards: A guard can regulate data storage or transit inside or across integrated circuits or logic modules, which might influence how Trojans interact with the data. Novel RTL-Level Architectures: According to researchers, modern processor and IC architectures can be modified in certain ways to safeguard against Hardware Trojans. The basic idea is to add or change logic gates to particularly detect the presence of Hardware Trojans or stop them from activating. Reconfigurable Logic: The significant advantage of reconfigurable logic is the distinct separation of hardware implementation and design execution. In reconfigurable logic, a standard programmable logic element or macro is first included in the semiconductor process. The concept is then implemented by programming these logic parts using a configuration bitstream. Unlike a standard integrated circuit (IC), the semiconductor process directly includes the design. Replication, Fragmentation, and Voting: Understanding the behavior of an electrical circuit design at several levels—from process and gate-level to RTL-level, IC-level, and electronic design—is critical for developing successful hardware Trojans.

Generic Hardware Trojan countermeasures that can be used at many of these levels include replication or duplication of logic and/or data; slicing or fragmentation of logic and/or data; scattering or distribution of logic and/or data; and gathering and combining of logic and/or data results, such as using a voting mechanism. These general countermeasures work on three fronts: preventing hardware Trojans from revealing confidential data by dividing the data and processing it with independent logic elements; preventing functional or specification changes to elements by using multiple replicated or duplicated logic; and preventing DoS attacks by ensuring that logic elements operate redundantly within the design. Countermeasures can be deployed at various levels, including IC and macro-level vices, RTL, gate-level, functional modules, IP cores, and logic design (Bellamy, A. J., 2005). The approaches for protecting replicated or copied design portions are based on anti-collusion concepts.

3.4 Problem Statement

A typical Hardware Trojan remains inactive most of the time in the modified device it is placed in, but its activation might result in catastrophic destruction. A hardware Trojan can alter a device's functionality, disable or damage it, disclose private information, or compromise security if activated. Traditional testing methods are inadequate for detecting these specialized pieces of malware as harmful alterations are positioned carefully to prevent discovery. Detecting such Trojans is crucial, as they have been reportedly used to target a country's defense and artillery equipment. According to CORDIS (European Commission)" Computer attacks are on the rise. According to some estimates, there were 3.2 billion attacks alone in the first half of 2020. While most of these are based on malicious software, attacks based on manipulated hardware, referred to as hardware Trojans, are particularly dangerous (Holaday, A., 1946). According to Eureka Alert," A small team of security researchers from Tallinn University of Technology (TalTech) has shown that hardware Trojan Horses may be installed into computer chips while they are being manufactured. After the researchers refined their insertion methods, the full layout adjustment to implant four Trojan Horses took over an hour (Chakraborty et al., 2009). The biggest issue for researchers in Hardware Trojan Security is the exclusivity of every Hardware Trojan. Unlike Software Trojans, Hardware Trojans are explicitly made for the targeted victim machines. Thus, it is hard to pinpoint similarities between Hardware Trojans and develop programs or algorithms to tackle these nuisances. One of the most effective solutions proposed (Bellamy, A. J., 2005; Ahmad, Z., Shahid Khan, A., Wai Shiang, C., Abdullah, J., & Ahmad, F., 2021; Choo, H. S., et al., 2020; Clements, J., & Lao, Y., 2018) is the training of machine learning models to detect patterns in different Hardware Trojans using feature extraction. The proposed solutions by various researchers were compared based on various parameters in Table 1, and the most prominent limitation is that the machine learning models either dealt with Gate-level netlists or Register Transfer Lists. Also, many models use the XGBoost algorithm as the basis for the development of their models, which makes bypassing all these models very convenient. Though multiple authors have proposed individual mechanisms, the possibility of a hybrid mechanism was not explored, and it is one area that authors could explore shortly and use the latest languages, such as LightBGM, to develop ML-based models.

3.5 Discussion of Existing Solutions

Overview: The Internet of Things (IoT) technology has received widespread praise from governments, academics, and corporations due to advancements in wireless communication, sensor technology, embedded system applications, and microelectronics technology. IoT applications can greatly enhance human-nature relationships and industrial productivity. Despite the IoT's rapid development, security concerns have taken center stage. The physical security of sensor layer devices is more vulnerable than that of the IoT's transport and application layers. The enemy may directly obtain the sensitive formation due to the widespread sensor deployment in industrial and agricultural settings if the sensors are not checked for an extended period. Because there are several unreliable producers of integrated circuits, malicious circuits can be inserted into IoT devices at any time. Various approaches to solving this problem were studied during the research tenure of this paper. After this, it was concluded that machine learning-based models provide the most reliable solutions to the problem. Thus, different machine learning-based models have been compared and analyzed in the upcoming section of the paper.

3.6 Evaluation Metrics

Aside from the choice of ML model, another key aspect is the metrics used to evaluate a model.

- **Accuracy:** Accuracy is used to evaluate the model's performance. It represents the ratio of total accurate instances to total instances.

Accuracy=(TP+TN)/TP+TN+FP+FN

- **Precision:** Precision measures how accurate a model's favorable predictions are. It is defined as the proportion of genuine positive predictions to total positive predictions made by the model.

Precision=TP/(TP+FP)

- **Recall:** The proportion of genuine malware that is accurately categorized.

Recall=TP/(TP+FN)

- **F1- score or F-measure:** The F1-score is used to assess the overall performance of a classification model. It is the harmonic average of accuracy and recall.

F1-score=(2*Precision*Recall)/(Precision+Recall)

Figure 3. ER diagram between evaluation metrics and ml models

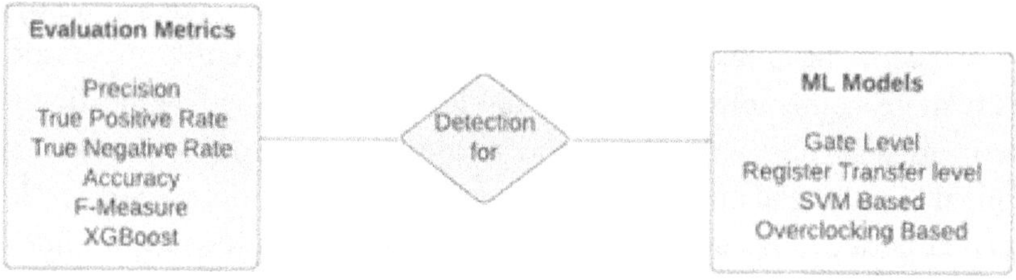

3.7 Anticipated Architecture

The proposed model is based on the XGBoost machine learning method, which gives it a lot of advantages, such as:

Figure 4. Gate-Level netlist detection mechanism

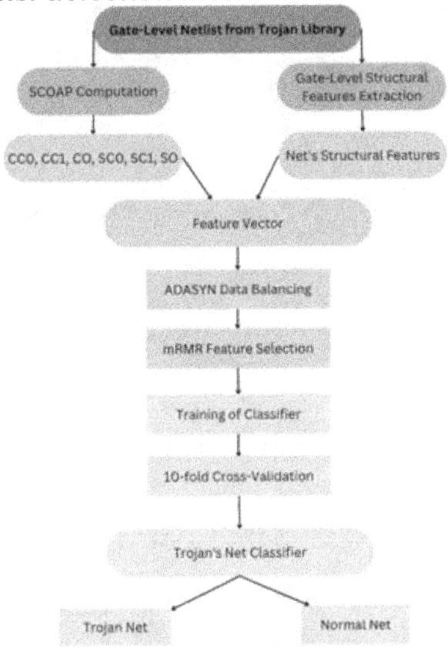

It has a high level of flexibility. It makes the use of parallel processing power. It works quicker than gradient boosting. The structure favors regularization. Its built-in features are designed to deal with missing data. The user can do cross-validation after each loop (Clements, J., & Lao, Y., 2018). The following architecture Figure 5 shows a skeletal model for a 'Gate-Level Netlist and RTL Hardware Trojan Detection Mechanism' that leverages the LightBGM framework instead of the XGBoost framework to get quicker results. Its ability to detect Hardware Trojans at both the gate and RTL levels distinguishes this approach from others. This model can be improved if government and defense organizations publicize the Hardware Trojan attack data they have, as this will provide a wealth of valuable inputs to the machine learning algorithm, allowing it to generate massive amounts of Hardware Trojan attack patterns (Dong et al., 2019; Han et al., 2019).

Figure 5. Gate-Level netlist and RTL hardware trojan detection mechanism

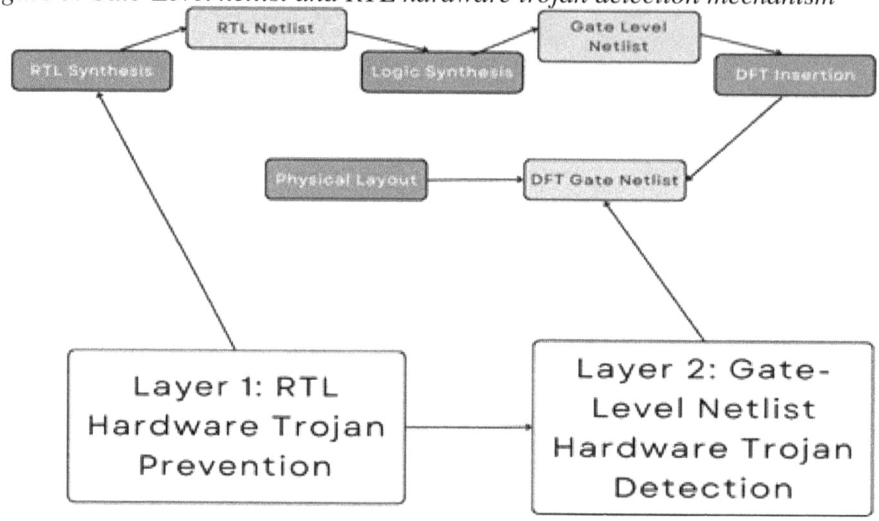

4. CRITICAL REVIEW DISCUSSIONS

Table 2. Benchmark of evaluation metrics.

Author & Year	Paper	TNR	TPR(Recall)	F-Measure	Precision	Accuracy
Chen Dong et al., 2019	A hardware-based technique for detecting Trojans using machine learning for Internet of Things chips.	99.87%	89.84%	86.75%	92.29%	99.83%
Chen Dong et al., 2019	Hardware Trojan Protection Framework for IoT Chips.	92.90%	99.10%	99.50%	99.80%	99%
Chen Dong et al.,2020	Unsupervised Detection Method for Hardware Trojans	97.52%	42.42%	33.56%	33.56%	96%
Xingyu Meng et al.,2021	Can Overclocking Identify Hardware Trojans?	x	87%	88%	89.33%	87.58%
Tatsuki Kurihara et al., 2020	Using Machine Learning Methods to Evaluate Hardware Trojan Detection at Gate-Level IP Cores	95.10%	84.60%	x	x	x

continued on following page

Table 2. Continued

Author & Year	Paper	TNR	TPR(Recall)	F-Measure	Precision	Accuracy
Taifeng Hu et al., 2019	Combining hardware Trojan detection with machine learning to create an SVM-based detection approach.	91.1%	92.5%	x	x	91.84%
Tao Han et al., 2019	Detecting hardware Trojans at the register transfer level using machine learning.	89.32%	100%	x	x	x
Chee Hoo Kok et al., 2019	Detecting hardware Trojans by Net Classification using Testability and Netlist Structural Features.	99.95%	99.85%	x	x	99.90%
Hau Sim Choo et al., 2020	Machine-Learning-Based Hardware Trojan Detection using Register-Transfer-Level Features.	91.44%	93.72%	x	x	91.91%

5 CONCLUSION AND FUTURE DIRECTIONS

Hybridization of models: Machine learning and deep learning techniques should be used in the next generation of hardware Trojan security models. They should detect the presence of Trojans at both the gate level and the register transfer level (RTL). Future research should also focus on mitigating or minimizing the harm caused by any hardware Trojan attacks.

LightBGM: XGBoost is one of the most widely used supervised machine learning algorithms. It improves the gradient-boosted decision tree's underlying boosting approach (GBDT). This algorithm is popular in data competitions like Kaggle, DataCastle, and Kesci because of its speed, accuracy, ability to handle large volumes of data, and support for several languages. Meanwhile, a distributed high-performance system developed by Microsoft called LightGBM employs decision trees for applications that include ranking, classification, and regression. LightBGM is a better alternative to XGBoost for the following reasons: Because LightGBM employs a histogram-based technique and values bucketing, it offers a quicker training time, more accuracy, and less memory. It also works with vast and complex datasets, but the training time is much faster. It supports both GPU and parallel learning. Because LightGBM uses a histogram-based approach and performs value bucketing, it has a faster training speed, more accuracy, and requires less memory. It also works with large and complicated datasets, but the training process is considerably quicker. It supports both GPU and parallel learning. The presence of Hardware Trojans in defense equipment and gear has been reported many times. Still, governments and defense organizations have always been secretive about it, which has resulted in a lack of information about Hardware Trojans. Thus, the government should publicize more information, and researchers should focus on tackling hardware Trojan attacks and threats to defense equipment and gear.

REFERENCES

Ahmad, Z., Shahid Khan, A., Wai Shiang, C., Abdullah, J., & Ahmad, F. (2021). Network intrusion detection system: A systematic study of machine learning and deep learning approaches. *Transactions on Emerging Telecommunications Technologies*, 32(1), e4150. DOI: 10.1002/ett.4150

Bellamy, A. J. (2005). Responsibility to protect or Trojan horse? The crisis in Darfur and humanitarian intervention after Iraq. *Ethics & International Affairs*, 19(2), 31–54. DOI: 10.1111/j.1747-7093.2005.tb00499.x

Blum, A., Hopcroft, J., & Kannan, R. (2020). *Foundations of data science*. Cambridge University Press. DOI: 10.1017/9781108755528

Chakraborty, R. S., Narasimhan, S., & Bhunia, S. (2009, November). Hardware Trojan: Threats and emerging solutions. In 2009 IEEE International high level design validation and test workshop (pp. 166-171). IEEE.

Chen, M., Li, Y., Zhou, S., Zou, L., Yu, L., Deng, T., Rong, X., Shao, S., & Wu, J. (2024). Establishment of a risk prediction model for olfactory disorders in patients with transnasal pituitary tumors by machine learning. *Scientific Reports*, 14(1), 12514. DOI: 10.1038/s41598-024-62963-7 PMID: 38822064

Choo, H. S., Ooi, C. Y., Inoue, M., Ismail, N., Moghbel, M., & Kok, C. H. (2020). Register-transfer-level features for machine-learning-based hardware trojan detection. IEICE TRANSACTIONS on Fundamentals of Electronics. *Communications and Computer Sciences*, 103(2), 502–509.

Clements, J., & Lao, Y. (2018). Hardware trojan attacks on neural networks. arXiv preprint arXiv:1806.05768.

DiMaggio, A. R. (2021). The Trojan Horse–"Conservative" Media and the Mainstreaming of Neofascistic Politics. In Rising Fascism in America (pp. 87-129). Routledge.

Dong, C., Chen, J., Guo, W., & Zou, J. (2019). A machine-learning-based hardware-Trojan detection approach for chips in the Internet of Things. *International Journal of Distributed Sensor Networks*, 15(12), 1550147719888098. DOI: 10.1177/1550147719888098

Dong, C., He, G., Liu, X., Yang, Y., & Guo, W. (2019). A multi-layer hardware trojan protection framework for IoT chips. *IEEE Access : Practical Innovations, Open Solutions*, 7, 23628–23639. DOI: 10.1109/ACCESS.2019.2896479

Dong, C., Liu, Y., Chen, J., Liu, X., Guo, W., & Chen, Y. (2020). An unsupervised detection approach for hardware trojans. *IEEE Access : Practical Innovations, Open Solutions*, 8, 158169–158183. DOI: 10.1109/ACCESS.2020.3001239

Han, T., Wang, Y., & Liu, P. (2019, May). Hardware trojans detection at register transfer level based on machine learning. In *2019 IEEE International Symposium on Circuits and Systems (ISCAS)* (pp. 1-5). IEEE. DOI: 10.1109/ISCAS.2019.8702479

Hasegawa, K., Shi, Y., & Togawa, N. (2018, August). Hardware trojan detection utilizing machine learning approaches. In 2018 17th IEEE International Conference On Trust, Security And Privacy In Computing And Communications/12th IEEE International Conference On Big Data Science And Engineering (TrustCom/BigDataSE) (pp. 1891-1896). IEEE. DOI: 10.1109/TrustCom/BigDataSE.2018.00287

Holaday, A. (1946). Heywood's" Troia Britannica" and the" Ages. *Journal of English and Germanic Philology*, 45(4), 430–439.

Hu, T., Wu, L., Zhang, X., Yin, Y., & Yang, Y. (2019, October). Hardware trojan detection combine with machine learning: an svm-based detection approach. In 2019 IEEE 13th international conference on anti-counterfeiting, security, and identification (ASID) (pp. 202-206). IEEE. DOI: 10.1109/ICASID.2019.8924992

Jain, A., Zhou, Z., & Guin, U. (2021, May). Survey of recent developments for hardware trojan detection. In 2021 ieee international symposium on circuits and systems (iscas) (pp. 1-5). IEEE.

Kindt, J. (2024). *The Trojan Horse and Other Stories: Ten Ancient Creatures that Make Us Human*. Cambridge University Press. DOI: 10.1017/9781009411332

Kok, C. H., Ooi, C. Y., Inoue, M., Moghbel, M., Dass, S. B., Choo, H. S., . . . Hussin, F. A. (2019, December). Net classification based on testability and netlist structural features for hardware Trojan detection. In 2019 IEEE 28th Asian Test Symposium (ATS) (pp. 105-1055). IEEE. DOI: 10.1109/ATS47505.2019.00020

Kundu, S., Meng, X., & Basu, K. (2021, April). Application of machine learning in hardware trojan detection. In 2021 22nd International Symposium on Quality Electronic Design (ISQED) (pp. 414-419). IEEE. DOI: 10.1109/ISQED51717.2021.9424362

Kurihara, T., Hasegawa, K., & Togawa, N. (2020, July). Evaluation on hardware-Trojan detection at gate-level IP cores utilizing machine learning methods. In 2020 IEEE 26th International Symposium on On-Line Testing and Robust System Design (IOLTS) (pp. 1-4). IEEE. DOI: 10.1109/IOLTS50870.2020.9159740

Liakos, K. G., Georgakilas, G. K., Moustakidis, S., Karlsson, P., & Plessas, F. C. (2019, November). Machine learning for hardware trojan detection: A review. In *2019 Panhellenic Conference on Electronics & Telecommunications (PACET)* (pp. 1-6). IEEE. DOI: 10.1109/PACET48583.2019.8956251

Meng, X., Hassan, R., Dinakrrao, S. M. P., & Basu, K. (2021, May). Can overclocking detect hardware Trojans? In *2021 IEEE International Symposium on Circuits and Systems (ISCAS)* (pp. 1-5). IEEE.

Mohammed, H., Hasan, S. R., & Awwad, F. (2020). Fusion-on-field security and privacy preservation for IoT edge devices: Concurrent defense against multiple types of hardware trojan attacks. *IEEE Access : Practical Innovations, Open Solutions*, 8, 36847–36862. DOI: 10.1109/ACCESS.2020.2975016

Mohammed, H., Howell, J., Hasan, S. R., Guo, N., Khalid, F., & Elkeelany, O. (2018, August). Hardware trojan based security issues in home area network: A testbed setup. In 2018 IEEE 61st International Midwest Symposium on Circuits and Systems (MWSCAS) (pp. 972-975). IEEE. DOI: 10.1109/MWSCAS.2018.8624048

Mondal, A., Karmakar, S., Mahalat, M. H., Roy, S., Sen, B., & Chattopadhyay, A. (2022). Hardware Trojan Detection using Transition Probability with Minimal Test Vectors. *ACM Transactions on Embedded Computing Systems*, 22(1), 1–21. DOI: 10.1145/3545000

Naveenkumar, R., & Sivamangai, N. M. (2024). Hardware Trojans Detection and Prevention Techniques Review. *Wireless Personal Communications*, 136(2), 1147–1182. DOI: 10.1007/s11277-024-11334-6

Sankaran, S., Mohan, V. S., & Purushothaman, A. (2021, December). Deep learning based approach for hardware trojan detection. In 2021 IEEE International Symposium on Smart Electronic Systems (iSES) (pp. 177-182). IEEE. DOI: 10.1109/iSES52644.2021.00050

Venugopalan, V., & Patterson, C. D. (2018). Surveying the hardware trojan threat landscape for the internet-of-things. *Journal of Hardware and Systems Security*, 2(2), 131–141. DOI: 10.1007/s41635-018-0037-2

Yang, Y., Ye, J., Cao, Y., Zhang, J., Li, X., Li, H., & Hu, Y. (2020, November). Survey: Hardware trojan detection for netlist. In 2020 IEEE 29th Asian Test Symposium (ATS) (pp. 1-6). IEEE.

Yasaei, R., Chen, L., Yu, S. Y., & Al Faruque, M. A. (2022). Hardware trojan detection using graph neural networks. *IEEE Transactions on Computer-Aided Design of Integrated Circuits and Systems*.

Yu, S., Gu, C., Liu, W., & O'Neill, M. (2020, October). A novel feature extraction strategy for hardware trojan detection. In *2020 IEEE International Symposium on Circuits and Systems (ISCAS)* (pp. 1-5). IEEE. DOI: 10.1109/ISCAS45731.2020.9180479

Chapter 12
Source Code Analysis With Deep Neural Networks

Rebet Keith Jones
https://orcid.org/0009-0008-0487-1301
Capitol Technology University, USA

ABSTRACT

In recent years, deep learning techniques have garnered considerable attention for their effectiveness in identifying vulnerable code patterns with high precision. Nevertheless, leading models such as Convolutional Neural Networks (CNNs) and Long Short-Term Memory (LSTM) networks require extensive computational resources, resulting in overhead that poses challenges for real-time deployment. This study presents VulDetect, an innovative transformer-based framework for vulnerability detection, developed by fine-tuning a pre-trained large language model (GPT) on a variety of benchmark datasets containing vulnerable code. Our empirical analysis demonstrates that VulDetect achieves a vulnerability detection accuracy of up to 92.65%, surpassing SyseVR and VulDeBERT, two of the most advanced existing techniques for identifying software vulnerabilities.

1. INTRODUCING

Cybersecurity aims to safeguard systems from increasingly sophisticated cyber-attacks, a growing challenge as businesses become more interconnected through technological advancements. The ability of organizations and individuals to defend against such widespread attacks is being strained, as highlighted in the 2023 Verizon Cost of Data Breach Report, which shows that companies take an average of

DOI: 10.4018/979-8-3373-0588-2.ch012

197 days to detect a security breach and 69 days to contain it. This delay exposes organizations to significant financial and operational risks, unscheduled downtime, and reduced productivity. Consequently, the need for automated systems capable of processing and analyzing vast volumes of language data—particularly for applications like software vulnerability detection—has become essential. Traditional methods of vulnerability detection, which depend on human experts to define vulnerabilities, are time-consuming and resource-intensive. Machine learning techniques, particularly Natural Language Processing (NLP) models like CodeBERT, present a more efficient alternative, enabling faster and automated detection of software vulnerabilities without extensive feature engineering (Healthcare, Business, & Technology, 2024; Basharat & Omar, 2024; Zangana, 2015).

Knowledge distillation (KD) is a technique that reduces neural network sizes for execution on devices with limited computational resources. KD involves training a smaller, lightweight model (the "student") to replicate the outputs of a larger model (the "teacher"), thus transferring the high performance of the teacher to a more compact architecture (Ahmed et al., 2023; Al-Sanjary et al., 2018; Arulappan et al., 2023). Remarkably, the student model may even surpass the teacher model in performance due to the "dark knowledge" embedded within the teacher's learned representations, such as insights into class similarities. This knowledge, often hidden in the teacher's outputs, can be more effectively utilized by the student than by the original labels (Dawson et al., 2019; Zangana, 2013; Zangana & Abdulazeez, 2023). As depicted in Figure 1, the student model is trained to mirror the teacher model's behavior, capturing its knowledge to achieve similar or even superior accuracy. The following section provides a comprehensive overview of the framework and components of knowledge distillation.

Transformer-based models like GPT-2 offer significant advantages for vulnerability detection, including improved accuracy and advanced natural language processing capabilities. These models reduce the need for manual inputs in static analysis tools, streamlining and automating the detection process (Basharat & Omar, 2024; Gholami & Omar, 2023; Jones & Omar, 2023). The proposed system, VulDetect, leverages the capabilities of Large Language Models (LLMs) such as GPT-2 to detect vulnerabilities in C and C++ source code. Specifically, VulDetect utilizes the power, speed, and precision of LLMs for software vulnerability detection. By leveraging benchmark datasets and a GPT-based large language model, VulDetect effectively identifies vulnerable code in multiple programming languages, including C/C++ and Java. Our empirical results demonstrate that VulDetect outperforms two leading state-of-the-art techniques in software vulnerability detection (Hamza & Omar, 2013; Huff et al., 2023; Zangana & Zeebaree, 2024).

2. RESEARCH METHOD

The Online Knowledge Distillation algorithm is designed for training a student network that has been trained on a smaller dataset of labeled examples compared to the original teacher model, yet achieves a comparable level of accuracy in detecting software vulnerabilities.

Input:

- A set of labeled training data.

Output:

- A trained student model.

Let DDD be the dataset of software code, where each example is represented as a tuple (x,y)(x, y)(x,y), with xxx being a piece of software code and yyy being a binary label indicating whether the code is vulnerable or not. Techniques such as "code gadgets," which extract library/API function calls from the source code, are employed to facilitate analysis.

In the context of cybersecurity, various approaches have been utilized to detect vulnerabilities. For instance, graph-based methods like Devign and DeepWukong employed Graph Neural Networks (GNNs) to learn data and control dependency code graphs, while DeepTective focused on detecting SQL injection, XSS, and command injection vulnerabilities in PHP source code by leveraging a combination of Gated Recurrent Units (GRUs) and Graph Convolutional Networks. Furthermore, researchers have addressed challenges posed by imbalanced datasets through resampling techniques and the use of curated benchmark datasets.

Transformer-based models, such as CodeBERT, have been utilized to automate program documentation generation and facilitate the search of natural language code. Additionally, the BERTBase model, fine-tuned with a database of C/C++ source files, has demonstrated potential in detecting vulnerabilities. Despite their promise, dynamic analysis techniques like fuzzing and taint analysis face challenges with increased runtime.

In a separate study, researchers explored the effectiveness of transformer-based models for detecting software vulnerabilities. By fine-tuning the BERTBase model with a database of C/C++ source files, they achieved a detection accuracy of 93.49%, surpassing the performance of standard LSTM and BiLSTM models. The dataset used in this study was relatively small, and vulnerability detection was framed as a task involving a set of labeled training data consisting of source code slices, where each slice represented a potential vulnerability.

Algorithm Overview

1. Input:
   - o A pre-trained teacher model: A larger and more accurate model used to generate soft labels for the training data.
   - o A smaller and less accurate student model: This model is trained to predict the soft labels generated by the teacher model.
2. Goal:
   - o The algorithm aims to transfer knowledge from the teacher model to the student model through knowledge distillation, thereby enhancing the student model's accuracy in detecting vulnerabilities.
3. Output:
   - o A trained student model capable of detecting vulnerabilities in software code.

     Specifically:

     - Let TTT be the set of KKK teacher models, where each teacher model TkT_kTk is trained on a different dataset or with a different configuration.
     - Let SSS be the student model, which is simpler and more lightweight compared to the teacher models.
     - Denote the parameters of the kkk-th teacher model by θk\theta_kθk, and the parameters of the student model by θS\theta_SθS.

The Online Knowledge Distillation with Dynamic Programming (OKDDP) algorithm can be outlined as follows:

1. Initialize the parameters of the student model θS\theta_SθS randomly.
2. For each teacher model TkT_kTk, compute the predictions pk(x)p_k(x)pk(x) for each example in the dataset DDD.
3. Initialize the student model's weights with the same values as the kkk-th teacher model.
4. Train the student model using a combination of the predictions from the teacher models as input and the true labels yyy as output.

The loss function for the student model can be defined as a combination of the cross-entropy loss and the knowledge distillation loss. In this code, the Kullback-Leibler divergence is denoted by DKLD_{KL}DKL, and the softmax output of the student model is denoted by σ\sigmaσ. The notation for the parameters of the student and teacher models remains consistent with the previous examples.

Security Automation and Orchestration

LLMs are increasingly being integrated into Security Orchestration, Automation, and Response (SOAR) platforms, where they play a key role in automating routine cybersecurity tasks. These tasks include triaging alerts, generating security reports, and correlating data from various sources to provide a comprehensive view of an organization's security posture (Abbasi et al., 2023; Al Harthi et al., 2023; Burrell et al., 2022). The automation provided by LLMs can significantly reduce the workload on security teams, allowing them to focus on more complex tasks, such as threat hunting and incident investigation (Jones & Omar, 2023; Zangana, 2022; Dawson et al., 2015).

Description

- **Step 1:** Data Collection - Security logs, network traffic, and other textual data are collected.
- **Step 2:** Data Processing - The collected data is processed and normalized for analysis.
- **Step 3:** LLM Analysis - The data is fed into an LLM, which analyzes the text for patterns and anomalies.
- **Step 4:** Threat Detection - The LLM identifies potential threats based on detected patterns.
- **Step 5:** Automated Response - The LLM generates automated recommendations or triggers an incident response.

Figure 1. An overview of defense framework

vulne

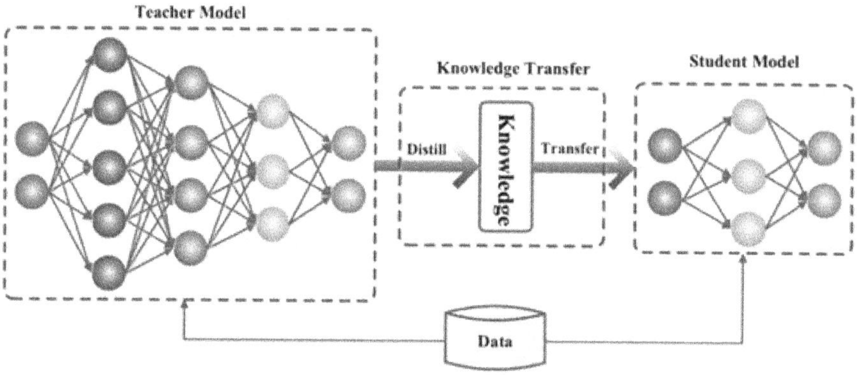

Figure 2. Showing the F1 score comparison for the different vulnerability detection models. The results indicate the performance of VulDetect, BERTBase, LSTM, and BiLSTM models in detecting vulnerabilities.

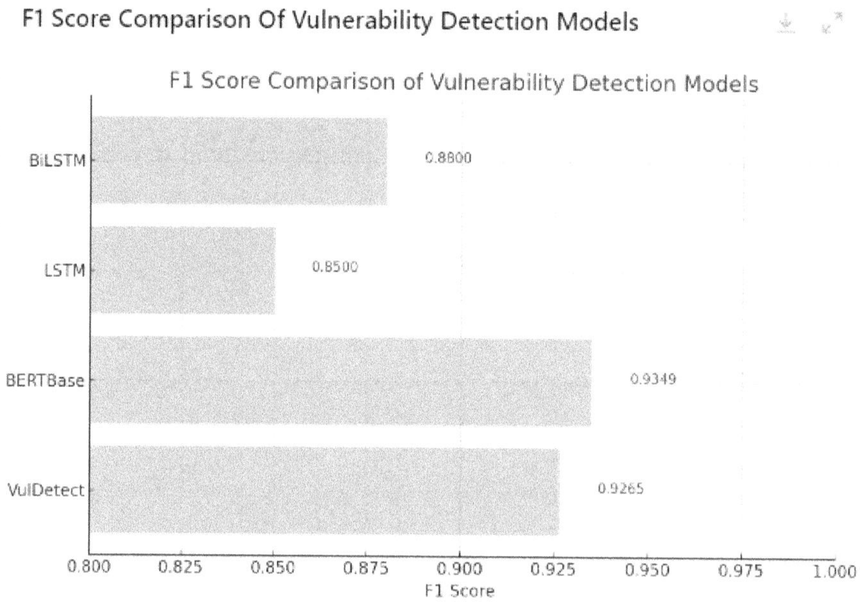

Figure 3. The pie chart displaying the accuracy distribution among the different vulnerability detection models. Each segment represents the proportion of accuracy achieved by VulDetect, BERTBase, LSTM, and BiLSTM

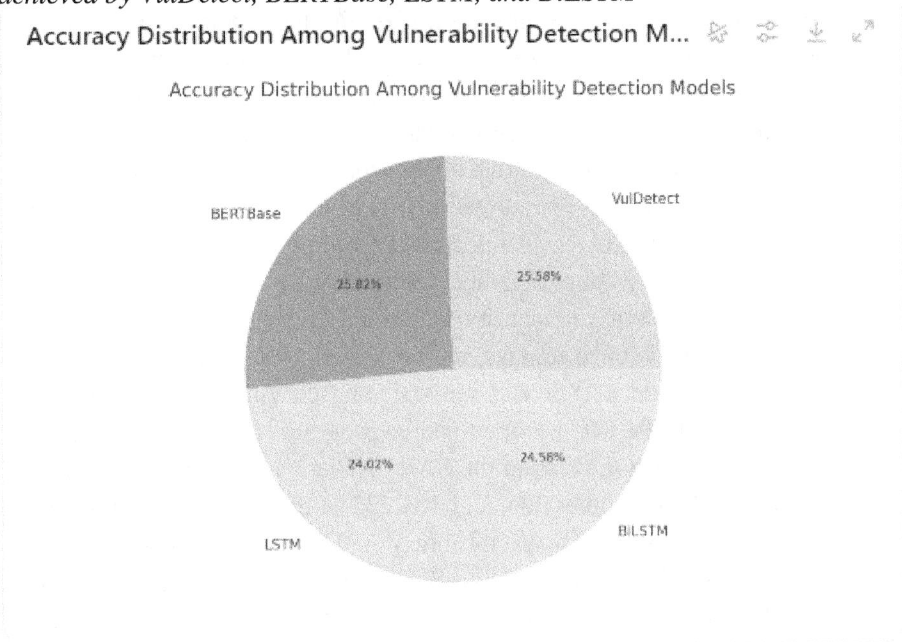

3. RESULTS

The technique of teacher-presented knowledge distillation involves training a student model using both soft and hard labels provided by the teacher. The soft labels, or targets, are calculated by applying the softmax function to the teacher's logits with a temperature parameter T. A higher T results in softer targets. In this study, we follow the suggestion of Lan, Zhu, and Gong (2018) and set T to 3 for all methods. To transfer knowledge from the teacher model to the student model, the predicted distribution q of the student model is aligned with the target distribution t, both calculated with a temperature of 3. The distillation loss function, which measures the difference between the two distributions, is represented by the KullbackLeibler (KL) divergence equation (3). The total loss for training the model with both hard and soft labels is given by equation (4), where the distillation loss Ldis is multiplied by T2 before combination to maintain its contribution roughly unchanged. It's important to note that the probabilities predicted by the student model q are computed from the logits with a temperature of 1 when aligning with hard labels, and with a higher temperature when aligning with soft targets. Throughout the paper, the notation q represents the T=1 version and q represents the high-temperature version. A. Datasets In this section, we present the datasets utilized in the remainder of this paper, which comprise function-level C/C++ source code obtained from diverse codebases such as opensource repositories and synthetic code samples. We categorize these datasets into two groups, based on their primary application for either pre-training or fine-tuning. It is important to note that all datasets mentioned in this section are publicly accessible and available for download. 1) SARD: The software assurance reference dataset (SARD) is SARD is especially appealing because it includes security vulnerabilities as well as nonvulnerable alternatives, which allows our models to learn the differences between security vulnerabilities. Afterward, we perform a preprocessing step in order to remove any unwanted artifacts that could lead to the overfitting of our models. 2) SeVC: Semantics-based Vulnerability Candidate: This dataset Contains 1,591 C/C++ open-source programs from the NVD, as well as 14,000 open-source programs from the SARD. There are 420,627 SeVCs in it, with 56,395 of them being vulnerable, and 364,232 of them not being vulnerable. Moreover, there are four types of SyVCs: Library/API Function Calls, Array Usage, Pointer Usage, and Arithmetic Expression. B. Devign The Devign dataset, which was first introduced in, is a real-world dataset for detecting software vulnerabilities. The dataset includes function-level C/C++ source code from two widely-used open-source software projects, QEMU and FFmpeg. The labeling and verification process was carried out by a team of security researchers in two rounds, and was done manually. 1) D2A: The IBM Research team introduced and curated the D2A dataset for real-world vulnerability detection [7]. This dataset includes various open-source software projects such as FFmpeg, httpd, Libav, LibTIFF, Nginx, and OpenSSL. To label the issues reported by static analyzers, the team utilized a differential analysis technique. V. EVALUATION AND RESULTS %beginitemize A. Configuration We Implemented our experiments using an ASUS TUF Gaming laptop with an Intel Core i7-8th generation CPU. The processor has six cores with a maximum operating frequency of 2.2 GHz for each core. sectionResult Model Score SARD SeVC Devign D2A VulBERTa 88.7 84.2 805 81.8 79.9 SyseVR DistilVulBERT 81.5 82.6 783 80.2 72.7 94.0 91.4 822 B. Defense Performance Evaluation 87.5 85.9 To evaluate the performance of our technique, we decided to test it on the same three classifiers (GPT-2, CodeBERT, and LSTM) using the same two benchmark datasets (SARD, and SeVC). The goal was to see how effective our technique is in detecting Vulnerabilities. Table I illustrates that models' classification accuracy is significantly higher when the VulDetect technique is implemented. In particular, we observe that our GPT-2 classifier fared the best with a classification accuracy of up to 92.59 when tested on the SARD dataset. On the other side of the spectrum, we noticed that LSTM fared the worst with a classification accuracy of 65.78 when evaluated on theSeVC dataset. To sum up, we observe that GPT-2 is consistently performing the best among the other two network architectures (CodeBERT, and LSTM). This is not surprising as GPT is a transformer-based learning model and is known to achieve state-of-the-art performance under various linguistic tasks including sentiment analysis and sentence classification. Table 2: DistilBERT yields comparable performance on downstream tasks. Comparison on downstream tasks: IMDb (test accuracy) and SQuAD 1.1 (EM/F1 on dev set). D: with a second step of distillation during fine-tuning.

4. FUTURE RESEARCH DIRECTIONS

Future research in the field of software vulnerability detection should focus on several key areas to further advance the capabilities and effectiveness of existing models. Firstly, exploring the integration of explainable AI (XAI) techniques with transformer-based models like VulDetect can provide deeper insights into the decision-making processes of these models, thereby increasing trust and transparency. This will be particularly important for critical applications where understanding why a particular piece of code is flagged as vulnerable is essential.

Another promising direction is the development of more efficient and scalable models capable of real-time vulnerability detection in large and complex codebases. This may involve optimizing current models or creating new architectures that balance accuracy with computational efficiency, making them more practical for use in production environments.

Additionally, the application of unsupervised or semi-supervised learning techniques in vulnerability detection could allow models to identify new, previously unseen vulnerabilities without requiring extensive labeled datasets. This could be particularly beneficial as software systems evolve and new types of vulnerabilities emerge.

Lastly, research should explore the use of synthetic data generation to enhance model training, especially in scenarios where labeled data is scarce. This approach could improve the robustness and generalizability of models, enabling them to perform well across diverse coding environments and programming languages.

5. CONCLUSION

In conclusion, the evolution of cybersecurity has necessitated the development of advanced techniques for detecting software vulnerabilities, particularly as cyberattacks become more sophisticated and pervasive. Traditional methods, while effective, are often labor-intensive and time-consuming, highlighting the need for automated solutions. The introduction of machine learning, specifically transformer-based models like GPT-2 and CodeBERT, has revolutionized vulnerability detection by providing faster, more accurate, and automated processes. These models leverage large datasets and fine-tuning techniques to identify vulnerabilities in various programming languages, significantly outperforming earlier models like LSTM and BiLSTM.

The implementation of knowledge distillation further enhances this process by allowing smaller, lightweight models to achieve performance levels comparable to their larger counterparts, making them suitable for deployment in resource-constrained environments. The VulDetect framework exemplifies the potential of these advancements, demonstrating superior accuracy in detecting vulnerabilities across different programming languages. As cybersecurity continues to evolve, the integration of these sophisticated machine learning techniques will be crucial in developing more resilient and proactive defense mechanisms, ultimately reducing the risk of breaches and ensuring the security and integrity of software systems.

REFERENCES

Abbasi, R., Bashir, A. K., Mateen, A., Amin, F., Ge, Y., & Omar, M. "Efficient Security and Privacy of Lossless Secure Communication for Sensor-based Urban Cities," *IEEE Sensors Journal*, vol. 2023.

Ahmed, H., Rasheed, H., Bashir, A. K., & Omar, M. (2023). Rasheed, A. K. Bashir, and M. Omar, "Millimeter-wave Channel Modeling in a VANETs Using Coding Techniques,". *PeerJ. Computer Science*, 9, e1374. DOI: 10.7717/peerj-cs.1374 PMID: 37346660

Ahmed, N., Mohammadani, K., Bashir, A. K., Omar, M., Jones, A., & Hassan, F. "Secure and Reliable Routing in the Internet of Vehicles Network: AODV-RL with BHA Attack Defense," *CMES-Computer Modeling in Engineering & Sciences*, vol. 139, no. 1, 2024.

Al Harthi, S., Al Balushi, M. Y., Al Badi, A. H., Al Karaki, J., & Omar, M. *"Metaverse Adoption in UAE Higher Education: A Hybrid SEM-ANN Approach," in 98 Mohammad Daradkeh, Boshra Aldhanhani, Amjad Gawanmeh, Shadi Atalla and Sami Miniaoui. Applied Research Approaches to Technology, Healthcare, and Business.* IGI Global.

Al-Karaki, J. N., Omar, M., Gawanmeh, A., & Jones, A. "Advancing CyberSecurity Education and Training: Practical Case Study of Running Capture the Flag (CTF) on the Metaverse vs. Physical Settings," in *2023 International Conference on Intelligent Metaverse Technologies & Applications (iMETA)*, pp. 1-7, IEEE, 2023. DOI: 10.1109/iMETA59369.2023.10294722

Al Kinoon, M., Omar, M., Mohaisen, M., & Mohaisen, D. "Security Breaches in the Healthcare Domain: A Spatiotemporal Analysis," in *Computational Data and Social Networks: 10th International Conference, CSoNet 2021, Virtual Event, November 15-17, 2021, Proceedings*, Springer International Publishing, pp. 171-183, 2021. DOI: 10.1007/978-3-030-91434-9_16

Al-Sanjary, O. I., Ahmed, A. A., Jaharadak, A. A. B., Ali, M. A., & Zangana, H. M. "Detection Clone an Object Movement Using an Optical Flow Approach," in *2018 IEEE Symposium on Computer Applications & Industrial Electronics (ISCAIE)*, pp. 388-394, 2018. DOI: 10.1109/ISCAIE.2018.8405504

O. I. Al-Sanjary, A. A. Ahmed, H. M. Zangana, M. Ali, S. Aldulaimi, and M. Alkawaz, "An Investigation of the Characteristics and Performance of Hybrid Routing Protocol in (MANET)," *International Journal of Engineering & Technology*, vol. 7, no. 4.22, pp. 49-54, 2018.

Alturki, N., Altamimi, A., Umer, M., Saidani, O., Alshardan, A., Alsubai, S., Omar, M., & Ashraf, I. "Improving Prediction of Chronic Kidney Disease Using KNN Imputed SMOTE Features and TrioNet Model," *CMES-Computer Modeling in Engineering & Sciences*, vol. 139, no. 3, 2024. DOI: 10.32604/cmes.2023.045868

Arulappan, G. (2023). Raja, A. K. Bashir, A. Mahanti, and M. Omar, "ZTMP: Zero Touch Management Provisioning Algorithm for the On-boarding of Cloud-native Virtual Network Functions,". *Mobile Networks and Applications*, •••, 1–13.

Ayub, M., Li, X., Mahmood, K., Shamshad, S., Saleem, M. A., & Omar, M. (2023). Secure Consumer-centric Demand Response Management in Resilient Smart Grid as Industry 5.0 Application with Blockchain-based Authentication. *IEEE Transactions on Consumer Electronics.*

M. Banisakher, D. Mohammed, and M. Omar, "A Cloud-Based Computing Architecture Model of Post-Disaster Management System," *International Journal of Simulation--Systems, Science & Technology*, vol. 19, no. 5, 2018.

Banisakher, M., Omar, M., & Clare, W. (2019). Critical Infrastructure—Perspectives on the Role of Government in Cybersecurity. *Journal of Computer Sciences and Applications*, 7(1), 37–42. DOI: 10.12691/jcsa-7-1-6

Banisakher, M., Omar, M., Hong, S., & Adams, J. (2020). A Human-centric Approach to Data Fusion in Post-Disaster Management. *Jurnal of Business Management and Science*, 8(1), 12–20.

Basharat, M., & Omar, M. "Adapting to Change: Assessing the Longevity and Resilience of Adversarially Trained NLP Models in Dynamic Spam Detection Environments," in *Innovations, Securities, and Case Studies Across Healthcare, Business, and Technology*, pp. 157-173, IGI Global, 2024. DOI: 10.4018/979-8-3693-1906-2.ch009

Basharat, M., & Omar, M. (2024). Harnessing GPT-2 for Feature Extraction in Malware Detection: A Novel Approach to Cybersecurity. *Land Forces Academy Review*, 29(1), 74–84. DOI: 10.2478/raft-2024-0008

M. Basharat and M. Omar, "SecuGuard: Leveraging Pattern-exploiting Training in Language Models for Advanced Software Vulnerability Detection," *International Journal of Mathematics and Computer in Engineering*, 2024.

Burrell, D. N., Nobles, C., Cusak, A., Omar, M., & Gillesania, L. (2022). Cybercrime and the Nature of Insider Threat Complexities in Healthcare and Biotechnology Engineering Organizations. *Journal of Crime and Criminal Behavior*, 2(2), 131–144. DOI: 10.47509/JCCB.2022.v02i02.04

Burrell, D. N., Nobles, C., Richardson, K., Wright, J. B., Jones, A. J., Springs, D., & Brown-Jackson, K. (2023). Allison Huff. In *Applied Research Approaches to Technology, Healthcare, and Business*. IGI Global. DOI: 10.4018/979-8-3693-1630-6

Davis, L., Dawson, M., & Omar, M. (2016). Systems Engineering Concepts with Aid of Virtual Worlds and Open Source Software: Using Technology to Develop Learning Objects and Simulation Environments. In *Handbook of Research on 3-D Virtual Environments and Hypermedia for Ubiquitous Learning* (pp. 483–509). IGI Global. DOI: 10.4018/978-1-5225-0125-1.ch020

Dawson, M. (2015). A Brief Review of New Threats and Countermeasures in Digital Crime and Cyber Terrorism. In *New Threats and Countermeasures in Digital Crime and Cyber Terrorism* (pp. 1–7). IGI Global. DOI: 10.4018/978-1-4666-8345-7.ch001

Dawson, M., Al Saeed, I., Wright, J., & Omar, M. "Technology enhanced learning with open source software for scientists and engineers," in *INTED2013 Proceedings*, IATED, 2013, pp. 5583–5589.

Dawson, M., Davis, L., & Omar, M. (2019). Developing learning objects for engineering and science fields: Using technology to test system usability and interface design. *Int. J. Smart Technol. Learn.*, 1(2), 140–161. DOI: 10.1504/IJSMART-TL.2019.097951

Dawson, M., Eltayeb, M., & Omar, M. (2016). *Security solutions for hyperconnectivity and the Internet of things*. IGI Global.

Dawson, M., Omar, M., & Abramson, J. (2015). Understanding the methods behind cyber terrorism. In *Encyclopedia of Information Science and Technology* (3rd ed., pp. 1539–1549). IGI Global.

Dawson, M., Omar, M., Abramson, J., & Bessette, D. (2014). *Information security in diverse computing environments*. Academic Press.

Dawson, M., Omar, M., Abramson, J., & Bessette, D. (2014). The future of national and international security on the internet. In *Information security in diverse computing environments* (pp. 149–178). IGI Global. DOI: 10.4018/978-1-4666-6158-5.ch009

Dawson, M., Omar, M., Abramson, J., Leonard, B., & Bessette, D. (2017). Battlefield cyberspace: Exploitation of hyperconnectivity and Internet of Things. In *Developing Next-Generation Countermeasures for Homeland Security Threat Prevention* (pp. 204–235). IGI Global. DOI: 10.4018/978-1-5225-0703-1.ch010

Dawson, M., Wright, J., & Omar, M. (2015). Mobile devices: The case for cyber security hardened systems. In *New Threats and Countermeasures in Digital Crime and Cyber Terrorism* (pp. 8–29). IGI Global. DOI: 10.4018/978-1-4666-8345-7.ch002

Dayoub and M. Omar. (2024). Advancing IoT security posture K-Means clustering for malware detection. In *Innovations, Securities, and Case Studies Across Healthcare, Business, and Technology* (pp. 221–239). IGI Global.

Dong, H., Wu, J., Bashir, A. K., Pan, Q., Omar, M., & Al-Dulaimi, A. "Privacy-preserving EEG signal analysis with electrode attention for depression diagnosis: Joint FHE and CNN approach," in *GLOBECOM 2023-2023 IEEE Global Communications Conference*, IEEE, 2023, pp. 4265–4270. DOI: 10.1109/GLOBECOM54140.2023.10436783

Fawzi, D., & Omar, M. (n.d.). *New insights to database security: An effective and integrated approach to applying access control mechanisms and cryptographic concepts in Microsoft access environments*. Academic Press.

Gholami, S. (2024). Can pruning make large language models more efficient? In *Redefining Security With Cyber AI* (pp. 1–14). IGI Global. DOI: 10.4018/979-8-3693-6517-5.ch001

Gholami, S. (2024). Do generative large language models need billions of parameters? In *Redefining Security With Cyber AI* (pp. 37–55). IGI Global. DOI: 10.4018/979-8-3693-6517-5.ch003

Gholami, S., & Omar, M. "Does synthetic data make large language models more efficient?" *arXiv preprint arXiv:2310.07830*, 2023.

Gholami, S., & Omar, M. (2024). Can a student large language model perform as well as its teacher? In *Innovations, Securities, and Case Studies Across Healthcare, Business, and Technology* (pp. 122–139). IGI Global. DOI: 10.4018/979-8-3693-1906-2.ch007

Hamza, Y. A., & Omar, M. D. (2013). Cloud computing security: Abuse and nefarious use of cloud computing. *International Journal of Computer Engineering Research*, 3(6), 22–27.

Huff, J., Burrell, D. N., Nobles, C., Richardson, K., Wright, J. B., Burton, S. L., Jones, A. J., Springs, D., Omar, M., & Brown-Jackson, K. L. (2023). Management practices for mitigating cybersecurity threats to biotechnology companies, laboratories, and healthcare research organizations. In *Applied Research Approaches to Technology, Healthcare, and Business* (pp. 1–12). IGI Global. DOI: 10.4018/979-8-3693-1630-6.ch001

Jabbari, H. Khan, S. Duraibi, I. Budhiraja, S. Gupta, and M. Omar, "Energy maximization for wireless powered communication enabled IoT devices with NOMA underlaying solar powered UAV using federated reinforcement learning for 6G networks," *IEEE Trans. Consum. Electron.*, 2024.

Jones, A., & Omar, M.Jones and M. Omar. (2024). Codesentry: Revolutionizing real-time software vulnerability detection with optimized GPT framework. *Land Forces Acad. Rev.*, 29(1), 98–107. DOI: 10.2478/raft-2024-0010

Jones, M., & Omar, M. (2023). *"Detection of Twitter spam with language models: A case study on how to use BERT to protect children from spam on Twitter," in 2023 Congress in Computer Science, Computer Engineering, & Applied Computing (CSCE).* IEEE.

Jones, M., & Omar, M. (2023). *"Measuring the impact of global health emergencies on self-disclosure using language models," in 2023 Congress in Computer Science, Computer Engineering, & Applied Computing (CSCE).* IEEE.

Jones, M., & Omar, M. (2023). *"Studying the effects of social media content on kids' safety and well-being," in 2023 Congress in Computer Science, Computer Engineering, & Applied Computing (CSCE).* IEEE.

Jones, R., & Omar, M. "Detecting IoT Malware with Knowledge Distillation Technique," in *2023 Congress in Computer Science, Computer Engineering, & Applied Computing (CSCE)*, pp. 131-135, IEEE, 2023. DOI: 10.1109/CSCE60160.2023.00026

Jones, R., & Omar, M. (2024). Codeguard: Utilizing Advanced Pattern Recognition in Language Models for Software Vulnerability Analysis. *Land Forces Academy Review*, 29(1), 108–118. DOI: 10.2478/raft-2024-0011

Jones, R., & Omar, M. (2024). Revolutionizing Cybersecurity: The GPT-2 Enhanced Attack Detection and Defense (GEADD) Method for Zero-Day Threats [INJIISCOM]. *International Journal of Informatics, Information System and Computer Engineering*, 5(2), 178–191. DOI: 10.34010/injiiscom.v5i2.12741

Jones, R., Omar, M., & Mohammed, D. "Harnessing the Power of the GPT Model to Generate Adversarial Examples," in *2023 Congress in Computer Science, Computer Engineering, & Applied Computing (CSCE)*, pp. 1699-1702, IEEE, 2023. DOI: 10.1109/CSCE60160.2023.00279

Jones, R., Omar, M., Mohammed, D., & Nobles, C. "IoT Malware Detection with GPT Models," in *2023 Congress in Computer Science, Computer Engineering, & Applied Computing (CSCE)*, pp. 1749-1752, IEEE, 2023. DOI: 10.1109/CSCE60160.2023.00288

Jones, R., Omar, M., Mohammed, D., Nobles, C., & Dawson, M. "Harnessing the Speed and Accuracy of Machine Learning to Advance Cybersecurity," in *2023 Congress in Computer Science, Computer Engineering, & Applied Computing (CSCE)*, pp. 418-421, IEEE, 2023. DOI: 10.1109/CSCE60160.2023.00074

Jones and M. Omar. (2023). *"Harnessing the efficiency of reformers to detect software vulnerabilities," in 2023 Congress in Computer Science, Computer Engineering, & Applied Computing (CSCE).* IEEE.

Jones and M. Omar. (2023). *"Optimized decision trees to detect IoT malware," in 2023 Congress in Computer Science, Computer Engineering, & Applied Computing (CSCE).* IEEE.

Jun, W., Iqbal, M. S., Abbasi, R., Omar, M., & Huiqin, C. "Web-Semantic-Driven Machine Learning and Blockchain for Transformative Change in the Future of Physical Education," *International Journal on Semantic Web and Information Systems (IJSWIS)*, vol. 20, no. 1, pp. 1-16, IGI Global, 2024. DOI: 10.4018/IJSWIS.337961

Khan, S. A., Alkawaz, M. H., & Zangana, H. M. "The use and abuse of social media for spreading fake news," in *2019 IEEE International Conference on Automatic Control and Intelligent Systems (I2CACIS)*, pp. 145-148, IEEE, 2019. DOI: 10.1109/I2CACIS.2019.8825029

V. A. Kumar, S. Surapaneni, D. Pavitra, R. Venkatesan, M. Omar, and A. K. Bashir, "An Internet of Medical Things-Based Mental Disorder Prediction System Using EEG Sensor and Big Data Mining," *Journal of Circuits, Systems and Computers*, vol. 2450197, World Scientific Publishing Company, 2024.

Majeed, H. (2020). Watermarking Image Depending on Mojette Transform for Hiding Information. *International Journal on Computer Science and Engineering*, 8, 8–12.

Mohammed, M. O., & Nguyen, V. (2017). Enhancing Cyber Security for Financial Industry through Compliance and Regulatory Standards. In *Security Solutions for Hyperconnectivity and the Internet of Things* (pp. 113–129). IGI Global. DOI: 10.4018/978-1-5225-0741-3.ch005

Mohammed, M. O., & Nguyen, V. (2018). Wireless Sensor Network Security: Approaches to Detecting and Avoiding Wormhole Attacks. *Journal of Research in Business, Economics and Management*, 10(2), 1860–1864.

Mohammed and M. Omar. "Decision Trees Unleashed: Simplifying IoT Malware Detection With Advanced AI Techniques," in *Innovations, Securities, and Case Studies Across Healthcare, Business, and Technology*, pp. 240-258, IGI Global, 2024.

V. Nguyen, D. Mohammed, M. Omar, and M. Banisakher, "The Effects of the FCC Net Neutrality Repeal on Security and Privacy," *International Journal of Hyperconnectivity and the Internet of Things (IJHIoT)*, vol. 2, no. 2, pp. 21-29, IGI Global, 2018.

V. Nguyen, M. Omar, and D. Mohammed, "A Security Framework for Enhancing User Experience," *International Journal of Hyperconnectivity and the Internet of Things (IJHIoT)*, vol. 1, no. 1, pp. 19-28, IGI Global, 2017.

Nguyen, V., Omar, M., Mohammed, D., & Dean, P. "Net Neutrality Around the Globe: A Survey," in *2020 3rd International Conference on Information and Computer Technologies (ICICT)*, pp. 480-488, IEEE, 2020. DOI: 10.1109/ICICT50521.2020.00083

Omar, M. *Smartphone Security: Defending Android-based Smartphone Against Emerging Malware Attacks* (Doctoral dissertation, Colorado Technical University), 2012.

Omar, M. "Insider Threats: Detecting and Controlling Malicious Insiders," in *New Threats and Countermeasures in Digital Crime and Cyber Terrorism*, pp. 162-172, IGI Global, 2015. DOI: 10.4018/978-1-4666-8345-7.ch009

Omar, M. "Cloud Computing Security: Abuse and Nefarious Use of Cloud Computing," in *Handbook of Research on Security Considerations in Cloud Computing*, pp. 30-38, IGI Global, 2015. DOI: 10.4018/978-1-4666-8387-7.ch002

Omar, M. (2019). A World of Cyber Attacks. *Survey (London, England).*

M. Omar, "New Insights into Database Security: An Effective and Integrated Approach for Applying Access Control Mechanisms and Cryptographic Concepts in Microsoft Access Environments," 2021.

Omar, M. "Application of Machine Learning (ML) to Address Cybersecurity Threats," in *Machine Learning for Cybersecurity: Innovative Deep Learning Solutions*, pp. 1-11, Springer International Publishing Cham, 2022. DOI: 10.1007/978-3-031-15893-3_1

Omar, M. *Machine Learning for Cybersecurity: Innovative Deep Learning Solutions*, Springer Brief, 2022. https://link.springer.com/book/978303115

Omar, M. "Malware Anomaly Detection Using Local Outlier Factor Technique," in *Machine Learning for Cybersecurity: Innovative Deep Learning Solutions*, pp. 37-48, Springer International Publishing Cham, 2022. DOI: 10.1007/978-3-031-15893-3_3

Omar, M. "VulDefend: A Novel Technique Based on Pattern-Exploiting Training for Detecting Software Vulnerabilities Using Language Models," in *2023 IEEE Jordan International Joint Conference on Electrical Engineering and Information Technology (JEEIT)*, pp. 287-293, IEEE, 2023. DOI: 10.1109/JEEIT58638.2023.10185860

Omar, M. "From Attack to Defense: Strengthening DNN Text Classification Against Adversarial Examples," in *Innovations, Securities, and Case Studies Across Healthcare, Business, and Technology*, pp. 174-195, IGI Global, 2024. DOI: 10.4018/979-8-3693-1906-2.ch010

Omar, M. "Revolutionizing Malware Detection: A Paradigm Shift Through Optimized Convolutional Neural Networks," in *Innovations, Securities, and Case Studies Across Healthcare, Business, and Technology*, pp. 196-220, IGI Global, 2024. DOI: 10.4018/979-8-3693-1906-2.ch011

Omar, M. *Defending Cyber Systems through Reverse Engineering of Criminal Malware*, Springer Brief, [n.d.][n.d.].https://link.springer.com/book/9783031116278

M. Omar, *Latina Davis Morgan State University 1700 E Cold Spring Ln. Baltimore, MD 21251, USA E-mail: latinaedavis@ hotmail.com*, [n.d.][n.d.].

M. Omar, *Machine Learning for Cybersecurity*, [n.d.][n.d.].

Omar, M.. (2024). Committee Members. *Journal of Physics: Conference Series*, 2711, 011001.

M. Omar and D. Burrell, "From Text to Threats: A Language Model Approach to Software Vulnerability Detection," *International Journal of Mathematics and Computer in Engineering*, 2023.

Omar, M., & Burrell, D. N. "Organizational Dynamics and Bias in Artificial Intelligence (AI) Recruitment Algorithms," in *Evolution of Cross-Sector Cyber Intelligent Markets*, pp. 269-290, IGI Global, 2024.

Omar, M., Choi, S., Nyang, D., & Mohaisen, D. "Quantifying the Performance of Adversarial Training on Language Models with Distribution Shifts," in *Proceedings of the 1st Workshop on Cybersecurity and Social Sciences*, pp. 3-9, 2022. DOI: 10.1145/3494108.3522764

Omar, M., Choi, S., Nyang, D., & Mohaisen, D. (2022). Robust Natural Language Processing: Recent Advances, Challenges, and Future Directions. *IEEE Access : Practical Innovations, Open Solutions*, 10, 86038–86056. DOI: 10.1109/ACCESS.2022.3197769

Omar, M., & Dawson, M. "Research in Progress-Defending Android Smartphones from Malware Attacks," in *2013 Third International Conference on Advanced Computing and Communication Technologies (ACCT)*, pp. 288-292, IEEE, 2013. DOI: 10.1109/ACCT.2013.69

Omar, M., Gouveia, L. B., Al-Karaki, J., & Mohammed, D. "Reverse-Engineering Malware," in *Cybersecurity Capabilities in Developing Nations and Its Impact on Global Security*, pp. 194-217, IGI Global, 2022. DOI: 10.4018/978-1-7998-8693-8.ch010

Omar, M., Jones, R., Burrell, D. N., Dawson, M., Nobles, C., & Mohammed, D. "Harnessing the Power and Simplicity of Decision Trees to Detect IoT Malware," in *Transformational Interventions for Business, Technology, and Healthcare*, pp. 215-229, IGI, 2023. DOI: 10.4018/979-8-3693-1634-4.ch013

Omar, M., & Mohaisen, D. "Making Adversarially-Trained Language Models Forget with Model Retraining: A Case Study on Hate Speech Detection," in *Companion Proceedings of the Web Conference 2022*, pp. 887-893, 2022. DOI: 10.1145/3487553.3524667

Omar, M., Mohammed, D., & Nguyen, V. (2017). Defending Against Malicious Insiders: A Conceptual Framework for Predicting, Detecting, and Deterring Malicious Insiders. *International Journal of Business Process Integration and Management*, 8(2), 114–119. DOI: 10.1504/IJBPIM.2017.083794

Omar, M., Mohammed, D., Nguyen, V., Dawson, M., & Banisakher, M. "Android Application Security," in *Research Anthology on Securing Mobile Technologies and Applications*, pp. 610-625, IGI Global, 2021. DOI: 10.4018/978-1-7998-8545-0.ch034

Omar, M., & Shiaeles, S. "VulDetect: A Novel Technique for Detecting Software Vulnerabilities Using Language Models," in *2023 IEEE International Conference on Cyber Security and Resilience (CSR)*, IEEE. https://ieeexplore.ieee.org/document/10224924

Omar, M., & Sukthankar, G. "Text-Defend: Detecting Adversarial Examples Using Local Outlier Factor," in *2023 IEEE 17th International Conference on Semantic Computing (ICSC)*, pp. 118-122, IEEE, 2023. DOI: 10.1109/ICSC56153.2023.00026

Omar, M., & Zangana, H. M. (2024). *Redefining Security With Cyber AI*. IGI Global., DOI: 10.4018/979-8-3693-6517-5

Pauu, K. T., Pan, Q., Wu, J., Bashir, A. K., & Omar, M. "IRS-Aided Federated Learning with Dynamic Differential Privacy for UAVs in Emergency Response," *IEEE Internet of Things Magazine*, vol. 7, no. 4, pp. 108-115, IEEE, 2024. DOI: 10.1109/IOTM.001.2400021

Peng, Y.. (2024). *"An Intelligent Resource Allocation Strategy with Slicing and Auction for Private Edge Cloud Systems," Future Generation Computer Systems* (Vol. 160). North-Holland.

Rajesh, R.. (2024). Threat Detection and Mitigation for Tactile Internet Driven Consumer IoT-Healthcare System. *IEEE Transactions on Consumer Electronics.*

Saleem, M. A.. (2023). Provably Secure Conditional-Privacy Access Control Protocol for Intelligent Customers-Centric Communication in VANET. *IEEE Transactions on Consumer Electronics.*

Sun, Y., Xu, T., Bashir, A. K., Liu, J., & Omar, M. "BcIIS: Blockchain-Based Intelligent Identification Scheme of Massive IoT Devices," in *GLOBECOM 2023-2023 IEEE Global Communications Conference*, pp. 1277-1282, IEEE, 2023. DOI: 10.1109/GLOBECOM54140.2023.10437203

Tao, Y., Wu, J., Pan, Q., Bashir, A. K., & Omar, M. (2024). O-RAN-Based Digital Twin Function Virtualization for Sustainable IoV Service Response: An Asynchronous Hierarchical Reinforcement Learning Approach. *IEEE Transactions on Green Communications and Networking*, 8(3), 1049–1060. DOI: 10.1109/TGCN.2024.3435796

Tiwari, N., Ghadi, Y., & Omar, M. "Analysis of Ultrasound Images in Kidney Failure Diagnosis Using Deep Learning," in *Transformational Interventions for Business, Technology, and Healthcare*, pp. 45-74, IGI Global, 2023. DOI: 10.4018/979-8-3693-1634-4.ch004

Tiwari, N., Omar, M., & Ghadi, Y. "Brain Tumor Classification From Magnetic Resonance Imaging Using Deep Learning and Novel Data Augmentation," in *Transformational Interventions for Business, Technology, and Healthcare*, pp. 392-413, IGI Global, 2023. DOI: 10.4018/979-8-3693-1634-4.ch023

Umer, M., Aljrees, T., Karamti, H., Ishaq, A., Alsubai, S., Omar, M., Bashir, A. K., & Ashraf, I. (2023). Heart Failure Patients Monitoring Using IoT-Based Remote Monitoring System. *Scientific Reports*, 13(1), 19213. DOI: 10.1038/s41598-023-46322-6 PMID: 37932424

Vitianingsih, V., Firmansyah, D., Maukar, A. L., Kacung, S., & Zangana, H. M. (2024, August). Recommendation System for Determining the Best Banner Supplier Using Profile Matching and TOPSIS Methods. *Intensif Jurnal Ilmiah Penelitian Teknologi Dan Penerapan Sistem Informasi*, 8(2), 246–262. DOI: 10.29407/intensif.v8i2.21635

Wright, J., Dawson, M. E.Jr, & Omar, M. (2012). Cyber Security and Mobile Threats: The Need for Antivirus Applications for Smartphones. *Journal of Information Systems Technology and Planning*, 5(14), 40–60.

Xu, X., Wu, J., Bashir, A. K., & Omar, M. (2024). Machine Learning and Zero Knowledge Empowered Trustworthy Bitcoin Mixing for Next-G Consumer Electronics Payment. *IEEE Transactions on Consumer Electronics*, 70(1), 2210–2223. DOI: 10.1109/TCE.2024.3361690

H. M. Zangana, "A New Skin Color Based Face Detection Algorithm by Combining Three Color Model Algorithms," *IOSR Journal of Computer Engineering*, vol. 17, pp. 06-125, 2015.

H. M. Zangana, "A new algorithm for shape detection," *IOSR Journal of Computer Engineering (IOSR-JCE)*, vol. 19, no. 3, pp. 71-76, 2017.

H. M. Zangana, "Library Data Quality Maturity (IIUM as a Case Study)," *IOSR-JCE*, vol. 29, Mar. 2017.

Zangana, H. M. (2017). Watermarking System Using LSB. *IOSR Journal of Computer Engineering*, 19(3), 75–79. DOI: 10.9790/0661-1903027579

Zangana, H. M. (2018). Design an information management system for a pharmacy. *International Journal of Advanced Research in Computer and Communication Engineering*, 7(10), 52–55. DOI: 10.17148/IJARCCE.2018.71012

Zangana, H. M. "Developing Data Warehouse for Student Information System (IIUM as a Case Study)," *International Organization of Scientific Research*, vol. 20, no. 1, pp. 09-14, 2018.

H. M. Zangana, "Implementing a System for Recognizing Optical Characters," 2018.

H. M. Zangana, "Issues of Data Management in the Library: A Case Study," 2019.

H. M. Zangana, "ITD Data Quality Maturity (A Case Study)," *International Journal Of Engineering And Computer Science*, vol. 8, no. 10, 2019.

Zangana, H. M. (2020). Mobile Device Integration in IIUM Service. *International Journal (Toronto, Ont.)*, 8(5).

Zangana, H. M. (2021). The Global Financial Crisis from an Islamic Point Of View. *Qubahan Academic Journal*, 1(2), 55–59. DOI: 10.48161/qaj.v1n2a39

Zangana, H. M. (2022). Creating a Community-Based Disaster Management System. *Academic Journal of Nawroz University*, 11(4), 234–244. DOI: 10.25007/ajnu.v11n4a1485

Zangana, H. M. (2022). Implementing New Interactive Video Learning System for IIUM. *Academic Journal of Nawroz University*, 11(2), 23–29. DOI: 10.25007/ajnu.v11n2a1281

H. M. Zangana, "Improving The Web Services for Remittance Company: Express Remit as a Case Study," *Academic Journal of Nawroz University (AJNU)*, vol. 11, no. 3, 2022.

Zangana, H. M. (2024). *Exploring Blockchain-Based Timestamping Tools: A Comprehensive Review*. Redefining Security With Cyber AI. DOI: 10.4018/979-8-3693-6517-5.ch006

Zangana, H. M. (2024). *Exploring the Landscape of Website Vulnerability Scanners: A Comprehensive Review and Comparative Analysis*. Redefining Security With Cyber AI. DOI: 10.4018/979-8-3693-6517-5.ch007

H. M. Zangana, "CHALLENGES AND ISSUES of MANET," 2024.

Zangana, H. M., & Abdulazeez, A. M. (2023). Developed Clustering Algorithms for Engineering Applications: A Review [INJIISCOM]. *International Journal of Informatics, Information System and Computer Engineering*, 4(2), 147–169. DOI: 10.34010/injiiscom.v4i2.11636

Zangana, H. M., & Al-Shaikhli, I. F. (2013). A new algorithm for human face detection using skin color tone. *IOSR Journal of Computer Engineering*, 11(6), 31–38. DOI: 10.9790/0661-1163138

Zangana, H. M., Al-Shaikhli, I. F., & Graha, Y. I. (2013). The Ethical Dilemma of Software Piracy: An Inquiry from an Islamic Perspective. *Creative Communication and Innovative Technology Journal*, 7(1), 59–76. DOI: 10.33050/ccit.v7i1.171

Zangana, H. M., Bazeed, S. M. S., Ali, N. Y., & Abdullah, D. T. (2024). Navigating Project Change: A Comprehensive Review of Change Management Strategies and Practices. *Indonesian Journal of Education and Social Sciences*, 3(2), 166–179. DOI: 10.56916/ijess.v3i2.735

Zangana, H. M., Graha, Y. I., & Al-Shaikhli, I. F. (2024). Blogging: A New Platform For Spreading Rumors! *Creative Communication and Innovative Technology Journal*, 9(1), 71–76.

Zangana, H. M., Khalid Mohammed, A., & Zeebaree, S. R. (2024). Systematic Review of Decentralized and Collaborative Computing Models in Cloud Architectures for Distributed Edge Computing. *Sistemasi: Jurnal Sistem Informasi*, 13(4), 1501–1509. DOI: 10.32520/stmsi.v13i4.4169

Zangana, H. M., Mohammed, A. K., & Mustafa, F. M. (2024). Advancements and Applications of Convolutional Neural Networks in Image Analysis: A Comprehensive Review. *Jurnal Ilmiah Computer Science*, 3(1), 16–29.

Zangana, H. M., Mohammed, A. K., & Mustafa, F. M. (2024). Advancements in Edge Detection Techniques for Image Enhancement: A Comprehensive Review [IJAIR]. *International Journal of Artificial Intelligence & Robotics*, 6(1), 29–39. DOI: 10.25139/ijair.v6i1.8217

Zangana, H. M., Mohammed, A. K., Sallow, A. B., & Sallow, Z. B. (2024). Cybernetic Deception: Unraveling the Layers of Email Phishing Threats [INJURATECH]. *International Journal of Research and Applied Technology*, 4(1), 35–47.

Zangana, H. M., Mohammed, A. K., Sallow, Z. B., & Mustafa, F. M. (2024). Exploring Image Representation and Color Spaces in Computer Vision: A Comprehensive Review. *The Indonesian Journal of Computer Science*, 13(3). Advance online publication. DOI: 10.33022/ijcs.v13i3.3998

Zangana, H. M., & Mustafa, F. M. (2024). From Classical to Deep Learning: A Systematic Review of Image Denoising Techniques. *Jurnal Ilmiah Computer Science*, 3(1), 50–65.

Zangana, H. M., & Mustafa, F. M. (2024). Review of Hybrid Denoising Approaches in Face Recognition: Bridging Wavelet Transform and Deep Learning. *The Indonesian Journal of Computer Science*, 13(4). Advance online publication. DOI: 10.33022/ijcs.v13i4.4209

Zangana, H. M., & Mustafa, F. M. (2024). Surveying the Landscape: A Comprehensive Review of Object Detection Algorithms and Advancements. *Jurnal Ilmiah Computer Science*, 3(1), 1–15.

Zangana, H. M., & Omar, M. (2020). Threats, Attacks, and Mitigations of Smartphone Security. *Academic Journal of Nawroz University*, 9(4), 324–332. DOI: 10.25007/ajnu.v9n4a989

Zangana, H. M., Omar, M., Al-Karaki, J. N., & Mohammed, D. (2024). *Comprehensive Review and Analysis of Network Firewall Rule Analyzers: Enhancing Security Posture and Efficiency*. Redefining Security With Cyber AI. DOI: 10.4018/979-8-3693-6517-5.ch002

Zangana, H. M., Omar, M., & Ali, N. Y. (2024). Harnessing Artificial Intelligence in Modern Marketing: Strategies, Benefits, and Challenges [BAMJ]. *Business, Accounting and Management Journal*, 02(02), 70–82.

Zangana, H. M., Sallow, Z. B., Alkawaz, M. H., & Omar, M. "Unveiling the Collective Wisdom: A Review of Swarm Intelligence in Problem Solving and Optimization," *Inform: Jurnal Ilmiah Bidang Teknologi Informasi dan Komunikasi*, vol. 9, no. 2, pp. 101-110, 2024.

Zangana, H. M., & Zeebaree, S. R. (2024). Distributed Systems for Artificial Intelligence in Cloud Computing: A Review of AI-Powered Applications and Services [INJIISCOM]. *International Journal of Informatics, Information System and Computer Engineering*, 5(1), 11–30. DOI: 10.34010/injiiscom.v5i1.11883

Zhang, H., Wu, J., Pan, Q., Bashir, A. K., & Omar, M. (2024). Toward Byzantine-Robust Distributed Learning for Sentiment Classification on Social Media Platform. *IEEE Transactions on Computational Social Systems*, 1–11. DOI: 10.1109/TCSS.2024.3361465

Zhang, H., Wu, J., Pan, Q., Bashir, A. K., & Omar, M. (2024). Toward Byzantine-Robust Distributed Learning for Sentiment Classification on Social Media Platform. *IEEE Transactions on Computational Social Systems*, 1–11. DOI: 10.1109/TCSS.2024.3361465

Zhou, S., Ali, A., Al-Fuqaha, A., Omar, M., & Feng, L. (2024). Robust Risk-Sensitive Task Offloading for Edge-Enabled Industrial Internet of Things. *IEEE Transactions on Consumer Electronics*, 70(1), 1403–1413. DOI: 10.1109/TCE.2023.3323146

Chapter 13
An In-Depth Analysis of a Cyber Attack: Case Study and Security Insights

Puya Pakshad
https://orcid.org/0000-0003-2834-2769
Illinois Institute of Technology, USA

ABSTRACT

Nation-sponsored cyberattacks pose a severe threat to national security, targeting critical infrastructure and disrupting essential services. Among the most impactful attacks on South Korea's banking sector and infrastructure was the DarkSeoul cyberattack, believed to have been conducted by North Korea state-sponsored hackers. Using spear phishing, DNS poisoning, and malware, this attack caused widespread disruption across critical systems. This paper presents an in-depth analysis of the DarkSeoul incident, detailing the techniques involved and offering insights and recommendations for the global cybersecurity community. The motivations and strategic objectives behind the attack are examined, as well as South Korea's response and the broader implications for cybersecurity policy. Our analysis highlights key vulnerabilities and underscores the urgency for enhanced defenses against state-sponsored cyber threats. This study emphasizes the necessity for robust national cybersecurity measures to counter such sophisticated attacks effectively.

INTRODUCTION

Cyber-attacks are increasingly reported worldwide, causing significant damage to software, networks, data, and infrastructure. Studying and analyzing these attacks enables us to better understand the technical damages and gain valuable experience,

DOI: 10.4018/979-8-3373-0588-2.ch013

allowing for more effective strategies in defense and countermeasures. One particularly dangerous cyberattack took place in South Korea during the final days of June 2013, coinciding with the anniversary of the start of the Korean War in 1950. The hackers appeared to mark occasion by disrupting websites associated with the South Korean president's office and several local newspapers. Although government officials have not officially attributed the attacks, other sources have linked at least one of them to a group known as DarkSeoul, which has been targeting South Korea for four years (Prince, 2013; Trim & Lee, 2010). This group is believed to be connected to the cyberattacks in March that resulted in the wiping of numerous hard drives at South Korean banks and television stations, as well as the more recent attacks on financial companies (Trim & Lee, 2010). The DarkSeoul cyberattack, which targeted major South Korean banks and broadcasting companies, is regarded as one of the most impactful cyber threats in the country's history. Allegedly orchestrated by North Korean state-sponsored hackers, this attack employed a range of malicious techniques, including spear-phishing, DNS poisoning, and destructive malware, to paralyze critical infrastructure. Over 48,000 computers were rendered inoperable, resulting in significant disruption of essential services for at least one day (Martin, 2016; Marpaung & Lee, 2013; Coleman, 2010). The attack's relatively low technical sophistication—compared to threats such as Stuxnet or 10 Days of Rain—was overshadowed by its high impact on South Korea's financial and media sectors. Despite using recycled malware from previous operations like Operation Troy, the attackers managed to penetrate multiple networks, pivot to critical systems, and erase data from both Windows and Unix-like operating systems. This paper aims to provide an in-depth analysis of the DarkSeoul attack, focusing on the techniques used, the impact on South Korea's infrastructure, and the broader cybersecurity lessons learned from the incident.

In general, the key focus areas of this paper are as follows:

- Provide an in-depth analysis of the DarkSeoul cyberattack scenario, including a comparison with other similar cyber warfare attacks.
- Analyze the South Korean government's response to the attack and its efforts to strengthen national cybersecurity defenses.
- Conduct a thorough and comprehensive exploration of the techniques employed in the DarkSeoul attack.
- Propose our recommendations for proactive strategies to prevent future state-sponsored cyberattacks.

The rest of the paper is organized as follows. Section 2 provides a background review of the DarkSeoul cyberattack, including its technical details and motivations. Section 3 presents a comparative analysis between the DarkSeoul attack and other similar nation-sponsored cyberattacks. Section 4 discusses the techniques used in the DarkSeoul attack and offers insights for future defense strategies. Finally, Section 5 provides conclusions and recommendations for proactive measures against state-sponsored cyberattacks.

Figure 1. Number of suspected cyber-attacks linked to North Korea from 2010-2020

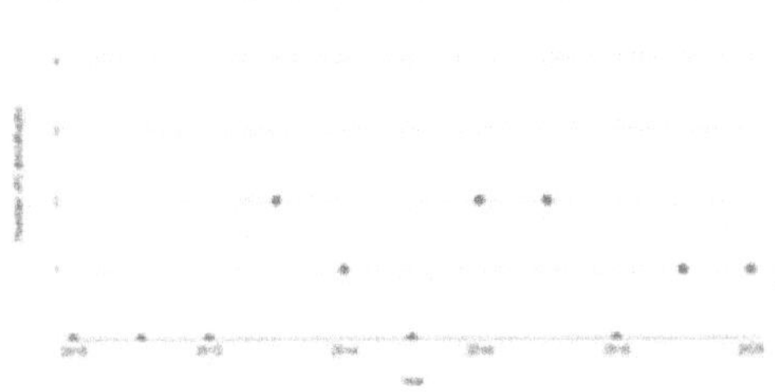

Background

Before delving into the analysis of the DarkSeoul attack, this section will provide an overview of malware within the cybersecurity domain. Malware, or malicious software, is a broad term that refers to any software intentionally designed to cause harm to a computer system, network, or device. It can take many forms, including viruses, worms, Trojan horses, ransomware, and spyware. The primary goal of malware is often to steal sensitive information, damage systems, or disrupt services, typically for financial gain, political motives, or personal reasons. In recent years, the complexity and frequency of malware attacks have increased, making them a significant threat to businesses, governments, and individuals worldwide. Three common motivations drive cyber-attacks: political, criminal, and personal. Politically motivated attacks often aim to disrupt or destabilize government entities or to protest certain policies (Trim & Lee, 2010; Nah, 2023; Shin et al., 2018). Criminal attacks focus on financial gain, such as stealing sensitive data or deploying ransomware. Personal attacks, on the other hand, can be driven by disgruntled employees or individuals seeking revenge. Regardless of the motive, attackers frequently use malware to exploit vulnerabilities and cause system-wide damage.

Understanding the nature and goals of malware is crucial for recognizing its role in various types of cyber-attacks. In this context, examining the methods employed in the DarkSeoul attack offers valuable insights into the evolving landscape of cyber warfare (North Korea's Cyber Operations, 2016; Park & Kim, 2024). This case illustrates how state-sponsored groups increasingly leverage relatively unsophisticated yet highly destructive techniques to achieve political and economic disruption. As such, it underscores the growing need for robust defensive strategies to safeguard critical infrastructure from similar threats. By analyzing such attacks, we can better appreciate the importance of advanced security measures in defending against emerging cyber risks (Desimone & Horton, 2017; Coleman, 2010).

DarkSeoul Impacts

The DarkSeoul cyberattack was a highly destructive event that revealed critical weaknesses in the nation's digital infrastructure. By targeting essential services such as banking and media, the attack demonstrated the far-reaching consequences of cyber warfare, where disruptions in key sectors can ripple across the entire economy. This incident showcased the vulnerability of both public and private institutions, which rely heavily on interconnected systems that, without strong security measures, can become single points of failure. Compounding these vulnerabilities is the reality that computer systems across various layers—software applications, operating systems, networks, and infrastructures—remain susceptible to security breaches (Pakshad et al., 2023; Sultana et al., 2023; Papain, 2011; Rossum, 2017). This is largely due to insufficient integration of comprehensive security policies during the development phase. In many cases, software vendors do not provide adequate documentation for assessing non-functional requirements, and security considerations are often limited to the basic principles of confidentiality, integrity, and availability (Pakshad et al., 2023; Sultana et al., 2023; Raska, 2022). These shortcomings create exploitable weaknesses, allowing attackers, like those responsible for DarkSeoul, to penetrate systems with relative ease. As this attack demonstrated, the failure to address such vulnerabilities during development can lead to severe consequences when systems are targeted. The DarkSeoul attack had both technical and psychological impacts. Technically, it caused widespread failures across crucial infrastructure systems, while psychologically, it undermined public trust in the government's ability to protect essential services. In the following sections, we will explore how the attack immediately affected key infrastructure and the broader implications it holds for cybersecurity strategy.

A. **Immediate Impact on Critical Infrastructure**

The DarkSeoul cyberattack had a significant and immediate impact on South Korea's critical infrastructure, particularly in the banking and media sectors. Approximately 48,000 systems were affected across key institutions, including Shinhan Bank, Nonghyup Bank, and major media outlets such as YTN, KBS, and MBC. Services were severely disrupted for over 24 hours, with widespread outages affecting ATMs, mobile banking, and online financial services, leaving millions of South

Koreans without access to essential resources. The attack, which rendered systems inoperable, created substantial public panic and resulted in considerable economic losses. This attack was both technical and psychological, aiming to undermine public trust in the country's digital infrastructure.

B. **Broader Cybersecurity Implications**

Figure 1 illustrates the number of cyberattacks attributed to North Korea as the perpetrator. It is important to note, however, that while some of these cyberattacks are officially linked to North Korea, others remain suspected rather than confirmed. As of 2024, the United Nations has identified North Korea as the suspected actor behind 58 attacks that are believed to have supported its nuclear weapons program. One notable cyber operation, attributed to North Korea state-sponsored actors, was designed to inflict both material and emotional damage. Although initially perceived as a low-sophistication attack due to its reliance on destructive malware, the scale of its impact revealed significant vulnerabilities within South Korea's cybersecurity defenses. By disrupting key financial services and media broadcasts, the attack highlighted the fragility of national infrastructure and demonstrated North Korea's growing cyber capabilities. This operation served a strategic purpose, aiming to erode confidence in the government's ability to protect critical infrastructure and amplify fear among the population (Martin, 2016; Jun et al., 2014; Kim, 2022).

Authorities' Challenges

Attributing the responsibility for the DarkSeoul cyberattack posed considerable challenges for South Korean authorities. While North Korea was the prime suspect, the country repeatedly denied involvement, and the attackers employed tactics that complicated the investigation. They reused malware from previous campaigns, including Operation Troy (2009–2013), which had targeted South Korea in earlier cyber threats. This reuse of malware, alongside the use of anonymizing techniques such as proxy servers and TOR exitnodes, obscured the origin of the attack, blurring lines of accountability (Martin, 2016; Mavroeidis et al., 2021; Iftikhar, 2024). Despite these obstacles, South Korean investigators ultimately attributed the attack to North Korea. The malware used in the DarkSeoul attack bore strong similarities to tools deployed in earlier cyber campaigns, and network logs revealed that some of the infrastructure used in the attack was linked to North Korean IP addresses. However, the attackers' use of proxy servers and anonymized networks made it difficult to conclusively trace the attack exclusively to North Korea (Martin, 2016; Mavroeidis et al., 2021; Iftikhar, 2024). A crucial part of the attack involved exploiting patch management systems, allowing the attackers to distribute malware across entire networks with minimal detection. This strategy of using legitimate infrastructure increased the complexity of both detecting and mitigating the threat. Investigators also noted that maintaining such a wide-reaching network of compromised infrastructure required significant time and resources, further implicating state-sponsored actors (Martin, 2016; Marpaung & Lee, 2013; Iftikhar, 2024; Siers, 2014). According to the spokesman for the Korea Internet and Security Agency (KISA), 22 of the IP addresses used in the DarkSeoul attack had been involved in previous attacks attributed to North Korean hackers since 2009 (Martin, 2016). The use of anonymizing tools and sophisticated malware distribution tactics demonstrated the attackers' operational sophistication. These challenges underscored the need for South Korea to strengthen its cyber-security defenses. In response to the growing threat of state sponsored cyber operations, South Korea established the Cyber Command, marking a significant step in enhancing its national cyber defense posture (Martin, 2016; Park, Rowe, & Cisneros, 2016; Chah, 2014).

A. **International Response**

The DarkSeoul cyberattack sent shockwaves through both national and international communities, emphasizing the growing need for cohesive and robust cybersecurity measures. While the attack was focused on a single nation, its broader implications highlighted the vulnerability of global interconnected systems and the potential for cyberattacks to destabilize critical infrastructures. This event served as a wake-up call for both national governments and the international community, urging them to rethink and strengthen their cybersecurity frameworks.

At the national level, the attack forced governments to consider the importance of both defensive and offensive cybersecurity capabilities. Defensive measures ensure that critical infrastructures such as financial systems, media networks, and public services are adequately protected from disruptive attacks. However, the attack also demonstrated the necessity of developing offensive capabilities to counter and potentially deter future state-sponsored cyberattacks (Baezner, 2018; Sultana, Boyd, & Williams, 2023; Kim, Alfouzan, & Kim, 2021; Nah, 2023). On the international stage, DarkSeoul highlighted the increasing prevalence of cyber warfare and the challenges associated with attributing attacks to specific state actors. The complexity of attribution made it difficult to respond decisively, but the attack ultimately galvanized international collaboration to enhance cybersecurity resilience. Below, we examine both the internal response of the affected nation and the broader international community's reaction to this pivotal event.

1) **South Korea's Internal Response**

The DarkSeoul cyberattack underscored the challenges faced by governments in responding to cyberattacks when the perpetrator is difficult to identify. The repeated cyber assaults on South Korea highlighted the urgent need for both offensive and defensive cybersecurity capabilities. South Korea had already started enhancing its cybersecurity posture before the DarkSeoul attack, focusing on strengthening strategic resources. Recognizing the rising cyber threats, the government began allocating sufficient institutional and financial resources to bolster its defenses. In January 2010, South Korea established the Cyber Command, and by March 2011, the Defense Ministry had set up a Cyber Policy Team. The Cyber Command played a central role in combating North Korea's online tactics, including counter-propaganda efforts such as posting on North Korean social media platforms and blocking access to North Korean broadcasts (Martin, 2016; Cybersecurity and Infrastructure Security Agency, 2013; Carnegie Mellon University, 2013). In 2013, the Cyber Policy Department was established to monitor cyberspace and telecommunications. That same year, South Korea announced an ambitious plan to train 5,000 cybersecurity experts and doubled its cybersecurity budget, aiming to reach $8.76 billion by 2017 (Martin, 2016; Kshetri, 2014; Kshetri, 2016; Kim & Polito, 2019).

2) **International Community's Response**

The international community responded to the DarkSeoul attack with growing concern over the increasing prevalence of state-sponsored cyber warfare. Although directly attributing the attack to North Korea posed significant challenges, many nations and cybersecurity experts condemned the incident for its devastating impact on critical infrastructure. Organizations like the United Nations pointed to the attack as part of a broader trend of North Korea's cyber aggression. In the aftermath, South Korea intensified its collaboration with international allies, focusing on enhancing its cybersecurity frameworks (National Cybersecurity and Communications Integration Center, 2013; Baezner, 2018). This cooperative response not only strengthened South Korea's defenses but also emphasized to the global community the importance of collective action in countering state-sponsored cyber threats. Collaborative efforts in intelligence sharing and policymaking were critical in shaping South Korea's defense strategies following the DarkSeoul attack. The incident highlighted the necessity for nations to stay vigilant in the face of evolving cyber threats from state actors (CISA, 2013; Carnegie Mellon University, 2013; National Cybersecurity and Communications Integration Center, 2013; Hwang & Choi, 2021).

Techniques Applied in DarkSeoul

The DarkSeoul cyberattack, a destructive cyber operation attributed to North Korean threat actors, demonstrated a complex, multi-stage infection scenario. Attackers employed a combination of spear-phishing campaigns and malware, sending emails embedded with malicious Trojan downloaders to various organizations. These emails tricked employees into downloading malware, often disguised as legitimate files like SimDisk.exe. The initial infection stage used a component called "Cast Off", which functioned as a downloader designed to bypass security defenses by masquerading as a harmless application. Upon execution, "Cast Off" established persistence mechanisms by modifying registry entries or adding startup scripts, ensuring its continued presence on infected systems. It then retrieved additional malicious payloads, including wiper malware that targeted both Windows and Unix-based systems. These wipers were designed to overwrite the Master Boot Record (MBR) or critical system files, rendering systems unbootable and causing extensive data loss (Prince, 2013; Martin, 2016; Ji-Young, 2019). In particular, the MBR wiper targeted the first 256 megabytes of the hard drive, which contains essential boot instructions needed to start the operating system. By overwriting this portion of the drive with random data, the malware destroyed the system's ability to boot, making recovery extremely difficult without specialized tools. Beyond simple downloading, "Cast Off" often fetched seemingly benign files, such as JPEG images, that contained hidden malicious code. This code was unpacked and decrypted by "Cast Off" and then executed from the system's temporary directory. A key secondary payload downloaded by "Cast Off" was the "Castdos" Trojan, which was used for Distributed Denial of Service (DDoS) attacks on targeted networks (Martin, 2016; see also Marpaung & Lee, 2013; Pasqualicchio, 2019; Klingner, 2021).

A. **Spear-Phishing and Malware Delivery**

In addition to spear-phishing, DNS poisoning played a crucial role in redirecting traffic from legitimate South Korean banking websites to fake servers controlled by the attackers, allowing them to harvest sensitive user data and disrupt financial services. The attack also incorporated advanced tactics, such as compromising patch management systems (e.g., AhnLab) by using stolen credentials to distribute malware across entire networks. These techniques allowed the attackers to deliver destructive payloads en masse. Deceptive tactics, including the use of fake hacktivist groups like the "Whois Crew," misled investigators and created false narratives, adding an extra layer of complexity to the attack. Through iterative processes, "Cast Off" continuously downloaded, unpacked, and executed new malicious components, expanding the attack's reach and impact (Prince, 2013; Martin, 2016; Ministry of National Defense, Republic of Korea, 1972).

B. **Advanced Tactics: Exploiting Vulnerabilities**

The scale and impact of the attack, which compromised both Windows and Unix systems, illustrated its broad scope, affecting multiple layers of infrastructure. Despite its relatively lower technical sophistication compared to advanced malware such as Stuxnet, the combination of spear-phishing, DNS poisoning, and data-wiping malware made the DarkSeoul attack devastatingly effective. It underscored the urgent need for robust cyber hygiene practices, especially improved patch management protocols, to prevent future breaches of this magnitude (Prince, 2013; Martin, 2016; Sanger et al. 2017).

C. **Possible Attack Vectors**

Several theories exist regarding how the Lazarus Group managed to execute the attack. One theory, published by Avast, suggests that the main attack vector was the Korea Software Property Rights Council (SPC) website. According to this theory, DarkSeoul was a watering hole attack, a cyber-attack that infects frequently visited websites to compromise user machines. The attackers compromised the SPC website and used it to redirect the victims' computers to another site, controlled by them, using a malicious JavaScript script. The attackers then exploited a known vulnerability in Internet Explorer, CVE-2012-1889. This vulnerability in Microsoft XML Core Services 3.0, 4.0, 5.0, and 6.0 allowed the attackers to run code remotely by accessing unused memory locations on the targeted machines (BetaFred., 2022; CISA, 2013; Boo, 2018). There is also a theory that the attackers took control of a patch management server used by many future victims to download updates. This theory asserts that the primary attack vector was a server running patch management software made by AhnLab. The attackers likely gained access to this server either by

Table 1. Comparison of DarkSeoul with major cyberattacks

Metric	DarkSeoul (2013)	WannaCry (2017)	NotPetya (2017)	Stuxnet (2010)	Shamoon (2012)
Sophistication	Moderate (known malware reuse)	High (used EternalBlue exploit)	High (EternalBlue & Mimikatz)	Extremely high (4 zero-days)	Moderate (destructive malware)
Scale (systems affected)	48,000 systems	300,000 globally	300,000 globally	1,000 nuclear centrifuges	35,000 computers
Impact	Disrupted South Korean banks, media	Global service disruption	Global economic damage ($10B)	Physical destruction	Destroyed data at Saudi Aramco
Economic Loss	$800 million	$4 billion	$10 billion	Undisclosed (nuclear damage)	Economic losses for Saudi Aramco
Propagation Method	Spear-phishing, DNS poi-soning	Worm, ransomware, Eternal Blue	Ransomware, worm	Worm, USB drives	Malware
Unique Aspects	Reused old malware, region-specific	Fast global spread, ransom demand	Wiper disguised as ransomware	Targeted industrial control systems	Targeted oi industry

obtaining credentials through spear-phishing or by compromising other systems and discovering stored data. Another theory, proposed by F-Secure, a Finnish cybersecurity firm, states that spear-phishing and email were the primary infection vectors. The attackers used long file names and double file extensions to trick users into opening infected files. F-Secure claims that the malware disguised itself as a fake Internet Explorer lookalike, tricking users into running it. The malware then targeted the System32 directory on Windows machines and executed its malicious code using a DLL file. Given the size of the attack and the numerous theories proposed by various organizations, it is reasonable to conclude that DarkSeoul was most likely a multi-vector attack, utilizing a variety of technologies. This is further supported by the involvement of a hacker group associated with the North Korean government. As a nation-state, North Korea has the resources and manpower to carry out such a complex attack, capable of targeting various computer systems and infrastructure.

D. **Attack Tactics**

The attackers employed several tactics to spread their malware and execute the attack. Social engineering was a key element of their operation. Spear-phishing was used to steal important credentials and gain access to critical systems like servers. Another tactic involved exploiting software bugs to access systems and execute malicious code. Once the attackers obtained the necessary information, they destroyed the infected systems' data to cover their tracks, making it difficult for investigators to determine exactly what happened and who was responsible. DNS poisoning, which redirects users to malicious websites, was another important tactic. The attackers likely used DNS poisoning to steal information or exploit the CVE-2012-1889 vulnerability to run malicious code on the victims' computers (BetaFred., 2022; CISA, 2013; Novetta, 2016).

E. **Attack Technologies**

The DarkSeoul cyberattack relied on three main pieces of malware to achieve its goals. The first was a dropper Trojan, designed to download additional malware onto the victim's computer. The second was a Master Boot Record (MBR) wiper, a destructive payload downloaded by the dropper Trojan that erased the data on infected PCs, rendering them unusable. The third was a Remote Access Trojan (RAT), used to compromise a patch management server. The RAT allowed attackers to control the patch management server and distribute the dropper Trojan and MBR wiper to other systems.

F. **Dropper Trojan**

Multiple versions of the dropper Trojan were employed in the DarkSeoul attack, targeting both Windows and Unix-based systems. The Windows version included executable files that placed malicious payloads in the %Temp% directory, bypassing detection. It also sought out antivirus programs commonly used in South Korea, such as AhnLab and Hauri, attempting to disable them by terminating related processes. Although initially tailored for South Korean antivirus software, experts suggest the malware could easily be adapted to target any antivirus product worldwide. Each variant of the dropper Trojan had unique payloads. For example, Dropper A contained both Windows and Unix components. On Unix systems, it used a Bash script to wipe hard drives by targeting the initial sectors of each partition, including the MBR, rendering the system unbootable. In Windows, Dropper A deployed a wiping executable designed to erase the hard drive and disable the system after shutting down any running antivirus processes. Dropper B included a similar Windows wiping executable but focused on disabling different antivirus programs before proceeding with the wipe. Dropper C operated by injecting its code into system memory, bypassing traditional antivirus detection.

G. **MBR Wiper**

The MBR wiper targeted both Windows and Unix-based systems like Linux and Solaris. On Windows, it wiped the MBR partition on each connected hard drive, then shut down the system, preventing it from booting. The Unix version used the "dd" shell command to wipe system data. Normally used for routine tasks like system backups, the "dd" command can cause irreparable damage if misused. In this case, the command was deliberately used to delete critical directories on the root partition of a Linux system, making it non-functional.

H. **Remote Access Trojan (RAT)**

To distribute the dropper Trojan and MBR wiper, the attackers used a Remote Access Trojan (RAT). This type of malware acts as a backdoor for attackers, giving them control over infected computers. In this case, the RAT was deployed on a server running patch management software developed by AhnLab. It is suspected that the attackers used this server to distribute their malware to other systems using the same patch management network.

I. **Attack Coordination and Procedures**

The DarkSeoul attack was highly coordinated, demonstrating meticulous planning and precision. The attackers effectively conducted a spear-phishing campaign to access numerous vital systems, collecting a vast amount of sensitive data from the South Korean government and major financial institutions. The destruction of these systems played a critical role in the overall attack, allowing the attackers to cover their tracks and make it harder for investigators to trace the attack back to them. The attack appeared to serve dual purposes: gathering intelligence and concealing previous cyber operations against South Korea. While the attackers initially focused on data collection, the destructive nature of the attack suggests an underlying motive to cripple critical infrastructure by wiping systems and rendering them non-functional.

Comparison with Major Cyber Attacks

While the DarkSeoul cyberattack was highly disruptive within its targeted region, it is essential to place its impact, scale, and sophistication within the broader context of other significant nation-sponsored cyberattacks. By comparing it to other well-known attacks like WannaCry, Not-Petya, Stuxnet, and Shamoon, we can better understand DarkSeoul's role in the evolution of cyber warfare and its standing among other landmark threats. Each of these attacks offers different insights into the strategies and objectives of state-sponsored hackers, ranging from espionage to outright destruction of critical infrastructure.

A. WannaCry (2017)

WannaCry was a global ransomware attack that affected over 300,000 systems across numerous regions. It spread rapidly using the EternalBlue exploit, a vulnerability in widely-used operating systems. The WannaCry attack primarily aimed to encrypt users' data and demand a ransom in cryptocurrency for its release. Although the attack did not specifically target critical infrastructure, its widespread reach caused massive disruptions in hospitals, businesses, and public services globally. Critical healthcare services in particular were significantly impacted, forcing cancellations of surgeries and diverting emergency patients.

In terms of scale, WannaCry dwarfs DarkSeoul in the number of systems affected and the geographical reach of the attack. However, while WannaCry caused chaos globally, it was less destructive than DarkSeoul because it did not aim to destroy data or disable critical systems permanently. DarkSeoul's focus on wiping data from critical financial institutions and media companies, combined with its targeted attack on the region's infrastructure, makes it more strategically focused and devastating in its local impact compared to the global, non-discriminatory spread of WannaCry.

B. NotPetya (2017)

Like WannaCry, NotPetya was another devastating attack that occurred in 2017. While it initially masqueraded as ransomware, its true objective was destructive. NotPetya targeted corporations during a period of heightened political tension in a specific region, but the malware quickly spread beyond its initial target, infecting global corporations. NotPetya exploited the same EternalBlue vulnerability as WannaCry but was far more destructive—rendering systems inoperable by overwriting the Master Boot Record (MBR), which controls system startup. Companies in various industries were hit, leading to $10 billion in global economic damages. While NotPetya caused substantial global damage, its impact on its initial target was similar to the DarkSeoul attack in its focus on destabilizing critical infrastructure. However, the global spread of NotPetya to major international companies magnified its overall impact far beyond its original regional borders. In contrast, DarkSeoul's primary impact remained confined to its targeted region, although the attack on media and financial sectors had profound consequences for internal stability and public trust in infrastructure.

C. Stuxnet (2010)

Stuxnet is often cited as the first known instance of a cyberattack that caused physical destruction. Widely believed to have been developed jointly by two collaborating nations, Stuxnet specifically targeted nuclear infrastructure in a particular region. The malware spread through infected USB drives and was designed to damage centrifuges used in uranium enrichment by causing them to spin out of control while providing normal readings to operators. Stuxnet's objective was clear: sabotage nuclear ambitions in its target region. In terms of sophistication, Stuxnet is unparalleled. It exploited four zero-day vulnerabilities in widely-used operating systems, a rarity in cyberattacks. Stuxnet was custom engineered to target industrial control systems (ICS), which made it highly specialized. While DarkSeoul employed known malware and more conventional attack vectors like spear-phishing and DNS poisoning, Stuxnet introduced a new frontier of cyber warfare where digital tools were used to cause real-world, physical damage. While Stuxnet had a clear military objective, DarkSeoul was designed more for psychological and economic disruption, targeting banking and media systems to sow panic and destabilize public trust. The two attacks differ in their focus—Stuxnet was a strategic military strike, while DarkSeoul was a nationwide disruption of civilian infrastructure—but both highlight the growing role of cyberattacks in achieving state-sponsored goals.

D. **Shamoon (2012)**

Shamoon, like DarkSeoul, was a destructive cyberattack designed to wipe data. Shamoon targeted the energy sector and infected 35,000 computers, effectively crippling operations for days. The malware wiped files and replaced them with politically charged images. Shamoon was likely motivated by regional political tensions and aimed at destabilizing the economy by disrupting critical energy production capabilities. When comparing Shamoon to DarkSeoul, both attacks share similarities in their destructive intent. Both targeted specific sectors of a country's economy and sought to destroy critical infrastructure. However, while Shamoon aimed at a single entity (in this case, an oil company), DarkSeoul targeted a broader spectrum of financial and media institutions, making it more widespread in its impact on civilian life. In terms of economic loss, Shamoon's attack had a significant impact on the global energy market, while DarkSeoul's focus was on the domestic economy and public infrastructure.

E. **Comparison Results**

In comparing DarkSeoul to other major cyberattacks, it becomes clear that while it was more regionally confined, it was highly destructive and strategically focused on key infrastructure sectors. Its targeted nature, particularly towards media and financial institutions, makes it distinct from more globally-oriented attacks like WannaCry and NotPetya. Furthermore, DarkSeoul's psychological and economic disruption tactics align it more closely with attacks like Shamoon, though it lacked the physical destruction characteristic of Stuxnet. DarkSeoul's significant impact on critical infrastructure and the public panic it generated underscore the evolving tactics in nation-sponsored cyber warfare. Though it didn't reach the global scale of attacks like NotPetya or WannaCry, its focused disruption of an entire country's essential services highlights the potential for future regional cyber conflicts to cause widespread damage without necessarily spilling over to other countries. The attack also emphasized the need for nations to strengthen their cyber defenses and to cooperate internationally in the face of increasingly sophisticated and destructive state-sponsored cyberattacks.

Defense Recommendations

Considering the pervasive use of phishing in the DarkSeoul attack, it is evident that a substantial portion of the attack was predicated on extracting sensitive information from unsuspecting users. The DarkSeoul incident is not an isolated case; numerous other cyber threats heavily rely on similar tactics. In fact, it can be reasonably asserted that a vast majority of cyber threats involve phishing and social engineering in some capacity. This leads to the conclusion that the most critical vulnerability in this cyberattack was the human element—employees working within the targeted organizations. Although the attack primarily exploited software vulnerabilities, its success hinged on the inability of key personnel in critical institutions to recognize that they were being deceived into divulging confidential information to unauthorized parties or opening email attachments that were malicious in nature. We contend that the success of this attack can largely be attributed to insufficient cybersecurity training within the affected organizations. It is imperative that all personnel handling sensitive computer systems and information receive comprehensive training in identifying common cyber threats. We recommend that organizations dealing with sensitive data implement thorough training programs, educating their employees on how to detect deceptive emails by providing instruction on identifying phishing attempts, and illustrating the potential consequences of failing to do so. Additionally, organizations should enforce a stringent email communication policy, mandating that all legitimate company emails follow a standardized format and are used exclusively for work-related communications. Moreover, employees should be discouraged from sending or opening files attached to emails, as more secure methods of file sharing, such as FTP servers, should be employed within the organization. Organizations must also perform regular security audits in collaboration with reputable cybersecurity consulting firms. These audits should be conducted covertly to properly assess the adherence of employees to established cybersecurity protocols, thus enabling organizations to accurately identify their vulnerabilities. Furthermore, it is essential that organizations employ an internal cybersecurity specialist with substantial expertise in identifying and responding to cyber threats in real time. This is crucial, as the delayed detection of the DarkSeoul attack allowed the Lazarus Group to compromise thousands of systems over an extended period. While this is not an exhaustive set of recommendations, it represents a pragmatic starting point that can be swiftly and efficiently implemented within any organization. The mitigation of software exploits used in such attacks presents a more complex challenge. No software is entirely immune to vulnerabilities, and most professional software is highly intricate, making it difficult to address flaws comprehensively. In many cases, resolving a particular vulnerability requires significant portions of the software to be rewritten from scratch. Therefore, to prevent attackers from exploiting software weaknesses, developers must adopt a proactive and security-centric approach throughout the software development lifecycle. In addition, Software developers must rigorously evaluate their code to ensure that it cannot be exploited for unintended purposes. Continuous and systematic checks throughout the development process are necessary to guarantee that the software is being developed securely from inception to completion. In addition, there must be more stringent regulatory oversight regarding software security. Large software companies, such as Microsoft, possess the requisite resources to prioritize the remediation of critical security flaws, yet often fail to allocate sufficient personnel to address these issues. This is largely due to the absence of legal mandates requiring companies to fix security vulnerabilities, which diminishes the perceived urgency of such issues. The obvious remedy for this problem would be to transition to a software provider that places a greater emphasis on security. However, in many cases, this is impractical due to the lack of viable alternatives for certain professional software. This dynamic grants significant leverage to software developers over both their users and the market, enabling them to neglect the remediation of vulnerabilities. While Microsoft is not the sole offender, it is certainly one of the most prominent. Given the lack of competition among many software companies, the only viable mechanism to compel them to address critical vulnerabilities is through the enactment of legislation mandating the prioritization of security patches. Furthermore, we propose that software service providers, such as Microsoft, offer real-time cybersecurity defense services to users who have purchased licenses for their products during critical cyber threats. For instance, in the DarkSeoul attack, the malware attempted to execute critical operations such as terminating processes and receiving remote code execution commands, as discussed in this paper. We recommend that Microsoft provide 24/7 online monitoring services for all licensed software connected to the network. Such a system would ensure that if a device exhibits signs of compromise, an immediate alert is sent to the support team through Microsoft's Windows Security plugin, allowing organizations to be notified of the attack in real time rather than retrospectively. The implementation of such mechanisms would facilitate timely responses, granting organizations critical time to deploy defensive strategies and safeguard compromised systems. By enabling real-time awareness of an attack, organizations can significantly enhance their capacity to mitigate the damage, which is crucial in minimizing the impact of cyberattacks.

CONCLUSION

DarkSeoul cyber-attack serves as a critical case study in state-sponsored cyber warfare, showcasing both the impact and complexity of such operations. Orchestrated by North Korean hackers, the attack used techniques like spear phishing, DNS poisoning, and MBR-wiping malware, crippling South Korea's financial and media sectors by disrupting over 48,000 systems. Although less sophisticated than attacks like Stuxnet, the operation highlighted the devastating consequences of exploiting vulnerabilities in critical infrastructure. Attribution was challenging due to anonymized infrastructures, but the Lazarus Group was identified as the likely perpetrator. The attack underscores the need for enhanced cybersecurity measures, including improved patch management, social engineering awareness, and stronger national cybersecurity frameworks. South Korea's response, through the creation of Cyber Command and increased resource allocation, demonstrates the importance of proactive defense strategies. The global response, led by international bodies like the United Nations, emphasized the importance of intelligence sharing and international cooperation to combat state-backed cyber threats. Ultimately, the DarkSeoul at- tack serves as a reminder of the need for continuous vigilance and collaboration against evolving cyber threats. The lessons learned should guide future efforts to strengthen resilience, particularly in protecting critical infrastructure.

REFERENCES

Baezner, M. (2018). ETH Library Cyber disruption and cybercrime: Democratic People's Republic of Korea Report. https://doi.org/DOI: 10.3929/ethz-b-000314511

BetaFred. (2022, October 14). Microsoft Security Advisory 2719615. Microsoft.com. https://learn.microsoft.com/en-us/security-updates/securityadvisories/2012/2719615

Boo, H. (2017). AN ASSESSMENT OF NORTH KOREAN CYBER THREATS. *The Journal of East Asian Affairs*, 31(1), 97–117. https://www.jstor.org/stable/44321274

Carnegie Mellon University. (2013). South Korean malware attack. Produced for US-CERT, a government organization. Retrieved from: https://www.cisa.gov

Coleman, K. (2010). The weaponry and strategies of digital conflict. International Conference on Information Warfare and Security. Retrieved from https://ezproxy.gl.iit.edu/login?url=https://www.proquest.com/conference-papers-proceedings/weaponry-strategies-digital-conflict/docview/869617526/se-2?accountid=28377

Desimone, A., & Horton, N. (2017). The 2014 North Korean Cyber Attack on Sony and Lessons for US Government Actions in Cyberspace NIGHTMARE National Security Report. https://www.jhuapl.edu/sites/default/files/2022-12/SonyNightmareBeforeChristmas.pdf

Hwang, J., & Choi, K.-S. (2021). North Korean Cyber Attacks and Policy Responses: An Interdisciplinary Theoretical Framework. *The International Journal of Cybersecurity Intelligence and Cybercrime*, 4(2), 4–24. DOI: 10.52306/04020221NHPZ9033

Iftikhar, S. (2024). Cyberterrorism as a Global threat: a Review on Repercussions and Countermeasures. PeerJ Computer Science, 10(e1772). https://doi.org/DOI: 10.7717/peerj-cs.1772

Jun, J., LaFoy, S., & Sohn, E. (2014, December 18). The organization of cyber operations in North Korea. Center for Strategic and International Studies. https://csis-website-prod.s3.amazonaws.com/s3fs-public/legacy_files/files/publication/141218_Cyber_Operations_North_Korea.pdf

Kim, C. W., & Polito, C. (2019). The evolution of North Korean cyber threats. Asan Institute for Policy Studies. https://www.jstor.org/stable/resrep20679

Kim, K., Alfouzan, F. A., & Kim, H. (2021). Cyber-Attack Scoring Model Based on the Offensive Cybersecurity Framework. *Applied Sciences (Basel, Switzerland)*, 11(16), 7738. DOI: 10.3390/app11167738

Kim, M. (2022). North Korea's Cyber Capabilities and Their Implications for International Security. *Sustainability (Basel)*, 14(3), 1744. DOI: 10.3390/su14031744

Klingner, B. (2021). North Korean cyberattacks: A dangerous and evolving threat (Special Report No. 247). The Heritage Foundation. https://www.heritage.org/sites/default/files/2021-09/SR247.pdf

Kshetri, N. (2014). Cyberwarfare in the Korean Peninsula: Asymmetries and Strategic Responses. *East Asia (Piscataway, N.J.)*, 31(3), 183–201. DOI: 10.1007/s12140-014-9215-1

Marpaung, J. A., & Lee, H. (2013). Dark Seoul cyber attack: Could it be worse? In *Conference of the Indonesian Studies Association in Korea*. Ji-Young, K., In, L. J., & Gon, K. K. (2019, May). The all-purpose sword: North Korea's cyber operations and strategies. In *2019 11th International Conference on Cyber Conflict (CyCon)* (Vol. 900, pp. 1–20). IEEE.

Martin, D. M. (2016). Tracing the lineage of DarkSeoul. Global Information Assurance Certification Paper. © The SANS Institute. https://www.giac.org/paper/gsec/31524/tracing-lineage-darkseoul/126346

Mavroeidis, V., Hohimer, R., Casey, T., & Jesang, A. (2021, May 1). Threat Actor Type Inference and Characterization within Cyber Threat Intelligence. IEEE Xplore. https://doi.org/DOI: 10.23919/CyCon51939.2021.9468305

Microsoft Updates for Multiple Vulnerabilities | CISA. (2013, January 24). Cybersecurity and Infrastructure Security Agency CISA. https://www.cisa.gov/news-events/alerts/2012/07/10/microsoft-updates-multiple-vulnerabilities

Ministry of National Defense. Republic of Korea. War History Compilation Committee. (1972). Cheonchaengsa [History of the Korean War]. Ministry of National Defense, Republic of Korea.

Nah, L. T. (2023). North Korean hackers: Vigilance against better than underestimation of. North Korean Review, 19(1), 91–98. https://www.jstor.org/stable/27217098

National Cybersecurity and Communications Integration Center. (2013, March 27). *South Korean malware attack*. U.S. Department of Homeland Security. https://www.nab.org/xert/scitech/pdfs/20130328_South%20Korean%20Malware.pdf

Niel Chah. (2014). North Korea: cyber threat perception and metadata analysis. https://doi.org/DOI: 10.14288/1.0165997

Nir Kshetri. (2016). Cybersecurity in South Korea. Springer EBooks, 171–182. https://doi.org/DOI: 10.1007/978-3-319-40554-4_10

North Korea's Cyber Operations. (2016). Google Books. https://books.google.com/books?hl=en&lr=&id=hUpQCwAAQBAJ&oi=fnd&pg=PR3&dq=Jun

Novetta. (2016). *Operation Blockbuster: Unraveling the long thread of the Sony attack*. Novetta Advanced Analytics. Retrieved from https://www.operationblockbuster.com

Pakshad, P., Shameli-Sendi, A., & Khalaji Emamzadeh Abbasi, B. (2023). A security vulnerability predictor based on source code metrics. *Journal of Computer Virology and Hacking Techniques*, 19(4), 615–633. DOI: 10.1007/s11416-023-00469-y

Papain, T. (2011). North Korea and cyberwarfare: How North Korea's cyber attacks violate the laws of war. In J. Korean L., 11, 29. Heinonline.org. https://heinonline.org/HOL/Page?handle=hein.journals/jkorl11&div=6&g_sent=1&casa_token=&collection=journals

Park, C., & Kim, H. (2024). A Study on the Change of Cyber Attacks in North Korea. *The Journal of the Convergence on Culture Technology*, 10(4), 175–181. DOI: 10.17703/JCCT.2024.10.4.175

Park, J. M., Rowe, N., & Cisneros, M. (2016). Responding to North Korean cyber-attacks. In *Eccws 2016 - Proceedings of the 15th European Conference on Cyber Warfare and Security* (pp. 245–251). Academic Conferences International Limited., https://books.google.com/books?hl=en&lr=&id=ijaeDAAAQBAJ&oi=fnd&pg=PA245

Pasqualicchio, V. T. (2019). Behind the Cyber Walls of North Korea (Order No. 27671005). Available from ProQuest Dissertations & Theses Global. (2378940811). https://ezproxy.gl.iit.edu/login?url=https://www.proquest.com/dissertations-theses/behind-cyber-walls-north-korea/docview/2378940811/se-2

Prince, B. (2013, June 27). South Korea Cyber Attack Tied to DarkSeoul Crew: Symantec. SecurityWeek. https://www.securityweek.com/south-korea-cyber-attack-tied-darkseoul-crew-symantec/

Raska, M. (2022). North Korea's evolving cyber strategies and operations: Toward weapons of mass effectiveness. In *North Korea's foreign policy*. Google Books., https://books.google.com/books?hl=en&lr=&id=mXufEAAAQBAJ&oi=fnd&pg=PA173

Raska, M. (2020). North Korea's Evolving Cyber Strategies: Continuity and Change. SIRIUS – Zeitschrift Für Strategische Analysen, 4(2), 1–13. https://doi.org/DOI: 10.1515/sirius-2020-3030

Sanger, D. E., Kirkpatrick, D. D., & Perlroth, N. (2017, October 15). The World Once Laughed at North Korean Cyberpower. No More. The New York Times. https://www.nytimes.com/2017/10/15/world/asia/north-korea-hacking-cyber-sony.html

Shin, Y., Lee, J., & Kim, M. (2018). Preventing State-Led Cyberattacks Using the Bright Internet and Internet Peace Principles. *Journal of the Association for Information Systems*, 19(3), 152–181. DOI: 10.17705/1jais.00488

Siers, R. (2014). NORTH KOREA: THE CYBER WILD CARD. *Journal of Law & Cyber Warfare*, 4(1), 1–12. https://www.jstor.org/stable/26441246

Sultana, K. Z., Boyd, C. B., & Williams, B. J.Kazi Zakia Sultana. (2023). A Software Vulnerability Prediction Model Using Traceable Code Patterns and Software Metrics. SN Computer Science. *SN Computer Science*, 4(5), 599. Advance online publication. DOI: 10.1007/s42979-023-02077-5

Trim, P. R. J., & Lee, Y.-I. (2010). A security framework for protecting business, government and society from cyber attacks. 2010 5th International Conference on System of Systems Engineering. https://doi.org/DOI: 10.1109/SYSOSE.2010.5544085

van Rossum, J. (2017). An Assessment of North Korean Threats and Vulnerabilities in Cyberspace. BearWorks. https://bearworks.missouristate.edu/theses/3212/

Chapter 14
Using Machine Learning to Identify High-Risk Employee Activity in Proactive Insider Threat Detection

M. Balasubramani
https://orcid.org/0000-0002-3030-8431
V.S.B. Engineering College, India

N. Selvamuthukumaran
Nalla Malla Reddy Engineering College, Hydrabad, India

P. Deepa
St. Joseph's college of Engineering, Chennai, India

R. Prathipa
Panimalar Engineering College, India

Sherly S. Irin
https://orcid.org/0000-0002-4518-3213
SIMATS Engineering, Saveetha Institute of Medical and Technical Sciences, SIMATS University, India

Joel M. Robinson
https://orcid.org/0009-0002-7633-8377
KCG College of Technology, India

ABSTRACT

Organizations continue to face a serious problem with insider threats, which frequently lead to data breaches, monetary losses, and harm to a brand's reputation. Because high-risk employee behaviors are complicated and usually subtle, traditional security measures often fail to uncover insider threats. By examining employee behavior patterns, this study explores the application of machine learning (ML) approaches to proactively identify possible insider threats. Our method simulates normal employee behavior and identifies deviations that point to unsafe behavior

DOI: 10.4018/979-8-3373-0588-2.ch014

by combining supervised learning for classification with unsupervised learning for anomaly identification. Network activity logs, email content, access history, and system usage are among the data sources that are processed to produce a thorough picture of employee behavior.

INTRODUCTION

Proactive insider threat detection is becoming increasingly important for firms looking to protect sensitive data and maintain operational integrity. Insider threats from workers, contractors, or anybody with legitimate access to company resources can cause severe data breaches, financial losses, and reputational harm. While some insider threats are deliberate, others occur unintentionally due to incompetence or a lack of understanding. Given the complex and frequently unpredictable nature of insider threats, typical rule-based techniques may be ineffective. Machine learning (ML) provides a powerful option for proactive insider threat identification by allowing for real-time analysis of massive amounts of employee activity data. Organizations can use machine learning to uncover patterns of high-risk behavior and discover anomalies before they become significant security problems. Anomaly detection, clustering, and supervised learning models can help security teams discern between normal activity and possibly malicious conduct. Machine learning models can improve their accuracy over time by continuously monitoring and adapting to new forms of behavior and threat vectors. Furthermore, these systems can be configured to generate risk scores, allowing security teams to prioritize cases based on the likelihood of a possible danger. This proactive, data-driven approach improves an organization's capacity to respond rapidly to possible insider threats, while also lowering false positives and increasing overall cybersecurity resilience. Detecting high-risk employee conduct in order to proactively handle insider threats is a fast expanding field in which machine learning (ML) can play an important role. ML algorithms can assist in detecting odd activity that may indicate insider threats by examining patterns of behavior within a company. Using machine learning to identify high-risk employee activity for proactive insider threat detection entails examining behavioral patterns, access logs, communication data, and other indications to detect abnormalities and potential security issues before they cause major harm. In this paper, we look at how machine learning models may be utilized to create effective, proactive insider threat detection systems, what sorts of data can be used, and how to identify high-risk employee activity with accuracy and speed.

Key Indicators of Insider Threats

Insider threats are a serious threat to organizational security, and recognizing key indications as shown in Figure 1, is critical for successful detection and prevention. Indicators might be classified as irregular access patterns, odd data transfers, behavioral changes, suspicious account activity, and personal stressors. Insider threats are frequently characterized by abnormal access patterns, such as unlawful attempts to access restricted files or systems. Employees that access data unrelated to their job tasks or attempt to log in during odd hours flag potential abuse of privilege (Rauf, et al., 2023). These access patterns differ from normal activity and may indicate an effort to circumvent security protocols. Furthermore, large-scale data transfers, such as excessive file downloads to external devices or attempts to relocate files outside of protected environments, are frequently connected with insider threats. Such activities can signal data exfiltration or data leaks, especially when personnel deal with sensitive material outside their normal scope.

Figure 1. Key indicators of insider threats.

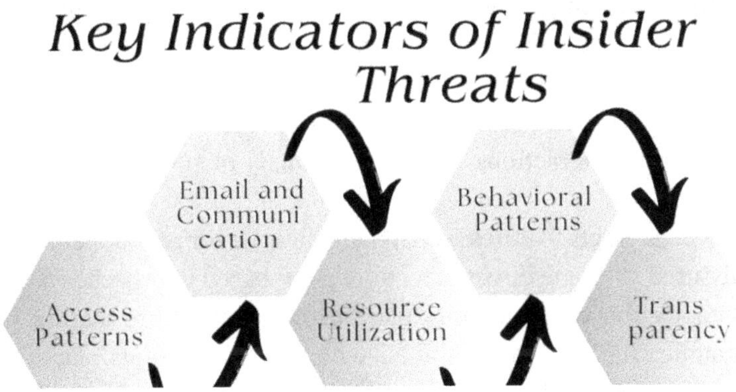

Access Patterns

Machine learning (ML) provides a disruptive technique to monitoring employee access patterns in order to identify high-risk actions in proactive insider threat detection. When access patterns such as login frequency, time of access, location changes, and frequency of access to specific data or apps deviate from established norms, possible security vulnerabilities emerge. Employees checking in at irregular times, particularly if this conduct differs from their normal access hours, may suggest an attempt to avoid notice. ML algorithms (Joel et al., 2023) that use historical access data to establish behavioral baselines may promptly detect these abnormalities.

ML models can incorporate behavioral and contextual data to generate a comprehensive risk profile, providing greater insight into high-risk access behaviors. Overall, machine learning offers a proactive, adaptable approach to monitoring access trends in insider threat detection (Katsikeas et al., 2020). By continuously evaluating employee behavior, machine learning models may quickly identify and analyze risk, allowing organizations to respond to threats with more speed and precision, ultimately boosting overall security.

Email and Communication

Sentiment analysis is a crucial indication in communication monitoring. ML algorithms can analyze the tone, sentiment, and intent of messages to detect shifts that may indicate disgruntlement, irritation, or hostility, potentially increasing the likelihood of insider threats (Mills et al., 2020). For example, an employee who typically exhibits positive engagement but suddenly begins delivering communications in a hostile or confrontational tone may demand additional investigation. Sentiment analysis models trained in natural language processing (NLP) can notify security teams to these shifts, providing vital information about an employee's emotional condition and possible risk. ML-driven models for communication monitoring are critical in proactive insider threat identification because they provide continuous analysis of employee interactions and detect signals of potential hostile activity before it escalates.

ML can detect attempts to utilize coded language, jargon, or euphemisms, which are commonly used to evade direct detection. NLP-based approaches (Chen et al., 2021) can decode context and identify patterns in language use that may indicate hidden communication. When combined with additional signs, such as abrupt surges in the use of specific keywords or phrases, these models can reveal attempts to conceal insider threats.

Resource Utilization

Unusually high network bandwidth usage is a common sign of resource utilization. Employees who access or download significant amounts of data may be seeking to remove sensitive information. ML models can track previous bandwidth usage and detect anomalies, such as spikes in data transfers or unexpected network access during off-hours (Katsikeas et al., 2020). These activities are frequently early indicators of unlawful data extraction and are particularly crucial to detect in personnel with access to sensitive information.

File access patterns are also important in detecting insider threats. Employees who view a large number of files in a short period of time, particularly sensitive or restricted files, may suggest possible data misuse. ML-based anomaly detection can monitor the frequency and timing of file accesses, detecting anomalous behaviors such as repeated access to certain files or unauthorized access to confidential data. When paired with contextual information (Chattopadhyay, A., & Das, A. 2020), such as an employee's function and prior access history, these insights improve the accuracy of insider threat detection.

Behavioral Patterns

An abrupt shift in an employee's mood or communication tone, which is frequently associated with increased stress or job discontent, is an important indicator of potential insider threats. Sentiment analysis based on natural language processing (NLP) can discover negative movements in employee communication, such as emails or chat messages, which may reveal underlying concerns. An employee who expresses dissatisfaction or hatred through digital communication channels may be more likely to participate in unsafe behavior, either purposefully or unintentionally.

Another crucial component is identifying anomalous interactions inside the company. Machine learning algorithms can monitor employee interactions and identify trends that depart from conventional relationships, such as greater communication with specific colleagues or external contacts. A sudden increase in interaction with colleagues in departments not connected to the employee's position could suggest collusion or an attempt to get unauthorized information access.

Transparency

Transparency in this context entails offering insight into the criteria, technique, and rationale used to flag high-risk staff activity, fostering fairness and avoiding biases in security monitoring. ML models may assist firms in understanding which employee behaviors are detected, how these behaviors correspond with specified risk thresholds, and how choices are made, ensuring that the process is visible and understandable to both security professionals and employees. This focused approach ensures that employees' privacy is protected, as ML models can be fine-tuned to detect only high-risk activities that depart from usual usage patterns, reducing unneeded surveillance.

Security teams can use interpretable machine learning techniques like decision trees or rule-based models to better explain why a specific activity is considered unsafe and how the model arrived at its result. This transparency builds (Ribeiro et al., 2026) trust in the system and allows security experts to make educated decisions when reviewing reported behaviors.

Data Processing and Feature Engineering

Data processing and feature engineering as shown in Figure 2, are critical components of applying machine learning (ML) to predict high-risk employee behavior in proactive insider threat detection. Effective data processing ensures that relevant information is retrieved, cleaned, and prepared for analysis by machine learning algorithms. Feature engineering, on the other hand, is the process of constructing meaningful input variables (features) from raw data, which can dramatically improve the model's ability to detect possible threats. These measures improve the accuracy, efficiency, and interpretability of ML models in detecting harmful insider behavior. Data processing starts with gathering and cleansing raw data from a variety of sources, including network logs (Joel, M at al., 2019), system access records, communication metadata, and staff resource consumption (Maloof, M. A., & Stephens, G. L. 2016). The raw data frequently contains noise, errors, and missing numbers, which might bias the conclusions. Preprocessing techniques including normalization, imputation, and outlier detection are required to guarantee the data is clean and ready for analysis.

Figure 2. Data processing feature engineering

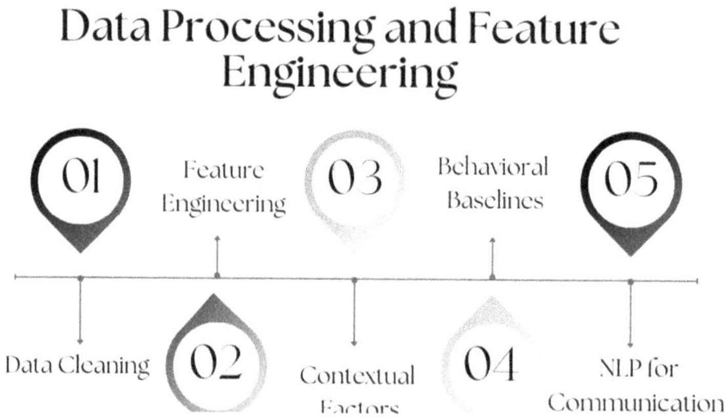

Data Cleaning

Data cleaning is an essential step in utilizing machine learning (ML) to discover high-risk employee activities in proactive insider threat detection. Raw data gathered from numerous sources, such as system logs, network activity, emails, and resource use, is frequently untidy and unstructured, with inconsistencies, errors, and noise. Cleaning this data guarantees that ML models can process and learn from it, hence boosting the accuracy and reliability of insider threat detection. Data cleaning consists of numerous processes, including resolving missing numbers, removing duplicates, addressing outliers, and converting data into a usable format.

Outlier detection is especially important when cleansing data for insider threat detection. Outliers are data points that deviate significantly from the overall trend and can sometimes indicate unexpected behavior. While outliers might occasionally reflect actual concerns, they can also be the result of data gathering flaws or discrepancies. As a result, ML models must be taught to discriminate between real outliers, which may indicate malevolent behavior, and those generated by data errors.

Feature Engineering

Feature engineering is an important step in utilizing machine learning (ML) to detect high-risk employee activities in proactive insider threat detection. It entails translating raw data into useful attributes that help ML models discover patterns suggestive of insider risks. Another important concern in feature engineering is the development of composite features, which combine numerous raw data points to produce more meaningful variables. For example, characteristics such as "number of unauthorized accesses" or "frequency of contact with external entities" (Vaughn, L. 2019) provide more detailed insights about an employee's activity and can assist identify suspicious activities more efficiently. This multidimensional method improves the precision of the ML model by capturing numerous aspects of employee activity, ensuring that high-risk behaviors are accurately identified.

Another important concern in feature engineering is the development of composite features, which combine numerous raw data points to produce more meaningful variables. Features such as "number of unauthorized accesses" or "frequency of contact with external entities" provide greater insights into an employee's behavior and can help expose questionable behaviors more effectively.

Contextual Factors

Contextual considerations are critical when applying machine learning (ML) to identify high-risk employee behavior for proactive insider threat identification. Contextual factors are the situational or contextual variables that influence employee activities, such as work location, time of day, organizational role, recent employment changes, and past behavior. By incorporating these characteristics, machine learning models obtain a more thorough picture of employee actions, enabling for more accurate detection of insider threats while lowering false positives. One critical contextual component is role-based access control, which sets the level of access that each person has based on their position within the organization. Employees in finance departments, for example, may have access to sensitive information that others should not have. ML models trained on contextual data can learn expected behavior patterns for each role, indicating instances where employees access information beyond their normal scope. This role-based context improves threat detection because accessing sensitive files may be suspect for some jobs but not for others.

Behavioral Baselines

Setting behavioral baselines is critical when utilizing machine learning (ML) to detect high-risk employee activities in proactive insider threat detection. A behavioral baseline is a profile of each employee's regular activity patterns, which allows ML models to detect deviations that could indicate possible hazards. This strategy aids in distinguishing between typical behavior and anomalies indicative of insider threats, such as strange access patterns, increased file downloads, or irregular working hours.

Another advantage of adopting behavioral baselines is that they provide a more targeted approach to threat identification, lowering the possibility of false positives. Rather than using a one-size-fits-all threshold for all employees, behavioral baselines enable ML models to detect deviations unique to each individual. For example, an IT administrator's baseline may naturally involve elevated access privileges and frequent database contacts, yet comparable activity by a financial professional may indicate a possible hazard.

NLP for Communication Analysis

Natural Language Processing (NLP) (Kang, Y et al., 2020) is an effective tool for employing machine learning (ML) to analyze employee communications in order to discover insider threats proactively. NLP can help identify high-risk behavior in emails, messages, and other text-based communications by analyzing the content, tone, and trends. NLP approaches allow machine learning models to detect not only blatantly suspect language, but also subtle alterations in tone, mood, and communication frequency, providing early warning signals of insider threats.

Sentiment analysis (Joel, M. R et al., 2023), which determines the emotional tone of texts, is one of the most common applications of NLP in communication analysis. For example, a rapid spike in negative sentiment in an employee's emails or chat messages could indicate job unhappiness, irritation, or disengagement, all of which are typically associated with insider threats. Studies have indicated that disgruntled employees are more likely to participate in hostile behaviors, making sentiment analysis an important component of insider threat identification.

Model Selection and Training

Model selection and training as shown in Figure 3, are critical phases in constructing machine learning (ML) systems for detecting high-risk employee behavior in proactive insider threat detection. Choosing the proper model entails analyzing several algorithms based on their suitability for anomaly detection and classification tasks, as well as their capacity to process huge amounts of employee behavior data efficiently. Decision trees, support vector machines (SVMs)(M, R. J et al., 2023), neural networks, and ensemble approaches are among the models often employed for insider threat identification, each with their own set of advantages and disadvantages when dealing with the intricacies of insider threat detection. Model selection has a considerable impact on the threat detection system's accuracy, interpretability, and responsiveness.

Decision trees, for example, offer excellent interpretability, which is critical for understanding the decision-making process underlying model predictions, particularly in scenarios needing forensic follow-up on flagged behaviors. SVMs, on the other hand, are adept at recognizing tiny anomalies and can handle high-dimensional data, making them ideal for detecting anomalous access patterns or changes in staff activity levels. Neural networks, particularly recurrent neural networks (RNNs), are well-suited to time-series data and may capture complicated behavioral patterns across time, although they may require a large amount of training data and computer resources.

Figure 3. Over view of model selection and training

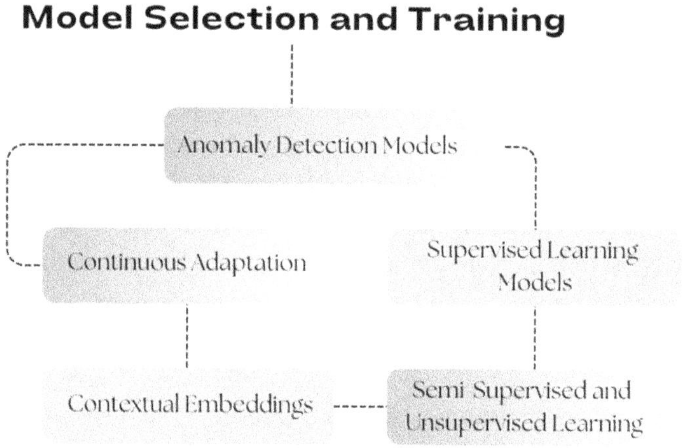

Anomaly Detection Models

Anomaly detection models are critical for applying machine learning (ML) to identify high-risk employee activities in proactive insider threat detection. These models excel at identifying patterns that differ from known standards, which is critical for detecting unexpected behavior that could suggest possible security issues. Unlike typical rule-based systems, anomaly detection models may discover subtle and complicated anomalies in behavior without predefined criteria, making them particularly effective in detecting both known and emergent danger patterns. Unsupervised learning is a popular approach to anomaly identification that does not require labeled data and instead discovers deviations from the dataset's underlying patterns. Clustering, autoencoders, and one-class support vector machines (SVMs) are popular methods. Clustering algorithms, for example, can group similar behavior profiles together; individuals whose activities fall outside of these clusters may be marked as engaging in odd conduct. Autoencoders are a form of neural network that compresses and reconstructs data to learn its underlying structure.

Supervised Learning Models

Supervised learning models are crucial for utilizing machine learning (ML) to detect high-risk employees (Costa et al., 2014) conduct in proactive insider threat detection. Supervised models are trained on labeled data, helping them to accurately spot and classify recognized patterns of malicious behavior. This strategy is particularly advantageous when there is a comprehensive dataset with labeled examples of both normal and anomalous actions, because it allows the model to "learn" the differentiating properties of harmful behaviors.

Neural networks, particularly deep learning models, are utilized when the intricacy of insider threats necessitates models that can deal with extensive, layered patterns. Although deep learning models often demand large, labeled data and processing resources, they can capture complicated correlations between behavioral features that simpler models may overlook. This ability to learn complex interactions can be critical for detecting multidimensional threats (Guo et al., 2022), such as coordinated acts across several systems or persistent access over time.

Semi-Supervised and Unsupervised Learning

Semi-supervised and unsupervised learning algorithms are useful in machine learning (ML) applications for detecting high-risk employee behavior, especially when labeled data is insufficient. Semi-supervised learning improves model performance by combining a small quantity of labeled data with a big number of unlabeled data. This approach is particularly useful in insider threat detection, when gathering full labeled data on hostile conduct is difficult due to its scarcity. Semi-supervised models can improve accuracy in recognizing harmful activities while minimizing the reliance on vast labeled datasets.

Self-training is a popular semi-supervised strategy in which a model is trained on a small, labeled dataset and then used to label the most confident predictions on unlabeled data. These freshly classified data points are then fed back to the training set, iteratively improving the model's performance. Self-training enables insider threat detection systems to recognize new behavioral trends and adapt to changing risks.

Contextual Embeddings

Contextual embeddings are a sophisticated natural language processing (NLP) technique that captures the subtle meanings of words based on their context, hence enhancing the performance of machine learning (ML) models in tasks such as insider threat identification and sentiment analysis. Unlike standard word embeddings such as Word2Vec and GloVe, which assign fixed vector representations to words, contextual embeddings modify these representations dynamically based on the context inside a sentence or document.

This adaptability enables contextual embeddings to capture more complicated linguistic nuances, such as polysemy (words with many meanings), which is critical for effectively analyzing employee communication data for insider threat detection (Peters et al., 2018). To summarize, contextual embeddings are an effective approach for improving the accuracy of NLP models in detecting insider threats by capturing linguistic meaning within context. Their capacity to change based on sentence structure and adjacent words allows models to better analyze communication data, offering a solid foundation for detecting potential security concerns in employee language and behavior.

Continuous Adaptation

Continuous adaptation is an important property of machine learning (ML) systems, particularly in dynamic applications such as insider threat detection, where behavior patterns and threat tactics change often. In the context of machine learning-based security systems, continuous adaptation refers to the continuing process of model updates and fine-tuning to ensure consistent accuracy and relevance in detecting high-risk actions. This adaptability is done by methods like incremental learning, transfer learning, and periodic retraining, enabling models to respond well to new data without the need for total retraining from scratch (Diethe et al., 2019).

Continuous adaptation is especially useful in proactive insider threat detection, as ML models must keep up with changing employee behavior to avoid false positives and false negatives. Without ongoing modification, models are likely to become obsolete and useless as habits change, lowering the system's security efficacy. Periodic retraining is also required for continual adaptation, especially in security-sensitive systems where new threats and techniques develop often. Organizations can keep their machine learning models (von Ziegler et al., 2021) up to speed with the most recent behavioral data by retraining them on a regular basis.

Model Evaluation and Tuning

Model evaluation and tuning are critical steps in constructing effective machine learning (ML) systems, particularly for sensitive applications such as insider threat detection. Proper evaluation ensures that the model correctly detects high-risk activities while avoiding excessive false positives and false negatives. Tuning (Provost, F., & Fawcett, T. 2013) is the iterative process of altering model parameters to optimize performance depending on evaluation measures. Both stages are crucial in constructing a robust, dependable machine learning system that balances precision, recall, and computing efficiency.

The Figure 4 explain about the Model Evaluation and Tuning. Accuracy, then the precision, also the recall, then the F1-score, and the area under the receiver operating characteristic (ROC-AUC) curve are standard evaluation measures for assessing a model's efficacy. Precision (the fraction of true positives out of anticipated positives) is critical in insider threat detection because it reduces the danger of false alarms, which can squander resources and cause employee distrust. Recall (the fraction of true positives versus actual positives) is also critical, as missing genuine threats can result in serious security breaches. Cross-validation (Bates et al., 2024) is particularly important in model evaluation and tuning since it eliminates overfitting and guarantees that the model applies well to new data. K-fold cross-validation, in which the dataset is divided into k subsets for training and validation over numerous rounds, gives a more reliable evaluation by averaging results from multiple data splits.

Figure 4. Model evaluation and tuning

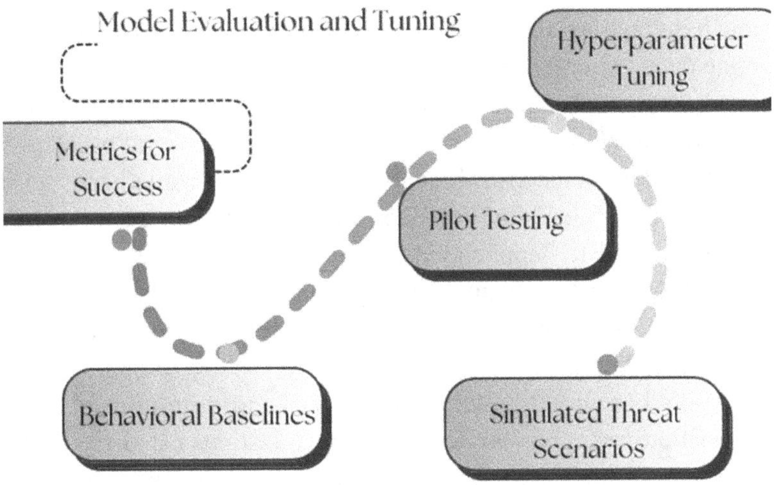

Metrics for Success

In machine learning (ML) applications, notably insider threat detection, selecting the correct success metrics is critical for evaluating models' efficacy in recognizing high-risk employee actions. These metrics provide insight into how well the model detects harmful behaviors while minimizing errors, ensuring that the deployed system is both accurate and efficient. Accuracy, precision, recall, F1-score, and area under the receiver operating characteristic (ROC-AUC) curve are some of the most commonly used measures for measuring model performance.

Accuracy (Rezvani, S., & Wang, X. 2023) is a fundamental metric that calculates the proportion of correct predictions (including true positives and true negatives) compared to the total number of forecasts. However, in imbalanced datasets where harmful behaviors are uncommon, accuracy alone might be deceiving, since a model can obtain high accuracy by predicting the majority class (non-malicious actions) most of the time. Precision is the proportion of true positive predictions (real threats successfully identified) to all positive predictions (including true and false positives). A high precision shows that the model is effective at identifying actual threats while avoiding false alarms (Naidu et al., 2023), which is critical for decreasing wasteful resource allocation and employee distrust. Recall, on the other hand, represents the proportion of actual threats that the model correctly identifies, emphasizing the model's capacity to detect the most threats conceivable.

Behavioral Baselines

Dynamic baselines are also a crucial part of this process, as employee behavior and corporate circumstances change over time. As an employee's function, project needs, or work patterns change, the baseline must be updated on a continuous basis. Machine learning models must be able to recalibrate behavioral baselines (Gama et al., 2014) to accommodate for these dynamic changes while being sensitive to new types of threats. Behavioral baselines are critical to detecting insider threats in machine learning (ML) applications, particularly in cybersecurity situations. Establishing a behavioral analyzing and comprehending regular patterns of activity inside an organization, allowing computers to detect abnormalities that could indicate malevolent behavior.

In conclusion, behavioral baselines are critical for spotting insider threats by detecting deviations from regular activities. Organizations can use a combination of statistical analysis and machine learning approaches to create adaptive models that continuously update these baselines, enhancing risk identification and assuring more accurate, prompt responses.

Hyperparameter Tuning

Hyperparameter tuning is a fundamental procedure in machine learning (ML) that involves modifying model parameters to increase performance. In contrast to model parameters, which are learnt from data during training, hyperparameters are specified before training begins and affect many aspects of the learning process, such as the model's complexity, learning rate, and regularization strength. Proper hyperparameter tuning (Bischl et al., 2023) can dramatically improve the model's performance, prevent overfitting, and boost its capacity to generalize to unseen data, making it an important step in constructing effective models for tasks like insider threat detection.

Random search, an alternative to grid search, selects hyperparameter values at random from predetermined ranges. Although this strategy does not cover the entire space as thoroughly as grid search, it has been found to be more efficient in practice, especially when only a few hyperparameters have a substantial impact on model performance. Random search is especially useful when dealing with models with a large number of hyperparameters since it can quickly uncover viable configurations without incurring the computational burden of grid search.

Pilot Testing

Pilot testing is an important step in the development and deployment of machine learning (ML) models, particularly in applications such as insider threat detection, where accuracy and dependability are critical. It entails testing a model on a smaller, controlled subset of data or in a restricted setting prior to full-scale deployment. This process enables businesses to detect possible flaws (Prvan et al., 2020), evaluate the model's performance in real-world settings, and collect useful input to improve the model and its underlying assumptions.

The fundamental purpose of pilot testing is to replicate real-world settings as precisely as possible, verifying that the ML model can manage the complexities of production data. This involves determining how successfully the model detects anomalies in employee behavior, such as unlawful access to sensitive data or strange communication patterns. It also aids in determining the model's capacity to reduce false positives (e.g., classifying typical activities as threats) and false negatives (e.g., failing to detect true threats). Pilot tests in a controlled environment allow businesses to fine-tune the model to balance these trade-offs and increase its overall performance (Tang et al., 2021).

Simulated Threat Scenarios

Simulated threat scenarios are an important part of developing, testing, and validating insider threat detection systems that use machine learning (ML). These scenarios entail developing realistic, controlled settings in which models are exposed to a number of potential threat scenarios that reflect real-world malicious activity. The goal of simulated threat scenarios is to determine how successfully the model detects and responds to insider threats while avoiding the dangers associated with genuine hostile conduct. By simulating various attack vectors and employee activities, organizations can guarantee that their ML-based detection systems are both robust and effective in recognizing a range of hazards.

Simulated threat situations are especially valuable for training and verifying anomaly detection algorithms because they help build the labeled datasets required for supervised learning. Furthermore, these scenarios allow for an assessment of how well the system handles various types of insider threats, such as insider espionage, in which an employee intentionally steals sensitive information, and unintentional threats, in which employees make mistakes that inadvertently reveal sensitive data. Insider threat detection (Shoeib et al., 2020) requires testing the system's response to both high-risk, overt malevolent activities and more subtle, less evident dangerous behaviors.

Implementation and Real-Time Monitoring

Machine learning (ML)-based insider threat detection systems must be implemented and monitored in real time to ensure their effectiveness in dynamic, production situations. After training and validating a model using historical data and simulated threat situations, it is deployed in a live environment to continually monitor and evaluate employee behavior (Liu et al., 2020). This phase involves not only the technical implementation of the model, but also its integration with current cybersecurity infrastructure to enable real-time threat detection and response capabilities.

The Figure 5 shows the clear idea about the implementation and real time monitoring system. The deployment step starts with integrating the ML model into the organization's security systems, making sure it has access to the necessary data streams such user activity logs, system access records, email conversations, and network traffic. Data from these sources must be continuously ingested, preprocessed, and loaded into the model for real-time analysis. This necessitates establishing powerful data pipelines capable of managing massive volumes of information, as insider threat detection systems must perform quickly in situations with substantial and rapidly changing data.

Once installed, real-time monitoring guarantees that the model is constantly evaluating employee behavior against established behavioral baselines, highlighting potential insider threats as they arise. Anomalies or suspicious activity, such as illegal access attempts or odd file transfers, generate alerts that security analysts can analyze for additional examinations. The ML model should be able to forecast and issue alerts with low latency, allowing security personnel to respond quickly to recognized risks.

Figure 5. Implementation and real-time monitoring

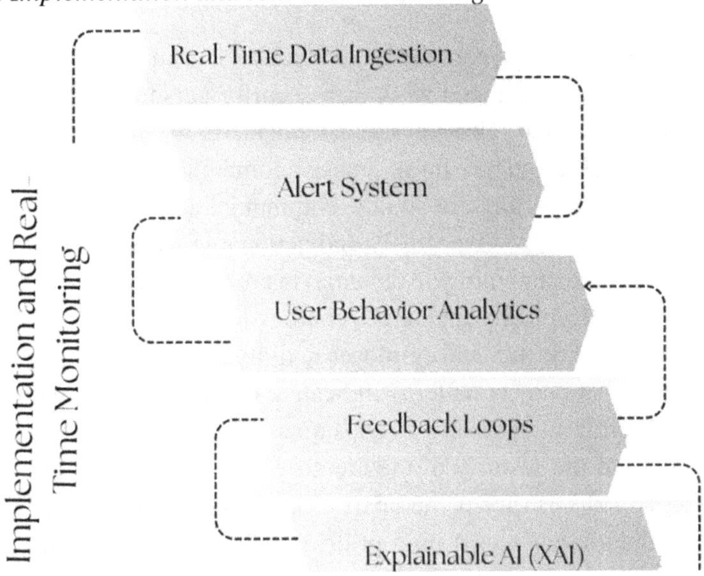

Real-Time Data Ingestion

Real-time data intake is an essential component of machine learning (ML)-based insider threat detection systems, since it allows for continuous monitoring of employee behavior and actions within an organization. This process entails continuous collecting, processing, and integration of enormous amounts of data in real time, guaranteeing that the system can analyze and act on new information as it is generated. Effective real-time data input is essential for recognizing and responding to insider threats as they occur, allowing rapid measures to prevent or reduce possible damage (Shoeib et al., 2020).

Real-time data ingestion in insider threat detection often entails collecting information from a range of sources, including as system logs, network traffic, employee communication patterns (e.g., email, messaging), and file access records. This data must be continuously fed into the detecting system in order to allow for near-instantaneous analysis. To manage the enormous amount and velocity of data, enterprises frequently use distributed data ingestion frameworks like Apache Kafka or Apache Flume (Vyas et al., 2021), which can handle large-scale, real-time data streams efficiently. These solutions are scalable enough to process data from thousands of employees across many systems and locations.

Alert System

An alert system is a critical component of machine learning (ML)-based insider threat detection systems, designed to inform security personnel to suspicious or unusual activity in real time. These systems issue alerts when they detect activity that deviates from established baselines, such as anomalous access to sensitive files, irregular data exfiltration efforts, or strange communication patterns. The primary goal of the alert system is to give timely and actionable notifications that enable security teams to analyze and mitigate potential insider threats before they escalate.

The warning system typically operates by continually monitoring data streams like as system logs, network traffic, and employee activity, and putting this information into an ML model that detects patterns indicative of normal or suspect behavior. When the system finds an anomaly, it sends an alarm. These notifications can be grouped according to the severity of the identified activity. For example, an alert may be labeled as low priority if the aberrant behavior is mild or occurs during normal working hours, whereas a high-priority alert may be generated if an employee accesses sensitive data outside normal working hours or exhibits indicators of data exfiltration.

User Behavior Analytics

User Behavior Analytics (UBA) (Nocera, F et al., 2022) is an important component of insider threat detection systems, especially when using machine learning (ML) approaches. UBA analyzes patterns of human behavior within an organization's systems to detect abnormalities that may signal possible dangers, such as deliberate or inadvertent activities. By modeling usual user actions, including as login times, data access patterns, and communication habits, UBA systems can spot variations from these baselines that may suggest risky conduct, allowing for prompt intervention to avert or minimize insider threats.

The basic role of UBA is to set behavioral baselines for users. These baselines indicate the typical patterns of activity for individual employees or groups within the organization. For example, a user may normally access specific files during business hours and interact primarily with a limited number of colleagues. When this behavior changes, such as accessing sensitive files late at night or engaging in unusual communication with external contacts, UBA might report those behaviors as anomalies.

Feedback Loops

Feedback loops are an important component of machine learning (ML)-based (Mahesh, B. 2020) insider threat detection systems since they increase the system's performance over time. A feedback loop is the ongoing process of collecting feedback from the model's predictions and using that information to refine and improve the model. Insider threat detection relies heavily on feedback loops to reduce false positives, improve detection accuracy, and adapt to changing threat environments. When an insider threat detection system raises an alert, security experts usually evaluate the highlighted activity to see if it is actually dangerous. If the alarm is valid, the analysts' feedback can be utilized to update the model, ensuring that the system improves its accuracy in future predictions. If the alarm is a false positive, the model can be changed to prevent similar alerts in the future. The act of updating the model based on real-world outcomes is critical for increasing the system's effectiveness.

Feedback loops can operate at several levels of the system. One stage involves modifying the model's parameters, such as alert thresholds. For example, if a specific sort of suspicious activity generates a large number of false alarms, security professionals might adjust the model's sensitivity to that activity, minimizing unneeded warnings. Another level of feedback is to improve the training data itself.

Explainable AI (XAI)

Explainable AI (XAI) (Dwivedi et al., 2023) is a set of strategies and procedures designed to make the decisions and behaviors of machine learning (ML) models more intelligible to humans. In the domain of insider threat detection, XAI is critical since security analysts must trust and evaluate ML model outputs in order to make informed decisions. Unlike traditional "black-box" models, which provide predictions without giving insight into how those predictions are made, XAI techniques enable transparency by providing explanations that clarify why certain actions, such as flagging a specific employee's behavior, are considered anomalous or suspicious.

Real-time feedback loops are particularly useful in insider threat detection because they allow the system to react to changes in user behavior and new methods used by malicious insiders. For example, if an insider threat actor's methods change or the organization suffers significant structural or operational changes, feedback loops ensure that the system remains sensitive to these changes, hence boosting its ability to detect new threats. Over time, the repetitive structure of feedback loops improves the system's ability to distinguish between regular and suspicious activity, even in complicated or ambiguous settings.

Related Work

Table 1. Some of the related survey on the concept

Study	Techniques / Models	Datasets	Key Findings	Citation
Insider Threat Detection Using ML Approach	One-Class SVM, Isolation Forest, Random Forest, Neural Networks	CERT dataset	Applied anomaly detection for identifying outliers as potential threats; tackled imbalanced data using SMOTE for enhanced performance in minority class detection	Abdulkareem et al., 2023
Machine Learning for Insider Threats	Data Mesh architecture with ML algorithms	Various organizational datasets	Emphasized using decentralized data to identify insider threats and streamline data accessibility, improving anomaly detection speed and accuracy	Booz Allen, 2023
Challenges in Malicious Insider Detection with ML	Hybrid approaches combining supervised/ unsupervised ML	Synthesized datasets from real insider threat scenarios	Highlighted challenges like imbalanced data and scalability, suggesting hybrid methods for more robust threat detection	IEEE Xplore, 2024
Deep Learning Techniques in Insider Detection	Deep Neural Networks, Decision Trees	Real-world and synthetic datasets	Showed deep learning's potential in detecting complex insider threat patterns, though noted high computational costs	IEEE Xplore, 2023

Table 1 shows some of the survey on the usage of High-Risk Employees and their solution explained by authors.

Proposed System

The Anomaly-Based Insider Security Identification System identifies irregularities in employee behaviour to identify insider risks. The technology is able to identify anomalous patterns or deviations that suggest possible risk by creating a baseline of typical activity for every employee. Unusual behaviours are found using anomaly detection techniques like autoencoders, one-class SVM, and isolation forests.

The Behavioural Risk Scoring System continuously determines each employee's risk score based on their activity in real time. A higher score is the result of actions like attempting to get around security measures, accessing data at odd times, or frequently accessing sensitive files. To give risk ratings to particular behaviours, supervised learning algorithms—such as decision trees, random forests, and gradient boosting—are trained using historical insider threat data.

The description of the Contextual Behaviour Monitoring System takes into account the role, place, and time of employees' actions. For example, accessing particular files could be dangerous in some positions but typical in others. Algorithms for contextual anomaly detection and clustering, such K-Means or DBSCAN, assist in classifying employee behaviours in pertinent situations and identifying abnormalities unique to a certain context. By employing anomaly detection to identify possible threats and a supervised classifier to confirm high-risk activities, the Hybrid Model for Insider Threat Prediction Description system integrates supervised learning and anomaly detection. Potential hazards are flagged by unsupervised models (like Isolation Forest) and then sent to supervised models (like SVM or logistic regression) for a final evaluation.

Using Time-Series Analysis to Monitor Activities. The description system tracks how employee behaviour changes over time and looks for questionable temporal trends by treating employee action as time-series data. Risk-signaling behavioural patterns can be captured by time-series models such as ARIMA and LSTM (Long Short-Term Memory) networks. efficient at identifying changing trends over time, especially in high-risk situations like access to sensitive data. Each user and entity (such as devices or apps) has a profile created by the User and Entity Behaviour Analytics (UEBA) System using machine learning, which is then used to compare current action to this profile. a mix of anomaly detection for profile deviations and clustering methods for behaviour profiling. reduces security blind spots by offering a comprehensive perspective of user and system behaviours.

Challenges

Data Privacy and Legal Concerns

Large volumes of data must be gathered in order to monitor employee activities, which may violate personal privacy. Such surveillance might be viewed as intrusive by employees, which could result in moral and legal dilemmas. Following data protection regulations, such as GDPR in the EU or HIPAA in the US, is crucial since they establish stringent rules for the gathering, storing, and using of data. Serious fines and harm to the organization's reputation might arise from breaking these rules.

Data Quality and Quantity

Since insider attacks are rather uncommon, there is frequently not enough data to build reliable machine learning models. Higher rates of false positives or missed threats may arise from models that are skewed towards non-threat behaviours as a result of this imbalance. Because it can be difficult to distinguish between ordinary and dangerous behaviours, especially when behaviours change over time, labelling data for insider threats can be difficult.

Detection of Subtle Threat Patterns

Because insider threats are frequently adaptable and subtle, it may be challenging for machine learning algorithms to identify subtle trends. Technically skilled insiders may purposefully steer clear of well-known trends or take part in "low-and-slow" operations, accumulating minor violations over time that pose a serious risk. Certain activities may be difficult for ML models to comprehend in their context. An employee who accesses confidential data outside of business hours, for instance, could be viewed as suspicious, but in practice, this could just be the result of a valid requirement.

High False Positive Rates

Security teams may get overloaded by high false positive rates, which might result in alert fatigue and decreased attentiveness. Because frequent false positives reduce the apparent intensity of alarms, this might lead to the overlooking of truly dangerous behaviours. Since employee behaviours are quite unique and can differ widely, it is challenging to define what constitutes "normal" behaviour. Changes in work routines, personal situations, or seasonal trends can all have an impact on behaviour in ways that machine learning models can mistakenly perceive as threats.

Adaptability and Scalability

Insider threat detection needs to be adaptable to different departments, positions, and organisational structures. Especially in organisations with a varied range of job responsibilities, models trained on one set of activities may not perform well when applied to another. Insider threat strategies change quickly, therefore in order for ML models to continue to be useful, they must be updated often with fresh information. However, organisations may find it difficult to maintain this over time due to the high cost and manpower requirements of regular changes.

Conclusion and Future Work

In conclusion, using machine learning (ML) for proactive insider threat detection provides significant benefits in identifying and reducing high-risk employee actions. ML models can discover small irregularities and suspicious actions that would otherwise go undetected by evaluating trends in user behavior, system access, communication, and resource use. Organizations can utilize advanced approaches such as anomaly detection, user behavior analytics, and explainable AI to continuously monitor and assess possible threats in real time, allowing for faster and more informed responses. The incorporation of continuous learning via feedback loops, data processing, and real-time data feeding improves the accuracy and adaptability of these systems, assuring their continued effectiveness as insider threat strategies evolve. Finally, ML-driven proactive detection systems not only minimize the danger of data breaches and sabotage, but they also contribute to a more secure and resilient corporate environment. Furthermore, machine learning models provide increased granularity in threat detection. Traditional methods may rely on static criteria or thresholds, which are frequently ineffective in detecting subtle or developing insider threats. In contrast, machine learning algorithms can distinguish more sophisticated patterns of behavior across numerous variables, making it easier to detect subtle activities that may suggest malevolent intent. This level of granularity improves the ability to discover insider threats early, before they cause major damage. one of the primary benefits of adopting machine learning in proactive insider threat identification is its capacity to scale with the growing complexity and volume of corporate data. As businesses grow, so does the number of interactions and activities that require monitoring. ML models, particularly those based on deep learning and ensemble approaches, can handle massive volumes of data fast and efficiently, making them perfect for large-scale deployments. This scalability ensures that insider threat detection systems can be applied in a variety of situations and adjusted to different levels of threat complexity.

REFERENCES

Abdulkareem, K. H., Ali, N. S., & Yunos, Z. (2023). *Insider Threat Detection Using Machine Learning Approach*. MDPI Applied Sciences.

Bates, S., Hastie, T., & Tibshirani, R. (2024). Cross-validation: What does it estimate and how well does it do it? *Journal of the American Statistical Association*, 119(546), 1434–1445. DOI: 10.1080/01621459.2023.2197686 PMID: 39308484

Bischl, B., Binder, M., Lang, M., Pielok, T., Richter, J., Coors, S., Thomas, J., Ullmann, T., Becker, M., Boulesteix, A.-L., Deng, D., & Lindauer, M. (2023). Hyperparameter optimization: Foundations, algorithms, best practices, and open challenges. *Wiley Interdisciplinary Reviews. Data Mining and Knowledge Discovery*, 13(2), e1484. DOI: 10.1002/widm.1484

Booz Allen Hamilton. (2023). *Leverage Machine Learning to Detect Insider Threats*. Booz Allen Perspectives.

Chattopadhyay, A., & Das, A. (2020). Insider Threat Detection Using Machine Learning. *Journal of Cyber Security Technology*, 4(3), 45–53.

Chen, J., Wang, Y., & Lu, C. (2021). Insider Threat Detection Using Natural Language Processing Techniques. *Computer Security Journal*, 7(2), 55–68.

Costa, D., Albrethsen, M., Collins, M., Perl, S., Silowash, G., & Spooner, D. (2014). *An Insider Threat Indicator Ontology*. Carnegie Mellon University, Software Engineering Institute.

Diethe, T., Twomey, N., & Flach, P. (2019). A Systematic Review of Machine Learning for Insider Threat Detection. *Journal of Information Security and Applications*, 46, 165–183.

Dwivedi, R., Dave, D., Naik, H., Singhal, S., Omer, R., Patel, P., & Ranjan, R. (2023). Explainable AI (XAI): Core ideas, techniques, and solutions. *ACM Computing Surveys*, 55(9), 1–33. DOI: 10.1145/3561048

Gama, J., Žliobaitė, I., Bifet, A., Pechenizkiy, M., & Bouchachia, A. (2014). A survey on concept drift adaptation. *ACM Computing Surveys*, 46(4), 1–37. DOI: 10.1145/2523813

Joel, M. R., Ebenezer, V., Jeyaraj, K. A., Navaneethakrishnan, M., Arunadevi, R., & Jenifa, D. R. (2023, February). Decoding and Analysing Consumer Feedback for Companies and Goods using Machine Learning. In *2023 Third International Conference on Artificial Intelligence and Smart Energy (ICAIS)* (pp. 1085-1091). IEEE. DOI: 10.1109/ICAIS56108.2023.10073801

Joel, M. R., Ebenezer, V., Karthik, N., & Rajkumar, K. (2019). Advance dynamic network system of internet of things. *International Journal of Recent Technology and Engineering*, 8(3), 6209–6212. DOI: 10.35940/ijrte.C5657.098319

Joel, M. R., Navaneethakrishnan, M., Sriram, K. P., & Manonmani, S. P. (2023, March). Machine Learning Algorithms for Predicting House Prices in a Smart city using its Real-Time Data. In *2023 Second International Conference on Electronics and Renewable Systems (ICEARS)* (pp. 1064-1070). IEEE. DOI: 10.1109/ICEARS56392.2023.10085090

Kang, Y., Cai, Z., Tan, C. W., Huang, Q., & Liu, H. (2020). Natural language processing (NLP) in management research: A literature review. *Journal of Management Analytics*, 7(2), 139–172. DOI: 10.1080/23270012.2020.1756939

Katsikeas, S., Lambrou, G., & Symeonidis, I. (2020). Proactive Insider Threat Detection through Contextual Behavioral Analysis. *Security and Privacy Journal*, 5(1), 21–35.

Liu, J., Huang, Q., Xia, X., Shihab, E., Lo, D., & Li, S. (2020, June). Is using deep learning frameworks free? characterizing technical debt in deep learning frameworks. In *Proceedings of the ACM/IEEE 42nd International Conference on Software* Engineering: Software Engineering in Society (pp. 1-10).

M, R. J., G, M., G, B., & P, S. (2023). SVM-RFE enabled feature selection with DMN based centroid update model for incremental data clustering using COVID-19. *Computer Methods in Biomechanics and Biomedical Engineering, 27*(10), 1224–1238. DOI: 10.1080/10255842.2023.2236744

Mahesh, B. (2020). Machine learning algorithms-a review. [IJSR]. *International Journal of Scientific Research*, 9(1), 381–386.

Maloof, M. A., & Stephens, G. L. (2016). Using machine learning techniques to identify unusual behavior for network security. *Journal of Machine Learning Research*, 3(5), 373–395.

Mills, R., Hussain, R., & Krishnamurthy, M. (2020). Sentiment Analysis for Insider Threat Detection in Email Communication. *Journal of Cybersecurity Insights*, 4(1), 33–47.

Naidu, G., Zuva, T., & Sibanda, E. M. (2023, April). A review of evaluation metrics in machine learning algorithms. In *Computer Science On-line Conference* (pp. 15-25). Cham: Springer International Publishing. DOI: 10.1007/978-3-031-35314-7_2

Nocera, F., Demilito, S., Ladisa, P., Mongiello, M., Shah, A. A., Ahmad, J., & Di Sciascio, E. (2022, May). A user behavior analytics (uba)-based solution using lstm neural network to mitigate ddos attack in fog and cloud environment. In 2022 2nd International Conference of Smart Systems and Emerging Technologies (SMART-TECH) (pp. 74-79). IEEE.

Peters, M. E., Neumann, M., Iyyer, M., Gardner, M., Clark, C., Lee, K., & Zettlemoyer, L. (2018). *Deep contextualized word representations.* NAACL-HLT. DOI: 10.18653/v1/N18-1202

Provost, F., & Fawcett, T. (2013). *Data Science for Business: What You Need to Know about Data Mining and Data-Analytic Thinking*. O'Reilly Media.

Prvan, M., & Ožegović, J. (2020). Methods in teaching computer networks: A literature review. [TOCE]. *ACM Transactions on Computing Education*, 20(3), 1–35. DOI: 10.1145/3394963

Rauf, U., Mohsen, F., & Wei, Z. (2023). A taxonomic classification of insider threats: Existing techniques, future directions & recommendations. *Journal of Cyber Security and Mobility*, 12(2), 221–252. DOI: 10.13052/jcsm2245-1439.1225

Rezvani, S., & Wang, X. (2023). A broad review on class imbalance learning techniques. *Applied Soft Computing*, 143, 110415. DOI: 10.1016/j.asoc.2023.110415

Ribeiro, M. T., Singh, S., & Guestrin, C. (2016). "Why should I trust you?" Explaining the predictions of any classifier. *Proceedings of the 22nd ACM SIGKDD International Conference on Knowledge Discovery and Data Mining*, 1135-1144.

Shoeib, M., Shalaginov, A., & Tian, Y. (2020). Insider threat detection using machine learning: A survey. *Computers & Security*, 92, 101736.

Tang, Y., Khatchadourian, R., Bagherzadeh, M., Singh, R., Stewart, A., & Raja, A. (2021, May). An empirical study of refactorings and technical debt in machine learning systems. In *2021 IEEE/ACM 43rd international conference on software engineering (ICSE)* (pp. 238-250). IEEE. DOI: 10.1109/ICSE43902.2021.00033

Vaughn, L. (2019). *Psychology and culture: Thinking, feeling and behaving in a global context.* Routledge. DOI: 10.4324/9781351268882 von Ziegler, L., Sturman, O., & Bohacek, J. (2021). Big behavior: Challenges and opportunities in a new era of deep behavior profiling. *Neuropsychopharmacology*, 46(1), 33–44. DOI: 10.1038/s41386-020-0751-7 PMID: 32599604

Vyas, S., Tyagi, R. K., Jain, C., & Sahu, S. (2021, July). Literature review: A comparative study of real time streaming technologies and apache kafka. In *2021 Fourth International Conference on Computational Intelligence and Communication Technologies (CCICT)* (pp. 146-153). IEEE. DOI: 10.1109/CCICT53244.2021.00038

Xplore, I. E. E. E. (2023). Detecting Insider Threats in Cybersecurity Using Machine Learning and Deep Learning Techniques. *IEEE Conference Publication.*

Xplore, I. E. E. E. (2024). *A Review of Recent Advances, Challenges, and Opportunities in Malicious Insider Threat Detection Using Machine Learning Methods.* IEEE Journals & Magazines.

Compilation of References

Abbasi, R., Bashir, A. K., Mateen, A., Amin, F., Ge, Y., & Omar, M. "Efficient Security and Privacy of Lossless Secure Communication for Sensor-based Urban Cities," *IEEE Sensors Journal*, vol. 2023.

Abdulkareem, K. H., Ali, N. S., & Yunos, Z. (2023). *Insider Threat Detection Using Machine Learning Approach*. MDPI Applied Sciences.

Addams, A., & Sasse, M. A. (1999). Users Are Not The Enemy. []. essay, CACM.]. *Communications of the ACM*, 42(12), 41–46.

Ahmad, Z., Shahid Khan, A., Wai Shiang, C., Abdullah, J., & Ahmad, F. (2021). Network intrusion detection system: A systematic study of machine learning and deep learning approaches. *Transactions on Emerging Telecommunications Technologies*, 32(1), e4150. DOI: 10.1002/ett.4150

Ahmed Alaa El-Din, E. (2022). Artificial intelligence in forensic science: Invasion or revolution? *Egyptian Society of Clinical Toxicology Journal*, 10(2), 20–32. DOI: 10.21608/esctj.2022.158178.1012

Ahmed, N., Mohammadani, K., Bashir, A. K., Omar, M., Jones, A., & Hassan, F. "Secure and Reliable Routing in the Internet of Vehicles Network: AODV-RL with BHA Attack Defense," *CMES-Computer Modeling in Engineering & Sciences*, vol. 139, no. 1, 2024.

Ahmed, H., Rasheed, H., Bashir, A. K., & Omar, M. (2023). Rasheed, A. K. Bashir, and M. Omar, "Millimeter-wave Channel Modeling in a VANETs Using Coding Techniques,". *PeerJ. Computer Science*, 9, e1374. DOI: 10.7717/peerj-cs.1374 PMID: 37346660

Ajzen, I. (1985). From intentions to actions: A theory of planned behavior. In Kuhland, J., & Beckman, J. (Eds.), *Action control: From cognition to behavior* (pp. 11–39). Springer. DOI: 10.1007/978-3-642-69746-3_2

Ajzen, I. (1991). The theory of planned behavior. *Organizational Behavior and Human Decision Processes*, 50(2), 179–211. DOI: 10.1016/0749-5978(91)90020-T

Ajzen, I. (2020). The theory of planned behavior: Frequently asked questions. *Human Behavior and Emerging Technologies*, 2(4), 314–324. https://publons.com/publon/10.1002/hbe2.195. DOI: 10.1002/hbe2.195

Ajzen, I., & Fishbein, M. (1975). A Bayesian analysis of attribution processes. *Psychological Bulletin*, 82(2), 261–277. Advance online publication. DOI: 10.1037/h0076477

Akbar, M. A., Smolander, K., Mahmood, S., & Alsanad, A. (2022). Toward successful DevSecOps in software development organizations: A decision-making framework. *Information and Software Technology*, 147, 106894. Advance online publication. DOI: 10.1016/j.infsof.2022.106894

Aksoy, C. (2024). Building a cyber security culture for resilient organizations against Cyber Attacks. *İşletme Ekonomi ve Yönetim Araştırmaları Dergisi, 7*(1), 96–110. DOI: 10.33416/baybem.1374001

Al Harthi, S., Al Balushi, M. Y., Al Badi, A. H., Al Karaki, J., & Omar, M. *"Metaverse Adoption in UAE Higher Education: A Hybrid SEM-ANN Approach," in 98 Mohammad Daradkeh, Boshra Aldhanhani, Amjad Gawanmeh, Shadi Atalla and Sami Miniaoui. Applied Research Approaches to Technology, Healthcare, and Business.* IGI Global.

Al Kinoon, M., Omar, M., Mohaisen, M., & Mohaisen, D. "Security Breaches in the Healthcare Domain: A Spatiotemporal Analysis," in *Computational Data and Social Networks: 10th International Conference, CSoNet 2021, Virtual Event, November 15-17, 2021, Proceedings*, Springer International Publishing, pp. 171-183, 2021. DOI: 10.1007/978-3-030-91434-9_16

Alam, S. S., & Sayuti, N. M. (2011). Applying the theory of planned behavior (TPB) in halal food purchasing. *International Journal of Commerce and Management*, 21(1), 8–20. DOI: 10.1108/10569211111111676

Alanazi, M., Freeman, M., & Tootell, H. (2022). Exploring the factors that influence the cybersecurity behaviors of young adults. *Computers in Human Behavior*, 136, 107376. Advance online publication. DOI: 10.1016/j.chb.2022.107376

Alghamdi, M. I. (2021). *Digital forensics in cyber security—recent trends, threats, and opportunities*. Cybersecurity Threats with New Perspectives. DOI: 10.5772/intechopen.94452

Al-Hajri, S. M., Al-Thonayan, Z. J., Alqattan, M. M., Alalyani, N. A., Alali, N. D., & Alnaim, N. (2023). Maximizing the Potential of Artificial Intelligence in Digital Forensics Investigations.

Ali, A. (2022). Cyber Crime Investigation and Forensics: Leveraging AI and Big Data for More Effective Solutions.

Ali, G., Shah, S., & ElAffendi, M. (2024). Enhancing Cybersecurity Incident Response: AI-Driven Optimization for Strengthened Advance Persistence Threat Detection.

Al-Karaki, J. N., Omar, M., Gawanmeh, A., & Jones, A. "Advancing CyberSecurity Education and Training: Practical Case Study of Running Capture the Flag (CTF) on the Metaverse vs. Physical Settings," in *2023 International Conference on Intelligent Metaverse Technologies & Applications (iMETA)*, pp. 1-7, IEEE, 2023. DOI: 10.1109/iMETA59369.2023.10294722

Almehdhar, M., Albaseer, A., Khan, M. A., Abdallah, M., Menouar, H., Al-Kuwari, S., & Al-Fuqaha, A. (2024). Deep learning in the fast lane: A survey on advanced intrusion detection systems for intelligent vehicle networks. *IEEE Open Journal of Vehicular Technology*, 5, 869–906. DOI: 10.1109/OJVT.2024.3422253

Almeida, M. C., Yoshikuni, A. C., Dwivedi, R., & Larieira, C. L. C. (2022). Do leadership styles influence employee information systems security intention? A study of the banking industry. Global Journal of Flexible Systems Management, 1–16. https://doi.org/DOI: 10.1007/s40171-022-00320-1

Alotaibi, N., Williamson, J., & Khamis, M. (2023). ThermoSecure: Investigating the effectiveness of AI-driven thermal attacks on commonly used computer keyboards. *ACM Transactions on Privacy and Security*, 26(2), 1–24. DOI: 10.1145/3563693

Al-Sanjary, O. I., Ahmed, A. A., Jaharadak, A. A. B., Ali, M. A., & Zangana, H. M. "Detection Clone an Object Movement Using an Optical Flow Approach," in *2018 IEEE Symposium on Computer Applications & Industrial Electronics (ISCAIE)*, pp. 388-394, 2018. DOI: 10.1109/ISCAIE.2018.8405504

Alturki, N., Altamimi, A., Umer, M., Saidani, O., Alshardan, A., Alsubai, S., Omar, M., & Ashraf, I. "Improving Prediction of Chronic Kidney Disease Using KNN Imputed SMOTE Features and TrioNet Model," *CMES-Computer Modeling in Engineering & Sciences*, vol. 139, no. 3, 2024. DOI: 10.32604/cmes.2023.045868

Alyami, A., Sammon, D., Neville, K., & Mahony, C. (2023). Critical success factors for Security Education, training and awareness (SETA) programme effectiveness: An empirical comparison of practitioner perspectives. *Information and Computer Security*, 32(1), 53–73. DOI: 10.1108/ICS-08-2022-0133

Amaro, R. M. D., Pereira, R., & da Silva, M. M. (2022). Capabilities and practices in DevOps: A multivocal literature review. *IEEE Transactions on Software Engineering*. Advance online publication. DOI: 10.1109/TSE.2022.3166626

Ani, U. D., He, H., & Tiwari, A. (2019). Human factor security: Evaluating the cybersecurity capacity of the Industrial Workforce. *Journal of Systems and Information Technology*, 21(1), 2–35. DOI: 10.1108/JSIT-02-2018-0028

Anjaria, D., & Kulkarni, M. **(2021).** Effective DevSecOps implementation: A systematic literature review. Revista Geintec-Gestao Inovacao E Tecnologias, 11(4), 4931–4945. http://revistageintec.net/wp-content/uploads/2022/03/2514.pdf

Antonucci, L., Kowalski, R., & Garamoni, M. (2020). *Manufacturing cyber security workforce and career development framework*. ManpowerGroup Milwaukee United States.

Arulappan, G. (2023). Raja, A. K. Bashir, A. Mahanti, and M. Omar, "ZTMP: Zero Touch Management Provisioning Algorithm for the On-boarding of Cloud-native Virtual Network Functions,". *Mobile Networks and Applications*, •••, 1–13.

Ask, T. F., Lugo, R. G., Knox, B. J., & Sütterlin, S. (2021, July). Human-human communication in cyber threat situations: A systematic review. In *International Conference on Human-Computer Interaction* (pp. 21–43). Springer, Cham. https://doi.org/DOI: 10.1007/978-3-030-90328-2_2

Aslam, M. (2024). AI and cybersecurity: An ever-evolving landscape. *International Journal of Advanced Engineering Technologies and Innovations*, 1(1), 52–71.

Ayub, M., Li, X., Mahmood, K., Shamshad, S., Saleem, M. A., & Omar, M. (2023). Secure Consumer-centric Demand Response Management in Resilient Smart Grid as Industry 5.0 Application with Blockchain-based Authentication. *IEEE Transactions on Consumer Electronics*.

Baezner, M. (2018). ETH Library Cyber disruption and cybercrime: Democratic People's Republic of Korea Report. https://doi.org/DOI: 10.3929/ethz-b-000314511

Banisakher, M., Omar, M., & Clare, W. (2019). Critical Infrastructure—Perspectives on the Role of Government in Cybersecurity. *Journal of Computer Sciences and Applications*, 7(1), 37–42. DOI: 10.12691/jcsa-7-1-6

Banisakher, M., Omar, M., Hong, S., & Adams, J. (2020). A Human-centric Approach to Data Fusion in Post-Disaster Management. *Journal of Business Management and Science*, 8(1), 12–20.

Banisakher, M., Omar, M., Hong, S., & Adams, J. (2020). A Human-centric Approach to Data Fusion in Post-Disaster Management. *Jurnal of Business Management and Science*, 8(1), 12–20.

Bartnes, M., Moe, N. B., & Heegaard, P. E. (2016). The future of information security incident management training: A case study of electrical power companies. *Computers & Security*, 61, 32–45. DOI: 10.1016/j.cose.2016.05.004

Basharat, M., & Omar, M. "Adapting to Change: Assessing the Longevity and Resilience of Adversarially Trained NLP Models in Dynamic Spam Detection Environments," in *Innovations, Securities, and Case Studies Across Healthcare, Business, and Technology*, pp. 157-173, IGI Global, 2024. DOI: 10.4018/979-8-3693-1906-2.ch009

Basharat, M., & Omar, M. (2024). Harnessing GPT-2 for Feature Extraction in Malware Detection: A Novel Approach to Cybersecurity. *Land Forces Academy Review*, 29(1), 74–84. DOI: 10.2478/raft-2024-0008

Bass, B. M., & Riggio, R. E. (2006). *Transformational leadership*. Lawrence Erlbaum Associates. DOI: 10.4324/9781410617095

Bates, S., Hastie, T., & Tibshirani, R. (2024). Cross-validation: What does it estimate and how well does it do it? *Journal of the American Statistical Association*, 119(546), 1434–1445. DOI: 10.1080/01621459.2023.2197686 PMID: 39308484

Bellamy, A. J. (2005). Responsibility to protect or Trojan horse? The crisis in Darfur and humanitarian intervention after Iraq. *Ethics & International Affairs*, 19(2), 31–54. DOI: 10.1111/j.1747-7093.2005.tb00499.x

BetaFred. (2022, October 14). Microsoft Security Advisory 2719615. Microsoft.com. https://learn.microsoft.com/en-us/security-updates/securityadvisories/2012/2719615

Betts, J., & Sezer, S. (2014, May). Ethics and privacy in national security and critical infrastructure protection. In *2014 IEEE International Symposium on Ethics in Science, Technology, and Engineering* (pp. 1-7). IEEE. DOI: 10.1109/ETHICS.2014.6893417

Bharathiraja, S., Rajesh Kanna, B., Geetha, S., & Anusooya, G. (2023). Unmasking the digital deception-a comprehensive survey on image forgery and detection techniques. *The Australian Journal of Forensic Sciences*, •••, 1–49.

Bischl, B., Binder, M., Lang, M., Pielok, T., Richter, J., Coors, S., Thomas, J., Ullmann, T., Becker, M., Boulesteix, A.-L., Deng, D., & Lindauer, M. (2023). Hyperparameter optimization: Foundations, algorithms, best practices, and open challenges. *Wiley Interdisciplinary Reviews. Data Mining and Knowledge Discovery*, 13(2), e1484. DOI: 10.1002/widm.1484

Blum, A., Hopcroft, J., & Kannan, R. (2020). *Foundations of data science*. Cambridge University Press. DOI: 10.1017/9781108755528

Blum, D. (2020). Institute resilience through detection, response, and recovery. In *Rational cybersecurity for business* (pp. 259–295). Apress., DOI: 10.1007/978-1-4842-5952-8_9

Bobbert, Y., & Chtepen, M. (2021). Research findings in the domain of CI/CD and DevOps on security compliance. In *Strategic approaches to digital platform security assurance* (pp. 286–307). IGI Global., DOI: 10.4018/978-1-7998-7367-9.ch008

Bonfanti, M. E. (2022). *Artificial intelligence and the offence-defence balance in cyber security. Cyber Security: Socio-Technological Uncertainty and Political Fragmentation*. Routledge.

Boo, H. (2017). AN ASSESSMENT OF NORTH KOREAN CYBER THREATS. *The Journal of East Asian Affairs*, 31(1), 97–117. https://www.jstor.org/stable/44321274

Booz Allen Hamilton. (2023). *Leverage Machine Learning to Detect Insider Threats*. Booz Allen Perspectives.

Boyce, M. W., Duma, K. M., Hettinger, L. J., Malone, T. B., Wilson, D. P., & Lockett-Reynolds, J. (2011). Human performance in cybersecurity: A research agenda. *Proceedings of the Human Factors and Ergonomics Society Annual Meeting*, 55(1), 1115–1119. DOI: 10.1177/1071181311551233

Briggs, P., Jeske, D., & Coventry, L. (2017). Behavior change interventions for cybersecurity. In *Behavior change research and theory* (pp. 115–136). Academic Press., DOI: 10.1016/B978-0-12-802690-8.00004-9

Brown, J. M., Greenspan, S., & Biddle, R. (2016). Incident response teams in IT operations centers: The T-TOCs model of team functionality. *Cognition Technology and Work*, 18(4), 695–716. DOI: 10.1007/s10111-016-0374-2

Brustolin, V. (2019). Comparative analysis of regulations for cybersecurity and cyber defense in the United States and Brazil. *Revista Brasileira de Estudos de Defesa, 6*(2).

Bures, O. (2017). Contributions of private business to the provision of security in the EU: Beyond public-private partnerships. *Crime, Law, and Social Change*, 67(3), 289–312. DOI: 10.1007/s10611-016-9650-6

Burrell, D. N., Aridi, A. S., McLester, Q., Shufutinsky, A., Nobles, C., Dawson, M., & Muller, S. R. (2021). Exploring system thinking leadership approaches to the healthcare cybersecurity environment. [IJEACH]. *International Journal of Extreme Automation and Connectivity in Healthcare*, 3(2), 20–32. DOI: 10.4018/IJEACH.2021070103

Burrell, D. N., Nobles, C., Cusak, A., Omar, M., & Gillesania, L. (2022). Cybercrime and the Nature of Insider Threat Complexities in Healthcare and Biotechnology Engineering Organizations. *Journal of Crime and Criminal Behavior*, 2(2), 131–144. DOI: 10.47509/JCCB.2022.v02i02.04

Burrell, D. N., Nobles, C., Richardson, K., Wright, J. B., Jones, A. J., Springs, D., & Brown-Jackson, K. (2023). Allison Huff. In *Applied Research Approaches to Technology, Healthcare, and Business*. IGI Global. DOI: 10.4018/979-8-3693-1630-6

Capuano, N., Fenza, G., Loia, V., & Stanzione, C. (2022). Explainable artificial intelligence in cybersecurity: A survey. *IEEE Access : Practical Innovations, Open Solutions*, 10, 93575–93600. DOI: 10.1109/ACCESS.2022.3204171

Carnegie Mellon University. (2013). South Korean malware attack. Produced for US-CERT, a government organization. Retrieved from: https://www.cisa.gov

Carr, M. (2016). Public-private partnerships in national cyber-security strategies. *International Affairs*, 92(1), 43–62. DOI: 10.1111/1468-2346.12504

Carturan, S. B. G., & Goya, D. H. (2019, September). A systems-of-systems security framework for requirements definition in cloud environment. In *Proceedings of the 13th European Conference on Software Architecture-Volume 2* (pp. 235–240). https://doi.org/DOI: 10.1145/3344948.3344977

Chadd, K. (2020) The History of Cybercrime and Cybersecurity, 1940-2020, Cybercrime Magazine https://cybersecurityventures.com/the-history-of-cybercrime-and-cybersecurity-1940-2020/ retrieved November 2, 2023

Chakraborty, R. S., Narasimhan, S., & Bhunia, S. (2009, November). Hardware Trojan: Threats and emerging solutions. In 2009 IEEE International high level design validation and test workshop (pp. 166-171). IEEE.

Chalmers, R. (2023, May 22). *Organizational culture*. StatPearls [Internet]. https://www.ncbi.nlm.nih.gov/books/NBK560543/

Charness, N., & Boot, W. R. (2016). Technology, gaming, and Social Networking. *Handbook of the Psychology of Aging, Eighth ed.*, 389–407. DOI: 10.1016/B978-0-12-411469-2.00020-0

Chattopadhyay, A., & Das, A. (2020). Insider Threat Detection Using Machine Learning. *Journal of Cyber Security Technology*, 4(3), 45–53.

Chen, J., Wang, Y., & Lu, C. (2021). Insider Threat Detection Using Natural Language Processing Techniques. *Computer Security Journal*, 7(2), 55–68.

Chen, M., Li, Y., Zhou, S., Zou, L., Yu, L., Deng, T., Rong, X., Shao, S., & Wu, J. (2024). Establishment of a risk prediction model for olfactory disorders in patients with transnasal pituitary tumors by machine learning. *Scientific Reports*, 14(1), 12514. DOI: 10.1038/s41598-024-62963-7 PMID: 38822064

CHILONGO, L., & KM, A. S. (2024). IMPACT OF ARTIFICIAL INTELLIGENCE ON CYBERSECURITY: A CASE OF INTERNET OF THINGS. *i-Manager's Journal on Digital Forensics & Cyber Security (JDF), 2*(1).

Choi, Y. H., Liu, P., Shang, Z., Wang, H., Wang, Z., Zhang, L., Zhou, J., & Zou, Q. (2020). Using deep learning to solve computer security challenges: A survey. *Cybersecurity*, 3(1), 1–32. DOI: 10.1186/s42400-020-00055-5

Choo, H. S., Ooi, C. Y., Inoue, M., Ismail, N., Moghbel, M., & Kok, C. H. (2020). Register-transfer-level features for machine-learning-based hardware trojan detection. IEICE TRANSACTIONS on Fundamentals of Electronics. *Communications and Computer Sciences*, 103(2), 502–509.

Choudhry, R. M., Fang, D., & Mohamed, S. (2007). The nature of safety culture: A survey of the state-of-the-art. *Safety Science*, 45(10), 993–1012. DOI: 10.1016/j.ssci.2006.09.003

Chowdhury, N., Katsikas, S., & Gkioulos, V. (2022). Modeling effective cybersecurity training frameworks: A delphi method-based study. *Computers & Security*, 113, 102551. Advance online publication. DOI: 10.1016/j.cose.2021.102551

Clements, J., & Lao, Y. (2018). Hardware trojan attacks on neural networks. arXiv preprint arXiv:1806.05768.

Coleman, K. (2010). The weaponry and strategies of digital conflict. International Conference on Information Warfare and Security. Retrieved from_https://ezproxy.gl.iit.edu/login?url=https://www.proquest.com/conference-papers-proceedings/weaponry-strategies-digital-conflict/docview/869617526/se-2?accountid=28377

Computer Security Division. I. T. L. (2020, October 21). DevSecOps | CSRC. *CSRC | NIST*. https://csrc.nist.gov/projects/devsecops

Conte, J., & Landy, F. (2019). *Work in the 21st Century: An Introduction to Industrial and Organizational Psychology* (6th ed.). Wiley.

Costa, D., Albrethsen, M., Collins, M., Perl, S., Silowash, G., & Spooner, D. (2014). *An Insider Threat Indicator Ontology*. Carnegie Mellon University, Software Engineering Institute.

Cyber Resilient Organization Study 2021. IBM. (2021). https://www.ibm.com/resources/guides/cyber-resilient-organization-study/

Das, R. (2024). *Generative AI: Phishing And Cybersecurity Metrics*. CRC Press. DOI: 10.1201/9781003503781

Davis, L., Dawson, M., & Omar, M. (2016). Systems Engineering Concepts with Aid of Virtual Worlds and Open Source Software: Using Technology to Develop Learning Objects and Simulation Environments. In *Handbook of Research on 3-D Virtual Environments and Hypermedia for Ubiquitous Learning* (pp. 483–509). IGI Global. DOI: 10.4018/978-1-5225-0125-1.ch020

Dawson, M., Al Saeed, I., Wright, J., & Omar, M. "Technology enhanced learning with open source software for scientists and engineers," in *INTED2013 Proceedings*, IATED, 2013, pp. 5583–5589.

Dawson, M. (2015). A Brief Review of New Threats and Countermeasures in Digital Crime and Cyber Terrorism. In *New Threats and Countermeasures in Digital Crime and Cyber Terrorism* (pp. 1–7). IGI Global. DOI: 10.4018/978-1-4666-8345-7.ch001

Dawson, M., Davis, L., & Omar, M. (2019). Developing learning objects for engineering and science fields: Using technology to test system usability and interface design. *Int. J. Smart Technol. Learn.*, 1(2), 140–161. DOI: 10.1504/IJSMART-TL.2019.097951

Dawson, M., Eltayeb, M., & Omar, M. (2016). *Security solutions for hyperconnectivity and the Internet of things*. IGI Global.

Dawson, M., Omar, M., & Abramson, J. (2015). Understanding the methods behind cyber terrorism. In *Encyclopedia of Information Science and Technology* (3rd ed., pp. 1539–1549). IGI Global.

Dawson, M., Omar, M., Abramson, J., & Bessette, D. (2014). *Information security in diverse computing environments*. Academic Press.

Dawson, M., Omar, M., Abramson, J., Leonard, B., & Bessette, D. (2017). Battlefield cyberspace: Exploitation of hyperconnectivity and Internet of Things. In *Developing Next-Generation Countermeasures for Homeland Security Threat Prevention* (pp. 204–235). IGI Global. DOI: 10.4018/978-1-5225-0703-1.ch010

Day, J., Kearney, P., Moor, J., Marshall, R., Bott, A., & Poyner, I. (2021). Vulnerability Disclosure: Best Practice Guidelines. IoT Security Foundation website.

Dayoub and M. Omar. (2024). Advancing IoT security posture K-Means clustering for malware detection. In *Innovations, Securities, and Case Studies Across Healthcare, Business, and Technology* (pp. 221–239). IGI Global.

Desimone, A., & Horton, N. (2017). The 2014 North Korean Cyber Attack on Sony and Lessons for US Government Actions in Cyberspace NIGHTMARE National Security Report. https://www.jhuapl.edu/sites/default/files/2022-12/SonyNightmareBeforeChristmas.pdf

Dhayanidhi, G. (2022). Research on IoT threats & implementation of AI/ML to address emerging cybersecurity issues in IoT with cloud computing.

Díaz, J., Pérez, J. E., Lopez-Peña, M. A., Mena, G. A., & Yagüe, A. (2019). Self-service cybersecurity monitoring as enabler for devsecops. *IEEE Access : Practical Innovations, Open Solutions*, 7, 100283–100295. DOI: 10.1109/ACCESS.2019.2930000

Diethe, T., Twomey, N., & Flach, P. (2019). A Systematic Review of Machine Learning for Insider Threat Detection. *Journal of Information Security and Applications*, 46, 165–183.

DiMaggio, A. R. (2021). The Trojan Horse–"Conservative" Media and the Mainstreaming of Neofascistic Politics. In Rising Fascism in America (pp. 87-129). Routledge.

Donaldson, S. E., Siegel, S. G., Williams, C. K., & Aslam, A. (2015). Enterprise cybersecurity and the cloud. In *Enterprise cybersecurity* (pp. 105–117). Apress., DOI: 10.1007/978-1-4302-6083-7_6

Dong, H., Wu, J., Bashir, A. K., Pan, Q., Omar, M., & Al-Dulaimi, A. "Privacy-preserving EEG signal analysis with electrode attention for depression diagnosis: Joint FHE and CNN approach," in *GLOBECOM 2023-2023 IEEE Global Communications Conference*, IEEE, 2023, pp. 4265–4270. DOI: 10.1109/GLOBECOM54140.2023.10436783

Dong, C., Chen, J., Guo, W., & Zou, J. (2019). A machine-learning-based hardware-Trojan detection approach for chips in the Internet of Things. *International Journal of Distributed Sensor Networks*, 15(12), 1550147719888098. DOI: 10.1177/1550147719888098

Dong, C., He, G., Liu, X., Yang, Y., & Guo, W. (2019). A multi-layer hardware trojan protection framework for IoT chips. *IEEE Access : Practical Innovations, Open Solutions*, 7, 23628–23639. DOI: 10.1109/ACCESS.2019.2896479

Dong, C., Liu, Y., Chen, J., Liu, X., Guo, W., & Chen, Y. (2020). An unsupervised detection approach for hardware trojans. *IEEE Access : Practical Innovations, Open Solutions*, 8, 158169–158183. DOI: 10.1109/ACCESS.2020.3001239

Dunsin, D., Ghanem, M. C., Ouazzane, K., & Vassilev, V. (2024). A comprehensive analysis of the role of artificial intelligence and machine learning in modern digital forensics and incident response. *Forensic Science International Digital Investigation*, 48, 301675. DOI: 10.1016/j.fsidi.2023.301675

Duque Anton, S. D., Fraunholz, D., Krohmer, D., Reti, D., Schotten, H. D., Selgert, F., Marosvölgyi, M., Larsen, M., Sudhakar, K., Koch, T., Witt, T., & Bassem, C. (2020, September 8). Creating it from SCRATCh: A practical approach for enhancing the security of IoT-systems in a DevOps-enabled software development environment. In *International Conference on Computer Safety, Reliability, and Security* (pp. 266–281). Springer, Cham. https://doi.org/DOI: 10.1007/978-3-030-55583-2_20

Du, X., Hargreaves, C., Sheppard, J., Anda, F., Sayakkara, A., Le-Khac, N. A., & Scanlon, M. (2020, August). SoK: Exploring the state of the art and the future potential of artificial intelligence in digital forensic investigation. In *Proceedings of the 15th international conference on availability, reliability and security* (pp. 1-10). DOI: 10.1145/3407023.3407068

Dwivedi, R., Dave, D., Naik, H., Singhal, S., Omer, R., Patel, P., & Ranjan, R. (2023). Explainable AI (XAI): Core ideas, techniques, and solutions. *ACM Computing Surveys*, 55(9), 1–33. DOI: 10.1145/3561048

Exec. Order No. 13035, 62 Fed. Reg. 7131 (Feb. 14, 1997), http://www.gpo.gov/fdsys/pkg/FR-1997-02-14/pdf/97-3992.pdf [https://perma.cc/D5WB-R4GJ].

Exec. Order No. 13133, 64 Fed. Reg. 43895 (Aug. 5, 1999), http://www.gpo.gov/fdsys/pkg/FR-1999-08-11/pdf/99-20924.pdf [https://perma.cc/W458-2QGZ]. 20 Id. 21 Exec. Order No. 13231, 3 C.F.R. § 13231 (2002), https://fas.org/irp/offdocs/eo/eo13231.htm [https://perma.cc/QAA4-ZF6T].

Faqir, R. S. (2023). Digital Criminal Investigations in the Era of Artificial Intelligence: A Comprehensive Overview. *International Journal of Cyber Criminology*, 17(2), 77–94.

Fawzi, D., & Omar, M. (n.d.). *New insights to database security: An effective and integrated approach to applying access control mechanisms and cryptographic concepts in Microsoft access environments*. Academic Press.

Fayyaz, Y., Almehmadi, A., & El-Khatib, K. (2024). A hybrid artificial intelligence framework for enhancing digital forensic investigations of infotainment systems. *Forensic Science International Digital Investigation*, 49, 301751. DOI: 10.1016/j.fsidi.2024.301751

Fearer, M. D. (2020). How to communicate to the C-level suite the need for security operations centers in fortune 1000 environments (Publication No. 28152440) [Doctoral dissertation, Capital Technology University]. ProQuest Dissertations and Theses Global.

Feng, C., Wu, S., & Liu, N. (2017, July). A user-centric machine learning framework for cyber security operations center. In *2017 IEEE International Conference on Intelligence and Security Informatics (ISI)* (pp. 173–175). IEEE. https://doi.org/ DOI: 10.1109/ISI.2017.8004902

Fowler, B. (2022, January 24). *Data breaches break record in 2021*. CNET. https://www.cnet.com/news/privacy/record-number-of-data-breaches-reported-in-2021-new-report-says/

Fu, M., Pasuksmit, J., & Tantithamthavorn, C. (2024). AI for DevSecOps: A Landscape and Future Opportunities. *arXiv preprint arXiv:2404.04839.*

Gama, J., Žliobaitė, I., Bifet, A., Pechenizkiy, M., & Bouchachia, A. (2014). A survey on concept drift adaptation. *ACM Computing Surveys*, 46(4), 1–37. DOI: 10.1145/2523813

Ghillani, D. (2022). Deep learning and artificial intelligence framework to improve the cyber security. *Authorea Preprints*. DOI: 10.22541/au.166379475.54266021/v1

Gholami, S., & Omar, M. (2023). Does Synthetic Data Make Large Language Models More Efficient? *arXiv preprint arXiv:2310.07830.*

Gholami, S., & Omar, M. (2024). Can a student large language model perform as well as its teacher? In *Innovations, Securities, and Case Studies Across Healthcare, Business, and Technology* (pp. 122-139). IGI Global. DOI: 10.4018/979-8-3693-1906-2.ch007

Gholami, S., & Omar, M. "Does synthetic data make large language models more efficient?" *arXiv preprint arXiv:2310.07830*, 2023.

Golda, A., Mekonen, K., Pandey, A., Singh, A., Hassija, V., Chamola, V., & Sikdar, B. (2024). Privacy and Security Concerns in Generative AI: A Comprehensive Survey. *IEEE Access : Practical Innovations, Open Solutions*, 12, 48126–48144. DOI: 10.1109/ACCESS.2024.3381611

Gordan, M. (2014). A Review of B. F. Skinner's 'Reinforcement Theory of Motivation'. *International Journal of Research in Education Methodology*, 5(3), 680–688. DOI: 10.24297/ijrem.v5i3.3892

Grant, J. (2010). Will there be cybersecurity legislation? *J. Nat'l Sec. L. & Pol'y*, 4, 103. https://www.dhs.gov/employee-resources/securing-cyberspace-and-critical-infrastructure and https://www.okta.com/identity-101/privacy-vs-security/

Guillén, J. H., Del Rey, A. M., & Casado-Vara, R. (2019). Security countermeasures of a SCIRAS model for advanced malware propagation. *IEEE Access : Practical Innovations, Open Solutions*, 7, 135472–135478. DOI: 10.1109/ACCESS.2019.2942809

Gupta, A. S., Shreneter, K. P., & Sehgal, S. (2024, March). Visual Veracity: Advancing AI-Generated Image Detection with Convolutional Neural Networks. In *2024 11th International Conference on Reliability, Infocom Technologies and Optimization (Trends and Future Directions)(ICRITO)* (pp. 1-6). IEEE.

H. M. Zangana, "A new algorithm for shape detection," *IOSR Journal of Computer Engineering (IOSR-JCE)*, vol. 19, no. 3, pp. 71-76, 2017.

H. M. Zangana, "A New Skin Color Based Face Detection Algorithm by Combining Three Color Model Algorithms," *IOSR Journal of Computer Engineering*, vol. 17, pp. 06-125, 2015.

H. M. Zangana, "CHALLENGES AND ISSUES of MANET," 2024.

H. M. Zangana, "Implementing a System for Recognizing Optical Characters," 2018.

H. M. Zangana, "Improving The Web Services for Remittance Company: Express Remit as a Case Study," *Academic Journal of Nawroz University (AJNU)*, vol. 11, no. 3, 2022.

H. M. Zangana, "Issues of Data Management in the Library: A Case Study," 2019.

H. M. Zangana, "ITD Data Quality Maturity (A Case Study)," *International Journal Of Engineering And Computer Science*, vol. 8, no. 10, 2019.

H. M. Zangana, “Library Data Quality Maturity (IIUM as a Case Study),” *IOSR-JCE*, vol. 29, Mar. 2017.

Hamza, Y. A., & Omar, M. D. (2013). Cloud computing security: Abuse and nefarious use of cloud computing. *International Journal of Computer Engineering Research*, 3(6), 22–27.

Han, C. H., Park, S. T., & Lee, S. J. (2019). The enhanced security control model for critical infrastructures with the blocking prioritization process to cyber threats in power system. *International Journal of Critical Infrastructure Protection*, 26, 100312. Advance online publication. DOI: 10.1016/j.ijcip.2019.100312

Haney, J. (2023), Users Are Not Stupid: Six Cyber Security Pitfalls Overturned, Cyber Security: A Peer-Reviewed Journal, [online], https://tsapps.nist.gov/publication/get_pdf.cfm?pub_id=935795

Haney, J., Cunningham, C., & Furman, S. M. (2024). Towards Integrating Human-Centered Cybersecurity Research Into Practice: A Practitioner Survey. *Symposium on Usable Security and Privacy (USEC) 2024*, 1–16. https://doi.org/DOI: 10.14722/usec.2024.23xxx

Han, T., Wang, Y., & Liu, P. (2019, May). Hardware trojans detection at register transfer level based on machine learning. In *2019 IEEE International Symposium on Circuits and Systems (ISCAS)* (pp. 1-5). IEEE. DOI: 10.1109/ISCAS.2019.8702479

Hardgrave, B. C., & Johnson, R. A. (2003). Toward an information systems development acceptance model: The case of object-oriented systems development. *IEEE Transactions on Engineering Management*, 50(3), 322–336. DOI: 10.1109/TEM.2003.817293

Hasegawa, K., Shi, Y., & Togawa, N. (2018, August). Hardware trojan detection utilizing machine learning approaches. In 2018 17th IEEE International Conference On Trust, Security And Privacy In Computing And Communications/12th IEEE International Conference On Big Data Science And Engineering (TrustCom/BigDataSE) (pp. 1891-1896). IEEE. DOI: 10.1109/TrustCom/BigDataSE.2018.00287

Hasib, M. (2022). *Cybersecurity leadership: Powering the modern organization* (Vol. 1). Tomorrow’s Strategy Today.

Hassan, S. K., & Ibrahim, A. (2023). The role of artificial intelligence in cyber security and incident response. *International Journal for Electronic Crime Investigation*, 7(2).

Hayes, D., & Kyobe, M. (2020, March). The adoption of automation in cyber forensics. In *2020 Conference on Information Communications Technology and Society (ICTAS)* (pp. 1-6). IEEE. DOI: 10.1109/ICTAS47918.2020.233977

Hays, D. G., & McKibben, W. B. (2021). Promoting rigorous research: Generalizability and qualitative research. *Journal of Counseling and Development*, 99(2), 178–188. DOI: 10.1002/jcad.12365

Heidari, A., Jafari Navimipour, N., Dag, H., & Unal, M. (2024). Deepfake detection using deep learning methods: A systematic and comprehensive review. *Wiley Interdisciplinary Reviews. Data Mining and Knowledge Discovery*, 14(2), e1520. DOI: 10.1002/widm.1520

Heifetz, R. A., Heifetz, R., Grashow, A., & Linsky, M. (2009). *The practice of adaptive leadership: Tools and tactics for changing your organization and the world.* Harvard Business Press.

Henneberg, A. (2019). ADDRR: A counter kill chain cyber security model. Cyber Security: A Peer-Reviewed Journal, 3(3), 233–255. https://www.ingentaconnect.com/content/hsp/jcs/2019/00000003/00000003/art00005

Herath, T., & Rao, H. R. (2009). Protection motivation and deterrence: A framework for security policy compliance in organisations. *European Journal of Information Systems*, 18(2), 106–125. DOI: 10.1057/ejis.2009.6

He, W., & Zhang, Z. (2019). Enterprise cybersecurity training and awareness programs: Recommendations for Success. *Journal of Organizational Computing and Electronic Commerce*, 29(4), 249–257. DOI: 10.1080/10919392.2019.1611528

Hewage, C. T., Khattak, S. K., Ahmad, A., Mallikarachchi, T., Ukwandu, E., & Bentotahewa, V. (2022). Multimedia privacy and security landscape in the wake of ai/ml. *Social Media Analytics, Strategies and Governance*, 203-228.

Holaday, A. (1946). Heywood's" Troia Britannica" and the" Ages. *Journal of English and Germanic Philology*, 45(4), 430–439.

Hossain, S. A., Bao, Y., Hasan, N., & Islam, M. F. (2020). Perception and prediction of intention to use online banking systems: An empirical study using extended TAM. International Journal of Research in Business and Social Science (2147-4478), 9(1), 112–116. https://doi.org/DOI: 10.20525/ijrbs.v9i1.591

Howley, C. (2023, April 12). *Gartner identifies the top cybersecurity trends for 2023.* Gartner. https://www.gartner.com/en/newsroom/press-releases/04-12-2023-gartner-identifies-the-top-cybersecurity-trends-for-2023

Hu, T., Wu, L., Zhang, X., Yin, Y., & Yang, Y. (2019, October). Hardware trojan detection combine with machine learning: an svm-based detection approach. In 2019 IEEE 13th international conference on anti-counterfeiting, security, and identification (ASID) (pp. 202-206). IEEE. DOI: 10.1109/ICASID.2019.8924992

Huang, K., & Pearlson, K. (2019). For what technology can't fix: Building a model of organizational cybersecurity culture. *Proceedings of the Annual Hawaii International Conference on System Sciences*, 6398–6407. DOI: 10.24251/HICSS.2019.769

Huff, A. J., Burrell, D. N., Nobles, C., Richardson, K., Wright, J. B., Burton, S. L., Jones, A. J., Springs, D., Omar, M., & Brown-Jackson, K. L. (2023). Management Practices for Mitigating Cybersecurity Threats to Biotechnology Companies, Laboratories, and Healthcare Research Organizations. In *Applied Research Approaches to Technology, Healthcare, and Business* (pp. 1-12). IGI Global.

Hwang, J., & Choi, K.-S. (2021). North Korean Cyber Attacks and Policy Responses: An Interdisciplinary Theoretical Framework. *The International Journal of Cybersecurity Intelligence and Cybercrime*, 4(2), 4–24. DOI: 10.52306/04020221NHPZ9033

Ifinedo, P. (2015). Effects of Organizational Citizenship Behavior and Social Cognitive Factors on Employees' Non-Malicious Counterproductive Computer Security Behaviors: An Empirical Analysis. *CONF-IRM 2015 PROCEEDINGS,* 1–13. https://aisel.aisnet.org/confirm2015/36/

Iftikhar, S. (2024). Cyberterrorism as a Global threat: a Review on Repercussions and Countermeasures. PeerJ Computer Science, 10(e1772). https://doi.org/DOI: 10.7717/peerj-cs.1772

Iqbal, S., & Alharbi, S. A. (2020). Advancing automation in digital forensic investigations using machine learning forensics. *Digital Forensic Science, 3.*

ISO/IEC 29147:2018, Information technology -- Security techniques -- Vulnerability disclosure

Jabbari, H. Khan, S. Duraibi, I. Budhiraja, S. Gupta, and M. Omar, "Energy maximization for wireless powered communication enabled IoT devices with NOMA underlaying solar powered UAV using federated reinforcement learning for 6G networks," *IEEE Trans. Consum. Electron.*, 2024.

Jain, A., Zhou, Z., & Guin, U. (2021, May). Survey of recent developments for hardware trojan detection. In 2021 ieee international symposium on circuits and systems (iscas) (pp. 1-5). IEEE.

Jarrett, A., & Choo, K. K. R. (2021). The impact of automation and artificial intelligence on digital forensics. *WIREs Forensic Science*, 3(6), e1418. DOI: 10.1002/wfs2.1418

Jbair, M. (2019). Security monitoring strategies for your OT infrastructure. Cyber Security: A Peer-Reviewed Journal, 3(3), 265–274. https://www.ingentaconnect.com/content/hsp/jcs/2019/00000003/00000003/art00007

Joel, M. R., Ebenezer, V., Jeyaraj, K. A., Navaneethakrishnan, M., Arunadevi, R., & Jenifa, D. R. (2023, February). Decoding and Analysing Consumer Feedback for Companies and Goods using Machine Learning. In *2023 Third International Conference on Artificial Intelligence and Smart Energy (ICAIS)* (pp. 1085-1091). IEEE. DOI: 10.1109/ICAIS56108.2023.10073801

Joel, M. R., Ebenezer, V., Karthik, N., & Rajkumar, K. (2019). Advance dynamic network system of internet of things. *International Journal of Recent Technology and Engineering*, 8(3), 6209–6212. DOI: 10.35940/ijrte.C5657.098319

Joel, M. R., Navaneethakrishnan, M., Sriram, K. P., & Manonmani, S. P. (2023, March). Machine Learning Algorithms for Predicting House Prices in a Smart city using its Real-Time Data. In *2023 Second International Conference on Electronics and Renewable Systems (ICEARS)* (pp. 1064-1070). IEEE. DOI: 10.1109/ICEARS56392.2023.10085090

Jones and M. Omar. (2023). *"Harnessing the efficiency of reformers to detect software vulnerabilities," in 2023 Congress in Computer Science, Computer Engineering, & Applied Computing (CSCE)*. IEEE.

Jones and M. Omar. (2023). *"Optimized decision trees to detect IoT malware," in 2023 Congress in Computer Science, Computer Engineering, & Applied Computing (CSCE)*. IEEE.

Jones, R., & Omar, M. "Detecting IoT Malware with Knowledge Distillation Technique," in *2023 Congress in Computer Science, Computer Engineering, & Applied Computing (CSCE)*, pp. 131-135, IEEE, 2023. DOI: 10.1109/CSCE60160.2023.00026

Jones, R., Omar, M., & Mohammed, D. "Harnessing the Power of the GPT Model to Generate Adversarial Examples," in *2023 Congress in Computer Science, Computer Engineering, & Applied Computing (CSCE)*, pp. 1699-1702, IEEE, 2023. DOI: 10.1109/CSCE60160.2023.00279

Jones, R., Omar, M., Mohammed, D., & Nobles, C. "IoT Malware Detection with GPT Models," in *2023 Congress in Computer Science, Computer Engineering, & Applied Computing (CSCE)*, pp. 1749-1752, IEEE, 2023. DOI: 10.1109/CSCE60160.2023.00288

Jones, R., Omar, M., Mohammed, D., Nobles, C., & Dawson, M. (2023). Harnessing the Speed and Accuracy of Machine Learning to Advance Cybersecurity. In *2023 Congress in Computer Science, Computer Engineering, & Applied Computing (CSCE)* (pp. 418-421). IEEE. DOI: 10.1109/CSCE60160.2023.00074

Jones, A., & Omar, M.Jones and M. Omar. (2024). Codesentry: Revolutionizing real-time software vulnerability detection with optimized GPT framework. *Land Forces Acad. Rev.*, 29(1), 98–107. DOI: 10.2478/raft-2024-0010

Jones, M., & Omar, M. (2023). *"Detection of Twitter spam with language models: A case study on how to use BERT to protect children from spam on Twitter," in 2023 Congress in Computer Science, Computer Engineering, & Applied Computing (CSCE)*. IEEE.

Jones, M., & Omar, M. (2023). *"Measuring the impact of global health emergencies on self-disclosure using language models," in 2023 Congress in Computer Science, Computer Engineering, & Applied Computing (CSCE)*. IEEE.

Jones, M., & Omar, M. (2023). *"Studying the effects of social media content on kids' safety and well-being," in 2023 Congress in Computer Science, Computer Engineering, & Applied Computing (CSCE)*. IEEE.

Jones, R. K., & Jones, A. J. (2024). Integration of LLMs With Traditional Security Tools. In *Application of Large Language Models (LLMs) for Software Vulnerability Detection* (pp. 295–334). IGI Global., DOI: 10.4018/979-8-3693-9311-6.ch008

Jones, R., & Omar, M. (2024). Codeguard: Utilizing Advanced Pattern Recognition in Language Models for Software Vulnerability Analysis. *Land Forces Academy Review*, 29(1), 108–118. DOI: 10.2478/raft-2024-0011

Jones, R., & Omar, M. (2024). Revolutionizing Cybersecurity: The GPT-2 Enhanced Attack Detection and Defense (GEADD) Method for Zero-Day Threats [INJIISCOM]. *International Journal of Informatics, Information System and Computer Engineering*, 5(2), 178–191. DOI: 10.34010/injiiscom.v5i2.12741

Jones, R., & Omar, M. (2024). Revolutionizing Cybersecurity: The GPT-2 Enhanced Attack Detection and Defense (GEADD) Method for Zero-Day Threats. *International Journal of Informatics* [INJIISCOM]. *Information System and Computer Engineering*, 5(2), 178–191.

Jun, J., LaFoy, S., & Sohn, E. (2014, December 18). The organization of cyber operations in North Korea. Center for Strategic and International Studies. https://csis-website-prod.s3.amazonaws.com/s3fs-public/legacy_files/files/publication/141218_Cyber_Operations_North_Korea.pdf

Jun, W., Iqbal, M. S., Abbasi, R., Omar, M., & Huiqin, C. "Web-Semantic-Driven Machine Learning and Blockchain for Transformative Change in the Future of Physical Education," *International Journal on Semantic Web and Information Systems (IJSWIS)*, vol. 20, no. 1, pp. 1-16, IGI Global, 2024. DOI: 10.4018/IJSWIS.337961

Kang, Y., Cai, Z., Tan, C. W., Huang, Q., & Liu, H. (2020). Natural language processing (NLP) in management research: A literature review. *Journal of Management Analytics*, 7(2), 139–172. DOI: 10.1080/23270012.2020.1756939

Katsikeas, S., Lambrou, G., & Symeonidis, I. (2020). Proactive Insider Threat Detection through Contextual Behavioral Analysis. *Security and Privacy Journal*, 5(1), 21–35.

Kaur, R., Gabrijelčič, D., & Klobučar, T. (2023). Artificial intelligence for cybersecurity: Literature review and future research directions. *Information Fusion*, 97, 101804. DOI: 10.1016/j.inffus.2023.101804

Khaleel, Y. L., Habeeb, M. A., Albahri, A. S., Al-Quraishi, T., Albahri, O. S., & Alamoodi, A. H. (2024). Network and cybersecurity applications of defense in adversarial attacks: A state-of-the-art using machine learning and deep learning methods. *Journal of Intelligent Systems*, 33(1), 20240153. DOI: 10.1515/jisys-2024-0153

Khan, N. (2017). Adaptive or transactional leadership in current higher education: A brief comparison. International Review of Research in Open and Distributed Learning, 18(3), 178¬–¬183. https://doi.org/DOI: 10.19173/irrodl.v18i3.3294

Khan, S. A., Alkawaz, M. H., & Zangana, H. M. "The use and abuse of social media for spreading fake news," in *2019 IEEE International Conference on Automatic Control and Intelligent Systems (I2CACIS)*, pp. 145-148, IEEE, 2019. DOI: 10.1109/I2CACIS.2019.8825029

Khimi, W., Albarqi, K., Saif, K., & Elhag, S. A Systematic Review on Deep Fake Image Generation, Detection Techniques, Ethical Implications, and Overcoming Challenges.

Khormali, A. (2022). Advanced Deep Learning Methodologies for Deepfake Detection.

Kim, C. W., & Polito, C. (2019). The evolution of North Korean cyber threats. Asan Institute for Policy Studies. https://www.jstor.org/stable/resrep20679

Kim, K., Alfouzan, F. A., & Kim, H. (2021). Cyber-Attack Scoring Model Based on the Offensive Cybersecurity Framework. *Applied Sciences (Basel, Switzerland)*, 11(16), 7738. DOI: 10.3390/app11167738

Kim, M. (2022). North Korea's Cyber Capabilities and Their Implications for International Security. *Sustainability (Basel)*, 14(3), 1744. DOI: 10.3390/su14031744

Kim, S. H., Yang, K. H., & Park, S. (2014). An integrative behavioral model of information security policy compliance. *TheScientificWorldJournal*, 2014, 1–12. Advance online publication. DOI: 10.1155/2014/463870 PMID: 24971373

Kindt, J. (2024). *The Trojan Horse and Other Stories: Ten Ancient Creatures that Make Us Human*. Cambridge University Press. DOI: 10.1017/9781009411332

Klimoski, R., & Murray, J. (2016). Cyber security executive leadership. In *Psychosocial dynamics of cyber security* (pp. 165–196). Routledge.

Klingner, B. (2021). North Korean cyberattacks: A dangerous and evolving threat (Special Report No. 247). The Heritage Foundation. https://www.heritage.org/sites/default/files/2021-09/SR247.pdf

Kok, C. H., Ooi, C. Y., Inoue, M., Moghbel, M., Dass, S. B., Choo, H. S., . . . Hussin, F. A. (2019, December). Net classification based on testability and netlist structural features for hardware Trojan detection. In 2019 IEEE 28th Asian Test Symposium (ATS) (pp. 105-1055). IEEE. DOI: 10.1109/ATS47505.2019.00020

Kruhlov, V., Latynin, M., Horban, A., & Petrov, A. (2019). Public-Private Partnership in Cybersecurity. In *CybHyg* (pp. 619-628).

Kshetri, N. (2014). Cyberwarfare in the Korean Peninsula: Asymmetries and Strategic Responses. *East Asia (Piscataway, N.J.)*, 31(3), 183–201. DOI: 10.1007/s12140-014-9215-1

Kumar, R., & Goyal, R. (2020). Modeling continuous security: A conceptual model for automated DevSecOps using open-source software over cloud (ADOC). *Computers & Security*, 97, 101967. Advance online publication. DOI: 10.1016/j.cose.2020.101967

Kundu, S., Meng, X., & Basu, K. (2021, April). Application of machine learning in hardware trojan detection. In 2021 22nd International Symposium on Quality Electronic Design (ISQED) (pp. 414-419). IEEE. DOI: 10.1109/ISQED51717.2021.9424362

Kurihara, T., Hasegawa, K., & Togawa, N. (2020, July). Evaluation on hardware-Trojan detection at gate-level IP cores utilizing machine learning methods. In 2020 IEEE 26th International Symposium on On-Line Testing and Robust System Design (IOLTS) (pp. 1-4). IEEE. DOI: 10.1109/IOLTS50870.2020.9159740

LaMorte, W. W. (2019). Behavioral change models: The theory of planned behavior. https://sphweb.bumc.bu.edu/otlt/mphmodules/sb/behavioralchangetheories/BehavioralChangeTheories3.html

Liakos, K. G., Georgakilas, G. K., Moustakidis, S., Karlsson, P., & Plessas, F. C. (2019, November). Machine learning for hardware trojan detection: A review. In *2019 Panhellenic Conference on Electronics & Telecommunications (PACET)* (pp. 1-6). IEEE. DOI: 10.1109/PACET48583.2019.8956251

Liu, J., Huang, Q., Xia, X., Shihab, E., Lo, D., & Li, S. (2020, June). Is using deep learning frameworks free? characterizing technical debt in deep learning frameworks. In *Proceedings of the ACM/IEEE 42nd International Conference on Software* Engineering: Software Engineering in Society (pp. 1-10).

Lubis, M., Wardana, C., & Widjajarto, A. (2020, December). The development of information system security operation centre (SOC): Case study of auto repair company. In 2020 6th International Conference on Interactive Digital Media (ICIDM) (pp. 1–8). IEEE. https://doi.org/DOI: 10.1109/ICIDM51048.2020.9339678

Lyu, S. (2024). *DeepFake the menace: mitigating the negative impacts of AI-generated content. Organizational Cybersecurity Journal: Practice*. Process and People.

M, R. J., G, M., G, B., & P, S. (2023). SVM-RFE enabled feature selection with DMN based centroid update model for incremental data clustering using COVID-19. *Computer Methods in Biomechanics and Biomedical Engineering, 27*(10), 1224–1238. DOI: 10.1080/10255842.2023.2236744

M. Banisakher, D. Mohammed, and M. Omar, "A Cloud-Based Computing Architecture Model of Post-Disaster Management System," *International Journal of Simulation--Systems, Science & Technology*, vol. 19, no. 5, 2018.

M. Basharat and M. Omar, "SecuGuard: Leveraging Pattern-exploiting Training in Language Models for Advanced Software Vulnerability Detection," *International Journal of Mathematics and Computer in Engineering*, 2024.

M. Omar and D. Burrell, "From Text to Threats: A Language Model Approach to Software Vulnerability Detection," *International Journal of Mathematics and Computer in Engineering*, 2023.

M. Omar, "New Insights into Database Security: An Effective and Integrated Approach for Applying Access Control Mechanisms and Cryptographic Concepts in Microsoft Access Environments," 2021.

M. Omar, *Latina Davis Morgan State University 1700 E Cold Spring Ln. Baltimore, MD 21251, USA E-mail: latinaedavis@ hotmail.com*, [n.d.][n.d.].

M. Omar, *Machine Learning for Cybersecurity*, [n.d.][n.d.].

Maalem Lahcen, R. A., Caulkins, B., Mohapatra, R., & Kumar, M. (2020). Review and insight on the behavioral aspects of cybersecurity. *Cybersecurity*, 3(1), 1–18. DOI: 10.1186/s42400-020-00050-w

Mahesh, B. (2020). Machine learning algorithms-a review. [IJSR]. *International Journal of Scientific Research*, 9(1), 381–386.

Maheshwari, R. U., & Paulchamy, B. (2024). Securing online integrity: A hybrid approach to deepfake detection and removal using Explainable AI and Adversarial Robustness Training. *Automatika (Zagreb)*, 65(4), 1517–1532. DOI: 10.1080/00051144.2024.2400640

Majeed, A., & Hwang, S. O. (2023). When AI meets information privacy: The adversarial role of AI in data sharing scenario. *IEEE Access : Practical Innovations, Open Solutions*, 11, 76177–76195. DOI: 10.1109/ACCESS.2023.3297646

Majeed, H. (2020). Watermarking Image Depending on Mojette Transform for Hiding Information. *International Journal on Computer Science and Engineering*, 8, 8–12.

Malatji, M., Von Solms, S., & Marnewick, A. (2019). Socio-Technical Systems Cybersecurity Framework. *Information and Computer Security*, 27(2), 233–272. DOI: 10.1108/ICS-03-2018-0031

Maloof, M. A., & Stephens, G. L. (2016). Using machine learning techniques to identify unusual behavior for network security. *Journal of Machine Learning Research*, 3(5), 373–395.

Mao, R., Zhang, H., Dai, Q., Huang, H., Rong, G., Shen, H., Chen, L., & Lu, K. (2020, December). Preliminary findings of DevSecOps from grey literature. In *2020 IEEE 20th International Conference on Software Quality, Reliability and Security (QRS)* (pp. 450-457). IEEE. https://doi.org/DOI: 10.1109/QRS51102.2020.00064

Marikyan, D., & Papagiannidis, S. (2023). Technology Acceptance Model: A review. In Papagiannidis, S. (Ed.), *TheoryHub Book.*, Available at https://open.ncl.ac.uk /

Maroukian, K., & Gulliver, S. (2020). Exploring the link between leadership and DevOps practice and principle adoption. *Advanced Computing: An International Journal*, 11(4), 1–18. DOI: 10.5121/acij.2020.11401

Marpaung, J. A., & Lee, H. (2013). Dark Seoul cyber attack: Could it be worse? In *Conference of the Indonesian Studies Association in Korea*. Ji-Young, K., In, L. J., & Gon, K. K. (2019, May). The all-purpose sword: North Korea's cyber operations and strategies. In *2019 11th International Conference on Cyber Conflict (CyCon)* (Vol. 900, pp. 1–20). IEEE.

Martin, D. M. (2016). Tracing the lineage of DarkSeoul. Global Information Assurance Certification Paper. © The SANS Institute. https://www.giac.org/paper/gsec/31524/tracing-lineage-darkseoul/126346

Masombuka, T., & Mnkandla, E. (2018, September). A DevOps collaboration culture acceptance model. In *Proceedings of the Annual Conference of the South African Institute of Computer Scientists and Information Technologists* (pp. 279-285). DOI: 10.1145/3278681.3278714

Maurushat, A. (2019). *Ethical hacking*. University of Ottawa Press.

Mavroeidis, V., Hohimer, R., Casey, T., & Jesang, A. (2021, May 1). Threat Actor Type Inference and Characterization within Cyber Threat Intelligence. IEEE Xplore. https://doi.org/DOI: 10.23919/CyCon51939.2021.9468305

McCord, M. (2007). Technology acceptance model. In *Handbook of research on electronic surveys and measurements* (pp. 306–308). IGI Global. DOI: 10.4018/978-1-59140-792-8.ch038

McDaniel, G. (Ed.). (1994). *IBM Dictionary of computing*.

McNeese, M., Cooke, N. J., D'Amico, A., Endsley, M. R., Gonzalez, C., Roth, E., & Salas, E. (2012). Perspectives on the role of cognition in Cyber Security. *Proceedings of the Human Factors and Ergonomics Society Annual Meeting*, 56(1), 268–271. DOI: 10.1177/1071181312561063

McNicholas, E., & Angle, K. (2022) Cybersecurity Laws and Regulations USA 2023, ICLG 2022-11-14 https://iclg.com/practice-areas/cybersecurity-laws-and-regulations/usa

Mehta, P. D., & Neale, M. C. (2005). People are variables too: Multilevel structural equation modeling. *Psychological Methods*, 10(3), 259–284. DOI: 10.1037/1082-989X.10.3.259 PMID: 16221028

Meng, X., Hassan, R., Dinakrrao, S. M. P., & Basu, K. (2021, May). Can overclocking detect hardware Trojans? In *2021 IEEE International Symposium on Circuits and Systems (ISCAS)* (pp. 1-5). IEEE.

Microsoft Updates for Multiple Vulnerabilities | CISA. (2013, January 24). Cybersecurity and Infrastructure Security Agency CISA. https://www.cisa.gov/news-events/alerts/2012/07/10/microsoft-updates-multiple-vulnerabilities

Millerd, P. (2022, June 7). *Edgar Schein - organizational culture: Artifacts, values & assumptions*. Boundless by Paul Millerd. https://think-boundless.com/edgar-scheins-anxiety-assumptions-powerful-ideas-on-culture/

Mills, R., Hussain, R., & Krishnamurthy, M. (2020). Sentiment Analysis for Insider Threat Detection in Email Communication. *Journal of Cybersecurity Insights*, 4(1), 33–47.

Ministry of National Defense. Republic of Korea. War History Compilation Committee. (1972). Cheonchaengsa [History of the Korean War]. Ministry of National Defense, Republic of Korea.

Mohammed and M. Omar. "Decision Trees Unleashed: Simplifying IoT Malware Detection With Advanced AI Techniques," in *Innovations, Securities, and Case Studies Across Healthcare, Business, and Technology*, pp. 240-258, IGI Global, 2024.

Mohammed, H., Howell, J., Hasan, S. R., Guo, N., Khalid, F., & Elkeelany, O. (2018, August). Hardware trojan based security issues in home area network: A testbed setup. In 2018 IEEE 61st International Midwest Symposium on Circuits and Systems (MWSCAS) (pp. 972-975). IEEE. DOI: 10.1109/MWSCAS.2018.8624048

Mohammed, D., Omar, M., & Nguyen, V. (2018). Wireless sensor network security: Approaches to detecting and avoiding wormhole attacks. *Journal of Research in Business. Economics and Management*, 10(2), 1860–1864.

Mohammed, H., Hasan, S. R., & Awwad, F. (2020). Fusion-on-field security and privacy preservation for IoT edge devices: Concurrent defense against multiple types of hardware trojan attacks. *IEEE Access : Practical Innovations, Open Solutions*, 8, 36847–36862. DOI: 10.1109/ACCESS.2020.2975016

Mohammed, M. O., & Nguyen, V. (2017). Enhancing Cyber Security for Financial Industry through Compliance and Regulatory Standards. In *Security Solutions for Hyperconnectivity and the Internet of Things* (pp. 113–129). IGI Global. DOI: 10.4018/978-1-5225-0741-3.ch005

Mohammed, M. O., & Nguyen, V. (2018). Wireless Sensor Network Security: Approaches to Detecting and Avoiding Wormhole Attacks. *Journal of Research in Business, Economics and Management*, 10(2), 1860–1864.

Mondal, A., Karmakar, S., Mahalat, M. H., Roy, S., Sen, B., & Chattopadhyay, A. (2022). Hardware Trojan Detection using Transition Probability with Minimal Test Vectors. *ACM Transactions on Embedded Computing Systems*, 22(1), 1–21. DOI: 10.1145/3545000

Montasari, R. (2023). *Countering cyberterrorism: the confluence of artificial intelligence, cyber forensics and digital policing in US and UK national cybersecurity* (Vol. 101). Springer Nature. DOI: 10.1007/978-3-031-21920-7

Moore, T. Introducing the Economics of Cybersecurity: Principles and Policy Options. Deterring Cyberattacks: Informing Strategies and Developing Options for U. S. Policy, https://www.nap.edu/read/12997/chapter/3, last accessed 2019/10/23.

Moustafa, N. (2022). *Digital Forensics in the Era of Artificial Intelligence*. CRC Press. DOI: 10.1201/9781003278962

Moustafa, N., Koroniotis, N., Keshk, M., Zomaya, A. Y., & Tari, Z. (2023). Explainable intrusion detection for cyber defences in the internet of things: Opportunities and solutions. *IEEE Communications Surveys and Tutorials*, 25(3), 1775–1807. DOI: 10.1109/COMST.2023.3280465

Mughal, A. A. (2019). A comprehensive study of practical techniques and methodologies in incident-based approaches for cyber forensics. *Tensorgate Journal of Sustainable Technology and Infrastructure for Developing Countries*, 2(1), 1–18.

Murphy, J. P. (2022). *Digital Forensic Investigations and Automated and Artificial Intelligence Technologies* (Master's thesis, Utica University).

Myrbakken, H., & Colomo-Palacios, R. (2017, October). DevSecOps: A multivocal literature review. In *International conference on software process improvement and capability determination* (pp. 17-29). Springer, Cham. DOI: 10.1007/978-3-319-67383-7_2

Nabil, M., Soukainat, S., Lakbabi, A., & Ghizlane, O. (2017, May). SIEM selection criteria for an efficient contextual security. In 2017 international symposium on networks, computers and communications (ISNCC) (pp. 1–6). IEEE. DOI: 10.1109/ISNCC.2017.8072035

Nah, L. T. (2023). North Korean hackers: Vigilance against better than underestimation of. North Korean Review, 19(1), 91–98. https://www.jstor.org/stable/27217098

Naidu, G., Zuva, T., & Sibanda, E. M. (2023, April). A review of evaluation metrics in machine learning algorithms. In *Computer Science On-line Conference* (pp. 15-25). Cham: Springer International Publishing. DOI: 10.1007/978-3-031-35314-7_2

Nair, M. M., Deshmukh, A., & Tyagi, A. K. (2024). Artificial intelligence for cyber security: Current trends and future challenges. *Automated Secure Computing for Next-Generation Systems*, 83-114.

National Cybersecurity and Communications Integration Center. (2013, March 27). *South Korean malware attack.* U.S. Department of Homeland Security. https://www.nab.org/xert/scitech/pdfs/20130328_South%20Korean%20Malware.pdf

National Institute for Cybersecurity Education Working Group (NICE). (2018). Cybersecurity is everyone's job. National Institute of Standards and Technology. Retrieved from https://www.nist.gov/system/files/documents/2018/10/15/cybersecurity_is_everyones_job_v1.0.pdf

Naveenkumar, R., & Sivamangai, N. M. (2024). Hardware Trojans Detection and Prevention Techniques Review. *Wireless Personal Communications*, 136(2), 1147–1182. DOI: 10.1007/s11277-024-11334-6

Nguyen, V., Omar, M., Mohammed, D., & Dean, P. "Net Neutrality Around the Globe: A Survey," in *2020 3rd International Conference on Information and Computer Technologies (ICICT)*, pp. 480-488, IEEE, 2020. DOI: 10.1109/ICICT50521.2020.00083

Nguyen, V., Mohammed, D., Omar, M., & Banisakher, M. (2018). The Effects of the FCC Net Neutrality Repeal on Security and Privacy. [IJHIoT]. *International Journal of Hyperconnectivity and the Internet of Things*, 2(2), 21–29. DOI: 10.4018/IJHIoT.2018070102

Niel Chah. (2014). North Korea: cyber threat perception and metadata analysis. https://doi.org/DOI: 10.14288/1.0165997

Nieles, M., Dempsey, K., & Pillitteri, V. Y. (2017). An introduction to information security. *NIST SP 800-12 Rev. 1.* DOI: 10.6028/NIST.SP.800-12r1

Nir Kshetri. (2016). Cybersecurity in South Korea. Springer EBooks, 171–182. https://doi.org/DOI: 10.1007/978-3-319-40554-4_10

Nobles, C. (2018). Botching human factors in cybersecurity in business organizations. *HOLISTICA–Journal of Business and Public Administration*, 9(3), 71–88. DOI: 10.2478/hjbpa-2018-0024

Nobles, C., Robinson, N., Cunningham, M., & Cunningham, M. (2022). Straight from the Human Factors Professionals' mouth: The need to teach human factors in cybersecurity. *Proceedings of the 23rd Annual Conference on Information Technology Education*, 157–158. DOI: 10.1145/3537674.3555782

Nocera, F., Demilito, S., Ladisa, P., Mongiello, M., Shah, A. A., Ahmad, J., & Di Sciascio, E. (2022, May). A user behavior analytics (uba)-based solution using lstm neural network to mitigate ddos attack in fog and cloud environment. In 2022 2nd International Conference of Smart Systems and Emerging Technologies (SMARTTECH) (pp. 74-79). IEEE.

North Korea's Cyber Operations. (2016). Google Books. https://books.google.com/books?hl=en&lr=&id=hUpQCwAAQBAJ&oi=fnd&pg=PR3&dq=Jun

Novetta. (2016). *Operation Blockbuster: Unraveling the long thread of the Sony attack.* Novetta Advanced Analytics. Retrieved from https://www.operationblockbuster.com

O. I. Al-Sanjary, A. A. Ahmed, H. M. Zangana, M. Ali, S. Aldulaimi, and M. Alkawaz, "An Investigation of the Characteristics and Performance of Hybrid Routing Protocol in (MANET)," *International Journal of Engineering & Technology*, vol. 7, no. 4.22, pp. 49-54, 2018.

Oakley Browne, T., Abedin, M., & Chowdhury, M. J. M. (2024). A systematic review on research utilising artificial intelligence for open source intelligence (OSINT) applications.

Omar, M. (2021). New insights into database security: An effective and integrated approach for applying access control mechanisms and cryptographic concepts in Microsoft Access environments.

Omar, M. (2022). *Machine Learning for Cybersecurity: Innovative Deep Learning Solutions.* Springer Brief. https://link.springer.com/book/978303115

Omar, M. (2024). From Attack to Defense: Strengthening DNN Text Classification Against Adversarial Examples. In *Innovations, Securities, and Case Studies Across Healthcare, Business, and Technology* (pp. 174-195). IGI Global.

Omar, M. (2024). Revolutionizing Malware Detection: A Paradigm Shift Through Optimized Convolutional Neural Networks. In *Innovations, Securities, and Case Studies Across Healthcare, Business, and Technology* (pp. 196-220). IGI Global. DOI: 10.4018/979-8-3693-1906-2.ch011

Omar, M. "Application of Machine Learning (ML) to Address Cybersecurity Threats," in *Machine Learning for Cybersecurity: Innovative Deep Learning Solutions*, pp. 1-11, Springer International Publishing Cham, 2022. DOI: 10.1007/978-3-031-15893-3_1

Omar, M. "Cloud Computing Security: Abuse and Nefarious Use of Cloud Computing," in *Handbook of Research on Security Considerations in Cloud Computing*, pp. 30-38, IGI Global, 2015. DOI: 10.4018/978-1-4666-8387-7.ch002

Omar, M. "From Attack to Defense: Strengthening DNN Text Classification Against Adversarial Examples," in *Innovations, Securities, and Case Studies Across Healthcare, Business, and Technology*, pp. 174-195, IGI Global, 2024. DOI: 10.4018/979-8-3693-1906-2.ch010

Omar, M. "Insider Threats: Detecting and Controlling Malicious Insiders," in *New Threats and Countermeasures in Digital Crime and Cyber Terrorism*, pp. 162-172, IGI Global, 2015. DOI: 10.4018/978-1-4666-8345-7.ch009

Omar, M. "Malware Anomaly Detection Using Local Outlier Factor Technique," in *Machine Learning for Cybersecurity: Innovative Deep Learning Solutions*, pp. 37-48, Springer International Publishing Cham, 2022. DOI: 10.1007/978-3-031-15893-3_3

Omar, M. *Defending Cyber Systems through Reverse Engineering of Criminal Malware*, Springer Brief, [n.d.][n.d.] https://link.springer.com/book/9783031116278

Omar, M. *Machine Learning for Cybersecurity: Innovative Deep Learning Solutions*, Springer Brief, 2022. https://link.springer.com/book/978303115

Omar, M. *Smartphone Security: Defending Android-based Smartphone Against Emerging Malware Attacks* (Doctoral dissertation, Colorado Technical University), 2012.

Omar, M., & Burrell, D. N. "Organizational Dynamics and Bias in Artificial Intelligence (AI) Recruitment Algorithms," in *Evolution of Cross-Sector Cyber Intelligent Markets*, pp. 269-290, IGI Global, 2024.

Omar, M., & Mohaisen, D. "Making Adversarially-Trained Language Models Forget with Model Retraining: A Case Study on Hate Speech Detection," in *Companion Proceedings of the Web Conference 2022*, pp. 887-893, 2022. DOI: 10.1145/3487553.3524667

Omar, M., & Shiaeles, S. "VulDetect: A Novel Technique for Detecting Software Vulnerabilities Using Language Models," in *2023 IEEE International Conference on Cyber Security and Resilience (CSR)*, IEEE. https://ieeexplore.ieee.org/document/10224924

Omar, M., & Sukthankar, G. "Text-Defend: Detecting Adversarial Examples Using Local Outlier Factor," in *2023 IEEE 17th International Conference on Semantic Computing (ICSC)*, pp. 118-122, IEEE, 2023. DOI: 10.1109/ICSC56153.2023.00026

Omar, M., Gouveia, L. B., Al-Karaki, J., & Mohammed, D. "Reverse-Engineering Malware," in *Cybersecurity Capabilities in Developing Nations and Its Impact on Global Security*, pp. 194-217, IGI Global, 2022. DOI: 10.4018/978-1-7998-8693-8.ch010

Omar, M., Jones, R., Burrell, D. N., Dawson, M., Nobles, C., & Mohammed, D. "Harnessing the Power and Simplicity of Decision Trees to Detect IoT Malware," in *Transformational Interventions for Business, Technology, and Healthcare*, pp. 215-229, IGI, 2023. DOI: 10.4018/979-8-3693-1634-4.ch013

Omar, M., Mohammed, D., Nguyen, V., Dawson, M., & Banisakher, M. "Android Application Security," in *Research Anthology on Securing Mobile Technologies and Applications*, pp. 610-625, IGI Global, 2021. DOI: 10.4018/978-1-7998-8545-0.ch034

Omar, M. (2019). A World of Cyber Attacks. *Survey (London, England).*

Omar, M. "VulDefend: A Novel Technique Based on Pattern-Exploiting Training for Detecting Software Vulnerabilities Using Language Models," in *2023 IEEE Jordan International Joint Conference on Electrical Engineering and Information Technology (JEEIT)*, pp. 287-293, IEEE, 2023. DOI: 10.1109/JEEIT58638.2023.10185860

Omar, M.. (2024). Committee Members. *Journal of Physics: Conference Series*, 2711, 011001.

Omar, M., Choi, S., Nyang, D., & Mohaisen, D. (2022). Robust Natural Language Processing: Recent Advances, Challenges, and Future Directions. *IEEE Access : Practical Innovations, Open Solutions*, 10, 86038–86056. DOI: 10.1109/ACCESS.2022.3197769

Omar, M., Choi, S., Nyang, D., & Mohaisen, D. "Quantifying the Performance of Adversarial Training on Language Models with Distribution Shifts," in *Proceedings of the 1st Workshop on Cybersecurity and Social Sciences*, pp. 3-9, 2022. DOI: 10.1145/3494108.3522764

Omar, M., & Dawson, M. "Research in Progress-Defending Android Smartphones from Malware Attacks," in *2013 Third International Conference on Advanced Computing and Communication Technologies (ACCT)*, pp. 288-292, IEEE, 2013. DOI: 10.1109/ACCT.2013.69

Omar, M., Mohammed, D., & Nguyen, V. (2017). Defending Against Malicious Insiders: A Conceptual Framework for Predicting, Detecting, and Deterring Malicious Insiders. *International Journal of Business Process Integration and Management*, 8(2), 114–119. DOI: 10.1504/IJBPIM.2017.083794

Omar, M., & Zangana, H. M. (Eds.). (2024). *Redefining Security With Cyber AI*. IGI Global., DOI: 10.4018/979-8-3693-6517-5

Onwubiko, C. (2020, June). Focusing on the recovery aspects of cyber resilience. In *2020 International Conference on Cyber Situational Awareness, Data Analytics and Assessment (CyberSA)* (pp. 1–13). IEEE. https://doi.org/DOI: 10.1109/CyberSA49311.2020.9139685

Orazi, G., Vallittu, K., Sainio, P., & Virtanen, S. (2020). Enhancing and integration of security testing in the development of a microservices environment. https://www.utupub.fi/bitstream/handle/10024/150701/orazi_master_thesis.pdf?sequence=1

Pakshad, P., Shameli-Sendi, A., & Khalaji Emamzadeh Abbasi, B. (2023). A security vulnerability predictor based on source code metrics. *Journal of Computer Virology and Hacking Techniques*, 19(4), 615–633. DOI: 10.1007/s11416-023-00469-y

Pan, C., Zhong, W., & Mei, S. (2015). Finding the weakest link in the interdependent security chain using the analytic hierarchy process. *Journal of Advances in Computer Networks*, 3(4), 320–325. DOI: 10.18178/JACN.2015.3.4.190

Pandey, A. (2019, June 14). Why do enterprises need Security operations center? https://www.proquest.com/magazines/why-do-enterprises-need-security-operations/docview/2239621832/se-2

Papain, T. (2011). North Korea and cyberwarfare: How North Korea's cyber attacks violate the laws of war. In J. Korean L., 11, 29. Heinonline.org. https://heinonline.org/HOL/Page?handle=hein.journals/jkorl11&div=6&g_sent=1&casa_token=&collection=journals

Park, C., & Kim, H. (2024). A Study on the Change of Cyber Attacks in North Korea. *The Journal of the Convergence on Culture Technology*, 10(4), 175–181. DOI: 10.17703/JCCT.2024.10.4.175

Park, J. M., Rowe, N., & Cisneros, M. (2016). Responding to North Korean cyber-attacks. In *Eccws 2016 - Proceedings of the 15th European Conference on Cyber Warfare and Security* (pp. 245–251). Academic Conferences International Limited., https://books.google.com/books?hl=en&lr=&id=ijaeDAAAQBAJ&oi=fnd&pg=PA245

Pasqualicchio, V. T. (2019). Behind the Cyber Walls of North Korea (Order No. 27671005). Available from ProQuest Dissertations & Theses Global. (2378940811). https://ezproxy.gl.iit.edu/login?url=https://www.proquest.com/dissertations-theses/behind-cyber-walls-north-korea/docview/2378940811/se-2

Patrascu, P. (2019). Promoting cybersecurity culture through education. *eLearning and Software for Education, Vol. II.* DOI: 10.12753/2066-026X-19-108

Pauu, K. T., Pan, Q., Wu, J., Bashir, A. K., & Omar, M. "IRS-Aided Federated Learning with Dynamic Differential Privacy for UAVs in Emergency Response," *IEEE Internet of Things Magazine*, vol. 7, no. 4, pp. 108-115, IEEE, 2024. DOI: 10.1109/IOTM.001.2400021

Pavlou, C. (2023, October 26). *The psychology of gamification: Motivating employees during Cybersecurity training*. eLearning Industry. https://elearningindustry.com/the-psychology-of-gamification-motivating-employees-during-cybersecurity-training

Pelgrin, W. (2014). A Model For Positive Change: Influencing Positive Change in Cyber Security Strategy, Human Factor, and Leadership. *Best Practices in Computer Network Defense: Incident Detection and Response*, 107–137. DOI: 10.3233/978-1-61499-372-8-107

Peng, Y.. (2024). *"An Intelligent Resource Allocation Strategy with Slicing and Auction for Private Edge Cloud Systems," Future Generation Computer Systems* (Vol. 160). North-Holland.

Peters, M. E., Neumann, M., Iyyer, M., Gardner, M., Clark, C., Lee, K., & Zettlemoyer, L. (2018). *Deep contextualized word representations*. NAACL-HLT. DOI: 10.18653/v1/N18-1202

Peterson, D. C., Adams, A., Sanders, S., & Sanford, B. (2018). Assessing and addressing threats and risks to cybersecurity. *Frontiers of Health Services Management*, 35(1), 23–29. DOI: 10.1097/HAP.0000000000000040 PMID: 30124511

Philip, J. (2021). Viewing digital transformation through the lens of transformational leadership. *Journal of Organizational Computing and Electronic Commerce*, 31(2), 114–129. DOI: 10.1080/10919392.2021.1911573

Pickford, H. (2024, March 12). *Organizational citizenship behaviours: Definitions and dimensions*. Economics of Mutuality Alliance. https://eom.org/literature-reviews/organizational-citizenship-behaviours/

Pijnacker, L. (2023, September 19). *HR analytics: Role clarity impacts performance*. Effectory. https://www.effectory.com/knowledge/hr-analytics-role-clarity-impacts-performance/

Piraianu, A. I., Fulga, A., Musat, C. L., Ciobotaru, O. R., Poalelungi, D. G., Stamate, E., Ciobotaru, O., & Fulga, I. (2023). Enhancing the evidence with algorithms: How artificial intelligence is transforming forensic medicine. *Diagnostics (Basel)*, 13(18), 2992. DOI: 10.3390/diagnostics13182992 PMID: 37761359

Pollini, A., Callari, T. C., Tedeschi, A., Ruscio, D., Save, L., Chiarugi, F., & Guerri, D. (2021). Leveraging human factors in cybersecurity: An integrated methodological approach. *Cognition Technology and Work*, 24(2), 371–390. DOI: 10.1007/s10111-021-00683-y PMID: 34149309

Prasad, N. S. (1989). *IBM mainframes: architecture and design*. McGraw-Hill, Inc.

Prince, B. (2013, June 27). South Korea Cyber Attack Tied to DarkSeoul Crew: Symantec. SecurityWeek. https://www.securityweek.com/south-korea-cyber-attack-tied-darkseoul-crew-symantec/

Provost, F., & Fawcett, T. (2013). *Data Science for Business: What You Need to Know about Data Mining and Data-Analytic Thinking*. O'Reilly Media.

Prümmer, J., van Steen, T., & van den Berg, B. (2024). A systematic review of current cybersecurity training methods. *Computers & Security*, 136, 103585. Advance online publication. DOI: 10.1016/j.cose.2023.103585

Prvan, M., & Ožegović, J. (2020). Methods in teaching computer networks: A literature review. [TOCE]. *ACM Transactions on Computing Education*, 20(3), 1–35. DOI: 10.1145/3394963

Rafi, S., Yu, W., & Akbar, M. A. (2020). Towards a hypothetical framework to secure DevOps adoption: Grounded theory approach. In *Proceedings of the evaluation and assessment in software engineering* (pp. 457-462). https://doi.org/DOI: 10.1145/3383219.3383285

Rajapakse, R. N., Zahedi, M., Babar, M. A., & Shen, H. (2021). Challenges and solutions when adopting DevSecOps: A systematic review. *Information and Software Technology*, 141, 106700. Advance online publication. DOI: 10.1016/j.infsof.2021.106700

Rajesh, R.. (2024). Threat Detection and Mitigation for Tactile Internet Driven Consumer IoT-Healthcare System. *IEEE Transactions on Consumer Electronics*.

Rane, N., Choudhary, S., & Rane, J. (2024). Machine Learning and Deep Learning: a Comprehensive Review on Methods, Techniques, Applications, Challenges, and Future Directions. *Techniques, Applications, Challenges, and Future Directions (May 31, 2024)*.

Raska, M. (2020). North Korea's Evolving Cyber Strategies: Continuity and Change. SIRIUS – Zeitschrift Für Strategische Analysen, 4(2), 1–13. https://doi.org/DOI: 10.1515/sirius-2020-3030

Raska, M. (2022). North Korea's evolving cyber strategies and operations: Toward weapons of mass effectiveness. In *North Korea's foreign policy*. Google Books., https://books.google.com/books?hl=en&lr=&id=mXufEAAAQBAJ&oi=fnd&pg=PA173

Rauf, U., Mohsen, F., & Wei, Z. (2023). A taxonomic classification of insider threats: Existing techniques, future directions & recommendations. *Journal of Cyber Security and Mobility*, 12(2), 221–252. DOI: 10.13052/jcsm2245-1439.1225

Redmiles, E., Malone, A., & Mazurek, M. L. (2015). How I learned to be secure: Advice sources and personality factors in cybersecurity. In *Proceedings of the 2016 ACM SIGSAC conference on computer and communications security* (pp. 666–677). https://doi.org/DOI: 10.1108/K-05-2018-0226

Reegard, K., Blackett, C., & Katta, V. (2019). Proceedings of the 29th European Safety and Reliability Conference (ESREL). *Proceedings of the 29th European Safety and Reliability Conference*, 4036–4043. DOI: 10.3850/978-981-11-2724-3_0761-cd

Regulation, G. D. P. (2018). General Data Protection Regulation (GDPR). *Intersoft Consulting, Accessed in October, 24*(1).

Rezvani, S., & Wang, X. (2023). A broad review on class imbalance learning techniques. *Applied Soft Computing*, 143, 110415. DOI: 10.1016/j.asoc.2023.110415

Ribeiro, M. T., Singh, S., & Guestrin, C. (2016). "Why should I trust you?" Explaining the predictions of any classifier. *Proceedings of the 22nd ACM SIGKDD International Conference on Knowledge Discovery and Data Mining*, 1135-1144.

Rizvi, S., Scanlon, M., Mcgibney, J., & Sheppard, J. (2022). Application of artificial intelligence to network forensics: Survey, challenges and future directions. *IEEE Access : Practical Innovations, Open Solutions*, 10, 110362–110384. DOI: 10.1109/ACCESS.2022.3214506

Robinson, N. (2023). Human Factors Security Engineering: The future of cybersecurity teams. *EDPACS*, 67(5), 1–17. DOI: 10.1080/07366981.2023.2211429

Rohatgi, S., Abinash, B., Joshi, S., Sushant, S., & Kumar, S. (2023). Introduction to Artificial Intelligence and Cybersecurity for Industry. In *Artificial Intelligence and Cyber Security in Industry 4.0* (pp. 1–22). Springer Nature Singapore. DOI: 10.1007/978-981-99-2115-7_1

Ron, F., & Porod, C. (2021). Motivating employees and organizations to adopt a cybersecurity-focused culture. *Journal of Organizational Psychology*, 21(1), 114–131. DOI: 10.33423/jop.v21i1.4030

Roshanaei, M., Khan, M. R., & Sylvester, N. N. (2024). Navigating AI Cybersecurity: Evolving Landscape and Challenges. *Journal of Intelligent Learning Systems and Applications*, 16(3), 155–174. DOI: 10.4236/jilsa.2024.163010

Rowse, M., & Cohen, J. (2021, January). A Survey of DevOps in the South African software context. In Proceedings of the 54th Hawaii international conference on system sciences (p. 6785). http://hdl.handle.net/10125/71435

Russo, K., & Rishikof, H. Cybersecurity: Executive Orders, Legislation, Cyberattacks, and Hot Topics, 19 Chap. L. Rev. 421 (2016). Available at: https://digitalcommons.chapman.edu/chapman-law-review/vol19/iss2/4

Sadiq Nasir, S. N., & Nasir, S. (2023). Exploring the effectiveness of cybersecurity training programs: Factors, best practices, and future directions. *Advances in Multidisciplinary and Scientific Research Journal Publication*, 2(1), 151–160. DOI: 10.22624/AIMS/CSEAN-SMART2023P18

Saleem, M. A.. (2023). Provably Secure Conditional-Privacy Access Control Protocol for Intelligent Customers-Centric Communication in VANET. *IEEE Transactions on Consumer Electronics*.

Samtani, S., Kantarcioglu, M., & Chen, H. (2020). Trailblazing the artificial intelligence for cybersecurity discipline: A multi-disciplinary research roadmap. [TMIS]. *ACM Transactions on Management Information Systems*, 11(4), 1–19. DOI: 10.1145/3430360

Sánchez-Gordón, M., & Colomo-Palacios, R. (2020, June). Security as culture: A systematic literature review of DevSecOps. In *Proceedings of the IEEE/ACM 42nd international conference on software engineering workshops* (pp. 266–269). https://doi.org/DOI: 10.1145/3387940.3392233

Sanger, D. E., Kirkpatrick, D. D., & Perlroth, N. (2017, October 15). The World Once Laughed at North Korean Cyberpower. No More. The New York Times. https://www.nytimes.com/2017/10/15/world/asia/north-korea-hacking-cyber-sony.html

Sankaran, S., Mohan, V. S., & Purushothaman, A. (2021, December). Deep learning based approach for hardware trojan detection. In 2021 IEEE International Symposium on Smart Electronic Systems (iSES) (pp. 177-182). IEEE. DOI: 10.1109/iSES52644.2021.00050

Sarros, J. C., & Santora, J. C. (2001). The transformational-transactional leadership model in practice. *Leadership and Organization Development Journal*, 22(8), 383–394. DOI: 10.1108/01437730110410107

Sayyafzadeh, S. (2024). *Thumbnail Image Forensic Acquisition and Analysis in the Age of Artificial Intelligence* (Master's thesis, Florida Agricultural and Mechanical University).

Settanni, G., Shovgenya, Y., Skopik, F., Graf, R., Wurzenberger, M., & Fiedler, R. (2017, June). Acquiring cyber threat intelligence through security information correlation. In 2017 3rd IEEE international conference on cybernetics (CYBCONF) (pp. 1–7). IEEE. https://doi.org/DOI: 10.1109/CYBConf.2017.7985754

Shillair, R. (2020a). Protection motivation theory. *The International Encyclopedia of Media Psychology*, 1–3. DOI: 10.1002/9781119011071.iemp0188

Shin, Y., Lee, J., & Kim, M. (2018). Preventing State-Led Cyberattacks Using the Bright Internet and Internet Peace Principles. *Journal of the Association for Information Systems*, 19(3), 152–181. DOI: 10.17705/1jais.00488

Shoeib, M., Shalaginov, A., & Tian, Y. (2020). Insider threat detection using machine learning: A survey. *Computers & Security*, 92, 101736.

Shukla, M., Tupsamudre, H., & Lodha, S. (2022). Enterprise security: Modern challenges and emerging measures. In *Research anthology on business aspects of cybersecurity* (pp. 441–470). IGI Global., DOI: 10.4018/978-1-6684-3698-1.ch021

Shutock, M., & Dietrich, G. (2022, January). Security operations centers: A holistic view on problems and solutions. In Proceedings of the 55th Hawaii international conference on system sciences. http://hdl.handle.net/10125/80249

Siangchokyoo, N., Klinger, R. L., & Campion, E. D. (2020). Follower transformation as the linchpin of transformational leadership theory: A systematic review and future research agenda. *The Leadership Quarterly*, 31(1), 101341. Advance online publication. DOI: 10.1016/j.leaqua.2019.101341

Siers, R. (2014). NORTH KOREA: THE CYBER WILD CARD. *Journal of Law & Cyber Warfare*, 4(1), 1–12. https://www.jstor.org/stable/26441246

Sikos, L. F. (2021). AI in digital forensics: Ontology engineering for cybercrime investigations. *WIREs Forensic Science*, 3(3), e1394. DOI: 10.1002/wfs2.1394

Sindiramutty, S. R., Prabagaran, K. R. V., Akbar, R., Hussain, M., & Malik, N. A. (2025). Overview of Generative AI Techniques for Cybersecurity. *Reshaping CyberSecurity With Generative AI Techniques*, 1-52.

Singla, J. (2024). Safeguarding the Future: Advancements in Cybersecurity. *Utilizing Generative AI for Cyber Defense Strategies*, 421.

Sinha, S., & Arora, D. Y. (2020). Ethical hacking: the story of a white hat hacker. *International Journal of Innovative Research in Computer Science & Technology (IJIRCST), ISSN*, 2347-5552.

Sobers, R. (2024, January 4). *161 cybersecurity statistics and trends [updated 2023]*. Varonis. https://www.varonis.com/blog/cybersecurity-statistics

Stutz, D., de Assis, J. T., Laghari, A. A., Khan, A. A., Andreopoulos, N., Terziev, A., ... & Grata, E. G. (2024). Enhancing Security in Cloud Computing Using Artificial Intelligence (AI). *Applying Artificial Intelligence in Cybersecurity Analytics and Cyber Threat Detection*, 179-220.

Sulaiman, N. S., Fauzi, M. A., Hussain, S., & Wider, W. (2022). Cybersecurity behavior among government employees: The role of protection motivation theory and responsibility in mitigating cyberattacks. *Information (Basel)*, 13(9), 413. DOI: 10.3390/info13090413

Sultana, K. Z., Boyd, C. B., & Williams, B. J.Kazi Zakia Sultana. (2023). A Software Vulnerability Prediction Model Using Traceable Code Patterns and Software Metrics. SN Computer Science. *SN Computer Science*, 4(5), 599. Advance online publication. DOI: 10.1007/s42979-023-02077-5

Sun, Y., Xu, T., Bashir, A. K., Liu, J., & Omar, M. "BcIIS: Blockchain-Based Intelligent Identification Scheme of Massive IoT Devices," in *GLOBECOM 2023-2023 IEEE Global Communications Conference*, pp. 1277-1282, IEEE, 2023. DOI: 10.1109/GLOBECOM54140.2023.10437203

Syed, F. M., & ES, F. K. (2024). AI-Driven Forensic Analysis for Cyber Incidents in Healthcare. *International Journal of Machine Learning Research in Cybersecurity and Artificial Intelligence*, 15(1), 473–499.

Takale, D. G., Mahalle, P. N., & Sule, B. (2024). Cyber Security Challenges in Generative AI Technology. *Journal of Network Security Computer Networks*, 10(1), 28–34.

Tang, Y., Khatchadourian, R., Bagherzadeh, M., Singh, R., Stewart, A., & Raja, A. (2021, May). An empirical study of refactorings and technical debt in machine learning systems. In *2021 IEEE/ACM 43rd international conference on software engineering (ICSE)* (pp. 238-250). IEEE. DOI: 10.1109/ICSE43902.2021.00033

Tao, F., Akhtar, M. S., & Jiayuan, Z. (2021). The future of artificial intelligence in cybersecurity: A comprehensive survey. *EAI Endorsed Transactions on Creative Technologies*, 8(28), e3–e3. DOI: 10.4108/eai.7-7-2021.170285

Tao, Y., Wu, J., Pan, Q., Bashir, A. K., & Omar, M. (2024). O-RAN-Based Digital Twin Function Virtualization for Sustainable IoV Service Response: An Asynchronous Hierarchical Reinforcement Learning Approach. *IEEE Transactions on Green Communications and Networking*, 8(3), 1049–1060. DOI: 10.1109/TGCN.2024.3435796

Terfloth, L., Budde, L., & Schulte, C. (2020). Combining ideas and artifacts: An interaction-focused view on computing education using a cybersecurity example. *Koli Calling '20:Proceedings of the 20th Koli Calling International Conference on Computing Education Research*. DOI: 10.1145/3428029.3428052

Tiwari, N., Ghadi, Y., & Omar, M. "Analysis of Ultrasound Images in Kidney Failure Diagnosis Using Deep Learning," in *Transformational Interventions for Business, Technology, and Healthcare*, pp. 45-74, IGI Global, 2023. DOI: 10.4018/979-8-3693-1634-4.ch004

Tiwari, N., Omar, M., & Ghadi, Y. "Brain Tumor Classification From Magnetic Resonance Imaging Using Deep Learning and Novel Data Augmentation," in *Transformational Interventions for Business, Technology, and Healthcare*, pp. 392-413, IGI Global, 2023. DOI: 10.4018/979-8-3693-1634-4.ch023

Tomas, N., Li, J., & Huang, H. (2019, June). An empirical study on culture, automation, measurement, and sharing of DevSecOps. In 2019 International conference on cyber security and protection of digital services (cyber security) (pp. 1–8). IEEE. https://doi.org/DOI: 10.1109/CyberSecPODS.2019.8884935

Trihinas, D., Tryfonos, A., Dikaiakos, M. D., & Pallis, G. (2018). DevOps as a service: Pushing the boundaries of microservice adoption. *IEEE Internet Computing*, 22(3), 65–71. DOI: 10.1109/MIC.2018.032501519

Trim, P. R. J., & Lee, Y.-I. (2010). A security framework for protecting business, government and society from cyber attacks. 2010 5th International Conference on System of Systems Engineering. https://doi.org/DOI: 10.1109/SYSOSE.2010.5544085

Trim, P. R., & Lee, Y. (2022). Combining sociocultural intelligence with artificial intelligence to increase organizational cyber security provision through enhanced resilience. *Big Data and Cognitive Computing*, 6(4), 110. Advance online publication. DOI: 10.3390/bdcc6040110

Tshilidzi, M. "Data Is the Lifeblood of the Global Economy, but Restrictions on Cross-border Data Flows Are a Reality," United Nations University, UNU Centre, 2023-08-17, https://unu.edu/article/data-lifeblood-global-economy-restrictions-cross-border-data-flows-are-reality

Tuli, F. A., & Thaduri, U. R. (2023). The Integration of Artificial Intelligence in Forensic Accounting: A Game-Changer. *Asian Accounting and Auditing Advancement*, 14(1), 12–20.

Turel, O., Xu, Z., & Guo, K. (2017). Organizational Citizenship Behavior Regarding Security: Leadership Approach Perspective. *Journal of Computer Information Systems*, 60(1), 61–75. DOI: 10.1080/08874417.2017.1400928

Tyagi, A. K., & Addula, S. R. (2024). Artificial Intelligence for Malware Analysis: A Systematic Study. *Artificial Intelligence-Enabled Digital Twin for Smart Manufacturing*, 359-390.

Tyagi, A. K., Kumari, S., & Richa. (2024). Artificial Intelligence-Based Cyber Security and Digital Forensics: A Review. *Artificial Intelligence-Enabled Digital Twin for Smart Manufacturing*, 391-419.

Uchendu, B., Nurse, J. R. C., Bada, M., & Furnell, S. (2021). Developing a cyber security culture: Current practices and future needs. *Computers & Security*, 109, 102387. Advance online publication. DOI: 10.1016/j.cose.2021.102387

Ukwen, D. O., & Karabatak, M. (2021, June). Review of NLP-based systems in digital forensics and cybersecurity. In *2021 9th International symposium on digital forensics and security (ISDFS)* (pp. 1-9). IEEE. DOI: 10.1109/ISDFS52919.2021.9486354

Umer, M., Aljrees, T., Karamti, H., Ishaq, A., Alsubai, S., Omar, M., Bashir, A. K., & Ashraf, I. (2023). Heart Failure Patients Monitoring Using IoT-Based Remote Monitoring System. *Scientific Reports*, 13(1), 19213. DOI: 10.1038/s41598-023-46322-6 PMID: 37932424

United States Department of Justice https://www.justice.gov/jm/jm-9-48000-computer-fraud#:~:text=The%20Department's%20goals%20for%20CFAA%20enforcement%20are%20to%20promote%20privacy,stored%20in%20their%20information%20systems

V. A. Kumar, S. Surapaneni, D. Pavitra, R. Venkatesan, M. Omar, and A. K. Bashir, "An Internet of Medical Things-Based Mental Disorder Prediction System Using EEG Sensor and Big Data Mining," *Journal of Circuits, Systems and Computers*, vol. 2450197, World Scientific Publishing Company, 2024.

V. Nguyen, D. Mohammed, M. Omar, and M. Banisakher, "The Effects of the FCC Net Neutrality Repeal on Security and Privacy," *International Journal of Hyperconnectivity and the Internet of Things (IJHIoT)*, vol. 2, no. 2, pp. 21-29, IGI Global, 2018.

V. Nguyen, M. Omar, and D. Mohammed, "A Security Framework for Enhancing User Experience," *International Journal of Hyperconnectivity and the Internet of Things (IJHIoT)*, vol. 1, no. 1, pp. 19-28, IGI Global, 2017.

Valani, A. (2018, September). Rethinking secure DevOps threat modeling: The need for a dual velocity approach. In 2018 IEEE cybersecurity development (SecDev) (pp. 136). IEEE. DOI: 10.1109/SecDev.2018.00032

van Rossum, J. (2017). An Assessment of North Korean Threats and Vulnerabilities in Cyberspace. BearWorks. https://bearworks.missouristate.edu/theses/3212/

van Steen, T., & Deeleman, J. R. (2021). Successful gamification of cybersecurity training. *Cyberpsychology, Behavior, and Social Networking*, 24(9), 593–598. DOI: 10.1089/cyber.2020.0526 PMID: 34491845

Vaughn, L. (2019). *Psychology and culture: Thinking, feeling and behaving in a global context*. Routledge. DOI: 10.4324/9781351268882

Venugopalan, V., & Patterson, C. D. (2018). Surveying the hardware trojan threat landscape for the internet-of-things. *Journal of Hardware and Systems Security*, 2(2), 131–141. DOI: 10.1007/s41635-018-0037-2

Vijga, L. (2024, February 12). *Cybersecurity gamification: Winning the cyberwar through play*. BYVI. https://byvi.co/2023/10/01/cybersecurity-gamification/

Vitianingsih, V., Firmansyah, D., Maukar, A. L., Kacung, S., & Zangana, H. M. (2024, August). Recommendation System for Determining the Best Banner Supplier Using Profile Matching and TOPSIS Methods. *Intensif Jurnal Ilmiah Penelitian Teknologi Dan Penerapan Sistem Informasi*, 8(2), 246–262. DOI: 10.29407/intensif.v8i2.21635

von Ziegler, L., Sturman, O., & Bohacek, J. (2021). Big behavior: Challenges and opportunities in a new era of deep behavior profiling. *Neuropsychopharmacology*, 46(1), 33–44. DOI: 10.1038/s41386-020-0751-7 PMID: 32599604

Vyas, S., Tyagi, R. K., Jain, C., & Sahu, S. (2021, July). Literature review: A comparative study of real time streaming technologies and apache kafka. In *2021 Fourth International Conference on Computational Intelligence and Communication Technologies (CCICT)* (pp. 146-153). IEEE. DOI: 10.1109/CCICT53244.2021.00038

Warren, S., & Brandeis, L. D. (1890, December 15). The right to privacy. *Harvard Law Review*, 4(5), 193. https://groups.csail.mit.edu/mac/class/6.805/articles/privacy/privacy_brand_warr2.html. DOI: 10.2307/1321160

West, R. (2008). The Psychology of Security. In *Communications of the ACM* (Vol. Vol. 51, Ser. No. 4, pp. 34–41). essay, Association of Computing Machinery. DOI: 10.1145/1330311.1330320

Whitman, M. (2018). *Management of Information Security* (6th ed.)., https://bookshelf.vitalsource.com/books/9781337671545

Wiewiorowski, W. (2023) Cybersecurity and Data Protection: a necessary and powerful duo. European Data Protection Supervisorhttps://edps.europa.eu/press-publications/press-news/blog/cybersecurity-and-data-protection-necessary-and-powerful-duo_en

Willie, M. M. (2023). The role of Organizational Culture in cybersecurity: Building a security-first culture. *Journal of Research* [JoRIT]. *Innovation and Technologies*, 2(16), 179–198. DOI: 10.57017/jorit.v2.2(4).05

Witts, J. (2024, March 21). *The top 10 security awareness training platforms*. Expert Insights. https://expertinsights.com/insights/the-top-security-awareness-training-platforms-for-businesses/

Workman, M. (2021). An exploratory study of mode efficacy in cybersecurity training. *Journal of Cybersecurity Education, Research and Practice, Volume*, 2021(1), 1–12. https://digitalcommons.kennesaw.edu/jcerp/vol2021/iss1/2/. DOI: 10.62915/2472-2707.1075

Wright, J., Dawson, M. E.Jr, & Omar, M. (2012). Cyber security and mobile threats: The need for antivirus applications for smartphones. *Journal of Information Systems Technology and Planning*, 5(14), 40–60.

Wright, J., Dawson, M. E.Jr, & Omar, M. (2012). Cyber Security and Mobile Threats: The Need for Antivirus Applications for Smartphones. *Journal of Information Systems Technology and Planning*, 5(14), 40–60.

Xplore, I. E. E. E. (2023). Detecting Insider Threats in Cybersecurity Using Machine Learning and Deep Learning Techniques. *IEEE Conference Publication*.

Xplore, I. E. E. E. (2024). *A Review of Recent Advances, Challenges, and Opportunities in Malicious Insider Threat Detection Using Machine Learning Methods*. IEEE Journals & Magazines.

Xu, X., Wu, J., Bashir, A. K., & Omar, M. (2024). Machine Learning and Zero Knowledge Empowered Trustworthy Bitcoin Mixing for Next-G Consumer Electronics Payment. *IEEE Transactions on Consumer Electronics*, 70(1), 2210–2223. DOI: 10.1109/TCE.2024.3361690

Yang, Y., Ye, J., Cao, Y., Zhang, J., Li, X., Li, H., & Hu, Y. (2020, November). Survey: Hardware trojan detection for netlist. In 2020 IEEE 29th Asian Test Symposium (ATS) (pp. 1-6). IEEE.

Yasaei, R., Chen, L., Yu, S. Y., & Al Faruque, M. A. (2022). Hardware trojan detection using graph neural networks. *IEEE Transactions on Computer-Aided Design of Integrated Circuits and Systems.*

Yu, S., Gu, C., Liu, W., & O'Neill, M. (2020, October). A novel feature extraction strategy for hardware trojan detection. In *2020 IEEE International Symposium on Circuits and Systems (ISCAS)* (pp. 1-5). IEEE. DOI: 10.1109/ISCAS45731.2020.9180479

Yusif, S., & Hafeez-Baig, A. (2021). A conceptual model for cybersecurity governance. *Journal of Applied Security Research*, 16(4), 490–513. DOI: 10.1080/19361610.2021.1918995

Zangana, H. M. (2024). Exploring Blockchain-Based Timestamping Tools: A Comprehensive Review. *Redefining Security With Cyber AI*, 92-110.

Zangana, H. M. (2024). Exploring the Landscape of Website Vulnerability Scanners: A Comprehensive Review and Comparative Analysis. *Redefining Security With Cyber AI*, 111-129.

Zangana, H. M. "Developing Data Warehouse for Student Information System (IIUM as a Case Study)," *International Organization of Scientific Research*, vol. 20, no. 1, pp. 09-14, 2018.

Zangana, H. M., Omar, M., Al-Karaki, J. N., & Mohammed, D. (2024). Comprehensive Review and Analysis of Network Firewall Rule Analyzers: Enhancing Security Posture and Efficiency. *Redefining Security With Cyber AI*, 15-36.

Zangana, H. M., Sallow, Z. B., Alkawaz, M. H., & Omar, M. "Unveiling the Collective Wisdom: A Review of Swarm Intelligence in Problem Solving and Optimization," *Inform: Jurnal Ilmiah Bidang Teknologi Informasi dan Komunikasi*, vol. 9, no. 2, pp. 101-110, 2024.

Zangana, H. M. (2017). Watermarking System Using LSB. *IOSR Journal of Computer Engineering*, 19(3), 75–79. DOI: 10.9790/0661-1903027579

Zangana, H. M. (2018). Design an information management system for a pharmacy. *International Journal of Advanced Research in Computer and Communication Engineering*, 7(10), 52–55. DOI: 10.17148/IJARCCE.2018.71012

Zangana, H. M. (2020). Mobile Device Integration in IIUM Service. *International Journal (Toronto, Ont.)*, 8(5).

Zangana, H. M. (2021). The Global Financial Crisis from an Islamic Point Of View. *Qubahan Academic Journal*, 1(2), 55–59. DOI: 10.48161/qaj.v1n2a39

Zangana, H. M. (2022). Creating a Community-Based Disaster Management System. *Academic Journal of Nawroz University*, 11(4), 234–244. DOI: 10.25007/ajnu.v11n4a1485

Zangana, H. M. (2022). Implementing New Interactive Video Learning System for IIUM. *Academic Journal of Nawroz University*, 11(2), 23–29. DOI: 10.25007/ajnu.v11n2a1281

Zangana, H. M. (2024). *Exploring Blockchain-Based Timestamping Tools: A Comprehensive Review*. Redefining Security With Cyber AI. DOI: 10.4018/979-8-3693-6517-5.ch006

Zangana, H. M. (2024). *Exploring the Landscape of Website Vulnerability Scanners: A Comprehensive Review and Comparative Analysis*. Redefining Security With Cyber AI. DOI: 10.4018/979-8-3693-6517-5.ch007

Zangana, H. M., & Abdulazeez, A. M. (2023). Developed Clustering Algorithms for Engineering Applications: A Review [INJIISCOM]. *International Journal of Informatics, Information System and Computer Engineering*, 4(2), 147–169. DOI: 10.34010/injiiscom.v4i2.11636

Zangana, H. M., & Al-Shaikhli, I. F. (2013). A new algorithm for human face detection using skin color tone. *IOSR Journal of Computer Engineering*, 11(6), 31–38. DOI: 10.9790/0661-1163138

Zangana, H. M., Al-Shaikhli, I. F., & Graha, Y. I. (2013). The Ethical Dilemma of Software Piracy: An Inquiry from an Islamic Perspective. *Creative Communication and Innovative Technology Journal*, 7(1), 59–76. DOI: 10.33050/ccit.v7i1.171

Zangana, H. M., Bazeed, S. M. S., Ali, N. Y., & Abdullah, D. T. (2024). Navigating Project Change: A Comprehensive Review of Change Management Strategies and Practices. *Indonesian Journal of Education and Social Sciences*, 3(2), 166–179. DOI: 10.56916/ijess.v3i2.735

Zangana, H. M., Graha, Y. I., & Al-Shaikhli, I. F. (2024). Blogging: A New Platform For Spreading Rumors! *Creative Communication and Innovative Technology Journal*, 9(1), 71–76.

Zangana, H. M., Khalid Mohammed, A., & Zeebaree, S. R. (2024). Systematic Review of Decentralized and Collaborative Computing Models in Cloud Architectures for Distributed Edge Computing. *Sistemasi: Jurnal Sistem Informasi*, 13(4), 1501–1509. DOI: 10.32520/stmsi.v13i4.4169

Zangana, H. M., Mohammed, A. K., & Mustafa, F. M. (2024). Advancements and Applications of Convolutional Neural Networks in Image Analysis: A Comprehensive Review. *Jurnal Ilmiah Computer Science*, 3(1), 16–29.

Zangana, H. M., Mohammed, A. K., & Mustafa, F. M. (2024). Advancements in Edge Detection Techniques for Image Enhancement: A Comprehensive Review [IJAIR]. *International Journal of Artificial Intelligence & Robotics*, 6(1), 29–39. DOI: 10.25139/ijair.v6i1.8217

Zangana, H. M., Mohammed, A. K., Sallow, A. B., & Sallow, Z. B. (2024). Cybernetic Deception: Unraveling the Layers of Email Phishing Threats [INJURATECH]. *International Journal of Research and Applied Technology*, 4(1), 35–47.

Zangana, H. M., Mohammed, A. K., Sallow, A. B., & Sallow, Z. B. (2024). Cybernetic Deception: Unraveling the Layers of Email Phishing Threats. [INJURATECH]. *International Journal of Research and Applied Technology*, 4(1), 35–47.

Zangana, H. M., Mohammed, A. K., Sallow, Z. B., & Mustafa, F. M. (2024). Exploring Image Representation and Color Spaces in Computer Vision: A Comprehensive Review. *The Indonesian Journal of Computer Science*, 13(3). Advance online publication. DOI: 10.33022/ijcs.v13i3.3998

Zangana, H. M., & Mustafa, F. M. (2024). From Classical to Deep Learning: A Systematic Review of Image Denoising Techniques. *Jurnal Ilmiah Computer Science*, 3(1), 50–65.

Zangana, H. M., & Mustafa, F. M. (2024). Review of Hybrid Denoising Approaches in Face Recognition: Bridging Wavelet Transform and Deep Learning. *The Indonesian Journal of Computer Science*, 13(4). Advance online publication. DOI: 10.33022/ijcs.v13i4.4209

Zangana, H. M., & Mustafa, F. M. (2024). Surveying the Landscape: A Comprehensive Review of Object Detection Algorithms and Advancements. *Jurnal Ilmiah Computer Science*, 3(1), 1–15.

Zangana, H. M., & Omar, M. (2020). Threats, Attacks, and Mitigations of Smartphone Security. *Academic Journal of Nawroz University*, 9(4), 324–332. DOI: 10.25007/ajnu.v9n4a989

Zangana, H. M., Omar, M., & Ali, N. Y. (2024). Harnessing Artificial Intelligence in Modern Marketing: Strategies, Benefits, and Challenges [BAMJ]. *Business, Accounting and Management Journal*, 02(02), 70–82.

Zangana, H. M., Omar, M., Al-Karaki, J. N., & Mohammed, D. (2024). *Comprehensive Review and Analysis of Network Firewall Rule Analyzers: Enhancing Security Posture and Efficiency*. Redefining Security With Cyber AI. DOI: 10.4018/979-8-3693-6517-5.ch002

Zangana, H. M., & Zeebaree, S. R. (2024). Distributed Systems for Artificial Intelligence in Cloud Computing: A Review of AI-Powered Applications and Services [INJIISCOM]. *International Journal of Informatics, Information System and Computer Engineering*, 5(1), 11–30. DOI: 10.34010/injiiscom.v5i1.11883

Zaydi, M., & Nassereddine, B. (2020). DevSecOps practices for an agile and secure IT service management. Journal of Management Information and Decision Sciences, 23(2), 1–16. https://www.proquest.com/openview/8fdf6472c3a73b00fed8ec83a3e97b76/1?pq-origsite=gscholar&cbl=38743\ 74.

Zeadally, S., Adi, E., Baig, Z., & Khan, I. A. (2020). Harnessing artificial intelligence capabilities to improve cybersecurity. *IEEE Access : Practical Innovations, Open Solutions*, 8, 23817–23837. DOI: 10.1109/ACCESS.2020.2968045

Zhang, H., Wu, J., Pan, Q., Bashir, A. K., & Omar, M. (2024). Toward Byzantine-Robust Distributed Learning for Sentiment Classification on Social Media Platform. *IEEE Transactions on Computational Social Systems*, 1–11. DOI: 10.1109/TCSS.2024.3361465

Zhao, C., Du, H., Niyato, D., Kang, J., Xiong, Z., Kim, D. I., Shen, X., & Letaief, K. B. (2024). Generative AI for secure physical layer communications: A survey. *IEEE Transactions on Cognitive Communications and Networking*, 1. DOI: 10.1109/TCCN.2024.3438379

Zhou, S., Ali, A., Al-Fuqaha, A., Omar, M., & Feng, L. (2024). Robust Risk-Sensitive Task Offloading for Edge-Enabled Industrial Internet of Things. *IEEE Transactions on Consumer Electronics*, 70(1), 1403–1413. DOI: 10.1109/TCE.2023.3323146

Zimmermann, V., & Renaud, K. (2019). Moving from a 'human-as-problem" to a 'human-as-solution" cybersecurity mindset. *International Journal of Human-Computer Studies*, 131, 169–187. DOI: 10.1016/j.ijhcs.2019.05.005

About the Contributors

Marwan Omar is an accomplished cybersecurity expert and academic, specializing in the intersection of artificial intelligence (AI) and cybersecurity. He currently serves as an Associate Professor of Cybersecurity and AI at the Illinois Institute of Technology, where he leads cutting-edge research on AI security, focusing on the detection and mitigation of advanced cyber threats. With over a decade of experience in the field, Dr. Omar has made significant contributions to the understanding and development of security frameworks for AI systems, particularly in the detection of adversarial inputs, data poisoning, and backdoor attacks. His research has been widely recognized for its innovative application of machine learning techniques to enhance the security and robustness of AI models. Dr. Omar holds multiple advanced degrees, including a PhD in Cybersecurity and a PhD in AI, and has earned numerous industry certifications such as Certified Ethical Hacker (CEH) and SANS Certified Smartphone Forensics Analyst (GASF). His extensive publication record includes books, peer-reviewed journal articles, and conference papers that explore the integration of AI in cybersecurity, with a particular focus on large language models (LLMs) and generalized AI (Gen AI). His recent work has pioneered the use of pruning techniques and anomaly detection to identify and neutralize hidden threats within AI models, establishing new benchmarks for security in AI research. Dr. Omar's ongoing research efforts continue to push the boundaries of how AI can be both a tool and a target in the cybersecurity landscape. In addition to his academic pursuits, Dr. Omar is actively involved in industry collaborations and has contributed to numerous high-profile projects aimed at securing AI-driven technologies. His expertise has positioned him as a sought-after advisor and thought leader in the cybersecurity community. As a first-generation American from the Yazidi community in Iraq, Dr. Omar is committed to serving as a beacon of hope and inspiration for underrepresented minorities in STEM fields. His dedication to advancing both the scientific and social aspects of cybersecurity makes him a unique and influential figure in the ongoing dialogue about the future of AI security.

Hewa Majeed Zangana is an Assistant Professor currently affiliated with Duhok Polytechnic University (DPU) in Iraq. He holds a Doctorate in Philosophy (PhD) degree in ITM, which he is currently pursuing at DPU. Prior to his current role, Hewa Majeed Zangana has held various academic and managerial positions. He previously served as an Assistant Professor at Ararat Private Technical Institute and a Lecturer at DPU's Amedi Technical Institute, and Nawroz University. He has also held administrative positions such as Curriculum Division Director - Presidency of DPU, Information Unit Manager of The Research Center at Duhok Polytechnic University, Head of the Computer Science Department at Nawroz University, and Acting Dean of the College of Computer and IT at Nawroz University. Hewa Majeed Zangana's research interests span a wide range of topics in computer science, including network systems, information security, mobile communication, data communication, and intelligent systems. He has published extensively in peer-reviewed journals such as IEEE, EAI, IGI-Global, Inform, Indonesian Journal of Education and Social Science, TIJAB, INJIISCOM, and AJNU. In addition to his research contributions, Hewa Majeed Zangana has been actively involved in editorial roles such as Editorial Board Member at Applied and Computational Engineering (ewapublishing.org), serving as a Reviewer for the Scientific Journals of Nawroz University. He has also been a member of various scientific committees and administrative bodies at Nawroz University, including the Scientific Curriculum Development Committee, the Student Follow-up Program Committee, and the Committee for the Preparation of the Rules of Procedure for Consultative Offices.

***

Luay Albtosh is a dedicated and accomplished professional currently pursuing a Ph.D. in Cyber Leadership. With a robust academic background and over a decade of industry experience, Luay Albtosh has established a strong foothold in the field of computer science. Luay Albtosh holds a master's degree in computer science, which laid the groundwork for a career marked by continuous learning and impactful contributions to the field. Throughout the years, Luay Albtosh has developed a profound expertise in various aspects of computer science, including cybersecurity, software development, and IT project management. In addition to academic achievements, Luay Albtosh has consistently demonstrated a commitment to excellence in professional endeavors. With more than 10 years of hands-on experience, Luay Albtosh has successfully led numerous projects, drove innovation and ensuring the seamless integration of technology solutions. This extensive experience has provided Luay Albtosh with a deep understanding of both the technical and strategic facets of the industry.

M.Balasubramani working as Assistant Professor in V.S.B. Engineering College,Karur.He has more than 13 years of experience in teaching and 8 years of experience in research. He has published more than 12 research papers in various international conference and reputed journals. He has published more than four books in various international publications. He has a strong passion in Data Science, Arificial Intelligence, Machine Learning and Deep Learning

M.Robinson Joel is working as an Associate Professor in the Department of Computer Science and Engineering, at KCG College of Technology, Chennai. He has 16 years of teaching experience. He received the Doctorate PhD in Computer and Information Technology from the Manonmaniam Sundaranar University, Tirunelveli in March 2019. He has more than 60 publications in reputed journals. He can be contacted at email: joelnazareth@gmail.com

Angel Jones is an Adjunct Professor At the University of Virginia School of Continuing and Professional Studies. Dr. Jones began his 20-year cybersecurity career as a special agent with the U.S. Coast Guard, investigating cybercrime. His expertise has made him the go-to subject matter expert for complex cybersecurity and cyber breach investigation matters. Dr. Jones' experience includes serving as the Chief Information Security Officer for several global firms, proactively protecting organizations from dynamic cyber threats. Further, Dr. Jones holds several industry certifications, including the Certified Information Systems Security Professional (CISSP), Certified Information Security Manager (CISM), Certified Information Systems Auditor (CISA), Certified Chief Information Security Officer (CCISO), Certified in Risk and Information Systems Control (CRISC), Certified Ethical Hacker (CEH), EnCase Certified Examiner (EnCE), Digital Forensics Certified Practitioner (DFCP), AWS Certified Solutions Architect – Professional and AWS Certified Security - Specialty and Project Management Professional (PMP).

Nilamadhab Mishra is an Associate Professor in the School of Computer Science and Engineering, AI-ML Division, at VIT Bhopal University, India. He received his Doctor of Philosophy (Ph.D.) in Computer Science and Information Engineering with a specialization in AI-data science and machine learning from Chang Gung University, Taiwan. He has over 23 years of national and international involvement in academic teaching and research at recognized Indian, Taiwanese, and African universities. He has over 100 publications in SCI/SCIE and SCOPUS-indexed journals, ISBN books and chapters, Indian and Australian patents, IEEE conference proceedings, etc. He has been a reviewer, associate editor, and editorial board member for SCI/SCIE-indexed journals and conferences. He has been involved with several professional bodies: "Fellow Member of "ISROSET"; Fellow Member of "ISRD"; Senior Member of "ASR" (Hong Kong); Senior Member of "IEDRC" (Hong Kong); and Member of "IEEE Collabratec". He is currently an Associate Editor for two SCOPUS-indexed journals, and his research interests span the areas of AI, Data Science, Machine Learning, and Cognitive Analytics & Applications.

Firas Mahmood Mustafa holds a Ph.D. in Computer Engineering from Mosul University, Iraq. His academic journey began with a B.Sc. in Electrical Engineering (Electronics and Communication), graduating in the top quarter of his class. He earned an M.Sc. in Computer Engineering from Mosul University in 2000. Mustafa joined the Computer Science Department at AlHadba University in 2003 and completed his Ph.D. in 2007. From 2013 to 2017, he was with DPU University, and from 2017 to 2020, he chaired the CCE Department at Nawroz University. An active participant in Erasmus+ and IREX programs, he now teaches at DPU University, shaping future computer engineering professionals.

Marwan Omar received a Master's degree in Information Systems and Technology from the University of Phoenix, 2009 and a Doctorate Degree in Digital Systems Security from Colorado Technical University, 2012. He is currently an associate professor at Illinois Institute of Technology where he teaches cyber security and digital forensics courses. His research interests fall in the broad area of cyber security with a recent focus on machine learning robustness. Among other services, he is currently an active reviewer for IEEE Access, IEEE Transactions on Parallel and Distributed Systems and a member of IEEE since 2021.

Puya Pakshad conducts research in the field of vulnerability/malware detection. With a solid educational foundation from his PhD studies in Information Technology, he leverages analytical skills to address complex security challenges.

Joel R. is working as an Associate Professor in the Department of Electronics and instrumentation Engineering,at St. Joseph's college of Engineering, Chennai. She has 27 years of teaching experience. she has published 15 journal papers in image processing in biomedical fields and control engineering areas. she has been chairperson in many conferences at engineering college.

R.Prathipa is currently working as Associate professor in the Department of Electronics and Communication Engineering, Panimalar Engineering College. She completed her under graduation in ECE from Madras University. Teaching being her passion, completed her Master of Engineering in Medical Electronics from Anna University and pursuing Doctorate in the field of Medical Image processing. She has about 21 years of teaching experience in which she has guided several student projects and has published papers in various Journals and conferences. Her areas of interest include Image Processing, Signal Processing and Deep Learning.

Index

A

B

C

D

E

F

Q

R

S

T

U

V

www.ingramcontent.com/pod-product-compliance
Lightning Source LLC
LaVergne TN
LVHW080612300926
849162LV00005B/1130

* 9 7 9 8 3 3 7 3 0 5 8 8 2 *